FROM THE TRINITY

FROM THE TRINITY

The Coming of God in Revelation and Theology

PIERO CODA

Foreword by Peter J. Casarella • Edited by William Neu

THE CATHOLIC UNIVERSITY OF AMERICA PRESS
WASHINGTON, D.C.

The original title in Italian of this work published by Città Nuova Editrice of P.A.M.O.M. Rome is:
Dalla Trinità: l'avvento di Dio tra storia e profezia

The paper used in this publication meets the minimum requirements of American National Standards for Information Science—Permanence of Paper for Printed Library Materials, ANSI Z39.48-1984.
∞

Library of Congress Cataloging-in-Publication Data
Names: Coda, Piero, 1955– author. | Casarella, Peter J., writer of foreword. | Neu, William, editor.
Title: From the Trinity : the coming of God in Revelation and theology / Piero Coda ; foreword by Peter J. Casarella ; edited by William Neu.
Other titles: Dalla trinità. English
Description: Washington, D.C. : The Catholic University of America Press, 2020.
Identifiers: LCCN 2020033883 | ISBN 9780813233017 (paperback)
Subjects: LCSH: Trinity—History of doctrines. | God—History of doctrines. Catholic Church—Doctrines.
Classification: LCC BT109 .C62813 2020 | DDC 231/.044—dc23
LC record available at https://lccn.loc.gov/2020033883

CONTENTS

FOREWORD TO THE ENGLISH EDITION

Peter Casarella

It is both a delight and special privilege to introduce *From the Trinity: The Coming of God in Revelation and Theology* to an English-speaking audience. For most readers this translation will be their first encounter with Fr. Piero Coda. That encounter gives me a welcome and long-awaited opportunity to introduce the author. He was born in 1955 in Cafasse near Turin, and his first doctorate was in philosophy from the University of Turin, the same faculty from which Primo Levi graduated in 1941 and Umberto Eco in 1954. In 1986 he was awarded the doctorate in theology from the Pontifical Lateran University in Rome. In spite of this exceptional pedigree, Coda is no household name, not even among theologians. To me it is actually strange that widely discussed post-Christian figures like Gianni Vattimo and Giorgio Agamben come immediately to mind when learned academicians in the North Atlantic turn to Italy's current intellectual heritage, but rarely the Catholic thinkers.[1] Moreover, students of the *aggiornamento* and *ressourcement* initiated by the *Concilium* and *Communio* "schools" respectively are trained to parse English, French, and German tomes of considerable weight and learning but are not even introduced to their Italian counterparts. Such an aversion might perhaps be justified were the theologians from Italy more ecclesiocentric and narrowly circumscribed in their intellectual outlook than other European writers, but this is clearly not the case. In his native Italy, however, Piero Coda belongs today to the very top tier of an eminent caliber of Catholic thinkers of theological renewal, along with Archbishop Bruno Forte, Angelo Cardinal Scola, and the ecclesiologist Severino Dianich.

In fact, Piero Coda's influence extends far beyond Italy, in the first case, because of his preeminence as a former collaborator with Chiara Lubich and expert interpreter of her spirituality, life, and witness to global unity. He accompanied Lubich together with the whole Abba School (in a mode of collaboration together with his senior colleague Klaus

Peter Casarella is professor of theology, Divinity School of Duke University.

1. A lonely exception is Robert Imbelli's fine review of Coda's work in *The Thomist* 69: 3 (Summer 2005): 472–75.

Hemmerle, the distinguished German theologian and beloved Bishop of Aachen). Drawing heavily from Lubich's mystical insights and inspiration, Coda's process of reflection deals with ecumenism, intercultural dialogue, and interreligious encounter.[2] Fr. Coda is the former president of the Italian Association of Theologians and recently stepped down as the president of the University Institute Sophia. He is also now a member of the International Theological Commission and is working concertedly with theologians in Latin America on a multivolume project on intercultural trinitarian anthropology.[3] It is high time that his work and his witness begin to have their impact in the English-speaking world!

Coda was a groundbreaking figure in late twentieth-century theological developments even though his contributions at that time were seldom noticed beyond a small but highly qualified coterie of international students at the Lateran University in Rome. His books engaged all of the dominant academic controversies through his reflection on the event of the Trinity: *Evento pasquale. Trinità e storia* (The Paschal event: Trinity and History) (1984), *Il negativo e la trinità. Ipotesi su Hegel* (Negativity and the Trinity: Hypotheses regarding Hegel (1987), *L'Altro di Dio. Rivelazione e kenosi in S. Bulgakov* (The Otherness of God: Revelation and Kenosis in Sergei Bulgakov) (1998), and *Il Logos e il Nulla* (*Logos* and Nothingness) (2003). All of these works focus on the relationship between reason, faith, and the experience of nothingness. As Robert Imbelli notes, the speculative title of the fourth work is deceptive, for it is a meditation not on an empty void but on a mystical path that opens up to a fullness of new life in the Trinity:

> An important consequence of Coda's sensitivity to the need to move towards a Trinitarian ontology is that the soteriology that permeates his work also exhibits ontological substance. In the face of so much impoverished exemplarism in contemporary soteriology, Coda offers a robust theology of salvation. The paschal mystery of Jesus Christ does not merely indicate a way to follow. Christ by his death and resurrection forges the Way. He himself becomes the Way into the new creation. Christians are called not so much to imitate the historical Jesus as to participate in the new life of their crucified and risen Lord, becoming, in the tradition's pregnant sense, "*filii in Filio*": sons and daughters in God's only Son.[4]

2. On the Abba School, one may consult *Introduction to the Abba School: Conversations from Focolare's Interdisciplinary Study Center*, ed. David L. Schindler (Hyde Park, N.Y.: New City Press, 2002).

3. See, for example, the volumes: *Antropología trinitaria para nuestros pueblos* (Bogotá: CELAM, 2014) and *Antropología trinitaria en clave afro-latinoamericana y caribeña* (Bogotá: CELAM, 2018). One of Coda's key collaborators on this project was the late Juan Carlos Scannone, SJ, Argentine philosopher and adviser to Pope Francis.

4. Robert Imbelli, "Review of Piero Coda's *Teo-Logia* and *Il Logos e la Nulla*," *The Thomist* 69: 3 (Summer 2005): 475.

The path that Coda maps out from absolute nothingness to living in the Trinitarian fullness of God's life passes through the paschal mystery. It is not an arid, conceptual path nor is it a flight into a faith that is nude and inscrutable to powers of rational reflection. The Trinity is a self-interrogating "place" from which one can confront a reality of world and community that appears at first glance groundless. At the same time, the same Trinitarian starting point is also a way to remain open to the possibility of being touched by a wounded but healing Other who offers new life in a way that fundamentally alters one's perspective on the course of life that one has already chosen.

I myself was caught off guard when I first met Piero Coda. We met in Rome in the year 2000 while I was on sabbatical from the Catholic University of America. I was stunned by his simplicity, eagerness to dialogue with a total newcomer from the other side of the Atlantic, and the vastness of his learning. Soon thereafter I devoured the two volumes of essays that he had just edited on Trinitarian reflection and contemporary metaphysical questions: *La Trinità e il pensare. Figure, Percorsi, Prospettive* (Trinity and thinking: Figures, trajectories, and prospects) (1997) and *Abitando la Trinità. Per un rinnovamento dell'ontologia* (Dwelling in the Trinity: Towards a renewal of ontology) (1998).[5] After reading these works, I could not understand why theologians in the United States had not yet paid more attention to his masterful appreciation of the Eastern and Western heritage of the inheritance of the church and its mystical tradition and his penetrating engagement of idealist, postidealist, and postmodern European philosophy (including his beloved Antonio Rosmini). By this point the revival of Trinitarian theology was galloping along in North America with Neo-Augustinian, Thomist, Barthian, Balthasarian, and Eastern Orthodox trailblazers but sadly without the benefit of Coda's lucid insights and new pathways.

What is Coda's most vital and distinctive contribution to contemporary theology, particularly to Trinitarian theology? First, Coda offers a dynamic and intellectually sustainable alternative to the great neo-Hegelian temptation of the twentieth-century Trinitarian revival, namely, that of joining the revealed Trinity to the dialectical unfolding of history so closely that the logic that guides the comprehension of the latter becomes *ipso facto* the logic that discloses the meaning of the former. Using the best of Russian Orthodox sophiology with prudence and discretion, Coda unveils the obvious limits of the Rahnerian identification of immanent and economic Trinity (and vice versa) while also laying out a path

5. *Abitando la Trinità: Per un rinnovamento dell'ontologia*, ed. Piero Coda and Lubomír Žak (Rome: Città Nuova, 1998).

for taking seriously the robust traces of the Trinity in the experience of individuals seeking a path for union with God and the social networks and realities that envelop and co-determine the lives of such individuals. Second, Coda reflects quite seriously upon the mystery of the Trinity qua ineffable mystery and thus names his proposal *Dalla Trinità*, "from the Trinity." He is still more generous to Rahner than was von Balthasar or Ratzinger, but not without laying his own cards on the table to demonstrate wherein the genuine strength of Rahner's post-liberal opponents actually lies. One school of Rahnerians interpreted the axiom that identified the immanent Trinity and the economic Trinity to be fully reciprocal (on the basis of the "vice versa"), and Coda judiciously surveys the critiques of this approach by contemporary theologians as well as by the International Theological Commission. Coda's revision and critique of a critical modern methodological principle thus aid in showing the proximity of his proposal to the great Eastern and Western Christian traditions of mystical theology, but his new path to the Trinity also opens up a sustained and multi-faceted reflection upon the relationship of the Triune communion of love with the human self-emptying lived in union by grace with the nothingness (*il nulla*) of Christ on the cross, which leads to receiving oneself renewed by the Love of God. His corrective of Rahnerianism is not so much a gentle critique as an appreciative inner development of the post-idealist and simultaneously Augustinian Thomist logic of Rahner's original starting point.

In complete alignment with this trajectory, Coda also grounds his theoretical reflection on the mystical insights and lived spirituality of communion of Chiara Lubich in its manifold socio-economic (e.g., her now global initiative for a new economy of communion) and interreligious dimensions, such that the final product is also a theology born of the act of living testimony. Coda performs academically and ecclesially the vibrant synthesis of theology and sanctity that Hans Urs von Balthasar once predicted would be the future of theology. Specifically, von Balthasar wrote eloquently in 1947 about the need to re-connect theology and sanctity.[6] In his own Trinitarian theology, the Swiss thinker shocked (and continues to shock) the guild of academic theologians by relying heavily and explicitly on the visions of a medical doctor and convert from Basel named Adrienne von Speyr. These visions treated Christ's descent into the realm of the dead on Holy Saturday. Adrienne was more than von Balthasar's muse. She was an authority whose work, in his view, merited ecclesial approbation. Coda insists that Lubich's mystical insights constitute an

6. Hans Urs von Balthasar, "Theology and Sanctity," in *Explorations in Theology I: The Word Made Flesh* (San Francisco: Ignatius, 1989), 181–209.

essential contribution to the theological renewal and development reflected in *From the Trinity*. These insights are inextricably linked to her life and work. There are similarities and differences between the two sets of collaborations. First, Chiara's life and work in her native Trent was fully public and unfolded fairly quickly onto the stage of the entire globe. The scale of Focolare is much larger than that of the Community of St. John, which centered on the city of Basel during Adrienne's lifetime but only slowly radiated outward. The charism of the Community of St. John was to live on a personal level the evangelical counsels of poverty, chastity, and obedience in the midst of the secular world in order to raze the bastions that have been artificially erected from both sides between Church and world. The accents of the Focolare are different. Focolare promotes a communitarian spirituality in which Jesus is encountered in the midst of the family of Foclarini gathered in his name.[7] Both ecclesial projects forge a theology that is lived and verified through the holiness of its followers. Coda too relies on a female spiritual authority in a way that could even be seen as imitating von Balthasar. In short, the witness of a holy, faithful, and charismatic woman of God is the engine that drives the vehicle of this first volume of a projected theological and institutional itinerary of great importance to the Church and the world.

From the Trinity occupies a unique place in Christian theology. In our day ecumenical, interreligious, intercultural, and socio-ecological concerns rise to the fore and press for ready-made answers. The renewal of Trinitarian thought by diverse groups of Protestant, Catholic, and Orthodox theologians in the twentieth century made it possible to rebut with a broad consensus of conviction both scientistic Deism and modern Gnosticism, but the precise contours of the revelation and contemporary significance of God as Father, Son, and Holy Spirit still remain more open to debate than ever.

The uniqueness of Coda's proposal lies in the first instance in his title. *From the Trinity* is the translation of Coda's own enigmatic title: *Dalla Trinità*. Not surprisingly and inevitably, something is lost in the translation. The English title sounds more artificial than might be desired. The translation is nonetheless both accurate and provocative. First of all, this work is *not at all* another contribution in the mould of scholastic or Neo-scholastic manuals labeled *De Trinitate*. The *da* of the Trinity is not the source of religious information, arcane *gnosis*, or even foundational knowledge *about* the Trinity. What, then, is the real sense of the preposition *da* that is here translated "from"? The preposition, in general, signals

7. Piero Coda, *Dalla Trinità: l'avvento di Dio tra storia e profezia,* 2d ed. (Rome: Città Nuova, 2012, ed.), 493–509.

movement from one place to another and is usually coupled with a verb of motion. But *da*, while different from the possessive *di* ("of"), can also signal the general context of which something arises. In this case, the context of a ubiquitous epiphany such as the Trinitarian self-disclosure is neither "from above" nor "from below." The Trinity arises from *within* the place that God has revealed God's very being as one of love and unity. God is Emmanuel. That wondrous and uncircumscribable "placing" of the divine into our midst signals a certain priority of experience but not in a modern and subjective sense of "my" experience. I, as a potential recipient of a gift, must seek out a community wherein the dynamic revelation of God has already found a home. As just one illustration of this Trinitarian placing, the name of the ecclesial movement founded by Chiara Lubich, "Focolare," means "hearth."

The preposition *da* can also have the strictly locative sense, as in *da noi*, "at our home," or the antiquated name: Jacopone da Todi. The medieval poet comes from the village of Todi, and the village of Todi marks the movement of his life and work from this place, not to mention the way in which he has been named by literary critics since the Middle Ages. By comparison, "I am a New Yorker" signals a similar sense of place, disposition, and identity. New York does not own the New Yorker in the sense of possession, but the New Yorker is still defined by being from there. The Trinity, therefore, is a revelation that gravitates towards a new definition of the "coming" of God's self-disclosure from within the vast and ultimately unmappable cartography of human experience, social networks, and relationships of empowerment and inequality on the globe.

The Trinity is found in the church in a uniquely privileged and ideally nonpossessive way. Through the communication of grace in baptism, which the church insists takes place in the name of Father, Son, and Holy Spirit, the gift becomes a form of identity as Christian for the catechumen who has just entered the "place" of the church. The arrival of God as *avvento* (which is rendered in the original Italian subtitle as "The Advent of God in the midst of History and Prophecy") is thus not without its historical and cultural spatial contours in the concrete places in which God is sought from afar, worshipped, loved, and known. Believers indwell the Trinity not by hovering above the world like a viewer of Google maps nor by their fixity in just one cultic temple or a pre-determined zip code of ethnic, cultural, or national origin. The place of the Trinity is one of positive, energizing freedom because God acts from within the abode of the Trinity to offer salvation to the world in the person of Jesus Christ as directly encountered in the very place in which one lives.[8] The God of

8. English-speaking readers may be learning for the first time about the ontology of freedom that Coda inherits from the Italian philosopher Luigi Pareyson (a teacher of Vattimo and Eco) and

Jesus Christ is everywhere and no place, but God as Father, Son, and Holy Spirit is never without a place to be discovered anew by those in search of the abiding (or aboding) love that the Triune God offers.

In *From the Trinity*, a principal source of spiritual renewal is Lubich's mysticism of unity. It is uniquely fitting that this work is published by the Catholic University of America Press. In the year 2000 Chiara Lubich was the recipient of an honorary doctorate from the Catholic University of America and spoke in that venue about the aim of education in our times.[9] I was privileged to be a member of the faculty of the Catholic University of America at that time. Chiara spoke eloquently about Catholic identity and a pedagogy of unity rooted in a mystical vision of the body of Christ.

It is important to note, especially for an English-speaking audience, that religious pluralism is also vigorously affirmed in *From the Trinity* in a manner consonant with the overall vision. This element stems in part from an encounter that took place on U. S. soil three years prior to the honorary doctorate ceremony in Washington, D.C. Coda had at that time accompanied Lubich in her historic visit to Black Muslims and, incidentally, prayed with Chiara at the tomb of Saint Mother Cabrini while visiting New York. On May 18, 1997, Chiara met with the charismatic Imam W. D. Mohammed in the Malcolm X Mosque in Harlem. That encounter marked the very first time a white Christian woman had spoken in that mosque.[10] In attendance were three thousand people, both Black Muslims as well as representatives of the Focolare Movement. Chiara spoke passionately from her heart and quoted both the Gospel and the Koran to illustrate the creative possibility of global unity. The crowd in the mosque interrupted her speech with shouts of "God is great." Later in a private meeting, W.D. Mohammed and Chiara made a pact in the name of the one God: to work unceasingly for peace and unity. Today the Focolarini in the U.S. continue to nurture this special kinship with the Muslim community.

I am grateful to the remarkable team of translators that made this work possible. The text *From the Trinity* may nonetheless seem strange and foreign to an English-speaking reader. The author did not write it with our tongue or our problems at the forefront of his consciousness. But the spirit of the work will bear fruit in many domains throughout the globe in which the English language is spoken and employed in theolog-

---

the way that this insight supplements the theo-dramatic rendering of freedom in Hans Urs von Balthasar's trinitarian anthropology (*Dalla Trinità*, 573–83).

9. Chiara Lubich, *Essential Writings* (Hyde Park, N.Y.: New City Press, 2007), 219–24.

10. For details, see the website https://www.focolare.org/en/news/2008/10/10/lultimo-saluto-allimam-della-pace-w-d-mohammed/ as well Piero Coda, *Nella Moschea di Malcolm X con Chiara Lubich negli Stati Uniti e in Messico* (Rome: Città Nuova, 1997).

ical education. The global impact that we anticipate for this work will be both welcome and fitting. The short stop made twenty-three years ago by Chiara Lubich and Piero Coda to pray at the tomb of Mother Frances Cabrini now seems prescient. In line with and in addition to the theology of concrete holiness, which the Italian immigrant Mother Cabrini taught many in this country, Chiara sowed a seed of insight that Piero is elaborating; today it still has the power to rejuvenate theology and philosophy.

Our fragmented world beckons for a new and unexpected form of unity, one that is wondrous in front of the novelty of difference and is to the same degree nurtured by the bread of Scripture and the wine of the Christian tradition. Coda plumbs those sources and has responded to this authentic and widespread cry by inviting us to enter the place in which God's self-disclosure has been definitively disclosed and made incarnate. These pages chart a path to enter into that mystery and to re-discover interiorly and exteriorly its delights and the healing power of Jesus of Nazareth as Son of God. The subtitle of this work in the original Italian reminds us that the event of the Triune God unfolds *tra storia e profezia*, "between history and prophecy," precisely because our histories find their abode in this "between." We are caught everyday between personal and social exigencies, on the one hand, and the hope for a new future, on the other. This text does not ask us to escape from this insuperable and sometimes unbearable tension but to dwell in it while recognizing that the God of Jesus Christ is in our midst and utters his cry of abandonment, his prophetic admonitions, and his message of salvation from this very same place.

Duke Divinity School
April 2020

PREFACE TO THE ENGLISH EDITION

Piero Coda

Among the many and often unsettling legacies left to us by the twentieth century, there was a vigorous and in many respects unforeseen rebirth of interest in the Trinity, God's face revealed in Jesus of Nazareth. And this was not only because theology was marked by a renewed focus on this central truth of the faith through various vicissitudes, thereby offering a true, precise readjustment of its course in terms of its content together with its form and its methodology. But it was also because Christian experience across the board was oriented to an unprecedented development in many respects of the trinitarian quality and form of its own life. This development was not only in its spiritual and even mystical roots, but also in its practical and even political and economic repercussions.

On the other hand, even though disaffection has persisted for God's image testified by the church's faith—indeed, it has intensified at times in today's world—there is also evidence of a nostalgia in this regard among both representatives of philosophical thought as well as spokespersons for the artistic and scientific world, not to mention its continuing prophetic significance in the Areopagus of religions and cultures, and even more so in view of the global pluralistic civilization clearly looming on the horizon.

A twofold consciousness came to maturation in me as a result of recognizing all this. First of all, that God's trinitarian face is not a secondary accessory, nor even less an undue deformation of Jesus' Gospel, but is its horizon of ultimate decisive truth, once it is understood and focused in its most authentic original theological and anthropological meaning. And at the same time, I understood that the Christian God's trinitarian form not only impacts the single person in the determination of his/her interior and religious life, but it says something crucial about the quality of his/her relationship with the other and with others in society, in the unfolding history of human existence within the cosmic scene of the universe and its destiny.

Taking into account this indisputable new element which was vividly outlined by the Second Vatican Council's magisterium, calls for a redefinition of the cultural expressions inspired by the Gospel, along with their renewed and more trenchant incorporation into our epoch's global public square. This is clearly evident in the pages of Benedict XVI's social encyclical, *Caritas in Veritate* (2009), for example, which was meant to relaunch the prophetic message of Paul VI's *Populorum Progressio* (1967). This is why it contains a wish for "a new trajectory of thinking" focused on "a metaphysical interpretation of the '*humanum*' in which relationality is an essential element" drawing its light from the Christian intuition about God the Trinity. For his part, Pope Francis does not tire of confirming the need to build a "new paradigm" of thought and practice today—see *Evangelii Gaudium* (2013) and *Laudato Sì* (2015)—a paradigm leading to "discovering in the whole of creation the Trinitarian imprint that makes the cosmos in which we live a 'network of relations' in which 'it is proper to every living being to tend towards other things.' This in turn fosters 'a spirituality of that global solidarity which flows from the mystery of the Trinity'" (*Veritatis Gaudium* [2018], par. 4).

The monograph that I am introducing here is meant to respond in its small measure in the theological sphere to this great and in many respects decisive appeal, which in itself calls upon all fields of knowledge. It is not a matter of a manual in the classical sense of the term. Books of this kind are not lacking fortunately, and some are even remarkably valuable insofar as they give the best organically coherent account of the theological renewal which came of age in the twentieth century. This essay is meant to be more modest while at the same time it may be more ambitious; it is meant to revisit the Christian tradition's legacy, delving into what I consider the determining contribution for the human family's future. This opinion was consolidated in me from the spiritual light and increasingly intense theological understanding resulting from the encounter with and sharing in the charism of unity given to our times by the Holy Spirit through Chiara Lubich's witness and spiritual and social doctrine.

The title and subtitle of this essay are meant to give an account of all that. The title, *From the Trinity*, makes an allusion more to the formal object than the material object. It is a matter of understanding in the Trinity, the interpretive key not only for the event of Jesus Christ, but for creation and history in him. You could say that each and every thing is to be seen "with the eyes of the Trinity." At the same time, the original subtitle, *l'avvento di Dio tra storia e profezia*, calls attention back to the fact that God's coming, which already happened once and for all in Jesus Christ at the center of time, is relaunched in the always new and pressing openness to and expectation of its accomplishment in the breath of the Spirit, which is awaited and dramatically built as our history unfolds among us today.

The English subtitle, *The Coming of God in Revelation and Theology*, encompasses this history in and through which God has been manifesting himself; it also includes the prophetic dimension as theology studies the Spirit's inspirations over the centuries and incorporates them into doctrinal development.

So even in the rich complexity and sometimes unavoidable technicalities of some of the topics faced, what I would love to come out of these pages is the itinerary and horizon through which the history of revelation, thought, and experience of God the Trinity passes in the context of humanity's present and future. This is without indulging the desire to comprehend all the documents, a daunting enterprise, nor the irresponsible wish for a definitive interpretation. It would rather be by welcoming the splash of fragments, accents, and paths that seemed the most precious and stimulating to me among many others. This should contribute to a picture of what awaits us from a perspective of trust and hope looking upon the memory of the event of freedom and truth offered to history in Jesus Christ while carefully, intensely listening to the breath of the Spirit without resistance.

I hope this intention will be easily grasped by the eye and heart of the attentive or even expert reader, in each of the sections in which this monograph is divided. To my grateful and astonished joy, this is what occurred with many of those to whom I had the chance to explain something of these pages over these years—in classes, dialogues, and conferences.

Each of the parts comprising this essay have a precise intent—to show a detail of the method in action, and so an outlook on and interpretation of the mystery of God the Trinity which leapt more vividly into my view, which was more enlightening to my mind and which was more warming to my heart. Essentially, it is a matter of the insurmountable fruitful ongoing interaction between understanding and experience, between faith and culture (part 1); it is a matter of the phenomenological approach in drawing out some of the principal lines of God's revelation attested in the First Testament (part 2), demonstrating the essential linkage (from a Christian point of view) with the New Testament, which is read from the same perspective as well. It reflects an effort to bring out the dramatic roles played by the Father and the Spirit in the event of the Son becoming flesh and bread for us (part 3). It is a matter of inventing the *golden thread* tracing out a path which can be perceived while listening to the Holy Spirit as testified by the documents and witnesses of his activity through history; this thread leads into the future (part 4). The last, just drafted part (part 5) is limited to describing the *platform* from which the leap can be made for a new proposal when the time comes.

Several of the intuitions and research hypotheses drawn out in these pages were verified and developed by friends and students as a result of their research and studies which are indicated along the way. My sincere gratitude to each one for this fellowship and trust. I am very grateful to each person that tenaciously worked for this English edition: Donald Mitchell, the publisher that accepted the proposal, and the translating team, which generously undertook the work in the communion of love flowing from the Trinity—Giovanna Czander, Thomas Norris, Declan O'Byrne, Paul O'Hara, and Brendan Purcell. Thanks for William Neu's editing and Julie Tremblay's coordination of the project.

The hope is that the outline drawn out in these pages will end up being useful and stimulating to proceed along the way, that it will provide pertinent, penetrating elements to understand and experience God the Trinity. It is offered as a contribution to the essential dialogue today among the fields of study and among cultures.

ABBREVIATIONS

CCC	*Catechism of the Catholic Church*
DH	Denzinger, *Compendium of Creeds, Definitions, and Declarations on Matters of Faith and Morals* (ed. Hünermann)
DV	*Dei Verbum* (Vatican Council II)
GLNT	*Grande Lessico del Nuovo Testamento*
GS	*Gaudium et Spes* (Vatican Council II)
LG	*Lumen Gentium* (Vatican Council II)
PG	Patrologiae Cursus Completus, Series Graeca (ed. Migne)
PL	Patrologia Latina, Cursus Completus (ed. Migne)
ST	Aquinas, *Summa Theologiae*

FROM THE TRINITY

Prologue

> I have desired to see intellectually what I have believed.
>
> —Augustine of Hippo, *De Trinitate* XV.28.51

Contemplating God who is Trinity with a pure heart and transparent intelligence, thus making the truth of his mystery—light that illuminates existence and satisfies the thirst—come to expression in words, opens onto the heart of the Christian faith. It is a demanding and fascinating undertaking, which is both a grace to be gratefully welcomed and a task to be fulfilled with commitment and perseverance. It is undoubtedly a demanding undertaking because it requires the most vigilant attention and our being's greatest effort, as it is called in its entirety to really encounter God who reveals and gives himself. But it is the most fascinating undertaking because the encounter with God the Trinity discloses the meaning and the beauty of existence.

Before anything else, it is grace, in other words, a gratuitous gift, because the Trinity cannot be known without the gift of Jesus' revelation, received in the church's living faith and enlightened by the Spirit's gifts. Jesus, the Son, affirms it with the emphatic words: "no one knows the Son except the Father, and no one knows the Father except the Son and anyone to whom the Son chooses to reveal him" (Mt 11:27). But it is also a demanding task because it is in the relationship with God in Jesus and in his Spirit—a relationship which is welcomed and sought with God who is known and loved for who he is, love—that human freedom and intelligence are called to express their truest nature and their highest vocation, all of themselves, as a gift.

Augustine of Hippo gave the undying masterpiece, *De Trinitate*, to the church and to the history of thought. This work may spontaneously come to mind when we think of the Trinity as the highest object, or better as the true subject, of theology.[1] This is what he writes in his famous book:

> Let us set out along Charity Street together, making for him of whom it is said, *Seek his face always* [Ps 105:4]. This covenant, both prudent and pious, I would wish to enter into in the sight of the Lord our God with all who read what I write, and with respect to all my writings, especially such as these where we are seeking the unity of the three, of Father and Son and Holy Spirit. For nowhere else is a mistake more dangerous, or the search more laborious, or discovery more advantageous.[2]

This brief text contains precious indications still today which can lead us into our journey as a stream of light to be followed with freedom of spirit and renewed creativity.

Before anything else, Augustine emphasizes that the way to knowledge of God the Trinity—in other words, the "method," in the etymological meaning of the Greek *méthodos*, the way to be tread to reach the goal before us—is the way of charity. In accordance with the precise dynamism of *fides quaerens intellectum* ("faith seeking understanding" of the One in whom it believes), it tends with intimate longing and confident hope to contemplation of the face of the beloved.

So it should undoubtedly be traveled first of all, *coram Deo*, in God's presence. But at the same time it demands being practiced together with brothers and sisters because the face of God's Son made flesh is hidden and appears in the face of men and women who are brothers and sisters. In fact, "those who do not love a brother or sister whom they have seen, cannot love God whom they have not seen" (1 Jn 4:20).

For Augustine, this is the starting point for the adventure of writing to put the search for God into words and to share the fruits of this quest; and for his readers, the adventure of listening and welcoming the gift of wisdom transmitted in this way, with pure and open hearts and minds, in such a way that they progress as well along the way of knowledge and love for God.

In fact, if charity is the main path to humbly and faithfully deal with any theological topic, Augustine adds, this is even more the case in the effort to penetrate that truth of unity and Trinity which the mystery of God himself encompasses and expresses, as he is love alone, in its entirety

1. See Piero Coda, *Teo-logia: La parola di Dio nelle parole dell'uomo* (Rome: Lateran University Press, 2004), 67.

2. Augustine, *De Trinitate* I.3.5, translated as *The Trinity*, ed. John E. Rotelle and trans. Edmund Hill (Hyde Park, N.Y.: New City Press, 1991): "Ita ingrediamur simul caritatis viam tendentes ad eum de quo dictum est: Quaerite faciem eius semper. Et hoc placitum pium atque tutum coram Domino Deo nostro cum omnibus inierim qui ea quae scribo legunt et in omnibus scriptis meis maximeque in his ubi quaeritur unitas Trinitatis, Patris et Filii et Spiritus Sancti, quia neque periculosius alicubi erratur, nec laboriosius aliquid quaeritur, nec fructuosius aliquid invenitur."

(1 Jn 4:8, 16). It is such a high and humanly impenetrable mystery that it is possible to run up against the most dangerous error in its regard. Therefore it requires the highest existential and intellectual, personal and communitarian commitment, precisely because it promises the most beautiful and substantial fruits for life and for thought.

But why did Augustine write his *De Trinitate*? And what route did he want to follow? At the end of a long and tormented journey, he embraces the Christian faith after the first Councils of Nicaea (325) and Constantinople (381) had been celebrated. They defined the trinitarian truth: not only is the Father God, but the Son, Jesus, is of the same substance as the Father as well, and the same is true of the Holy Spirit.

It is thus that Augustine feels strongly urged from within to write a work, *De Trinitate*, to fulfill an ecclesial task which the Spirit had suggested to him. That task was to illustrate and penetrate the truth about God expressed in the church's faith. He is pushed and urged by the desire to know this God better, God the Trinity, so that he can love him not only with the heart that "believes," but also with the intellect that "sees," inasmuch as life allows on earth: *Desideravi intellectu videre quod credidi.*[3]

But what way should be followed to be able "to see," in other words to contemplate, the beauty and the truth of God the Trinity? Augustine journeys almost twenty years—the time it took him to write his work—broken down into three points that are interwoven while remaining distinct: *regula fidei, intelligentia fidei, experientia fidei*. The *regula fidei* is the firm launching pad, the truth that the church believes and transmits, having received it from God's revelation culminating in Jesus, the truth which is condensed and articulated in the symbol of faith professed by the church. According to this symbol, God is both one and triune: Father, Son, and Holy Spirit.

The second point is the *intelligentia fidei*. This means making this truth enlighten and almost transfigure the intellect, inasmuch as it is humanly possible. It does not mean wanting to understand it, in other words to "contain" it in the limited and fragile space of human reason, but "to purify the mind" so that the light of the truth transforms it little by little into a clear and faithful mirror of itself. This calls to mind the episode narrated in the hagiographical tradition. Along the seashore, Augustine encounters a child trying to pour the limitless seawater into a little hole dug in the sand. This remarkable doctor intuits that only God's gift, the Holy Spirit, can achieve the impossible miracle of enabling us to receive the infinite of divine life in us. An audacious thinker among Augustine's interpreters recognized the Son of God made flesh in that child, because

3. Ibid., XV.28.51.

it is only in smallness and humility—that of Bethlehem and Calvary—that the amazing immensity and the inaccessible glory of the most high shine out to human eyes.

Augustine proceeded with rigor and speculative audacity in the first books of *De Trinitate*, enabling him to achieve an intuition, due to the intellect's docility to the Spirit's breath, which was an extraordinary illustration of the trinitarian truth marking the subsequent tradition of Christian thought. But this was not yet enough for him. In fact, he had an intense desire to be able to "touch" in some way God who is Trinity; in other words, he wanted to enter into vital communion with him already down here on earth. This leads to the third point of his journey, the *experientia fidei* which he tenaciously pursued beginning with Book VIII.

The question he sought to answer was the following: What is the "way" I must pursue to meet God the Trinity in my concrete existence? Where is the "place" in which I can contemplate him already here and now, with the confident hope of seeing him one day "face to face" (see 1 Cor 13:12), according to the promise of eternal life? In short, where in this life on earth can I experience him, the God revealed by Jesus? The answer is not difficult. And Augustine discovers it in its disturbing simplicity in John's first Letter: "God is love, and those who abide in love abide in God, and God abides in them" (1 Jn 4:16). Dazzled by this light, he then exclaims: "There you are, *God is love*. Why should we go running round the heights of the heavens and the depths of the earth looking for him who is with us if only we should wish to be with him?"[4] As he explains, when I sincerely love the brother according to Jesus' precept, I experience a love inside of myself, and yet it does not come from me. Loving the brother, I experience God's love like a source of that love which enables me to love, that love which is bigger than my heart even though it dwells within me (see 1 Jn 3:20).

Thanks to the gift of the Spirit in fact, in Jesus God is no longer far away, outside of ourselves, nor are we far away, outside of him. But he really dwells in us and we in him. He dwells precisely in the love for the brother which is born from and expresses God's love for us and ours for him. This is with the confident hope that one day, "we will see him as he is" (see 1 Jn 3:2).

Like Augustine along with his readers, we are called to journey along the way of charity as well, to know God the Trinity with the mind and to touch God the Trinity with the heart. This way of love (*agápe*, *caritas*) is God himself who gives himself to us in Jesus Christ, as Benedict XVI re-

4. Ibid., VIII.7.11: "Ecce: Deus dilectio est. Utquid imus et currimus in sublimia caelorum et ima terrarum quaerentes eum qui est apud nos, si nos esse velimus apud eum?"

called.[5] The Son illustrates this way by inviting us to follow him in loving the Father, "with all your heart, and with all your soul, and with all your mind, and with all your strength" (Mk 12:28) and in loving one another as he personally loves each one of us (Jn 15:12). But looking at the effort to contemplate, together with study, research, and dialogue (to which these pages are dedicated), what does it mean concretely to love God and to love one another in Christ in order to know God and to be able to "see" us and the world in him?

Love God, before anything else. We may have never paid attention to the fact that the commandment to love God which Jesus recovers from the First Testament (see Dt 6:4–5), does not only ask that he be loved with all one's heart, with all one's soul, with all one's strength, but also with all one's mind (*diánoia* is the term that recurs in Mk 12:19, Mt 22:38, Lk 10:27).

In reality, our journey to contemplation and knowledge of God the Trinity is an expression and fruit of our *loving God with intelligence.* First comes the heart, which for the Bible, means the center of our being. Then the soul, which means our life concretely in its humanity (*psyché*), which we have to be ready to postpone and indeed to radically put at risk to follow Jesus: "For those who want to save their life [*psyché*] will lose it, and those who lose their life for my sake, and for the sake of the gospel, will save it" (Mk 8:35). Then further still, one's strength, in other words our energy and our talents. Finally, the intellect. Loving God *with intelligence,* in other words with an increasingly pure, deep, and transparent knowledge of him.

If our faith does not sink into, which means if it does not participate in our flesh and our intelligence, in addition to our life, it is not possible to say that it has reached the center of our being and of our existence to then permeate all its expressions from this point. John Paul II emphasized it incisively: "A faith that does not become culture is a faith which is not fully welcomed, nor is it fully thought out, nor is it faithfully lived."[6]

On the other hand, our knowledge of God is not a sterile fact functioning on its own, independent of the existential and spiritual conditions in which it is exercised. Rather, it requires education and maturation. It

5. This is the theme of his *Deus Caritas Est* (Encyclical Letter, December 25, 2005; available at www.vatican.va). Among other things, Benedict XVI writes, "Love is 'divine' because it comes from God and unites us to God; through this unifying process it makes us a 'we' which transcends our divisions and makes us one, until in the end God is 'all in all' (1 Cor 15:28)" (par. 18); "Love is possible, and we are able to practice it because we are created in the image of God. To experience love and in this way to cause the light of God to enter into the world—this is the invitation I would like to extend with the present Encyclical" (par. 39).

6. "Letter to Cardinal A. Casaroli for the Institution of the Pontifical Council for Culture," May 20, 1982, in *Insegnamenti di Giovanni Paolo II* (Vatican City: LEV, 1982), 2:1777; available at www.vatican.va.

also requires purification because it is always undermined by that temptation to self-affirmation which is idolatry, the opposite of knowing and recognizing God.

So the object is to love God with all one's intelligence so that our knowing God "becomes love."[7] For the disciple of Jesus therefore, that means opening one's mind to Christ before anything else. He is the light illuminating the Father's face. Being united to him does not only mean making room for and welcoming in ourselves his heart, but also his mind. As the apostle Paul attests in fact, by grace, "we have the mind [*noûs*] of Christ" (1 Cor 2:16).

For our intellect to welcome the knowledge of Christ within itself, to progressively make itself "one" with it, our mind must also be "baptized" in his death and resurrection (see Rom 6:3). In other words it must die to itself and live in Christ, of Christ, in accordance with the "formula" of Christian existence which Benedict XVI describes this way: "Paul reveals in the Letter to the Galatians: 'It is no longer I who live, but Christ who lives in me' (Gal 2:20). Hence, the essential identity of my life is changed."[8]

That occurs on the basis of the grace of faith, when the intellect offers itself to Christ out of love in response to his prior, always greater, gift manifested on the cross: "In this is love, not that we loved God but that he loved us and sent his Son to be the atoning sacrifice for our sins" (1 Jn 4:10). So our intelligence "know[s] nothing among you except Jesus Christ, and him crucified" (1 Cor 2:2). And in him it is reborn by the Spirit, in order to know the Father's face with amazement and gratitude.

Thus crucified and risen with Christ, the intellect is purified and enlightened little by little by the Spirit, "that we may understand the gifts bestowed on us by God" (1 Cor 2:12). This is what the apostle Paul describes and testifies in the first Letter to the Corinthians:

> But, as it is written, "What no eye has seen, nor ear heard, nor the human heart conceived, what God has prepared for those who love him." These things God has revealed to us through the Spirit; for the Spirit searches everything, even the depths of God. For what human being knows what is truly human except the human spirit that is within? So also no one comprehends what is truly God's except the Spirit of God. Now we have received not the spirit of the world, but the Spirit that is from God, so that we may understand the gifts bestowed on us by God (1 Cor 2:9–12).

7. This is how Benedict XVI incisively expressed it: "knowing God is not enough. For a true encounter with him one must also love him. Knowledge must become love." "Address during the visit to the Pontifical Gregorian University," November 3, 2006; available at www.vatican.va.

8. Benedict XVI, "Address to the Participants in the Fourth National Ecclesial Convention," Verona, October 19, 2006; available at www.vatican.va.

The Spirit poured out "without measure" (Jn 3:34) by Christ crucified and risen, not only touches the heart and turns it to the Father, not only opens the mind's eyes to contemplate his mystery shining out in Jesus, but with his gifts he makes us penetrate more and more in the bottomless abyss of trinitarian Love.

So knowing God, loving him with all one's mind, means sharing in Christ by grace, in the life and in the knowledge that God has of himself, knowing and loving the Father of light as true children in the Son, in the Spirit's transfiguring communion. Paul writes, "And because you are children, God has sent the Spirit of his Son into our hearts, crying, 'Abba! Father!'" (Gal 4:6).

So the knowledge of God the Trinity essentially is the trinitarian event, in other words, real participation in the Trinity's life. Justly considered the church's first theologian, Irenaeus of Lyons had already written in the second century:

> For this reason the baptism of our regeneration ... takes place through these three articles,[9] granting us regeneration unto God the Father through His Son by the Holy Spirit: for those who bear the Spirit of God are led to the Word, that is to the Son, while the Son presents [them] to the Father, and the Father furnishes ... incorruptibility. Thus, without the Spirit it is not [possible] to see the Word of God, and without the Son one is not able to approach the Father; for the knowledge of the Father [is] the Son, and knowledge of the Son of God is through the Holy Spirit, while the Spirit, according to the good-pleasure of the Father, the Son administers, to whom the Father wills and as He wills.[10]

But another step is still needed. In fact, knowledge of the Trinity is not only a trinitarian event in our own personal and irreplaceable rapport with God. Augustine emphasizes that it is inseparably united with our journey as a community of disciples along the way of reciprocal charity and charity toward everyone, beginning with the smallest (see Mt 25:40). This is the church's "way" marked out by Jesus "once for all" (see Heb 7:27) as he reveals the mystery of the Trinity to us.

The fact is that faith in Jesus attests that love for God—and indissolubly linked with that, love for neighbor—establish the precise and original "theological place" for knowledge of God. Love for neighbor, the commandment promulgated by God in the First Testament (Lv 19:18) on the basis of the universal progressive experience of the "golden rule" known in

9. Irenaeus of Lyons is referring to Christ's mandate which is in the rhythm of the three verbs (to go, to teach, to baptize); it is specified by faith in the Father, in the Son and in the Holy Spirit: "Go therefore and make disciples of all nations, baptizing them in the name of the Father and of the Son and of the Holy Spirit" (Mt 28:19).

10. Irenaeus of Lyons, *Epideixis* 7; *On the Apostolic Preaching*, trans. John Behr (Crestwood, N.Y.: St. Vladimir's Seminary Press, 1997).

all the religious traditions ("do not do to others what you would not want done to yourself"), gets its perfection in fact with the New Testament (see 1 Jn 4:12) in the Gospel law of reciprocal love.

This is the commandment which Jesus defines as his and new—the commandment of the fullness of times, shaped by the measure of Jesus' love for us. "This is my commandment, that you love one another as I have loved you. No one has greater love than this, to lay down one's life for one's friends" (Jn 15:12–13). "Beloved, since God loved us so much, we also ought to love one another. No one has ever seen God; if we love one another, God lives in us, and his love is perfected in us" (1 Jn 4:11–12). So the fruit and the evidence of God's love for us, and of our love for God, is love among brothers and sisters: "We know that we have passed from death to life because we love one another" (1 Jn 3:14); "No one has ever seen God; if we love one another, God lives in us, and his love is perfected in us" (1 Jn 4:12).

This is a love that takes initiative and it is gratuitous because it expresses the Father's and the Son's love; they were the first to love us (see Jn 4:19). It is a love that attains its "perfection," in other words its complete expression (see Jn 4:12), there where it becomes reciprocal upon enkindling a response.

Because it is love, it is loving and being loved, becoming one in love: Father, Son, and Holy Spirit. This is what God's being indicates; being love (see 1 Jn 4:8, 16), it is Trinity. This is not to be closed within this circle of love, which would not be true love in such a case, love which is from God, love which is God. On the contrary, it is to be communicated, poured out, and intensified to infinity. So the *via caritatis* toward God and among us, in reciprocity and toward everyone, is the royal way to knowledge of God the Trinity, as Augustine sensed.

In fact reciprocal love expresses a specific experience and in itself it is the cause of some precise, demanding requirements on the level of the exercise of knowing as well. In fact, dialogue—the exercise of knowing and saying (*lógos*) in the reciprocity of research and communion among (*diá*) those who journey together along the way of the truth (Plato's seventh letter teaches this in a masterly way)—is the privileged path leading to knowledge of the truth.[11] When it is lived in Christ, it releases his truth and trinitarian treasure.

In fact, what does speaking become when it is lived in Christ, if not a gift of love of what is sought in God and what comes to be known by

11. "For it [the highest truths, philosophy's object] does not admit of exposition like other branches of knowledge; but after much converse about the matter itself and a life lived together, suddenly a light, as it were, is kindled in one soul by a flame that leaps to it from another, and thereafter sustains itself" (*Epistle VII*, 341C–D, trans. J. Harward). See also my *Teo-logia*, 18–19.

grace? And what is listening in Christ if not welcoming such a gift in love, to then offer a gift in turn of what the Spirit inspires in us? And what is the dialogical relationship that comes to be established among those that speak and those that listen reciprocally, if not communion and communication in the Holy Spirit?

"That they may all be one. As you, Father, are in me and I am in you, may they also be in us" (Jn 17:21). As his "hour" was approaching, Jesus' prayer to the Father said in an extraordinary synthesis that the unity of the Father, Son, and Spirit in love is the source, the dwelling, and the goal of our life. At the same time, he said that reciprocal love lived in Christ to the point of unity, is the place where the unity of the Father and the Son in the Holy Spirit is made manifest and tangible in the world.

Even better, it could undoubtedly be affirmed that the pertinent subject for knowledge of God the Trinity is being "one in Christ Jesus" (Gal 3:28). Benedict XVI explains:

> "It is no longer I who live, but Christ who lives in me" (Gal 2:20). Hence, the essential identity of my life is changed through Baptism, and I continue to exist only in this changed state. My own self is taken away and I am filled with a new and greater subject, in which my "I" is still there but transformed, purified, "open" through the insertion into the Other, who acquires new space in my existence. Thus, we become "one in Christ" (Gal 3:28), a unique new subject, and our "I" is freed from its isolation.[12]

Only in this way can someone truly be in Christ as Christ is in the Father: "so that the love with which you have loved me may be in them, and I in them" (Jn 17:26). So even the dialogue among the disciples, like each one's dialogue in prayer with the Father, must acquire Christ's form and breathe the Spirit's breath in order to open access to the Father.

This means once more passing by means of faith—in relationship with the faith community—through an ever new and true Paschal mystery of the death and resurrection of our existence. This includes our knowledge consequently as well. When Paul wants to offer a model and measure for the life of communion (*koinōnía*) among the disciples in accordance with God's design, it is not by chance that he looks to Christ and to Christ crucified who "empties" himself even of what is most precious to him—union with the Father—to identify himself with us and thus communicate the life he had received from the Father (Phil 2:1–10):

> If then there is any encouragement in Christ, any consolation from love, any sharing in the Spirit [*koinōnía*], any compassion and sympathy, make my joy complete: be of the same mind, having the same love, being in full accord and of one

12. Benedict XVI, "Address to the Participants in the Fourth National Ecclesial Convention."

mind. Do nothing from selfish ambition or conceit, but in humility regard others as better than yourselves. Let each of you look not to your own interests, but to the interests of others. Let the same mind be in you [*toûto phroneîte*] that was in Christ Jesus, who, though he was in the form of God, did not regard equality with God as something to be exploited, but emptied himself [*eautòn ekénōsen*], taking the form of a slave, being born in human likeness. And being found in human form, he humbled himself and became obedient to the point of death—even death on a cross. Therefore God also highly exalted him and gave him the name that is above every name, so that at the name of Jesus every knee should bend, in heaven and on earth and under the earth.

For Paul, "thinking and acting" (*phroneîn*) like Christ means considering the others as superior to oneself. It seems a paradox: to love the other *as* oneself, it is necessary to lower oneself, to put oneself on a lower level, like he who came down from heaven to put himself on our level. Out of love indeed, he stripped himself of what belonged to him because of his divine condition in order to "identify himself" with us and thus, from underneath and from within, to bring us with him into communion with the Father.

Dialogue as an expression of the *via caritatis* to know God, lived in the school of Christ as teacher (see Mt 23:8), is a demanding way. It requires death to self, to the "old man" with his thoughts and his desires, in the ongoing exercise of love for God and the brothers and sisters, and in the ability to recognize and love Christ's cross, even more the face itself of Christ crucified in the inevitable difficulties, exhaustion, trials, and shadows.

So dialogue, woven with words and listening in that constantly renewed communication which is an effusive experience of reciprocity, becomes the trinitarian event. It becomes a fragile and humble dwelling where the risen Jesus becomes present himself to walk in the midst of his own (see Mt 18:20), with his Spirit enlightening minds and warming hearts, as it happened to the disciples on the way to Emmaus: "Were not our hearts burning within us while he was talking to us on the road, while he was opening the scriptures to us?" (Lk 24:32).

Ultimately, knowledge of God the Trinity is nothing other than the understanding and the communication about gradually becoming participants in that ecclesial "we" which is being "one in Christ Jesus" and in him, one with the Father. This is my prayer. This is my wish: that the journey undertaken along these pages could be a journey taken together, a journey of life and light, because it is nourished and enlightened by the love of Jesus who introduces us in the Holy Spirit into the Father's bosom to make us see each reality anew, from him.

Faithful to this subject, enlightened by the Spirit, we will try to listen to the witness of what God has communicated to us about himself in Jesus and what the experience and the intelligence of men and women have lived and said about him through the centuries: in the church, through scripture and tradition. And this pertains not only to theology but to the spiritual and mystical dimensions as well. We will also listen and learn from the church's encounter with culture, religious wisdom, and philosophy.

Our journey will take us through five stages. Each of these will be articulated through one principal development of the discussion, and within a few breaks dedicated to studying specific emerging themes little by little. In the first stage I will try to offer a general introduction of a methodological character regarding the Christian understanding of the mystery of God. In particular, I will articulate what characterizes an approach of faith. I will contextualize the discussion in the present, focusing on the method required to be followed, taking into consideration the gains and issues brought out by the trinitarian theology of our times.

Then I will develop three stages, recovering and updating the memory of the revelation of the Christian God, initially dwelling on the First Testament promise, and will then concentrate on the fullness of times in the event of Jesus Christ, the living and always present center of our entire journey, to finally retrace the important episodes and some of the more significant figures in Christian tradition and in the history of thought that dialogues with revelation. Enriched by the journey undertaken, returning to the point from where we took our first steps, I will offer in the fifth and last stage some perspectives for integration, study, and relaunching, with an attentive look at the challenges of our history. We will be open with hope to the happy goal and promise of our common destiny.

PART I

THE LOCUS

The Meaning and Method of Trinitarian Theology

For where two or three are gathered in my name, I am there among them.

—Matthew 18:20

I explain below the first stage of the journey as a perspectival outlook: (1) on the specific and original meaning along with the theological locus of the trinitarian truth; (2) on the historical and cultural context for this truth today; and (3) on the theological method to understand and communicate this truth. I begin with the faith professed by the church. From a methodological perspective, I begin with what twentieth-century trinitarian theology has left us: with its positive contributions, but also its unresolved questions.

Reflection on the meaning of trinitarian faith is aimed at appreciating what distinguishes the Christian approach to the mystery of God and its original interpretive key. Recalling the theological locus and its context will help us to locate ourselves with relevance respectively in the ecclesial and historical-cultural horizon of our investigation. Thirdly, my comments on method will provide some data needed to structure the later stages in the journey, both in its historical and systematic aspects. This first part will set out the coordinates for the point of departure and prospects for the development of trinitarian theology in the context of the church's faith as lived in our time.

CHAPTER 1

The Meaning and Theological Locus of Faith in God the Trinity

The specific object of this book is God revealed in Jesus Christ. The point of departure is the Christian faith lived in the church. This is expressed in the following profession: we believe in one God: Father, Son, and Holy Spirit. For this, all we have to do, along with the *Catechism of the Catholic Church*, is to point to the Apostles' Creed, to the baptismal creed of the church of Rome, and to the Nicene-Constantinopolitan Creed that emerged from the first two Ecumenical Councils (325 and 381) common to all the churches and ecclesial communities of the East and West.[1]

The ancient baptismal formula placed by Matthew in the mouth of the risen Jesus as he sends forth his disciples to the nations (see Mt 28:29) confirms the centrality of trinitarian faith as defining the Christian identity. According to this formula, "Christians are baptized in the name of the Father and of the Son and of the Holy Spirit: not in their names, for there is only one God, the almighty Father, his only begotten Son, and the Holy Spirit: the Most Holy Trinity."[2] In a particular and clear way, Christian existence bears with it the indelible seal of the Trinity, as shown by both the sacrament of baptism giving entry to the life and community of Jesus Christ, and the Creed professing the central content of faith. The sign of the cross too like a summary of Christian prayer traces the trinitarian movement of baptism and of the profession of faith. The gesture is clearly linked with the cross of Jesus, suggesting that the cross is the expressive image in history of the trinitarian face of God; it should shine out from our existence.

It should be clear that, starting from the Christian faith in God, one and three, I do not intend to exclude other ways and manners of approaching the mystery of God, whether philosophical or religious. Later I will say something about these in order to acknowledge what distin-

1. See the *Catechism of the Catholic Church* [hereafter *CCC*], nos. 194–95.
2. *CCC*, no. 233.

guishes them, along with their relation to the Christian and theological approaches. I intend to consciously start with my own specific adherence to and experience of faith. This kind of beginning can also be doubly justified from an epistemological viewpoint, where discourse on God should express publicly the reasons why it makes sense and claims to be true.

On the one hand, there is a hermeneutic justification: every human discourse, including discourse on God, starts off from a presupposition, a given vital intellectual horizon within a human and cultural tradition within which each of us responsibly thinks and acts. On the other hand, this starting point also has—before everything, from my specific viewpoint—a theological justification belonging to the Christian faith of which I am fully aware. According to this, Jesus Christ is the unique, universal, and eschatological revelation of God the Trinity faithfully conserved and handed on by the faith of the church.

For the most part I have to take as presupposed these two distinct and related justifications, basic to my whole discussion, because they are taught, articulated, and justified in another disciplinary context, that of fundamental theology.[3] While I will not explicitly focus on them, this does not rule out that they can be confirmed and verified throughout this journey.

The Two Assertions of Christian Faith in God the Trinity

Let us now turn to the formula I have already quoted. Already in a first analysis, the profession of faith in God revealed by Jesus Christ—Father, Son, and Holy Spirit—inseparably connects two theological assertions expressing God's revelation of himself, and how as such they are received in faith. The first affirms the uniqueness and unity of God: God is one and only one. Monotheism is the great inheritance that, as Christians, we receive from the revelation of the First Testament which we thus have in common with Judaism and also, though in a different form, with Islam.[4] The second affirms the specific originality of Christianity in relation to any other form of monotheism, particularly compared to Judaic and Islamic monotheism, as Christian monotheism is a trinitarian monotheism: we believe in a God who is unique and one and as such is Father, Son, and Holy Spirit.[5]

3. See particularly, on all of this, the solid and well-argued approach in Pierangelo Sequeri's fine essay, *Il Dio affidabile: Saggio di teologia fondamentale* (Brescia: Queriniana, 1996).

4. The *CCC* remarks on this: "The confession of God's oneness, which has its roots in the divine revelation of the Old Covenant, is inseparable from the profession of God's existence and is equally fundamental" (no. 200).

5. Caesar of Arles (fifth-sixth century): "Fides omnium christianorum in Trinitate consistit" /

The Various Meanings of Monotheism

The concept of monotheism is undoubtedly basic for understanding and expressing the identity of the revelation of and in Jesus Christ in relation to its trinitarian aspect.[6] Further on, regarding the First Testament (see part 2, below), I will discuss biblical monotheism, but it will be useful to distinguish here between the various meanings that are given to monotheism and to its principal expressions. The notion of monotheism is rather vague, often used imprecisely and even ambiguously. Because of the frequently indiscriminate critique it receives at present, it is worth examining. To try to clarify and begin a deeper study, we can place the question of monotheism in at least three distinct contexts: (1) the history of religions, (2) Greek-Hellenistic philosophy, and (3) the event of revelation. Then we can proceed and clarify its explicit relationship with Judeo-Christian revelation.

According to the History of Religions

The term and notion of monotheism were imposed and disseminated in the history of religion from the second half of the nineteenth century. But it is found for the first time in the second half of the seventeenth century, in the wake of terms like polytheism and atheism, in the work of Cambridge Platonist Henry More (1614–87).[7] He meant by monotheism the kind of religion that was not quantitatively different from polytheism, as recognizing only one god rather than a plurality of gods, but qualitatively: monotheism affirms that unicity is an essential attribute of such a god (indicated by the choice of *mónos* rather than *eís*). Research

"The faith of all Christians rests on the Trinity" (*Expositio symboli* [*sermo 9*], in Corpus Christianorum, Series Latina no. 103.48); see *CCC*, no. 232.

6. For a thematic and bibliographic introduction to the question, see the entries on "Monotheism" by R. Hülsewiesche, in *Historisches Wörterbuch der Philosophie*, ed. J. Ritter et al. (Basel: Schwabe, 1971), 142–46; T. M. Ludwig, in *The Encyclopedia of Religion*, ed. M. Eliade (New York: Macmillan, 1987), 10:68–76; B. Lang, in *Handbuch der religionswissenschaftlicher Grundbegriffe*, with G. Kehrer, H. G. Klippenberg, M. Laubscher, H. Cancik, B. Gladigow and K.-H. Kohl (Stuttgart: Kohlhammer, 1998), 4:146–65; Th. Birkheuser, in *Nuovo Dizionario delle Religioni*, ed. H. Waldenfels (Cinisello Balsamo: San Paolo, 1993), 621–23; and in *Grande Dizionario delle Religioni*, ed. P. Poupard (Casale Monferrato: Piemme, 2000). Among recent theological reassessments, see *Concilium* 21, no. 1 (1985): *Il monoteismo*; Yves Labbé, *Essai sur le monothéisme trinitaire* (Paris: Cerf, 1987); Paul Beauchamp et al., *Monothéisme et trinité* (Brussels: Facultés universitaires Saint-Louis, 1991); Italian Theological Association, *Monoteismo cristiano e monoteismi*, ed. G. Cereti (Cinisello Balsamo: San Paolo, 2001); Vittorio Possenti et al., *Il monoteismo* (Milan: Mondadori, 2002); Mariano Crociata (ed.), *Il Dio di Gesù Cristo e i monoteismi* (Rome: Città Nuova–Facoltà di Sicilia, 2003); and my "Trinità e monoteismo," in *Il logos e il nulla: Trinità, religioni, mistica* (Rome: Città Nuova, 2003), 288–316.

7. Henry More, *An Explanation of the Grand Mystery of Godliness* (Bristol: Thoemmes, 1997); see Roberto Bondì, *L'onnipresenza di Dio: saggio su Henry More* (Soveria Mannelli: Rubbettino, 2001).

into the relation between polytheism and monotheism continued in the eighteenth century. It tended to show monotheism's superiority, and in the atmosphere of the Enlightenment, its consonance with the supreme and universal principles of reason. As it was considered by David Hume (1711–76) in his *The Natural History of Religion*, Voltaire (1694–1778) in his *Dictionnaire philosophique*,[8] Jean-Jacques Rousseau (1712–78) in his *Emile*,[9] and Immanuel Kant (1724–1804) in his *Critique of Pure Reason*.[10]

These clearly aprioristic historical-religious propositions are taken up in the nineteenth century by Auguste Comte in his *Cours de philosophie positive* (1830–44). With his three progressive stages of the development of reason (theological, metaphysical, positive) he notes the passage in the first stage from fetishism to polytheism to arrive finally at monotheism. This evolutionistic framework is developed, from a positivistic viewpoint, by the newborn sciences of religion, particularly by cultural anthropology, which attempts to verify the proposition by ethnographic field research. For example, one of the founders of cultural anthropology, Edward Burnett Tylor (1832–1917) saw in "animism" the basis for all religious belief, from which polytheism emerged, and finally, monotheism.[11]

In contrast to this approach, which prevailed for a long time, Andrew Lang (1845–1912) and especially Wilhelm Schmidt (1868–1954) through their ethnographic research sought to establish the existence of an "originary monotheism."[12] This would be consistent with the affirmation and worship of a supreme being in many, if not in all, primitive cultures, originating—according to Schmidt—in a primitive revelation. Raffaele Pettazzoni (1883–1959), a historian of religions, opposed Schmidt's "originary monotheism" because of its apologetic aims, and because this hypothesis lacked historical evidence.[13] Pettazzoni can be credited in par-

8. "Polytheism was the first religion of men ... they began by believing in many gods, before reason became more illuminated, until they came to recognize one supreme Being." *Réligions* (Paris, 1764).

9. "Polytheism was their first religion and idolatry, their first cult. They would only have been able to recognize one God when, gradually generalizing their ideas, they were able to get back to a first cause, uniting the complete system of reality under just one idea." *Émile ou de l'éducation* (1762), in *Oeuvres complètes* (Paris: Gallimard, 1969), 4:552.

10. "In all peoples we see shimmering a few sparks of monotheism, to which they have been led not by reflection and deep speculation, but only in accordance with a natural course of common understanding becoming gradually more intelligible." Immanuel Kant, *The Critique of Pure Reason*, trans. and ed. Paul Guyer and Allen W. Wood (Cambridge: Cambridge University Press, 1998), "Transcendental dialectic," §3: "The grounds of proofs of speculative reason inferring the existence of a highest being" (563). F. W. J. Schelling opens up a speculative perspective in his Munich lectures on monotheism from 1828 published posthumously in his *Sämmtliche Werke* (Stuttgart: Cotta, 1856–61), 12:3–131.

11. See Edward B. Tylor, *Primitive Culture* (1871), in *The Collected Works of Edward Burnett Tylor*, vols. III–IV (London: Routledge, 1994).

12. Wilhelm Schmidt, *Der Ursprung der Gottesidee* (Münster: Aschendorff, 1912).

13. See especially Raffaele Pettazzoni, *Dio: Formazione e sviluppo del monoteismo nella storia delle religioni* (Rome: Athaeneum, 1922); *L'onniscienza di Dio* (Turin: Einaudi, 1955); *L'essere supremo nelle religioni primitive* (Turin: Einaudi, 1957).

ticular with demonstrating the strict connection between the affirmation of monotheism and the notion of an omniscient and transcendent God, a notion which is not the result of an evolution, but of a true and real "revolution," "a historical fact rarely occurring, and each time it does it is due to the intervention of a great religious personality (Moses, Jesus, Mohammed, Zoroaster)."[14]

At present, the originary monotheism and evolutionist approaches are both rejected because of their one-sidedness and their polar opposition. Both have ideological starting points. Originary monotheism is a projection backward from Judeo-Christian monotheism, while the evolutionist approach interprets the movement from the less to the more defined only as an increase of human self-awareness. In fact we can find the cult of a supreme god in populations still at their very first cultural stage, often represented by the sky or the sun. Among the Indo-European languages, for example, *div-* and *dyu* indicate light, splendor, day, from which are derived the Latin *dies* and *deus*. St. Francis of Assisi too, in his *Canticle of the Creatures*, recognizes that the sun is "porta significatione" of the most high.

In other cases, recognition of a supreme god comes from the negation of an earlier polytheistic cult. This happens with the religious reform of Pharaoh Akhenaton (Amenophis IV) in Egypt (1364–1347 BCE). He professed belief in only one god, Aton, who manifested himself in the solar disk and in the light emanating from it. Aton was however inaccessibly distanced from all men except the Pharaoh, who represented him on earth. This kind of monotheism, however, quickly died out along with its founder.[15] Zoroaster's monotheism in Iran (between the seventh and sixth centuries BCE), adored as supreme divinity the Lord Wisdom (*Ahura Mazda*), who is at the origin of the universe, of which he is sovereign, despite the aggressive antagonism of the evil spirit (*Angra Mainyu*, then *Ahriman*).[16]

A separate, more recent approach, "inclusive" monotheism, can be found in some modern streams of Hinduism, which sets off from more ancient polytheistic representations, either through the fusion of different divinities or through the quest for an originary foundation of the universe.

14. Raffaele Pettazzoni, "Monoteismo," in *Enciclopedia Italiana* (Treccani), XXIII (1949), col. 699; about Pettazzoni, see Giuseppe Mihelcic, *Una religione di libertà* (Rome: Città Nuova, 2003).

15. Erik Hornung, *Gli dèi dell'antico Egitto* (Rome: Salerno, 1992), 158; see also his *Akhenaton: La religione della luce nell'antico Egitto* (Rome: Salerno, 1998); Jan Assmann, *Mosè l'egizio* (Milan: Adelphi, 2000).

16. Zoroastrian researchers however do not agree on Zoroastrian monotheism, as a dualistic interpretation is possible: see James W. Boyd and Donald A. Crosby, "Is Zoroastrianism Dualistic or Monotheistic?," *Journal of the American Academy of Religion* 47, no. 80 (1979): 577–88; Giovanni Filoramo, "La risposta dualistica al problema del male," in *Male, Bibbia e Occidente*, ed. P. Lombardi (Brescia: Morcelliana, 2000), 11–20.

This latter quest most often links the characteristics of the metaphysical principle of reality with personal traits, at least from the viewpoint of human perception. "This divinity alone exists before the world and the other gods, constituting itself as the source of all being. Without beginning, incorruptible, it is all knowing and all powerful, independent and in control of everything."[17] Vishnuism linked with the cult of Vishnu was especially affirmed in this context, along with Shivaism linked with the cult of Shiva.

We definitely have to study each religious form without constructing *a priori* notions of them. What can be concluded, thanks to the contribution by the sciences of religion, is that there is an original form of perception, representation, and cult of the supreme being.[18] Along with this there are later conscious forms of recognition of it, where wisdom reflections and political and state interests also enter into play (for example, justification of the political institution of the monarchy based on the "monarchy" of the first principle of the universe).[19] But in both cases we cannot speak of explicit, rigorous monotheism, definitively professed by a religious faith, in the sense that will gradually develop in the history of Israel. From the viewpoint of phenomenology and the religious history of humanity, what is decisive in monotheism's appearance and establishment, is in fact revelation—that is, the personal, precise, and progressive intervention of God himself in human history.[20]

In Greek Philosophy

The question of the unity of God takes another form when we enter the world of Greek philosophy.[21] Here, it is the critique of religion and its

17. Heinrich von Stietencron, *Der Hinduismus* (Munich: Beck, 2001), 38–39.

18. The most characteristic form of this is the "heavenly God" with the attributes of transcendence and morality. Starting from R. Pettazzoni's suggestions, both Eliade and Goetz agree: see Mircea Eliade, *Patterns in Comparative Religion* (London: Sheed and Ward, 1971), and Joseph Goetz, *L'esperienza di Dio nei primitivi*, trans. Bruno Marra (Brescia: Morcelliana, 1983).

19. See the classic essay on this by Erik Peterson, *Der monotheismus als politischen Problem?* (Leipzig: Hegner, 1935).

20. In the context of his specific hermeneutic of religious reality, Mircea Eliade also notes this in his *Storia delle credenze e delle idee religiose*, where, referring to Abraham, he remarks that, "here we are faced with a new kind of religious experience: 'Abrahamic faith,' as it was understood after Moses, which gradually becomes the religious experience specific to Judaism and Christianity" and that "the transformation of the cosmic type of religious structure through the events of sacred history characteristic of Yahwist monotheism will then be taken up and brought ahead by Christianity" (Florence: Sansoni, 1990), 1:191, 199. On his part, A. Di Nola says that "the term monotheism refers to the religious ideologies that affirm the oneness of God and are based on the cult of one God alone. Rigorous application of the term leads to the conclusion that only the religions deriving from Judaism (Christianity, Islam and related movements) can be called monotheistic, since only Judaism, in terms of textual documentation and theological elaboration, arrives at an *absolute* monotheism." "Monoteismo e idea di Dio," in *Enciclopedia delle Religioni*, 4:658.

21. See the classic study of the notion of God in the Greek world by Werner Jaeger, *The Theology of the Early Greek Philosophers* (1936), trans. Edward S. Robinson (Eugene, Ore.: Wipf and Stock Publishers, 2003); W. Bröcker, *Politische Theologie* (Frankfurt a.M.: Klostermann, 1980);

mythological expression (beginning with Xenophanes of Colophon, 570/65–475 BCE) that opens the way to the affirmation of God as the *hèn kaì pân*, the all-one: "One God is greatest among gods and men, not like mortals in body or thought."[22] Similarly, for example, in Parmenides's mystic-speculative vision (520–440 BCE).[23]

Plato (427–348/47 BCE) and Aristotle (384/83–322 BCE) arrive at an explicit affirmation of the unique principle of the *kósmos* with decisive consequences for the development of Western thought. In Plato this is the Good, not by chance assimilated to the Sun in the great *Republic* dialogue,[24] and the One, present especially in the so-called unwritten doctrines[25] further taken up and clarified by Plotinus (203/4–269/70 CE). Aristotle writes of the "unmoved mover" in *Metaphysics* XII.[26] But in neither case can we speak of monotheism.

For example, Aristotle admits a certain number of divinities (forty-seven or fifty-five, according to the number of heavenly spheres) that, while ontologically subordinate to the first mover, have the same divine rank. Elsewhere he speaks constantly of other gods.[27] Nor, as N. Abbagnano, historian of philosophy points out,

> should we confuse the insistence of Plotinus and the Neoplatonists in general on the *unity* of God with a recognition of the *unicity* of God. God is one, rather he is the one, because he is the unity of the world and the source of all the orders of reality that derive or emanate from it. But this is precisely because it is not alone: unity does not eliminate multiplicity but gathers it into itself.[28]

---

and, in general, "Gli dei e il Dio: La teologia greca," in *Il sapere degli antichi*, ed. M. Vegetti (Turin: Boringhieri, 1985), 295–318.

22. Diels, 21 B 23.

23. Parmenides describes what he calls "IS" like this: "IS uncreated and imperishable, whole, unmoved, and without end. And it was not, and it will not be, for it is altogether now . . . one [*hén*], continuous" (*Perì phýseōs*, fr. 7/8).

24. See Plato, *Republic* VI.508c: "As goodness [*tagathòn*] stands in the intelligible realm to intelligence and the things we know, so in the visible realm the sun stands to sight and the things we see." As translated by Robin Waterfield (New York: Oxford University Press, 1994).

25. The Platonic *Parmenides* dialogue is full of consequences; it all turns on the metaphysical question of the "one." See Massimo Donà, *Aporie platoniche: Saggio sul "Parmenide"* (Rome: Città Nuova, 2003).

26. On one hand Aristotle affirms that, "first essence [*tò tí hên heinai*] has not matter, for it is pure act. So the unmovable first mover is one both in definition and in number, and thus is one whatever is moved always and continuously by Him" (1074a36–39). On the other hand, he says that, "we must regard this [mythical] affirmation that the first substances are gods as an inspired utterance" (1074b9–10). It is also significant that he concludes the treatment of Book XII with a quotation from Homer's *Iliad* II.204): "The rule of many is not good; let there be one ruler" (1076a4).

27. See Aristotle, *Nicomachean Ethics* X.9.1179a24; *Metaphysics* I.2.983a11 and III.2.907b10. Besides, as Barbera Botter has recently shown in her *Dio e Divino in Aristotele* (Sankt Augustin: Academia Verlag, 2005), in Aristotle and generally in the other Greek philosophers, the term "god" is not used as a proper name, nor generally as a substantive, but as an attribute or predicate indicating a grade of excellence in an ordered scale of beings. So it can be attributed to the gods of the traditional religions, but also to the stars, to the entire cosmos, to the human intellect and even to the first unmoved mover.

28. Nicola Abbagnano, "God," in *Dizionario di Filosofia* (Turin: UTET, 1971), 243.

For example, Plotinus writes:

It is not by crushing the divine [*tò Theîon*] into a unity [*eis hén*] but by displaying its exuberance [*polý*]—as the Supreme himself has displayed it—that we show knowledge of the might of God, who, abidingly what He is, yet creates that multitude, all dependent on Him, existing by Him and from Him. This Universe, too, exists by Him and looks to Him—the Universe as a whole and every god within it—and tells of Him to men, all alike revealing the plan and will of the Supreme.[29]

In Greek philosophy, then, we cannot speak of monotheism proper, as (1) there is not unicity of God, (2) nor a definitive and recognized otherness of his personality in relation to the cosmos and to man, (3) nor, finally, as a result, is there an affirmation of the principle of creation.

In Abrahamic Revelation

For Israel there is the unforeseen and unforeseeable event of the revelation of God, which gives rise firstly to the experience and then the conscious and formal affirmation of the uniqueness and the unity of God. Without going into a detailed discussion,[30] it is enough here to emphasize that what is decisive is the initiative of the living God and Lord, who inaugurates a covenant of salvation in history with his people, and through this covenant, reveals himself as the unique, true God. The historical and dialogical nature of the covenant marks the space in which the following is perceptibly and explicitly affirmed: (1) the otherness of God in relation to the world, (2) his gratuitous nearness to man but also to the world, (3) his absolute and universal lordship over the world and history, expressed in the principle of creation, and (4) the resulting nullity of the other gods. In a word, the unicity of God is revealed to Israel (YHWH) as savior and creator.

As a result, if "revelation" is strictly defined, then monotheism refers to Jewish, Christian, and also Islamic faith. All of these recognize themselves in that story of God's revelation that begins with the calling

29. Plotinus, *Enneads* II.9.9.35–40; trans. Stephen MacKenna, fourth edition revised by B. S. Page (London: Faber and Faber Limited, 1969), 141 (parentheses added in reference to the original in Greek).

30. The formation of the historic emergence of monotheism in Israel, as is well known, is a difficult and complex issue. For an introduction, see N. Lohfink, E. Zenger, G. Braulik, and J. Scharbert, *Dio l'Unico: Sulla nascita del monoteismo in Israele* (Brescia: Morcelliana, 1991), the Italian translation of *Gott, der einzig: Zur Entstehung des Monotheismus in Israel* (Freiburg: Herder, 1985), 9–53 and 115–92; G. L. Prato, "L'attuale ricerca sul monoteismo ebraico biblico," in Italian Theological Association, *Monoteismo cristiano e monoteismi*, 37–57, with extensive bibliography on 58–65; O. Loretz, *Des Gottes Einzigkeit: Ein altorientalisches Argumentationsmodell zum 'Schma Jisrael* (Darmstadt: Wissenschaftliche Buchgesellschaft, 1997). R. Albertz conducts a fascinating investigation in *Religionsgeschichte Israels in alttestamentlicher Zeit*, 2, *Vom Exil zu den Makkabäern* (Göttingen: Vandenhoeck and Ruprecht, 1997).

of Abraham, narrated in the Book of Genesis, then taking shape in the later history of Israel. Onto that story were grafted in different ways the revelation of Jesus Christ as well as the Koranic tradition.

As I have said, Christian monotheism relates differently to Hebrew than it does to Islamic monotheism. With Jewish monotheism there is a common root and an inalienable continuity, even if the revelation of Jesus Christ brings with it a new, specific, and determining element of originality—the Trinity—along with an eschatological factor, insofar as Jesus Christ is recognized as the full and definitive revelation of God in history.[31] The case with Islam is more complex, as on the one hand we have to appreciate what the Koran, Islam's sacred book, derives from the preceding Hebraic and Christian revelations, and on the other hand, what is specific to Mohammed's religious inspiration, as delivered to the Koran itself.[32]

Between Reason and Revelation

Taking into account what I have said up to now, a question arises that is worth at least noting: is a rigorous, convinced, rational affirmation of the unicity of God possible, prescinding from his historical revelation? Christian tradition, on biblical grounds (see Wis 13:1–9; Rom 1:20), clearly affirms this as intrinsically connected with the rational affirmation of the existence of God.[33]

It is enough to quote one dogmatically authoritative text, the dogmatic constitution *Dei Filius* of Vatican I (1870). This takes up Thomas Aquinas's argument. Having said that "the holy apostolic Roman Church believes and confesses that there is *only one God* living and true (*unum Deum verum et vivum*), Creator and Lord of heaven and earth," it specifies:

> The same Holy Mother Church holds and teaches that God, the beginning and end of all things, can be known with certainty by the natural light of human reason from created things; "Ever since the creation of the world his eternal power and divine nature, invisible though they are, have been understood and seen through the things he has made" [Rom 1:20]; nevertheless, it has pleased His

31. See the relevant interpretive approaches offered in Pontifical Biblical Commission, "The Jewish People and their Sacred Scriptures in the Christian Bible" (2001); available at www.vatican.va.

32. See Claude Geffré, "Il Dio Uno dell'Islam e il monoteismo trinitario," *Concilium* 37, no. 1 (2001): 116–26. On the difference between these various forms of monotheism, even though deriving from a single source, see Rémi Brague, *Il Dio dei cristiani: L'Unico Dio?* (Milan: Raffaele Cortina, 2009).

33. Wis 13:1: "For all people who were ignorant of God were foolish by nature; and they were unable from the good things that are seen to know the one who exists, nor did they recognize the artisan while paying heed to his works"; Rom 1:20: "Ever since the creation of the world his eternal power and divine nature, invisible though they are, have been understood and seen through the things he has made. So they are without excuse."

wisdom and goodness to reveal Himself and the eternal decrees of His will to the human race in another and supernatural way, as the Apostle says: "Long ago God spoke to our ancestors in many and various ways by the prophets, but in these last days he has spoken to us by a Son" [Heb 1:1–2]. Indeed, it must be attributed to this divine revelation that those things, which in divine things are not impenetrable to human reason by itself, can, even in this present condition of the human race, be known readily by all with firm certainty and with no admixture of error. Nevertheless, it is not for this reason that revelation is said to be absolutely necessary, but because God in His infinite goodness has ordained man for a supernatural end, to participation, namely, in the divine goods which altogether surpass the understanding of the human mind.[34]

Human beings are defined here with special vigor, as *capax Dei*: insofar as they are created by God to know him and freely share in his life. In itself, this includes, in the very dynamism of the human person's existence, the capacity and intentionality of perceiving, recognizing, and affirming through a correct exercise of intellect and freedom the existence and unicity of God as the being that is the principle and final end of the created word. St. Thomas—assumed by *Dei Filius* in this as well—realistically explains that in fact such knowledge is possible only for a few, after a long time and with mistakes. Because of this, with his revelation, God came to the aid of man wounded by sin to open up for him the sure way of knowing his existence and will.[35] This does not mean misunderstanding or repressing man's cognitive potential, but redeeming and strengthening its full and correct exercise. On the other hand, God's revelation that culminates with Christ illuminates those depths of the mystery of God (see 1 Cor 2:10) which in themselves are inaccessible to reason alone, but which God gratuitously wishes his creatures to share in, which is the end for which they were created by him.

Vatican I's affirmation, understood historically, means concretely that certain knowledge of the existence of the unicity of God, even if possible for reason in its natural exercise, is strictly bound to revelation. The path of Western thought shows this in capital letters. In fact, the precise and conscious affirmation of the unicity of God, creator and Lord of the universe, thanks to revelation, matures in the history of the people of Israel up to Jesus Christ, to then be transmitted to successive theological and philosophical reflection of Christian inspiration. In dialogue with Greek philosophy, this reflection leads to the theoretically rigorous affirmation

34. Heinrich Denzinger, *Compendium of Creeds, Definitions, and Declarations on Matters of Faith and Morals*, ed. Peter Hünermann for the original bilingual edition and ed. Robert Fastiggi and Anne Englund Nash for the English edition, 43rd ed. (San Francisco, Calif.: Ignatius Press, 2012), nos. 3001 and 3004–5 [hereafter DH]; what is essential in this doctrine is taken up in Vatican Council II, *Dei Verbum*, November 18, 1965 [hereafter *DV*], no. 6 (available at www.vatican.va.).

35. See *Summa Theologiae* I, q. 1, a. 1 [hereafter *ST*]; *Summa Contra Gentiles* I, chap. 4.

of the existence and unicity of God as *ipsum esse per se subsistens*, along with God's freedom and gratuity in the act of creation.

Thus, Thomas Aquinas, in questions 2 to 26 of the first part of the *Summa Theologiae*, dedicated to the (positive) knowledge of God's existence and (negative, as by reason we can know not what God is, but what he is not) knowledge of his essence. This shows that the human spirit, healed and strengthened by divine revelation, can and should be led to "develop taking possession of his own rational faculty to the point in fact of arriving at what by right man's natural reason has the capacity to reach."[36] It is not by accident that, for Thomas, the fundamental truth that reason can reach regarding God is exactly the unicity/unity strictly bound to the very truth of his existence.

The Neo-Pagan Critique

A new phenomenon that has developed in our time consists of an even sharper criticism of monotheism. As a matter of fact, its roots are in the nineteenth century, but it can be grasped in its essence even earlier: in the growing nostalgia for the Greco-Roman classics, even religiously in humanism and in the renaissance, and in the Romantic period with some typical accents of Friedrich Hölderlin's thought (1770–1843), and more recently, in Friedrich Nietzsche (1844–1900) and Martin Heidegger (1889–1976), who should be interpreted carefully for their often hidden meaning of protest and invocation. According to an influential thread in contemporary thought with various origins and results, this is due to the notion that a God who is one and unique implies in itself the negation of the values of otherness and freedom, values that are implied by and presuppose plurality, both in theory and in practice. And history provides many examples, even if they take different directions as soon as the question is posed about monotheism's supposedly idiosyncratic relationship with pluralism and freedom.

On the one hand, an excessive narcissistic identification fostered by monotheism is recognized, thus generating intolerance, violence, and conflict,[37] which are connected, among other things, with a patriarchal and authoritarian notion of religion and society. Monotheism is then seen as a powerful and arrogant ideology, as described by the novelist M. Yourcenar through the words of Emperor Hadrian: "No people besides Israel has the arrogance to enclose the whole truth within the restricted limits of a unique divine conception, thereby insulting the multiplicity

36. Dominique Dubarle, *Dieu avec l'être: De Parmenide à Saint Thomas. Essai d'ontologie théologale* (Paris: Beauchesne, 1986), 268.

37. See Enrico Ferri (ed.), *Monoteismo e conflitto* (Naples: CUEN, 1997).

of the God that contains everything; no other God has inspired in his worshipers contempt and hatred for those who pray at different altars."[38]

On the other hand, we can recognize the cause of monotheism's congenital inability to make space for otherness can be found in its own endemic weakness. This stems from the impoverishing abstraction from the vital and varying multiplicity of the divine from which it is born. For example this is Friedrich Nietzsche's provocation expressed in *Thus Spake Zarathustra*: "What is divine, is it not perhaps that there are gods but no God?"; and in *Antichrist*: "Two thousand years have come and gone—and not a single new god! ... But this pitiful god of Christian monotono-theism! This hybrid image of decay, conjured up out of emptiness, contradiction and vain imagining, in which all the instincts of decadence, all the cowardice and weariness of the soul find their sanction!" So monotheism would interrupt and then prevent the dance of otherness, ending with the impoverishment of the human and the betrayal of the divine, reducing the multiform expressions of reality to the lowest common denominator of a rarefied and demanding unity, thus defending a fatally bloodless or oppressive God.

Much of the disaffection and distancing from the monotheist traditions in favor of a return to paganism,[39] along with many fascinating calls for a more welcoming and multiform divinity like what is proposed often in an idealized and syncretistic form by the oriental religions, is derived today in the secularized, postmodern West in a New Age or Next Age atmosphere, from the vulgarization of these currents, connected with a vague anti-authoritarian sentiment. What really must be asked is what notion of monotheism and what image of God is being targeted by such positions. Are they not perhaps caricatures of a genuine religious and philosophic understanding of God? On the other hand, what notion of truth and reason can be invoked to support this claim of pluralism and tolerance? And finally, what does an intolerant and exclusive God have to do with the face of the trinitarian God of love revealed in Jesus Christ? We have to take account of these questions in order to offer a relevant and articulate reply to the critiques of monotheism briefly noted here.

Two Clarifications

What provisional conclusions can we draw from our discussion regarding the question of monotheism up to this point? I will limit myself to two methodological clarifications.

38. Marguerite Yourcenar, *Mémoires d'Hadrien* (Paris: Gallimard, 1974), 254.

39. See Marc Augé, *Génie du paganisme* (Paris: Gallimard, 1982). On these approaches, see K. Müller's lucid essay, "Cristianesimo e occidente: quale universalismo?," *Il Regno*, supplement to no. 6 (March 15, 2004): 6–11, with its relevant bibliography.

On the notion of monotheism First we need to reflect semantically on the notion of monotheism in its relationship to what is specifically new in the revelational event and on the connection/distinction between the notions of the unicity and unity of God to which they refer. The notion of monotheism is defined in a rather general and negative manner, as simply excluding its opposite, polytheism—so much so that normally it is duly specified either in relation to extrabiblical forms (e.g., Hinduism or Zoroastrianism), or to the three great religions referring back to Abraham's faith (when Abrahamic or revealed monotheism is considered) or to the revelation of Jesus Christ (when Christian or trinitarian monotheism is considered).

Regarding the usage of the notions of unicity and unity, we need to differentiate what is specific to each, where each at least partly differs from the other. This holds whether from the viewpoint of the history of salvation or of theory (this second viewpoint is well covered in the manuals' treatment of *De Deo Uno* which we will discuss later).[40] From the viewpoint of the history of salvation in fact, the unicity of God is first revealed and accepted by faith. That is why Israel confesses having one God alone, YHWH, in exclusion of the other gods; then as a consequence, his being one and one alone in himself is revealed and confessed in faith. So the notion of unicity in itself immediately indicates the exclusivity of the God that reveals himself. That is why YHWH alone is the God of Israel, for Israel; while the notion of unity expresses God's essence precisely as God, his being Lord and creator—to say it with biblical terms—or his "nature" or "essence" in the terminology of the later theological tradition. The unity of God, then, should not only be understood in its metaphysical meaning, in a sense before revelation (where unity is the basis for unicity), but in terms of its original form as gradually proposed by revelation itself.

On the logic of revelation of the unique and one God There is also a second consideration: to receive in faith and to theologically penetrate the meaning of monotheism, we must be faithful to the history of revelation and the logic it gradually comes to exhibit. Revealed monotheism is not a datum of faith acquired from the beginning once for all, but an unfolding event in time, in its authentic and even unforeseeable meaning.[41] God

40. See André Manaranche, *Il monoteismo cristiano* (Brescia: Queriniana, 1988), 188–90.

41. The International Theological Commission writes: "Old Testament monotheism owes its origin to a supernatural revelation and is therefore intrinsically related to trinitarian revelation." *Theology, Christology, Anthropology* (1982), I.B.3; available at www.vatican.va. Luis F. Ladaria notes: "In a certain sense the revelation of the fullness of the divine 'common' essence and the revelation of God as Father, as Son (Word), and as Holy Spirit almost run parallel. Or, better yet, both revelations make up a unity, grow at the same time and in the same understanding, because they

comes to be known for who he is in the very act of revealing himself progressively to humanity as the living God, he who makes an alliance with his people.[42] What is amazingly new about the New Testament is that in the fullness of time the "I am" spoken by God in the First Testament (see Ex 3:14) discloses itself from within as the "I am" of Jesus Christ; that is why he can say: "I and the Father are one" (Jn 10:30). In this affirmation—which, in the Easter light of his death and resurrection takes on the meaning of the whole Christological event—Jesus not only simply reaffirms the monotheism of the forefathers as he has done when explicitly recalling the *Shema' Israel* (see Mk 10:18; 12:29, 32), but introduces us into the inner life of God.

This implies two intrinsically connected consequences. On one hand, that Jesus comes to define the face of God, whose being one and unique can no longer be understood without or outside of the distinction in unity between Jesus and God/*Abbà* in the Spirit. On the other hand, precisely that we are gratuitously introduced, through the gift of the Spirit who sparks off faith, to contemplation, even to participation in the relation of unity/otherness that Jesus lives as Son with the Father and the Spirit. "And because you are children, God has sent the Spirit of his Son into our hearts, crying, "Abba! Father!'" (Gal 4:6). This is definitively the goal of the coming of the Son of God into the world: "to gather into one [*eís hén*] the dispersed children of God" (Jn 11:52). For this Jesus prays to the Father at the Last Supper: "that they may all be one. As you, Father, are in me and I am in you, may they also be in us, so that the world may believe that you have sent me" (Jn 17:21).

This basic reality of the Christian faith has a fundamental methodological implication for the theology of the unicity and unity of God: it cannot be understood outside of God, but only from within the filiation given by Jesus thanks to the gift of the Spirit. Christian monotheism, as trinitarian, is not simply exclusive, in the sense that it affirms God's absolute sovereignty—certainly it does this. But it is also outpouring and participative,[43] in the sense that it opens and shares with human creatures its

constitute the *sole* self-revelation of God who is one, Father, Son, and Holy Spirit.... a progressive manifestation of the one and only God in the history of salvation of the Old and the New Testament." *The Living and True God: The Mystery of the Trinity*, ed. Rafael Luciani, trans. Maria Isabel Reyna and Liam Kelly (Miami, Fla.: Convivium Press, 2010), 405.

42. See Bastiaan van Iersel, *The Bible on the Living God*, trans. H. J. Vaughan (Del Pere, Wis.: St. Norbert Abbey Press, 1965).

43. Rather than "inclusive" I prefer the term "participative," sometimes used in this context. In both cases, it is a matter of an inclusiveness—if we must use this term—different from what we have found in the monotheism of some kinds of Hinduism. While in the Trinity it is a matter of inclusion by grace in the life of God, the one God of Hinduism understands unity in terms of the absolute as absorbing all reality which, in various forms and levels, are its expressions without there being real and definite otherness.

own mystery through the revelation of Jesus Christ as the only-begotten Son and the gift of the Holy Spirit as the Spirit of filiation. God does not cease to be the one true God: on the one hand, in other words, the Son and the Spirit do not multiply the being of the one God. On the other hand, the divinity of God and human createdness are not confused.

The fact is that in Jesus Christ, Son of God made flesh, we are called to approach the mystery of God, which undoubtedly remains a mystery, infinitely transcending us as God transcends creation. We are not placed in front of the mystery, but introduced into it by the gift of the Holy Spirit. In this sense, the Christian religion—as John Paul II has written—is "the religion of 'dwelling in the heart of God'" (*Tertio Millennio Adveniente*, par. 8).

Jesus Christ: Unique, Universal, and Eschatological Revelation of God the Trinity

Having given an approximate clarification of the notion of monotheism in relation to Christological revelation, we can turn to the second assertion contained in the Christian profession of faith. On the basis of what I have said, this is intrinsically connected with the first as its gratuitous and specific explication. The originality of the Christian faith in the unique and one God, inherited from the First Testament has its principle, its center, and its standard in fact in Jesus Christ, in other words in the unique, universally effective, and eschatological revelation he offers, indeed that he himself is, about God. Let us thoroughly examine and elaborate this statement in some affirmations sustaining it and flowing from it.

The Reciprocal and Indissoluble Connection between Faith in Jesus Christ and Faith in God the Trinity

The revelation of the trinitarian God is indissolubly connected to the person of Jesus Christ. The way of revelation of the trinitarian God passes through him. On the basis of First Testament revelation it is Jesus of Nazareth—and he alone and in definitive fullness—who shows in himself the face of God/*Abbà*, handing on the gift of his own Spirit. In its turn, the revelation of the Father illuminates, in the Spirit, the face of Jesus as that of the only-begotten Son and Word of the Father sent into the world for our adoption as sons in the communication of the Holy Spirit.

In a word: Jesus, by revealing, in the Holy Spirit, God as the *Abbà*, in his turn is revealed by the *Abbà,* in the Spirit, as the Son.[44] Christological

44. This reciprocity between the knowledge of the Father and the knowledge of the Son is affirmed by both the synoptic and the Johannine traditions; see Mt 11:27: "All things have been handed over to me by my Father; and no one knows the Son except the Father, and no one knows the

faith and trinitarian faith mutually refer to each other, standing or falling together: without Jesus the Christ there is no revelation of God the Trinity; without Trinity there is neither Christian faith in the identity of Jesus Christ as only begotten Son of the Father in the Holy Spirit, having come into the world to make us "sons in the Son" in the breath of the Spirit.

The Centrality of the Paschal Event in the Revelation of God the Trinity

Such a revelation is not offered to us as a truth expressed in the first place through a formula or a doctrine, but through the event itself of Jesus in his unity and in his entirety: as witnessed by the Son coming into the flesh in the Spirit about God/*Abbà*, and by God/*Abbà* about the Son in the Spirit (see Mt 11:27). This comes about through the announcement that Jesus makes about the coming of the kingdom of God, the praxis that witnesses to and fulfills such an announcement, his same person and the vicissitudes of his ministry—which first experiences his being welcomed, then being misunderstood and rejected up to his condemnation to death on the cross and his resurrection in the outpouring of the Spirit.[45] It is the Paschal event of death, resurrection, and outpouring of the Spirit which definitively is the constitutive locus of the Christological truth fully laid out, and consequently of the trinitarian truth.

In light of and starting from the Paschal event, the Christian faith confesses that Jesus of Nazareth, the crucified messiah, is risen and is Lord as only-begotten Son of the Father in the Holy Spirit's effusive communion. As a result, the Paschal event is the permanent source and standard of the definitive truth about the trinitarian faith: in Jesus' *pascha*, God reveals himself and communicates as Father of the crucified/risen Son

---

Father except the Son and anyone to whom the Son chooses to reveal him"; Mt 16:16–17: "Simon Peter answered, 'You are the Messiah, the Son of the living God.' And Jesus answered him, 'Blessed are you, Simon son of Jonah! For flesh and blood has not revealed this to you, but my Father in heaven'"; Jn 6:44–47: "No one can come to me unless drawn by the Father who sent me; and I will raise that person up on the last day. It is written in the prophets, 'And they shall all be taught by God.' Everyone who has heard and learned from the Father comes to me. Not that anyone has seen the Father except the one who is from God; he has seen the Father. Very truly, I tell you, whoever believes has eternal life." But the Holy Spirit is also intrinsically involved in this reciprocal knowledge, showing precisely in this his divine identity, bound in a trinitarian way to that of the Father and of the Son. So, for example, the apostle Paul can assert: "no one can say 'Jesus is Lord' except by the Holy Spirit" (1 Cor 12:3). If God/*Abbà* reveals himself as such in the Son made man, Jesus, it is the Holy Spirit poured into our hearts who recognizes in Jesus the Lord, as Son of the Father.

45. *Dei Verbum* puts it like this: "To see Jesus is to see His Father (Jn 14:9). For this reason Jesus perfected revelation by fulfilling it through his whole work of making Himself present and manifesting Himself: through His words and deeds, His signs and wonders, but especially through His death and glorious resurrection from the dead and final sending of the Spirit of truth. Moreover He confirmed with divine testimony what revelation proclaimed, that God is with us to free us from the darkness of sin and death, and to raise us up to life eternal" (no. 4).

who gives the Holy Spirit "without measure" (see Jn 3:36) for the salvation of humanity—that is, to redeem us from sin and introduce us into the fullness of the communion of life with himself.[46]

Christological Originality of Trinitarian Monotheism

This is how the originality of Christianity stands out in relation to the other revelational monotheisms, along with the unexpected and explosive newness of the God of Jesus Christ. The Christian God is not only the unique and one God (Judaism and Islam); nor only the God of the covenant and the promise, a "God of humankind" (Judaism). But he is the God who in his only-begotten Son becomes man, is crucified, rises, and gives the fullness of the Spirit.[47]

In other words, the God witnessed by the Christian faith is not only freely and gratuitously bound to humanity through the history of the covenant and the promise of which Israel is the partner on behalf and in view of all humanity: he is bound forever to the life and death of Jesus Christ. What is new in Christianity is this: that God's revelation is offered fully to us in his only-begotten Son becoming man and in his *pascha* of cross and resurrection. The Pauline dictum: "I know nothing ... except Christ Jesus and him crucified" (1 Cor 2:2) also means: I do not know God except in the faith of Jesus Christ crucified.

So the death on the cross of Jesus the Christ becomes either the unsurmountable reef that shatters the '"good news," the "Gospel," of which he is the champion, because that death of the one proclaimed and sent as son of God but who dies on the cross crying out his forsakenness (see Mk 15:34; Mt 27:46) makes it impossible to deny the failure of his message. Or else it implies the reduction of Jesus' message and existence to an ethical-religious model, however elevated and demanding, of fidelity to God and solidarity with humanity. But it still says nothing about the truth of God and our final destiny. Or, finally, in the faith springing from meeting him as risen, it witnesses to the definitive and universal truth about God's revelation of himself in Jesus, together with the vocation of each human being.[48]

46. See *DV*, no. 2.

47. In the fourth Gospel, Jesus says: "For this reason the Father loves me, because I lay down my life in order to take it up again. No one takes it from me, but I lay it down of my own accord. I have power [*exousía*] to lay it down, and I have power to take it up again. I have received this command from my Father" (Jn 10:17–18).

48. See Vatican Council II, *Gaudium et Spes*, December 7, 1965, available at www.vatican.va [hereafter *GS*]: "The truth is that only in the mystery of the incarnate Word does the mystery of man take on light. For Adam, the first man, was a figure of Him Who was to come, namely Christ the Lord. Christ, the final Adam, by the revelation of the mystery of the Father and His love, fully reveals man to man himself and makes his supreme calling clear" (no. 22)

The Trinitarian Truth of the Confession of Faith

The truth of the revelation of God the Trinity is professed by the apostolic church in John's first Letter, expressed in a pregnant confession of faith: "God's love was revealed among us in this way: God sent his only Son into the world so that we might live through him.... So we have known and believe the love that God has for us. God is love, and those who abide in love abide in God, and God abides in them" (1 Jn 4:9, 16). The mystery of the covenant and of the promise, of the incarnation and of the death/resurrection of Jesus Christ and of the Pentecostal gift of the Holy Spirit, the very mystery of God revealed in the history of salvation—the Father who sends the Son in the Holy Spirit for humanity—is condensed and expressed by this confession of faith flowing from the Paschal event. At the same time it constitutes the relevant and unsurpassable theological explanation.

We can put it as follows: God is a gratuitous, unconditional, inexhaustible, and definitive self-dedication in the reciprocity of the *agápe* of the Father and Son lived and shared with humanity in the breath of the Spirit. The truth of God the Trinity is the unfolding content of the faith in God's *agápe* revealed in the *pascha* of Jesus Christ and so discloses the ultimate truth of humanity, of history, and of creation.

If by now we are giving sufficient attention to these basic data of Christian faith, we can recognize—with amazement and thankfulness—the extraordinary gift and the huge task consisting of thinking, in faith, of the face of God revealed in Jesus Christ. As the *Catechism of the Catholic Church* affirms, in the confession of faith in God one and triune there is acknowledged without any doubt the center of revelation and of Christian existence:

> The mystery of the Most Holy Trinity is the central mystery of Christian faith and life. It is the mystery of God in himself. It is therefore the source of all the other mysteries of faith, the light that enlightens them. It is the most fundamental and essential teaching in the "hierarchy of the truths of faith." The whole history of salvation is identical with the history of the way and the means by which the one true God, Father, Son and Holy Spirit, reveals himself to men "and reconciles and unites with himself those who turn away from sin."[49]

49. *CCC*, no. 234. The principle of the "hierarchy of truths" of faith referred to here by the *CCC* was formulated by the Second Vatican Council in the decree on ecumenism, *Unitatis Redintegratio*: "Moreover, in ecumenical dialogue, Catholic theologians standing fast by the teaching of the Church and investigating the divine mysteries with the separated brethren must proceed with love for the truth, with charity, and with humility. When comparing doctrines with one another, they should remember that in Catholic doctrine there exists a 'hierarchy' of truths, since they vary in their relation to the fundamental Christian faith" (no. 11). This principle governs the structure of *CCC* and finds the center and basis for Christian faith precisely in the Christological revelation of the trinitarian God. Allow me to refer to part 4, "La verità di Dio in Cristo," in my *Teo-logia*, 385–410.

Throughout the whole journey of listening and understanding in faith the Word of God written down and handed on, all that we will be doing is introducing ourselves into the contemplation of this truth as it radiates upon the whole of reality. Having clarified the center of trinitarian discourse, we now need to reflect—as a first step—on the "theological locus" as the starting point from which we confess faith in the trinitarian God as disciples of Christ.

The Church: Locus of the Knowledge of God the Trinity

To say that knowledge of God the Trinity finds its undeniable and permanent way of access through faith in Jesus Christ means to say it cannot occur in its genesis and living fullness outside the church. In other words, just as it is impossible to arrive at true and full knowledge of God except by the mediation of Jesus Christ, so it is impossible to arrive at true and full knowledge of Jesus Christ except by the mediation of the church.[50] In fact, the church is defined as the locus of testimony in faith to God's revelation, eschatologically offered to the world in Jesus Christ, and as such lived and transmitted in the Holy Spirit.[51]

This mediation is objectively proposed in the canon of scripture and the sacramental signs, interpreted and carried out by the ordained ministry, in the authenticity of their form and meaning. And it is made effective through the action of the Holy Spirit, making the event of Jesus Christ crucified/risen contemporary in every place and time. This, then, is not a merely verbal but a real and substantial mediation, fully actualized in the Eucharistic presence of Christ.

50. The theological meaning of mediation originates in Christology insofar as Jesus Christ is the only mediator between God and humanity (see Gal 3:20; 1 Tm 2:3–6), as he is the one who brings about immediate communion between the Father and those who, in and through him, are made "sons in the Son" by the Spirit. Depending on Christ's unique mediation, we can and should also speak of the church's mediation, insofar as it is through her that Christ is made present and brings about, in the Spirit, communion with the Father. *Lumen Gentium* puts this succinctly: "Christ, present to us in His Body, which is the Church, is the one Mediator and the unique way of salvation" (no. 14). On the intrinsic connection between the Christological and ecclesiological forms of mediation, see J. Feiner, "Rivelazione e Chiesa: Chiesa e rivelazione," in *Mysterium Salutis* (Brescia: Queriniana, 1977), 2:11–67; M. Löhrer and Basil Studer, "Portatori della mediazione," in ibid., 69–144; A. Stenzel, Karl Rahner, and Hans Urs von Balthasar, "Modi attraverso i quali la mediazione si realizza," in ibid., 145–293; and Sequeri, *Il Dio affidabile*.

51. The intrinsic theological connection between mediation and witness in Christology and consequently in ecclesiology is at the center of von Balthasar's systematic proposal: see Marcello Neri, *La testimonianza in H.U. von Balthasar: evento originario di Dio e mediazione storica della fede* (Bologna: EDB, 2001); Gianluca Zurra, *Mediazione ecclesiale e testimonianza: In dialogo con l'estetica teologica di H.U. von Balthasar* (Rome: Pontificia Università Lateranense, 2003). On the category of witness, see also Piero Ciardella and Maurizio Gronchi (eds.), *Testimonianza e verità: Un approccio interdisciplinare* (Rome: Città Nuova, 2000), with bibliography by Francesco Gaiffi.

Objective mediation in itself implies, gives rise to, and regulates the subjective mediation of the faith that receives it and lives it, as this is the significance and final aim of objective mediation. Without the correct and vital subjective reception of the objective tradition, the event of Jesus Christ does not become present to the world and for the world. In reality, subjective mediation or reception is also the work of the Holy Spirit. The Spirit not only freely arouses faith in Jesus Christ, in cooperation with human freedom, not only does he support and guide it with his gifts, but from time to time he illuminates, strengthens, and orients the faith with special charisms[52] aimed at actualizing the people of God's reception and living penetration of and in the event of Jesus Christ.

In a word, the life of the church presupposes and at the same time carries out the transmission (*parádōsis*) of the event of Jesus Christ: "remember, I am with you always, to the end of the age" (Mt 28:20), in the ever reproposed and ever new encounter between the objective mediation of the word of God and the sacraments with the subjective mediation of the faith receiving and living them.[53]

The Presence of the Risen Jesus to the Church

The actual presence of the risen Jesus is decisive in Christian faith for the church's mediation. It is in him that "God, who spoke of old, uninterruptedly converses with the bride of His beloved Son" (see *DV*, no. 8).[54] This presence is grace (*cháris*), offered by the word of God and by the sacraments, which becomes subjectively and therefore historically effective where the freedom of the disciples recognizes it in faith and practices it existentially in the exercise of an *agápe* both reciprocal and universal (see 1 Jn 2:23).

52. See *Lumen Gentium*, no. 12. I have attempted a further examination of this ecclesiological theme in my *Teo-logia*, 364–67.

53. In this context Gerald O'Collins's distinction between "past-foundational" revelation and "present-actualizing" or "participant" revelation is not only fully acceptable but shows itself to be theologically necessary; see Gerald O'Collins, "Revelation: Past and Present," in *Vaticano II: bilancio e prospettive venticinque anni dopo (1962–1987)*, ed. René Latourelle (Assisi: Cittadella, 1987), 1:125–35. It is enough to reflect on the fact that revelation can only be received and understood as such if it is actually given through faith. As Pierangelo Sequeri has written, "the Church as communion/community of believers, instituted through the apostolic tradition of the founding event, is not an entity separate from revelation, added on in a second time. Rather, it belongs to the historic aim of the incarnation and mission of the Son and in view of its unfolding over time, is originally inscribed in the *parádōsis* of that very founding event. Such an aim, guided by the Spirit of the risen Lord, is not limited to the ancient kerygma, but entails a web of *stable relations*, where the communion with God, inaugurated by Jesus and the hospitality of the Kingdom inaugurated by the incarnation of the Son continues." *L'idea della fede: Trattato di teologia fondamentale* (Milan: Glossa, 2002), 127.

54. No doubt the risen Christ is present to history through the action of the Holy Spirit, even through other ways "known only to God" (see *GS*, no. 22), but his effective presence is manifested and fulfilled in its fullness where the Word is preached and lived, the Eucharist is celebrated and made effective in life and reciprocal love toward all, building this community of communion as sign and instrument of the presence of Christ in and through his disciples.

Agápe's reciprocity leads the dynamic of faith to perfection (as its aim and fulfillment: in the full meaning of the Greek *teleioûn*),[55] actualizing the communion among the disciples where the risen Christ dwells (see Mt 18:20). Because of this, St. Bonaventure was able to say: "Ecclesia mutuo se diligens."[56] Mutual love is the full subjective reception of the grace objectively participated in by the church from the word of God and from the sacraments. Thus, commenting on John 17, St. Thomas Aquinas describes a dual unity among the disciples as the completed form of their being in Christ: the unity fulfilled objectively by grace and the unity fulfilled subjectively by reciprocal love, where the objective fulfilment is finalized in accordance with the ontological dynamic of *agĕre sequitur esse*.[57] As a result, where the objective gift of *communio* in Christ is existentially actuated—through mutual and universal love—there the church fulfills and manifests the form it receives from Christ as a lived and witnessed *communio*, in him, with God the Trinity and with humanity. So the church becomes in fact what it is through grace: the relevant and adequate locus of the knowledge of God revealed in Christ as *agápe*.

Access to Jesus Christ, Word of the Father, and the way to knowledge of him in the Spirit (see Jn 14:9) is located and actualized within the dynamic circularity between the self-giving of his historical-eschatological event, witnessed to by scripture and offered through the sacramental signs on the one hand, and on the other, by the actual presence of the crucified/risen one, by the power of the Holy Spirit, in the life of communion. That communion emerges from the lived Word and the Eucharist, received in the practice of mutual and universal love.[58] It is he himself who, present among his own,[59] through the mediation of the word of God transmitted by the church and through the Eucharist, opens out access to the Father in the Spirit. The evangelist Luke affirms this concretely in his account of the disciples at Emmaus (see Lk 24:13–35), where his narrative is meant to describe exactly how the crucified/risen one alone is the permanent

55. See my *L'agape come grazia e libertà: Alla radice della teologia e prassi dei cristiani* (Rome: Città Nuova, 1994), 66 and 124.

56. St. Bonaventure, *Collationes in Hexaemeron* 1.4; see Klaus Hemmerle, *Partire dall'unità: La Trinità come stile di vita e forma di pensiero* (Rome: Città Nuova, 1998).

57. Thomas Aquinas, *Super Evangelium S. Ioannis lectura*, 3, XIII–XXI.

58. Pottmeyer notes: "The eschatological 'once for all' of the event of Christ is the basis for the two dimensions of the apostolic and ecclesial tradition: in the *horizontal dimension* of the historical transmission this is the anamnetic witness of what occurred once in Jesus Christ; in the *vertical dimension* there is the actualizing witness of the once for all in the pneumatic presence of the glorified Lord in the 'Body of Christ' composed of many members (see Eph 1:23; 5:30)." H. J. Pottmeyer, "Norme, criteri e strutture della tradizione," in *Corso di teologia fondamentale*, ed. Walter Kern, Hermann J. Pottmeyer, and Max Seckler, vol. 4: *Trattato di gnoseologia teologica* (Brescia: Queriniana, 1990), 158.

59. See Mt 18:20; Gérard Rossé, *L'ecclesiologia di Matteo: Interpretazione di Mt 18:20* (Rome: Città Nuova, 1987).

source and specific form of ecclesial existence,[60] how it is he who introduces us into the authentic knowledge of himself, and in himself, of the Father.

The disciples live in Christ by faith (see Jn 15:5: "I am the vine, you are the branches"), becoming his living body through mutual love (see 1 Cor 12:12; Rom 12:5; *LG*, no. 1).[61] By receiving the Spirit, they share in the eschatological existence of the crucified/risen one and in his knowledge of the Father.[62] Being-in-Christ, as church, then defines the theologically relevant locus for the knowledge of the Father in the Spirit. A sign of this is the heart opening out in amazement in the invocation suggested by the Spirit: "*Abbà*, Father!"[63]

The Communion Dynamic of Tradition

Communion not only describes the existence of the disciples in Christ as a presupposition which is both objective and subjective, reflecting their knowledge of *Abbà* in the Spirit, but it describes the dynamic of their access to such knowledge by means of the *traditio* as well. The Second Vatican Council teaches in this regard that, "Sacred Tradition, Sacred Scripture and the Magisterium of the Church, in accord with God's most wise design, are so linked and joined together that one cannot stand without the others" (*DV*, no. 10). This statement underlines that the objective mediations making possible the church's dwelling in and ever new penetration into the truth of Christ are of value in each being related to the crucified/risen one in the Holy Spirit, and are consequently also in reciprocal relation with each other. Thus they are intrinsically designated to place each single form of mediation and its single historic moment

60. The 18th National Congress of the Italian Theological Association focused on this theme in 2003: *Annuncio del Vangelo, "forma Ecclesiae,"* ed. Dario Vitali (Cinisello Balsamo: San Paolo Edizioni, 2005).

61. *LG* = Vatican Council II, *Lumen Gentium*, November 21, 1964; available at www.vatican.va.

62. Bernhard Casper writes: "The community of believers, or the Church, constituted in a historico-dialogical manner, is presented as the hermeneutic totality regenerating herself in history, where the perennially valid call of the Gospel keeps her continually open within her lived existence." *L'ermeneutica e la teologia* (Brescia: Morcelliana, 1974), 56.

63. See Rom 8:15; Gal 4:6. On the relation between a Christology of the actual presence of the risen one in the church and a pneumatology of the Spirit's effective action in and through the church, see Marcello Bordoni, *La cristologia nell'orizzonte dello Spirito* (Brescia: Queriniana, 1995); also Valentino Maradi, *Lo Spirito e la Sposa: Il ruolo ecclesiale dello Spirito Santo dal Vaticano I alla Lumen Gentium del Vaticano II* (Casale Monferrato: Piemme, 1992), who relevantly writes that the Holy Spirit is given and "gives himself, as an effective power of renewal and unity: where he is present, there arises community; there humanity is gathered into the unity of the Father, Son and Spirit; there the Church is present: *ubi Spiritus Dei, illic Ecclesia*. On the other hand, he is present in the Church as fruit. Where ecclesial activities are carried on *en agápe*, he becomes in a certain way something that was not there before: person-in-the-midst of ecclesial communion; shared, and therefore unifying space of action.... Where believers live in communion, the Spirit receives a new objectification, a new concretization, there he becomes shared Spirit, there he is transmitted by the ecclesial communion itself: *ubi Ecclesia, ibi et Spiritus Dei*" (342).

of realization in communion with the other forms and moments of the transmission. This occurs in a dynamic tasked in the "now" of faith and history with safeguarding and expressing the eschatological singularity of the Word of God in Christ.

H. J. Pottmeyer writes:

The supreme norm of Christian faith and its tradition is only the Word of God which was made flesh in Jesus Christ, remaining present in the Holy Spirit, and not merely one of its forms of witness. In fact, the Word of God is certainly affirmed in Sacred Scripture, in the doctrine, liturgy and life of the Church and in the hearts of believers (see 2 Cor 3:3; 1 Th 4:9; 1 Jn 2:28); due to its eschatological character however, none of these forms of testimony exhaust the Word—it produces, rather, the multiplicity and the fruitfulness of ever new witnesses.[64]

As Max Seckler showed in the systematic notion of the *loci theologici*, already elaborated by Melchior Cano in the sixteenth century, and then becoming standard for subsequent theology, the *traditio* of the Christ-event was guaranteed by "an interactive organism of the subjects of Tradition" (scripture, tradition, the church, the pope, theologians, the patristic writers, and so on). This occurred in such a way that each of them "potentially represent the whole, but with their own means and starting from their particular viewpoint." In this way, "the whole *veritas catholica*, because it is *veritas catholica*, is realized only through the cooperation of this whole." What limits this notion is the fact that the various subjects could, in fact, become "ever more autonomous."[65]

Vatican II's theological perspective matured with reference to Christ's presence in mystery in *Sacrosanctum Concilium*, and to the Christological-trinitarian concept of revelation set forth in *Dei Verbum*, and to the concept of church-communion presented in *Lumen Gentium*. Without mixing up the identity and function proper to the various forms and the various moments of mediation, this perspective opens out to a vision which comprehends and promotes the convergence and connections based on the one root from which they flower and the one goal toward which they tend: the *parádōsis* in the Holy Spirit of the event of the Word of God made flesh "once for all" in Jesus Christ.[66] As D. Wiederkeher explains:

64. Hermann J. Pottmeyer, "Tradizione," in *Dizionario di Teologia Fondamentale* (Assisi: Cittadella, 1990), 1347.

65. Max Seckler, "Il significato ecclesiologico dei 'loci theologici,'" in his *Teologia, scienza, Chiesa* (Brescia: Morcelliana, 1988), 171–206, esp. 188–89 and 193–94; see Bernhard Körner, *Melchior Cano, De locis theologicis: Ein Beitrag zur theologischen Erkenntnislehre* (Graz: Styria, 1994), which not only reconstructs the genesis and structure of Cano's work, but also shows its reception in our own time up to *Dei Verbum*, finishing by proposing an epistemological application.

66. See Pottmeyer, *Norme, criteri e strutture della tradizione*, 137–72.

The people of God (the Church) [are the] subject for the promise concerning the transmission and tradition (of the Christ event) insofar as the single subjects do not separate themselves from the others, but remain in dialogical relation with each other: the magisterium with the community of believers including the prophetic dimension, and vice versa; the local Church with the universal Church; the central Roman Church in synodal "communio" with the worldwide Church.... A condition for a healthy process of tradition and of the promise is the responsible understanding among the single forms and concretizations of life and religious language, therefore among existential praxis, liturgical assembly and theological reflection, between the inner life of the most intimate mystery of the Church and its presence in concrete and effective social diaconia.... Finally, this dialogue of the Church should take place between the single forms and the temporal-historical epochs.[67]

The theological criterion regulating such a multiple relationality is the one Vincent of Lerins[68] had already noted: consensus. This must now be studied and understood more deeply in light of the ecclesiology of communion. The diachronic consensus is expressed in this context in fact, binding the church of all times with the apostolic church, and with the constitutive value of the tradition of the word of God which it transmits. On one hand, the synchronic consensus is expressed in this same context, informing the relations between the local churches united to their bishops and the universal church, the unity of which is signified and visibly expressed by the bishop of Rome, shepherd of the whole church (*communio ecclesiarum*). On the other hand, the synchronic consensus informs the relationships among the magisterium, the *sensus fidelium*, the charisms, and theology (*communio fidelium*).

In the context of the relational dynamic of the subjects of transmission of the word of God, scripture and the magisterium have a particular role on the basis of the Catholic notion of consensus,[69] that is, insofar as they manifest and guarantee, in different ways, what is eschatologically definitive in the revelation of God in Jesus Christ. So we can speak of the written Word of God as normative and unsurpassable testimony to the event of revelation, and of the magisterium as the certain and authentic exercise of interpretation of the Word of God. However, Vatican II clar-

67. D. Wiederkeher, "Il principio della tradizione," in *Corso di teologia fondamentale* (ed. Kern et al.), 4:107–36, at 133.

68. We owe to him the well-known formula which holds that the church must maintain what has been believed: *quod ubique, semper, ab omnibus* (everywhere, always and by all). *Commonitorium*, II.5.

69. See Seckler, "Il significato ecclesiologico dei *loci theologici*," 192 and 196. M. Seckler particularly notes that "it belongs as much to the Catholic conception of magisterial authority and the Church's government in the end, that there is no higher human authority to which appeal can be made in its officially binding decisions of faith; as the fact that such power requires no further consent beyond itself for the binding nature of these decisions" (196).

ifies this: "This Magisterium is not above the word of God, but serves it, teaching only what has been handed on, listening to it devoutly, guarding it scrupulously and explaining it faithfully in accord with a divine commission and with the help of the Holy Spirit" (*DV*, no. 10).

With regard to synchronic consensus, to express and guarantee the fidelity and vitality of the Word of God's *traditio/receptio*, what is needed is effective communication among the various interacting elements to reach its expression. These elements should listen to and welcome one another, respecting their functions with an attitude of reciprocal openness and service. By doing so, the whole church, through the transparency of the various elements and subjects which are building it, can readily and openly accept the event of the word of God,[70] in an unfiltered hearkening to what "the Spirit says to the Churches" (see Rv 2:7). The origin and form of ecclesial *parádōsis* is definitely the trinitarian *parádōsis* itself, in virtue of which the Father gives the Son for the salvation of humankind and the Son gives the Spirit, thus making us sharers in divine sonship.[71] The ecclesial tradition is located, then, in the prolongation of the trinitarian *parádōsis*; it transmits and actualizes it insofar as it expresses the intrinsic trinitarian *rhythm* and form.[72]

Tradition, Communion, Mission

In this light we have to thoroughly reflect on the deep roots, internal to the ecclesial experience itself, while at the same time drawing from the sociocultural context—the greater difficulty the church finds today in

70. Pottmeyer explains: "The true and faithful witness of Jesus Christ takes second place to what is being testified, becoming transparent vis a vis what is greater than the witness. This occurs specifically by not depriving himself of his own personality, but by sharing the self-giving of Jesus Christ in a personal way.... The bearer of the tradition becomes competent insofar as he is converted from selfishness to other-centeredness. Through that conversion he and his testimony become the sign actualizing the love of God.... In this way, authentic tradition comes about through the identification of the witness with what is testified, within the community of witnesses, thus becoming the epiphany of the kingdom of God in history." Pottmeyer, *Norme, criteri e strutture della tradizione*, 171–72. For a clear study of this dynamic in its existential and juridical repercussions, see Christoph Hegge, *Rezeption und Charisma: Der theologische und rechtliche Beitrag Kirchlicher Bewegungen zur Rezeption des Zweiten Vatikanischen Konzils* (Würzburg: Echter Verlag, 1999).

71. See the Johannine description of the risen Christ's appearance to the disciples in the upper room, where he gifts them the Holy Spirit (*lábete pneûma hágion*) so that, as the Father has sent him (*kathòs apéstalkén me ho patèr*), he may, in turn, send them too (*kagò pnémpō hymâs*) (Jn 20:19 23).

72. Irenaeus of Lyons is the one who uses the metaphor of "rhythm" with regard to the dynamic of trinitarian revelation and its reception by the faithful: see Bart Benats, *Il ritmo trinitario della verità: La teologia di Ireneo di Lione* (Rome: Città Nuova, 2006). Bernhard Körner writes that theological epistemology should take as its starting point "the fact that the origin of revelation, revelation itself, its transmission and understanding in faith should be understood as Trinitarian event." "La gnoseologia teologica alla luce di una teologia trinitaria," in *Abitando la Trinità: Per un rinnovamento dell'ontologia*, ed. Piero Coda and Lubomir Žak (Rome: Città Nuova, 1998), 79–93, at 84.

transmitting the faith, that is, in making an experience and knowledge of the God of Jesus Christ accessible and livable in a way that is existentially meaningful and objectively authentic. In reality, transmission of the meaning and forms of life is the primary and fundamental anthropological infrastructure of human existence with an intrinsic religious value. This is because it is accomplished in the context of the transmission of humans' own experience with respect to the ultimate truth of their being, anchored in God making himself present to them.[73] In the faith-event corresponding to revelation, such a structure assumes by grace a determined and determining qualification, both redemptive and fulfilling of our humanity. For this reason, it would be fatal to reduce *traditio* understood theologically to a mere vehicle or instrument through which something is communicated as if separate from the act of communication itself; rather, it should be understood at root as the form and content of the anthropological in its Christic fulfillment.[74]

The primacy of personal relations with reciprocal transparency in the witness and communication of the faith is derived from this. This is not an extrinsic and accidental issue, as ends up being thought too often.[75] Rather it is intrinsic and substantial, ultimately founded on the trinitarian structure of revelation. To separate the dimension of personal relations from the notion and task of Christian *traditio* means to ultimately reduce this tradition to a functional aspect. This would show, among other things, a failure to grasp the theological meaning of the intrinsically personalizing dynamic in itself of the faith.

The anthropological crisis at the diachronic level in advanced Western societies affecting communication between the generations in reality

73. See Karl Rahner and K. Lehmann, "Storicità della mediazione," in *Mysterium Salutis*, 295–366.

74. In recent times, there have been worthwhile and consistent theological attempts at reading the tract on ecclesiology in terms of communication. To take just a few examples: M. Kehl, reformulating K. O. Apel's and J. Habermas's theory of communicative action, taken up in a theological context by H. J. Höhn, has proposed "a model for understanding inspired by the theory of communication." *La Chiesa: Trattato sistematico de ecclesiologia cattolica* (Cinisello Balsamo: San Paolo, 1995). With this, Kehl wishes to offer a realistic and incisive presentation of Vatican II's ecclesiology of communion. There is also Severino Dianich's and Serena Noceti's *Trattato sulla Chiesa* (Brescia: Queriniana, 2002), which focuses more on the decisive theological and pastoral question of the communication of the faith, while emphasizing that "the communication of the faith in Jesus from person to person, is not only the generative principle of the Church in its originary meaning, where it did not previously exist. It is also the permanent dynamic principle by which the living Church as already constituted is truly the Church of Jesus Christ" (191) (own trans.).

75. M. Neri writes: "Witness is not a trigger for posterity (in a kind of chain reaction), from the Christological occurrence of God's truth. Rather, the truth of the Father-God of the man of Nazareth is always shown uniquely *in* witness and occurs *as* witness. The *testimonium* is the originary form of the *veritas* and not an external consequence of it, or its result in the inconsolable and uncertain time of its unavailability" (*La testimonianza in H.U. von Balthasar*). See the clear account spelled out by Adriano Fabris in his *TeorEtica: Filosofia della relazione* (Brescia: Morcelliana, 2009).

mirrors a wider and deeper crisis at the synchronic level: the crisis in relations among persons, beginning, at the microsocial level, with relations between men and women. The crisis of communication of the faith is in itself connected with this historic crisis of tradition as an anthropological fact. The modernization process of what are defined as traditional societies[76] implies the increasing expulsion of religion as an adequate context for the transmission of values and meanings, insofar as they are ultimately anchored precisely in a religious foundation. When this foundation begins to fade away, the connection—up to now plausible and taken for granted—between transmission as an anthropological-social reality and the *traditio* of the Christian faith as a religious reality, becomes problematical. The immediate relation between the partners of the transmission becomes the exposed nerve both of social life and of the ecclesial mission. This fact undoubtedly has problematical repercussions and implications from an ethical and cultural viewpoint, but it can also offer unexpected opportunities not least at an ecclesial level, insofar as the Christian faith shows itself capable of freeing up and fulfilling the meaning and dynamic of human relations.

The concrete possibility of taking advantage of this opportunity and so offering a responsive framework in response to the Western cultural crisis depends on being able to manifest lived relations in the ecclesial community in their more characteristic and original quality of witness in concrete existence, in the existence set free and fulfilled in Christ. The ecclesiology of communion thus stands out in the wide backdrop of this epochal transition. In other words, *communio* not only constitutes an unavoidable evangelical requirement that the church is recognizing today. At the same time, this is a specific historical demand connected to the possibility that it has to live its mission today, in the credible communication of the event of grace by which it is continually regenerated. *Traditio*, *communio*, and *missio* are closely bound together, in other words. There cannot be an incisive and effective *traditio* of the faith in God the Trinity, thus actuating the *missio*, without a mature choice and experience of *communio* in the church.

76. See Carlo Prandi, *La tradizione religiosa: Saggio storico-sociologico* (Rome: Borla, 2000).

CHAPTER 2

The Historical Context

What clearly emerges from this discussion is that the ecclesial locus of the knowledge of God is not torn from the historical and cultural context of the time in which the community of Christ's disciples lives. Because of this, as Vatican II teaches, the church "is in Christ like a sacrament or sign and instrument both of a very closely knit union with God and of the unity of the whole human race" (*Lumen Gentium*, no. 1). So the church "realizes that it is truly linked with mankind and its history by the deepest of bonds," such that the "joys and the hopes, the griefs and the anxieties of the men of this age, especially those who are poor or in any way afflicted, these are the joys and hopes, the griefs and anxieties of the followers of Christ. Indeed, nothing genuinely human fails to raise an echo in their hearts" (*GS*, no. 1).

The Demanding Task of Discernment

As men and women of our time, then, we find ourselves immersed in the context of today and its demanding challenges. It is a matter of situations and questions arising from the world in which we live, from the cultural currents running through it and from the social, ethical, and spiritual problems facing us. These are situations and questions coming to our experience of faith and ecclesial life. And these come not only from the outside, precisely because we carry them within ourselves as persons of our time, if for no other reason than our solidarity and common destiny.[1]

We are called as disciples of Jesus in this matter to exercise the demanding and challenging task of discernment.[2] As Vatican II shows, this

1. For example, proclaimed a doctor of the church by John Paul II, and as such definitely having something to teach us, St. Thérèse of Lisieux experienced in herself the trial of the absence of God lived by many of her contemporaries as a peculiar form of sharing in the life of Christ himself, who "sat at table with sinners."

2. On this topic, see A. Barruffo, "Discernimento," in *Nuovo dizionario di spiritualità*, ed. S. De Fiores and T. Goffi (Rome: Paoline, 1982), 419–30; José M. Castillo, *Il discernimiento cristiano: Por una conciencia crítica* (Salamanca: Ediciones Sígueme, 1984); "Discernimento dello Spirito e degli spiriti," ed. C. Duquoc and C. Floristan, in *Concilium* 9 (1978): 13–139; Rino Fisichella,

is nothing more than the specifically theological method—as exercised in Christ under the guidance of the Holy Spirit—through which the church reads history in the light of the Word of God in order to effectively fulfill its own mission. It is for the precise aim of exercising its own mission—"Christ entered this world to give witness to the truth, to rescue and not to sit in judgment, to serve and not to be served" (*GS*, no. 3)—that the church regards it as its own the inalienable duty of "scrutinizing the signs of the times and of interpreting them in the light of the Gospel" (*GS*, no. 4). Two passages from *Gaudium et Spes* illustrate the task and the method of discernment:

The People of God believes that it is led by the Lord's Spirit, Who fills the earth. Motivated by this faith, it labors to decipher authentic signs of God's presence and purpose in the happenings, needs and desires in which this People has a part along with other men of our age. For faith throws a new light on everything, manifests God's design for man's total vocation, and thus directs the mind to solutions which are fully human.[3]

With the help of the Holy Spirit, it is the task of the entire People of God, especially pastors and theologians, to hear, distinguish and interpret the many voices of our age, and to judge them in the light of the divine word, so that revealed truth can always be more deeply penetrated, better understood and set forth to greater advantage.[4]

Both passages emphasize the perspective "in the Spirit" within which discernment is to be understood and exercised. In the first passage discernment is directed at integral human development, while the second focuses on the proclamation of the truth of Christ in the concrete cultural situation of our time.

Today, the human race is involved in a new stage of history. Profound and rapid changes are spreading by degrees around the whole world. Triggered by the intelligence and creative energies of man, these changes recoil upon him, upon his decisions and desires, both individual and collective, and upon his manner of thinking and acting with respect to things and to people. So we can already speak of a true cultural and social transformation, one which has repercussions on man's religious life as well.[5]

This has lost nothing of its bite but has become even more pressing today. What is now appearing is a new perspective, full of unknowns, with dramatic implications, from which indications of its meaning and the direc-

---

"Discernimento," in *Enciclopedia di pastorale*, ed. C. Floristan and J. J. Tamayo (Vatican City: Libreria Editrice Vaticano, 1999), 1:275–78; Walter Kasper, "Discernimento dello Spirito e degli spiriti come modello di intelligenza ecclesiale," in *Dilexit Ecclesiam* (Rome: Las, 1999), 663–94.

3. *GS*, no. 11.

4. *GS*, no. 44.

5. *GS*, no. 4.

tions of its development emerge with ever increasing clarity and urgency. By now it has become convenient to label this as "globalization," with a wider signification than its original, simply economic, meaning.[6] Vatican II already spoke of this phenomenon, underlining the increasing interdependence among peoples and cultures as a characteristic of our times (see *GS*, nos. 25–26).[7]

Obeying the requirement to discern, I will try to outline some of the more relevant challenges involved in the wider context of globalization, which relate to the discourse that I wish to carry on. Without that context, my speaking of the God of Jesus Christ runs the risk of sounding empty and distant.

The Horizon of the Human Family

I will start by saying something about the universalistic horizon characterizing our time. If it is beyond doubt that globalization constitutes the central challenge of today, it is equally clear that we are dealing with a challenge attaining an unprecedentedly radical level, in the sense that it touches the roots of human identity. The fact is that we have not succeeded in mastering, even though we may intuit it, the *novum* that such a phenomenon brings into history. It is the space where for the first time and irreversibly, the different identities through which human experience is expressed enter into a relationship of mutual visibility and communication. This is a cultural event of enormous anthropological importance. We must bear in mind moreover that it is mediated and largely made possible by two closely connected processes: the technological results made available through scientific research, and globalization of the market and production that has taken over the economy.

Global communication as the place to manage existence in an ideal reciprocity of relationships made available to individuals, to social institutions, and to cultural and religious traditions ends up being sustained and

6. On the topic of globalization, see Ulrich Beck, *Cos'è la globalizzazione: Rischi e prospettive della società planetaria* (Rome: Carocci, 1999); Clifford Geertz, *Local Knowledge: Further Essays in Interpretive Anthropology* (New York: Basic Books, 2008); Maria Rosaria Ferrarese, *Le istituzioni della globalizzazione: Diritto e diritti nella società transnazionale* (Bologna: Il Mulino, 2000); Ph. de Woot and J. Delcourt, "Finalités du développement: Valeurs chrétiennes," in *Les défis de la globalisation: Babel ou Pentecôte?*, ed. J. Delcourt and Ph. de Woot (Louvain-la-Neuve: Presses universitaires de Louvain, 2001); Peter Sloterdijk, *L'ultima sfera: Breve storia filosofica della globalizzazione* (Rome: Carocci, 2002); Federico Bonaglia and Andrea Goldstein, *Globalizzazione e sviluppo* (Bologna: Il Mulino, 2003); Agostino Giovagnoli, *Storia e globalizzazione* (Rome-Bari: Laterza, 2003).

7. This is a situation calling for a specific theological reflection: see Johann B. Metz, "Proposta di programma universale del cristianesimo nell'età di globalizzazione," in *Prospettive teologiche per il XXI secolo*, ed. R. Gibellini (Brescia: Queriniana, 2003), 389–402.

regulated primarily by the media network and by the economic dynamic. This has two effects: first, the displacement of traditional anthropological issues, which run the risk of finding themselves left behind—if not pushed aside—in their capacity to provide discernment and direction to what is happening at a pace beyond their control. Second, there is the danger of an ideological drift, where the processes within a specific economic and scientific-technological logic come to constitute the meaning of globalization themselves, and finally its determining goal. Too often, the means ultimately assume the role of the ends.

The challenge posed to human experience in this way takes the form of risking the transformation of what in itself is in function of the development and growth of human identity into a radical misconception of the same. In fact, it ends up being subjected to a process which not only does not respect anthropological and ethical criteria, but in the end prioritizes efficiency and economic and technical-scientific results over the human. To paraphrase Francis Fukuyama's thesis, this can be described as a kind of tragic "end of history,"[8] if what is in function of the human person ends up subordinating this same person to itself. Maria Zambrano has written that history "would make no sense unless as the progressive revelation of man. If man were not a hidden being who had to reveal himself little by little."[9]

This is confirmed and made even more obvious because of the effects of such processes at the political level. On one hand, there is the difficulty and definite, almost structural incapacity of national and international political institutions to manage the new situation which has already begun to establish and impose itself with a logic that escapes political governance inspired by social justice and pursuit of the common good at a universal level. On the other hand, there are various kinds of reactions looming with respect to the process in its gestation stage, having recognized in this one part of humanity's (the West's) brutal power to impose, assimilate, and homogenize the other.[10] As Amartya Sen, the well-known Nobel Prize-winning economist, has noted:

> The contemporary presence of great wealth and suffering in the world in which we live makes it hard to avoid basic questions on the ethical acceptability of

8. See Francis Fukuyama, *The End of History and the Last Man* (New York: The Free Press, 1992).

9. María Zambrano, *Persona e democrazia: La storia sacrificale* (Milan: Mondadori, 2000), 29 (own trans.).

10. What is involved in the fundamentalist impulses affecting various religious universes—including dangerous and deviant impulses—is the defense of their own specific identity. In the movements of resistance and opposition to globalization, there is in play—here too in forms that are questionable—the need to introduce decisive correctives at the anthropological and social level to how globalization is managed.

the prevailing social organization and on our values.... There is a pressing need to question not only the economics and politics of globalization in today's world, but also its values and the ethics underlying our conception of the global world.[11]

This is not a merely theoretical challenge of limited importance—rather what lodged it into our heart was the tragedy of 9/11 in 2001. Not only because, for a moment of time, it made visible countless 9/11s—small or big, but always tragic insofar as human beings were involved—who too often are silently consumed and too quickly forgotten. But also because it has become a universal media symbol, kneaded from flesh and blood, of what is only made possible by the economy and technology which can transform the promise of communication and encounter they make possible into an extreme conflict of death. A great Italian poet, Mario Luzi, with the prophetic glance of the seer, has given us these verses:

> Those planes which hurled themselves down
> on the haughty towers,
> that headlong flight of human lives
> against other lives ...
> The mind wavers, the soul is overpowered, oppressed ...
>
> Times are foreboding, maybe they've already come,
> when men will be asked to be other
> than how we've been. How?[12]

This question is the complex horizon within which we have to consider the challenges that at various levels today assail the witness and proclamation of the God of Jesus Christ insofar as they are the carriers of an anthropological and social proposal able to orient us toward a realistic and promising solution.

The Modern Question of Freedom between Critical Distance and Indifference

A first challenge is represented by the persistent anthropological and cultural phenomenon of a critical distance with respect to religion in general and specifically with respect to Christian faith. Even if today this is to be found less in the form of militant atheism, theoretical or practical,[13] the

11. Amartya Sen, *Globalizzazione e libertà* (Milan: Mondadori, 2002). For an examination of the relation between globalization and economics with regard to human well-being, see Tibor Scitovsky, *The Joyless Economy: An Inquiry into Human Satisfaction and Consumer Dissatisfaction* (Oxford: Oxford University Press, 1976); Benedetto Gui and Robert Sugden, *Economics and Social Interaction: Accounting for Interpersonal Relations* (Cambridge: Cambridge University Press, 2005).

12. Mario Luzi, *Contro le altere torri* (2001) (own trans.).

13. As is known, nos. 19–21 of *Gaudium et Spes* offer a reading and discernment of the phe-

space of religious indifference and the increasing detachment from the forms of institutional religion continues to expand. And all this while indications are not lacking of a sincere quest—sometimes in suffering—for the face of God. This is a matter of a challenge which matured in the time of modernity and which therefore developed in a context pervasively marked by the Christian religion. From Europe and, more generally, from the West, this skeptical culture with respect to God, or painfully orphaned of experience of him, has spread throughout the world by now.

The phenomenon of the critical distance and indifference in reality covers really different ways of relating to the fact of religion. However, it seems to express its vitality starting from at least three issues characterizing the event of modernity as a process of the *secularization* of the cultural, social, and political forms from the religious sphere: (1) the desire for *emancipation* from religious guardianship, which is perceived as a tendency to keep humans in the state of childhood, impeding the autonomous expression and fulfilment of their rationality and freedom; (2) the desire for *defense* against the regressive and conflictual charge of irrationality, or if nothing else, intolerant exclusivism, recognized as proper to many if not all the positive religious traditions, and in particular, of the monotheistic religious traditions as we noted earlier; and (3) the resulting desire to seek in a consensual way the criteria and forms of an ethical rationality and communication that, prescinding from specific religious affiliation, would be able to respect legitimate individual and social identities, promoting an effective local and global network of public relationships.

The radical question thus directed to Christianity and to the religions has to do above all with respect and the promotion of personal identity, in its inalienable *freedom* and in its basic rights. Their ultimate root should be seen—as Vatican II recognizes—as the right to religious freedom, demanding recognition both at the civil and religious levels (see *Dignitatis Humanae*). A second issue is connected with this: the affirmation of the distinction between the religious sphere and the civil one, along with the proper autonomy of temporal realities (see *GS*, no. 36).

The Christian discourse on God must take account of these issues, also because at root they are really intrinsically connected to Judeo-Christian revelation. We should not underestimate the view that sees a connection between the fading of the trinitarian image of the God of Jesus Christ—or at least of its philosophical and anthropological-social relevance—in Christian doctrine and piety over the last few centuries,

nomenon of modern atheism, seeking to discover its real causes, ancient and recent. So much so that Joseph Ratzinger in his commentary on the Council's Pastoral Constitution in *L.Th K.* saw these pages as among the most important parts of its teaching.

and the sharpening criticism of the Christian religion in its supposed authoritarian, imposing position, a criticism fed by the phenomenon of division among Christians and by the wars of religion at the dawn of modernity.

On the other hand, if the anthropocentric turn of modern thought was meant to affirm the rights of reason and freedom in opposition to the principle of revelation and of authority, the theological response has been shown to be insufficient; it considered revelation to be a doctrinal issue primarily. And it has justified faith especially in apologetic terms, as occurred with the advent of Neoscholasticism following upon Leo XIII's encyclical *Aeterni Patris* (1879). Only the gradual recovery during the twentieth century—expressed authoritatively in *Dei Verbum*—of the notion of revelation as a historical event, gratuitously calling out to human reason and freedom, can show a way out of this impasse.

From this perspective we should evaluate the significance of the crisis that—in its most clear and conscious self-awareness—by now definitively affects Western culture's form of reason and freedom in its tendency to be distanced from Christian faith, or at least from wisdom in its religious matrix, and from the same Greek philosophical tradition from which it originally emerged. We have to ask ourselves if the crisis of the Western *lógos* will implode into scattered, weak, and declining fragmentation of meaning as the still manageable outcome of nihilism, while surrendering in fact to the impersonal process of economic and technocratic rationalization? Or can it open up again and in a new way—and along which path then—to a real relationship with that ethical and wise otherness of which religions, particularly Christianity, are guardians and mediators? Could it do this without losing its own identity and autonomy, but definitively saving the source of its own secularity?[14] So the issue of freedom, a generating and synthetic marker of modernity, is called today to decisively face in a new way the gratuitous offer of the truth of the trinitarian God revealed in Jesus Christ and witnessed in a mature, credible, and dialogical way by the community of his disciples.[15]

14. On this, see Benedict XVI, "Faith, Reason and the University: Memories and Reflections," discourse to the representatives of science at the University of Regensburg, September 12, 2006; available at www.vatican.va.

15. So *Gaudium et Spes* can say: "The remedy which must be applied to atheism ... is to be sought in a proper presentation of the Church's teaching as well as in the integral life of the Church and her members. For it is the function of the Church, led by the Holy Spirit Who renews and purifies her ceaselessly, to make God the Father and His Incarnate Son present and in a sense visible" (no. 21).

The Seduction of the Postmodern and the Return of the Sacred

A second challenge—somehow dialectically related to the preceding one—is the reawakening of an interest in religious experience, or as it is often said, in a return of the sacred. This is an unexpected phenomenon of great importance. In fact, it appears to contradict the fundamental direction of modernity, which aimed for what seemed to be a definitive surpassing, or at least a tendency to privatize the religious dimension. So much so that today, also in the context of the reawakening of attention to the sacred, that the use of the term postmodernity has become widespread—referring precisely to the period denoting the end and the overcoming of the modern adventure.

A more careful discernment leads to reflection on the fact that such a reawakening does not automatically mean a return to Christian faith, but rather to an opening of trust in other religious and often pseudo-religious forms of ancient or recent origin. These are presumed to be more original or more futuristic, as the case may be, compared to the by-now irreversible decline of Christian faith. This phenomenon, alongside the development of the affective, experiential, and even mystical dimension over against the rationalistic and reductionist tendency of modernity, often brings with it a regressive and disturbing anthropological effect. Very often in fact, the primacy of subjectivity degenerates into a facile subjectivism vulnerable to impulses and projections, that are without spiritual and ethical consistency, when they are not dehumanizing.

In this context, the understanding of the trinitarian God is shown to have particular weight and urgency—not only from the theological angle, in other words, showing the authentic face of God, but also from the anthropological angle, promoting the authentic face of the person. J. Sudbrack notices an analogy in this sense, allowing for the obvious difference, between the phenomenon of the new religiosity and that of the Gnostic challenge to the faith in the first centuries of the Christian era.[16] G. Filoramo supports this thesis in the framework of the history of religions. In particular, Sudbrack emphasizes that only the truth and the experience of God offered by trinitarian revelation—the incarnation of the Son of God and his death/resurrection with all that implies for the understanding of human destiny, the universal fatherhood of the transcendent God, the Holy Spirit's healing and divinizing action on human spirit and flesh—can and should unmask the current Gnostic temptation

16. See Josef Sudbrack, *La nuova religiosità: Una sfida per i cristiani* (Brescia: Queriniana, 1988).

and give a positive response to the questions advanced in an ambiguous form by the new religiosity.

Religious Pluralism and the Imperative of a Dialogical Identity

A third challenge is posed by religious pluralism, in the sense of the multiple reality of the great religious traditions of humanity in their by-now inescapable face-to-face meeting with one another. In fact, we are living in an unprecedented historical situation where the world religions have become both historically and geographically contemporaries of one another. The question is not the fact of the plurality of religions, as old as the world, but the awareness of this and the need for an effective way of dealing with the new situation as it is manifested today.

Up to now in fact, the great religions did not generally share the same geographic area, to such a degree that it was possible to mark out more or less exactly the Christian, Islamic, Hindu, Buddhist, Confucian, etc., areas. They were almost impermeable to each other, or at most simply contiguous with each other. Increasingly in recent decades, due especially to the means of communication and the huge migration movements affecting the whole planet, religions have come face to face with one another.

But there is also a historic contemporaneity among them today. In the Eurocentric Western culture prevalent until now—enlightened, evolutionist, or generally progressive—the more ancient religions were usually interpreted as belonging to a now-surpassed stage of humanity's religious development in order to arrive at Christianity, defined by Hegel as the "religion of modern times," finally leading to its becoming true as celebration of the humanization of man. Thus Feuerbach's anthropocentrism, Comte's positivism, and Bloch's neo-Marxism. Today we are aware that the religions coexist beside each other, and they often exhibit a surprising vitality—Islamic expansion, Hindu reawakening, and the West's fascination with Hinduism and Buddhism.

All of this happens within a cultural atmosphere of a crisis of the experience and the very notion of truth. In this unprecedented situation, there is a chance that Jesus Christ will no longer be seen, even by Christians, as the definitive and universal revelation of the truth of God, but only as one of many roads leading to him.[17] The temptation is to say that every experience and religious tradition has an absolute value in itself: a form of radical relativism that can be dressed up as an apparently more innocent

17. This is the risk that is identified in the declaration of the Congregation for the Doctrine of the Faith, *Dominus Iesus* (available at www.vatican.va), on the unicity and salvific universality of Jesus Christ and of the church.

and tolerant syncretism. This would hold at the end of the day that there would be a lowest common denominator summing up the meaning and function of all religions, without identifying with any of them. Rather, this common synthesis would contain the inner and essential truth, the common source, understood and expressed in different forms together with the common destiny.

This poses a formidable challenge to Christian theology, which is called to revive the principle from the originality of the Christological event to understand the meaning of religious plurality in the unique divine plan of salvation, with its eschatological center in Jesus Christ. That call is to open up sincere and personal relationships of dialogue, without lessening faith in the unicity and universality of Christ himself, but precisely through this, becoming believable and radical witnesses of this faith. The truth of the image of God flowing from Christological revelation is gauged in this context not so much in terms of the capacity it shows to exclude the other religious traditions, but to bring out their positive theological meaning—even if partial and provisional—and their intrinsic relation to Christ through the Spirit, who, by ways known only to God, reaches all humanity (see *GS*, no. 22).

Before everything, this means coherently and creatively starting out from the Christological and trinitarian center of the faith to a deep and broad study of the categories of understanding and expression of Christian truth itself on a more universal scale. Until now this truth has generally taken shape in relation to Greek philosophy and the cultures of the peoples of the West.

Social Injustice, the Question of Evil, and the Ecological Crisis

A further and radical challenge is that of poverty, of oppression, and of the impending ecological crisis. A dramatic and pressing appeal to God and the rest of humanity for justice, solidarity, peace, and the protection of creation arises from millions and millions of men and women. This emerges from the "upending of the history" of a progress, development, and well-being which only regards one part, and that a minority, of the human family. It is the cry generated by political oppression and economic inequality that gives rise to often despairing apathy, or revolt tragically leading even to terrorism in the face of the apparent impossibility of escaping the perverse logic of exploitation of humans by humans, of poor countries by the rich, which seems to become inescapable by a certain interpretation of the process of globalization.

Emerging from this cry are many radical, burning questions to Christian faith and the image of God it proposes: On whose side is the Christian God? Is the God that the Christians proclaim truly the God of exodus and liberation, the God of Jesus who proclaims, "blessed are the poor," who has come to announce the good news particularly to them, and who has, on the cross, shared the destiny of those unjustly rejected and eliminated? Or is he an instrumentalized, ideological God, integral to the status quo of privileged Western society and of the classes dominating the countries of the third and fourth world? And again, is it not perhaps in the name of the Christian God that the indiscriminate exploitation of nature foreshadowing the ecological disaster has been justified?

Closely connected to these questions is the tragic experience suffered in the twentieth century: two world wars in which humanity underwent countless atrocities and sufferings, the *shoah* of the Jewish people, Hiroshima and Nagasaki's atomic mushroom, the *lagers* and *gulags*, and then, nearer to us, the atrocities of "ethnic cleansing" and the despicable trafficking of innocents. Then there has been the disturbing menace, spread all over the planet after September 11, 2001, followed by repeat attacks both on a small and large scale, by the unprecedented form of permanent and total war represented by terrorism. Even if the temptation is strong to forget, to avoid, to approve, perhaps never more than now is the human conscience taken up with the personal and social question of good and evil, of happiness and suffering, of the future of humanity and of the cosmos.

Philosophical theodicy and its theological restatement are shipwrecked. What remains is the eternal and universal cry of Job. It has become more raw and anguished, with an epochal and collective dimension. It is a cry that calls out for the revelation of God in Jesus and Christian experience and witness. Only a disarmed listening to another cry, that of Jesus at the ninth hour—"My God, my God, why have you forsaken me?" (see Mk 15:34; Mt 27:46)—can open the way for theology to witness to a word and a praxis that express the nearness and all-powerfulness of God's love, stronger than any evil, stronger than death itself.

In *Salvifici Doloris* (1984), John Paul II emphasized that in Jesus, God offers an answer to the piercing questions of suffering and evil by lowering himself down into them, making them his own, illuminating and redeeming them with the light and power of love. And in his *Novo Millennio Ineunte*, recalling the passage in the Gospel about the final judgment (see Mt 25:31–46), he makes a strong and decisive statement: "This Gospel text is not a simple invitation to charity: it is a page of Christology which sheds a ray of light on the mystery of Christ. By these words, no less than by the orthodoxy of her doctrine, the Church measures her fidelity as the Bride of Christ" (par. 49).

The theology of the God of Jesus Christ is called to express an interpretive horizon and a project for human development and transformation of history that does not escape any of these questions, nor any of these responsibilities. Rather, faithful to the truth of that God of Jesus Christ, they witness to the liberation and integral salvation of every human being and of the entire human being. Again it is John Paul II who forcefully says (par. 29):

> It is not therefore a matter of inventing a "new program." The program already exists: it is the plan found in the Gospel and in the living Tradition, it is the same as ever. Ultimately, it has its center in Christ himself, who is to be known, loved and imitated, so that in him we may live the life of the Trinity, and with him transform history until its fulfilment in the heavenly Jerusalem.

The Unprecedented Frontiers Favored by Science and Technology

A final challenge is raised by a question that has become ever more pressing for contemporary humanity—not just for theoretical reasons, like deciphering the meaning and destiny of history and the cosmos but also ultimately for ethical concerns affecting behavior and human existence. Questions like: What is the relation between on one hand, the image of the world constructed by the sciences and formed by technology, within which human dignity and the development of human existence is placed, and on the other hand, the image of God put forward by Christian revelation? Or how do theories about the beginning, expansion, and end of the universe, along with theories and technologies dealing with the origin, growth, and ending of human life, connect with the basic truths of revelation—creation and sin, the incarnation of Christ, the Holy Spirit's action in the world, "the new heavens and the new earth," and the resurrection of the body?

The relation between modern science—or better, the sciences—with their related technological implications, and Christianity, proceeds through two thousand years of Western history with various ups and downs, through reciprocal stimulation and sharp conflicts as well. And the relationship continues today within a changed, historically unprecedented horizon. We can outline three organically linked perspectives—historical, epistemic, and ethical-anthropological—where this relationship has been and is at play.

Historical Perspective

Regarding the historical perspective it is essential to bear in mind how the understanding of the meaning and significance of God's revelation, as testified by scripture, has been expressed and has developed in Christian consciousness over the course of centuries. What was decisive in that was acquiring the concept that affirmation of the truth stemming from revelation pertains to the context of "salvific" truth, in other words it concerns the ultimate meaning and destiny of humanity with respect to God. If understood correctly, this includes the implications concerning the understanding of human being and action in the world; it does not directly and intentionally concern historical or scientific truth.

In fact, the Christian vision of the world as God's creation, entrusted by him to human responsibility, has constituted a decisive horizon or frame of reference for the cultural and scientific development of the West. The notion of creation, while affirming that the world depends for its coming into being and its continuing existence on God alone, brings out from this very fact that it is other than God and as such has its own identity. Two consequences flow from this which have no little importance in favoring scientific research: firstly, the intensification of the principle of the inner intelligibility of creation on its various theoretical levels, a principle that is already available from Greek philosophy in the Western cultural tradition. Secondly, there is the affirmation of its autonomy from the fact that it enjoys its own laws, inscribed in it by the creator (see *GS*, no. 36).[18] So much so that it has become normal in the cultural tradition of Christian inspiration, to speak of a "book of nature" alongside the "book of scripture."

The case of Galileo and the sharp nineteenth-century polemic about evolution should be understood within this rich and complex framework of mutual relations and stimulations, marked by a difficult but constructive process of maturation of each side's respective epistemic awareness. Speaking of the Galileo case, John Paul II remarked:

> Thus the new science with its methods and the freedom of research which they implied, obliged the theologians to examine their own criteria of scriptural interpretation.... The birth of a new way of approaching the study of natural phenomena demands a clarification on the part of all disciplines of knowledge. It obliges them to define more clearly their own field, their approach, their methods, as well as the precise import of their conclusions.[19]

It is significant that both the Galileo case as well as the quarrel about evolution which is closer to us in time have become the objects of more serene consideration in the last century, reflecting a more attentive understanding of the concept of revelation. It is enough to mention in this

18. As *Gaudium et Spes* clearly explains, it is not a matter of absolute autonomy, precisely because it is God who creates the world with its own ontological identity, to be investigated with methodologies appropriate to its various levels of expression.

19. *Dizionario Interdisciplinare di Scienza e Fede*, 2216–18: "Discorso di Giovanni Paolo II alla Pontificia Accademia delle Scienze," October 31, 1992 (own trans.).

regard Teilhard de Chardin's pioneering attempt; he tried to show the possibility not only of the integration but also of the convergence of the evolutionary vision of the universe proposed by modern science and the Christocentric and Christ-finalized interpretation of the *historia salutis* proposed by faith. The same conviction can be found in many pages of *Gaudium et Spes.* Nor is Teilhard de Chardin an isolated example; today an emphasis is even beginning concerning what the grammar of trinitarian revelation can offer as a contribution to illuminate the understanding of the genesis and the dynamic and relational structure of created reality, on its various levels and in its different forms.

Epistemic Perspective

Within a correct epistemological context and in the light of what I have discussed above, we can affirm the possibility and necessity of a dialogue between theology and science. In this dialogue, on the one hand, theology acknowledges the sciences' right to investigate the specific dimension of reality falling under their own methodology; on the other hand, the sciences recognize that theology deals with its own dimension of reality which it manifests and justifies, a dimension that transcends their observational and verificational criteria.

Human beings strive to interpret their relationship with the original data of reality by means of a plurality of approaches, each of which can be described as a distinct context of knowledge. From the viewpoint of theology, philosophy, and of the sciences, to speak of an "interpretation of reality" means to put forward a point of reference and of verification on the basis of which they can meet one another, respecting their distinct methodological autonomies. On one hand there is the objective reference to reality, understood in a dynamic, open, perspectival, and multidimensional sense, around which the various kinds of knowledge can be harmonized. On the other hand, there is the subjective reference to the person, incorporated in and expressing the community and the tradition of human knowledge, in the person's capacity and effort to receive, interpret, and shape reality in its widest horizon of meaning.

This double reference brings out the correlation between the unity and the multiplicity intrinsic both to human knowledge and to the reality which offers itself to that knowledge as its object. It is precisely reality's multidimensionality that requires a plurality of approaches and interpretations of that same reality, just as the constitutive openness of humans to reality makes possible the rich ontological and semantic appreciation and expression of that reality.

So the double reference to the objective principle of reality and to the subjective principle of interpretation makes room for the recognition of the epistemic status and correlative investigatory method of the various disciplines, overcoming any undue temptation for one kind of knowledge to reduce or dominate another. John Paul II underlined this at the University of Bologna in 1982:

> Since reason can grasp the unity which binds the world and truth to their origin only within partial modes of knowledge, each single science—including philosophy and theology—is a limited attempt which can grasp the complex unity of truth only in diversity, that is, within a system of open and complementary areas of knowledge.

The reciprocal autonomy and complementarity of the different spheres of knowledge pushes us at the same time toward the recovery from within, and in the appreciation of, the multiplicity and unity of reality known, as well as of the subject that interprets it. This is one of the topics in John Paul II's 1988 message to Fr. George Coyne, director of the Vatican Observatory:

> When human beings seek to understand the multiplicities that surround them, when they seek to make sense of experience, they do so by bringing many factors into a common vision. Understanding is achieved when many data are unified by a common structure. The one illuminates the many: it makes sense of the whole. Simple multiplicity is chaos; an insight, a single model, can give that chaos structure and draw it into intelligibility.

Ethical and Anthropological Perspective

Finally, with regard to the ethical and anthropological perspective, the new frontiers opened up by scientific exploration and technology, especially in the fields of information technology and genetics, bring the question of humanity back to the center in an unprecedented way, requiring its responsible incorporation into the history of the universe. What makes this question different from the past is that it is not only a matter of interpreting what is human but of transforming it. Nor is the question limited to our economic and social relations, but more radically to our own biological and psychological reality, from human generation to brain function. A disturbing danger really threatens the age of technology: "Where the world of life is completely generated and made possible by technical means, man becomes a functionary of these means and his identity becomes completely determined by his functionality. That is why it is possible to say that in the age of technology man is in himself only insofar as he is in function of that other-than-himself which is technology."[20]

20. Umberto Galimberti, *Psiche e téchne: L'uomo nell'età tecnica* (Milan: Feltrinelli, 1999), 41 (own trans.).

So the technological enterprise becomes the subject with the human as its predicate. In a certain sense, it is a matter of human history's entering an era of technological virtual reality, not only able to create effective prosthetics to support humanity, but even able to transform what is human, making it support something which from a human product appears to become a producer of what is "beyond" (where?) it. Philosophers like Martin Heidegger and Emanuele Severino have made us aware of this frontier.[21] So the inescapable question that is asked again not only concerns the uniqueness of the human in the concert of reality, but also regards how each human enterprise relates to the respect and promotion of human identity, dignity, and freedom. This is the context where, by rereading the question regarding the human within the new understanding of the universe, the vision of the universe in light of its relation to the human, and of both in the horizon of the revelation of God in Christ, the knowledge of faith and the knowledge of the sciences can and should be measured and should encounter each other in a new way.

It is a matter of appreciating the demand for meaning that each vision discloses in a positive form, placing them in mutually respectful dialogue with one another. For example, if science is essential to define the biological conditions for the human person's physical existence, philosophical reflection and theology have the task of disclosing the person's integral and transcendent meaning, the coordinates of his or her ethos, the moral obligations which should be at the basis of scientific experimentation and genetic engineering. In the end, the knowing and acting human person is one, even in the multiplicity of ways that each person discovers, imagines, and pursues to access and transform the reality in which we dwell. Similarly there is one human family in space and time, involved in this magnificent and dramatic adventure of knowledge, freedom, and fraternity that makes up history. And there is one divine light in the rich variety of its expressions and appeals illuminating the journey even if it is perceived and named in different ways.

Discourse on the Christian God must take account of these demanding challenges and radical questions. Pursuant to these, and in dialogue with each authentic quest for truth and for goodness, it must map out the paths for a meaningful and constructive proposal which can draw its truth and its strength from God's revelation in Jesus Christ.

21. See especially by Martin Heidegger: *Il cammino verso il linguaggio* (Milan: Mursia, 1973) and "La questione della tecnica," in *Saggi e discorsi* (Milan: Mursia, 1976). By Emanuele Severino, see *Gli abitatori del tempo: Cristianesimo, marxismo, tecnica* (Rome: Armando, 1981); *Téchne: Le radici della violenza* (Milan: Rizzoli, 2002); *Il destino della tecnica* (Milan: Rizzoli, 2009); and *Democrazia, tecnica, capitalismo* (Brescia: Morcelliana, 2009).

CHAPTER 3

The Method and the Rhythm of Trinitarian Theology

Taking account of what has been said up to now, we can return to the issues under consideration in terms of these questions: (1) How, in the understanding of the faith, can we relevantly articulate the first and second affirmations in the Christian profession of faith in God, one and three? (2) How can we speak of God in the social and cultural context of our time? (3) Therefore what is the way to follow in order to receive gratefully and express responsibly God's gift of his self-revelation in Jesus Christ, from which the church lives, with words that are understandable to people today and at the same time which also move their minds and hearts by offering them believable and practical paths to respond to their deepest questions and expectations?

In fact, during the twentieth century the question of method has become more and more central for trinitarian theology. This is due both to the recovered awareness of what is specific to the knowledge of the faith and to the newness and gravity of the cultural and social challenges affecting us just now outlined with broad strokes. To arrive at a definition of this treatise's method and structure we have to go over the principal stages that trinitarian theology has passed through in recent decades.

From *De Deo Uno* and *De Deo Trino* to the Christocentrism of Revelation

In the centuries of modernity, beginning with the second Scholastic period of the sixteenth century and even later, after the reproposal of Neoscholasticism favored by Leo XIII with his *Aeterni Patris* encyclical (1879) toward the end of the nineteenth century, the mystery of God was treated systematically by Catholic theology according to the classic distinction of the two treatises: *De Deo Uno* and *De Deo Trino*. This drew from the plan of Thomas Aquinas's *Summa Theologiae*,[1] which in turn was inspired, if not by the structure, at least by the speculative approach of Augustine's *De Trinitate*, or more specifically by one of his interpretations that prevailed in Latin theology.[2]

The Manualist Treatment

In the first treatise, *De Deo Uno*, this kind of systematic approach provided for an exposition of the topics of God's existence and essence with a primarily philosophical argument. Because of this, the coincidence was shown between what a correct metaphysical speculation can say about God as *ipsum esse per se subsistens*—thus one and unique—and what is attested to by the revelation of Israel on the unicity of the living God. This too was generally read in a metaphysical key, starting from the revelation of the name of God on Sinai.[3]

The second treatise, *De Deo Trino*, went on to indicate that the Trinity of Persons was not in contradiction but profoundly in harmony with the unity and unicity of the divine being as Spirit that is the highest good, and thus full and inexhaustible communication of oneself to oneself within oneself. And this was on the basis of the revelation of the Father, Son,

1. In the prologue to *ST* I, q. 2, Thomas writes: "In treating of God there will be a threefold division:—For we shall consider (1) Whatever concerns the Divine Essence; (2) Whatever concerns the distinctions of Persons; (3) Whatever concerns the procession of creatures from Him." All references in this section are to Thomas Aquinas, *Summa Theologica*, trans. Fathers of the English Dominican Province (New York: Benziger Bros., 1981). It is worth noticing that the act of creation is explained, even if only in a third moment, as qualifying the treatise on God himself: unlike the case with the event of the incarnation. This can be seen in its positioning and in the significance of the treatise on the mystery of God in Thomas's *ST*; see Ghislain Lafont, *Structures et méthode dans la "Somme Théologique" de Saint Thomas d'Aquin* (Paris: Desclée de Brouwer, 1960), chap. 1. In reality, Thomas, as we will see in detail below, while distinguishing the discourse on God's essence from the divine Persons, does not separate them—neither from the viewpoint of the treatise that continuously unfolds nor from the viewpoint of the formal object of theology that, for both viewpoints, is the *ratio fide illustrata*.

2. According to the historiographic thesis proposed by Theodore de Régnon in *Études de théologie positive sur le Sainte Trinité* (Paris: V. Retaux et fils, 1892–98), starting from the Augustinian framework of *De Trinitate*, the approach beginning with the divine *essentia* (i.e., from Augustine's viewpoint, from the singularity of the divine *esse*) prevailed in the West. In a second moment, this arrived at the Persons, while in the East, the opposite approach was made, beginning with the persons to arrive at the *ousía*. K. Rahner made this approach his own, as we will see below, when we reflect on his proposal to reframe trinitarian theology. This thesis has been largely reconsidered or even substantially refuted today however. We shall return to the relevance of this interpretation in part 4, dedicated to the history of dogma. It is enough to say here that, leaving aside the profound aims both of St. Augustine and of St. Thomas, the prevailing thesis, especially for Neoscholasticism, was precisely this.

3. We remember what E. Gilson wrote on "the metaphysics of the exodus" linked with the revelation of the name of God at Sinai (Ex 3:14), according to the Greek translation of the Septuagint: *egó eimi ho ón*, in Latin: *Ego sum qui sum*, interpreted with Greek philosophical categories, even though already leavened, at least indirectly, by revelation. See also Klaus Obenauer, *Thomistische Metaphysik und Trinitätstheologie: Sein, Geist, Gott-Dreifaltigkeit, Schöpfung, Gnade* (Münster: Lit Verlag, 2000).

and Holy Spirit attested by the New Testament. All of this was illustrated drawing from the verbal witnesses of this truth contained in scripture. It is from there that the speculative understanding of the mystery, in terms of the categories worked out by the theology of the Church Fathers was adopted into church dogma and refined and developed by the Scholastics as unity of the essence, trinity of the Persons, processions, relations, missions, and so on.[4]

What was thus clarified was that while the unity of God is a truth attainable by reason and confirmed by revelation, the Trinity of persons is the specific object of revelation. While such a distinction is in principle justified in itself, in fact it runs the risk of a rigidity unknown to Thomas, but fostered by the conflict between *fides* and *ratio* emerging with ever greater sharpness in modernity. And this distinction found authoritative justification in the manualistic interpretation of theology, based on the viewpoint of the *duplex ordo cognitionis*—precisely of *fides* and *ratio*—outlined in Vatican I's *Dei Filius*.[5]

Toward a Rereading of Thomas Aquinas's *De Deo*

In addition to its intrinsic speculative value, it is at all events important for the sake of historiographical accuracy to provide some kind of criterion for a rereading of *De Deo* by Thomas Aquinas in the *Summa Theologiae* that goes beyond manualistic rigidity, to bring out its richness and qualities. As I mentioned in introducing *quaestio* 2, Thomas presents the enormous triptych of the *Summa* (God, man, Christ) with the first panel outlining the *consideratio de Deo*, which itself has three parts: "We

4. For example, see the *De Deo Uno* prepared by R. Garrigou-Lagrange as a commentary on the *prima pars* of Aquinas's *Summa Theologiae* (Paris: Desclée de Brouwer, 1937): in the comment on q. 11, *De unitate Dei*, he explains how "St. Thomas first treated of the divine nature, metaphysically considered in itself, and then asked whether this divine nature could exist in many gods" (234); he then (240) underlines that "God is most one" insofar as "he is most being and most undivided" and that "unity is the foundation of unicity." He clarifies that this affirmation "on the basis of reason" is confirmed "by faith." Having quoted the *Shemà* (Dt 6:4), he comments that "Monotheism is inscribed on almost every page of the Old and New Testaments. Similarly, the Creed begins: 'Credo in unum Deum ...' In the IV Lateran Council: 'We firmly believe that there is only one true God ... one principle of all things ...' (Denz. 428). In C. Vatic (Denz. 1782, 1801)." Garrigou-Lagrange in his *De Deo Trino et Creatore*, (Turin / Paris: Marietti / Desclée de Brouwer, 1943), starts from q. 27 of the *prima pars*: "having considered from what pertains to the unity of the divine essence, it remains to consider what pertains to the trinity of the divine Persons," and taking up again the conclusion of the *corpus* of the first article, he explains: "St. Thomas says: 'and so the Catholic faith affirms the divine processions.' From this last line it is clear that it is a matter of explaining the faith" (54). In this way, the principle of the knowability of the Trinity of divine Persons is found in revelation, and following that, is theologically explained.

5. Chap. 4 of *De fide et ratione* speaks of a "*duplex ordo cognitionis* distinct not only in principle but also in object: in principle, indeed, because we know in one way by natural reason, in another by divine faith; in object, however, because, in addition to things to which natural reason can attain, mysteries hidden in God are proposed to us for belief which, had they not been divinely revealed, could not become known" (DH 3015).

shall consider (1) Whatever concerns the Divine Essence; (2) Whatever concerns the distinctions of Persons; (3) Whatever concerns the procession of creatures from Him."[6] So, first the divine essence, then the divine Persons, and finally creation, insofar as it has its principle in God. Why according to Thomas does the *ordo disciplinae* require this division into three? Meanwhile, we have to first try to understand the precise contents of these three moments of the *De Deo*. It is simpler for the third moment—creation seen as God's *operatio ad extra*, constituting into existence whatever is created, and also for the second moment: the doctrine of the divine Persons deduced from revelation.

The determination both of the material and formal object of the treatise's first moment, regarding the divine essence, at first seems more difficult. We could initially ask ourselves: because the treatise on the divine Persons is based on revelation, does it not follow that the treatise concerning the *essentia divina* is developed on the basis of reason alone? But this would not make sense, given that we are doing theology. Rather, we should remember what Thomas clarified in the first *quaestio*, concerning the nature, rule, and method of theology: that nothing prohibits that those same realities which in themselves are the object of philosophy should also be, from another viewpoint, the object of theology. Theology, therefore, not only presupposes a correct exercise of reason with which it reaches some truths which are accessible to it, the *preambula fidei*. But it makes use of a reason from within that is redeemed and illuminated by the gift of grace in the exercise proper to it. Having clarified this, what then is the proper object of the treatise regarding the essence of God? To answer this important question we need to examine the development of the *ordo disciplinae* proposed by Thomas concerning this first moment of the *De Deo*: "Concerning the divine essence, we must consider: (1) Whether God exists? (2) The manner of His existence, or, rather, what is *not* the manner of His existence; (3) Whatever concerns His operations—namely, his knowledge, will, power."[7]

First of all, Thomas does not mean to place *De Deo Uno* before *De Deo Trino*; following the *ordo disciplinae* instead, he intends to initially clarify the meaning of the word "God," the realistic scope of the knowledge that reason can have of him, and the correct and sensible conditions for speaking about him. The first part of the treatise (*an Deus sit*,

6. "Primo namque considerabimus ea quae ad essentiam divinam pertinent; secondo, ea quae pertinent ad distinctionem Personarum; tertio, ea quae pertinent ad processum creaturarum ab ipsc" (*ST* I, q. 2, prologue).

7. "Circa essentiam vero divinam, primo considerandum est an Deus sit; secondo, quomodo sit, vel potius quomodo non sit; tertio considerandum erit de his quae ad operationem ipsius pertinent, scilicet de scientia et de voluntate et potentia" (ibid.).

the existence of God) and the second (*quomodo sit, vel potius quomodo non sit*) are the response to this quest. After affirming his existence, God's essence—what God is—is only determined negatively, in the sense that he specifies the conditions reason must obey to be prepared in an opportune way to acquire the knowledge of God in his mystery toward which the human being is oriented, along with the language to be able to speak about him correctly. Thomas explains: "Because we cannot know what God is, but rather what He is not, we have no means for considering how God is, but rather how He is not. Therefore, we must consider (1) How He is not; (2) How He is known by us; (3) How he is named." So Thomas begins by considering God as he is in himself, starting from what we can know of him by reason. It concerns his perfect transcendence in relation to all created reality. In this first moment, his essence is only negatively defined therefore, through a kind of purification of reason which comes to know him *tamquam ignotum*, and only in this way can it become certain of really finding itself before him.[8] Thomas then examines the same question of God's essence in a complementary way in *quaestio* 12, but this time from the viewpoint of the knowledge humans can have of it. He shows how, *per se*, human reason cannot know the divine essence—as he has already pointed out—but also how, on the basis of revelation, we have to affirm that by grace God enables humans in eternal life to know him "as he is" (see 1 Jn 3:2), that is, in his essence. Thus, on the solid basis of revelation attained in faith, theology finds itself on the way that anticipates and prepares, in time, for the full knowledge of God to be had in the vision.

Analysis of the approach Thomas proposes confirms the view therefore that he does not first premise *De Deo Uno* where the divine essence is defined, to then approach *De Deo Trino* derived from revelation, so as not to change the metaphysical framework he has already traced out. Quite the opposite. Thomas, rather, outlines the conditions for a correct knowledge of God as God (the *quomodo sit* or rather the *quomodo non sit*), to then engraft within this framework the treatment of the divine Persons as object of God's self-revelation, a revelation anticipating the knowledge of God's essence which will be fully revealed *in patria*. In other words, the treatises on the essence and on the persons do not mark out two distinct areas of the knowledge of God (as later became a tendency). Rather they were two articulated and progressive moments in the *ordo disciplinae*: first, a negative approach to God's essence (the *quomodo non sit*), then the divine Persons beginning from New Testament revelation,

8. Such negative knowledge of the absolute transcendence of God's being does not lead to nothingness, to the void, but preserves the knowledge of God from anthropomorphism, from idolatry, and from rationalism. Positively, it opens up to the knowledge of God's perfection (qq. 4–6).

where something of the mystery of God is unveiled. This puts off the positive, "face to face" knowledge of the divine essence to the *visio beatorum*. Following this order we can even expect a positive determination of the divine essence after the treatment of the Persons. Thomas does not do this explicitly and extensively, but he seems aware of this perspective. Clear evidence of this is in q. 12, a. 13: "utrum per gratiam habeatur altior cognitio Dei quam ea quae habetur per rationem naturalem."

Thomas begins with a strong objection, drawn from Dionysius in *De Mystica Theologia*. According to the Areopagite, it should be held that whoever is better united to God in this life is united to God as to one who is completely (*omnino*) unknown. Here is how Thomas answers the objection:

> Although by the revelation of grace in this life we cannot know of God *what He is*, and thus are united to Him as to one unknown; still we know Him more fully according as many and more excellent of His effects are demonstrated to us, and according as we attribute to Him some things known by divine revelation, to which natural reason cannot reach, as, for instance, that God is three and one.[9]

The text is full of significance. Being really united to God by grace must have consequences regarding the knowledge of God: that is, to be brought—even with our reason—beyond the threshold of the mystery concealing the *quid est* and *qui est* of God himself. This occurs under two profiles: in the first place, as more numerous and more excellent effects of God's action are manifested in us by the grace of revelation, and—according to the well-known principle Thomas made his own—because from the quality and nature of the effect we can know something about the cause that has constituted it in being.

In the second place, "insofar as we start from divine revelation, we are able to attribute to Him some perfections which natural reason cannot reach, as for instance, that God is three and one." Obviously it is not by chance that of all the truths inaccessible to our reason but offered by revelation, Thomas recalls precisely that of the threeness and oneness of God, as, more than any other, this truth leads us into the heart of the mystery of God. Nor do I think it was by chance that Thomas connects the unknowability in this life of God's essence (the object of the first moment in the *De Deo*) with the affirmation of God three and one (the object of the second moment). It is as if to say that a first, incipient, but real introduction into the mystery of God is accessible precisely with the revelation of

9. "Licet per revelationem gratiae in hac vita non cognoscamus de Deo quid est, et sic quasi ignoto coniungamur; tamen plenius ipsum cognoscimus, inquantum plures et excellentiores effectus eius nobis demonstrantur; et inquantum ei aliqua attribuimus ex revelatione divina, ad quae ratio naturalis non pertingit, ut Deum esse trinum et unum" (*ST* I, q. 12, a. 13, ad 1).

the Trinity. As he fully shows later in the treatment of the divine Persons, thanks to revelation and respecting the transcendence of the mystery, the *ratio fide illustrata* is called to penetrate to the depths of the mystery of God, expressing it in human words—that is, to communicate the truth by indicating its greater intelligibility. Finally, it is important to emphasize that in speaking of the Trinity, Thomas spontaneously mentions first the truth according to which God is triune and then that according to which he is one. He seems to suggest that the Trinity of God leads to a new understanding of his being one, already known by reason, at least negatively. Thomas does not develop this intuition. But it is important that it should be explicitly mentioned here.

The Christocentrism of Revelation

Karl Barth's dialectical revolution The theological renewal that began at the beginning of the twentieth century has an undisputed protagonist at its start in the Reformed theologian, Karl Barth. In fact he forcefully reaffirmed the centrality of Christ and the cross in the interpretation of revelation put forward by Martin Luther.[10] Regarding our access to and understanding in faith of the trinitarian mystery, this renewal is expressed above all by the overcoming of the intellectualist notion of revelation prevalent during modernity and systematized in the manuals. It places at the center once again the historical-salvific and eschatological event of Jesus Christ as the relevant epistemic principle for theology. It is not by chance that Barth's *Kirchliche Dogmatik* (1932) is structured to begin from the doctrine of revelation, the content of which is the exposition of the mystery of God one and three.[11]

The *history of salvation* is thus reproposed as the original and unsurpassable locus of trinitarian revelation. It is particularly from here that the unexpected highlighting of the Christological opening to discourse on God occurs, according to St. John's graphic affirmation: "No one has ever seen God. It is God the only Son, [or *the only-begotten God*, according to some reliable readings], who is close to [*projected toward*] the Father's heart, who has made him known" (Jn 1:18). The one who is God, in his revealed face and inner life, cannot be theologically presupposed before Christological revelation and the Pentecostal outpouring of the Holy Spirit.

10. On this, see the representative theses 19 and 20 of the *Heidelberg Disputations*: "19: *Non ille digne theologus dicitur, qui invisibilia Dei per ea, quae facta sunt, intellecta conspicit* (He who, on the basis of intellect, knows the invisible perfections of God through created realities, should not be regarded as a worthy theologian); 20: *Sed qui visibilia et posterior Dei per passione et crucem conspecta intelligit* (but he who penetrates visible realities with the intellect through the trials of the passion and the cross that [the revelation of God] shows as from behind" (*WA* 1:353.17–20).

11. Karl Barth, *Die Kirchliche Dogmatik*, I, 1. *Die Lehre vom Wort Gottes: Prolegomena zur Kirchlichen Dogmatik* (Munich, 1932).

Michael Schmaus's theological reform All of this gradually led Catholic theology as well to reconsider the relationship between *De Deo Uno* and *De Deo Trino*. It is indeed true that there is an anthropological precomprehension of the mystery of God, insofar as humans are able to arrive with certainty at an affirmation of his existence (as Vatican I states in *Dei Filius*), through the concrete exercise of the reason the creator has given them. But it is also true that the understanding not only of the Trinity of the divine Persons, but also of the unity of God, is only fully opened up by the culminating revelation of Jesus Christ.

Already in the first volume of his *Katholische Dogmatik*, first appearing in 1938,[12] Michael Schmaus was aware of the need to "overcome, from the beginning, the danger of considering the Trinity of persons as a complementary adjunct to the essence of God," and so was led to, "lightly change the usual division of the treatises of God one and three." Following St. Augustine, and as an expert in his thought, he intended thus "to interweave the treatment of the unity of nature with that of the trinity of the persons."[13] Following from this, the division of the materials treated was: (1) the self-revelation of God one and three regarding his existence; (2) the self-revelation of God one and three regarding his personality (Trinity); and (3) the self-revelation of God one and three regarding the fullness of his life.[14]

The Christocentric perspective of Dei Verbum The teaching put forward by *Dei Verbum* is authoritative and decisive in this process of renewal, where the revival of the notion of revelation in this renewed theological context comes to mature expression.[15] The conciliar Constitution (at no. 2), in historic-salvific, Christocentric, and trinitarian terms, describes the event and the object precisely of revelation,[16] by defining Jesus Christ as "mediator simul et plenitudo totius revelationis." At no. 3, it proposes again the notion of witness (*testimonium*) rendered by God to himself by means of creation carried out in his Word, along with the manifestation of himself granted by God from the beginning to our ancestors and the

12. The first edition of 1938 was in three volumes, re-edited in five volumes up to the fifth edition of 1947; trans. T. Patrick Burke as *Dogma*, 6 vols. (London: Sheed and Ward, 1968–83).

13. Schmaus, *Katholische Dogmatik*, 136 (own trans.).

14. See ibid., 137.

15. On this issue, see H. Waldenfels, "La comprensione della rivelazione nel XX sec," in *La Rivelazione* (*Storia della dottrina Cristiana I*), ed. M. Seybold and H. Waldenfels, trans. G. Ruggieri (Palermo: Edizioni Augustinus, 1992), 405–558, esp. 552–54 and bibliography, 534–36.

16. "In His goodness and wisdom God chose to reveal Himself and to make known to us the hidden purpose of His will (see Eph 1:9) by which through Christ, the Word made flesh, man might in the Holy Spirit have access to the Father and come to share in the divine nature (see Eph. 2:18; 2 Pt 1:4). Through this revelation, therefore, the invisible God (see Col 1:15, 1 Tm 1:17) out of the abundance of His love speaks to men as friends (see Ex 33:11; Jn 15:14–15) and lives among them (see Bar 3:38), so that He may invite and take them into fellowship with Himself" (*DV*, no. 2).

manifestation of the uninterrupted care carried out by him for all humanity after the Fall, so as to arrive at the call of Abraham and the special history of salvation at his initiative and witnessed by the First Testament.[17] At no. 4, it illustrates the eschatological fullness of God's revelation in the Son made flesh, "especially through His death and glorious resurrection."[18] Finally, at no. 5, it thematizes the notion of faith as a free act, with awareness of the correspondence to revelation where man "commits his whole self freely to God."

What is the relation between Jesus and God's revelation? The crisis of the rigid manualistic distinction between *De Deo Uno* and *De Deo Trino* and the need to overcome it through the affirmation of revelation's Christocentricity ended up putting a crucial question on the table. The International Theological Commission in its document, *Theology, Christology, Anthropology*, put it like this: "What is the relation between the event of Jesus Christ and God's revelation?" "To avoid all *confusion* and all *separation* of the two aspects of this question, the complementary character of the two approaches to it must be maintained. The first descends from God to Jesus: the other returns from Jesus to God."[19]

Regarding the speculative dangers of confusion and of separation, the ITC explains:

> *Confusion* between Christology and Theology results if one supposes that the name of God is totally unknown outside of Jesus Christ, and that there exists no other Theology than that which arises from the Christian revelation. This does not respect the mystery of man the creature in whom there wells up a fundamental desire for God, intimated in religious and in philosophical teachings all throughout history. It also neglects the importance of the traces of God in creation (cf. Rm 1:20). In addition, it denies the economy of the revelation of the unique character of God in the Old Testament, which the Church recognized from the very beginning, as well as the theocentric attitude of Jesus, who asserted that the God of the Old Law was his own Father. Furthermore, one creates a serious ambiguity in the understanding of the confession, "Jesus is the Son of God"—an ambiguity that, in the last analysis, can result in an atheistic Christology. A *separation* between Christology and Theology supposes the idea that in any part of the body of Theology, the notion of God elaborated by philosophical wisdom can take the place of reflection upon revealed faith. It also misunderstands the originality of the revelation given to the people of Israel—revelation

17. See Anthony Abela, *The Themes of the Abraham Narrative: Thematic Coherence within the Abraham Literary Unit of Genesis 11:27–25:18* (Malta: Studia Editions, 1989).

18. "To see Jesus is to see his Father (see Jn 14:9). For this reason Jesus perfected revelation by fulfilling it through his whole work of making himself present and manifesting himself: through his words and deeds, his signs and wonders, but especially through his death and glorious resurrection from the dead and final sending of the Spirit of truth. Moreover he confirmed with divine testimony what revelation proclaimed" (*DV*, no. 4).

19. International Theological Commission, *Theology, Christology, Anthropology*.

embodied in the Christian Faith with radical newness—while diminishing the importance of the event of Jesus Christ. Paradoxically, this separation can lead to the opinion that Christological investigation is sufficient of itself and is turned in on itself, with no reference to God.[20]

Contemporary theology has clearly grasped that there had been a great insistence on seeing Jesus starting from God, especially in the Latin and Catholic post-Tridentine and Neoscholastic tradition, which missed out on the reverse and complementary journey: that of seeing God starting from Jesus. This second movement, however, has been affirmed in the modern period, particularly beginning from the *theologia crucis* inspired by Martin Luther. It is an approach definitely aimed in this direction, running the risk opposite to the Catholic approach, to put in brackets or even to deny the possibility of the complementary movement descending from God to Jesus. This has occurred also because the Christological focus of Protestant theology, realized in the twentieth century starting with the Barthian change of direction, tended to deny the possibility of an authentic access to the mystery of God prescinding from faith in Jesus Christ.

What is needed then, is to recover the balance between the two movements. We have to take into account the universal anthropological pre-comprehension of the mystery of God in the desire for him testified by the wisdom of the religions and by philosophy. Secondly, we must take into account the history of revelation related by the First Testament. On this basis the discussion should be focused on God in the Christological revelation of the Father, the Son, and the Holy Spirit. In this way, we see and express not only the truth of the Trinity of Persons, but precisely with that, the truth of God's being one. Because of this, having overcome the manualistic distinction between *De Deo Uno* and *De Deo Trino*, what we are doing is developing a single treatise that organically links the understanding of the unity and the Trinity of God both from the viewpoint of its progressive manifestation on the historic-salvific level as well as from the viewpoint of its theological thematization. This is in the context of revelation which fulfills the cognitive openness and the human desire for God.

Rahner's "Fundamental Axiom," "Economy," and "Theology"

A second important moment in twentieth-century trinitarian thought, closely connected to and following on the first, has developed in the

20. Ibid., I.A.1.1–2. The ITC also connects this theme with the relation between theocentrism and Christocentrism, showing how in reality they are false alternatives as "Christian Theocentrism [revealed, trinitarian] and Christocentrism are in fact one and the same" (I.B.1–3).

Catholic tradition, but has been widely accepted in the theology of other traditions too. It is marked by the proposal of the "fundamental axiom" (*Grundaxiom*) formulated by Karl Rahner at the end of the 1950s. It is aimed at offering a foundational principle for the realignment of the treatise on trinitarian theology required by the renewal being carried out at that time.

Rahner committed himself to recover the perspective of the Church Fathers, especially the Greek Fathers, at the source of Scholastic speculation and of the Christocentrism of the Protestant Reformation. In accordance with this perspective, it is necessary to ascend from the *oikonomía* (the revelation of God in the history of salvation) to the *theología* (the contemplation of God the Trinity in himself). Rahner wished to make this approach more rigorous undoubtedly in order to overcome the separation, developed in modernity, between *De Deo Uno* and *De Deo Trino*, but more in general the separation between the history of salvation and the ontological understanding of the trinitarian truth. So he proposed this axiom: "The 'economic' Trinity is the 'immanent' Trinity and the 'immanent' Trinity is the 'economic' Trinity,"[21] where "economic" refers to the Trinity as revealed in the history of salvation and "immanent" refers to the Trinity in its existence in itself. It should be noted that the "vice versa" used by Rahner to specify the formulation of the axiom is, as we shall see, still hotly debated.

Genesis and Meaning

The fundamental axiom was meant to respond to the concrete situation characterizing, in Rahner's opinion, believers' perception and the theological formulation of the trinitarian mystery over the time of modernity, especially among Catholics. He saw the risk of the practical irrelevance of the trinitarian mystery, at the levels of ordinary existence, of theological isolation at the level of doctrine. He made the well-known declaration that one could have the accurate impression that

> Christians are, in their practical life, almost mere "monotheists." We must be willing to admit that, should the doctrine of the Trinity have to be dropped as false, the major part of the religious literature could well remain virtually unchanged.... One has the feeling that, for the catechism of head and heart (as contrasted with the printed catechism), the Christian's idea of the incarnation would not have to change at all if there were no Trinity.[22]

21. See Rahner's formulation in *The Trinity*, trans. Joseph Donceel (London: Burns and Oates, 2001), 22, which takes up the formulation first given in "Bemerkungen zum dogmatischer Traktat *De Trinitate*," in Rahner, *Schriften zur Theologie* IV (Einsiedeln-Zürich-Köln: Benziger, 1960), 103–33. On this, it is enough to return to the detailed work of Marcelo González, *La relación entre Trinidad económica e inmanente: el 'axioma fundamental' de K. Rahner y su recepción. Lineas para continuar la reflexión* (Rome: Libreria Ed. della Pontificia Università Lateranense, 1996).

22. Rahner, *The Trinity*, 10–11.

An obvious symptom of this situation can be found under two aspects: on one hand, in ordinary language we tend to speak generally and even generically of God who is made man, rather than speaking pertinently of the Son/Word of God who is incarnated. On the other hand, theological language has tended to emphasize that Jesus' mission has a soteriological meaning (he is redeemer of humanity), undervaluing or not even mentioning its revelational meaning (in the first place, as Son/Word he is the one who reveals the Father). For Rahner, this can be related to the peculiar form in which Western theology ended up outlining its understanding of the relation between God and the history of salvation, too often leaving the organic connection between the two out of the picture. As a result, it has gone on to elaborate a theology of the immanent Trinity prescinding from the dynamic of the history of salvation, though it is only by starting from the economy of revelation that we can adequately ascend to the being of the Trinity in itself. This kind of approach is clearly expressed in two propositions that came to be gradually affirmed in theology and ended up being interpreted in a rigid and reductive manner.

The question of the incarnation The first thesis affirms that "each of the divine persons (if God freely so decided) could have become man."[23] According to Rahner, this proposition goes back to St. Augustine[24] (which

23. See ibid., 11.

24. In reality, in the *De Trinitate*, and especially in Book IV, Augustine illustrates the trinitarian reason for the incarnation as mission of the Son precisely from the fact that he is Son generated by the Father: "Non quia ille major est et ille minor; sed quia ille Pater est, ille Filius; ille genitor, ille genitus; ille a quo est qui mittitur, ille qui est ab eo qui mittit. Filius enim a Patre est, non Pater a Filio. Secundum hoc iam potest intelligi, non tantum ideo dici missus Filius quia *Verbum caro factum est*, sed ideo missus ut Verbum caro fieret, et per praesentiam corporalem illa quae scripta sunt operaretur; id est ut non tantum homo missus intellegatur, quod Verbum factum est, sed et Verbum missum ut homo fieret, quia non secundum imparem potestatem vel substantiam, vel aliquid quod in eo Patri non sit aequale missus est, sed secundum id quod Filius a Patre est, non Pater a Filio. Verbum enim Patris est Filius, quod et Sapientia eius dicitur. Quid ergo mirum si mittitur, non quia inaequalis est Patri, sed quia *est manatio quaedam claritatis omnipotentis Dei sinceris*? [Not because one is greater and the other less, but because one is the Father and the other is the Son; one is the begetter, the other begotten; the first is the one from whom the sent one is; the other is the one who is from the sender. For the Son is from the Father, not the Father from the Son. In the light of this we can now perceive that the Son is not just said to have been sent because the Word became flesh, but that he was sent in order for the Word to become flesh, and by his bodily presence to do all that was written. That is, we should understand that it was not just the man who the Word became that was sent, but that the Word was sent to become man. For he was not sent in virtue of some disparity of power or substance or anything in him that was not equal to the Father, but in virtue of the Son being from the Father, not the Father being from the Son. The Son of course is the Father's Word, which is also called his Wisdom. Is there anything strange, then, in his being sent, not because he is unequal to the Father, but because he is *a certain pure outflow of the glory of almighty God?*]" (20.27). The terms of the problem can be summed up like this: is it accurate to hold that Augustine in his theological illustration of the trinitarian dogma emphasized that the starting point is the essential unity of God, in order to then derive from that the distinction of the Father, Son, and Holy Spirit? And that this choice should have determined the approach of Western trinitarian theology in a direction opposite to Eastern theology, which starts from the Father

in fact, is something that needs to be proven), but in any case it is expressly stated by Thomas.[25] In *ST* III, q. 3, a. 5, Thomas asks the question explicitly: "Utrum alia persona divina potuerit humanam naturam assumere praeter personam Filii." He explains that the cause of the act of assuming human nature is the *virtus divina*, which is the same in all three persons, along with the same *ratio personalitiatis*, although the *proprietates personales* are different. He concludes: "Sic ergo divina virtus potuit naturam humanam unire vel personae Patris vel Spiritus Sancti, sicut univit eam personae Filii." Thomas's thesis is definitely questionable, as it hinges exclusively on two ontological notions which need further clarification: that of the divine *potentia* or *virtus*, common to the three persons, and that of the *ratio personalitatis*, which is also common to them, without taking into account the concrete dynamic expressed by the event of revelation in this matter.

However, a tension within the Thomas's overall theological perspective should be noted. Elsewhere (see *ST* I, q. 45, a. 6; and also q. 37, a. 2) he defines the intra-trinitarian processions as *ratio* and *causa* of creation: insofar as created realities are thought/configured by God in the Word and willed/loved in the Holy Spirit. So what we should expect is that the same *ordo* of the divine processions would be respected and reproposed in the economy of salvation, as the redemption/fulfillment of creation, which Thomas himself does quite explicitly. While referring to the incarnation, the trinitarian order is recovered moreover when he speaks of the *convenientia* of the incarnation of the second person of the Trinity: "Utrum fuerit magis conveniens Filium Dei incarnari quam Patrem vel Spiritum Sanctum."[26] In fact Thomas writes: "congruum fuit ut per eum qui est Filius naturalis, homines participarent similitudinem huius filiationis secundum adoptionem: sicut Apostolus dicit: 'quos praescivit et praedestinavit conformes fieri imagini Filii eius' (Rm 8:29)"; and again: "prima rerum creatio facta est a potentia Dei Patris per Verbum. Unde et recreatio per Verbum fieri debuit a potentia Dei Patris, ut recreatio creationi responderet."[27]

---

and therefore immediately moves toward the distinction of persons, faithfully reading the history of salvation? Rahner (see *The Trinity*), following Theodore de Régnon (see *Études de théologie positive sur la Sainte Trinité* [Paris, 1892–98]), is decisively inclined toward making a doubly positive answer to these questions, even if the real polemical objective of his thesis is not Augustine's theology, but that of the Scholastic manualists. On the contrary, B. Studer has shown analytically that the issue is more complex, that in Augustine there are precise affinities with the Eastern theological tradition and that, in any case, Augustine's position cannot be simplistically traced back to a single paradigm, but is in itself rich in tensions and possibilities. See "La teologia trinitaria in Agostino d'Ippona: Continuità della tradizione occidentale," in *Cristianesimo e specificità regionali nel Mediterraneo latino (sec. IV-VI). 22° Incontro di studiosi dell'antichità cristiana (Roma, 6–8 maggio 1993)* (Rome: Ist. Patristico Augustinianum, 1994), 161–77.

25. It is worth noting that Rahner prudently does not explicitly refer to Thomas in *The Trinity*, probably to avoid the polemics still prevalent in the manualist approach at that time.

26. *ST* III, q. 3, a. 8.

27. Ibid.

Among other things, the notion of *convenientia* at the ontological level has an important and even decisive significance in describing the deep structural truth of the relations between God and creation. At all events, a perspective from above prevails in article 5 (from the notion of God to the history of salvation) which leaves in the background the complementary perspective from below (from the history of salvation to the understanding of the mystery of God). There is a more unitary vision as a result, but also more undifferentiated, of the salvific being and action of the Father, Son, and Holy Spirit. On all this, there is the balanced analysis of G. Lafont in his *Peut-on connaître Dieu en Jésus Christ?* which suggests a discernment within Thomas's theology between

> his metaphysical and critical analysis of the Trinitarian reality ... and the "regrettable" option of the unreal hypotheses concerning the Incarnation. In the first case, he makes the necessary effort of analysis, starting from the dogma of Nicaea; at the same time out of fidelity to what is without doubt less solidly based in the post-Nicene tradition (a static conception of the *hypóstasis*) and in acquiescence to the customary scholastic spirit of the irreal suppositions, he yields in the second case to a current developed after St. Anselm, the inadequacy of which he believed he could demonstrate.[28]

On the other hand, as this was done with indisputable awareness and intention, we can draw from two important elements in the Thomistic approach: (1) the freedom/gratuity of redemption (deliberately expressed in terms of the notion of *convenientia*, which in Scholastic language undoubtedly has a precise and strong meaning which subsequently was disempowered); (2) the principle according to which each divine Person in their own manner (and this should be more emphasized) can unite themself to the created person—think of the indwelling in the human person of the Holy Spirit, who is one, identical in all his gifts and in all those who receive them (see 1 Cor 12:1–2), and of God the Father being "all in all," of which the apostle Paul speaks from the viewpoint of the completed *eschaton* (see 1 Cor 15:28). This holds even though only the Son/Word is incarnate, in other words, hypostatically assumes a human nature according to the language hallowed by tradition.

The question of the missions ad extra The second thesis affirms that in God, "all are one when not prevented by the opposition of relation."[29] As M. González points out, this principle is oriented toward "reaffirming the inseparability of the Trinity in its action *ad extra* as the necessary expression

28. Ghislain Lafont, *Peut-on connaître Dieu en Jésus Christ?* (Paris: Cerf, 1969), 165 (own trans.).

29. This axiom was attributed to St. Augustine but it was explicitly formulated by St. Anselm in *De processione Spiritus Sancti* 2, in *Patrologia Latina, Cursus Completus*, ed. J.-P. Migne (Paris, 1841–55) [hereafter PL], 158:288c, as well as the Council of Florence (1442) (see DH 1330).

of its unity of essence *ad intra*. However, it came to be interpreted in such a way as to conceal, or at least weaken, consideration of the missions *ad extra* of the Son and of the Spirit, according to what was proper to them as persons and to their reciprocal relationship."[30] On the other hand, an unbiased reading of the history of salvation shows instead not only God's unity of saving action, but also the order of relations among the three divine Persons along with the singularity of the missions of the Son and of the Holy Spirit.

Concretely, the result of the two theological theses mentioned above becomes clear in the tendency to obscure the originality of the personal relations that God—in the language of Rahner, the "absolute Mystery" from which human beings gratuitously originated and to whom they are freely destined—establishes with us through the incarnation of the Son/Word and the Pentecostal outpouring of the Holy Spirit. And it is worth repeating that this is because of the accentuation of the unity of God's being and of an undifferentiated interpretation of the notion of person in God. Rahner wants to remedy this tendency by putting in the forefront again the peculiarity of the missions of the Son and of the Holy Spirit which are the only way for access to the knowledge of and communion with the trinitarian God.

God's trinitarian self-communication In fact, the incarnation—the mission of the Son/Word into history—marks the original and radically new presence of God with respect to creation from the tradition expressed through the notion of the hypostatic union affirming the personal unity in Christ of the divine and human natures. This is why Christ is the redeemer of humanity and the eschatological revealer of the Father—precisely because he is the Son/Word made flesh. In his turn, the Pentecostal outpouring of the Holy Spirit on the part of the incarnate, crucified, and risen Word constitutes the fulfillment of God's saving revelation, as it is thanks to the Holy Spirit that humans recognize and receive into themselves the gift God makes of himself in the Son/Word made flesh.

Rahner expresses all this through the synthetic concept of self-communication, *Selbst-Mitteilung*, which in his thought comes in this way to constitute theology's principle. This implies that (1) God freely and gratuitously reveals and communicates himself to humans, (2) that he himself, in his incarnate Word, is the content of the truth of his revelation; and (3) that in the Holy Spirit he really gives himself as love, welcomed by human freedom through a causality which is not extrinsic but "almost formal," such as to make itself gratuitously interior to the one who freely receives it and exercises it as his or her own.

30. González, *La relación entre Trinidad economica e immanente*, 346.

So God is revealed in the history of salvation in the triple manner by which he subsists in himself: as the Father who communicates himself to humans through the Son in the Holy Spirit. "God relates to us in a threefold manner, and this threefold, free, and gratuitous relation to us is not merely a copy or an analogy of the inner Trinity, but this Trinity itself, albeit as freely and gratuitously communicated."[31]

Critical Reception and Reformulation

In his fundamental intuition, Rahner's proposal tending to organically rearticulate economy and theology in a trinitarian framework, has in fact been received by contemporary theology. The rather formal dimension of his concept of revelation has also been correctly noted nevertheless. That is why in the end the reciprocal relations among the divine Persons, as they act in the history of salvation and are attested by scripture, are not adequately emphasized. This comes out most clearly at the level of the immanent Trinity because of the need, strongly noted by Rahner, to safeguard the mystery of God by avoiding any kind of naïve anthropomorphism.[32]

Criticism of the "vice versa" However, as I have already mentioned, it is especially the "vice versa" that has given rise to a vigorous debate, including Y. Congar, H. U. von Balthasar, G. Lafont, W. Kasper, P. Schoonenberg, W. Pannenberg, J. Moltmann, and E. Jüngel. The question touches upon how the identity between the economic and the immanent Trinity is to be understood, and consequently, between the immanent Trinity and the economic Trinity. Is there a simple and perfect reversibility of the axiom, and therefore an absolute identity between the two? In fact, the quarrel that has been touched off concerning the "vice versa" ended by drawing attention to the true problem: what is the identity/distinction between the economic and immanent Trinity expressed by the predicate connecting them by identifying them (by which one "is" the other) but at the same time distinguishing them (by which one "is not" simply and tautologically the other). Besides, the very fact that we speak of the "economic" Trinity (with reference to us) and of the "immanent" Trinity (with reference to God in and for himself) brings out that there is a distinction which as such should be correctly made and understood.

31. Rahner, *The Trinity*, 35.

32. As we shall see further on during my systematic reflection (see part 5), the critique of Rahner's use of the notion of person emerges at this point within the contemporary hermeneutic context, with respect to the immanent Trinity, his preference for the concept of *Lógos* over that of the Son, and his refusal to speak of an "intra-trinitarian You." See *Mysterium Salutis*, 3:488–89.

The International Theological Commission's proposal Bearing this debate in mind, the International Theological Commission in its already cited document, *Theology, Christology, Anthropology* (1982), has certainly reaffirmed the *Grundaxiom*'s relevance, but reformulated it to avoid any ambiguity of interpretation: "Therefore a fundamental axiom of modern Theology is best put in the following terms: the Trinity that manifests itself in the economy of salvation is an immanent Trinity, and it is this Trinity that gives itself freely and graciously in the economy of salvation."[33] In addition, the Commission has clarified the relation between the economic and immanent Trinity, which "is to be understood according to the way of affirmation, negation, and eminence."[34] The new formulation brings out that the immanent and the economic Trinity are the same Trinity in two distinct "situations": the in-itself of God and the revelation of God in history. So recourse to the principle of analogy is meant to express a relation of identity, but at the same time of distinction between the economic and the immanent Trinity. This is a relation that can be expressed in the form of analogical language, through which we can truly speak of God, but whose mystery ultimately transcends our capacity of understanding and expression.

The identity is to be affirmed in the sense that it refers to the one true God: he who is in himself Father, Son, and Holy Spirit is revealed and given to us precisely as Father, Son, and Holy Spirit, and in accordance with the "order" of that relation. But this should be said, safeguarding the distinction between God in himself and God for us: (1) the *freedom* and *gratuity* of the relation God establishes with us, and as a result, the otherness that remains in each case between God in himself and his being for us and in us; (2) we have to take account of the fact that when he is revealed and communicated in the history of salvation, God, while remaining himself and in himself, transcends himself in a free *kénosis* of self with reference to the partner to whom he turns (this partner has to be realistically considered in his creaturely limits and in the concretely sinful situation in which he finds himself), and God's *kénosis* is manifested both in the incarnation of the Son and in the gift of the Holy Spirit; (3) finally, we should not forget that God's self-communication in the history of salvation, through the Son and the Holy Spirit, is intrinsically eschatological. In other words, it will achieve its fulfillment only in the kingdom of heaven: and even then, he will keep communicating himself in a trinitarian way to humans in ever new and inexhaustible ways.

Therefore, the uneasiness caused by the use of "vice versa" is ultimately

33. ITC, *Theology, Christology, Anthropology*, I.C.2.
34. Ibid., I.C.3.

derived from the perception of faith that we can and should say that the economic Trinity is the immanent Trinity: because it is God himself who in Jesus Christ and in the Holy Spirit really reveals and gives himself to us, even if we immediately need to clarify that the immanent Trinity "transcends" its self-revelation in the economic Trinity. From this it follows that we cannot affirm the "vice versa" without further clarifications, that is, that the immanent Trinity is the economic Trinity. This is because the Trinity in itself, while definitely being identical to the Trinity for us, is not only and necessarily for us.

The ITC opportunely guards against a double danger in the representation of the relationship between the economic and immanent Trinity: first, that of separation, which has a Neoscholastic form (isolation of the Trinity from the whole Christian mystery, without taking adequate account of the event of revelation in the understanding of the mystery of God, that is, of the incarnation of the Son and of the deification of human beings through the Holy Spirit). It also has a modern form (agnosticism of the trinitarian God in himself, when the economy is taken as a starting point). A second danger is that of confusion (of the economy as constitutive of and founding the trinitarian immanence itself, "as if God needed a historic process in order to become trinitarian"). The modern form of separation can perhaps be recognized in P. Schoonenberg's position in his study of the Rahnerian *Grundaxiom*[35]; in the confusion, the danger can lead to a viewpoint like that of J. Moltmann in *The Crucified God*.[36]

With Rahner beyond Rahner From the viewpoint of theological epistemology, it remains to be asked what pushes Rahner to affirm the identity between the economic and immanent Trinity without the opportune nuances—at least in the best known formulation of the *Grundaxiom*—thus postulating the "vice versa." In my opinion this can be detected in his privileging of the anthropological-transcendental method. This consists in moving *a priori* from the viewpoint of man, focusing on the conditions for the possibility that make man the recipient of God's revelation.[37] If pushed to an extreme, such an approach can lead to overvaluing man as the unique and definitive "measure" of God's revelation. It is the penal-

35. See especially *Un Dio di uomini: Questioni di cristologia* (Brescia, 1973); "Trinität – Der vollendete Bund: Thesen zur Lehre von dreipersönlichen Gott," *Orientierung* 37 (1973): 115–17. The thesis of trinitarian agnosticism paradoxically results from a wide interpretation of the Rahnerian *Grundaxiom*: where, to safeguard the transcendence of the mystery of God, a distinction is postulated between God's being in himself, which remains inaccessible, and his self-revelation, contravening in this way Rahner's most genuine intention, however.

36. In its turn, it is impacted by the Hegelian dialectical conception of the relationship between the infinite and the finite.

37. This is basically von Balthasar's frequently voiced criticism of the epistemological framework of Rahnerian theology.

ty paid for assuming the anthropological turn. While allowing emphasis on the *pro nobis* of revelation, there is the danger of reducing it to the pre-comprehension of something to which in fact human beings neither have nor can have a right. It is a risk that cannot be ascribed to Rahner's trinitarian theology taken as a whole, as he is extremely careful to tenaciously safeguard the quality of the mystery *per se* inherent in God, but which can come from an inattentive and unbalanced reading of the *Grundaxiom*. In fact, this is what happened.

Rahner strives to offer a new appreciation of Christian revelation for modern consciousness; so he offers a recovery of the great Thomist tradition, grafting his thought on its trunk. This is shown by his first work, *Geist in Welt*,[38] but also by the rest of his writing, where he seeks to open up to positive new contributions offered by modern thought. From this viewpoint, there are no problematic issues regarding orthodoxy in Rahner. If there is a question, it is that this delicate and necessary operation is still in the middle of a passageway because it is excessively conditioned by modernity's theoretical preconceptions. Rahner does not really carry out that complete exodus from the primacy of subjectivity, which is only possible by drawing from and fully expressing the Christological originality again. In this sense it is possible to grasp how the Rahnerian speculation could lead to results which, from a theoretical viewpoint, are not pertinent to fully expressing revelation. And this could be seen in the Rahnerian formula of the *Grundaxiom*, and still more, from some of its various interpretations. As I have shown, pure and simple reversibility between the economic and immanent Trinity is unacceptable in reality. Not for nothing has the most informed trinitarian theology, while taking on board the unavoidable aspect of the rearticulation of economy and theology, put its finger on the wound of the "vice versa," and therefore a circularity of idealist flavor, which can emerge beginning with a certain conception of the transcendental. Basically, a Christological application is necessary, which even in its theoretical dimension is expressed and determined in a trinitarian manner—an application for which Rahner deserves credit because he brought it to the center of attention, but he failed to think it through all the way in the end.

At all events—and this is not to be missed in the debate sparked off by the *Grundaxiom*—the Rahnerian principle emphasizes that God is in himself as revealed in Jesus Christ through the Holy Spirit. Or better yet, that in his revelation, God really communicates himself and makes himself known by us for who he is in truth. In this way the truth and ontological consistency is affirmed both of God's self-giving to humans and of

38. Karl Rahner, *Spirit in the World* (New York: Continuum, 1994).

his becoming known and received by humans as he is in himself. If these acquisitions are connected to the not merely verbal or doctrinal understanding of revelation, but as God's self-communication to his creation in Christ through the Holy Spirit, authoritatively received and expressed by Vatican II in *Dei Verbum*, you have the framework for the new perspective in which *De Trinitate* is to be placed. This must recover its principle—both in terms of form and content—within the historic-salvific revelation of the Son and of the Spirit in order to truly touch upon the transcendent and inexhaustible mystery of God, one and three.

The Paschal Event as Eschatological Act of the Trinity's Self-Communication

A third moment in the twentieth century's trinitarian renewal can be characterized, especially from the 1970s on, by the concentration of interest in the Paschal event of Jesus Christ as eschatological event of trinitarian revelation.[39] This was a true rediscovery in itself of Christ crucified/risen who pours out the Holy Spirit "without measure" as the definitive and incomparable epiphany and communication of the Trinity in history. It is a rediscovery that should be seen as rooted in the cultural and spiritual experience and in the theological self-awareness maturing during the previous decades.

Reasons and Images

Above all, what are the reasons that have led us in this direction? From a theological viewpoint, we should certainly mention: (1) attention to an effective and concrete unfolding of the history of salvation, (2) the earlier recovery of Christocentrism, linked to a more accurate exegetical and historical reconstruction of the event of Jesus Christ, and (3) the focus on the eschatological meaning of Jesus' death and resurrection not only in its soteriological importance—as was often done in the past—but also together with the revelation and self-communication of God to human history.[40]

39. My own personal theological research on this topic has unfolded in three stages, exploring the Catholic, Protestant, and Orthodox theological approaches and aiming at getting to the roots of these traditions and their specific epistemologies. So, in *L'evento pasquale* (1984), I particularly focused on the Catholic tradition in the light of a creative rethinking of the principle of *analogia*; this was followed by *Ipotesi su Hegel: Il negativo e la Trinità* (1987), which was meant to probe the origin and the meaning of the dialectic stemming from Luther and Hegel as a tool for conceptual understanding and expression, arriving then at *L'altro di Dio: Rivelazione e kenosi in S. Bulgakov* (1998), articulating the iconic and sophiological perspective employed in a significant current of Russian Orthodoxy in the nineteenth and twentieth centuries.

40. Wolfhart Pannenberg's reflections are significant here: both with reference to the principle

In addition, from the social and cultural viewpoint: (1) the challenge to the image of God, put on the table by the metaphysical crisis, by the ontotheological critique, by the philosophy of the "death of God" (Hegel, Nietzsche, and Heidegger), (2) along with the burning questioning emerging from suffering, from the inevitability of death, from existential anxiety and from the tragedies of history—questioning sharpened by the tragic experience of the Second World War.

The often decisive contribution of new sensibilities and spiritual ways linked with these signs of the times[41] cannot be forgotten: from Thérèse of Lisieux to Edith Stein,[42] from Simone Weil[43] to Adrienne von Speyr[44] and Chiara Lubich.[45] In this context, it is not by chance that Thérèse of Lisieux was declared a doctor of the church in 1997 by John Paul II.[46]

Besides, the centrality of the *mysterium paschale* brings together, with different emphases, the four constitutions of the Second Vatican Council: I am thinking particularly of *Dei Verbum*, inviting us to consider in

of revelation as history (*Offenbarung als Geschichte*) as well as with reference to the Paschal event as anticipation (*prolepsis*) of the eschatological meaning of revelation itself. See especially Pannenberg's "Dogmatic Theses on the Doctrine of Revelation," in *Revelation as History*, ed. Wolfhart Pannenberg et al., trans. David Granskou (New York: Macmillan, 1968), 123–58.

41. See François-Marie Léthel, *Connaître l'amour du Christ qui surpasse toute connaissance: La théologie des Saints* (Venasque: Ed. du Carmel, 1996).

42. Edith Stein, *Kreuzeswissenschaft* (Louvain: Nauwelaerts, 1950).

43. Simone Weil, *La connaissance surnaturelle* (Paris: Gallimard, 1950).

44. Adrienne von Speyr, *Das Wort und die Mystik*, I, *Subjektive Mystik*, II, *Objektive Mystik* (Einsiedeln: Johannes Verlag, 1970).

45. Chiara Lubich, *Essential Writings: Spirituality Dialogue Culture* (Hyde Park, N.Y.: New City Press, 2007).

46. John Paul II, Litterae Apostolicae Sedis *Sancta Teresa a Jesu Infante e Sacro Vultu, Doctor Ecclesiae universalis renuntiatur*, October 19, 1997; available at www.vatican.va. What John Paul II wished to emphasize in his Apostolic Letter *Novo Millennio Ineunte* (January 6, 2001) is particularly interesting on this, recalling Thérèse of Lisieux, who "lived her agony in communion with the agony of Jesus" (par. 27), sharing with whoever is far from God the weight of the obscurity and of the night of faith. John Paul also, in a theologically highly significant discourse given in Segovia (Spain), in reference to John of the Cross's mystical theology of the "dark night," said: "The dark night, the trial that makes us touch the mystery of evil, requiring the openness of faith, at times acquires an epochal dimension and a collective character," and the Pope saw a similar epochal and collective "dark night" "in the abyss of forsakenness, in the temptation of nihilism, in the absurdity of so many physical, moral and spiritual sufferings" affecting contemporary humanity. John Paul II thus concluded: "Christians too and the Church itself can feel themselves *identified* with the Christ of St John of the Cross, at the highpoint of his suffering and his forsakenness, to reveal to the contemporary world, in faith, in hope and especially in love, from within that very dark night, the dawn of a new resurrection" (see *Osservatore Romano*, Italian edition, November 6. 1982). Recently Benedict XVI, with his own sensibility, has returned to this topic in his *Jesus of Nazareth: From the Baptism in the Jordan to the Transfiguration* (London: Bloomsbury, 2007): "But should it not put us in mind of the fact that God has placed a particularly heavy burden of temptation on the shoulders of those individuals who were especially close to him, the great saints, from Anthony in the desert to Thérèse of Lisieux in the pious world of her Carmelite monastery? They follow in the footsteps of Job, so to speak; they offer an apologia for man that is at the same time a defense of God. Even more, they enjoy a very special communion with Jesus Christ, who suffered our temptations to the bitter end. They are called to withstand the temptations of a particular time in their own skin, as it were, in their own souls. They are called to bear them through to the end for us ordinary souls and to help us persist on our way to the One who took upon himself the burden of us all" (164).

Jesus' *pascha* the summit of revelation (no. 4), of *Lumen Gentium* which sees the birth of the Church in that event, of *Sacrosanctum Concilium* which sees flowing from it the river of divine grace, and of *Gaudium et Spes* which recognizes there the permanent center of the history of salvation which has the vocation to reach out toward all of humanity. It is from here that the rediscovery of the crucified God has been made, a discovery read and proposed once again in each of the great Christian traditions, according to the richness and uniqueness of their own history and their own theology. The names illustrating the theological flowering of this renewed trinitarian period are especially, in the world of the Reformation, those of J. Moltmann with the essay bearing this title,[47] and of E. Jüngel with his *God as the Mystery of the World*;[48] and in the Catholic world, of G. Lafont in *Peut-on connaître Dieu en Jésus Christ*,[49] of H. U. von Balthasar in *Mysterium Paschale*,[50] and of B. Forte in his *Gesù di Nazareth, storia di Dio, Dio della storia*.[51] Nor should F. X. Durwell's earlier work from a biblical perspective be forgotten,[52] and even earlier, S. Bulgakov's presentation in the Orthodox world.[53]

Gains and Perspectives

The refocusing on the Paschal event as the highpoint and eschatological horizon of trinitarian revelation has gradually favored the gain of important results; it widened the horizon of stimulating perspectives. In particular, it has permitted (1) the most intense and determined historical-salvific concreteness to the principle of revelation, earlier taken up from its eschatological highpoint constituting the relevant hermeneutic key in the meantime;[54] (2) taking up the provocation of the *scandalum cru-*

47. Jürgen Moltmann, *Der gekreuzigte Gott: Das Kreuz Christi als Grund und Kritik christlicher Theologie* (Munich: Kaiser, 1972). This perspective becomes the hermeneutical key to Moltmann's later extensive theological publications with regard to the Trinity. It is enough to think of his *Trinität und Reich Gottes: Zur Gotteslehre* (Munich: Kaiser, 1980).

48. Eberhard Jüngel, *Gott als Geheimnis der Welt: Zur Begründung der Theologie des Gekreuzigten im Streit zwischen Theismus und Atheismus* (Tübingen: J. C. B. Mohr, 1977); *God as the Mystery of the World: On the Foundation of the Theology of the Crucified One in the Dispute Between Theism and Atheism*, trans. Darrell L. Guder (Grand Rapids, Mich.: Eerdmans, 1983).

49. Lafont, *Peut-on connaître Dieu en Jésus Christ.*

50. Hans Urs von Balthasar, *Mysterium Paschale: The Mystery of Easter*, trans. Aidan Nichols (San Francisco, Calif.: Ignatius Press, 2005).

51. Bruno Forte, *Gesù di Nazareth, storia di Dio, Dio della storia* (Rome: Edizioni Paoline, 1981).

52. François-Xavier Durrwell, *The Resurrection: A Biblical Study* (London: Sheed and Ward, 1986).

53. Sergius Bulgakov, *The Lamb of God*, trans. Boris Jakim (Grand Rapids, Mich.: Eerdmans, 2008); *The Comforter*, trans. Boris Jakim (Grand Rapids, Mich.: Eerdmans, 2004).

54. This was also emphasized in *DV*: insofar as Jesus Christ, is Word made flesh, so that "to see Jesus is to see His Father (John 14:9). For this reason Jesus perfected revelation by fulfilling it through his whole work of making Himself present and manifesting Himself: through His words and deeds, His signs and wonders, but especially through His death and glorious resurrection from

cis et resurrectionis, that is, of the uniqueness and excess (see 1 Cor 1:24) constituted for the understanding of the mystery of God from the event of the crucifixion, forsakenness, death, descent into hell, and resurrection of Jesus Christ, Son of the Father come in the flesh, and from the event of the Pentecostal outpouring of the Holy Spirit; (3) focusing on the interpersonal dynamism of God's self-communication, expressed in the trinitarian "handing on" (*parádōsis*) by the Father of the Son and of the Holy Spirit, achieving its fulfillment in the Paschal event; (4) a reconsideration of the mystery of God's unity/Trinity in the light of God's name revealed in the new alliance sealed by Jesus' *pascha*: "God is *Agápe*" (1 Jn 4:8, 16), expressing not simply a divine attribute but God's own being;[55] (5) an organic connection of the trinitarian "rhythm" of revelation with the trinitarian "rhythm" of "faith working through love" (Gal 5:6); a rhythm that involves not only the relation between God and humans in Christ, but also the mutual relationships among humans in him, with the related foreshadowing of a trinitarian ontology.[56]

The Critical Reception of the International Theological Commission

The ITC's 1982 document, to which I have frequently referred, summed up the result of this inquiry in a condensed and beautiful passage:

> In the economy of salvation we see the Eternal Son take on in his own life the "kenotic" event of birth, of human life, and of the death on the Cross.... For not alone in the mystery of Jesus Christ does God the Father reveal and communicate himself to us freely and graciously through the Son and in the Holy Spirit; but also, the Father leads a Trinitarian life with the Son and the Holy Spirit in a manner most profound and almost new, according to our way of speaking, insofar as the Father's relationship to the incarnate Son, in the communication of the gift of the Spirit, is the very relationship that constitutes the Trinity. In the intimate life of the Triune God the very potential exists for the realization of these events, which, through the inexplicable freedom of God, take place for us in the history of salvation brought by our Lord Jesus Christ. These great events in the life of Jesus clearly make applicable to us, and make efficacious in a new way, the eternal word of generation, in which the Father says to the Son: "You are my Son: this day have I begotten you."[57]

---

the dead and final sending of the Spirit of truth. Moreover He confirmed with divine testimony what revelation proclaimed" (no. 4).

55. Ladaria, for example, notes that "*God is Love*. The whole of Trinitarian theology can be understood as commenting on this phrase" (*The Living and True God*, 23–24).

56. It is not by chance that the edition of Klaus Hemmerle's *Thesen zu einer trinitarischen Ontologie* (Einsiedeln: Johannes Verlag) bears the date of 1976, envisioned as a homage to von Balthasar for his seventieth birthday (Rome: Città Nuova, 1996).

57. ITC, *Theology, Christology, Anthropology*, C.3.

At least the following points should be emphasized in this text; (1) the trinitarian life, as life of love and mutual giving by the Father, by the Son, and by the Holy Spirit, is the condition of the possibility (and living archetype) of the economy of salvation (and so of the *kainè ktísis*, the new creation, as the gratuitous fulfillment to which creation is destined); (2) the trinitarian economy of salvation, culminating in the Paschal event, proposes the relation of the Father to the incarnate Son in the communication of the gift of the Holy Spirit as identical to the constitutive relation of the Trinity; (3) the trinitarian relation of "generation" between the Father and the Son (in the Holy Spirit), reproposed to us in the history of salvation, is, properly considered, a "dialogical" relation; (4) the trinitarian life in the economy of salvation is somehow conducted in a new way because it is translated into a human event for humans—even if it is a human which, by grace, is fulfilled in the act of self-transcendence in his or her definitive vocation in God.[58]

John Paul II's magisterium, in the encyclical *Fides et Ratio* (1998), along with earlier documents—see especially the trinitarian trilogy: *Redemptor Hominis* (1979), *Dives in Misericordia* (1980), and *Dominum et Vivificantem* (1986), but also *Salvifici Doloris* (1984) and *Novo Millennio Ineunte* (2001)—testifies to a substantial reception of this perspective, while also inviting a deeper exploration. For example, we read in par. 93 of *Fides et Ratio*:

The chief purpose of theology is *to provide an understanding of Revelation and the content of faith*. The very heart of theological enquiry will thus be the contemplation of the mystery of the Triune God. The approach to this mystery begins with reflection upon the mystery of the Incarnation of the Son of God: his coming as man, his going to his Passion and Death, a mystery issuing into his glorious Resurrection and Ascension to the right hand of the Father, whence he would send the Spirit of truth to bring his Church to birth and give her growth. From this vantage-point, the prime commitment of theology is seen to be the understanding of God's kenosis, a grand and mysterious truth for the human mind, which finds it inconceivable that suffering and death can express a love which gives itself and seeks nothing in return. In this light, a careful analysis of texts emerges as a basic and urgent need: first the texts of Scripture, and then those which express the Church's living Tradition. On this score, some problems have emerged in recent times, problems which are only partially new; and a coherent solution to them will not be found without philosophy's contribution.[59]

58. St. Bernard of Clairvaux stated that the Word of God "quod ab aeterno sciebat per divinitatem, hoc aliter didicit experimento per carnem" (see *De gradibus humilitatis et superbiae*, III.6–10).

59. John Paul II clarifies this necessary reference to philosophy at par. 97: "If the *intellectus fidei* wishes to integrate all the wealth of the theological tradition, it must turn to the philosophy of being, which should be able to propose anew the problem of being—and this in harmony with the demands and insights of the entire philosophical tradition, including philosophy of more

As I have already mentioned, it is worth noting that John Paul II in *Novo Millennio Ineunte*, originally reproposing the reading of H. U. von Balthasar, indicates "the lived theology of the Saints," that indispensable *scientia amoris*, in particular, for a balanced, concrete and deep understanding of the mystery of God as revealed and communicated to us in the abyss of Jesus' forsakenness on the cross and death out of love: "The saints offer us precious insights which enable us to understand more easily the intuition of faith, thanks to the special enlightenment which some of them have received from the Holy Spirit, or even through their personal experience of those terrible states of trial which the mystical tradition describes as the 'dark night'" (par. 27).

The Method of Trinitarian Theology between History and Ontology

The phases depicted so far, marking out the twentieth-century trinitarian renewal, encourage a rereading, freed from limiting pre-comprehensions, of the richness of the event of Christological-trinitarian revelation attested by scripture and consequently of the dogma and theological tradition, both Western and Eastern. This favors a more direct comparison with philosophical issues, and in general, with modern and contemporary culture; it stimulates a hermeneutics and a renewed expression of dogmatic language. This should be done without losing what is essential and unchanging in the transmission of the *depositum fidei*. Bearing these developments in mind, we can plot out some indications regarding the method to follow in the framing and articulation of trinitarian theology.

Phases in the Way to the Knowledge of God in Jesus

The approach to the mystery of God the Trinity is eschatologically offered to us in the event of Jesus Christ crucified and risen, the definitive and permanent historical highpoint of God's revelation witnessed by the New Testament and made contemporary to each time in the Spirit, by the life of the church in human history. The event of Jesus presupposes the openness and the ontological and existential intentionality of the human person toward the mystery of God who created him "in his image and likeness" (Gn 1:26). It also presupposes the free and gratuitous initia-

recent times, without lapsing into sterile repetition of antiquated formulas. Set within the Christian metaphysical tradition, the philosophy of being is a dynamic philosophy which views reality in its ontological, causal and communicative structures. It is strong and enduring because it is based upon the very act of being itself, which allows a full and comprehensive openness to reality as a whole, surpassing every limit in order to reach the One who brings all things to fulfillment."

tive of God who, through the Spirit's mediation, prepares and guides humanity along the history of salvation, toward the full revelation of himself in Jesus Christ.

Perception of and desire for God It must be borne in mind in the first case that on the human side, there is the simple and profound perception and the inner and radical desire for God as mystery and meaning grounding, enveloping, and directing personal, communitarian, and cosmic existence. This mystery is the principle and goal, guarding within itself the reply, awaited and promised, to the ultimate questions about the destiny and history of humanity.

This is a matter of that knowledge of God, in his existence and mystery, starting from humans and their experience in the world, which is testified by scripture (see Wis 13:1–9; Rom 1:18–21) and expressed and objectified in various forms in religions, wisdom traditions, and philosophy. In such knowledge, the Spirit of God is already at work, stimulating the human spirit from within by directing human understanding and freedom to that meeting with God by whom humanity is created and to whom it is destined. This humanity is fully realized in Jesus Christ.

This invites us to take sufficiently into account, in theological understanding, humanity's religious experience both in its universality and in its multiple particularity, in other words in the traditions by which it is expressed beyond the historical radius of Israel and of Christian revelation,[60] along with the essential reference of humanity's reason/freedom to the mystery of God, intentionally directed toward the event of Jesus Christ. At the same time, by turning our gaze to the social, cultural, and spiritual context of our time, we are bid to bear the existential situation of contemporary humanity in mind, in its concrete historical position before the mystery of God.

The revelation of God in Jesus Christ Such a perception and expectation is in itself oriented toward the knowledge of God, actuated in faith, beginning from the initiative of God's grace. This occurs insofar as he, in revealing himself, enters into human history to make himself known in his Son/Word made flesh and to give himself in the Holy Spirit, poured out "without measure" (see Jn 3:34) by Christ crucified/risen, decisively appealing to human freedom. But this precisely presupposes our perception of and desire for God: how is it possible to recognize that the one

60. As I am unable to deal at sufficient length with this issue explicitly here, please refer to the pathways suggested in my *Il Logos e il nulla*, parts 1 and 3. Regarding the human constitutive openness to the mystery of God and the possibility of knowing his existence, the dogmatic statements of the First Vatican Council's *Dei Filius*, mentioned earlier, remain fundamental.

revealing himself and given in Jesus Christ is in fact God himself? As a matter of fact however, the face that God reveals of himself in Christ and in the Spirit fulfills and judges the expectations and the preceding cognitions of him, and gives new meaning to the understanding of his mystery by opening out horizons of truth and good unforeseen and inexhaustible for human understanding and freedom.[61]

Hence the need to reread the history of salvation more directly preparing for the coming of Jesus Christ. The God of Jesus Christ freely took the initiative of revealing himself: from Abraham to Moses, from the prophets to Israel's teachers of wisdom. This is why the experience of revelation and the promise made to Israel do not represent something in the past or external with regard to the revelation of Jesus, but remain contemporary with and interior to it, as their constitutive presupposition.

With the Spirit "toward the complete truth" Finally, we have to take into consideration the witness to the event of Jesus Christ handed on by the New Testament and, based on its normative testimonial foundation, the church's spiritual and practical experience along with its theological and dogmatic understanding, listening to the Spirit who "will guide you into all the truth" (Jn 16:13). This experience and understanding must also be considered with respect to the different cultural contexts in which it has developed throughout the ages.

The revelation of God needs a partner who receives it, who makes it their own and lives it: otherwise there would not be a revelation of someone to someone else. All this is demonstrated in the case of Israel, where YHWH's revelation is mediated by great interlocutors of the dialogue of salvation (Abraham, Moses, Isaiah), and by the experience of a whole people. The same happens eschatologically with Jesus in the life of the church: beginning—in an individual and normative way—with the apostles who hand on the experience of Jesus they themselves have lived up to its Paschal outcome in death and resurrection; and then, through the ages, in the journey of the community of disciples until the present time. As *Dei Verbum* puts it (no. 8): "God, who spoke of old, uninterruptedly converses with the bride of His beloved Son; and the Holy Spirit, through whom the living voice of the Gospel resounds in the Church, and through her, in the world, leads unto all truth those who believe and makes the word of Christ dwell abundantly in them (see Col 3:16)."

61. In fact in every authentic knowledge of God, grace is always already at work as God's self-communication, even if not yet in the historical and explicit form of consciousness it assumes in the course of biblical revelation. In any case, such grace is oriented toward Christ and definitely emanates from him (see *GS*, no. 22).

The Way to the Knowledge of God in Jesus in Its Various Forms

The experience and understanding of God in Jesus Christ are expressed and articulated in the faith of the church in multiple forms which are connected with one another. Their succession should not be thought of in a simply chronological and ascending way. In fact, the order can be inverted and the forms can be combined with one another in various manners.

Existential knowledge Before everything the existential and experiential knowledge of God is given in faith, which matures in the dialogue of freedom with Jesus as a living and personal presence which, in the identification of grace with itself through the Spirit, reveals the knowledge of the Father. Starting from being grafted into the life of Jesus—through baptism, the Eucharist, prayer, discernment of his will during the journey of existence, experience of ecclesial *koinōnía*—the participation in the knowledge he himself has, and is, of the Father in the Spirit is realized.[62]

Doctrinal knowledge The knowledge of God mediated by the truths handed on by the church's living tradition is given, along with this existential knowledge which is its presupposition and its effect. The lived experience and acquired understanding of God's revelation in Christ is verbally crystallized in these truths. It is a matter of the conceptual knowledge of the *doctrina fidei* as objectively proposed.[63]

Spiritual knowledge Finally there is the spiritual, even mystical knowledge of God, flowering from the experience and understanding of faith, corroborated by the gifts of the Spirit and enjoyed through the "spiritual senses." This kind of knowledge, through God's grace and for building up the church (often due to a "charism" granted by the Spirit for a specific "mission"), constitutes a gratuitous illumination and intensification of the life and understanding of faith. In this kind of experience, it is God who takes the decisive initiative, informing with himself the knowledge he himself gives of himself in Christ through the Spirit. He is intensely

62. Antonio Rosmini speaks of a synergy between God's "immense interior action" in the human spirit and the "positive experience of the divine persons": "the august Trinity's interior revelation of himself in souls hallowed by grace—to some more, to others less—we have called this manifestation the *Triniform God* because it brings to us a triple experience, and in such a way that each one has as much as is desired of the three modes of this effect so that they lack nothing, an experience where we are aware of having such support, lacking nothing, and where there is all being, God." *Antropologia soprannaturale* (Rome: Città Nuova, 1983), 1:222–23 (own trans.).

63. In his *Antropologia soprannaturale*, Rosmini defines this as a "negative" faith, consisting of simple notions and concepts. See also J. H. Newman.

anticipating the full and definitive communion with the Trinity which will be enjoyed in the kingdom of heaven.

Contemporaneity and synergy If we look from the perspective of the history of the church and of dogma, we can speak of a certain contemporaneity and of a reciprocal synergy among these three forms. At the point of origin, starting from the eschatological event of Jesus Christ, there is the experiential and existential knowledge of God the Trinity nourished by scripture, celebrated in baptism and in the Eucharist, and lived in the ecclesial *koinōnía*.[64] Such knowledge is gradually expressed at a conceptual level in the formulation of the *regula fidei* and then in the dogmatic definitions of the Christological and trinitarian councils of the first centuries, to then be deepened through the reflections of the great theologians and illuminated and almost existentially proven in the experiences of the mystics. Once the doctrinal formulation is consolidated, the knowledge of the Trinity could begin, starting either from doctrinal knowledge, or from a more existential approach; but, in an integral and balanced growth of the faith, neither approach can develop without the other.

The place and role of theology If theology is faithful to its vocation and its integral meaning, it consists of an intellectual illumination—critical, orderly, and culturally relevant—of the knowledge of God the Trinity carried on in faith, exercised in existence and expressed in dogma, with the awareness that it leads to a gratuitous fulfillment in history, as a real anticipation of the *eschaton* of "God all in all," which is the constitutive perception of and desire of human destiny. In working out trinitarian theology, it is therefore necessary to accept and give value not only to what is testified by the First and the New Testaments, by the church's dogmatic tradition, by the living experience of the people of God, but also what has been handed on by the saints and mystics, as passionate knowers and witnesses of the living God. Nor should the treasury of religious experience and philosophical inquiry carried out through the ages by human wisdom be forgotten.

History and Ontology

The method of trinitarian theology, then, is definitely historical, because God reveals himself in human history, which as the locus of God's ac-

64. On this, see the Pauline texts, like 2 Cor 13:13: "The grace of the Lord Jesus Christ, the love of God [the Father], and the communion of the Holy Spirit be with all of you"; Gal 4:6: "And because you are children, God has sent the Spirit of his Son into our hearts, crying, 'Abba! Father!'"; or John 17:21–23: "that they may all be one. As you, Father, are in me and I am in you, may they also be in us.... The glory that you have given me I have given them, so that they may be one, as we are one, I in them and you in me, that they may become completely one."

tion with and for humanity, is pertinently defined as salvation history. But it is also, and precisely because of this, ontological; this is insofar as it draws from and expresses in history the truth of God who, in Christ Jesus, becomes event for us through the Spirit, appealing to and realizing our freedom.

History and ontology however should not be understood as two separate dimensions or moments in the understanding of the faith, as Jesus Christ is the advent of God, really revealing and bestowing himself through the Spirit to historically and socially situated human freedom, as promise and real anticipation of the complete and definitive gift of himself in the kingdom of heaven. It is an event which occurred in the history of Jesus of Nazareth crucified and risen "once for all" and made contemporary for all times and for all humans, by the work of the Holy Spirit, in virtue of Christ's *pascha* of death/resurrection.

In this way, Jesus Christ, truth both of God and of man, is made present in the Spirit to the church and through the church to the world, reaching and appealing to each free person mysteriously related to Jesus Christ and the church, by virtue of the same Spirit who, "in a manner known only to God offers to every man the possibility of being associated with the paschal mystery [of Jesus Christ]" (see *GS*, no. 22). Both the person who explicitly and deliberately welcomes the self-offering of the Christological revelation as well as those who are open and live with justice in truth and goodness, really enter therefore, in different ways, into relation with God, living and holy: Father, Son, and Holy Spirit, who is eschatologically given to the world in Jesus Christ.

CHAPTER 4

The Journey

Some years ago, Ghislain Lafont drew up a precise itinerary to reach the mystery of God the Trinity, the center and interpretive light of the Christian faith, and within this, of the truth of God and of creation. This journey seems to me to encompass synthetically and relevantly the meaning of all that has emerged in our inquiry up to now.[1] It can be articulated in three stages.

The Three Movements of One Rhythm

The first movement goes over salvation history again until it reaches its Christological completion; it is focused on the Paschal event by which access is available to the Father through Jesus Christ crucified and risen in the Spirit, by participating through grace in the trinitarian life as church. The second movement contemplates the mystery of God, one and three in himself—Father, Son, and Holy Spirit—as revealed and communicated in the Paschal event, and starting from there, contemplated as the infinite and inexhaustible life of *agápe* in the mutual communion of the three divine Persons. Finally, the third movement, in the light of the trinitarian God's *agápe*, rereads the event of creation, of the incarnation, death, and resurrection of the Son of God and of the Spirit's outpouring as self-communication of the trinitarian life to the church. The church, as sacrament of Christ's kingdom, is called to freely and dialogically leaven all of humanity and the cosmos, in a progressive dynamic of "trinitization" and in the eschatological perspective of God "all in all" (see 1 Cor 15:28) as fulfillment of the gift of God. Therefore, the approach's three movements traced out here are articulated in accordance with this rhythm: economy > theology > economy. In creation's gratuitous vocation to share in the very life of God, this is how, starting from the Paschal event of Jesus Christ, the trinitarian dynamic of God's *agápe*, received and

1. Lafont, *Peût-on connaître*, 229.

contemplated, is revealed as the light illuminating the mystery of God and the mystery of creation, in themselves and in their relationship.

The Five Stages of a Journey

Fitting in with Lafont's contribution and with the viewpoint just sketched out, I will try to synthesize what has been achieved in this methodological introduction by describing concretely the journey awaiting us. First, it is a matter of starting off from the present day, that is, from the experience and theological understanding of the mystery of God revealed/actuated in Christ as church, within the social and cultural context of our time: this is exactly what I have been trying to do up to now (part 1).

From this point, a second stage is needed to draw from the permanent source and center of revelation—the Paschal event of the crucified/risen one. This stage is to approach the universal religious experience of humanity in its multiple expressions, and in a definite form, the immediate preparation/promise of this source and center in the First Testament (part 2). Thus it will be possible to focus our study on the "fullness of times" eschatologically realized in the event of Jesus Christ testified by the New Testament (part 3).

After that, I will review the path taken by the church's theological understanding in dialogue with the development of human experience and reflection through history, in the progressive return from the economy to theology and in the correlated and gradual illumination of the creative-salvific economy in the light of theology (part 4).

Finally, we reach today again: in an attempt to come to a synthetic perspective, where, having reread trinitarian theology starting from the economy, I can articulate in a relevant way some prospects for theological understanding of creation and of the history of salvation in the light of God the Trinity (part 5).

We can only live and grasp the present, the today of our faith in the contemporaneity of a conscious and responsible assumption of the memory of what God has fulfilled eschatologically for us in Christ crucified and risen, along with an equally responsible and committed projection into the history we are living—all this with the confident hope that it will be fulfilled definitively in the parousiac advent of the Lord crucified and risen at the end of time.

PART 2

THE PROMISE

YHWH, the God of Israel

Then you will know that I am YHWH.

—Exodus 6–7; Ezekiel 20:44

CHAPTER 5

God's Revelation from the First to the New Testament

Our starting question is: Who is the God manifested by Jesus? In order to answer, we need to remember and keep in mind the following point: Jesus of Nazareth does not start from scratch nor does he proclaim any God. He appears on the dramatic scene of the history of humanity as the one sent according to the promise made by the God of Israel, YHWH, and awaited by the chosen people. If we approach Jesus' message, we are reminded in so many ways of the God of the patriarchs (Abraham, Isaac, and Jacob), the God revealed by Moses, the God of the prophets and of wisdom and apocalyptic literature. However, Jesus undoubtedly brought with him a radical novelty.

In order to adequately enter into the truth of God's revelation in Jesus, we need to retrace the way that leads to Jesus. The reading and theological interpretation of God's revelation witnessed by and transmitted in the First Testament are not simple and immediate, however. They require a careful critical analysis so that this reading and interpretation can be framed and carried out adequately and fruitfully.[1]

Three specific methodological issues need to be addressed and made

1. To identify the issues that I will engage with, it is useful to consult some introductory tools on the theology and history of the First Testament. As an example, see the following: first of all, the classic general illustration of First Testament theology in Walther Eichrodt, *Theologie des Alten Testamentes*, I–III (Göttingen, 1961–62); Edmond Jacob, *Théologie de l'Ancien Testament* (Neuchâtel, 1955); Paul Van Imschoot, *Théologie de l'Ancien Testament*, 2 vols. (Tournai, 1954–56); Gerhard Von Rad, *Old Testament Theology*, 2 vols., trans. D. M. G. Stalker (New York: Harper and Row, 1965); Theodorus Christian Vriezen, *Theologie des Alten Testaments in Grundzügen* (Neukirchen, 1956); Rolf Rendtorff, *Theologie des Alten Testaments: ein kanonischer Entwurf* (Neukirchen-Vluyn: Neukirchener Verlag, 1995). Second, more directly related to trinitarian revelation in the New Testament, the essays in *MySal*, III: R. Schulte, *La preparazione della rivelazione trinitaria*, 61–110; Alfons Deissler, *L'autorivelazione di Dio nell'A.T.*, 285–344; see also, on the relationship between diachronic and synchronic approaches to biblical texts, Paul Beauchamp, *L'un et l'autre Testament: Essai de lecture* (Paris: Seuil, 1976), and *L'un et l'autre Testament*, vol. 2: *Accomplir les Écritures* (Paris: Éditions du Seuil, 1990). Finally, on the religious history of Israel, especially related to the image of God: Rainer Albertz, *Religionsgeschichte Israels in alttestamentlicher Zeit*, vol. 1: *Von den Anfängen bis zum Ende der Königszeit*, vol. 2: *Vom Exil bis zu den Makkabäern*, 2nd ed. (Göttingen: Vandenhoeck and Ruprecht, 1996–97).

explicit at the outset. The most general issue concerns the concept and characteristics of the revelation event in the Jewish and later in the Christian perspective. The second methodological issue concerns the relationship between God's revelation in the First Testament and God's revelation in Jesus Christ. The third issue regards the criterion for a theological understanding (and therefore a historical and systematic criterion) of God's revelation within the First Testament as well as its inherent openness to be fulfilled in the New Testament. At this point an initial description becomes viable of the forms of God's revelation which are offered in the figure of the covenant (synchronic approach), and then some highlights of its history (diachronic approach) will be addressed.

God's Revelation Attested by Faith

When we approach the First Testament, we notice some features typical of the event that, in the theological tradition—especially in its modern forms—we call revelation or, more recently, God's self-disclosure. The term is certainly limited and even inadequate to express the originality and richness of our intended theme. It represents the breaking in "from outside" and "from above"—that is, by God perceived as utterly other and transcendent—and at the same time "from within" and "from below"—that is, in the history of human consciousness and of the human religious quest—of a mysterious God who is however close and can be perceived, desired, and longed for by human beings.

Historical-Phenomenological Concept and Theological Concept

We need first of all to keep in mind a dual concept of revelation and its two-pronged use.[2] The first concept is elaborated particularly by religious sciences, especially by phenomenology and the history of religions. In this context, revelation indicates every manifestation of the divine or of God recognized as such by a religious tradition: visions, ecstatic experiences but also natural events carrying a mysterious meaning, powerful signs, divination, etc. This is therefore a very broad concept which has undergone several attempts at classification according to various criteria. However, all these attempts are more or less centered around an essential criterion: the distinction between the sphere of the "profane" (related to the daily worldly existence) and the sphere of the "sacred," which is the

2. See Max Seckler's contribution about the concept of revelation in *Handbuch der Fundamentaltheologie, 2. Traktat Offenbarung*, ed. W. Kern, H. J. Pottmeyer, and M. Seckler (Freiburg im Breisgau: Herder, 1985–88).

intervening of the divine in the first sphere. The second concept of revelation, the one elaborated by the Christian theological tradition on the other hand, is more narrow and specific, because it recognizes as a specific and uniquely revelatory event the manifestation of God which, starting from Abraham, challenges human beings, establishing with them a covenant and initiating a specific salvation history.

The theological concept of revelation, therefore, is limited to the series of God's interventions in history which, starting from Abraham, generated a particular salvation history (though universal in its address) which, for Christian faith, is fulfilled in Jesus Christ. This is the specific theological meaning I refer to here. Its use does not entail a preconceived negative assessment of different religious traditions from an exclusively Judeo-Christian perspective—as if outside of the horizon of revelation and of its actualization there was no possibility of an active and efficacious work of God in human history. In every authentic religious experience, which becomes the principle and inspiration of a tradition that is linked to it, God's presence needs to be acknowledged. Religious experience is not simply intellectual knowledge of the existence of God achieved through the proper use of human reasoning but somehow it entails awareness of God's presence in one's existence. In principle, it is not a revelatory event like those that took place in Judeo-Christian salvation history; rather it is an inner understanding through which God attracts the conscience to Godself. This of course does not mean to exclude a revelatory event properly understood, such as the ones mentioned above.

From a theological perspective, such an efficacious presence of God in determining each authentic religious experience should be understood as the work of the Holy Spirit, who opens the individual's mind and heart to the encounter with God. God, however, remains unknown until he freely initiates his own revelation in history. The Spirit, in any event, does not work separately from the unifying design of salvation history but prepares and directs toward it and, in the end, toward its fulfillment in Christ Jesus; the Spirit, who comes from the Father, prepares the advent of Christ and from him crucified and risen irradiates "without measure" (Jn 3:34). The Spirit irradiates in such a way that, as stated in *Gaudium et Spes*, "we ought to believe that the Holy Spirit in a manner known only to God offers to every man the possibility of being associated with this paschal mystery" (no. 22). Finally, it is worth remembering that the theological concept of revelation does not rule out a "phenomenological" reading of what revelation offers, as testified in the Judeo-Christian tradition. This is actually what I intend to do, especially in the footsteps of the attempt carried out by Hans Urs von Balthasar.

In order to explain in a more balanced and holistic way the meaning of the theological concept of revelation we need to take into consideration an essential fact: revelation is not exclusively or primarily an intellectual and doctrinal reality but it is first of all *existential and historical*. Although it primarily concerns God, at the same time it concerns human beings because it is an *encounter* and a *mutual relationship*, even though the initiative and the priority is and remains God.

Objectivity and our (prejudice-free as much as possible) assent to the narratives in the First Testament call us to take seriously the following: the God whom human beings seek and confusedly perceive as surrounded in mystery took the first step toward us. The revelation of God occurred progressively, and in such a way that we can identify—through the pages of scripture, where it is attested—its key milestones and unique characteristics.

God's Initiative

First of all, it is God who takes the initiative. Compared to the various religious traditions, in which what comes to the fore are human beings in search of God, Israel's faith is characterized as the answer (faith) to God who first seeks humanity.[3] This shows from the start that at the origin of revelation there is a living and holy God who, establishing a privileged relationship with Israel, testifies to his uniqueness and character.

Ever since the First Testament, the experience of revelation is expressed with two claims that can be stated as follows: it is God who called, it is God who chose, it is God who spoke, it is God who promised, to finally arrive at the apex, in the New Testament, where it is God who "first loved us" (see 1 Jn 4:9–19). This summarizes the meaning of the Christ-event. First of all, God is the subject who testifies, beginning with Godself, God's own working and word: "I have observed the misery of my people … I have heard their cry" (Ex 3:7); "I, I am the Lord," up to God's self-revelation on Sinai: "I am who am" (Ex 3:14), which will be echoed in surprising ways in Jesus' "I am."

Establishing Salvation History

The second aspect is that revelation is the event which takes place in history or, better yet, establishes salvation history as the history of the cove-

3. At this point, as it is impossible to explore this theme in depth, a general clarification is needed. A manifestation and presence of God with human beings needs to be recognized in every authentic religious experience, which is so precisely because in some way it expresses an encounter between God and human beings. What is typical of the Hebrew revelation is God's intervening in history through words and actions. This intervening establishes a new history and allows for a dialogic relationship between humanity and God, albeit in God's transcendence and mystery.

nant between God and God's people and, through it, in perspective, with all of humanity. In revelation, God invites human beings to enter, with a free decision, into a relationship with God, trusting in God's word and entrusting themselves to God's promise. God cannot be welcomed and known starting from the revelation that God discloses other than through a response of faith.

Because it is an event, revelation is not simply a verbal fact, that is, it does not concern only doctrine communicated by God about Godself or about the world. Nor can it be reduced merely to the facts that took place. God calls and speaks, intervenes and works personally in the history of God's people. Scripture is the written testimony of God's words and salvific works which delineates a journey, by disclosing, little by little, a coherent logic—though at the same time always surprising and unexpected. The description offered by *Dei Verbum* is accurate and appropriate: "This plan of revelation is realized by deeds and words having an inner unity [*fit gestis verbisque intrinsece inter se connexit*]: the deeds wrought by God in the history of salvation manifest and confirm the teaching and realities signified by the words, while the words proclaim the deeds and clarify the mystery contained in them" (no. 2).

A Progressing Rhythm

Thirdly, God's revelation has a *progressive* character. God does not reveal Godself completely at the beginning but according to a rhythm of stages and waiting, interventions, pauses, and sudden irruptions. This rhythm expresses the realization of God's free loving design and at the same time respect for human needs, through a kind of philanthropic pedagogy, which the Church Fathers later called divine "acceptance" (*synkatábasis*). St. John of the Cross states that there is a rhythm typical of God and a rhythm typical of human beings in their communication with each other. While God gives all of Godself each time, human beings can accept God only little by little, with increasing fullness.[4] This says much about the identity of the God we are dealing with in revelation: this God seeks out human beings and respects them and the time they need to grow because God loves them and wants them to be free and mature partners. Irenaeus of Lyons even says that this divine acceptance aims not only at letting human beings learn to live with God but also to allow God to "get used to" living with human beings![5]

4. As St. John of the Cross observes, the marriage between God and the soul is on the one hand "attained at the soul's pace, and thus little by little, and the other at God's pace, and thus immediately." *The Spiritual Canticle*, Stanza 23.6, in *The Collected Works of St. John of the Cross*, trans. Kieran Kavanaugh and Otilio Rodriguez (Washington, D.C.: Institute of Carmelite Studies, 1979), 500.

5. See, respectively, *Adversus haereses* IV.38.1; V.8.1; V.32.1; III.20.2; V.5.1; III.17.1; IV.12.4.

The Dynamic Uniqueness of the Design of Salvation

An additional characteristic of God's revelation concerns the uniqueness of God's design which is realized in history through revelation. This sheds light on the dynamics, consistency, and finality of revelation itself, beyond what at a first superficial glance or close reading of the particulars may seem inconsistent and even contradictory. In fact, a stage presupposes the other, even if it goes beyond it. Therefore, we never find, for example, an irreconcilable contrast among the various images of God that are found in scripture, though we may note some tensions and even stark differences among them. At times, God is presented as absolutely transcendent, while at other times God is intimately close to humanity. At times, God is strong and even violent; at other times God is fatherly and merciful. However, these opposites are reconciled in a greater synthesis and harmony, which goes beyond the human ability to understand and yet is intuited as true and needs to be interpreted as such. The historical development of revelation is therefore characterized by continuity in discontinuity, from innovation within tradition. The reason for this lies in God as transcendent and free subject of the revelatory event. God is always the same and always new in God's full self-revealing and self-giving for who God is.

A Personal and Communal Experience

Again: revelation's addressees are individuals (Abraham, Moses, the prophets) but at the same time, through them, a whole people, the people of Israel, which was shaped by revelation and ultimately—in perspective—all of humanity. We are then dealing with a personal experience which involves individuals and at the same time is communal, because revelation is addressed and progresses through the involvement of an entire people, called to live out in the concreteness of its ethical and social relationships the novelty of its encounter with the living God. Israel is called to become as a whole the sign and instrument through which God's revelation will reach all peoples. This paradigm will appear again in the discussion about Jesus and his church.

A Unique Temporal Structure

Finally, revelation shows and develops a unique temporal structure. It starts from a foundational event (exodus/covenant in the First Testament and the Paschal event of Jesus in the New Testament) which is remembered and which sheds light on the preceding stages of salvation history.

The salvific event is constantly re-actualized and so it shapes the present, while at the same time it is projected toward a future, promised, and expected fulfillment. This dynamic—already present in the First Testament and without which it is impossible to understand the New Testament—takes on an unprecedented meaning and tension in the New Testament. Revelation is projected toward a culminating and definitive event, like a golden thread aiming toward a decisive point that will take place in history and beyond it.

In other words, the theological and anthropological locus in which Israel enters into a relationship with a self-revealing God is history, not an inner exploration or contemplation of what is beyond the world. This is not just any history but the history created and shaped by the relationship freely established by God with God's people: the history of the covenant in which the initiative, absolute and free, is God's and only God's.

The Theological Relationship between the First and New Testament

How can we express correctly and efficaciously the relationship between the revelation of God in the First Testament and the Christ-event, which Christian faith understands and gives witness to as the eschatological revelation of the God of Israel? Far from eliminating the witness of the First Testament as superseded or even unrelated (as Marcion would have liked in the second century),[6] the church embraced it fully and constantly since the beginning as relevant and intimately connected to the Christ-event. The very label of "New" Testament reflects Christian revelation's self-understanding as *télos* and fulfillment of the "First" or "Old" Testament.

This means that between the First and the New Testament there is an unavoidable hermeneutic circularity. This circularity is first of all asymmetrical, because the priority, in Christian faith, is given to the Christ-event insofar as it expresses an essential reference point for the premise/promise of the First Testament, to which it refers. From the perspective of Christian faith, it is only starting from the eschatological event of Christ, attested in the New Testament, that it is possible to have a unified and efficacious reading of the deep and full meaning of the First Testament. Conversely, it is only thanks to the First Testament that one can show how the New Testament is its freely given fulfillment. In this sense, the execution of a theology of God's revelation in the First Testament is nec-

6. In the second century, Marcion established his own church, rejecting all the books of the First Testament, claiming that the image of God presented in them was irreconcilable with the image of God proclaimed by Jesus in the New Testament.

essary and intrinsic to the project of a theology of the eschatological revelation of God in Jesus Christ.

The document of the Pontifical Biblical Commission entitled "The Jewish People and Their Sacred Scriptures in the Christian Bible" (2001) offers a clear and balanced hermeneutical perspective. First of all, it underscores that "the New Testament recognizes the authority of the Old Testament as divine revelation and that the New Testament cannot be properly understood apart from the Old Testament and the Jewish tradition which transmits it" (no. 1). Christian faith, explains the document, "is not based solely on events, but on the conformity of these events to the revelation contained in the Jewish Scriptures" (no. 7). This takes place so that "this relationship [between the two Testaments] is reciprocal: on the one hand, the New Testament demands to be read in the light of the Old, but it also invites a 're-reading' of the Old in the light of Jesus Christ (see Lk 24:45)" (no. 19).

On account of this fact, there is the need to be aware of two opposed risks: one is the risk of separating the two Testaments, assuming that reading the First in light of the New would deprive it of its own essence or would force its meaning. The other risk is to confuse the two Testaments, without respecting the specific essence and journey of the First with respect to the New.[7] On the positive side, the relationship between the First and New Testaments is to be structured—within the logic of revelation acknowledged by the church document—according to the dynamics of continuity, discontinuity, and progression (see nos. 64–65).

Concerning the topic addressed here, God's revelation (addressed especially in nos. 64–65), the document of the PBC states the following about continuity: "The New Testament fully appropriates the great themes of the theology of Israel.... A universal perspective is always present: God is one; it is he who, by his word and spirit, created and sustains the whole universe, including human beings" (no. 64). Concerning progression, the document recalls especially the novelty by which the Word and Spirit of YHWH, through and in the Jesus-event, show their belonging to the very mystery of God in an unprecedented form (no. 65):

> The New Testament firmly holds on to the monotheistic faith of Israel: God remains the One (Mk 12:29; 1 Cor 8:4; Eph 4:6; 1 Tm 2:5); nevertheless, the Son participates in this mystery that from now on will be expressed in a ternary symbolism, already opaquely foreshadowed in the Old Testament (Ps 33:6; Prv 8:22–31; Sir 24:1–23, etc.). God creates by his word (Gn 1), but this Word pre-exists "with God" and "is God" (Jn 1:1–5), and after entering history through a line of

7. These directions are also very important to establish correct and productive relationships of dialogue with our "elder brothers," the Jews.

authentic spokespersons (Moses and the prophets), is now incarnate in Jesus of Nazareth (Jn 1:14–18; Heb 1:1–4). God also creates "by the breath of his mouth" (Ps 33:6). This breath is "the Holy Spirit" sent from the Father by the risen Christ (Acts 2:33).

Along these lines, the incarnation event of the Son of God up to its Paschal outcome of crucifixion-resurrection which coincides with the eschatological effusion of the Holy Spirit "without measure" underscores the discontinuity and even a certain rupture between the First and the New Testament. Even though "the radical replacement in the New Testament was already adumbrated in the Old Testament" (no. 64).

The decisive dynamics of the relationship between First and New Testament is ultimately that of the promise. The First Testament progressively displays a promise made by God which anticipates being fulfilled by God even if such fulfillment, in its concrete happening, certainly goes beyond human expectations and understanding of the promise. With an extraordinary paradox, Psalm 138:2 can even state: "You have so exalted your solemn decree that it surpasses your fame."[8]

The Christian reading is therefore grounded on the faith perception that the inner movement within the First Testament leads beyond itself and is fulfilled in Jesus: "This is a retrospective perception whose point of departure is not in the text as such, but in the events of the New Testament proclaimed by the apostolic preaching." Therefore, Christians, "in the light of Christ and in the Spirit, discover in the text an additional meaning that was hidden there" (no. 21)—the so-called *sensus plenior*. The Christian interpretation of the First Testament is therefore theological because it moves from the faith in Jesus Christ and at the same time essentially historical because it is committed to finding the original meaning of the events and words that are handed down in scripture by applying the historical-critical method (no. 21). In a particular way after the tragedy of the Shoah, a new awareness has emerged: "The Jewish reading of the Bible is a possible one, in continuity with the Jewish Sacred Scriptures from the Second Temple period, a reading analogous to the Christian reading which developed in parallel fashion. Both readings are bound up with the vision of their respective faiths, of which the readings are the result and expression. Consequently, both are irreducible" (no. 22).

8. New International Version translation.

Diachronic and Synchronic Readings of the Biblical Revelation

Diachronic Reading and Historical-Critical Method

In order to approach the First Testament and the history of God's revelation attested in it, I need to address another topic. In its current shape, the First Testament is the result of a progressive sedimentation and literary and theological organization of the attestation of revelation, collected from and expressed in the experiences of ancient Israel. The order of the books that are part of the First Testament does not reflect the chronology of their composition. To reconstruct the origin and development of the revelation of the faith in God that it witnesses, a careful assessment of the traditions that are part of it and of the theological meaning underlying the final redaction are necessary, all the while trying—as much as possible—to go back from them to the very events of revelation and salvation in which and from which they originated.[9] This is not at all easy because obviously tradition constantly enriches and rereads what it hands down, while the final redaction offers an interpretive framework which is not perceivable as such in the individual moments collected and referred to.

Furthermore, especially in the case of the most ancient stages of this tradition, it is not always easy to verify what was original compared to the religious experiences and traditions of the other ancient Near Eastern peoples who lived in contact with ancient Israel and with whom there had been many exchanges. Archaeological discoveries of the last few centuries have unearthed an abundance of information that needs to be carefully decoded and assessed. In any event, the analysis of historical sources and the exegetical method are necessary and valuable in order to identify the historical context and theological meaning of the main stages of the history of ancient Israel from the perspective of God's self-revelation.

This is the goal of the diachronic reading of the First Testament in which the historical-critical method, developed especially in the twentieth century, offered and still offers an absolutely necessary contribution. Below is what the Pontifical Biblical Commission writes in the document "The Interpretation of the Bible in the Church" (1993) concerning the nature of the principles and use of the historical-critical method (I.A, 2):[10]

> It is a historical method, not only because it is applied to ancient texts—in this case, those of the Bible—and studies their significance from a historical point

9. I am referring not only to the Yahwist, Elohist, Priestly, and Deuteronomistic traditions which are intertwined in the Pentateuch but also to the various historical, prophetic, and wisdom traditions which are part of the First Testament.

10. In *The Interpretation of the Bible in the Church*, EV/13, nos. 2846–3150.

of view, but also and above all because it seeks to shed light upon the historical processes which gave rise to Biblical texts.... It is a critical method, because in each of its steps (from textual criticism to redaction criticism) it operates with the help of scientific criteria that seek to be as objective as possible. In this way, it aims to make accessible to the modern reader the meaning of Biblical texts, often very difficult to comprehend.

Without entering into scholarly details and in issues that are still debated in the field, we can say that from this perspective it becomes possible to reconstruct, though only in a basic sense, the origin and development of—starting from God's freely given self-revelation—the faith in God experienced by ancient Israel throughout its history. We cannot forget or underestimate the fact that at the basis of the narrated events there are original experiences of God initiated by God himself. The witness of Abraham, Moses, and the prophets cannot be explained from a simple anthropological, cultural, and social perspective. These individuals had an authentic experience of God who reveals Godself; they witness to and transmit this experience. The faith of Israel, in other words, cannot be explained aside from God's intervention.

It may be difficult and at times impossible to reconstruct such experiences in their original freshness because often the literary documents that hand them down were composed much later and as such they interpret the preceding stages of revelation in light of what happened afterward. However, this does not mean that the living essence of these experiences does not resound through the biblical pages and from them it could be found and revisited thanks to the biblical text itself. In fact, the tradition of the foundational events of salvation history—supported and guided by God's Spirit—needs to be welcomed and understood as assuring the transmission and interpretation of their original tone and of their original and lasting theological meaning.

Therefore, we can dare to use the metaphor according to which all of the First Testament is presented like a symphony which shares the same essential theme, the covenant of God with God's people, which is constantly actualized, reinterpreted, and shared in light of the various and subsequent stages of God's revelation and of the maturation of Israel's consciousness—one single theme, with many variations, consistent and progressive, always more complex and rich, in a constant movement of transcendence toward the promised and expected fulfillment.

Synchronic Reading and Canonical Approach

For the above reason, in the interpretation of the First Testament it is helpful, or rather necessary, to employ—along with a diachronic reading proposed by the historical-critical methods—also a synchronic reading, fostered especially by the canonical approach to biblical texts.[11] This approach starts from the realization that the testimony of God's revelation is presented to us as one corpus of texts recognized as normative for our faith and codified in the canon that, as Christians, we define as Old or First Testament. In it, what is handed down is an overall organization of the written testimony of revelation, in which the final redactions of the various books are reflected, which in turn present in an organized way several earlier traditions.

The canon of scripture, in other words, offers a criterion of organization and interpretation of the truth and of the development of revelation which has both historical and theological value. Historical value, because it creates the framework and succession of the key events of the history of revelation; theological value, because it specifies the shape and intentionality of the current arrangement, situating them in a mutual relationship with each other within the open perspective of the promise.

The classic tripartite structure is found in the prologue to the Book of Ecclesiastes 1:8 (in it there is explicit mention of "the Law, the Prophets, and the other Writings") which dates back to the scribes of the Second Temple (founded ca. 537 BCE) when the overall architecture of scripture began to be delineated and which would subsequently be recognized and finalized in the canon: Law or Torah, prophets, and other writings (indicated also as wisdom writings). This tripartite structure, according to the canonical approach, has not only literary value but is also a theological hermeneutics of revelation.

The Law, in this perspective, shows the foundational event (the revelation of the name, exodus, the covenant) which establishes the beginning and sets up the historical space in which the unique revelation of God to Israel as covenant takes place. This is all increasingly retrojected, from the history of the patriarchs to the liminal point of creation: the principle, the *alpha*. At the same time, it is also projected ahead according to the eschatological dynamics of the promise: the fulfillment, the *omega*.

The prophets, on their end, linking back to the original form of reve-

11. The synchronic reading focuses on the study of the biblical text just as it is in its final form. It takes into account the fact that "the Bible does not appear as a collection of texts with no relationship among them but as a collection of witnesses in the same great tradition" (ibid., no. 2911). The synchronic reading uses, specifically, an approach defined as canonical: "starting from the realization that the historical-critical method sometimes finds it difficult to get to theological conclusions, the canonical approach ... intends to contribute positively to the theological task of interpretation, starting from the explicit framework of faith: the Bible overall in order to do this interprets each biblical text *in light of the canon of Scriptures, that is, of the Bible received as norm of faith from a community of believers*. It seeks to locate each text *within the unique design of God*, to achieve a realization of Scripture for our times. It does not aim at substituting the historical-critical method but aims at complementing it" (nos. 2912–13).

lation, keep open the space of the covenant and constantly renew it. They criticize Israel's infidelities and promote the Law as Word of God in its dynamic character as efficacious principle of salvation history and criterion to judge it. Thus, the foundational event—especially after the exile, a tragic consequence of Israel's infidelity—is projected ahead toward a new and decisive advent of God's liberating action in the midst of God's people within a universal horizon (the "new" exodus, the "new" covenant, the coming of the messiah).

On the other hand, while the Law and the prophets narrate God's intervention directly and suggest God's Word to challenge and judge, the wisdom books testify to the answer and discernment carried out by Israel, thanks to which God's people intercept the search for the truth and meaning which dwells in and moves all of human history. This is the case in the prayer of the Psalms, the meditation on the meaning of individual and societal experience, the meaning and destiny of creation and history proposed by the Wisdom texts within a universalistic horizon. In this holistic and evolving context, *apocalyptic* in some way, the last and summarizing Word is situated as the imminent announcement of the expected event, within history but also at the boundaries of it (the end, the *omega*) according to the eternal and universal design of God which is displayed throughout time.

CHAPTER 6

God's Revelation in the Figure of the Covenant—a Phenomenology

The two readings of scripture briefly described above—synchronic and diachronic—are not mutually exclusive but complementary. Before exposing diachronically the main stages and contents of God's revelation event to Israel, we should attempt, through a synchronic reading, a phenomenology of the shape of revelation expressed in a unique and paradigmatic way in the image of the covenant.

God's Revelation as Covenant

When I speak of a shape of revelation—freely inspired by the terminology used by H. U. von Balthasar[1]—I am talking about the offer and exercise of that unique relationship between God and Israel which is created in and as history thanks to the event of God's revelation embraced by faith as an efficacious sign of encounter destined to be universally spread. It is precisely within this relationship that the identity of the living God is demonstrated and given.

By "figure" I mean the historical embodiment that the shape of revelation increasingly takes in the history of Israel on a symbolic, ritual, ethical, juridical, and prophetic level. In other words, it is the covenant which emerges in all its facets in the theological narrative of the Sinai event, is dynamically made current by the prophets, is projected retroactively onto the interpretation of the preceding stages of the history of Israel up to the liminal point of creation, underlies the universalistic reflection of the wise men, and is launched toward eschatological fulfillment by apocalyptic literature.

Dei Verbum fittingly and concisely expresses the theological meaning of the First Testament, stating that God

1. See Hans Urs von Balthasar, *The Glory of the Lord: A Theological Aesthetics*, vol. 1: *Seeing the Form* (Edinburgh: T and T Clark, 1982).

entered into a covenant with Abraham (see Gn 15:18) and, through Moses, with the people of Israel (see Ex 24:8). To this people which He had acquired for Himself, He so manifested Himself through words and deeds as the one true and living God that Israel came to know by experience the ways of God with men. Then too, when God Himself spoke to them through the mouth of the prophets, Israel daily gained a deeper and clearer understanding of His ways and made them more widely known among the nations (see Ps 21:29; 95:1–3; Is 2:1–5; Jer 3:17).[2]

God's revelation, in this dense text, is linked to the foundational event in salvation history (the covenant with Abraham and especially with Moses) and to the message of the prophets, in the inextricable connection of deeds and words, and at the same time it is understood as the principle and space of the original experience which the people of Israel is called to fulfill by walking along the pathway traced by the covenant, to open themselves to God's design being fulfilled in history and *per se* addressed to all peoples.

From the perspective of historical-critical analysis of the First Testament, the concept of covenant (*berith*)[3] in the most mature formulation offered by the Deuteronomistic, prophetic, and Priestly theologies cannot be simplistically dated back to the most ancient times of Israel's tradition. It is clear, for example, that reading God's revelation to Abraham in the Book of Genesis through the lens of the covenant is produced by a retroactive theological interpretation, starting from the concept of covenant which emerges at a later point in time. However, it is precisely this interpretation which allows access to the deeper meaning of what in a nutshell is already present in Abraham's experience. The historical context of this experience needs to be reconstructed insofar as this is possible. This can be done not only through the historical-critical analysis of the most ancient traditions, traces of which can be found in the texts as they have come to us, but also through the historical-religious studies on the cultural environment within which this original experience took place.

From the perspective of the canonical approach, it should be recognized that the central item in the Jewish canon is certainly the Law. However, as pointed out by N. Lohfink, "the covenant is the *locus* of the Law, in which it opens toward multiple directions." So that

through the diversity of theologies, this concept (of covenant) allows to link all the essential themes in the Bible. With the covenant of Noah and Abraham and with the other covenants throughout history, the concept itself is linked to the

2. *DV*, no. 14.

3. On the theme of the covenant, from a biblical viewpoint, see G. Quell, "*diathékē*, A. *berith nell'AT*," in *Grande Lessico del Nuovo Testamento* [hereafter *GLNT*], 2:1017–65; J. Guhrt, "*diathékē*," in *Dizionario dei concetti biblici del NT*, ed. L. Coenen, E. Beyreuthen, H. Bietenhard; N. Lohfink, "Alleanza," in Lacoste (ed.), *Dizionario critico della teologia*, Italian edition, 68–74.

overall narrative of salvation history. Through the pericope of Sinai and Deuteronomy this narrative is linked to the Law. Through Jer 30–33 and parallel texts, it takes up the prophetic promises. Since it designates the Decalogue and especially its first commandment, it recalls the essence of the relationship with God.[4]

Lohfink concludes: "Thus, the covenant becomes a comprehensive feature of the biblical canon." In light of this, I will offer a phenomenological summary of the shape of revelation represented by the image of the covenant.

The Covenant: Image and Dynamics

According to the paradigmatic narrative of exodus,[5] the institution of the covenant entails the following moments: the deed of grace and salvation implemented by God (liberation and exodus); the self-attestation of the living, personal, historically active, and promising identity of the God of the patriarchs (revelation of the name); God's promulgation and Israel's acceptance of the rules of the covenant (law expressed in the Decalogue); God's promise of faithfulness; and the sacrifice which seals the covenant. The event of revelation creates and shapes Israel's existence in her communal and at the same time individual dimension, thanks to the experience of the unique relationship with the living God through the image of the covenant which entails God's offer and Israel's acceptance of the Law—acceptance sealed by the sacrifice as guarantee of the promise.

The image of the covenant is articulated according to some polarities which delineate its identity in tension toward a novel fulfillment: the first expresses the uniqueness of the relationship between God and Israel (grace and Law); the second establishes the intrinsic temporal stretch of memory/presence and at the same time of promise and fulfillment; and the two are combined in delineating the dynamic encounter between God's coming and human exodus. These three polarities are in accord among themselves by being manifested and fulfilled symbolically and prophetically in the sacrifice of communion which directly involves the two partners in the covenant.

4. Lohfink, "Alleanza," 71.

5. Ultimately, the entire Book of Exodus frames the establishing of the covenant. After the narrative of the call of Moses, of the revelation of the name (which I shall examine later) and of liberation from Egypt, one can focus on the story from the arrival of Israel to Sinai (Ex 19) to the renewed gift of God of the tablets of the law (Ex 34) after the golden calf event; the redaction of chapters 19–40 are attributed to the Priestly tradition on the basis of previous literary units of the Yahwist and Elohist traditions.

Grace and Law

The first polarity is that of grace and Law. Grace expresses God's freely given initiative, God's faithfulness to the covenant (even when the human partner breaks it), the active and constant proximity of God to the history of God's people, God's mercy forgiving and opening to a new beginning. The Law, on the other hand, expresses the request of a free and responsible answer by human beings, to God's grace.

The Law, therefore, is not originally an alternative to grace but springs from it as a sign and instrument through which Israel can respond to grace by realizing her existence in being faithful to the covenant. God's grace, in other words, demands and supports obedience to the Law, which in turn guarantees a responsible and persevering acceptance by Israel, of grace itself. This will come to the fore in the prophetic message of a law interiorized in the hearts of human beings thanks to being given the very Spirit of God (Ezek 36:26–27; Jer 31:33).

Memory and Presence

The second polarity, which is a consequence of the first one, is related to time: memory and presence. The revelation event which establishes the covenant is a specific historical event and, as such, once it happened, it becomes past. But because it is the living God who, engaging God's people, establishes with them a relationship that shapes history, the memory of the foundational event becomes a way in which God challenges in the present in which it is efficaciously actualized. This is guaranteed and made possible especially by the renewed narration of the foundational event and by its ritual celebration (in the Temple liturgy).

From this comes a further temporal stage connected to revelation: promise and fulfillment. Because God in the covenant is committed to Israel through a promise of faithfulness, the history of the covenant is projected toward a fulfillment which, taking place already in history, at the same time stretches history beyond itself toward a fulfillment that still has to take place. God's faithfulness to the covenant in a certain sense is multiplied: it is faithfulness of God to the covenant and faithfulness of God to the content of the covenant—God's commitment to be present on the side of God's people. The foundation of the faithfulness to the covenant is ultimately God's faithfulness to Godself and therefore to God's design of salvation for humankind.

In a few words, what is the content of the promise established in the covenant? God's salvific presence among God's people in a way that goes beyond all expectations. Thus, God shows fully and definitively God's face, answering positively to the unfaithfulness of God's people, that is, healing with God's grace and mercy the wound of sin stemming from having broken the covenant.[6] This is the meaning of the new and conclusive covenant. The dynamics that permeate the covenant are that of *magis*, the "more": "Where sin increased, grace abounded all the more" (Rom 5:20).

Advent of God, Exodus of Humankind

A polarity that somehow summarizes the two preceding ones is that of the advent of God and the exodus of humankind. It highlights the dynamic of a developing and growing relationship between God who reveals Godself and humankind which, in Israel, accepts it. The advent of God: God descends into history, frees Israel, establishes a covenant, and promises God's presence among human beings. God is and wants to be the God-with-us, Emmanuel. Exodus of humankind: human beings come out of their "land," obeying a calling from God, walking and following God's Word, then settle down in the "promised land" where God wants to pitch God's tent in the midst of the people. However, human beings continue to wander, always waiting. The promised land toward which they are called to walk, without losing any of its realistic concreteness, is offered as a simple down payment. In a way, it avoids being completely absorbed by Israel in order to be given back more fully and beyond expectations.

There are two movements. One is originating and constitutive, so to speak, from the top down; the other is replying, longing and desire, from the bottom up. These two movements are both projected ahead, according to a specific temporal line along which they will eventually meet in the final event of the covenant. It is possible also to talk about a double ecstasy of love stretched throughout time: the ecstasy of God toward humanity, which in turn generates humanity's ecstasy toward God. In both cases, ecstasy means going out of oneself to live with and for the other. This is best expressed by the metaphor of conjugal love celebrated both realistically and mystically in the Song of Songs. The image of the covenant there becomes personal, revealing its most intimate meaning and ultimate intention in the image of conjugal love. In itself, it is inscribed in the grammar of the creation of man and woman in the image and likeness of God: "they become one flesh" (Gn 2:24). This is then understood as the universal grammar which expresses the relationship of grace, longing, and promise between God and humanity.

6. Paul Beauchamp observes: "The transgression of the law cannot be reversed and healed other than by an *excess*. . . . To the people who will break the covenant, God will answer by giving more than what the people had given." "Dio, Teologia biblica," in *Dizionario critico di Teologia* (ed. Lacoste), 415.

The Sacrifice for Communion

The covenant and the mutual conjugal ecstasy of love stemming from it, maintained in it and promised by it, are expressed in sacrifice. Sacrifice symbolically represents the encounter between God's grace and Israel's reply as memory, presence, and prophecy of God's advent and of the exodus of humanity which already happened in the covenant at Sinai. It was proleptically announcing the new and final covenant.

Moses proclaims, "This the blood of the covenant," after having read the book of the covenant and having sprinkled the blood on the people gathered there (Ex 24:6–8). The blood is the principle of life, whose only guarantor is YHWH: hence the prohibition from ingesting it (Gn 9:4; Dt 12:23–24) and the sprinkling of blood around the altar of sacrifice to acknowledge God's right (Lv 17). "The blood means not only that *the covenant is more valuable than life*, but also that *the covenant gives greater value to life*, transforming it."[7] In the sacrifice the encounter takes place between humanity's free reply and commitment to God's covenant offer and God's acceptance of the offer. Sacrifice therefore seals and makes tangible and efficacious the communion between the two covenant partners. The blood poured out, symbol of the offer of one's life, is sprinkled on the people as a sign that God accepted the offer and therefore Israel belongs to God, is God's people, and God is the God of Israel.

While, originally, blood is the symbol of the blood of a sacrificial victim, it becomes increasingly understood—linked to the prophetic promise that the first covenant would be fulfilled in a "new" and final covenant—that the sacrifice is no longer ritual but existential, the sacrifice of the servant of YHWH (in the songs in Second Isaiah: Is 42:1–7; 49:1–6; 50:4–9; 52:13; 53:12), who takes on, though innocent, the sin of the multitudes (Is 50:9), suffers pain and mistreatment to the point of seeming to be "beaten by God" and suffers meekly an unjust death like a lamb lead to slaughter (Is 53:7). In this way, the protagonist himself becomes the sacrifice in which the definitive covenant is sealed.

Somehow, his sacrifice expresses not only Israel's answer to God for the sake of all of humanity but also, symbolically, what has always been implicitly in God's offer of the covenant to Israel. For God, entering into a relationship with human beings is a sacrifice, a giving up of God's absolute power, making Godself vulnerable, taking risks, in order to be faithful to God's people to the very end and no matter what.

7. Beauchamp, *L'uno e l'altro Testamento*, 282 (emphasis added; own trans.).

Summary

The revelation event expressed in the image of the covenant is such because it challenges, prompts, and shapes the answer of faith understood as self-entrusting to the self-revealing God. This entails a mutual commitment between God and human beings expressed in the sacrifice of communion, a mutual "giving of oneself in pledge" ("pledge" meant as the down payment for a larger payment which is going to be given as agreed upon). This is an anticipation and promise of the full gift of oneself: the commitment of God who intervenes in human history and giving Godself to humanity and the commitment of human beings who entrust themselves to God giving God credit and behaving accordingly.

CHAPTER 7

YHWH, the Only True and Living God

A Brief Diachronic Overview

The key theme emerging from a diachronic reconstruction of God's revelation in the First Testament is definitely that of the unique identity of the God of Israel. Bracketing the more general issues on the origin and forms of monotheism, already briefly mentioned, here I will just underscore that when I approach the biblical witness we cannot talk of monotheism from the onset—at least not as something already explicitly and fully achieved, understood as the formal claim of the uniqueness and universal lordship of God. Scholars, using a technical language borrowed from the history of religions prefer to talk—when referring to the most ancient stage of Israel's history—of henotheism or monolatry. In these perspectives, only one God is recognized and venerated first by Abraham's clan and later by the people who originated from him in light of the exodus from Egypt and thanks to Moses's mediating role. They include at least implicitly the premise and promise of revelation and acknowledgment of the one and only true God; they increasingly matured through the history of ancient Israel to the point of blossoming into an authentic monotheism. From this, often the distinction is being made—with some approximation and not without some linguistic and conceptual variations—among four main stages of development:

(1) The first period of henotheism or monolatry, which more or less corresponds to the time of the patriarchs (ca. 1850 to 1250 BCE).

(2) The following period is of Yahwhism proper, which includes the revelation of God's name (YHWH) to Moses and the acknowledgment by Israel that God is the only God (ca. 1250 BCE).

(3) During the period of settling and of monarchy there is a movement from poly-Yahwhism as worship rendered to YHWH in various shrines, and with the risk of syncretistic contaminations, to mono-Yahwhism and

the related centralization of worship in the Jerusalem Temple (ca. 1100 to 900 BCE).

(4) Explicit and official monotheism, theoretically and practically, is proclaimed solemnly only in the time between the Babylonian exile (which takes place in 598–597 BCE), especially with the *Shema* recorded in Deuteronomy (Dt 6:4) and the message of Second Isaiah.

These distinct stages, and the very concept, which is ultimately generic and abstract, of monotheism, should not obscure the fundamental data attested to and increasingly theologically elaborated by the First Testament tradition. It is, as we saw when discussing the covenant, the unique relationship that God established, starting from Abraham, with what will then become during exodus the people of Israel. Through this relationship, God attested increasingly God's identity through salvific acts and bringing about the increasing acknowledgment as true and living God by Israel as representative of all of humanity.

Two Levels of God's Name

In the pages of the First Testament, there is a distinction found throughout the experience and understanding of God starting from revelation, even from a merely linguistic perspective. There are two different names used to designate God, which are related, in the final canonical redaction, to two distinct historical stages.[1] The first dates back to the time of the patriarchs until Moses. In this stage, God is known as *El*, whose plural is *Elohim* or as the God of Abraham, Isaac, and Jacob. In the second stage, the "proper" name of the God of Israel becomes more relevant: YHWH, the name revealed, according to a consistent and strong tradition, to Moses on Mount Horeb.[2]

The most ancient name, *El*, derives from the Semitic root (*'l*) which designates the king or father of the gods. To label the God who reveals Godself to them, Abraham and the patriarchs use therefore a term found among surrounding Semitic peoples bringing to it their own unique experience starting from God's own intervening in their own lives. In order to express this unique experience:

1. This is evident also from the fact that the Yahwist tradition uses the name "YHWH" also before the Mosaic covenant.

2. The development from the more archaic stage to the more recent one is found in Dt 32, where Israel explicitly becomes aware that her God is YHWH, while *El* is the name used for the deity that Israel shares with other peoples. "When the Most High apportioned the nations, when he divided humankind, he fixed the boundaries of the peoples according to the number of the gods; the Lord's own portion was his people, Jacob his allotted share" (Dt 32:8–9)

(1) They qualify *El*, by adding an adjective *El Elion*, God most high (see Gn 14:19–22); (*El Shaddaii*), omnipotent God or God of the Mountain (see Gn 17:1); (*El Olam*), eternal God (see Gn 21:33), and so on.

(2) They use the plural of *El*, which is *Elohim* to express the power, grandeur, fullness of life of the God of Israel, who is the God *par excellence*.[3]

(3) The designation of God with the name of YHWH is linked to the chosenness of Israel through Moses. It is God, the God of the Father, in dialogue with Moses while calling him and in view of the liberation from Egypt and the covenant established on Sinai, who reveals the name.

Here is how the Priestly account describes Moses's calling: "God also spoke to Moses and said to him, 'I am YHWH. I appeared to Abraham, Isaac and Jacob as God Almighty [*El Shaddai*], but by my name of YHWH I did not make myself known to them'" (Ex 6:2–3). Therefore, "the consciousness of Israel is determined by the two levels of the divine name: YHWH/God. The universality of God and God's unique presence to God's people come together."[4] Israel expresses thus the awareness that "her" God, the one who called Abraham and revealed Godself to Moses, is the God that other people worship without knowing God, giving God various names and often confusing God with "idols" with which they represent God—they are all one and the same God. While God remained hidden from the other peoples, God showed Godself to Israel: "For what other great nation," we read in the Book of Deuteronomy, "has a god so near to it as the Lord our God [*Adonai Eloheinu*] is whenever we call to him?" (Dt 4:7).

YHWH is therefore the name of election and relationship with which God—the God all peoples grope to find and to whom somehow they give form and worship—introduces and gives Godself to the people God chose in order to be revealed to all of humanity as the only true God.

The God of Abraham and of the Patriarchs

As we begin our journey through the First Testament, let us briefly pause to consider the first moment of this history of revelation: the God of the patriarchs. It is insightful to point out that God, in God's actions and manifestations, establishes a relationship with the individuals God chooses and calls and who, in reply, welcome and follow God. In other words:

3. This plural becomes typical for Israel, to talk about "her" God, who will later reveal the name of YHWH. While the term *El* appears 240 times in the First Testament, *Elohim* appears 2,600 times!

4. Beauchamp, *L'uno e l'altro Testamento*, 272 (own trans.).

God makes Godself known through the experiences of Abraham, Isaac, and Jacob with God.

In its most ancient version, the story of the Patriarchs is handed down to us in summary form through the ancient "creed" in Dt 26:5–8:

> A wandering Aramean was my ancestor; he went down into Egypt and lived there as an alien, few in number, and there he became a great nation, mighty and populous. When the Egyptians treated us harshly and afflicted us, by imposing hard labor on us, we cried to the Lord, the God of our ancestors; the Lord heard our voice and saw our affliction, our toil, and our oppression. The Lord brought us out of Egypt with a mighty hand and an outstretched arm, with a terrifying display of power, and with signs and wonders.

Gerhard von Rad, eminent First Testament exegete, comments:

> Between this very simple formulation, which is probably also the most concise, and the form in which the history of the patriarchs now appears in Genesis, there lies a very long road in the history of tradition, the main stages of which can however, be approximately reconstructed.... The Israel which had become conscious of her peculiarity now felt the need to visualize how she came into being. Thus, there lies behind the patriarchal history ... a mighty amazement at the far-reaching preparations which Jhwh had made to summon Israel into being.[5]

The arrival of Abraham in Canaan is estimated to have occurred around 1850 BCE. What was the actual experience Abraham had of God? The text under consideration is the history of the patriarch narrated in Genesis 12–36. It is difficult and complicated to examine this literary topic to identify the original kernel of revelation behind it. However, there is at a minimum the memory of a pre-Exodus tradition and of the increasing shaping of Israel's faith in the God of Israel. The clues of its ancient origin are still discernible in the final redaction of Genesis. Genesis suggests a theology of God's revelation in a specific way, which prepares the following moment/stage which was in many ways decisive for salvation history: the revelation to Moses and the exodus from Egypt. On this ground, we can say that the God of Abraham enters the nomads' routes and transforms the destiny of those who are nomads and foreigners into a vocation and a promise. Thus, the call of Abraham, narrated in Genesis 12:1–9, revisits the experience of the leader of a nomad Aramean clan, opening this experience up through God's intervention, to the journey toward an unexpected destination indicated by God.

The God of Abraham, then, is above all a God who calls to go out, to walk in space and time, a God who makes history, breaking the ever

5. Gerhard von Rad, *Old Testament Theology*, vol. 1: *The Theology of Israel's Historical Traditions*, trans. D. M. G. Stalker (New York: Harper and Row, 1962), 166 and 170.

self-renewing cycle of the natural order with its seasons and the rhythm of human life, with the habits and customs which shape personal and communal experiences in tune with the cycle of nature. It is a God who takes the initiative to dialogue: God's calling assumes two partners who enter into a relationship. It is a God who, calling and dialoguing, shows Godself as a friend of human beings, guiding and sustaining them, so much so that God is being described with metaphors like "rock" and "shield." It is a God who promises, who is committed to the future of Abraham (whom God chose and to whom God manifested the call) and that of his descendants. Since the beginning, God is a God of promise and covenant.[6]

At the same time, the God of Abraham and the patriarchs remains mysterious and transcendent. Otherwise, this would not be God but an idol, a mere projection of human longing and desires. Let us consider for example the episode of the struggle between God and Jacob (Gn 32:25–31). In this narrative, the dramatic dialectic of God's closeness-remoteness is represented, along with the hiddenness of God's name which conceals, for Semitic peoples, the secret of God's life and the possibility of knowing and possessing God.

In the most ancient stage of the history of Israel (it is noteworthy that in the very name of the chosen people there is a reference to God, El) within a predominantly polytheistic context like the one of the peoples among whom the patriarchs lived, we witness the establishing and renewing of a lively and unique relationship between God and Abraham, Isaac, and Jacob. The most relevant aspect is that it is a personal God: this should be understood in the double meaning of God showing Godself to human beings and that God being the God of Abraham, not of just any human being. Abraham's experience of God, starting from God's revelation, relates to God's same definition and to the possibility of bearing witness to it. However, this personal relationship is addressed, through Abraham, to the many. The very act of revealing oneself in the calling addressed to Abraham is a sign of benevolence, it shows that God is good and has a design of goodness not only for Abraham and his descendants, but through him for all peoples: "in you all the families of the earth shall be blessed" (Gn 12:3).

Abraham's reply to God's calling, to God's self-revealing through the covenant, is faith. In both the Jewish and Christian traditions, Abraham is known as the "father" of all in faith (Rom 4:11–16). It is in faith that Abraham knows God, that is, walks in God's ways and presence. His is a faith which becomes more mature, grows, is purified: it goes from en-

6. The Book of Genesis talks about the event of this covenant, projecting onto it the light of the future (paradigmatic for Israel) covenant of exodus (see Gn 17:1–8).

trusting himself to God's word, to persevering obedience, to the crucial test of the sacrifice of his son Isaac (Gn 22:1–18).

Noteworthy also is the narrative of Genesis 18:1–15, with the story of God's appearing to Abraham accompanied by two "men" who, according to Genesis 19:1 are "angels" (messengers). The text vacillates between singular and plural. Because of this, the Church Fathers will consider these "three," whom Abraham addresses in the singular, a prophetic foreshadowing of the mystery of the Trinity. Notable, and closer to the original intention of the text, is the mention of the "angels." They are constantly present in the story of God's revelation in the First Testament, from Abraham to late-Judean apocalyptic literature. As we will soon discover, they denote God's coming close to humanity while preserving God's mystery.

Moses and the Revelation of the Name

Within the Context of Exodus

Like in Abraham's case, Moses's mission (about 1250 BCE) is presented within the framework of the freeing of Israel from Egyptian captivity as a calling and at the same time as a powerful intervention of God in history. The story is articulated in three moments, closely interconnected: (1) the call of Moses and the revelation of the name on Mount Horeb (Ex 3:13–15; 6:2–3); (2) the liberation and exodus from Egypt; and (3) the covenant on Horeb. The God who calls, reveals Godself, and acts is presented in the Exodus narrative as the God of the patriarchs who, having heard Israel's cry for help, descends to free her (Ex 2:23–25). In a new way, compared to previous experiences, God displays a universal and historically decisive power for the future of God's people, by revealing Godself as the mysterious and powerful "I" who becomes close to Israel and who, after establishing a covenant with Israel, guides her toward a land of freedom and justice.[7]

God's personal encounter with Moses is recounted as an unexpected event which gives Moses a unique mission, the tone of which Moses conveys to his people, initiating a process from which Israel is shaped as a people thanks to the intervention of God who frees her and, through Moses, ties her to Godself with the covenant.

> Jhwh becomes Israel's "primary God" only thanks to the fact that God creates for Godself a people, who owes God her land and freedom and therefore worships God as her God. The "ascent" of Jhwh to Israel's main God is a pre-historic event, not connected with the monarchy, the priesthood and the temple, but with

7. All this is expressed, for example, in the victory song of Moses and the Israelites in honor of YHWH after the powerful crossing of the Red Sea (see Ex 15:1–6).

the origins of a people who frees herself from Pharaoh's enslavement. From the historical-religious perspective, Jhwh came to be accepted in the world of the ancient Near Eastern gods, not with limitations like other gods but as the "mover" of the complex process by which Israel became a people.[8]

The revelation of the name, therefore, is decidedly understood within the context of liberation from Egypt and the covenant established on Horeb. In other words, YHWH manifests Godself as the God of the patriarchs (Ex 3:6; 3:15, 16) who, in the sanctity and power of his ministry, draws near to enslaved Israel to free her and lead her to the promised land. This is God's unique identity, attested and communicated by God's name.

The Theophany at Horeb

In order to adequately understand the meaning that the First Testament tradition gives to the revelation of the name it is essential to closely read the text in Exodus where it is told (3:1–15):

Moses was keeping the flock of his father-in-law Jethro, the priest of Midian; he led his flock beyond the wilderness, and came to Horeb, the mountain of God. There the angel of the LORD appeared to him in a flame of fire out of a bush; he looked, and the bush was blazing, yet it was not consumed. Then Moses said, "I must turn aside and look at this great sight, and see why the bush is not burned up." When the LORD saw that he had turned aside to see, God called to him out of the bush, "Moses, Moses!" And he said, "Here I am." Then he said, "Come no closer! Remove the sandals from your feet, for the place on which you are standing is holy ground." He said further, "I am the God of your father, the God of Abraham, the God of Isaac, and the God of Jacob." And Moses hid his face, for he was afraid to look at God.

Then the LORD said, "I have observed the misery of my people who are in Egypt; I have heard their cry on account of their taskmasters. Indeed, I know their sufferings, and I have come down to deliver them from the Egyptians, and to bring them up out of that land to a good and broad land, a land flowing with milk and honey, to the country of the Canaanites, the Hittites, the Amorites, the Perizzites, the Hivites, and the Jebusites. The cry of the Israelites has now come to me; I have also seen how the Egyptians oppress them. So come, I will send you to Pharaoh to bring my people, the Israelites, out of Egypt." But Moses said to God, "Who am I that I should go to Pharaoh, and bring the Israelites out of Egypt?" He said, "I will be with you; and this shall be the sign for you that it is I who sent you: when you have brought the people out of Egypt, you shall worship God on this mountain."

But Moses said to God, "If I come to the Israelites and say to them, 'The God of your ancestors has sent me to you,' and they ask me, 'What is his name?' what shall I say to them?" God said to Moses, "I AM WHO I AM." He said further,

8. E. Zenger, "L'opera jahvista – un precursore del monoteismo jahvista?," in *Dio l'Unico: sulla nascita del monoteismo in Israele*, ed. N. Lohfink et al. (Brescia: Morcelliana, 1991), 45 (own trans.).

"Thus you shall say to the Israelites, 'I AM has sent me to you.'" God also said to Moses, "Thus you shall say to the Israelites, 'The LORD, the God of your ancestors, the God of Abraham, the God of Isaac, and the God of Jacob, has sent me to you': This is my name forever, and this my title for all generations."[9]

The final canonical redaction which gave us this narrative certainly does not intend to report the exact historical event of the theophany witnessed by Moses. However, the narrative cannot be reduced to a mere literary and theological reconstruction without reference to the historical event of revelation attested by YWHW. And this, not only because tradition (both oral and written) and the ritual celebration have handed down and recreated for centuries the foundational event. But also because a phenomenological analysis of the narrative shows clearly its intrinsic reference—not merely exterior—to a theophanic event, at least in the sense that the redactor, receiving and handing down the story of the event, somehow relived it himself in order to be able to hand it down in its original revelatory tone/power. In fact, this is what I also wish to convey when I talk about "inspiration" of biblical texts.

The revelation of the name, in the narrative in Exodus 3, is surrounded by the theophany of the "burning bush" in which is narrated the story of God's coming closer and introducing Godself: (1) through God's angel (2) in the sign of the burning fire (3) in addressing the word to Moses.[10] The angel of YHWH is not an entity distinct from God but simply God's coming closer while preserving God's sanctity and transcendence,[11] as underscored by the command not to come closer, to remove the sandals (3:5) and by Moses's covering his face (3:6). The "burning fire" is the dynamic symbol of God's sanctity: "the Lord your God is a devouring fire" (Dt 4:24), who is utterly other than anything that is experienced: each

9. The first account of the call of Moses (chapters 3 and 4) combines Yahwist elements (theophany and Moses's mission) and Elohist elements (revelation of the name).

10. See Jörg Jeremias, *Theophanie: Die Geschichte einer alttestamentlichen Gattung* (Neukirchen-Vluyn: Neukirchener Verlag, 1977).

11. What is the theological meaning of the presence of angels in relation to the development of Israelite monotheism? Manaranche gives an excellent explanation: "Since Israel's religion is prophetic in nature, it has to harmonize two needs: to proclaim God as God is, in God's mystery, rejecting any form of idolatry; and to proclaim God to a people in whose favor God intends to intervene and with whose mindset it is important to be familiar. Now, monotheism, if it carries out well the first part of this plan, runs the risk of neglecting the second part, by becoming too abstract. Herein lies the problem. The concept of the angel of Yhwh contributes to resolve it. Far from being a concession to polytheism, it is a protection against monotheism so pure that it becomes unapproachable by human beings. Thanks to this protection, the only One, without ceasing to be so, can communicate Godself a number of times. The utterly Other can, without ceasing to be so, become more familiar. The angel represents a figure difficult to identify: he is approachable like a human being and can slip away like a spirit; the angel is at the same time close and far away. However, his presence is necessary so human beings can relate to the utterly Other; and it is necessary also to explain the mysterious events which leave them perplexed and anxious." *Il monoteismo cristiano* (Brescia: Queriniana, 1988), 101–2 (own trans.).

worldly reality, in contact with the Lord is as if it were devoured by a burning fire, albeit without being destroyed (the bush is not consumed).[12]

God, however, is not making Godself sensibly present only in the sign of the fire: God addresses Moses with words and calls him by name, thus attesting to his being alive and his will to enter into a personal relationship with him. It is remarkable that the narrative insists repeatedly on saying that God "sees" Moses approaching (Ex 3:4, like before God "saw" and "heard" the oppression of God's people in Egypt: Ex 2:24–25; 3:7, 9, 16) and calls him (Ex 3:4) to send him to Pharaoh (Ex 3:10). From this point on, through a "relatively complex" exegesis (E. Jenni), the story offers an interpretation of God's name which is at the same time etymological and theological. The name of God, YHWH, is etymologically linked to an ancient form of the verb *hayah*, to be. This is close by root and meaning to the verb *ḥayah* (with the first "h" being a sharp "h"), to live, exist, show oneself, act. The entire pericope thus aims at suggesting that the name YHWH derives from the third-person singular of the indicative imperfect of this verb, thus meaning: he is, he is making himself present, he shows himself to be active. This meaning is made explicit by God's self-introduction which towers like a peak upon the text: *ehjeh asher' ehjeh*, I am who I am (3:14), where it is God himself introducing himself, and it becomes precisely "he is" when he is spoken about in the third person.

The commandment in the Decalogue prohibiting pronunciation of God's name in vain (Ex 20:7)—of which I will say something later—was intensified after the Babylonian exile, embodying the absolute respect for divine transcendence. So much so that, possibly during the Maccabean time (in the second century BCE), the name of YHWH was no longer pronounced except once a year (by the great priest, in the solemn liturgy in the Temple on the day of atonement, Yom Kippur), so as not to profane its sanctity. When we encounter the Tetragrammaton (the four letters יהוה, YHWH) in the Bible, the term is read aloud as *Adonai* (my Lord) or *Hashem* (the name). Adonai is translated in the Septuagint (third-century BCE) as *Kýrios*. As the name is no longer pronounced, with time the exact pronunciation was lost, because the original vocalization was not written down in the Hebrew text. The Masoretes, in later times (from the sixth to tenth century CE) added to the consonants in the text the vowels taken from *Adonai*, from which is derived the reading, *Jehovah*. However, the authentic pronunciation was most likely Yahweh: this

12. The "fire," on the other hand, becomes increasingly a symbol of YHWH's "jealous" love. It should be noted also that in other religious contexts, fire becomes a symbol for God, though mostly described as something which consumes in itself what it finds so as to absorb in itself the identity of the one who is consumed. This is not what happens in the Exodus account. Is the language of Exodus a symbolic means to express the experience that YHWH respects the identity of the other-than-himself even when confronted with YHWH's holiness?

is preserved by the Samaritans and was known to the Church Fathers. More recently, the Congregation for Divine Worship and the Discipline of the Sacraments, upon the request of Pope Benedict XVI and in agreement with the Vatican Congregation for the Doctrine of the Faith, sent a letter to the bishops' conferences on "the Name of God" (June 29, 2008), in which the statement of the Instruction *Liturgiam Authenticam* (no. 41) is reiterated:

In accordance with immemorial tradition, which indeed is already evident in the above-mentioned "Septuagint" version, the name of almighty God expressed by the Hebrew Tetragrammaton (YHWH) and rendered in Latin by the word *Dominus*, is to be rendered into any given vernacular by a word equivalent in meaning.... Avoiding pronouncing the tetragrammaton of the name of God on the part of the Church has therefore its own grounds. Apart from a motive of a purely philological order, there is also that of remaining faithful to the Church's tradition, from the beginning, that the secret tetragrammaton was never pronounced in the Christian context nor translated into any of the languages into which the Bible was translated.

"This Is My Name Forever"

In light of the context and exegesis from etymological and theological perspectives argued above, what is the meaning of the name and the characteristic features of God's face attested by it?

The Septuagint translation and the "metaphysics of Exodus" The meaning of Exodus 3:14 understood as decisive by the tradition, of Judaism of the Hellenistic diaspora first and afterward of Christianity, is the one expressed by the Greek translation of the Septuagint: *egó eimi ho ón*, I am who am (Ex 3:14), which translates the second *I am* (see also Ex 3:14b) as the one who is. In Latin, this was rendered as *ego sum qui sum* (in the first person) and *qui est* (third person), which render explicitly also in the second verb the reference to the "I" of God, which in Greek, in this case, is maintained only by the masculine article before the participle. This translation opens the way to the interpretation in a metaphysical key of the name of God (the "metaphysics *of* Exodus," as E. Gilson defines it).[13] God is the being *par excellence*, transcendent and omnipotent, the *ipsum esse per se subsistens*, as Thomas Aquinas will describe God.[14] This demon-

13. Etienne Gilson, *The Spirit of Mediaeval Philosophy (Gifford Lectures 1931–1932)*, trans. A. H. C. Downes (New York: Charles Scribner's Sons, 1936), 51n9.

14. See *ST* I, q. 13, a. 11, where St. Thomas, referring precisely to Ex 3:13–14, affirms, "This name HE WHO IS," "Hoc nomen 'Qui est' est maxime proprium nomen Dei," "primo quidem, propter sui significationem. Non enim significat formam aliquam, sed ipsum esse. Unde, cum esse Dei sit ipsa eius essentia, et hoc nulli alii conveniat, ut supra ostensum est (see q. 3, a. 4), manifestum est quod inter alia nomina hoc maxime proprie nominat Deum."

strates a certain correspondence between the God of Greek philosophy and the God of the Mosaic tradition[15] even though the verb to be (*eînai*) of the Greek translation actually sets the meaning of the Hebrew YHWH in a partially new context.

The original semantics The original semantics of the name, in tune with the tone of the Hebrew text, immediately underscores the mysterious and holy "I" and at the same time the efficacious proximity and mercy of God as the one who establishes a relationship with Israel to free her, asking her to respond with exclusive love and faithfulness. The name therefore should be translated as follows: "I am the One Who is here with and for you" (as explained in Ex 3:12). YHWH, as the Psalms sing, is the one who sits on high but at the same time "bows the heavens and comes down," to save Israel and "bring them up to a good and broad land" (Ex 3:8; Ps 144:3). The proper ontological meaning of the revelation of the name is not therefore to be eliminated but—as P. Ricoeur pointed out—it should be expressed in all its pregnancy, without being flattened upon preestablished metaphysical categories.[16]

The verb in question, in fact, manifests the transcendent and sovereign being of God as relationship of freely given and liberating benevolence. Because it is in the imperfect, it entails permanence and at the same time openness to the future. It can be translated as: "I am always with you," and also, "I will be with you" (see Ex 3:12: where in the Hebrew it has simply *ehyeh*, which is correctly translated in the future both in Greek, *ésomai*, and in Latin, *ero*). The name of God contains therefore a promise which is realized in history. So much that in the Palestinian *Targum* (Aramaic version and paraphrase of the First Testament), probably dated in pre-Christian times, its meaning is made explicit through a three-staged temporal rhythm: the one who is, who was, and who will be—a phrase reiterated in the New Testament, slightly modified, in Revelation: *ho ón kaì ho ên kaì ho erchómenos*, "he who is and who was and who is to come" (Rv 1:4; 4:8).

Reaffirming God's transcendence and hiddenness The doubled construction is noteworthy: I am who I am, where the predicate is identical to the

15. On this, Joseph Ratzinger has offered important insights in his *Introduction to Christianity*, trans. J. R. Foster (San Francisco, Calif.: Ignatius Press, 2004).

16. See Paul Ricoeur, "From Interpretation to Translation," in André LaCocque and Paul Ricoeur, *Thinking Biblically: Exegetical and Hermeneutical Studies*, trans. David Pellauer (Chicago: The University of Chicago Press, 1998), 337–59. Ricoeur recalls "the exceptional hermeneutic situation" of the burning bush story; linking the revelation of the name in Ex 3:14 to the profession of faith in 1 Jn 4:8, 16 ("God is *agápe*"), he states that "it still needs to be shown that thinking in terms of love does not demand a new *sacrificium intellectus*, but rather another reason" (359).

subject. It can underscore a strengthening of YHWH's self-introduction: I am precisely who am. More deeply, it hints at a reaffirmation of God's transcendence and hiddenness at the same time when God is making Godself present: only I know who I am. It is an invitation not to stop at the name for what it sounds like and which expresses all we have mentioned but to go through it to let God establish, through the name, a living and personal relationship with us. Otherwise, one may fall into the temptation of wanting to take possession of God's name and even to turn it into an idol. Because of this, YHWH commands not to utter his name in vain and not to fashion any image of him. God reveals Godself, as Beauchamp points out, "through a meaning which is not part of the internal organization of the discourse but grounds it like a signature. 'I am who am' as a signature external to the text, though it is in the text: these two words 'pierce through the page,' give the text an exceptional emphasis.... The name revealed to Moses places the entire Bible under the first person of God as the subject."[17]

A name of relationship In other words, YHWH does not offer in the name a self-definition but introduces himself as the one who is recognizable as the one who cares, with power and absolute faithfulness, for Israel. Those whom YHWH addresses as those who listen to YHWH's voice and are faithful to the covenant enter into a new sphere of existence, established by the relationship with YHWH. It is in this personal relationship that YHWH reveals who YHWH really is. The name makes it possible to experience the constant relationship of God with God's people. It has sacramental value: it is an effective sign of God's presence, God's entering into a relationship with Israel and saving her. This in itself attests and guarantees that God will continue to make Godself known, through grace and with faithfulness, within this relationship: "This is my name forever, and this my title for all generations" (Ex 3:15).

Summary Through the revelation of the name the following aspects are attested: God's intervening character contained in the sovereign sanctity of God's being and in the freely given mercy of God's freeing work toward Israel; God's transcendence, for God, in God's incandescent and unique mystery, makes Godself present regardless of places and times, becoming close to Israel wherever she is and forever; God's unstoppable efficacy and power, far superior to those of Egypt's gods, freely given toward God's people; and God's uniqueness, as God is the only God in the full and true sense, as expressed in God's self-introduction: I am who am.

17. Beauchamp, *L'uno e l'altro Testamento*, 182 (own trans. from the Italian).

In all this, as it happened for the God of the patriarchs, there continues to be a mysterious sovereignty, attested by the name itself and compellingly testified by, for example, the episode narrated in Ex 33:17–23:

The Lord said to Moses, "I will do the very thing that you have asked; for you have found favor in my sight, and I know you by name." Moses said, "Show me your glory, I pray." And he said, "I will make all my goodness pass before you, and will proclaim before you the name, 'The Lord'; and I will be gracious to whom I will be gracious, and will show mercy on whom I will show mercy. But," he said, "you cannot see my face; for no one shall see me and live." And the Lord continued, "See, there is a place by me where you shall stand on the rock; and while my glory passes by I will put you in a cleft of the rock, and I will cover you with my hand until I have passed by; then I will take away my hand, and you shall see my back; but my face shall not be seen."

Moses, as the Exodus narrative illustrates in various occasions, is the one who spoke with God "face to face." He is "God's friend" (Ex 33:11) and at the same time—more than any other—experienced the impossibility of contemplating God's face: "because no human being can see God and live" (see Ex 33:20).

Trust, Advent, Recognition

In the narrative in Exodus 3 it is important to consider especially a section of the dialogue between YHWH and Moses, in verses 11 and 12: "Moses said to God, 'Who am I that I should go to Pharaoh, and bring the Israelites out of Egypt?' He said, 'I will be with you; and this shall be the sign for you that it is I who sent you: when you have brought the people out of Egypt, you shall worship God on this mountain.'"

The sign confirming Moses's mission, which guarantees the credibility of the mission received and the reliability of God who testifies and of whom Moses is the spokesperson, is not immediately given. It is delayed and connected to the covenant. Meanwhile, God is asking to trust God's Word: only in this way will God show the authenticity of the mission given to Moses and the efficacy of God's closeness to Israel. Once achieved by a "strong arm," the liberation of Israel from Egypt will lead to establishing the covenant with her on Mount Horeb. This specific dynamic shows that the knowledge of God that God offers requires human faith and is displayed in a history of increasingly full communion, by God, and an increasingly more mature trust and awareness by Israel. This dynamic is expressed and included in God's name: YHWH is the one who is and will be with and for God's people, opening Godself to the people and letting Godself be inasmuch as the people will trust and recognize God as their God.

In this perspective, the self-introductory formula used by God and attested in several First Testament texts is quite unique: *anì YHWH,* I am YHWH, related to the promise of recognition by Israel at the moment of God's coming: "You will know that I am YHWH."[18] For example, we read in Exodus (6:1, 6–8):

The Lord said to Moses: ... "Say therefore to the Israelites, 'I am the LORD, and I will free you from the burdens of the Egyptians and deliver you from slavery to them. I will redeem you with an outstretched arm and with mighty acts of judgment. I will take you as my people, and I will be your God. You shall know that I am the YHWH, your God, who has freed you from the burdens of the Egyptians. I will bring you into the land that I swore to give to Abraham, Isaac, and Jacob; I will give it to you for a possession. I am YHWH.'"

In Ezekiel 20, which elaborates on this intuition,[19] the entire history of Israel is interpreted in light of the revelation of the name by God and the recognition of the name by Israel. Thus, the promise of the new exodus culminates in the following statement: "You shall know that I am YHWH when I bring you into the land of Israel.... You shall know that I am YHWH when I deal with you for my name's sake" (Ezek 20:42–44). The rhythm of the history of the relationship between YHWH and Israel takes place in the faithfulness of God to the covenant and, ultimately to God's name revealed to Moses. This alternates with Israel's infidelity, which God always forgives, and, faithful to God's name, this allows Israel to begin anew, renewing the covenant and moving it ahead toward its freely given fulfillment. Zimmerli concludes as follows:

All that YHWH intends to say and proclaim to God's people appears to be a longer display of the foundational statement "I am YHWH".... The deepest intention of God's working with the people will take place when the people will engage in an act of knowledge: "You know that I am YHWH" ... The entire historical action for which Moses was sent carries its meaning as intended by God, not only in its happening but precisely because of the challenge to know this fundamental truth of revelation: knowledge of the Name of YHWH as a

18. See Walther Zimmerli, *Ich bin Jahwe,* in *Geschichte und Altes Testament, A. Alt zum 70. Geburstag* (Tübingen: J. C. B. Mohr, 1953), later collected in his *Gottes Offenbarung* (München: C. Kaiser, 1963); Richter, *Anì hu und egò eimì: Die Offenbarungsformel "Ich bin es" in der biblischen Welt und Umwelt* (PhD diss., University of Erlangen, 1956); Heinrich Zimmermann, "Das Absolute 'egò eimì' als Neutestamentliche Offenabrungsformel," *Biblische Zeitschrift* 4 (1960): 54–69; see also E. Stauffer, "Ego," in *GLNT* III:41–93; see also Anja Angela Diesel, *«Ich bin Jahwe»: Der Aufstieg der Ich-bin-Jahwe Aussage zum Schüsselwort des alttestamentlichen Monotheismus* (Neukirchen-Vluyn: Neukirchener Verlag, 2006).

19. "Thus says the Lord God: On the day when I chose Israel, I swore to the offspring of the house of Jacob—making myself known to them in the land of Egypt—I swore to them, saying, 'I am the Lord your God' ... But they rebelled against me and would not listen to me.... Then I thought I would pour out my wrath upon them.... But I acted for the sake of my name, that it should not be profaned in the sight of the nations among whom they lived, in whose sight I made myself known to them in bringing them out of the land of Egypt" (Ezek 20:5–9).

fulfillment of YHWH's self-introduction ... [Israel] through this revelation is situated in a process of knowledge which was not a state of beatific vision but life, event, development toward a goal.... The history of Israel is the place in which, for its fulfillment, the truth of YHWH's revelatory word becomes knowable.... Ex 20 shows how it is thought that in the revelation of the name of YHWH all the contents of revelation are already contained.[20]

These comments immediately point to the New Testament. The name of YHWH is manifested in the very event of YHWH's coming and intervening in history for the sake of God's people: and this is the promise of God's final salvific coming. From this perspective, we can understand the unusual use by Jesus—emphasized in the fourth Gospel but already apparent, even if less explicitly, in the synoptic Gospels—of the expression *egṓ eimi* (I am) without the nominal predicate (Jn 8:24, 28, 58; 13:19; and also 4:26; 6:20, 35; 18:5, 8; and in the synoptic Gospels, Mt 28:20 and Mk 6:40) which reminds one of Exodus 3:14–15. Jesus introduces himself, and is recognized as such in the Paschal faith, as YHWH's eschatological coming promised by YHWH while revealing YHWH's name. Jesus, therefore, can tell the Father, "I have made your name known to those whom you gave me from the world. They were yours, and you gave them to me, and they have kept your word. I made your name known to them, and I will make it known, so that the love with which you have loved me may be in them, and I in them" (Jn 17:6, 26). Jesus makes known God's name in his ministry and in his person—"whoever sees me, sees him who sent me" (Jn 12:45)—but makes God known definitively and fully in the Easter event, "When you have lifted up the Son of Man, then you will realize that I am he" (Jn 8:28). The Spirit of truth, the Paraclete, promised by the Son will keep the disciples in this name.[21]

Anthropological and Social Implications

The revelation of the name happens, as I pointed out, within the context of the ratification of the covenant, thanks to which Israel became the Lord's people. From here, specifically, comes the anthropological and social relevance of this event. A specific and unalienable implication of the covenant as commitment to an exclusive relationship with YHWH is not only the commandment to love God "with all your heart, and with all your soul, and with all your might" (Dt 6:5), but also the precept of love of neighbor: the one who belongs to the covenant, but also the foreigner who lives among the Israelites.

The love of neighbor is the foundation and rule which is the source of

20. Zimmerli, *Rivelazione di Dio*, 24–28 (own trans.).
21. See part 3.

all the social legislation of the First Testament (see Ex 23:4–5; Dt 22:1–4; Lv 19:17–18). A unique expression of it is the command of solidarity with the poor (see Dt 15:7–8; Lv 19:11–15). YHWH, as the prophets will reiterate, is their protector and avenger. J. Alfaro writes: "The earth, gift of God for the entire people, had to be the 'sacrament' which gave a sense of reality to freedom, dignity and security achieved through the exodus.... The purpose of the exodus was perfect fraternity and freedom among the Israelites who, thanks to the gift of the land, would have as final result the elimination of all forms of oppression, injustice, and poverty."[22]

Rules such as those of the sabbatical and jubilee years (Dt 15; Lv 25; Ex 23) have the clear purpose of establishing the principle that every certain amount of years the history and life of Israel need to begin again from exodus, to eliminate discriminations that in the meantime had occurred and to constantly transform from within the social life of the chosen people and shape it according to YHWH's design. The meaning of exodus and the covenant, therefore, is at the same time theological: because it reveals the face of YHWH as an omnipotent God who freed God's people; and socioanthropological because it shows and protects, through the covenant, the dignity of each member of the covenant community, especially of the poor, proposing the ideal law of a free and cohesive people. God's name, in other words, guarantees the true name of humanity.

From Mono-Yahwism to Monotheism

A consequence and, at the same time, an expression of the revelation of the name and of the establishing of the covenant is the exclusive relationship established between YHWH and YHWH's people. The revelation of the name and liberation from Egypt promote the advent of *mono-Yahwism*,[23] in the sense that YHWH is recognized as the only God for Israel, who reveals Godself with a power that practically reduces to nothing the gods venerated by the Egyptians. What emerges is a unique logic, named by Manaranche as *monogamic monotheism*, generated as a free reciprocating response by the free and exclusive choice by YHWH—election, according to the Book of Deuteronomy—of Israel as partner in the covenant.

Yahwist Faith in the Decalogue

Mono-Yahwism is expressed clearly and with its multiple practical implications in the text of the Decalogue as reported in Exodus 20:1–11:

22. Juan Alfaro, "Dio protegge e libera i poveri," *Concilium* 22, no. 5 (1986): 54.

23. As mentioned previously, the technical term *mono-Yahwism* (as opposed to *poly-Yahwism*) is used when the worship is centralized in one place, the Temple in Jerusalem.

Then God spoke all these words: I am the LORD your God, who brought you out of the land of Egypt, out of the house of slavery; you shall have no other gods before me. You shall not make for yourself an idol, whether in the form of anything that is in heaven above, or that is on the earth beneath, or that is in the water under the earth. You shall not bow down to them or worship them; for I the LORD your God am a jealous God, punishing children for the iniquity of parents, to the third and the fourth generation of those who reject me, but showing steadfast love to the thousandth generation of those who love me and keep my commandments. You shall not make wrongful use of the name of the LORD your God, for the LORD will not acquit anyone who misuses his name. Remember the sabbath day, and keep it holy. Six days you shall labor and do all your work. But the seventh day is a sabbath to the LORD your God; you shall not do any work—you, your son or your daughter, your male or female slave, your livestock, or the alien resident in your towns. For in six days the LORD made heaven and earth, the sea, and all that is in them, but rested the seventh day; therefore the LORD blessed the sabbath day and consecrated it.

Here we find some unique features of the Yahwist faith, which will increasingly become more defined and affirmed. Consider the commandment not to make images of God, in order to acknowledge on the one hand God's transcendence and holiness and to avoid, on the other hand, confusion between God and the idols. In parallel, the prohibition is given against pronouncing God's name in vain. The affirmation of YHWH's "jealousy" is important as well, and typical; it stems from the unique covenantal relationship established with Israel and, indirectly, it stems from the uniqueness of God: "you shall worship no other god, because the Lord, whose name is Jealous, is a jealous God" (Ex 34:14; Dt 4:24; Gn 24:16).

Mono-Yahwism of the Prophets

The period of the monarchy, established around the year 1000 BCE, coincides with the emergence of that unique and decisive phenomenon for the history of Israel: prophetism. That period of time, from the standpoint of revelation and the experience of God, is marked by at least two events. On the one hand, Israel became organized as a political unit which promoted the strengthening of Yahwism as the only faith of the entire people of Israel. This faith was expressed in particular through the building and dedication of the Temple in Jerusalem, by King Solomon, as the specific and distinct place for YHWH's presence amongst his people. On the other hand, Israel interacted with the neighboring cultures and religions and its monarchy tended to follow the example of their sacred traditions. From there, evident traces of religious syncretism and even tolerant polytheism appeared, not necessarily at a theoretical level but certainly at a practical level. These dangers were met by the prophetic reaction (from Elijah to Amos and Isaiah) which engendered a truly ideal and militant movement aiming at reestablishing and promoting Yahwism. This entailed a hard struggle against pagan cults and the always looming risk of idolatry. Just consider, as a notable example, the challenge launched by the prophet Elijah to the priests of Baal on Mount Carmel.[24]

Within this sensitive context, the preaching of the prophets is undoubtedly a reinforcement and deepening of the Yahwistic faith. It is in continuity with the Mosaic faith, because they experience personally YHWH's presence, manifestation, and guidance through their calling and being sent to his people. While maintaining and in some ways even increasing the historical efficacy of YHWH's revelation, the prophets, through the experience of the Word addressed to them in the Spirit, interiorize the quality and meaning of God's revelation and soften its cosmic connotations with which revelation had previously been manifested and perceived. Thus, God's revelation is disclosed as the inner dynamics of penetration and transformation of human existence, both personal and social. Compare, for example, YHWH's theophany on Mount Horeb, as narrated in the Book of Exodus and the theophany experienced by the prophet Elijah as narrated in 1 Kings 19:8, 11–13:

> He got up, and ate and drank; then he went in the strength of that food forty days and forty nights to Horeb the mount of God ... [The Lord] said, "Go out and stand on the mountain before the LORD, for the LORD is about to pass by." Now there was a great wind, so strong that it was splitting mountains and breaking rocks in pieces before the LORD, but the LORD was not in the wind; and after the wind an earthquake, but the LORD was not in the earthquake ... and after the earthquake a fire, but the LORD was not in the fire; and after the fire a sound of sheer silence.... When Elijah heard it, he wrapped his face in his mantle and went out and stood at the entrance of the cave. Then there came a voice to him ...

Manaranche well illustrates the meaning of this narrative and of the image of YHWH emerging from it. It is a question, he argues,

24. This takes place in the ninth century and King Ahab had married Jezebel, daughter of the king of Tyre and Sidon. Therefore, syncretism with the Phoenician gods is a real threat. "Elijah then came near to all the people, and said, 'How long will you go limping with two different opinions? ... At the time of the offering of the oblation, the prophet Elijah came near and said, 'O Lord, God of Abraham, Isaac, and Israel, let it be known this day that you are God in Israel, that I am your servant, and that I have done all these things at your bidding. Answer me, O Lord, answer me, so that this people may know that you, O Lord are God, and that you have turned their hearts back.' Then the fire of the Lord fell and consumed the burnt offering, the wood, the stones, and the dust.... When all the people saw it, they fell on their faces and said, 'The Lord indeed is God; the Lord indeed is God.' Elijah said to them, 'Seize the prophets of Baal; do not let one of them escape.' Then they seized them; and Elijah brought them down to the Wadi Kishon, and killed them there" (1 Kgs 18:17–40).

of liberating God from the cosmic phenomena with which God could be confused. That is why there is the need of proclaiming that the only existing God is Jhwh (or Adonai). No shape or face is attributed to him: Jhwh is content with simply working or "passing by." Jhwh is distinct from destructive forces: the hurricane, the earthquake, and the fire. At most, Jhwh is a "a still small voice"—a voice, certainly, but a soft voice, a quiet whisper. The presence, the contact, need to be affirmed while at the same time conserving in the same concrete language, the non-material aspect. It is the "utterly delicate and refined subtlety of the word" which presupposes the believer's "hi-fi" listening. Therefore, Elijah needs to be detached from everything, and to "go out" and "wrap his face." In this experience, he is alone, and Jhwh reveals himself without other witnesses. In this monotheism, human beings reach their limit. They are "on the tips of their toes," or, as one may say "on the tips of their souls."[25]

Monotheistic Faith in Deuteronomy and Second Isaiah

The Deuteronomistic tradition consistently attests and provides evidence of monotheism's openly establishing itself. This tradition, beginning from a more ancient origin faithful to Yahwism, coalesced during the period of the religious reform promoted by King Josiah (621 BCE) and then continues up to post-exilic times. As Braulik notes: "The texts in Deuteronomy, if arranged in chronological order, show a constant development of the doctrine on God. This doctrine goes from the statement, 'Jhwh is the only one' (6:4) within a still polytheistic referential system of the late monarchic period up to the monotheistic formulation of the Babylonian exile: 'Jhwh is God and there is no-one besides Him' (4:35)."[26]

One only needs to recall two pericopes which attest these two main stages in the development of monotheism. The first is the beginning of the *Shema* ("listen"), Israel's prayer *par excellence*. YHWH, it says, is the only God to whom Israel should feel linked with all of herself, in exclusive love (Dt 6:4–5, 14–15):

> Hear, O Israel: The LORD is our God, the LORD alone. You shall love the LORD your God with all your heart, and with all your soul, and with all your might.... Do not follow other gods, any of the gods of the peoples who are all around you, because the LORD your God, who is present with you, is a jealous God. The anger of the LORD your God would be kindled against you and he would destroy you from the face of the earth.

The second attestation is offered by the other well-known theological synthesis of Israel's faith which illustrates the goal of the divine working as "allowing Israel to understand its history as a people, a history lived

25. Manaranche, *Il monoteismo cristiano*, 94 (own trans.).

26. Georg Braulik, "Il Deuteronomio e la nascita del monoteismo," in N. Lohfink et al., *Dio l'Unico: sulla nascita del monoteismo in Israele* (Brescia: Morcelliana, 1991), 55–102 (own trans.).

and handed down by Israel and to identify it as revelation of YHWH, fully understood as the only God" (Braulik). Here, with determination and clarity, YHWH is designated no longer as *Elohim* (God, though *par excellence*) but as *hā Elohim* ("the" God, the only one). See Deuteronomy 4:32–40:

For ask now about former ages, long before your own, ever since the day that God created human beings on the earth; ask from one end of heaven to the other: has anything so great as this ever happened or has its like ever been heard of? Has any people ever heard the voice of a god speaking out of a fire, as you have heard, and lived? Or has any god [*Elohim*] ever attempted to go and take a nation for himself from the midst of another nation, by trials, by signs and wonders, by war, by a mighty hand and an outstretched arm, and by terrifying displays of power, as the LORD your God [*YHWH Eloheykem*] did for you in Egypt before your very eyes? To you it was shown so that you would acknowledge that the LORD is God [*YHWH hu hā Elohim*]; there is no other besides him. From heaven he made you hear his voice to discipline you. On earth he showed you his great fire, while you heard his words coming out of the fire. And because he loved your ancestors, he chose their descendants after them. He brought you out of Egypt with his own presence, by his great power, driving out before you nations greater and mightier than yourselves, to bring you in, giving you their land for a possession, as it is still today. So acknowledge today and take to heart that the LORD is God [*YHWH hu hā Elohim*] in heaven above and on the earth beneath; there is no other. Keep his statutes and his commandments, which I am commanding you today for your own well-being and that of your descendants after you, so that you may long remain in the land that the LORD your God is giving you for all time.

Thus we arrive at the explicit and formal statement of monotheism during the Babylonian exile and right after the exile. When succumbing before the great powers (Assyrians and Babylonians were the powerful forces throughout the entire ancient Near East and beyond), Israel discovered in a new way, thanks to the prophets, the faithfulness and omnipotence of her God and Lord. The polemical texts on the nothingness of the idols are developed during this time. They declare unquestionably that only YHWH is the living and true God and that his omnipotence extends to all the peoples, the entire created world and history. The prophet who stretches himself the most is Second Isaiah, who was active in Babylon before King Cyrus's edict freeing Israel (538 BCE) and whose work includes chapters 40–55 of the Book of Isaiah in its present form. See Isaiah 40:18, 21–23; 44:6–9:

To whom then will you liken God, or what likeness compare with him? . . . Have you not known? Have you not heard? Has it not been told you from the beginning? Have you not understood from the foundations of the earth? It is he who sits above the circle of the earth, and its inhabitants are like grasshoppers; who stretches out the heavens like a curtain, and spreads them like a tent to live in; who brings princes to naught, and makes the rulers of the earth as nothing.

Thus says the LORD, the King of Israel, and his Redeemer, the LORD of hosts: I am the first and I am the last; besides me there is no god. Who is like me? Let them proclaim it, let them declare and set it forth before me. Who has announced from of old the things to come? Let them tell us what is yet to be. Do not fear, or be afraid; have I not told you from of old and declared it? You are my witnesses! Is there any god besides me? There is no other rock; I know not one. All who make idols are nothing, and the things they delight in do not profit.

A consequence of the theoretical proclamation of monotheism is the doctrine according to which YHWH is creator or all things: "Have you not known? Have you not heard? The Lord is the everlasting God, the Creator of the ends of the earth." (Is 40:28).

Faith in Creation as Consequence and Expression of Monotheism

Given the relevance of the concept of creation, and its intrinsic link with monotheism, it is helpful to focus, albeit briefly, on its origin and meaning. In the narrative of creation in Genesis (Priestly redaction Gn 1:1–2:4a, whose basic elements date back to the monarchic period) the act of creation is expressed with both solemnity and simplicity by the verb *bārā* which has become, in biblical language, the only specific and technical verb used to express the act of creating which is uniquely God's. In order to preserve this meaning, the Greek translation of the First Testament, the Septuagint, does not use the verb *demiourgeîn*. After Plato's *Timaeus*, this verb was commonly used to express the transformative and organizing work of the material world. The Septuagint uses rather the nonloaded verb *ktízein*, which indicated the act of the will before the building of a city or the establishment of a feast day.[27] The use of the verbs *bārā* and *ktízein* meant that only God creates, as creating is a "doing" so unique according to which reality different from God in God's unity and multiplicity, enters on the scene of existence. The fact is significant that God creates through word or wisdom, as expressed in numerous texts of the First Testament (see especially Prv 8:22–31). This underscores the omnipotence, freedom, wisdom, and goodness of God, who does not need to associate anything to Godself in the act of creating.

Only in later texts do we find formulas which expressly allude to creation from nothing. Thus, in the period after the Babylonian exile, Second Isaiah joins tightly faith in the one God to faith in creation: "I am

27. Foerster, in *Theologisches Wörterbuch zum Neuen Testament* III:1022–27.

the Lord, who made all things, who alone stretched out the heavens, who by myself spread out the earth; who is with me?" (Is 44:24).[28] In the second Book of Maccabees (from the second century BCE) we find an even more explicit statement: "I beg you, my child, to look at the heaven and the earth and see everything that is in them, and recognize that God did not make them out of things that existed [*ouk ex hóntōn*]" (2 Mc 7:28). But the Book of Wisdom (second half of the first century BCE, the most recent of the First Testament books), with an expression inspired at least in part by Plato's *Timaeus*, still talks of the "omnipotent hand" of the Lord who "created the world out of formless matter [*ex amórphou*]" (Wis 11:17), assuming an unspecified and chaotic state of matter to which God, creating, gave shape and order.

In spite of these inconsistencies, we should emphasize that both in the Genesis account and in the post-exilic prophets, and in the later wisdom tradition, the unique horizon of experience and understanding emerges within which the original meaning of biblical creation comes increasingly to the fore. This is the horizon of the historical, salvific, and dialogical covenant between YHWH and his people and through them, with the whole of humanity and creation. God freely and without expectations freed the children of Israel from slavery in Egypt and established them as God's people, in a relationship which is made both of grace and justice, mercy and faithfulness. It is this paradigm, the paradigm of exodus, which sheds light on the Hebrew cosmogony, which is distinct from that of other religions, though culturally advanced, which surrounded Israel.

Creation is the first and original covenant: it is calling into being, establishing a relationship, expressing a freely given gift. It is not only an offer of salvation and friendship to this human partner: human beings created in God's image and likeness in order that they may freely respond to the calling of their creator and Lord, welcoming the grace of communion with God. Paul the apostle will later express this concept in the Letter to the Romans, addressing God as the One "who gives life to the dead and calls into existence the things that do not exist [*toû Theoû kaloûntos tà mè ónta hōs ónta*]" (Rom 4:17). The horizon of creation in light of the covenant is therefore that of the gift, of the most basic gift that can be conceived: existence. The meaning of creation related to nothingness is manifested precisely to express on one hand, the free and absolute springing up of this gift, and on the other hand, its radicality.

In Christian theological tradition, the concept of creation was explored in depth since the beginning, on the basis of First Testament biblical texts revisited and reread in light of the Christ-event, while also

28. American Standard Version translation.

taking on the Greek philosophical tradition and the religious and cosmogonic currents of the Hellenistic period.[29] In Greek thought in particular a principle had arisen and was held which had a general meaning valid on various levels, for all the expressions of the *episteme*. It was the principle of *ex nihilo nihil fit*. Aristotle, in *Metaphysics* XI, expressed it with great clarity, summarizing the principle held by previous thinkers: "that nothing comes to be out of that which is not, but everything out of that which is, is a dogma common to nearly all the natural philosophers [*tò gár mēdèn ek mè óntos gígnesthai, pân d'ex óntos, schedòn apántōn estì koinòn dógma tôn perì phýseōs*]."[30] This principle is considered evident from an essentially cosmological and physiological perspective. If the horizon of being of what is, is the horizon of *phýsis* and *kósmos*—in the deep meaning these terms have in Greek—and this not only in the dimension of what appears (the *daimónenon*) and is material but also in what "underlies" (*hypokeímenon*, the *substantia*) and is immaterial, the consequence is that nothing comes from nothing and everything is aware of its own being and becoming (though the two begin to diverge, starting with Heraclitus and Parmenides) within what somehow always is. For Plato and Aristotle, we cannot speak of a nothingness of being with respect to which the demiurge or the unmoved mover exercise their cosmogonic activity. Although Plato's *chóra*[31] and Aristotle's *prótē hýlē*[32] are the ultimate boundaries of being, the empty space and primal virtuality from which the cosmos is shaped and ordered, they are not "nothingness," sheer nothingness. Somehow, they too are, as they are coextensive with being, almost its shadow or, better yet, the very horizon of its becoming being that is, and is what is, in what is other than itself (Plato) or becoming (Aristotle).

This is why for Christian thought, to state that God is the creator of all things specifies that creating means drawing being from nothingness. The Christian tradition does not mean to argue—which would be a contradiction—that nothingness is, next to God, almost a metaphysical space totally void of being (the absolute nothingness) within which God brings about the things that are. Rather, it means to say that next to God

29. On the genesis of this formula as continuation of the doctrine contained in the Judeo-Christian revelation in the patristic era, see J. Fantino, "L'origine de la doctrine de la création ex nihilo," *Révue des Sciences philosophiques et théologiques* 80 (1996): 589–602, which addresses the essay by Gerhard May, *Creation ex nihilo: The doctrine of 'Creation out of Nothing' in Early Christian Thought* (Edinburgh: T and T Clark, 1994).

30. Aristotle, *Metaphysics* XI.6.1062b.

31. See *Timaeus* 48–53. Plato himself states that it is difficult to express this third *eídos* which is *anóratou kaì ámorphos* and therefore he only makes reference to it through a series of metaphors, "recipient of everything that is generated" (49a; see 51a–b and 53a); "space" (52a-d); "wet nurse" (49a, 52d, 88d); "mother" (50d, 51a); "that which is generated" (50d); "nature which receives all the bodies" (50b); "matter which shapes everything" (50a–e).

32. Aristotle, *Metaphysics* IX.7.1049a18.

and before (understood ontologically) creation, there is nothing but God. From the perspective of the "metaphysics *of* Exodus" (E. Gilson), which reads ontologically the revelation of God's name to Moses, "I am Who I am" (Ex 3:14), only God originally is. The *Shepherd of Hermas*, already at the beginning of the second century CE, maintains that faith in God who "dwells in the heavens and created out of nothing [*ek toû mè óntos*] the things that are."[33] Shortly after, the first true Christian theologian, Irenaeus of Lyons, clearly argues this truth in his work against the Gnostics, "Ipse a semetipso fecit libere et ex sua potestate et disposuit et perfecit omnia et est substantia omnium voluntas eius."[34] Thus the *creatio ex nihilo* formula becomes a technique to express the properly theological concept of creation.

33. *Shepherd of Hermas* I.1, in Michael W. Holmes (ed.), *The Apostolic Fathers*, trans. J. B. Lightfoot and J. R. Harmer, 2nd ed. (Grand Rapids, Mich.: Baker Book House, 1992), 194–290.

34. *Adversus haereses* II.30.9.

CHAPTER 8

Attributes and Names of YHWH

Beginning from the experience of exodus and the covenant, somehow condensed and handed down through the revelation of the name, two unique attributes of the God of Israel are delineated: sanctity and mercy.[1] They attest to the multifaceted richness and at the same time the intrinsic tension of the experience Israel has of YHWH in his self-revealing and which stems from his very being. Two names increasingly come to the fore which reveal YHWH's identity with respect to his people through the anthropologically intense—and decisive—metaphors of parenthood and sponsality. We could say that the attributes say "how God is" stemming from how God manifests Godself in the relationship with Israel; the names express "who God is" derived from the analogy with the most meaningful human experiences.

Holiness and Mercy

To say that YHWH is holy (*qadósh*) means to state first and foremost his utter otherness with respect to human beings and all creatures,[2] therefore his transcendence and mystery before which human beings become aware of being "dust and ashes" (Gn 18:27) and are filled with holy fear. Human beings also recognize YHWH's absolute perfection, YHWH's ontological and ethical goodness and truth which become an imperative duty toward holiness for the Israelites, according to the precept in Leviticus, "I

1. I am using the term "attributes" derived from the Scholastic treatise *De Deo* applying it to the more typical properties of God's salvific work, which show God's intimate being in action. See M. Laher, "Riflessioni dogmatiche sugli attributi e sui modi di agire di Dio," in *Mysterium Salutis*, ed. J. Feiner and M. Löhrer (Brescia: Queriniana, 1969), 3:370–400.

2. A reality expressed in the frequent statement found in the First Testament: "I am God, no mortal" (Hos 11:9; Nm 23:19, 42; etc.). Note the difference between the designation "holy" applied to YHWH and "sacred" from Latin religious language (*Sacer*) and from Greek (*hierós*) often used in the phenomenology of religions to designate a divine manifestation to human beings. See, for example, R. Otto, *Das Heilige: Ueber das Irrationale in der Idee des Göttlichen und sein Verhältnis zum Rationalen* (Breslau, 1917), which illustrates the characteristics of the "numinous" as both "*fascinans*" and "*tremendum*." The holy one of Israel and the living, personal God, omnipotent and ethically perfect. The holy is tendentially impersonal and, in itself, without any moral characteristics.

am the Lord your God; sanctify yourselves ... and be holy, for I am holy" (Lv 11:44).

To say that YHWH is merciful means that YHWH is "tender and gracious, slow to anger, and abounding in steadfast love and faithfulness" (Ex 34:6). YHWH's mercy is revealed first of all to Israel through the paradigmatic experience of the exodus, but it describes the constant trait of God's work toward God's people throughout history. In order to express such experience, the First Testament uses two terms that attempt to reveal, with different nuances, the deeper content.

The first term is *ḥesed*, an "attitude of goodness." It indicates what in human experience is the benevolence of a man toward another man or toward a subject and the faithfulness to this attitude which ends up expressing faithfulness of a man to himself. Betraying one's partner is, ultimately, betraying oneself. For YHWH, showing *ḥesed* toward Israel means establishing with Israel a covenant freely given, having compassion for his own people in its difficulties and trials and even more: forgiving its unfaithfulness. Being faithful to the covenant means, ultimately for YHWH, being faithful to himself. Hence the two traits which appear very often together in the First Testament when speaking of YHWH: *ḥesed we'emet*, mercy (grace) and faithfulness (Ex 34:6; 2 Sm 2:6; 15:20; Ps 25:10; 40:11, etc.). Because God is God, God is holy, merciful. Better yet, God is merciful because God's holiness is actually mercy.

The second term is *raḥamím*, from *reḥem*, inner guts. This indicates the love of a mother for the fruit of her womb. YHWH shows the people of Israel also this expression of love. While *ḥesed* has a more masculine nuance of mercy, as faithfulness of the man to himself and to his word, *raḥamím* has a more feminine nuance as maternal goodness and tenderness, patience and compassion, readiness to forgive and patiently wait.

Holiness and mercy say something about the mystery of the living God as can be gleaned from how God works/acts. YHWH is ungraspable and very close, majestically transcendent and undeniably a protagonist of human history. Ultimately, YHWH's name summarizes these two traits, so much that one could say that Israel's experience of God, beginning from exodus, is but the constant deepening and discovery of YHWH's holiness and mercy. "Can a woman forget her nursing child, or show no compassion for the child of her womb? Even these may forget, yet I will not forget you" (Is 49:15). "How can I give you up, Ephraim? How can I hand you over, O Israel? My heart recoils within me; my compassion grows warm and tender" (Hos 11:8). So sanctity and mercy say the same thing about the mystery of the living God, as his action attests. YHWH cannot be grasped and yet he is very close; he is sovereignly transcendent and undeniably a protagonist of human history as well. Deep down, his name summarizes these two attributes. This is so much the case that it is possible to say that Israel's experience of God, starting with the exodus, is nothing other than a constant study of the continuing discovery of YHWH's sanctity and mercy.

YHWH as Father and Spouse

This same experience is described in the more mature texts of the First Testament with a double name attributed to YHWH: that of father and of spouse. Both these terms, with different nuances, express the quality of the relationship that the Lord establishes freely and without strings attached with God's people. The metaphorical meaning of these two terms, therefore, aims at making concrete and dynamically personal what, in more pregnant but distant terms, is expressed in and by the name.

The Paternity Metaphor

Initially, God is not invoked by Israel as father. In many contemporary religions, this felt quite natural. The supreme being was often seen as the forefather almost in a natural sense, so much so that a genealogy of continuity of human beings and the gods would be established. For Israel, however, God is God: first and foremost, God reveals God's own absolute transcendence and only from there would God reveal Godself as father. YHWH is father, not because he generates children but because he freely chooses Israel and cares for it as if Israel were his child. YHWH's paternity is not according to nature but stems from having chosen Israel and established a covenant with it. "When Israel was a child, I loved him, and out of Egypt I called my son" (Hos 11:1). "They shall come with weeping; and with supplications will I lead them: I will cause them to walk by rivers of waters, in a straight way wherein they shall not stumble; for I am a father to Israel, and Ephraim is my first-born" (Jer 31:9; see also Ps 103:13; Is 63:15; 64:7). To manifest this paternal relationship, YHWH declares first his infinite distance. An authentic loving relationship—even on a human level—presupposes and requires otherness as essential. Otherwise, an authentic communion would not be not possible and the relationship would become an illusory and destructive fusion.

God's love is also expressed through maternal symbols (see Is 49:15; 66:13). But even in this case Israel's experience is original. For other neighboring and contemporary peoples speaking of a goddess, in addition to a male god, was quite normal, but it was a projection of human experience onto the divine realm. In his absolute transcendence, YHWH cannot be said to be either male or female—that would be blasphemous. Rather, YHWH discloses in his relationship with Israel traits that express the uniqueness and richness pertaining to both males and females. To think of it, were men and women not created "in the image and likeness" of YHWH?

In this context, it is easier to understand the relevance and meaning of the so-called anthropomorphism used in the First Testament to describe the identity and work of God (hence the mention of hands, eyes, ears, face, nose; God is described as laughing, whistling, listening, yelling, rejoicing, being jealous, repenting). These qualities and verbs aim at underscoring dynamically the involved personality of YHWH and therefore they should not be naïvely understood as absolute, let alone be interpreted literally.

The Marriage Metaphor

With the preaching of the prophets, another metaphor begins to emerge and becomes prominent to express YHWH's relationship with the people of Israel: the marriage metaphor. The relationship traditionally expressed, beginning from the powerful exodus event, in political and juridical terms through the covenant, is now described in more personal terms as the covenant between a man and a woman, the bridegroom and the bride.

It is the prophet Hosea (seventh century BCE) who brings to the forefront in a powerful way the marriage metaphor to describe the relationship between YHWH and his people: beginning from the story (a real event or a parable?) of the prophet himself.[3] He marries a woman, Gomer, who abandons him and is a prostitute going with other men: this is an allusion to the sacred prostitution practiced by the Canaanites and the cultic worship of other gods, which the prophets name as prostitution with idols. YHWH orders Hosea to go and look for her, his wife, and again entice her to come back home with mercy and renewed love. This is to express what YHWH feels for the people, who prostituted themselves with foreign gods. Thus, the relationship between YHWH and Israel is described with the intense flavors of a marriage relationship, strengthened by the overcoming of infidelity and always ready to begin anew.[4]

3. See *Hosea*, trans. J. Jeremias (Brescia: Paideia, 2000).

4. "Therefore, I will now allure her, and bring her into the wilderness, and speak tenderly to her. From there I will give her her vineyards, and make the Valley of Achor a door of hope. There she shall respond as in the days of her youth, as at the time when she came out of the land of Egypt. On that day, says the Lord, you will call me, 'My husband' and no longer will you call me, 'My Baal'.... And I will take you for my wife forever; I will take you for my wife in righteousness and in justice, in steadfast love, and in mercy. I will take you for my wife in faithfulness; and you shall know the Lord.... I will sow him for myself in the land. And I will have pity on Not-pitied and I will say to Not-my-people 'You are my people' and he shall say 'You are my God'" (Hos 2:14–16, 19–20, 23).

Starting from Hosea, the theme continues to be revisited and elaborated upon incessantly: from Jeremiah (see Jer 2:2; 3:1–5) to Ezekiel, who use an amazingly rich and realistic language to revisit the entire history of Israel in light of the marriage parable of unfaithfulness of the chosen people and of God's ever renewed faithfulness (see Ezek 16).[5] Second Isaiah uses the metaphor as well (see Is 54:5–8, "for your Maker is your husband" [54:5]) as does Third Isaiah (Is 61:10; 62:2–5, "For as a young man marries a young woman, so shall your builder marry you, and as the bridegroom rejoices over the bride, so shall your God rejoice over you" [62:5]).

Ultimately, we can find an implicit connection—or at least an anthropological foundation of this rich marriage metaphor—in the Yahwist tradition, and specifically in the description of the creation of man and woman (Gn 2:23–34). We find it even more powerfully in the Priestly tradition (Gn 1:26–28, 31) during the post-exilic period, where the creation of the two in their reciprocity, in "the image and likeness of God," recalls the marriage relationship as a living analogy of God's actions toward God's people.

The highest and most sophisticated expression of this metaphor appears later (fifth or fourth century BCE) in a book which belongs to wisdom literature: the Song of Songs.[6] Here we find the intense and poetic celebration of the marriage relationship between King Solomon and the beautiful Shulamite woman. It is a song, or better yet, a marriage poem, which describes moments and stages of light and darkness, of seeking and encounters between the two lovers. In light of the positive value of

5. "The word of the Lord came to me: Mortal, make known to Jerusalem her abominations, and say, Thus says the Lord God to Jerusalem: Your origin and your birth were in the land of the Canaanites; your father was an Amorite, and your mother a Hittite. As for your birth, on the day you were born your navel cord was not cut, nor were you washed with water to cleanse you, nor rubbed with salt, nor wrapped in cloths. No eye pitied you, to do any of these things for you out of compassion for you; but you were thrown out in the open field, for you were abhorred on the day you were born. I passed by you, and saw you flailing about in your blood. As you lay in your blood, I said to you, 'Live! and grow up like a plant of the field.' You grew up and became tall and arrived at full womanhood; your breasts were formed, and your hair had grown; yet you were naked and bare. I passed by you again and looked on you; you were at the age for love. I spread the edge of my cloak over you, and covered your nakedness: I pledged myself to you and entered into a covenant with you, says the Lord God, and you became mine. Then I bathed you with water and washed off the blood from you, and anointed you with oil. I clothed you with embroidered cloth and with sandals of fine leather; I bound you in fine linen and covered you with rich fabric. I adorned you with ornaments: I put bracelets on your arms, a chain on your neck, a ring on your nose, earrings in your ears, and a beautiful crown upon your head. You were adorned with gold and silver, while your clothing was of fine linen, rich fabric, and embroidered cloth. You had choice flour and honey and oil for food. You grew exceedingly beautiful, fit to be a queen. Your fame spread among the nations on account of your beauty, for it was perfect because of my splendor that I had bestowed on you, says the Lord God. But you trusted in your beauty, and played the whore because of your fame, and lavished your whorings on any passer-by" (Ezek 16:1–15).

6. See Gianfranco Ravasi, *Cantico dei Cantici* (Cinisello Balsamo: Paoline, 1987); H. Gollwitzer, *Il poema biblico dell'amore tra uomo e donna: Cantico dei Cantici* (Turin: Claudiana, 2004).

marriage relationships—as the creation of man and woman was willed by God—this book was later interpreted in the Jewish and then in the Christian traditions as the sublime song of the love story between God and God's people.

The marriage metaphor, with its apex in the Song of Songs, represents the greatest expression of the sharing and intimacy that YHWH intends and wishes to experience with Israel. At the same time, it emphasizes, surprisingly, not only the infinite mercy of God, who forgives and transforms even the most intimate and painful betrayals but also the reciprocity of a relationship to which God, though sole initiator, calls God's creatures.

CHAPTER 9

YHWH's Presence in History and Creation

Between Otherness and Closeness

The suggested phenomenology of the shape of revelation claims that YHWH reveals himself and communicates himself in history for who he is in the figure of the covenant: that is, in establishing and gradually accomplishing the unconditional and free, but also demanding and empowering relationship with humanity through Israel. Within the space of grace and faithfulness (*ḥesed we'emet*) of this relationship, I argued that YHWH makes himself known increasingly as other and transcendent (*qadósh*, "holy") with respect to humanity and the world. At the same time, quite astonishingly, YHWH reveals himself as increasingly close to them and present through his grace and mercy (*ḥesed*). These two attributes of God's working and ultimately being are intrinsically related and in some way inversely proportional. The closer that God draws to Israel, the more God shows God's otherness; the more God shows God's otherness—as God, not a human being—the more God manifests God's omnipotent and merciful love.

This dialectic of otherness/proximity is disclosed in history through the multiple character of mediations between God on one side and Israel, humanity and creation on the other.[1] These mediations ensure both God's otherness and God's presence and proximity to humanity "with-

1. The term and concept of mediator, understood in a specific and precise sense, are not found in the First Testament (see O. Becker, "mesitēs," in *Dizionario di concetti biblici del Nuovo Testamento*, 73–76). However, the function of mediation between God and the people is certainly present, especially in the priest and the prophet, less so in the king, where it will become more defined in the messianic perspective. There are also two unique mediators, one at the beginning of the history of Israel, the other waited for in the promised kingdom: Moses (mediator in the revelation of the Name, the exodus from Egypt, the covenant) and the servant of YHWH in Second Isaiah, who brings God's revelation (Is 42:1–4) and is the keeper of the message of salvation to the Gentiles (Is 49:1–6) and takes upon himself and atones for human sin (Is 52:13–53:12). Actually, a careful theological reading will find that the function, better yet, the identity of mediation is implicit in the figure of Word/Wisdom and of the Spirit of YHWH.

out separation and without confusion." Their meaning is precisely that of "mediating" the relationships, that is, making it possible and direct, without getting in between the partners. These mediations, according to the polarity of the advent and exodus previously described, can be labeled with two titles: mediations that come from above, from God toward human beings; and those which rise from below, from human beings toward God (though also generated by God).

Among the mediations from above, we find: the angel, the name, the glory, the Law, the Word, Wisdom, the Spirit. Among the mediations from below, we find the witnesses and mediators of revelation and of the liberating actions of YHWH: Abraham, Moses, the judges, the kings, the prophets, and the priests, the individuals entrusted with being mediators because the word of God is addressed to them. They become mouthpieces of the Word because they are inhabited and anointed by the Spirit and instructed by wisdom—as the figure of the messiah and suffering servant gradually begin to emerge. With apocalyptic literature, we arrive at an understanding of human beings (see especially Dn 7:9–14) which is undoubtedly human—as attested by his designation and features—but at the same time is mysteriously close to the realm of God's transcendence, where he is introduced because of his unique mission entrusted to him by the most high "from heaven." Once again, everything leads toward an unpredictable point of encounter, a decisive coincidence, we would say, between mediation from above and mediation from below.

In the variety and progression typical of revelation of YHWH through this multiple experience of his mediations several points can be gleaned. First of all, there is an absolute preeminence of mediations "from above" because they express the presence and work of God so that, as noted above, the mediations "from below" stem from and are shaped by the mediations "from above." Second, the increasing emergence of two tracks according to which the mediations from above coalesce: the track of the Spirit of YHWH, on the one hand, and that of his Word/Wisdom, on the other. However, this coalescing of the two will become more clearly evident only with the Christ-event and the theological experience-interpretation given by the New Testament. On the other hand, this double mode of mediation by God shows an anthropological correspondence in the experience of the two privileged mediations of interpersonal relationships: language, that is, communication through words; and empathy, that is, being on the same spiritual wavelength.

Finally, there is the increasing development, evident especially in the most recent stages of the history of Israel (as per the post-exilic prophets and wisdom literature written during the Hellenistic period) of the personalist and ontological dimensions of the mediations of the Spirit and the Word/Wisdom. These remain emanations of YHWH but also express his presence and work in history and constitute a real and effective ec-stasy of God into human beings. In this way, human beings are attracted into the sphere of existence and life of God. This too will become fully intelligible only by being grounded in the Christ-event attested in the New Testament.

In light of this, let us explore the concrete defining of the mediation of the breath/Spirit and that of the Word/Wisdom by introducing them briefly through that unique form of YHWH's manifestation to and presence with Israel and creation which in some way precedes them and at the same time is their fruit: glory. Glory recalls the universal symbol of light, shared among all religious traditions as a way to express the irradiation of the divine onto the world, but with a remarkable originality in this case.

The Glory of YHWH

God's glory, in Hebrew *kabód* (*dóxa* in Greek, *claritas* in Latin) literally means "weight." It expresses the perceived and almost touched immensity, holiness, and beauty of God who makes Godself present to human beings in going toward them. Glory is the way in which God manifests God's holiness and at the same time the sign of God's presence among Israel. Glory is described in the Book of Exodus as follows (Ex 13:21–22; 24:15–17):

> The LORD went in front of them in a pillar of cloud by day, to lead them along the way, and in a pillar of fire by night, to give them light, so that they might travel by day and by night. Neither the pillar of cloud by day nor the pillar of fire by night left its place in front of the people.
>
> Then Moses went up on the mountain, and the cloud covered the mountain. The glory of the LORD settled on Mount Sinai, and the cloud covered it for six days; on the seventh day, he called to Moses out of the cloud. Now the appearance of the glory of the LORD was like a devouring fire on the top of the mountain in the sight of the people of Israel.

This is clearly figurative language, which illustrates dynamically the real and perceived presence of God who manifests Godself and leads God's people. At the time of the kings, the Temple in Jerusalem was built by Solomon to provide a symbolic dwelling for YHWH in the midst of his people and offer a worthy place for the ark of the covenant which during the wandering in the desert had preserved the tablets of the law given on Mount Sinai.[2] Thus the Temple became the place of YHWH's

2. The consecration of the Temple is described in 1 Kgs 8:10–13, 22–23, 27–29.

presence manifested by the descending of his glory. God is not portrayed, like the gods of other peoples, by a statue placed in the Temple: God remains transcendent (so much so that "emptiness" could be used to describe the typical form of YHWH's presence) though, in some mysterious way, YHWH truly dwells among his people.

From the motif of glory and YHWH's presence in the Temple stems the *shekinah* motif (from the verb *shākan*, to pitch a tent, dwell) found in rabbinical texts. "This is an abstract feminine noun which comes to signify all modes of God's presence in the past, the present, and the eschatological future."[3] The glory motif is also pervasive among the prophets. Just think of Isaiah's recalling the grandiose vision which occurred when he was called in roughly 740 BCE (Is 6:1–3):

In the year that King Uzziah died, I saw the Lord sitting on a throne, high and lofty; and the hem of his robe filled the Temple. Seraphs were in attendance above him; each had six wings: with two they covered their faces, and with two they covered their feet, and with two they flew. And one called to another and said: "Holy, holy, holy is the LORD of hosts; the whole earth is full of his glory."

During the exile, Ezekiel too recalls the reality of glory to describe the initial vision of his ministry (Ezek 1:4–5, 26–28):

As I looked, a stormy wind came out of the north: a great cloud with brightness around it and fire flashing forth continually, and in the middle of the fire, something like gleaming amber. In the middle of it was something like four living creatures ... And above the dome over their heads there was something like a throne, in appearance like sapphire; and seated above the likeness of a throne was something that seemed like a human form. Upward from what appeared like the loins I saw something like gleaming amber, something that looked like fire enclosed all around; and downward from what looked like the loins I saw something that looked like fire, and there was a splendor all around. Like the bow in a cloud on a rainy day, such was the appearance of the splendor all around. This was the appearance of the likeness of the glory of the LORD.

The glory of the Lord appears here, unexpectedly, in human form. The preceding description, with the symbol of the throne and the reference to the splendor, says that we are in the divine sphere. But then there is mention of human features. The vision is mysterious, almost undecodable in itself, expressed in very vivid apocalyptic language. It is almost as if we are faced with the maximum metaphorical tension to express, on the one hand, that God is transcendent holiness and, on the other hand, that God is intimately close to human beings, in which God's glory is mirrored.

3. Joseph Sievers, "'Where Two or Three ...': Shekhinah and Mt 18:20: Foundations for Jewish-Christian Dialogue and Beyond?," in *Claritas: Journal of Dialogue and Culture* 6, no. 1 (March 2017): 25–39.

This gives us the vision of a future, unexpected, and abundant manifestation of YHWH.

In the Book of Sirach, this prayer is found. "Fill Zion with your majesty, and your Temple with your glory" (Sir 36:19) and the psalm sings of the certainty that the Glory of the Lord will "dwell in our land" (Ps 85:9). It will be through his servant that YHWH will "be glorified" (Is 49:3). In other words, the glory is the manifestation of God's holiness who is present among Israel: glory fills nature, the cosmos, history, and especially the people of Israel, and wants to fill and transform into herself the holy city and God's chosen one.

Connected to this tradition, the Gospel of John, in the prologue, later states that the *Lógos* "lived among us" (literally, established his tent, *eskénosen*) and we "have seen his Glory" (Jn 1:14). Jesus is recognized as the splendor of God's glory who dwells among human beings. Better yet, for John, the divine glory which is manifested to Isaiah is the same glory which will burst forth in Jesus (Jn 12:41).

An aspect of God's revelation—parallel to the experience of the covenant, which characterizes YHWH's act of creation and care for it and which is promised by the prophets as decisive and universal for messianic times—is God's becoming present and self-communicating in and through God's own breath or Spirit. The experience of the divine Spirit or of the divine as Spirit, in reality is a complex religious phenomenon we need to briefly address before focusing on its original meaning in the First Testament.

The Experience of the Spirit

Leaving aside a specific interpretation connected to the individual cultural and religious *Sitz im Leben*, we can say that the symbol of the spirit by its own vocation and intrinsic semantic structure, is in itself in tension. It is at the same time cosmological or anthropological and also typically theological; it expresses at the same time, and in its intrinsic correlation, the principle of unity-totality of being and of its multiplicity-multifacetedness; it typifies the ecstasy of the divine in relationship to the world (and the divine's exhaustive immanence in the world) and, dialectically, the divine's transcendent and holy/sacred otherness with respect to the world; and it denotes the personality (of God and human beings) and at the same time a sort of impersonality or better yet, super-personality. And the list could go on.

From this observation, questions can be raised about the possibility of establishing a sort of *symbolic net* which, without forcing the phenomenological and historical data, may identify the shared and universal semantic field of the experience of the spirit of God and of God as spirit, through the multiplicity, both diachronic and synchronic, of the Spirit's expressions and unique nuances. This is challenging. H. Kleinknecht, for example, in his contribution to the term *pneûma* in Kittel's dictionary, finds in the Western context a parallel/simultaneous development of Greek *pneûma*, Latin *spiritus*, and Germanic *Geist*, which would express the perception of the same reality.[4] Di Nola does not hide the difficulty given by the remaining ambiguity of the term, of which he lists eleven meanings, though he ends up establishing an original convergence (the result, in his view, of a stage of deepening the religious experience). This convergence goes beyond the dynamic reference to the Greek root *pne-* and the Latin root *sp-*, which relate to rhythm of breathing to approach what is expressed in Sanskrit by *ātman* and in Hebrew by *rūah*.

In any event, the term *spirit*, which comes from the Latin *spiritus* (from *spirare*, "to blow," "exhale") corresponds to the Greek *pneûma*, "breath," "blow," similar to the term *anima*. In Sanskrit we find *ātman* (possibly from *áni-ti*, "he blows"), "blow," "exhalation," and "breath," semantically similar to the Hebrew *rūah* which clearly indicates "air in motion," "wind" (Gn 3:8; Ex 10:13–19), "exhalation" (Gn 45:27) of a powerful being (Ex 15:8; 2 Sm 22:16; Ps 18:16; Is 30:28; Hos 13:15). All these terms carry traces of the experience of the physiological phenomenon which has struck human beings since the beginning of history, especially in connection with the moments of birth and death, when the baby has come out of the mother's womb and takes the first breath of air and the dying person gives "the last breath." The terms discussed above also attest to the religious intuition that that breath of life comes from and returns to the one who originally gave it: God, the principle of life, who—as gradually perceived and expressed—is "pure and superior Spirit." This is in spite of the fact that the connection to the image of the wind or of human breath at first has a physical background, though quite subtle and movable; their terms of comparison are fire and air. Only slowly and gradually the meaning of the incorporeal reality has taken over.

Through the symbol of the spirit, human beings perceive and describe the indwelling—in themselves, in others, in the world—of life and power coming from God and belonging to God and at the same time being grasped by God in privileged moments of personal existence and in the history of the community in view of a specific mission. Within this perspective, Louis Bouyer, looking at the original religious experience, emphasizes:

4. H. Kleinknecht, "pneûma," in *GLNT* X:784.

> The shaman is the primal type of the inspired person. It seems that the shaman's inspiration is found at the origins of every culture and religion worthy of this name. It is a sort of primal phenomenon which is equivalent, from the perspective of primitive cultures, to what we have come to recognize as the great mystics in developed cultures.... A formula like Saint Augustine's of a God who is more intimate to myself than I to myself and yet is ungraspable by human beings has always been felt by Taoists, who came in contact with the West, as the expression which best expresses their experience and their understanding of it.[5]

He continues, concerning Hinduism: "Some texts present the situation in a way that is not very different from the second Biblical story of the creation of human beings: things develop as if the *ātman* were blown into the nostrils of the first human being by the divine Brahman."[6] In the Greek tradition we find for example Socrates's *daimon*, the divine voice in the heart of humans and the "enthusiastic" *pneûma* which takes hold of human beings and makes it possible for the deity to dwell within them: this is according to Plato. Not to mention Stoicism, which sees in the reality of the *pneûma*, the vital and unifying principle in the cosmos, the foundational concept; or Plotinus and the Neoplatonists' insight of the *anima mundi* (*psyché*).

The Spirit of YHWH

The uniqueness of the First Testament is that the anthropological experience of the "vital breath" and the inner religious experience of being touched and taken hold by God are understood as related to the action and presence of YHWH in the history of his people as creator and liberator. This means that the space of perception and understanding of the Spirit becomes, with increasing awareness, the covenant between YHWH and his people. The Spirit is no longer experienced and understood merely as the "life breath" which animates the world but the "breath" which belongs to YHWH and only to him; it comes from him and is freely communicated to human beings and the world, giving them life and enveloping them in beauty. The Spirit is the life breath of a face, of an "I." It is the Spirit of YHWH. Psalm 104:29–30 expresses it beautifully: "When you hide your face, they are dismayed; when you take away their breath, they die and return to their dust. / When you send forth your spirit, they are created; and you renew the face of the ground." The presence and action of the spirit of YHWH, therefore, are experienced *first* and originally on the level of the religious and ethical relationship that YHWH establishes with his people (the covenant). Only *afterward*,

5. Louis Bouyer, *Il Consolatore: Spirito Santo e vita di grazia* (Rome: Paoline, 1983), 20 and 24 (own trans.).

6. Ibid., 27.

in light of this horizon of meaning, it is experienced also on the level of the relationship of God with the world, including human beings, as a result of his creative and free action. All this entails, more or less implicitly, the overcoming and critique of an understanding of the spirit as cosmic force, or as a certain autonomous anxiety, or even something lending itself to magical manipulation for human use. The spirit of YHWH is rather a mediating modality to make God present and active outside of Godself, in creation and history.

In Genesis, for example, the encounter between YHWH and human beings is described poetically as "at the time of the evening breeze" (Gn 3:8) after the command had been given to Adam: "of the tree of the knowledge of good and evil you shall not eat" (Gn 2:17). Creation is a work of the Word ("God said") and of the Spirit ("a wind from God swept over the face of the waters," Gn 1:2). If YHWH's word expresses what he wants to communicate, the spirit gives life, so much that without the spirit, human beings are merely "flesh" (*bāśār*) and so are all the other creatures. The being of man who is an "image" of God (Gn 1:26) and lives because the Lord "breathed into his nostrils the breath of life" (Gn 2:7) subsists only by being in front of the creator, in his capacity of encountering the creator, by accepting an invitation to do so. It is the vital spirit shared by YHWH at creation which allows human beings to be the "you" of YHWH, his interlocutor and partner in the covenant. When human beings refuse to live a life entirely of communion with YHWH (in mystery and in being open to a greater future), YHWH is forced to proclaim: "My spirit shall not abide in mortals forever" (Gn 6:3).

Therefore, the Spirit is the vital atmosphere of God's communion with human beings. Because it is the Spirit who works and renews the encounter of human beings with YHWH, we could say that the people of the covenant is the space which God creates in history so that his Spirit may act in it, guiding it, as a sign attracting everyone toward the promised land of the fulfilled communion with God.

The Messiah and the Eschatological Effusion of the Spirit

From this derives a second feature of the experience of the Spirit in the First Testament: its link to the promise. The covenant designs the space within which the Spirit, coming from YHWH and being welcomed by creatures, works as a principle of liberation and justice. Thus God's presence/action in the history of God's people and prospectively in the history of all of humanity, takes place along a journey marked by a specific and increasing irruption of the Spirit. This journey is in tension toward an eschatological and abundant effusion of the Spirit at the appointed time, as a living principle of full communion between God and God's people and of the liberating justice among human beings.

The irruption of the Spirit becomes active and palpable through the word and power of YHWH given to people chosen by YHWH not to be made holy but to be sent as messengers and mediators of the covenant and the promise. YHWH allows a unique effusion of his Spirit to human beings such as Moses (see Nm 16:17), the judges (as in the Book of Judges), kings (see Ps 8:7; 9:16), prophets (see Ezek 3:12, 14, 24; Is 59:21). They are made aware of God's designs and power to bring them about; they are called to lead the people through the challenges of history while keeping their eyes fixed on the goal. It will be the anointed one *par excellence*, the promised messiah (*mashiah*, in Hebrew, *Christós* in Greek) who will receive onto himself an overly abundant effusion of the Spirit of YHWH (see Is 61:1). The Spirit will rest upon him and will bring him the fullness of divine gifts: "A shoot shall come out from the stump of Jesse, and a branch shall grow out of his roots. The spirit of the Lord shall rest on him, the spirit of wisdom and understanding, the spirit of counsel and might, the spirit of knowledge and the fear of the Lord" (Is 11:1–2).

According to the logic of the promise, messianic expectations become the "backbone" of Israel's history. Within the space of messianic hope, throughout the centuries, different strands emerge: the kingly, the prophetic, the Priestly, and the apocalyptic strands. However, because these are based upon the memory of the character of Moses, they tend to be concentrated into one character and in only one decisive intervention of YHWH. Thanks to the overly abundant effusion of the Spirit upon him, the messiah will lead the chosen people to full communion with YHWH, making it possible for the other peoples to be part of it as well: "Here is my servant, whom I uphold, my chosen, in whom my soul delights; I have put my spirit upon him; he will bring forth justice to the nations" (Is 42:1). This effusion will involve the entire people, or rather, all of creation. Thus, it will be proclaimed from the Babylonian exile by Jeremiah and Ezekiel, Joel and Zachary: "Then afterward I will pour out my spirit on all flesh; your sons and your daughters shall prophesy, your old men shall dream dreams, and your young men shall see visions" (Jl 2:28). The distinctive eschatological gift of the Spirit is his effusion within the hearts of human beings, upon which the Spirit will inscribe the Law/Word of YHWH, enabling human beings to observe it and revealing himself as the principle of a new and full covenant which will never again be broken. Ezekiel writes (Ezek 36:24–28; see also Jer 31:3):

> I will take you from the nations, and gather you from all the countries, and bring you into your own land. I will sprinkle clean water upon you, and you shall be

clean from all your uncleannesses, and from all your idols I will cleanse you. A new heart I will give you, and a new spirit I will put within you; and I will remove from your body the heart of stone and give you a heart of flesh. I will put my spirit within you, and make you follow my statutes and be careful to observe my ordinances. Then you shall live in the land that I gave to your ancestors; and you shall be my people, and I will be your God.

As the principle of the new and final covenant, the "new" Spirit given in "the last days" will purify human beings from every sin (see Ps 51), will give them life anew, even after death (see the vision of the dry bones in Ezek 37:1–4), will give the gift of prophecy to the entire people, without class distinctions (see Jl 3:1–2). The eschatological effusion of the Spirit will have repercussions at a social and even cosmic level, renewing all of creation: "a spirit from on high is poured out on us and the wilderness becomes a fruitful field.... Then justice will dwell in the wilderness, and righteousness abide in the fruitful field. The effect of righteousness will be peace, and the result of righteousness, quietness and trust forever. My people will abide in a peaceful habitation, in secure dwellings, and in quiet resting places" (Is 32:15–18).

Summary

The Spirit of YHWH, which brings about a sense of grace and communion between God and human beings, will be fully given to each and all, in the end times. The messiah (the servant of YHWH) will have an essential role in extending to the peoples the fruits of this communion with God, through a universal effusion of the Spirit. The Spirit, interiorized in human hearts, will prompt a new and final covenant and a renewal of all of creation. The Spirit will thus become the inner principle of communion with God and among human beings as a freeing, freely given, and abundant gift.

The Word and Wisdom of YHWH

Closely linked to Israel's experience of the Spirit of YHWH, is the experience of his Word. Here too, there is a unique creativity. In relationship with human experience, in Semitic culture the word (*dābār*) is not at all a *flatus voci* nor does it merely express an abstract concept, but it is an expression of the "heart," that is, the unifying and personal core of human beings. It expresses what in Greek is represented by the concepts of *lógos* (thought, word) and *prágma* (event, action). This is even more true of YHWH, whose Word comes from his transcendent being and communicates his all-powerful will: it is a Word which is alive and effective, bringing about what it expresses.

The Word

In this perspective, the Word is above all mediator of God's revelation and action in salvation history. God manifests Godself with words to Abraham, Moses, the prophets; through them, God pronounces in history the words which interpret and guide events, causing them through the free collaboration of human beings (see Is 44:26; 55:10–11). In this light, the Word is increasingly understood also as mediator for creation: in the sense that it is through the word that God sets into being and orders what is other than Godself: what, in itself, simply is not (see Gn 1: "God said ... and it happened"; Ps 33:6: "By the Word of the Lord the heavens were made").

The Law

In a certain way, and certainly linked to the Word, is the Law (*torah*).[7] In the Torah, given by YHWH to Moses, are condensed the "words" which express the will of YHWH for his people in the context of the covenant (see Dt 28:6–9): the Decalogue (see Ex 34:28; Dt 4:13; 10:4).[8] Therefore, the Law is an efficacious sign of the constant presence of YHWH among his people, as it is tangibly symbolized by the ark of the covenant which contains its tablets and the Temple in Jerusalem where it is jealously kept. At first carved on "tablets of stone," it would then be carved in the new covenant on the "tablets of flesh" of human hearts (see Gn 31:31; Ezek 36:26).

Wisdom

The First Testament is familiar with God's Wisdom, with which YHWH created and sustains the universe (see Jb 28:20–28). The Hebrew term is *ḥōkmah*, translated in Greek with *sophía* and Latin *sapientia*. In post-exilic times, the meditation on wisdom became increasingly relevant and developed, as in the Book of Proverbs, of which the most ancient parts date back to the times of the kings, and in the Book of Wisdom, probably redacted in Alexandria in the first century BCE, very close to the time of Jesus Christ.[9]

7. See Paul Beauchamp, *La legge di Dio* (Casale Monferrato: Piemme, 2000); F. Dal Bo, *La Legge e il volto di Dio: La Rivelazione sul Sinai nella letteratura ebraica e cristiana* (Florence: Giuntina, 2004); Frank Crüsemann, *La torà: Teologia e storia sociale della legge nell'Antico Testamento* (Brescia: Paideia, 2008).

8. See Marc-Alain Ouaknin, *Les Dix Commandements* (Paris: Seuil, 1999).

9. See, respectively, *Libro dei proverbi. Tradizione, redazione, teologia*, ed. G. Bellia and A. Passaro (Casale Monferrato: Piemme, 1999); and Victor Morla Asensio, *Libros sapienciales y otras escritos* (Estella: Editorial Verbo Divino, 1994).

Three Different Charisms

Word, Law, and Wisdom, though originally distinct, are actually converging mediations of the presence and action of God among God's people: while the oracular Word is the charism of the prophet, the interpretation of the Law is the charism of the priest and the advice of Wisdom the charism of the wise (Jer 18:18). These are interconnected, to the point of becoming synonyms: thus, in the Book of Baruch, Wisdom is identified with "the book of the commandments of God, the Law that endures forever" (Bar 4:1), and in the Book of Sirach with "the book of the covenant of the Most High God, the law that Moses commanded us" (Sir 24:23). With them, God's communication of truth and meaning to humanity is integrated into one design. In this communication, God effectively reveals and shares the design (*mystérion*) which God conceived from the foundation of the world and which increasingly and efficaciously unfolds in creation and history. Therefore, the Word and Wisdom deal primarily with YHWH but at the same time with creation and history.

The Personification of Wisdom

Beginning from the most recent sections of the Book of Proverbs, we find a unique process of personification of Wisdom which governs the universe and guides history. This is certainly a literary device but quite meaningful for various reasons (Prv 8:22–24, 29–31):

> The Lord created me at the beginning of his work, the first of his acts of long ago. Ages ago I was set up, at the first, before the beginning of the earth. When there were no depths I was brought forth, when there were no springs abounding with water.... when he assigned to the sea its limit, so that the waters might not transgress his command, when he marked out the foundations of the earth, then I was beside him, like a master worker; and I was daily his delight, rejoicing before him always, rejoicing in his inhabited world and delighting in the human race.

Further emphasis in this direction is given in the Book of Wisdom, consistent with theological developments influenced by Hellenism (Platonism and Stoicism). In the Book of Wisdom, Wisdom is portrayed not only as God's creature and instrument in creation and revelation—as in the Book of Proverbs—but it is presented in such a close relationship with God that some of the characteristics and actions typical of God end up being applied to Wisdom (Wis 7:25–27):

> For she is a breath of the power of God, and a pure emanation of the glory of the Almighty [*atmìs gár estin tês toû theoû dynámeōs kaì apórria tês toû pantokrátoros dóxēs*] therefore nothing defiled gains entrance into her. For she is a reflection of eternal light, a spotless mirror of the working of God, and an image of his

goodness [*apaúgasma gár estin phōtos aidíou kaì ésoptron akēlídōton tês toû Theoû energeías kaì eikòn tês agathótētos autoû*]. Although she is but one, she can do all things, and while remaining in herself, she renews all things; in every generation she passes into holy souls and makes them friends of God, and prophets.

Finally, still in the Book of Wisdom, we find the description of creation of the cosmos through the Word and of humanity through God's Wisdom, along with mention of the sending of the Spirit with Wisdom so that human beings may know the thoughts of YHWH (Wis 9:1–2, 4, 9–10, 17):

O God of my ancestors and Lord of mercy, who have made all things by your word, and by your wisdom have formed humankind ... give me the wisdom that sits by your throne, and do not reject me from among your servants.... With you is wisdom, she who knows your works and was present when you made the world; she understands what is pleasing in your sight and what is right according to your commandments. Send her forth from the holy heavens, and from the throne of your glory send her, that she may labor at my side, and that I may learn what is pleasing to you.... Who has learned your counsel, unless you have given wisdom and sent your holy spirit from on high?

The Unity of the Origin and Destiny of Creation

P. Beauchamp has acutely interpreted this broad process of development of the biblical character of wisdom as an expression of the increasing understanding, in light of revelation, of the ontological unity which contains in itself the truth and destiny of everything that has been created by God. This unity is present in creation because it is the work of YHWH and creation goes toward unity through the mediation of human freedom. This unity has its ultimate roots and destiny in God, of whom wisdom is an effective reflection. Wisdom, therefore, is not confused with God and God's being one but comes from God, manifesting God and almost projecting God outward:

The characteristics given to this amazing unity, called Wisdom, are pretty specific: they express what is before the beginning and present at the time of creation, what is present in all historical periods, what, coming from God, dwells always with God and human beings, what is defined as a subsistent being.... Wisdom is the unity of all divine manifestations and no aspect of creation is outside of the attraction of her essential simplicity, so that God may be known. God would not be known if Wisdom was self-involved or if Wisdom did not emanate from God.... Here we find what allows us to think about something that can be said about God's essence: God is manifested in a unity which exits from God and returns to God.[10]

10. Beauchamp, *L'uno e l'altro Testamento*, 130 and 140–41 (own trans.).

CHAPTER 10

The Image of YHWH Tested

Krisis, *Pathos*, Apocalypse

The exile in Babylon (sixth century BCE) is a time of extreme suffering, rather, of a real collective "night" for Israel. It was overcome thanks only to the message of the prophets who promoted faith and hope in the liberating and recreating action of God. However, once Israel returned home, even the promise of a new exodus and a new covenant clashed with a harsh reality. This generated a true crisis within the religious consciousness of Israel, attested in the post-exilic period, by the Books of Job and Ecclesiastes.

Job's Cry and Qoheleth's Vanity

After the exile, the interest in the destiny of the individual—in facing the dramatic and universal questions of human existence: suffering, death, the final destiny of the righteous, the lack of intervention by God to defend the righteous—comes to the fore. The Book of Job attests to the crisis of Israel's traditional wisdom when faced with these issues. Yet this leads to a deepening of traditional wisdom and to deeper and more authentic answers.

In the Book of Psalms and in the prophets we encounter the signs of violent tests which take place and which purify the faith of Israel, while posing the most painful questions of individual and communal existence. In its most ancient formulation, the expression, "It is the Lord. Let him do what seems good to him" (1 Sm 3:18), expressed the unflinching conviction which prompted "hope in YHWH" while awaiting YHWH's liberating intervention. Toward the end of the monarchic period, with its political and social catastrophes, this logic seemed to no longer work. To the point that—as found in Ezekiel 18—disillusion leads to the conclusion that "the way of the Lord is unfair" (Ezek 18:25).

The prophet Jeremiah,[1] during the exile, experiences something similar—being seduced, almost forcefully, by God, tragically suffering to adhere to God's will, then feeling abandoned: "Lord, you have enticed me, and I was enticed; you have overpowered me and you have prevailed" (Jer 20:7). It is not just being seduced by YHWH and not being successful in his ministry that torment Jeremiah. It is also the fact that God is not answering the prophet's burning questions. G. von Rad remarks: "It is still Jeremiah's secret how, in the face of growing skepticism about his own office, he was yet able to give an almost superhuman obedience to God.... If God brought the life of the most faithful of his ambassadors into so terrible and utterly uncomprehended a night and there to all appearances allowed him to come to utter grief, this remains God's secret."[2]

Job and the Struggle with God

Jeremiah's question underlies the Book of Job (ca. early fifth century BCE).[3] In Job, the problem of suffering and evil explodes with unprecedented intensity and starkness in Israel. The anonymous author describes the drama of a righteous man who, having served the Lord, is being tested in unimaginable ways in all that he has and is. He experiences in his faith "the grotesque contrast of an omnipotent God who turns against the very fragile being, man, who is marked by death, and does not give him a little respite even in the little life he has been given."[4]

In the narrative portion of the book—the most ancient—Job is still so strong in his faith that he can rhetorically ask whether we only accept what God gives but not also what he takes back from what he has given: "The Lord gave, and the Lord has taken away; blessed be the name of the Lord" (Jb 1:21) and "Shall we receive the good at the hand of God, and not receive the bad?" (Jb 2:10).

In the poetic portion of the book—the most recent—the question of divine justice, facing the humanly unjust suffering of Job, opens a real theological abyss. Job, who knows he has already lost his struggle with God and that it is pointless to even attempt it—"For he is not a mortal, as I am, that I might answer him, that we should come to trial together. There is no umpire between us, who might lay his hand on us both"

1. See Dreston, "Geremia, un uomo in mezzo," in *Dio e il suo avvento*, 62–96; Michael P. Maier, *Jeremia: Die Geschichte eines Berufenen* (Bad Tölz: Verlag Urfeld, 2004).

2. Gerhard von Rad, *Old Testament Theology*, vol. 2: *The Theology of Israel's Historical Traditions*, trans. D. M. G. Stalker (Harper and Row, 1962), 206.

3. See Roland E. Murphy, *The Psalms, Job* (Philadelphia: Fortress Press, 1977); Gerald Janzen, *Job* (Atlanta: John Knox Press, 1985).

4. Gérard Rossé, *La rivelazione di Dio nell'Antico Testamento: il periodo post-esilico*, in Università Popolare Mariana, *Il Dio di Gesù Cristo, Corso di teologia II* (Rome: Città Nuova, 1982), 76 (own trans.).

(Jb 9:32–33)—still engages in the impossible enterprise of the *rîb* (confrontation, struggle, trial) with YHWH.

Against stereotypical talks of Job's friends, which are abstract and ultimately too human, he gives witness to an all-enduring justice, "I put on righteousness, and it clothed me; my justice was like a robe and a turban" (Jb 29:14). This does not entail absence of sin but presupposes a relationship of acceptance and grace on God's part which Job never rejected or withdrew by refusing it. Job's confrontation with YHWH is therefore a dramatic and almost desperate prayer of invocation with which he begs the Lord to save the image of holiness and justice which Job has of him, in the hope of having some sort of satisfaction beyond the boundaries of the human mortal condition (Jb 7:17–21):

> What are human beings, that you make so much of them, that you set your mind on them, visit them every morning, test them every moment? Will you not look away from me for a while, let me alone until I swallow my spittle? If I sin, what do I do to you, you watcher of humanity? Why have you made me your target? Why have I become a burden to you? Why do you not pardon my transgression and take away my iniquity? For now I shall lie in the earth; you will seek me, but I shall not be."

The real issue in the Book of Job is that of the image of God, and, as a consequence, of the relationship between God and human beings. The rationales that Job's friends bring out to defend God's actions, expressing a naïve anthropomorphic concept of retributive justice, do not explain Job's suffering. The struggle of Job with God (like the struggle of Jacob and the angel) is carried out to grasp God's secret, going beyond an accepting and insufficient theological perspective. Even in the most excruciating suffering, Job affirms in spite of everything, his faith in the God of his life: "For I know that my Redeemer lives, and that at the last he will stand upon the earth; and after my skin has been thus destroyed, then in my flesh I shall see God, whom I shall see on my side, and my eyes shall behold, and not another. My heart faints within me!" (Jb 19:25–27).

Precisely because of this, Job awaits—and almost expects—a reply from his transcendent interlocutor: "Let the Almighty answer me!" (Jb 31:35). Finally, God agrees. God displays, while also hiding behind, God's own mysterious omnipotence: "Where were you when I laid the foundation of the earth? Tell me, if you have understanding!" (Jb 38:4). God cannot be trapped into any human comprehension. It is only in the deepest depths of human existence, where the most excruciating questions are harbored, that Job can encounter God not superficially but directly, not to hear a satisfying answer to his questions but to recognize God as the one in whom is hidden the secret of existence. The celebration of the sovereign justice of God which sustains the universe, God's saving and benevolent participation in creation, in modes and times which go beyond human understanding, closes the confrontation and invites to adoration: "Will you even put me in the wrong? Will you condemn me that you may be justified?" (Jb 40:8).

> I know that you can do all things, and that no purpose of yours can be thwarted. "Who is this that hides counsel without knowledge?" Therefore I have uttered what I did not understand, things too wonderful for me, which I did not know. "Hear, and I will speak; I will question you, and you declare to me." I had heard of you by the hearing of the ear, but now my eye sees you; therefore I despise myself, and repent in dust and ashes." (Jb 42:2–6)

"Just as you do not know how the breath comes to the bones in the mother's womb, so you do not know the work of God, who makes everything" (Eccl 11:5; 3:11; 8:17). The ultimate entity one has to deal with is death, which calls for the revelation of the face of a God who would give an answer to the supreme enigma of life. Job's cry remains without an answer and settles into adoring the utter mystery of the most high. The confrontation is over. But if the faith of Job settles down, the burden of an answer to the crisis of God's justice in history (which would more recently be called theodicy) remains in God's secret, because God has so established. This is ultimately in tune with the prophetic strands of a messianic promise. YHWH himself will establish the holy city upon justice (see Is 54:13–14) and will "cause righteousness and praise to spring up before all the nations" (Is 61:11).

Job's crisis and the suffering of the righteous person—which seems inevitably to compromise the experience of justice and the promise of the covenant between YHWH and his people—gain in a certain way some meaning and delineate how exemplary is the messianic character of the righteous servant of YHWH. He "shall make many righteous" and will have "a portion with the great ... because he poured out himself to death and was numbered with the transgressors; yet he bore the sin of many and made intercession for the transgressors" (Is 53:12). The development of the concept of justice in the First Testament "ends with this wonderful and amazing paradox."[5] As C. G. Jung wrote in *Answer to Job*, only the cry of God made man will actually answer the cry of Job.[6]

5. Nynfa Bosco, *Idea e concezioni della giustizia nelle civiltà occidentali*, vol. 1: *L'antichità* (Turin: Edizioni di "Filosofia," 1983), 15.

6. See Carl Gustav Jung, *Antwort auf Hiob* (Zurich: Rascher and Cie A. G., 1952).

Qoheleth and the "Fear of God"

Qoheleth (ca. late third century BCE) is situated in a context of social and cultural transition as well as of mutual influence of two cultural traditions. On the one hand, there was the Hellenistic world in its full expression—Palestine being under the Ptolemies—and on the other hand the Hebrew world living faithfully according to the traditions of the forefathers but witnessing the dissolution of the reference points and ethical categories to understand reality and the existential attitudes which had supported it through the centuries. Qoheleth is at the crossroads of these two worlds. He is between the Hebrew world, the originality of which he does not want to suppress, and the Hellenistic world, from which come questions and cosmological and ethical perspectives stemming, for example, from Stoic or Epicurean philosophies. The book of Qoheleth achieves an extraordinary and unprecedented synthesis of these two worlds in light of the tradition of the patriarchs.

On the one end, Qoheleth is an extremely sophisticated text, modern, radically existentialist. On the other hand, it is not afraid of showing a strong critique of a worldly vision of life and also of a markedly religious vision which runs the risk of becoming fossilized. Actually, there is nothing more corrosive in the book than the critique of a religious vision which reduces faith to an ideological veneer. Qoheleth removes from religiosity every superstructure and channels a theological meaning which is certainly not easy to decipher but is open and allusive.

Superstructures are what Qoheleth terms as *vanitas vanitatum*, vanity of vanities, understood by Norbert Lohfink as vapor.[7] Life, the very essence of reality, is "vapor," a simple and innocent "weaving of air." It is a beautiful metaphor, which alludes to the fact that life lasts only an instant because it does not have roots in itself. We are faced with a vision that disintegrates the sense of reality in which we are immersed: not to avoid it, not to build an alternative reality, but rather to lead to the awareness that the essence of everything is but "vapor." This is so that we may decide to live intensely each present moment. This is the discovery and advice of Qoheleth: only in the present moment can we find the grace of finding the reliable foundation which is the hidden and mysterious, but also very real, presence of God.

Only in the mystery of God the meaning of everything is hidden: it eludes us because it is, by definition, ungraspable. Facing this, human beings entrust themselves to God by embracing immediately each present

7. Norbert Lohfink, *Kohelet* (Würzburg: Echter Verlag, 1980); see also *Il libro del Qohelet: Tradizioni, redazione, teologia*, ed. G. Bellia and A. Passaro (Milan: Paoline, 2001).

moment, whether it is a moment of darkness or light, joy or suffering. Death is the ark which contains the secret of everything. From there, from God, the meaning gives true flavor—even in the temporary earthly existence—to what we experience. Experiencing the transiency of life does not deprive it of its essence, nor its beauty. On the contrary, it is the only horizon which makes it possible for human beings to experience it. Therefore, one should not flee from the world or separate the body from the soul. Living the present: this is, for Qoheleth, the authentic "fear of the Lord."

In a certain way, Qoheleth is a preparation for the Gospel of Jesus at the advent of God in human existence, which is fulfilled in his death and resurrection. This is because it fosters the attitude of one living the present moment, linked to the living relationship freely given by God in the breath of the Spirit.

The Suffering Servant and the Pathos of YHWH

Within the prophetic perspective, the theme of suffering and trial is emphasized to the breaking point in the figure of YHWH's "suffering servant." On the one hand, this thread seems to emerge in a sort of absolute solitude in Second Isaiah. On the other hand, it represents the sudden coalescing, and almost personification, of a constant in YHWH's work with respect to his people, through the one sent to them as message and instrument of redemption. In the four servant songs,[8] we actually find ourselves facing the mysterious emergence of an unexpected answer from God to Job's cry (Is 53:3–6, 10–12):

> He was despised and rejected by others; a man of suffering and acquainted with infirmity; and as one from whom others hide their faces he was despised, and we held him of no account. Surely he has borne our infirmities and carried our diseases; yet we accounted him stricken, struck down by God, and afflicted. But he was wounded for our transgressions, crushed for our iniquities; upon him was the punishment that made us whole, and by his bruises we are healed. All we like sheep have gone astray; we have all turned to our own way, and the LORD has laid on him the iniquity of us all.... Yet it was the will of the LORD to crush him with pain. When you make his life an offering for sin, he shall see his offspring, and shall prolong his days; through him the will of the LORD shall prosper. Out of his anguish he shall see light; he shall find satisfaction through his knowledge. The righteous one, my servant, shall make many righteous, and he shall bear their iniquities. Therefore, I will allot him a portion with the great, and he shall divide the spoil with the strong; because he poured out himself to death, and was numbered with the transgressors; yet he bore the sin of many, and made intercession for the transgressors.

8. Is 42:1–4; 49:1–6; 50:4–11; 52:13–53:12.

Who is the servant? Among the many answers attempted, the most plausible is that it is the one to whom a prophetic and redemptive mission with universal scope has been entrusted. However, it is also clear that there is a reference to the entire people of Israel and especially the "remnant," which is the ideal seed of the new covenant. It is a prophetic mediator, as Moses was, and is similar in various ways to some of the prophets, but is superior to them all, just like the new exodus and the new covenant will be superior to the first exodus and the first covenant. What is unique, beyond the universal scope of his mission, is that the servant freely takes on a subordinate function. He "took it upon himself to act vicariously, that submissively and unresistingly, and therefore deliberately, he took this mediating office upon himself even unto death, and that in so doing he complied with Jhwh's purpose."[9] He will go through full suffering and will experience death, but this is precisely how he will reestablish a full and lasting relationship of all with YHWH.

Thus a prophetic theme emerges clearly: the mediator whom YHWH will send and who will be faithful to the end to YHWH's salvific plan will suffer the consequences of Israel's and humanity's iniquity to establish the new and final covenant. However, this remains quite enigmatic: how and by whom will this be brought about? Suffering and trial, experienced with faithfulness to the unchangeable will of YHWH toward his people (and all of humanity) take on an atoning and redemptive value and seem to be connected to the ministry of the messiah-servant. But this is not all. YHWH does not only use the vicarious suffering of the one he sent; somehow, YHWH participates in it. At the beginning of the twentieth century, Abraham Joshua Heschel described the theology of the prophets as a "theology of divine *pathos*."[10] YHWH is not impassible and distant but is close to his people, comes down toward them and suffers—while remaining free, in his holiness—because of the offenses and infidelity by Israel but also because of the trials and suffering that Israel has to go through. Ultimately, many anthropomorphisms used in the First Testament (such as YHWH being portrayed as angry, feeling betrayed, suffering for and with his people) aim at expressing this deep participation and compassion of God for and with his people.

This does not mean that YHWH is no longer the holy one and Lord. But his holiness and his very divinity are not in contradiction with his free relating to human history. Rather, it is thanks to his omnipotence that YHWH, almost transcending himself, comes to encounter human

9. Von Rad, *Old Testament Theology*, 2:257.

10. His book *Die Prophetie* was published in 1936: see what J. Moltmann says about it both in *Der gekreuzigte Gott*, and in *Trinität und Reich Gottes*; see also Paolo Gamberini, *Pathos e logos in Abraham J. Heschel* (Rome: Città Nuova, 2009).

beings and descends toward them. According to Greek philosophy, which maintains divine immutability and apathy, it is difficult and ultimately impossible to reconcile these aspects of God's being and working which are so different and seemingly contradictory. The First Testament is not interested in philosophical clarity but in expressing the authentic face of YHWH as he himself reveals it in the relationship with his people.

This time too, the New Testament, with an incredible leap forward, in light of the Jesus-event, talks about a God who becomes flesh (Jn 1:19), who humbles himself and takes on the form of a servant (Phil 2:7–8). This unforeseeable event—which unsettles the First Testament's image of YHWH, shedding light at the same time on its otherwise irreconcilable tensions—was anticipated by the rabbinic teachings on the *shekinah*, which we already mentioned. The philosopher Franz Rosenzweig describes it in the early twentieth century as follows:

> Mysticism bridges the gap between "the God of our Fathers" and the "Remnant of Israel" with the doctrine of the Shekhina. The Shekhina, God's descent upon man and his sojourn among men, is pictured as a dichotomy taking place in God himself. God himself separates himself from himself, he gives himself away to his people, he suffers in their sufferings, sets forth with them into the agony of exile, joins their wanderings.... Nothing would be more natural for the "God of our Fathers" than that he should "sell" himself for Israel and share its suffering fate. But by doing so, God himself puts himself in need of redemption. In this suffering, therefore, the relationship between God and the remnant points beyond itself.[11]

YHWH's mysterious divine *pathos* and the vicarious suffering of his servant seem to meet in the unique, stubborn purpose of saving Israel and all human beings, welcoming them in the Lord's dwelling of grace.

YHWH's Universal Design of Salvation Entrusted to the Son of Man

A final, faster but decisive chapter in the history of YHWH's revelation to his people is given to us by apocalyptic literature.[12] The main canonical text where it is documented, the Book of Daniel, can be dated to the second century BCE. Beauchamp writes: "The Old Testament is raised up to the very end by the apocalypses, and it is precisely in them that the generation of Jesus will encounter Scriptures."[13]

11. Franz Rosenzweig, *The Star of Redemption*, trans. William W. Hallo (New York: Holt, Rinehart and Winston, 1971), 409–10.

12. Mathias Delcor, *Studi sull'apocalittica*, trans. A. Zani (Brescia: Paideia, 1987).

13. Beauchamp, *L'uno e l'altro Testamento*, 231 (own trans.).

As the term *apocálypsis* (revelation) indicates, the subject of apocalyptic literature is precisely revelation by God of God's own mysterious design on the coming of the kingdom and the conclusion or fulfillment of history. God is defined as "the one who reveals mysteries" (*ho anakalýptōn mystéria*; see Dn 2:28–29, 47). The term *mystérion*, which will become a key term in the New Testament thanks to Paul's interpretation of the Jesus-event, expresses the perspective of God's universal plan of salvation which will be fulfilled in the fullness of time. This is mysterious because it is not managed by human beings but is hidden in God's foreknowledge and free will and later is unveiled in human history. The distinctive features of *mystérion* as understood in the First Testament are: (1) the perspective of divine decision and the freely given design of salvation; (2) the assured promise of a future fulfillment; (3) the dramatic dimension of the final conflict between the powers of good and the powers of evil; and (4) the universal perspective, which involves Israel and through Israel, all peoples, in participating in the grace and plan of God.

Even by saying that YHWH is Lord, Israel testifies that YHWH is the author and sustainer of history (see Ps 77:14–21; 78:1–72; 135; 136; Is 44:6) and also of creation, in the sense that he made everything that is out of nothing (Is 40:21–28; Gn 1:1; 2 Mc 7:20–29). The prophets express God's lordship over history by using terms related to royalty. In Micah, for example, the Lord judges Samaria and Jerusalem; in Isaiah, the Lord reigns, his glory fills the earth and it is promised that the Lord will finally be the king through his consecrated one. In apocalyptic literature (Is 24–27; Ezek 38–39, and especially in the Book of Daniel), God exerts his royal sovereignty on all of history and all human beings through the ministry of the Son of Man.

Along these lines, the author of the Book of Daniel, who lives during the dramatic time of the persecution of Israel by the King Antiochus IV Epiphanes of Syria, situates himself through a literary fiction in the time of the Babylonian exile. He goes back to past centuries of history up to his present time, finally projecting himself into the future. The lesson he draws is that YHWH, in spite of all appearances, is truly the Lord of the cosmos and of history, who holds in mysterious but efficacious ways the strings of the events and is faithful to his project, ensuring the achievement of the goal: the coming of his kingdom. This is through the mysterious mediation of the Son of Man, who brings to mind the figure of human features in which the glory of YHWH in the vision of Ezekiel[14] is

14. See Franz Sedlmeier, *Studien zu Komposition und Theologie von Ezechiel* 20 (Stuttgart: Verlag Katholisches Bibelwerk, 1990), and *Das Buch Ezechiel: Kapitel 1–24* (Stuttgart: Verlag Katholisches Bibelwerk, 2002).

reflected and which is found in the inter-testamental literature (especially in the second Book of Enoch and fourth Book of Ezra). Here is what the Book of Daniel says about him (Dn 7:9–10, 13–14):

> As I watched, thrones were set in place, and an Ancient One took his throne, his clothing was white as snow, and the hair of his head like pure wool; his throne was fiery flames, and its wheels were burning fire. A stream of fire issued and flowed out from his presence. A thousand thousands served him, and ten thousand times ten thousand stood attending him. The court sat in judgment, and the books were opened.... As I watched in the night visions, I saw one like a human being coming with the clouds of heaven. And he came to the Ancient One and was presented before him. To him was given dominion and glory and kingship, that all peoples, nations, and languages should serve him. His dominion is an everlasting dominion that shall not pass away, and his kingship is one that shall never be destroyed.

The promise of the messianic fulfillment, already proclaimed by the prophets, acquires a new and full meaning: the establishment of the kingdom of God, in fact, does not only have a historical dimension but also points toward a dimension of definitiveness which is beyond history. In this context, the message on the destiny of resurrection of the just emerges: "You, go your way, and rest; you shall rise for your reward at the end of the days" (Dn 12:13; see also Dn 12:2–3; 2 Mc 7:9, 11, 14, 46). The faith in the resurrection is a consequence of the deepened understanding of the revelation of the face of God in history and in one's life. YHWH is not only the God of the living but calls back to life the faithful and the righteous ones, not back into time but into eternity.

CHAPTER 11

Summary

Looking at the First Testament overall, we can conclude that everything starts from and converges around a center: the event/coming of YHWH's freely-given revelation, which develops and becomes increasingly more decisive and imminent—YHWH, the God of Abraham, Isaac, and Jacob, the God of exodus who revealed God's name to Moses and the people of the covenant, the God of prophets and wise men. The living God, who is personal, holy, and merciful.

He is the living God because YHWH has the fullness of life and freely communicates it to creation and history, entering dynamically into relationship with creation and participating in its history from within. He is the personal God because YHWH, though in mysterious ways and utterly transcending any human experience and understanding, is the center of infinite personality and not an absolute anonymity dominating everything. He is the merciful God, because God manifests Godself as neighbor and liberator of his people, faithful to the covenant, always ready to be merciful and forgive and capable of infinite welcoming and tenderness toward everything he created.

The revelation of YHWH therefore manifests an intimate and indestructible paradox. By revealing Godself in what he is and does, YHWH reveals his insuperable otherness, that is, his divinity. YHWH has his measure of his being and doing only within himself. At the same time, his being utterly other, infinitely beyond everything is manifested precisely in his being close to human beings and creation, closer to human beings than they are to themselves. From this paradox stems the dynamics of his increasing self-communication to human beings in the history of salvation which he establishes with Israel while keeping his gaze toward everyone else as well.

By manifesting himself as other (and what other people experienced God's divinity as clearly and powerfully as Israel?), YHWH challenges and presses to enter human history as protagonist. He challenges with his Word/Law and encourages with his Spirit human freedom—not to crush it but to make it more intense, to free it, to unfold from within a covenantal relationship and ever deeper communion with himself. He does this so much that the promise of the new covenant, in the post-exilic prophets, is presented as a "creative grafting of the will of God on the hearts of men."[1]

Thus, in an increasingly intense fashion, YHWH communicates himself and manifests his will in a variety of ways to live among and with human beings, so that human beings may enjoy his peace (*shalom*). Each manifestation of YHWH is revelation and at the same time a guarantee of his being-God and his will to live in the midst of his people. However, it is a variety of mediations which, within the eschatological horizon of the promise, converges dynamically toward unity. From above, the Word/Wisdom and the Spirit; from below, the promised messiah, the servant of YHWH and the Son of Man. The two movements seem to be destined to ultimately converge. The book of the promise, the First Testament, is therefore presented as the intertwining of many different threads which, if they appear distinct and at times even in tension, in reality are increasingly and with increasing speed showing that they are tied into the same golden thread which goes through the entire history of the covenant.

On the one end of the thread, we find the mysterious, involved, and attractive identity of YHWH, the one who is, who was, and who is coming. On the other end, we find YHWH's persevering will to live with and among human beings. The deeper we go into the abyss of suffering and the heart-rending questions in human hearts (Job), so much more does God descend with compassion into the abyss, to release human beings—through his servant who takes upon himself the experience of trial and sin of Israel and humanity—and to take them by infusing God's Spirit into a humanly unimaginable communion with Godself. This communion is to be played out in history, fully and conclusively but at the same time it is destined to transcend history and endure forever.

YHWH, the God of the promise is, in a word, the true and living God, the only and holy one. God communicates Godself to human beings in a universal design of wisdom and salvation, aiming at establishing among them God's kingdom through God's servant, the Son of Man, in the abundant and universal effusion of God's Spirit.

1. Von Rad, *Old Testament Theology*, 2:215.

PART 3

THE EVENT

The *Abbà* of the Son Made Man in the Spirit

When you have lifted up the Son of Man, then you will realize that I am.

—John 8:28

CHAPTER 12

The God Revealed in Jesus the Christ

Who is the God revealed in Jesus the Christ? This question, properly understood, has a double meaning. On the one hand, it invites us to recognize the God that Jesus announces and witnesses as the God of the patriarchs, the God who revealed his name to Moses, the God who has spoken through the prophets (Heb 1:1), the God of the promises. On the other hand, it invites us to open ourselves to the newness that Jesus brings, in reference to the decisive coming of *this* God into the history of human beings through his eschatological messenger and only-begotten Son.

The Historical and Theological Centrality of the Paschal Event

In the second part of this work I looked at the most direct premise of the history of Jesus constituted by the First Testament promise. In this part, I examine the New Testament and immediately note that the heart of the revelation of God in Jesus is the *Paschal event*, his death on the cross and resurrection, to which is connected the pouring out "without measure" of the Holy Spirit. The Paschal event represents the turning point of the Christological event and the revelation of God therein contained, and as such is transmitted by the apostolic testimony. This affirmation has decisive value both from the *historical-exegetical* and *theological-systematic* points of view.

From the first point of view, we must recognize a fundamentally important fact: the composition of the New Testament came about in the wake of the Paschal event. The evangelists gathered apostolic traditions regarding Jesus of Nazareth and shaped their Gospels in the light of this event. The same is true of all of the other New Testament writings: each in their own way reflecting and transmitting the newness of life and understanding of the mystery of God springing from the Paschal event. From the second point of view, it is clear that the original and definitive meaning of the event of Jesus Christ and of the revelation that he is of God can—from a theological point of view—be penetrated and articulated correctly only on the basis of the Paschal event, and within the new horizon of existence and thought opened up by this event.

This does not mean underestimating or bracketing the importance of the rest of the story of Jesus. Not at all. The Paschal event, as a matter of fact, throws light both backward onto the whole event of Jesus, in the sense that it permits us to reread the integral meaning of his existence and historical mission, and forward in a deeper sense, because it illuminates the eschatological meaning of his mission and the protological meaning of his identity as the only-begotten Son of the Father.

It is not possible to develop an exhaustive Christological perspective here, nor to deal with all of the methodological or substantial questions that this implies. I refer to other works from the past couple decades for this purpose.[1] It is enough to recall certain methodological indications that are essential in order to correctly deal with the question of the face of God that Jesus Christ proposes and reveals.

The Newness of the Event of Jesus in the Context of the First Testament

First of all, my treatment of the Christological event should be placed against the whole background of the First Testament premise/promise. In this way, the event emerges in all its unprecedented newness, but also as the fulfillment of the promise and, therefore, as the coming of God among human beings in the fullness of time (see Gal 4:4). Indeed, it is only in the light of a full understanding of the event of Jesus Christ that it becomes possible to fully comprehend the dynamic and meaning of the golden thread that runs through and directs the First Testament. For this reason, we need to bear in mind the Jewishness of Jesus, his being heir and expression of the most genuine tradition of Israel. This point has been carefully studied in recent years thanks to the so-called third quest for the historical Jesus.[2] While it would be incorrect to try to understand the whole message of Jesus in terms of the preceding First Testament tra-

1. I gratefully acknowledge my indebtedness with respect to two prestigious colleagues from the theology faculty of the Lateran Pontifical University: Romano Penna for biblical exegesis, in particular, *I ritratti originali di Gesù Cristo: Inizi e sviluppi della cristologia neotestamentaria*, 2 vols. (Cinisello Balsamo: San Paolo, 1996–99), as well as Marcello Bordoni's *Gesù di Nazareth: Presenza, memoria, attesa* (Brescia: Queriniana, 1988) and *Gesù di Nazareth: Signore e Cristo. Saggio di cristologia sistematica* (Roma: Herder-PUL, 1982–86). Regarding the relationship between Jesus and his historical, religious, and cultural environment, the essay by Paolo Sacchi is stimulating and pertinent: *Gesù e la sua gente* (Cinisello Balsamo: San Paolo, 2003).

2. For an introduction, see Giuseppe Segalla, "La verità storica dei vangeli e la 'terza ricerca' su Gesù," *Lateranum* 61 (1995): 195–234.

dition, it is nevertheless essential to grasp the dynamic of continuity and innovation, even rupture, that characterizes it, even in relation to the revelation of God.

In the second place, and precisely in order to correctly understand the place and meaning of the event of Jesus Christ in the horizon of biblical revelation, it is important to recall the analogy, in faith, with the principal events of the self-revelation of YHWH to Israel. These, in fact, represent the unique form of revelation and trace out the clear direction of development according to God's plan: the *mystērion* of which Paul speaks, taking up a symbol dear to First Testament apocalyptic literature[3] and illuminating it in the light of the event of Jesus Christ. As I noted above, each of these events is in continuity with the preceding events and each constitutes, once it happens, a logical step ahead with respect to those. Each step represents a greater measure of gratuity and excess. Continuity of the tradition goes together with irruption of the new. This is true in a decisive way for the event of Jesus Christ, for whom, in the space of the analogy of faith, we can certainly speak of *maior dissimilitudo in tanta similitudine* (the greater the similarity, the greater the dissimilarity)[4] to underline thus the newness of the Christ-event coherent with the earlier revelation of God in the First Testament.

In the third place, we can already affirm that all of the newness of the New Testament in Jesus himself consists, properly speaking, in the identity of his person that becomes manifest from the unique meaning of his mission, consumed in the Paschal event of death and resurrection. As the Church Fathers incisively affirm, Jesus "brought all possible newness, by bringing himself."[5] This newness is so new that, though it is in continuity with what came before, it can be read both by Jews and Christians as discontinuity and rupture. The reaction of the first-century establishment in Israel to Jesus is the clearest and most tragic witness to this.

It is Jesus of Nazareth—his message, his existence, his person, the event of his death and resurrection—who forces the rereading and reinterpretation of the First Testament faith in the one and only God that bring about the trinitarian form proper and unique to the Christian faith. As Hegel wrote, the death of Jesus is the hinge around which the history of the world now rotates: so much so that whoever does not know of God that he is three does not know anything of Christianity. We should not fear the affirmation that the event of Jesus Christ enters decisively into

3. See Romano Penna, *Il "Mysterion" paolino: Traiettoria e costituzione* (Brescia: Paideia, 1978), and *Paolo di Tarso: Un cristianesimo possibile* (Milan: San Paolo, 2000).

4. The formula is drawn from the Fourth Lateran Council (1215): "quia inter creatorem et creaturam non potest tanta similitudo notari, quin inter eos maior sit dissimiltudo notanda" (DH 806).

5. Irenaeus of Lyons, *Adversus haereses* IV.34.1: "omnem novitatem attulit, semetipsum afferens."

the "definition" that God freely offers of himself, constituting the culmination of his self-communication to humanity.

Access to the Historicity of Jesus of Nazareth

Our historical access to the figure and message of Jesus of Nazareth is given to us through written documents, both extrabiblical and biblical. He is known, first of all, from certain extrabiblical writings, roughly contemporary with the events themselves, which refer indirectly to the events by speaking of the movement that Jesus' preaching gave rise to. Roman historiography attests that, during the period between the second half of the first century and the early second century, a new religious identity, distinct from Judaism, appears and develops. This identity is linked to a person who did not have a significant public impact during his lifetime, but was to give rise to a movement that grew rapidly and in a capillary manner. The name of this movement was "Christians," from his name, Christ (see Acts 11:26, "and it was in Antioch that the disciples were first called 'Christians'").

A first witness, from 112 CE, is the letter addressed by Pliny the Younger, then-governor of the Roman province of Bithynia, to Emperor Trajan (*Epistles* 10.96). Coming into contact with a group of Christians, and not knowing how to behave toward them, Pliny informs Trajan that they "were accustomed to meet together on a fixed day, before dawn, to sing hymns to Christ as to a god," with clear reference to the first day after the sabbath (sacred for the Jews), in which the memorial of the resurrection of Jesus was celebrated.

A second witness, from 116 CE, is from Tacitus, who in his *Annals* (15.44.2–5) narrates the great fire of Rome during which Nero, in order to deflect accusations of his involvement, blames those whom he calls *Chrestians* (confusing, maybe, the name "Christ" of Jewish origin, with another name, commonly used in Rome, of Chrest, or perhaps deriving the name from the Greek *Chrestos*, mild, pleasant, gentle). This reference in Tacitus is important for the support it gives to a fundamental datum of the New Testament: the death on the cross of Jesus, in Judea, under Pontius Pilate. The fact that the historian defines the Christian religion as a "superstition," and that he considers it among "vulgar and ignominious" things, is perhaps explained by the disconcerting idea of a would-be crucified messiah. For the Romans, death by crucifixion was an ignominious end.

A third witness comes from 120 CE: this is the witness of Suetonius who narrates an episode that took place under the emperor Claudius (*Claudius* 25), when a certain number of Christians and Jews were expelled from Rome because of continuous conflicts between them. A final document, this time from a Jewish source, is that of the historian Flavius Josephus, who, in his *Antiquitates iudaicae* (18.109–19), presenting the prophetic figure of John the Baptist, also recalls Jesus (the parts in italics are considered to be later interpolations):

> About this time arose Jesus, a wise man, *if indeed it be lawful to call him a man.* For he was a doer of wonderful deeds, and a teacher of men who gladly receive the truth. He drew to himself many both of the Jews and of the Gentiles. *He was the Christ*; and when Pilate, on the indictment of the principal men among us, had condemned him to the cross, those who had loved him at the first did not cease to do so, *for he appeared to them again alive on the third day,* the divine prophets having foretold these and ten thousand other wonderful things about him. And even to this day the race of Christians, who are named from him, has not died out.[6]

As these extrabiblical witnesses tell us very little about Jesus of Nazareth, for greater access to him we need to go to the New Testament, and in particular to the four Gospels. The other New Testament writings—the Book of Acts, the Pauline epistles, the apostolic letters, and the Book of Revelation—do not directly regard the historical figure of Christ, but the movement born of him, and witness in various ways to the life, doctrine, and development of the church. In this context, we should also inquire about the reliability and usefulness as historical sources of the so-called apocryphal Gospels more or less contemporaneous with the New Testament. It is enough to say here that the progressive formation of the New Testament canon—the expression of the ecclesial tradition stemming from the Jesus-event—constitutes by itself a clear principle of discernment in this regard. Some of the apocryphal Gospels are, in effect, the fruit of an interpretation of the message and the figure of Jesus corrupted by a pre-comprehension not in conformity with the Christian faith (as, for example, with Gnostic interpretations). In any case, any of the elements not present in the canon that might be gathered from these writings should always be placed in relation and judged in the light of the witness of the New Testament. Assured of his underlying historicity on the basis of the extrabiblical documents, it is important to make primary use of the biblical texts to approach the figure of Jesus.

This raises the question of access to the history of Jesus of Nazareth through the Gospels, bearing in mind that they witness to the Christian faith. As Christianity imposed itself in Europe, up until modern times the historicity of the Gospels was taken for granted, and they were inter-

6. Translation in Charles K. Barrett, *New Testament Background: Selected Documents* (London: SPCK, 1987), 277–78.

preted as a chronological narration of the history of Jesus. From the seventeenth century onward, questions began to be raised about discrepancies and even contradictions present in the evangelical accounts. Modern criticism therefore gave rise to the so-called quest for the historical Jesus (*Leben Jesu Forschung*), which attempts to offer reconstructions of the life of Jesus on the basis of the Gospels.

The first phase, known as the *Old Quest*, lasted from 1774, when G. E. Lessing (1729–81) began to publish some posthumous fragments of H. S. Reimarus (1694–1768), to 1906, with the publication by A. Schweitzer (1875–1965) of a summary of the research on the life of Jesus to that point. This period includes authors such as J.-E. Renan (1823–92) and D. F. Strauss (1808–75), who share the conviction according to which the reconstruction of the figure and story of Jesus of Nazareth is corrupted by the prejudice of his messianicity and divinity, thereby making an exact and objective historical reconstruction necessary apart from the interpretation of faith. Various moments, first the Enlightenment and, then, in the nineteenth century, the idealistic school (the Hegelian Left and Right), then positivism, and finally scientific Marxism each in their own way move in this direction, provoking a true "historiographical revolution" related to the question of the historical Jesus.

The first half of the twentieth century was characterized by a contrast between the historical Jesus and the Paschal Christ advanced by R. Bultmann (1884–1976). This contrast meant distancing oneself from historical research, and concentrating one's attention on the Jesus professed by faith. Any attempt to move from the Christ to faith to the Jesus of history was considered impossible, theologically secondary, and even misleading, because the faith is founded exclusively on the *kérygma* that Jesus is alive and present. The rediscovery of the historical Jesus on the part of the so-called post-Bultmannians, in the 1950s—in particular, E. Käsemann (1906–98) and G. Bornkamm (1905–90)—mark the beginning of the *New Quest*. In contrast with Bultmann, they affirm not only the possibility, but also the need to search for and reconstruct the identity of the earthly Jesus, inasmuch as it is he who is the risen one proclaimed by the church.

In the 1980s, finally, the third quest gets underway (M. J. Borg, E. P. Sanders, B. F. Meyer, R. W. Funk, C. A. Evans), a quest characterized by its attention to the historicity of Jesus seen in the historical-religious-cultural context of his time. These developments, closely followed by theologians, exegetes, historians, and philosophers, show that in order to approach Jesus of Nazareth, we need to bring together the approach of faith with a historiographically and methodologically founded approach, and which through a correct use of the historical-critical method is capable of reconstructing the three principal phases which stand behind the composition of the Gospels, by which we have access to his message and his destiny.

The first phase directly reflects the historical existence of Jesus, and can be found in sayings (*logía*) and in facts related to his preaching and life. These sayings and facts are embedded in the Gospel narratives that have come down to us. Jesus, who did not leave any writings of his own, used a method well-known in the rabbinic schools: the oral transmission of the doctrines of the Jewish faith or, in his case, central points of his teaching. Thus, the group of disciples that formed around him were able to use known memory techniques to record the basic outlines of his teaching and the main steps of his life. Not only did Jesus constitute a stable community (in particular the "twelve"), but he sent them out to preach, associating them in this way with his own mission, which meant that they needed to assimilate very precisely the teachings of their master. Because they were eyewitnesses, the disciples carry the witness of his teachings and actions impressed in their memories and lives, which had received an indelible imprint from their meeting with him. It is this that then finds expression when others record their testimony in written form.

A second phase is that immediately after the death of Jesus, and consists in the preaching notes used by the apostles and early communities. The event that founds the Christian community is the faith in the resurrection of Jesus. The witnesses to the events of the life of the Nazarene, the apostles, transmit his teaching to the community, rereading the meaning of what he had said and done through the lens offered by his death and resurrection. In this second moment, then, narrative units are brought together for kerygmatic and dogmatic purposes, which synthesize the preaching of Jesus and the principal moments of his life. These are used by the community in three contexts (*Sitz im Leben*): in worship and especially at the Eucharist which remembered the Paschal meal of Jesus and his disciples before his death; that of preaching, the announcement of Jesus of Nazareth as the crucified and risen messiah, the fulfillment of the "good news" that he himself had given of the coming of the kingdom of God; and the context of catechesis, or the Christian formation of those who had joined the community.

The third phase consists in the bringing together of the material from the preceding phases through the final redaction of the Gospels. The Gospels have as their primary function the proclamation of the Christian gospel, and as such they are kerygmatic writings. They present the historical density of the event of Jesus and its definitive salvific meaning unleashed from the cross and resurrection. Each Gospel tells the event of Jesus of Nazareth to a particular Christian community: the Gospel of Mark, for example, is directed to the community of Rome, Matthew's Gospel to a community of Jewish origin, Luke's Gospel to a community of a Hellenistic background. In each case, the presentation expresses the theological interpretation of the evangelist, which is a fruit of the progressive maturation of the Christian experience and faith.

Thus we have the diversification of the Gospels, in which there is a basic theological given and a shared narrative structure, but also important differences on the level of the arrangement of the materials and the theological interpretation of the same. Through the use of specific literary, linguistic, and hermeneutical techniques, historical-critical exegesis allows us to identify the elements which arose at the first, second, or third of these strata. The criteria which allow us to identify materials coming from the actions or preaching of the historical Jesus are multiple attestation; discontinuity with regard to the Jewish culture of the time, or with regard to what we know about the earliest church; conformity with Jesus' time and environment, but above all with his fundamental teaching; and the intrinsic coherence of a saying or fact with the whole picture. These criteria should not be absolutized, nor should they be used one against the other. They are used in a converging way, and above all are used on the basis of the underlying unity of the life and message of Jesus. More recently, the techniques of hermeneutics, philosophy of language, and phenomenological analysis are pressed into service so as to grasp and express what derives from Jesus himself in the Gospel narratives.

Two Moments of the Jesus-Event and Three Stages of New Testament Christology

Obeying the established canons of historical research about the mission of Jesus of Nazareth and the determination of its theological meaning, we need to distinguish two organically linked moments, both of which are constitutive of the event fully and correctly understood. These two moments are distinguished and united by the Paschal event. I will call them the pre-Paschal and post-Paschal periods.

Rudolf Bultmann's dialectic, mentioned above, between the "Jesus of history" and the "Christ of faith," is misleading. There is never a Jesus who is an exclusively historical personality, just as there is no such thing as a Christ of faith different from—because of the cross and resurrection—the historical Jesus. Once this separation is made, it is no longer possible to cross the ditch between them. As I showed in the first part of my treatment, history and faith need always to be thought in their constitutive relation to the other. Jesus of Nazareth cannot be simply reduced to his historicity in the sense that he always reveals in himself and his history, his "coming from the Father" and his "returning to the Father." He reveals therefore his filial identity in a theological sense. Precisely for this reason, it is impossible to reach his identity without freely involving ourselves in his event through faith. On the other hand, the risen Christ is not only the object of an act of faith in one who transcends history, but, more exactly, it is the faith in him as historically present, in his coming from God into the history of human beings. The concept of faith itself needs to be understood correctly, taking precisely its reference to Jesus Christ as its starting point, so as to move beyond groundless oppositions and simplistic identifications.

The first moment of the Christ-event concerns the preaching Jesus, that is, the *kérygma* (proclamation) of Jesus himself: a *kérygma* that, as happens throughout the biblical story, is intimately linked to the acts that Jesus himself carried out. The second concerns the preached Jesus, that is, the *kérygma* about Jesus: on his death on the cross and his resurrection or, better, on him crucified and risen and, in this light, on the full meaning of his message, his life, and his presence.

The connection between these two moments of the Christ-event is essential if we are to grasp and fully express the truth of Jesus Christ according to the logic of the faith. The risen Christ, without the historical Jesus and the crucified Jesus, becomes a myth. The historical and crucified Jesus, without the resurrection, remains simply a great prophet or the supreme ideal of humanity.

Once we have a correct and complete reading of the New Testament in the light of these indications, it becomes possible to trace a line of development of Christology that is of itself intrinsically trinitarian. There is a hermeneutical circle between the event of Jesus Christ and the revelation of God, a revelation which the New Testament—in the very attesting of the event of Jesus Christ—then indicates as the necessary point of access to the true and full meaning of the Christ-event. This development involves three stages which, as stated, have their point of departure and criterion of truth in the Paschal event.

The Eschatological Perspective

In a first stage, the appearances of the risen Jesus uncover, to the faith of the apostles, in a full and definitive manner the revelation of the identity of Jesus of Nazareth as the crucified messiah and the Lord (*Kýrios*) in whom God, in the "fullness of time," actuated his promise: he came among human beings. This is the eschatological dimension of the event of Jesus Christ, that is, the understanding of it as the final and definitive event (*éschatos*) of the plan of revelation and salvation of God in history.

This dimension works itself out in two directions. On the one hand, in fact, Jesus of Nazareth is recognized as the Christ and the Son of the *Abbà* who announced, realized in his ministry and brought to completion at Easter the event of the kingdom of God promised for the fullness of times and announced by him. On the other hand, in the light of his Passover of death and resurrection, the profession is made in the faith that he will return "soon" from God to complete, among the nations and in a definitive way, the coming of the kingdom that was already realized by him in his Passover (*parousia* of the risen Lord). This is the origin of the dialectic between the "already" and "not yet" typical of eschatology which breaks into history in virtue of the Christological event.

The Protological Perspective

In a second stage, the presence of the crucified and risen Lord, welcomed and lived by the community of disciples who await his glorious return, thanks to the superabundant gift of the Holy Spirit, draws the church into the theological penetration of the filial identity of Jesus Christ which had already been given—in essence and in its determining historical expression—in the pre-Paschal phase of his ministry. This leads to the contemplation of the protological dimension of the event of Jesus Christ: recognized as the only begotten Son and the *Lógos* of the Father who always lives with and in him, in the beginning (*arché*), so that he is the first (*prôtos*) by means of which and in view of which the Father brings about his plan of love on creation and salvation.

The Perspective of the Incarnation

In the third stage, closely linked with the previous, theological focus is brought to the event of the coming in the flesh of the only-begotten Son: both from the point of view of God, who sends the Son into the world, and from the point of view of humanity, which welcomes him in Mary. This is the incarnation as an expression of the dynamic identity of the only-begotten Son of the Father with Jesus of Nazareth, the messiah and crucified and risen Lord.

In this way the story comes full circle. The Paschal event discloses the filial-trinitarian identity of Jesus Christ in a definitive way, and his filial-trinitarian identity gives foundation and illuminates the event of the incarnation to the point of its Paschal consummation. This development favors and brings about the recognition in faith that Jesus Christ is the Son/*Lógos*: the eschatological revealer of God the Father in the light and in the power of the Spirit, determining the trinitarian understanding of

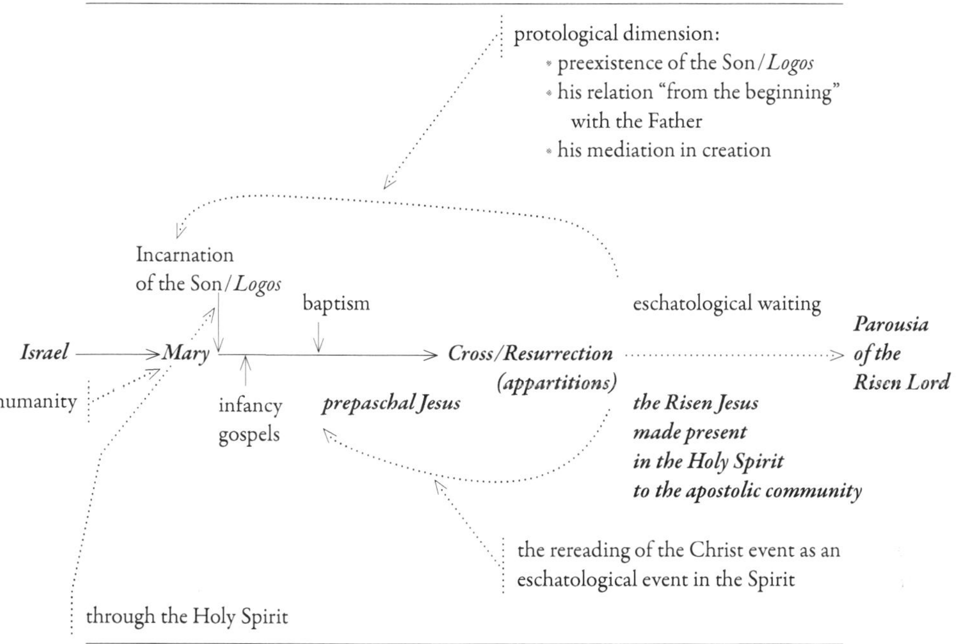

FIGURE 1. The Development of New Testament Christology

God in his eschatological self-communication to humanity (see figure 1). Bearing the development of New Testament Christology in mind (in the historical analysis and theological interpretation of the revelation of God that occurs in Jesus), we can follow an itinerary with three main stages.

In the first, I examine the *pre-Paschal* Jesus, reconstruct his message, praxis, and destiny, in relation to the face of God/*Abbà* that in them and through them is eschatologically manifested; to the mission and identity of Jesus himself, the Son, which thus become clearly discernible; to the presence and the action, in him, of the Holy Spirit promised for the fullness of times in a full measure and in a permanent way; and framing the whole in the two crucial and paradigmatic events of the baptism and transfiguration. In the second, I concentrate on the Paschal event understood in the light of the pre- and post-Paschal apostolic witness, as an act of the Father, of the Son, and of the Holy Spirit. In the third, finally, I offer a synthetic glance at the revelation of God given to us through the New Testament through the event of Jesus Christ, the Son of God become flesh, in the Holy Spirit. In conclusion, I will say something about the essential role in the event carried out by his mother, Mary.

CHAPTER 13

Jesus of Nazareth and the Event of the Kingdom of God in the Power of the Spirit

Contemporary exegesis invites caution in relation to the interpretation of the events of the baptism and transfiguration. It is stressed that in the Gospel passages that recount these events, the light of the resurrection of Jesus is anticipated. It is important nonetheless not to exaggerate this caution in such a way as to make the events themselves disappear. In both cases, we are dealing with real experiences of Jesus and—by extension—of the disciples, with precise and crucial significance as revelation. The underlying experiences should themselves be considered as the origin and criterion of the narratives in question and their constant transmission as documented by the New Testament sources. This is true not only of the account of the baptism, which is unanimously attested to in the various traditions as the beginning of Jesus' messianic ministry, but also of the transfiguration, which has a precise and important meaning in the economy of the Christ-event.

Faithful to this tradition, the theology of the Church Fathers and Scholastics places great emphasis on the theme of the "mysteries of Christ" often in the context of Christological discourse.[1] Liturgical praxis, further, such as in the tradition of the Eastern churches, has always attributed great significance to both the baptism and the transfiguration as places in which the identity and mission of Christ, as well as the closely connected mystery of the Trinity are manifested. As is well-recognized, the *lex orandi* of the church corresponds to its *lex credendi*. A retrieval of this attention, renewed by the results of historical-critical exegesis, would be welcome today. Thus, we can think of the baptism and the transfiguration as, respectively, the *terminus a quo* and the *terminus ad quem* of the mystery of Jesus prior to Easter.

1. St. Thomas, for example, dedicates two questions of *ST* to the baptism (III, qq. 38–39) and one to the transfiguration (III, q. 45).

The Baptism of Jesus

A central role in the attestation of the event of the revelation of God in Jesus, as found in the New Testament, is undoubtedly played by the baptism in the River Jordan. In this event the singularity of the relationship of Jesus with God/*Abbà* in the Holy Spirit is presented almost as an interpretive prism of the whole story of Jesus. The event of the baptism of Jesus in the Jordan constitutes the point of intersection of a whole series of relationships: (1) first of all, the relationship between the preaching of John the Baptist and the ministry of Jesus; (2) the relationship between the beginning of the mission of Jesus and its Paschal fulfillment (which the New Testament witness also interprets as a baptism: the eschatological baptism); and (3) the relationship, finally, between the baptism received by Jesus as an historical event and the baptism in the name of Jesus, crucified and risen, imparted by the apostolic church. Our intent is to understand the historical substance of the event of the baptism of Jesus in its relation to the face of the God who is Trinity. In order to do this, however, it is obviously necessary to bear in mind the fact that in the Gospel accounts the original event has been reread and represented both in the light of Jesus' Paschal event and secondarily in relation to the baptismal praxis of the church. There are however many factors that can be gleaned from the New Testament (the multiple attestation, the embarrassment about the fact that Jesus had submitted himself to a penitential rite such as that proposed by John the Baptist, and the baptism of the cross) that lead one to not only grasp the importance, but also the decisive nature of this event as an initial moment in Jesus' ministry, and also to discern something of what that event meant in the ministry of Jesus received from the Father and sealed by the descent of the Holy Spirit.[2]

Regarding the significance of Jesus' messianic choice to submit himself to baptism by John, it is important to emphasize at least the fact that this is to be grasped from within the religious and social context of his time. At the time, the religious life of Israel is dominated at an official level by two groups: the Pharisees and the Sadducees. The first group represents the middle and high bourgeoisie in society, and strongly emphasizes the scrupulous observance of the Law; the second group represents the Priestly class, a group that is more aristocratic and conservative, with their center of influence in the Temple of Jerusalem. Further, the Roman

2. For an introduction to the complexity of the question and its many implications, we refer back for example to *Alle origini del battesimo cristiano*, ed. P. R. Tragan (Rome: Pont. Ateneo Sant'Anselmo, 1991); *La Santisima Trinidad y el bautismo cristiano*, Semanas de "Estudios Trinitarios" 26 (Salamanca: Secretariado Trinitario, 1992); Simon Légasse, *Naissance du baptême* (Paris: Cerf, 1993).

dominion and the periodical flaming up of messianic hopes, sometimes with apocalyptic overtones, made the whole situation very varied and unstable. Then there are the Essenes, pious Israelites who regarded those who officially held religious power to be irredeemably compromised with the Roman domination, thus distancing themselves from civic society and constituted a kind of messianic community characterized by a strong asceticism, projected toward the coming one of YHWH who would restore the kingdom of God (see the writings of Qumran). In a politico-messianic perspective instead there was the group of Zealots, who interpreted the coming of the kingdom in political terms, thinking armed revolution to be the only means of removing the unjust oppressors and reestablishing the Davidic monarchy.

Within this complex and agitated situation, the preaching of the Baptist is rather unique. The themes of his preaching, as witnessed by the Gospels, are peremptory: the time is about to be fulfilled, the day of the judgment with which, before the inauguration of his kingdom, YHWH would condemn the sinful without appeal. In order to avoid this judgment and open oneself to the salvation from God, the only path is conversion (see Mk 1:1–8; Mt 3:1–6, 11–12; Lk 3:1–6, 15–18; Jn 1:19–34). John thus places himself in the long line of First Testament prophecy and seems to close a period (that of the long silence of the prophetic spirit in Israel) in order to inaugurate another, of unique importance. By becoming at least a passing member of the penitential movement of the Baptist, Jesus opens the path of novelty that John anticipated and for which he prepared.[3]

The Gospel tradition attaches a decisive importance to the event of the baptism. The precise and concrete event with which Jesus inaugurates his ministry is the first witness in the New Testament of his vocation and his messianic choice and, by consequence, of awareness of a mission entrusted to him by God, who invites him to announce and bring about the coming of his kingdom among men in the power of the Spirit. Jesus, accepting the invitation to penance and in expectation of the imminent and eschatological intervention of God announced by the Baptist, recognizes in this baptism the symbolic expression of his unconditional "yes" to carrying out of the will of God. In this way, he adopts as his own the path of the servant of YHWH preannounced by Deutero-Isaiah: the path of solidarity with human beings, to the point of self-sacrifice in expiation of sins, and—as one would say today—a preferential option for the poor

3. The studies by Edmondo Lupieri constitute a fundamental reference point regarding the figure of the Baptist and his relationship with Jesus of Nazareth: *Giovanni Battista fra storia e leggenda* (Brescia: Paideia, 1988); *Giovanni Battista nelle tradizioni sinottiche* (Brescia: Paideia, 1988); *Giovanni e Gesù: Storia di un antagonismo* (Milan: Mondadori, 1991).

and marginalized.[4] The Gospels frame the event as an event of revelation and messianic investiture: the opened heavens, indeed ripped open (see Is 64:1); God is pleased with Jesus; the descent of the Spirit. The difference among the Gospel redactions[5] leaves open the possibility of two lines of interpretation, in which the experiences of Jesus and the witness of the Baptist are drawn together: (1) Jesus begins his messianic ministry in faithfulness to the investiture by God who attests—in a precise event of revelation that occurs in connection with the baptism in the Jordan that Jesus receives from the Baptist—to the messianic mission and the filial identity of Jesus, sending the Spirit which the prophets had experienced and which was promised in superabundance to the servant in the fullness of time, to Jesus in a stable and permanent way. (2) The Baptist recognizes and points out—to those penitents gathered on the banks of the Jordan and to his own disciples (many of whom would then follow him)—Jesus, the one whom the Lord was to send at the fullness of time.

The account of the baptism appears therefore as a theophany of apocalyptic style, which although it is modeled on analogous accounts of vocation and revelation in the First Testament, nevertheless bears an absolute novelty. The theophany is extraordinarily intense and new, both in its dynamics and in its contents. Whether one reads the account from the point of view of the revelatory act of God (attested to by the Baptist) or from the point of view of the personal experience of Jesus (lived in prayer, as Luke suggests, and then communicated to the disciples), or whether it is better to think of it in terms of the coincidence of the two, this account clearly indicates the singularity of the mission that God entrusts to Jesus and his filial identity. The event of the baptism gives witness, in brief, to the immediate, unique, and eschatological relation manifested and realized precisely in this way between God and Jesus as Son.

The voice that comes "from the heavens" indicates that it is already through Jesus and in him only that God speaks eschatologically, acts, and shows his face. This is emphasized by the descent on Jesus and of

4. Bruno Maggioni explains: "submitting to John's baptism (a baptism of conversion in remission for sins)—participating in this way in the renewal and conversion movement aroused by the Baptist in his people – Jesus shows that he understands his life to be a life of solidarity with respect to human persons.... In Jesus's gesture whereby he mixes with the crowd of sinners seeking conversion, that logic guiding his entire existence is hidden. It will make it possible for him to understand his death as a death in 'ransom for many' (Mk 10:45)." "Il battesimo di Gesù," in *Battesimo, Purificazione, Rinascita*, Dizionario di spiritualità biblico-patristica 6 (Rome: Borla, 1992), 76–93 (own trans.); see André Feuillet, "La personalité de Jésus a partir de sa soumission au rite de repentence du Précurseur," *Revue Biblique* 77 (1970): 30–49.

5. Mk 1:9–11; Mt 3:13–17; Lk 3:21–22; Jn 1:29–34. Mark and Matthew say that Jesus "saw" (*eîden*). Luke presents the event as an objective fact which happens while Jesus is at prayer. John quotes the witness of the Baptist who, as had been preannounced, sees the Holy Spirit descend and remain on Jesus.

the remaining on him of the Spirit which, from this moment onward, will guide and illuminate his ministry.[6] In John especially the remaining (*ménien*) of the Spirit on Jesus is made explicit. Regarding the image of the dove, it is important to emphasize that the evangelists attest that the Spirit descended on Jesus "like a dove" (see Mk 1:10; Mt 3:16; Lk 3:22; Jn 1:32), by which the authors intend to underline not only the modality of the event but also its objective and visible reality, that all could perceive (as is emphasized by the word *sōmatikô*, "bodily," in Lk 3:22), even though it remains shrouded in sovereign mystery. Paraphrasing the passage from the fourth Gospel where Philip asks Jesus to show him the Father, it is clear that from that point on "whoever sees Jesus sees the Father" (see Jn 12:45). Obviously, the meaning of the mission of Jesus and his identity will gradually become more clear—dramatically—in the course of his messianic ministry, and reach fulfillment in the Paschal event.

Jesus and God/*Abbà*

The account of the baptism, as with an *ouverture*, sets out the basic theme on the basis of which the action will unfold. The protagonists of the event which Jesus of Nazareth will produce in the history of salvation are God who intervenes eschatologically to realize the promise; Jesus, the Son, who is sent to carry out the divine plan; and the Spirit, breath of life and power of God, who descends on Jesus and who lives in him to sustain him and guide him in his decisive ministry. Let us now read some determining passages of the story that takes off from this starting point, placing under the lens each of the three actors in the intervention of God in order to understand the respective identities and reciprocal relations on the basis of a phenomenological reading of the communication of the message and praxis of Jesus.

The mission of Jesus and the manifestation which—from him and in him—the God of Israel makes of himself in the power of the Spirit, in reality are fulfilled thanks to some peculiar expressions of his existence, closely correlated with one another: his *kerygma*, his praxis, his self-consciousness, his destiny. In a word, it is the person of Jesus himself, the Son, who is the locus/event of the eschatological revelation of God as the *Abbà*.

6. See, for example, in Mark's account, the scene immediately following this one, where the Spirit "drives" Jesus into the desert: Mk 1:12. I will return to the important theme of the relationship of Jesus and the Spirit, on the basis of the event of the baptism, below.

The Advent of the Kingdom of God

The Gospels attest that the original *kérygma* of Jesus was the coming of the kingdom of God. Here is the Gospel of Mark's summary statement: "Now after John was arrested, Jesus came to Galilee, proclaiming the good news of God, and saying, 'The time is fulfilled, and the kingdom of God has come near; repent, and believe in the good news [*Peplḗrōtai ho kairòs kaì éngeken he basileía Theoû metanoeîte kaì pisteúete en tô euangelíō*]'" (Mk 1:14–15). Announcing the coming of the kingdom, Jesus announces the fulfillment of the promise: and that is the coming of the God of the patriarchs, of Moses, and of the prophets into the midst of human beings. The concept of *basileía Theoû*—which should be understood in the active sense of the efficacious exercise of the kingship of God—belongs completely to the tradition of Israel.[7] It indicates the sovereignty of YHWH over Israel, over the nations, over the whole of creation and stands for, especially in the prophets and in the apocalyptic writings, the promise of the eschatological coming of his lordship. He then would reveal his name, and with that would bring about the liberation of human beings according to the dynamic of revelation and recognition well-known from the First Testament: "Then you will know that I am." We should note three unique characteristics in the *kérygma* and in the praxis of Jesus in this context.

The first relates to the tone of novelty which Jesus' announcing of the kingdom assumes compared with the previous tradition, and especially in relation to the preaching of John the Baptist. Whereas in John's case—as in the prophetic announcement of the "Day of the Lord"—the threat of judgment ("the wrath to come" of which the Baptist speaks; see Mt 3:7 and Lk 3:7), for Jesus the announcement of the kingdom expresses and represents an unprecedented and definitive intervention of mercy and salvation on the part of God in favor of his people. For this reason, the coming of the kingdom is an event of joy, because it represents the fulfillment of the promise from which Israel was born and in which it lived. It is precisely *eu-angélion*, good news.

This fact introduces us to a second point of novelty in the *kérygma* of Jesus and in the face of God which is announced therein. The coming of the kingdom of God—all of the teaching and praxis of Jesus witness to this—is intimately linked with the coming and with the ministry of Jesus himself, with his being present here and now, with his acting in the name of and with the authority of God. It is in him and by means of him

7. See Rudolf Schnackenburg's classic, *God's Rule and Kingdom* (London: Burns and Oates, 1968); Helmut Merklein, *Jesu Botschaft von der Gottesherrschaft* (Stuttgart: Verlag Katholisches Bibelwerk, 1983); for a rapid overview, Penna, *I ritratti*, 1:102–13.

that the kingdom of God makes itself present: "The time is fulfilled, and the kingdom of God has come near," he announces (Mk 1:15). As Origen expressed so succinctly, Jesus is the *autobasileía*: the kingdom in person. It is only by studying his face, his words, his actions, only by looking at his way of living, his solidarity with men and women that one can perceive who the coming God is.

A third characteristic, linked to the previous, is the dynamic tension—unprecedented prior to Jesus—between the announcement of the future coming of the kingdom and the actuation of that kingdom already in his presence. This actuation is irreversible, despite the harsh difficulties that it encounters in being actualized, precisely in the *kérygma* and praxis of Jesus. God, therefore, comes close to us eschatologically in the promise of a perfect and definitive coming communion. From the very beginning, Jesus' preaching of the coming of the kingdom raises a crucial question: what relationship is there between Jesus, the one who announces the imminent coming of the kingdom, and YHWH who sent him? This question directs one's gaze toward the center of the announcement of Jesus and of his praxis, in order to gather the beating heart of the unique relationship with God that he lived and gave witness to. The God who is coming is the *Abbà* of Jesus. This is attested, in a privileged way, by the prayer of Jesus.

Jesus' Prayer

The concept of the fatherhood of God is certainly to be found in the religious tradition of Israel prior to Jesus. As I have noted, it refers to a fatherhood of salvific election and not a fatherhood of natural genealogy as would be the case in cosmic religions. It concerns the whole people of Israel,[8] but also, in a special way, the king[9] and messiah.[10] Only rarely do we find God addressed by the individual as "my father" (*abî*).[11] This invocation is original and spontaneous on the lips of Jesus, and it offers a unique point of entry to the personal experience of God that he lived

8. Ex 4:22; Nm 11:12; Dt 32:6, 18; Is 63:16; 64:7; Jer 31:9, 20; Hos 11:1; Mal 1:6; 2:10. See Romano Penna, "La Paternità di Dio nel Nuovo Testamento: natura e condizionamenti culturali," *Rassegna di Teologia* 40 (1999): 7–39; among other things he remarks that this idea can also be traced to post-biblical Judaism. This appears in the two synagogue prayers in Jesus' time—that of the "Eighteen Blessings" ("Our Father") and that of the "*Qaddish*" ("The Our Father who is in the heavens").

9. See 2 Sm 7:14; Ps 89:27.

10. See Ps 2:7.

11. Romano Penna notes that the designation "Our Father" is "never present in Mark (who affirms however the expression 'his Father' from Jesus' lips referring to the Son of Man: Mk 8:38; Mt 16:27), it is very rare in the Q source (Mt 11:27/Lk 10:22; possibly Mt 26:29/Lk 22:29) and also in Lk (2:49; 24:49), whereas it is very frequent in Mt (7:21; 10:32–33; 12:50; 15:13; 16:17; 18:10,14,19,35; 20:23; 25:34; 26:53) and it also frequently appears in John (24 times)." *I ritratti originali di Gesù il Cristo*, 1:113.

and transmitted. This experience can be discerned through an attentive phenomenology of the various expressions of his existence and mission, but appears most clearly in his prayer. In this prayer we have the most direct testimony of the unique quality of the relation of Jesus with God who is Father.

The "hymn of jubilation" The Gospels attest to at least fourteen different moments in which Jesus prays.[12] These are spread throughout the itinerary that goes from the baptism to the cross. The Gospel according to Matthew gives us one significant example, densely meaningful and revelatory, known in the Christian tradition as the "hymn of jubilation" (Mt 11:25–27; see also Lk 10:21–22):

> At that time Jesus said, "I thank you, Father, Lord of heaven and earth, because you have hidden these things from the wise and the intelligent and have revealed [*apekálypsas*] them to infants; yes, Father, for such was your gracious will. All things have been handed over to me by my Father; and no one knows the Son except the Father, and no one knows the Father except the Son and anyone to whom the Son chooses to reveal him [*apokalýpsai*]."

The substance of this prayer, interpreted closely, can almost certainly be attributed to the pre-Paschal Jesus, even if some exegetes have in the past compared it to a "Johannine thunderbolt" that fell into the synoptic tradition. In reality, it can be considered as the "most precious pearl of the tradition according to Matthew"—thus Lagrange[13]—because it declares that the heart of the life and mission of Jesus is his relationship with the Father, the intimacy of a trusting, full, and permanent communication. This theme will underpin the theological reflections developed in the fourth Gospel.

What should be noted is the unequivocal primacy that Jesus gives to the Father. He stresses first of all that it is the Father and only he who knows the Son, which is to say that it is only the Father who knows and recognizes the deepest and truest identity of the Son, and therefore also his mission. It is therefore in this context that the Son, on the basis of the knowledge that the Father has of him, in turn knows the Father as he truly is. This is what gives him the unique possibility of revealing the mystery of the Father to whomever he wants through his mission. He reveals this mystery to those to whom he addresses his proclamation and those who open themselves in faith to it.

If we ask ourselves why Jesus began to preach, where the strength and

12. See Petr Mareček, *La preghiera di Gesù nel vangelo di Matteo: Uno studio esegetico-teologico* (Rome: Pontificio Università Gregoriana, 2000).

13. Marie-Joseph Lagrange, *Évangile selon saint Mathieu* (Paris: Gabalda, 1923), 226 (own trans.).

inner light of his message and ministry came from, we would unhesitatingly respond that it is all born of his unique relationship with God known as the Father who sent him to humans. Indeed, this Matthean *logíon* tells us not only that Jesus is moved—in all that he says and does—by the relationship of intimate communion with God, by whom he has the awareness of having been sent, and indeed of being the Son; but also that he conceives his ministry as the gratuitous transmission of this relationship to human beings.[14]

Abbà, Father! Without entering into the details of Jesus' use of the word "Father" in the various Gospel redactions, it is fundamental that we underline the uniqueness of the Aramaic word that he uses. The word is *Abbà*, and is preserved for us in the Gospel according to Mark (14:36, Jesus' prayer at Gethsemane) and recurs also in Paul (Rom 8:15; Gal 4:6) where it is applied to believers who have already been made participants through the gift of the Spirit in that same relationship of sonship that Jesus lives with the Father.[15]

Abbà looks at the Father with that spontaneous and trusting familiarity, respect, and quick and full adhesion to his will. It speaks of deep gratitude, complete trust, and responsible freedom, nourished by the joyful experience of reciprocity and communion. There are no documented cases in the rabbinic tradition where this term is used in reference to God, whereas in Jesus' use it is central, and filled with the newness of the experience that he lived. "Although the Aramaic invocation is only attributed to Jesus himself in Mark 14:36, in all likelihood, it constituted the habitual way in which he addressed God in prayer."[16]

The "Our Father" Returning to the proclamation of the kingdom, we encounter the deep and transparent link between the originality of Jesus' prayer and the central content of the *kérygma* of the kingdom in the prayer of the "Our Father" (see Mt 6:9–13; Lk 11:2–4), taught to the disciples by the master. Through the technique of mirror reading, we can recognize that which is being said directly, but also intuit something of

14. Romano Penna writes: "Certainly nothing is said about the pre-existence nor the divinity of the Son, but an equality of nature between the Father and the Son is clearly suggested, as appears both from the exclusive nature of the reciprocal relationship, as well as from the semitic-experiential connotation of the verb, 'to know,' which implies both the concepts of knowing and loving. The Son's relationship with the Father is not something accidental, but it belongs to the ontology of the persons, however one interprets the 'all' that was entrusted to him." *I ritratti originali di Gesù Cristo*, 1:153.

15. See Gottlob Schrenk, "Patér," in *GLNT* IX:1211–1306; Joachim Jeremias's classic, *Abbà* (Göttingen: Vandenhoeck and Ruprecht, 1966); François-Xavier Durrwell, *Le Père: Dieu en son mystère* (Paris: Cerf, 1987); "Abbà Padre," in *Dizionario di spiritualità biblico-patristica*, ed. S. A. Panimolle (Rome: Borla, 1992).

16. Penna, *Gesù di Nazareth e la sua esperienza di Dio*, 502–3 (own trans.).

the experience of the one who is reflected in it, indirectly, as its author. In brief: what is the relationship with God and his face that Jesus lives in his personal experience?

Following this criterion, H. Schürmann[17] emphasizes that what is most typical in the prayer of Jesus derives from a double synthesis between aspects dynamically in tension: first, the synthesis of theology (the invocation of God who is Father, the gaze upward) and eschatology (the sanctification of his name, the coming of the kingdom, the gaze forward); second, the synthesis between doxology (the praise of God) and soteriology (the entrusting of human needs to God). The dynamic connection of these components delineates Jesus' personal attitude of prayer and the face of God to which he witnesses: the holy and merciful God who is now finally coming to act for the salvation of humanity, loved and redeemed as sons.

It is useful, therefore, to offer a brief theological exegesis of the individual "petitions," indeed of the individual expressions that are gathered in extraordinary simplicity in the prayer that Jesus teaches his disciples. I favor Matthew's version (6:9–13) because of its wider and more universal reception in the praxis of faith of the church and because of the semitizing character of some of its literary features similar to two Hebrew prayer formulae from the first century: the *Qaddish* (holy) and the *Shemoneh eshrei* (the eighteen blessings).[18] In the Matthean version Jesus' prayer is clearly structured in three parts: the initial invocation, addressed to the Father, three petitions formulated with the verb in the second person and addressed to the Father, four petitions also formulated in the second person (that is, addressed to the Father) in favor of the "we" of the community, which however is inherently universal, and without boundaries. What emerges is, on the one hand, the trusting openness to God's activity and, on the other hand, the recognition of the "we" as the subject in whose favor and in whom his action is to be realized.

Our Father. What trust in, and responsibility toward God these words express! On their own they already express the novelty and grace of the revelation in Jesus. Even when they are recited without full understanding of the importance of calling God "Father," but recited with love and trust, they address God as a "you" who is love, only and completely love. These words state most of all and in the most radical way possible the

17. Heinz Schurmann, "Das 'eigentümlich Jesuanisch' im Gebet Jesu. Jesu Beten als Schlüssel für das Verständnis seiner Verkündigung," in his *Jesu: Gestalt und Geheimnis. Gesammelte Beiträge*, ed. Klaus Scholtissek (Paderborn: Bonifatius, 1994), 45–63, and *Praying with Christ: the "Our Father" for Today* (New York: Herder and Herder, 1964); along this same line, see his *Das hermeneutische Hauptproblem der Verkündigung Jesu* (Freiburg: Herder, 1964).

18. For example, see the beautiful commentaries to the two versions of the "Our Father" offered respectively by Gérard Rossé, *Il vangelo di Luca: Commento esegetico e teologico* (Rome: Città Nuova, 1992) and by Rinaldo Fabris, *Matteo: Traduzione e commento* (Rome: Borla, 1982).

faith in God who is love (see 1 Jn 4:8, 16). Everything changes in the light of this faith and acquires meaning. The adjective "our" speaks of the link between God and us, our God, the God of our people. Thus, we recognize ourselves as a "we," a multitude of beings, each one kissed personally by a ray of this love, and in this way drawn together into one by and in the witness of love of Jesus the Christ. This "we" is and wishes to manifest itself as universal.

Who art in heaven. Heaven is the dwelling place of God. And it is ours in him. It is different from the earth, but is in relationship with it. It is not the ultimate depth of heaven, because in that case we would never definitively leave the earth itself. But that which is on high, beyond, *in excelsis*. That which transcends, infinitely, our self-transcendence, in desire and thought: "You were more inward than my own interior self and loftier than my most lofty self" (St. Augustine). But, precisely for this reason, it is that alone in which we foresee with certainty, that we will finally find ourselves "at home" (Chiara Lubich).

Hallowed be your name. This is the first thing that Jesus invites us to ask the Father in prayer, because it coincides with his deepest desire: that God's name be made holy, and that it is manifested and recognized in its truth and glory. It is in this way that human beings recognize God as who he is, entrusting oneself and welcoming in oneself the sanctity that from his name he illuminates the world. As God promised in the words of the prophet Ezekiel: "So I will display my greatness and my holiness and make myself known in the eyes of many nations. Then they shall know that I am the Lord" (Ezek 38:23). God's holiness is revealed in power, with the power of love, in Jesus, the Son: he is the holiness of the Father, one with his being Father, that is love. And, through Jesus and in him, he should show himself in the disciples, sons in the Son: "You shall be holy, for I the Lord your God am holy" (Lv 19:2).

Your kingdom come. The sanctification of the name, *Abbà*, coincides and is one with the coming in the Son of the kingdom among human beings. It is important to see how Jesus, teaching the prayer to his disciples, reveals his relationship with the Father. All of his being is addressed to the Father. He teaches them to pray, first of all, that the name of his Father, who is also our Father, be sanctified and, consequently, that his kingdom might come where this happens: where God, that is, is glorified by human beings who recognize him as Father, and become what they are called to be—sons. Truly, "the glory of God is a living man, and the life of man is the vision of God" (Irenaeus of Lyons). This kingdom begins in history and is completed in eternity, at the return of Jesus.

Your will be done. What is the coming of the kingdom if not the fulfillment of the will of the Father? His name, that of the Father, is glorified when his sons and daughters fulfill his will, showing themselves thus to be true children. Nothing else. It is not even necessary to specify the content of this will, so evident is it. The recognition of the Father implicitly points to the reciprocal recognition of the children as brothers and sisters of each other. This is, in the final analysis, the meaning of the double commandment of love (see Mt 22:37–39; Mk 12:29–31) and of the new commandment of Jesus (see Jn 13:34).

On earth as it is in heaven. The "as" (*hōs*) is the true link, the only link between heaven and earth. The life of heaven is to be transferred to the earth. This earth is to remain, not only in this present time, but also in the definitive time to come. We hear of "new heavens and new earth." This "as" means that the life which is lived in heaven—the sanctification of the name of the Father on the part of the Son, that infinite breath of reciprocal glorification that is the Holy Spirit—is to be lived on earth. This is the will of the Father.

Give us this day our daily bread. Here is the request of sons. As sons the Father wills us to ask. This request to the Father comes after the entrusting of ourselves without reservation to him: "But strive first for the kingdom of God and his righteousness, and all these things will be given to you as well" (see Mt 6:33; Lk 12:31). The first thing that is given to us "as well"—which from the human point of view might seem to be a precondition for the rest is our daily bread. The request is for today, and is valid for today only. The Father concedes bread to his sons only day by day, as he had done with the manna in the desert for Israel. Otherwise, it would rot. "Do not accumulate treasures" (see Mt 6:19–20). Is that not a new principle of economics and prudent management of resources? *Today*: only today exists. The rest is vanity: what has already passed and what is yet to come. And yet, how much trust in God, and how much care on his part in this "daily bread"! Bread stands here for that which is truly essential, that to which human beings correctly aspire. Bread which is an existence worthy of human beings, and which therefore is also the work with which we earn our bread, the houses above our heads in which we can eat it together, in peace and joyous conviviality, but also the social relations, from culture to art and prayer without which the bread would be tasteless. It is bread that is also the responsibility of those who have toward those who do not. This bread is described as "supersubstantial" (*epiousios*) bread of life (see Jn 6:33) which, in the final analysis, is the Eucharist in which the infinite joy of eternal life together is anticipated.

Forgive us our trespasses. Forgiveness is for the spirit what bread is for the body. Without forgiveness, the spirit does not live, it is dead, even if it seems alive. Forgiveness—"for-give-ness"—in its ultimate principle is a gratuitous gift of God which receives its proper response in the gratitude of human beings alone. This is the first and insoluble debt that we have with God because he thought of us, wanted us, created us, loved us. But what Jesus suggests is that we ask God for the forgiveness for trespasses that we have committed through the course of our lives. Missed opportunities, graces to which we did not correspond, refusals, closures, wickedness, obstinacy; to be able to look God in the eyes, every day anew, as if for the first time. We must be able to recognize ourselves before him for what we are, sinners, like the publican who went to the Temple, and not parading our inexistent merits, like the Pharisee (see Lk 18:10–14). To recognize that "all is grace" without quietistic self-flagellation or whining.[19] We must do this with realism, simplicity, and humility. Then God's gaze will bring us to new birth and will make us immaculate.

As we forgive those who trespass against us. Here is another "as" (*hōs*). God forgives us our debts "as": and that is if and in the measure that we forgive those who are in debt to us. The parable of the wicked servant (see Mt 18:21–35) spells out this requirement clearly and directly. We, however, are capable of forgiving others only if we first discover ourselves forgiven by God. The "as" works in both directions. It is striking that Jesus invites his listeners to ask the Father for precisely this. This is basically the only petition of the Our Father that explicitly regards our interpersonal relationships. Jesus does not urge us to be capable of loving, welcoming, serving. Instead he urges us to forgive. This is because the gratuity of forgiveness is the only one which, by repairing the relation broken by evil, brings about the rebirth of the other, a rebirth that is experienced in his heart and in the heart of the one who forgives. It has been said: if loving is like generating a son, forgiving is like raising the dead to new life. Forgiveness is, therefore, the highest image of who God is. It is the possibility of birth and growth in the relations among human beings, both of individuals but also of groups and among peoples. The ability to forgive is born of the ability—an ability given to us by God—to look at other human beings as God sees them.

And lead us not into temptation. What does a son, who believes in the love of the Father and lives for his kingdom, fear? Obviously not "those who can kill the body, but not the soul" (see Mt 10:28). The only thing that he or she fears is betraying the love and trust of the Father, whenever, having been lead into temptation by circumstances or by his or her own foolishness—without the protection of God, who thereby puts him or her to the test—he or she might finally give in to compromise and aposta-

19. "Tout est grace": Georges Bernanos, *The Diary of a Country Priest*, trans. Pamela Morris (New York: Macmillan, 1937), 298: "Grace is everywhere," everything is grace.

sy. Nothing is easier. Jesus himself was "tempted" and in the most terrible way: in the desert, at Caesarea Philippi, and right up to the cross. But he always won, because he believed in the Father. For the disciples the risk is far greater. This is why Jesus invites us to ask, with the correct fear of God that is the principle of wisdom (Ps 111:10), to keep us safe from temptation. We are weak. When we are able, when it will be for our good, God will know when to leave us in those situations in which with his help we can show him our faithfulness, in deeds and not only in words. Whatever the cost might be, to the point of martyrdom.

But deliver us from evil. The evil from which Jesus invites us to ask for deliverance is true evil: wickedness, perversion. Not that which we often call evil—sickness, trials, sufferings—which, certainly, are not a good in themselves, but which can become a good. It all depends on how these are lived. He is speaking of the evil that infects the soul, the heart—see Mk 7:20–21: "And he said, 'It is what comes out of a person that defiles. For it is from within, from the human heart, that evil intentions come'"—the evil that brings one to true and definitive, eternal death. The original and sprawling evil behind which the blasphemous and mocking face of the evil one lurks. The evil which rejects the *Abbà*, love. Destruction and hate. It is like a succubus that strikes whoever is not careful to stay distant, and enslaves them: the individual, society, the world. Only God, the Father, can free us radically forever. In Jesus, the crucified and risen Son, who overcame it once and for ever.

The Fatherhood of the *Abbà* Revealed in the Son

The "Our Father" prayer, as with the hymn of jubilee found in Matthew and Luke, tells us that God reveals himself not only and uniquely as the Father of Jesus, but also through him, as the Father of all and in the first place Father of the marginalized, the forgotten and sinners. The paternity of God to which Jesus witnesses and which he announces is expressed first of all and in a singular way in its fundamental form in the unique relationship between God/*Abbà* and Jesus. It is in this relationship, in its concreteness and historical realization, that both the paternity of God/*Abbà* and the Sonship of Jesus are revealed. Jesus, in reality, never says "Our Father" together with his disciples: the prayer that he teaches is for them, not for himself (see Mt 6:9; Lk 11:2). He often uses, however, the expression "My Father." He therefore distinguishes between the relationship that he lives with God/*Abbà* from the one that he transmits by grace to human beings in such a way as to implicitly affirm that he is the "way" by which this true and transcendent sonship can be communicated to all human beings.

The sonship of Jesus in reference to the *Abbà* is unique, it exists eternally and is permanent: it invests and expresses the very identity of Jesus, who reveals and actualizes himself entirely in his relationship with God/*Abbà*. The sonship that Jesus transmits is a gift: it is manifested and communicated by him, in the name of the Father, through his *kérygma* and his praxis, so that the coming of the kingdom through the mission of Jesus consists precisely in the witnessing to and transmission of that relationship.

All of this is fulfilled in the Easter event, through the superabundant communication of the Spirit of Jesus. Thanks to this, as the risen one proclaims in the fourth Gospel, the "my Father" (of Jesus) is manifested also as "your Father" (Jn 20:17: "I am ascending to my Father and your Father, to my God and your God"). In this way the disciples, as the apostle Paul claims, can address themselves to God using the name *Abbà* (see Gal 4:6) and do so with full justification.

A Universal Fatherhood Beginning with the Least

In the messianic ministry of Jesus the proclamation of the liberating paternity of God is addressed first of all to the poor (beatitudes) and to the sinners (Lk 15: the parables of mercy). In his praxis, which reflects the *kérygma* and is coherent with it, Jesus becomes close to the most humble (the parable of the good Samaritan, Lk 10:29–37), and dines with sinners (the meeting with the woman who was a sinner, Lk 7:36–50, and that with Zacchaeus, Lk 19:1–10), in such a way that the mercy of God as Father is directly experienced. The *kérygma* and praxis of Jesus in relationship with the marginalized and the sinner become the privileged place of the revelation of the universal paternity of God. It is worth emphasizing in particular two points in this regard.

First of all, we must ask ourselves: what meaning does this preference for the poor have for Jesus himself? It is not difficult to respond to this question. The fatherhood of God is certainly universal, and this is shown precisely because he shows particular favor to the least. Just think of a mother who has many children: she loves them all in the same way, but if one of them—for whatever reason—has need of greater help in whatever way, whether that be material or moral, she will certainly love that one more, in the sense that she will manifest the love that is needed more directly and concretely. "Just so, I tell you, there will be more joy in heaven over one sinner who repents than over ninety-nine righteous persons who need no repentance" (Lk 15:7). There is no partiality in this or exclusion of those who are better off. There is, instead, realistic and impartial closeness to all, most concretely to those who are in greater need.

In the second place, the paternity of God is superabundant and gratuitous: it goes beyond what is deserved, presumptively or actually, by human beings. As Luther writes, taking up an affirmation of Augustine, the love of God does not direct itself toward an object which is worthy of being loved, but rather creates the beauty in its object of love through the very fact of loving it.[20] Thus, for example, the parable of the workers sent at different hours of the day into the vineyard (Mt 20:1–15) portrays God as one who pays everyone equally, because God is good, and because goodness is not envious. We find the same concept expressed in another form in the parable of the Pharisee and the publican who go to the Temple (Lk 18:10–14a). What is essential, on the human side, is simple, total, and unexacting trust—the trust of a child toward his father and mother (see Mt 18:3).

God therefore clearly shows in a tangible and concrete way, through the message and action of Jesus, that the human being is not an orphan in the world, but is always sustained and protected by his hand (see Jn 10:28–29), surrounded by and guided by his love. It is enough to think of chapters 6 and 7 of Matthew's Gospel, the true *magna carta* of God's Fatherhood.[21]

The revelation of God/*Abbà* that Jesus offers is certainly in continuity with the central message of the First Testament. But the paternity of God to which Jesus witnesses is deeper and more radical, not only because it is fully universal, but also because it is absolutely personifying, in the sense that it touches every single human being in his or her real situation, both

20. "Amor hominis fit a suo diligibile," "amor Dei non invenit sed creat suum diligibile"; "ideo enim peccatores sunt pulchri, quia diliguntur, non ideo diliguntur, quia sunt pulchri.... Et iste est amor crucis ex cruce natus, qui illuc sese tranfert, non ubi invenit bonum quo fruatur, sed ubi bonum conferat malo et egeno [Human love starts out from what is lovable; God's love does not find, but it creates what is lovable; thus in fact, sinners are beautiful because they are loved, not that they are loved because they are already beautiful.... And this is the love of the cross, born from the cross, which is placed not where it finds a good to be loved, but where it can give a good to the one that is bad and poor]." *WA* 1:365.1–5; see Augustine's *Homily on the First Letter of John* 9.9.

21. "Therefore I tell you, do not worry about your life, what you will eat or what you will drink, or about your body, what you will wear. Is not life more than food, and the body more than clothing? Look at the birds of the air; they neither sow nor reap nor gather into barns, and yet your heavenly Father feeds them. Are you not of more value than they? And can any of you by worrying add a single hour to your span of life? And why do you worry about clothing? Consider the lilies of the field, how they grow; they neither toil nor spin, yet I tell you, even Solomon in all his glory was not clothed like one of these. But if God so clothes the grass of the field, which is alive today and tomorrow is thrown into the oven, will he not much more clothe you—you of little faith? Therefore do not worry, saying, 'What will we eat?' or 'What will we drink?' or 'What will we wear?' For it is the Gentiles who strive for all these things; and indeed your heavenly Father knows that you need all these things. But strive first for the kingdom of God and his righteousness, and all these things will be given to you as well. So do not worry about tomorrow, for tomorrow will bring worries of its own. Today's trouble is enough for today" (Mt 6:25–34). "Ask, and it will be given you.... If you then, who are evil, know how to give good gifts to your children, how much more will your Father in heaven give good things to those who ask him!" (Mt 7:7–11).

body and soul, in the concreteness of his relations and affections, his work and the community in which he lives: "even the hairs of your head are all counted" (see Mt 10:30; Lk 12:7). In the final analysis, the paternity of God is measured by the sonship of Jesus: in which all are called to participate by gift.

A Nonpaternalistic Fatherhood

This constant, direct, and crystal-clear accent on the paternity of God should not make us think of a paternalistic God, protective and invasive, who suffocates or limits human freedom. Anything but! The God/*Abbà* that Jesus witnesses to is a Father who invites us to attain responsibility, who guarantees and promotes human freedom and stimulates the human capacity to decide and take risks. This, for example, is the image that emerges from the parable of the talents: "Then the one who had received the one talent also came forward, saying, 'Master, I knew that you were a harsh man, reaping where you did not sow, and gathering where you did not scatter seed; so I was afraid, and I went and hid your talent in the ground'" (Mt 25:24–25). The attitude of this man toward God cannot be fear that paralyzes, but neither should it conclude from God's goodness and mercy that it can let itself off the hook or become lax. The paternity of God implies responsibility and concrete personal commitment. It is demanding and stimulates growth. This is also true of God's mercy. Certainly, God is the Father who forgives and brings the sinner back to the original state prior to sin, and indeed brings the sinner to the unforeseeable condition of communion with himself. But only when one recognizes one's sin does he offer the grace to be fully welcomed back as son (see the Lukan parable of the prodigal son in Lk 15:11–32). This is a grace that, as Dietrich Bonhoeffer writes, even if it is gratuitous, is "not cheap."[22]

Jesus' entire life speaks of the character of God's paternity. From the messianic choice carried out at the moment of the baptism which, as the episode of the temptations shows us (see Mk 1:12 and parallels), is not a glorious and theocratic form of messianism, but one made of that solidarity with human beings that implies a making oneself one with them to the point of sharing their distance from the Father. And then, especially in the episode at Gethsemane (see Mt 26:36–46 and parallels), it shows that Jesus' life is the revelation of a nonmanipulative and nonpaternalistic paternity of the *Abbà*. Jesus experiences solitude, anguish, and all of the difficulty of having to bring his will into alignment with that of the Father. This paternity, therefore, is one that does not spare us the darkness, suffering, and even the risk of losing our lives. The face of the *Abbà* pro-

22. Dietrich Bonhoeffer, *The Cost of Discipleship* (London: SCM Press, 2001), 3–9.

claimed and witnessed to by Jesus pushes us, in the final analysis, to look at the cross as the culminating event which reveals the true meaning of God's paternity.

The "Paternal Phantasm" and the Maternity of God

A brief word on at least two important questions regarding the paternity of God that Jesus announces, correctly emphasized in our time. The first, representing the sensitivities of the fields of psychology and psychoanalysis, alerts us to the need to distinguish between the authentic symbol of God as *Abbà*/Father and the "paternal phantasm"—a distorted and dangerous projection onto God of an improper image of paternity. The "paternal phantasm" refers to the perception of father either as "patron" who stands over the child, or as a "protector" in whom the child seeks security abdicating his or her personal responsibility. In both cases, the father ends up being one who blocks the child's move beyond childhood toward maturity. It is clear that such a "paternal phantasm," fatally regressive from the anthropological point of view, can be projected onto the relationship between human beings and God. A phenomenology aware of the kind of paternity which Jesus experiences and announces in relation to the *Abbà*, however, makes it clear that here we are faced with something radically different. Not only does the experience of *Abbà* that illuminates and guides the preaching and action of Jesus not have anything regressive about it, it has as its horizon full liberation and authentic maturation.

The second question comes from the absolutely justified concern about female identity and specificity. Is the language of fatherhood Jesus uses to refer to God conditioned by a culture marked by the primacy of patriarchy? The question should be raised, but the answer should not be arrived at too quickly or simplistically. The answer should be capable of comprehending two fundamental data of the Judeo-Christian revelation: that God is by definition beyond male and female, because God holds within Godself the roots and vocation of both men and women; and that the human being is created "according to the image and likeness" of God precisely as male and female (Gn 1:27). The symbol of fatherhood which Jesus uses should be understood, in this perspective, not as a one-sided privilege of the male compared to the female, but as the recognition in God of that peculiarity that the role of a human father has toward his child—loving care and promotion of otherness—enriching this symbol also with aspects of maternity: tenderness, intimacy, mercy. It is no accident that the New Testament, like the First Testament, contains maternal imagery to speak of God. Thus, in describing the relationship between the Father and the Son, the author of John speaks of the "bosom" of the

Father (Jn 1:18), while the attitude of God toward Israel is represented as that of a hen toward its chicks (see Mt 23:37). Similarly the relationship between Jesus and people he meets and to whom he turns with compassion is described using the imagery of "guts." See, for example, Lk 7:13, where the attitude of Jesus in meeting the widow of Nain is described with the verb *splanchnizomai* which recalls precisely the "guts of mercy" with a female connotation, a term already used in the First Testament to express the mercy of God toward his people. I think that it is improper to try to change the language of Jesus, speaking for example of God as "mother" rather than "father," but also that it is important to respect the intentional depth of his experience of his message. It is more necessary than ever today to introduce into our understanding of his message and the language that expresses it, the symbolic density of essential reference to the female too. Such reference to maternity is intrinsically part of what Jesus is invoking even as he speaks of the paternity of God.

Jesus, the Son

Everything that has been said about God/*Abbà* that Jesus testifies and so reveals, inevitably determines and unequivocally expresses the unique quality of his mission, of the self-consciousness and, finally, the identity itself of Jesus. But one can also say the inverse, or rather affirm what is implicit in this reciprocal relationship, namely that Jesus in the way in which he lives his life and mission as expression of sonship refers one to God's paternity. In his sonship he is the mirror of God's paternity. Only the Son can reveal the Father. Only one who has the unique experience of God who is *Abbà*—as does Jesus—can communicate this experience: with words, deeds, life, and death.

The Filial Identity in Obedience to God/*Abbà*

First of all it is necessary to more closely study the suggestion, which has already appeared above, according to which the closeness, indeed the eschatological urgency of the coming of the kingdom, is to be seen in immediate and intrinsic relationship with Jesus himself. It is in Jesus that God announces and brings about the coming of the kingdom among human beings. The *kérygma* and the praxis of Jesus, and his very personal identity, are indissolubly linked to the coming of God/*Abbà* among humankind.[23]

23. In this regard, Luke gives us an important *logion* of Jesus: "Once Jesus was asked by the Pharisees when the kingdom of God was coming, and he answered, 'The kingdom of God is not coming with things that can be observed; nor will they say, Look, here it is! or There it is! For, in fact, the kingdom of God is among you'" (Lk 17:20–21). Other sayings reported by Luke regarding the coming of the kingdom present in Jesus are 10:23–24 ("Blessed are the eyes that see what you

In this way the quality of the mission and the self-awareness of Jesus are made clear, and become unique, precisely because he knows himself to be, and acts as, the Son of God/*Abbà* sent for the salvation of humanity. As Son he receives everything and gives everything to God, who—being *Abbà*—keeps nothing for himself but communicates all of himself to the Son. The identity of Jesus consists in his ex-isting, in his coming to existence from the Father, and his living for the Father in the carrying out of his mission in favor of humanity. He therefore knows himself to be Son in the face of—indeed in the relationship of intimate communion with—the Father: "The Father and I are one" (Jn 10:30).

This relationship is expressed in the living perception and conscious knowledge of God as *Abbà* and, consequently, in the trust and unconditional self-entrustment to him. It is actualized as the free and creative adhesion of the Son to the Father's will. Obedience (*hypakoé*) is the fundamental and permanent attitude that the experience and actions of Jesus express. It constitutes the form of his existence as a man who in making the relationship with the *Abbà* the determinant of all that he ever does, presents himself to the world as "the" Son in the mission of announcing and bringing about the coming of the kingdom. Jesus' mission, the consciousness that he has in carrying out this mission in obedience to the will of the Father, is the place in which his identity as Son is revealed. As H. U. von Balthasar writes:

> More and more the man Jesus understands and learns to understand himself for what he is: as the Word of the Father directed to the world, in whose mission is contained the destiny of the grain of wheat, which is to die for the world and thus to bring forth fruit. And as he does so Jesus experiences God, not in an "objectivised" vision which is separated from his own reality, but rather in his humility, which does not reflect on itself (and does not seek its own honor, 5.41f.), which opens itself up wholly to God and which in its own functionality experiences the reality of the God who sends him forth, disposes over him, and begets him eternally out of himself.[24]

The faith "of" Jesus In the context of the relationship of obedience that Jesus lives before the *Abbà* it is worth exploring the theme of faith from a specifically Christological point of view. Here I refer not only to the obvious aspect of concentrating on Jesus as the full and definitive path of access to God who is the Trinity of love. I also refer to the need to

see! For I tell you that many prophets and kings desired to see what you see, but did not see it, and to hear what you hear, but did not hear it"); 11:20 ("But if it is by the finger of God that I cast out the demons, then the kingdom of God has come to you"); 16:16 ("The law and the prophets were in effect until John came; since then the good news of the kingdom of God is proclaimed, and everyone tries to enter it by force"); etc.

24. Von Balthasar, *Seeing the Form*, 325.

discover and explore the centrality of the faith "of" Jesus, recognizing the subjective dimension of this faith. Jesus is described as *archēgòs kaì teleiōtès tês písteōs*, "Jesus the pioneer and perfecter of our faith," following the affirmation of Hebrews 12:2.[25]

The theological tradition, in reality, did not speak of the faith "of" Jesus, both because of the danger of a reduction of his unique identity to the status of a mere man, and because of the concept of faith that has been affirmed since Augustine.[26] This was influenced by the encounter between the Jewish-Christian faith and Greek philosophy, and the resulting idea of faith emphasized especially the assent to what is not in itself evident, an assent understood as submission to the authority of God who reveals himself. Following Augustine, Thomas Aquinas explicitly asks the question in his *Summa Theologiae* III, q. 7, a. 3: "*Utrum in Christo fuerit fides*" ("Whether in Christ there was faith"), and his response was negative. Naturally his full response is full of nuance: Thomas, for example, recognizes that in Jesus there is the *meritum fidei*, that which makes faith meritorious, the act of faithful obedience to God, and the response needs to be understood in the context of his overall thought. Nevertheless, after Thomas, the response becomes so obvious that it is not even dealt with in the great commentators or in the theology of the manuals.

The question reemerged in the last fifty years, first of all thanks to an essay by Hans Urs von Balthasar in 1961, "Fides Christi,"[27] which had been born as a response to a book by Martin Buber, *Zwei Glaubensweise* (1950),[28] where the author distinguishes faith as self-entrusting, a Jewish understanding that emphasizes the subjective dimension, from faith as knowledge—the Christian understanding—with the accent on the objective dimension. Balthasar strives to overcome this reductive binary opposition and to interpret Thomas's negative response by opening a positive path in a Christological key. The question is thereby relaunched in the context of a focus on a phenomenology of the experience of Jesus that aims at highlighting the subjective dimension of his experience as both archetype and foundation. This leads to a renewal of two inquiries: the biblical research into Hebrews 12:2[29] cited above and discussion about

25. For a documented and lucid historical and systematic introduction to the question, see Flavio Campagnoli, *"Fides Jesu": Storia della questione e ripresa teologica* (PhD diss., Lateran Pontifical University, 2009).

26. See Magnus Löhrer, *Der Glaubensbegriff des hl. Augustinus in seinen ersten Schriften bis zu den Confessiones* (Einsiedeln: Benzinger, 1955).

27. "*Fides Christi*: An Essay on the Consciousness of Christ," in *Explorations in Theology*, vol. 2: *Spouse of the Word* (San Francisco, Calif.: Ignatius Press, 1991), 43–79.

28. Martin Buber, *The Two Types of Faith* (New York: Macmillan, 1951).

29. See Albert Vanhoye, "La fede di Gesù? A proposito di Eb 12, 2," in *PATH* 2 (2003): 401–15. Vanhoye writes, "In itself, faith implies different levels within the anthropological dimension: from the highest expressing the free and conscious relationship with God, to others that

pístis Christoû (the faith of Christ) as object and as subject in the Pauline correspondence.[30] Together with this the systematic question related to this theme is renewed.

In point of fact, it is the relation to the Father that Jesus lives that constitutes the foundation and concrete example of the attitude of faith that the Christian is called to follow. The New Testament and especially the Johannine literature describes it most clearly as constant openness and filial obedience toward the Father and total trust in the only relationship which is truly capable of giving a foundation to the human being in his or her call to become son in the Son. In John 6:38, Jesus affirms: "I have come down from heaven, not to do my own will, but the will of him who sent me." This expression sets out in the clearest way possible the structure of the faithful obedience of Jesus. "My food is to do the will of him who sent me and to complete his work" (Jn 4:34). Such obedience has an active character; it is a free choice: "I glorified you on earth by finishing the work that you gave me to do" (Jn 17:4). It is the relationship with the Father, therefore, which represents the essential presupposition of the unfolding of Jesus' story as the coming of the kingdom of God among human beings, and it is the relationship with the Father (and its extension

---

invest human nature in its diverse volitional, intellectual and psychic dynamisms. Now on the highest level, the relationship lived by Jesus with the Father was very particular, whereas on other levels, Jesus shared our situation because of his human nature of flesh and blood (Heb 2:14). He was a pioneer in the faith, as demonstrated by his prayers of petition to the One that could save him from death (Heb 5:7)" (ibid., 415; own trans.). That is particularly expressed by the affirmation: "Although he was a Son, he learned obedience through what he suffered" (Heb 5:8). Such apprenticeship was necessary "to become like his brothers and sisters in every respect, so that he might be a merciful and faithful high priest" (Heb 2:17). In this way, he was "made perfect" in his human nature (Heb 5:9), and "he became the source of eternal salvation for all who obey him, having been designated by God a high priest according to the order of Melchizedek" (Heb 5:9–10).

30. See Roberto Vignolo, "La fede portata da Cristo. '*Pístis Christoû*' in Paolo," in *La fede di Gesù*, ed. Giacomo Canobbio (Bologna: EDB, 2000), 43–67. The genitive in question is interpreted by Vignolo as a "complex" or "relational" genitive which makes it possible "to interpret the *fides Christi* as faith instituted by Jesus, or else directly inaugurated by him in singular, unmistakable and irreplaceable fullness, and on the strength of the universal inclusion guaranteed by the subject and by the act of this event, established *pro nobis* as something which could be shared universally. Even before that, the *pístis Christoû* contains the unique trust and radical obedience of Jesus in front of the Father all the way to death on the cross; then there is the subsequent intrinsic possibility of sharing his same trust and obedience, the same passion, death and resurrection (see the verbs constructed with *sun-*), as a trustworthy and attractive foundation stimulating faith. It is because of the *pístis Christoû* that we are *en Christoû*" (ibid., 66; own trans.). So the *pístis Christoû* is an attribute which is both Christological and anthropological; it is "faith borne by Christ," in the sense that he is the unique and only subject establishing in us, his rapport with the Father, in the participation given through the Spirit. From the theological standpoint therefore, Marcello Bordoni's affirmation ends up undoubtedly being plausible; in fact it is essential for the determination of a pertinent and integral definition of Christian faith. According to Bordoni, "Jesus incarnates in his earthly life both the 'Way' in which each true knowledge of the Father comes down to man, as well as the 'Way' that one is elevated to the Father under the action of the Spirit (Heb 9:14), in the sacrificial, obedient response to his will (Mk 14:36)." Marcello Bordoni, "Gesù di Nazareth, un modello di uomo religioso?," *Ecclesia Mater* 41, no. 3 (2003): 142 (own trans.).

to his brothers and sisters) which Jesus is fulfilling by offering his life on the cross.

It is precisely this radical faithfulness of Jesus to the Father, leading to that death on the cross which in itself might seem to be a failure (see the cry of forsakenness: Mt 27:46; Mk 15:34), but instead turns out to be the highest point of the faith/obedience that he lives, despite everything. It is this that is vindicated by the *Abbà* in the resurrection, not only as the fulfillment of the life of the only-begotten Son made flesh, but also as the event on the basis of which this fulfillment is made available to all human beings as a participation in the *fides Jesu* in the new experience disclosed by the Holy Spirit.

Filial Identity and *exousía*

The unique filial relationship that Jesus has toward the *Abbà* brings fulfillment to the image of messiah that had been developing in the religious consciousness of Israel, but does so in a way that was unforeseeable, and which thereby purifies and even corrects that image. His mission and identity, in effect, both in the perception that his contemporaries had and even more so in the consciousness of his disciples and apostles, and in his own self-consciousness, exceed the interpretive categories available in Judaism regarding the mission and identity of the one whom God would send.

It is true that Jesus presents himself—or is presented, as the case may be—as teacher,[31] or prophet[32] and even as messiah,[33] but the uniqueness of his announcement and praxis transcend such designations. He is a teacher, but a charismatic teacher—he teaches without exclusively relying on the previous tradition. He is prophet, but with a decisive and new quality: he interprets the word of God authoritatively and definitively. He is the expected messiah, but not in any simple or prevalently earthly way, nor in a historical-political and national way: he fulfills the hopes of the people and the promise of God in an eschatological and universal way, relating himself explicitly to the prophecy of the suffering servant of YHWH.

What emerges as evident and unique in the ministry of Jesus is especially the exercise of his sovereign authority (*exousía*), which he presents without hesitation or reserve as the immediate, unquestionable and authentic authority of God himself. This places Jesus, in his proclamation, attitudes, and deeds, on the level of YHWH himself. YHWH, in and

31. As the title of "teacher," rabbi, with which he is addressed.

32. See Mk 1:15; Mt 16:10, 14; Lk 16:39; 24:19.

33. See the paradigmatic episode known as the confession of Caesarea Philippi (Mk 8:27–33).

through Jesus, proclaims his word and carries out his deeds of salvation in the history of Israel. From the outset, the proclamation and teaching of Jesus strike and amaze his listeners for their revolutionary novelty.

The synoptics record the reaction of those confronted with his "new teaching with authority" (see Mk 1:22, 27; Mt 7:28–29; Lk 4:32, 36). Accordingly, his praxis is characterized by great signs and exorcisms, clear evidence of his unquestionable messianic power. The fact that he regally dispenses forgiveness—something correctly understood to be a prerogative of YHWH alone—underlines his *exousía*.[34] The stories of the calling of the disciples and the convocation of the messianic community further confirm the unprecedented authoritativeness of Jesus. In contrast to the teachers of his time who were chosen by their disciples, Jesus calls his own disciples with the same authority by which YHWH himself called the prophets to His service.[35]

It is this claim to authority, implicit in the proclamation and praxis of Jesus, that explains the dramatic conflict that is gradually unleashed, to the point of the inevitable break with the religious, social, and political establishment of Israel. Such claims were unacceptable to both Pharisees and Sadducees. Jesus presents himself as the authoritative and definitive interpreter and provider who brings the Law to fulfillment (see Mt 5:17) and as the normative and final guide to the will of God for Israel.[36] Even the holiness of the Temple, the place of the presence of YHWH in the midst of his people, is relativized by the message and praxis of Jesus: indeed by his very person which is proposed as the eschatological location of the presence of YHWH among human beings.[37]

The exousía *of Jesus in relation to Law and Temple* The Gospels witness to the rapid growth in the conflict between Jesus and the Jewish establishment. There are two religious currents that oppose Jesus: the Pharisees and scribes on the one hand, and the Sadducees on the other. The first represent the Law; the latter the Temple. The Torah—composed by a central nucleus and by a precise and well-articulated series of prescriptions of an ethical, juridical, and ritual character—was considered the greatest gift that God had given in the Sinai covenant. It expressed God's will and regulated social and religious life. By contesting the standard interpreta-

34. See the account of the healing of a paralytic in Mk 2:1–12, where the thought of the scribes is reported: "Why does this fellow speak in this way? It is blasphemy! Who can forgive sins but God alone?" (2:7), and the bystanders' reaction of marvel and amazement after the miracle of his healing: "We have never seen anything like this!" (2:12).

35. See, for example, Mk 1:16–20; 2:13–14; 3:13–15; Jn 1:35–51, etc.

36. See the typical "antitheses" used by Jesus ("it was said.... But I say to you ...": Mt 5:21–22, 27–28, 43–44), and the emphasis Jesus put on his own teaching ("Truly I tell you ...").

37. See Mk 11:15–17; Mt 12:1; Jn 2:19–21.

tions, Jesus presents himself as the authoritative interpreter of God's original intention and of the definitive manifestation of this intention in the eschatological coming of the kingdom (see Mt 5:17–20). He thus places himself in the line of the prophets (especially Jeremiah and Ezekiel) who had announced the coming of a new covenant.

In this new covenant the human person would be finally capable of carrying out the Law, which would no longer be a merely exterior prescription, but something that would guide him interiorly to a true and right relationship with God and with his brothers and sisters. Faced with the absolutization of the *shabàth*, Jesus takes up and radicalizes a criterion already known to rabbinic exegesis: "The sabbàth was made for humankind and not humankind for the sabbàth" (Mk 2:27). As far as the practice of ritual purity was concerned, Jesus brings about an even more radical reversal, emphasizing that the important thing is the intention rather than the exterior act—see, for example, Mk 7:15: "there is nothing outside a person that by going in can defile, but the things that come out are what defile." What the Pharisees contest about Jesus, especially following the episodes of the violation of the sabbàth (see Mk 2:23–28 and parallels; Mk 3:1–6 and parallels; Lk 13:10–17), is the interpretation that he gives of the Law that is so innovative as to appear subversive. Two fundamental criteria guide Jesus' reinterpretation: (1) following the will of God, which is to announce and inaugurate the kingdom (the new covenant), and (2) the salvation and liberation of humanity, so that the Law might be solely in the service of integral human growth and liberation.

The relationship with the Temple, the place of the presence of God among his people and of prayer addressed to him, is equally decisive if we are to understand the mission and identity of Jesus. While it is true that he does visit the Temple, and more than once, it is also true that he indirectly but also explicitly declares the overcoming of the economy of the Temple. For this reason, one of the accusations, perhaps even the decisive one which brought about his condemnation to death, is related to his affirmations about the Temple. Thus, in Mark's account: "We heard him say, 'I will destroy this Temple that is made with hands, and in three days I will build another, not made with hands'" (14:58). This text immediately recalls the dialogue between Jesus and the Samaritan in John 4, where Jesus declares the overcoming not just of the cult of the Samaritans on Mount Gerizim (where in the fifth century a rival Temple to that of Jerusalem had been built, and had then been converted to the worship of Jupiter by Antiochus Epiphanes and destroyed in 108 BCE), but also that regarded by the Jews themselves as the true Temple of God in Jerusalem (Jn 4:21–24):

Woman, believe me, the hour is coming when you will worship the Father neither on this mountain nor in Jerusalem. You worship what you do not know; we worship what we know, for salvation is from the Jews. But the hour is coming, and is now here, when the true worshipers will worship the Father in spirit and truth, for the Father seeks such as these to worship him. God is spirit, and those who worship him must worship in spirit and truth.

The meaning of this affirmation should be drawn out from the whole of Jesus' message and praxis and from the final outcome of the story of Jesus. If we examine these and their interrelation, we can intuit that according to Jesus the economy of the Temple, and that is the presence of YHWH in the midst of his people that it symbolized, and which was expressed in the cult and in the sacrifices, is definitively passed. The episode which attests to this fact is the vigorous polemic that Jesus unleashes against the traders in the Temple area, narrated by the synoptics (see Mk 11:15–17 and parallels). This does not only have the simple meaning of the purification and restoration of the cult, but reveals a prophetic and even eschatological intention: according to Jesus the time has come for another and now definitive presence of God among human beings, and consequently the prayer and cult to God should take on a new form. Here Jesus places himself in the line of prophets who criticize the inadequacy of the Temple, and the danger of formalism and particularism connected with the Temple cult (see, for example, Am 5:25–27). This implies, positively, an emphasis on interiority and universality in the adoration that should be addressed to God. Therefore, when Jesus affirms decisively, "Go and learn what this means, 'I desire mercy, not sacrifice'" (see Mt 9:13; 12:7), he does no more than recall Hosea's message "For I desire steadfast love and not sacrifice, the knowledge of God rather than burnt offerings." (6:6; see also 1 Sm 15:22).

The evangelists Mark and Matthew describe the scene of the rending in two of the veil of the Temple (see Mk 16:38; Mt 27:51) in the moment in which "Jesus gave a loud cry and breathed his last" (Mk 16:37; Mt 27:50). The closure of one period and the definitive opening of another is symbolized in this moment. It is as if the presence of God abandoned the Holy of Holies at the heart of the Temple in order to concentrate itself outside the walls of Jerusalem, in that profane place, in that crucified one hanging between two thieves. The fourth Gospel, for its part, places the deepest meaning of what happens to him in relation to the economy of the Temple: "Destroy this Temple and in three days I will raise it up" (Jn 2:19). The affirmation is cryptic, like so many others in the pre-Paschal Jesus. What does it mean regarding his identity and eschatological destiny? The fourth Gospel explicates the dynamics of the hermeneutics disclosed by the event of the death and resurrection of Jesus and the effusion of the Spirit in the hearts of believers, responding with conviction: "But he was speaking of the temple of his body. After he was raised from the dead, his disciples remembered that he had said this and they believed the scripture and the word that Jesus had spoken" (Jn 2:21–22). In this perspective, there is a passage from Matthew which he links to the polemic against the absolutized sabbàth, the heart of the Law of Israel, and the polemic against the Temple (Mt 12:1–8):

> At that time Jesus went through the grainfields on the sabbath; his disciples were hungry, and they began to pluck heads of grain and to eat. When the Pharisees saw it, they said to him, "Look, your disciples are doing what is not lawful to do on the sabbath." He said to them, "Have you not read what David did when he and his companions were hungry? He entered the house of God and ate the bread of the Presence, which it was not lawful for him or his companions to eat, but only for the priests.... I tell you, something greater than the Temple is here. But if you had known what this means, 'I desire mercy and not sacrifice,' you would not have condemned the guiltless. For the Son of Man is lord of the sabbath."

What then, in brief, is the meaning of the conflict that inevitably develops between Jesus and the social and religious establishment of Israel? Here are some interrelated elements that we should bear in mind: Jesus contests the absolutization of laws and cultic institutions, both in relation to the original plan of God which with his proclamation was coming to fulfillment, and in relation to the salvation of humanity which is the purpose of the ethical and cultic laws given by the Lord in the old covenant ("The sabbath was made for humankind, and not humankind for the sabbath," see Mk 2:27). He contests the status quo of the functioning of the Temple: the risk that the Temple might lose its original meaning, and become a simple (ideological) prop to other interests. Through his contestation, Jesus announces the fulfillment of these institutions, the Law and the Temple in the perspective of the coming of the kingdom and the new covenant. Both the Law and the cult are interiorized: the ritual prescriptions are relativized with respect to the inner intention of the worshipper; the supreme Law is condensed into love of God and neighbor; the Temple, the place of adoration of God, is no longer tied to a sacred place, but is there wherever human beings exercise their obedience to the Father and service of their brothers. Finally, Jesus universalizes the particularism implicit in the interpretation of the covenant of God with Israel. By giving fulfillment of the Law and the Temple, the experience of God offered by Jesus shows itself *in nuce* as a universalistic experience, open to and capable of being shared with all nations, as the apostle Paul will later show.

Filial Identity and Temptation

Jesus' identity as Son, rooted in the awareness of his unique relationship with God/*Abbà*, is clearly evident throughout the story of the Gospels in the temptations to which Jesus is constantly subject. The relationship of communion and obedience in relation to the *Abbà* is perceived immediately, but is also lived out historically, which means in a history of growth, risk, freedom, and trial. Jesus adheres to the will of the Father in the various circumstances in which he lives as his relationship takes shape in the dramatic concreteness of his mission, faced with the reactions and responses that his proclamation of the kingdom in Israel provokes, whether these be positive or even more if they are indifferent or negative.

It is no accident that in the synoptics, immediately following the baptism, there is the account of the forty days in the desert where Jesus is "tempted by Satan" (Mk 1:13). Mark limits himself to announcing the fact in unadorned fashion, while Matthew and Luke dramatize the dialogue between Jesus and the tempter and spell out the context (see Mt 4:1–11; Lk 4:1–13). But even in Mark we find an explicit reference to the basic theme of the temptation in the central moment of the ministry of Jesus when, following Peter's confession at Caesarea Philippi (Mk 8:31–33), Jesus begins his journey toward Jerusalem where the final conflict with the adversary awaits him. At Caesarea, Peter confesses that Jesus is messiah (8:29–30), and Jesus manifests what awaits him in Jerusalem—suffering and rejection. Peter draws him away from the others and expresses his perplexity: it is not possible that the one sent by God, the chosen one of God should be submitted to such an ignoble fate. But Jesus reproaches him bitterly "Get behind me, Satan! For you are setting your mind not on divine things but on human things" (Mk 8:33). The temptation to which Jesus' freedom is subjected is not that of turning to evil, but of exercising his messianic *exousía* in his own way, according to human ways of thinking, rather than according to the will of the Father.

The temptation of Jesus, therefore, has a Christological quality. It is the temptation to not live fully the discernment of the will of the Father and obedience to him, in full dedication to the mission which was given to him, according to the form that the Father wished for the Son, that of being the filial witness to the true face of divine paternity. This temptation is faced and overcome repeatedly, in a life of ever more profound communion with the Father, as the episode at Gethsemane on the vigil of the passion demonstrates (Mk 14:32–36 and Mt 26:36–39). Even when he is raised on the cross, the temptation of betraying his filial identity/mission represents itself in the sarcastic invitation to save himself

(Mk 15:31–32). But, as the centurion exclaims from the foot of the cross, it will be precisely in seeing how he dies that we can recognize in faith that he is truly the Son of the *Abbà* (see Mk 15:39).

Filial Identity as Ex-istence and Pro-existence

In brief, the form in which and the style with which Jesus lives his mission express his filial identity. The Father sent him for the salvation of humankind. The being of Jesus, being a "being-from" (the Father) is for that very reason a "being-for" (the Father and, in fulfillment of his mission, for human beings). His identity/mission is therefore an ex-istence which is expressed in pro-existence, first of all in relation to the Father and, in adhering to the will of the Father, in relation to his brothers and sisters.

This is already clear in the first period of Jesus' ministry in Galilee, centered on the proclamation of the kingdom of God, but even more explicitly in his Jerusalem ministry. Thus, in the Markan *logíon*: "the Son of Man came not to be served but to serve, and to give his life as a ransom for many" (Mk 10:45). Indeed the particle *hypér* (for, in favor of) can stand as expression of the quality and most proper dynamic of the mission of Jesus, as revelation of his filial identity. We find it, for example, and in a highly significant way, in the account of the Last Supper: "This is my blood of the covenant, which is poured out for many" (Mk 14:24).[38] The being of Jesus from and for the Father is concretely expressed in his being to the very end, and that is to the point of the gift of life, for humanity in fulfillment of the will of the one who sent him.

Filial Identity and Self-Consciousness

All of the expressions of the ministry of Jesus then refer one to his unique filial identity. The question then arises: what awareness does Jesus have of himself? In order to respond, it is important first of all to bear in mind the title that he uses of himself and his mission, often indirectly: the Son of Man.[39] It is not easy to interpret this expression. On the one hand it emphasizes the full and true humanity of Christ. On the other hand it is connected with the prophecies contained in the Book of Daniel (7:9–14) and in the apocalyptic literature of the inter-testamental period. As we know, in these texts the expression refers to an eschatological persona who is welcomed into the sphere of the divine, and to whom God entrusts a mission, unique in the history of salvation, in view of the inauguration of God's kingdom. It is a title then that certainly highlights the true

38. See also Lk 22:19–20; Jn 6:51; 10:11, 15; 11:50–52; 13:37–38; 15:13; 17:19; 18:14.

39. The title "Son of Man" appears eighty-two times in the Gospels, and eighty of these are from the mouth of Jesus, referring at least indirectly to himself.

humanity of Christ, born of a woman (Gal 4:4), but at the same time it places him decisively in relationship with the coming of YHWH among human beings, through the one whom he has chosen.

All of this leads us to the conclusion that the title was used by Jesus, especially in the period of his ministry in Jerusalem. Using it, he could translate and announce what had been the symbol typically used in his Galilean ministry—the coming of the kingdom of God—into more personal terms, explicitly and directly related to himself and the events of which he was protagonist. This fact alone expresses clearly the fact that the self-consciousness of Jesus overcomes the purely intra-historical messianic perspective, in an eschatological line that involves the final and definitive times of the coming of the kingdom in a horizon that transcends history itself.[40]

It is also important to highlight the fact that in both the proclamation and praxis of Jesus an authoritative and strong "I" emerges quite clearly. Just think of those episodes where Jesus emphatically says: "I say unto you" to carry out a miracle, or to give authority to his teaching.[41] Or think of the typical antithetical style with which Jesus intentionally opposes his teaching to the interpretation of the law of the ancient teachers: "it has been said, but I say unto you . . ."

Jesus' "I" is so authoritative that it is paralleled in the First Testament only by the "I am" with which the Word of YHWH and his actions in the midst of human beings are sealed and confirmed, from the revelation of the name to Moses (Ex 3:14) onward. Consequently the rereading that the evangelist John offers becomes particularly significant. It is based on some affirmations of the synoptics (see Mk 6:50, the episode of the storm on the lake in Mk 14:62, Jesus in front of the high priest). He presents the "I" of Jesus when he refers in an absolute way to Jesus' use of the affirmation *egó eimi*, "I am,"[42] in which the sovereign and transcendent "I" of YHWH is re-echoed.[43]

40. This meaning becomes fully clear in the Gospel of John, where the title "Son of Man" appears twelve times. According to one author, on Jesus' lips, this expression "means his humanity which possesses the fullness of the Spirit, the divine project on humanity realized in Him, the model of humanity, the culmination of humanity. It is the reality of Jesus seen from below, from its human roots, raised to the most complete realization by means of the communication of the Spirit. The corresponding title is Son of God, which indicates the same reality seen from above, from God, designating the one who is totally similar to and who possesses the divine condition." Juan Mateos and Juan Barreto, *Il vangelo di Giovanni* (Cittadella: Assisi, 1982), 876 (own trans.). The vivid expression of this Johannine interpretation is given in the verse where Pilate presents Jesus to the Jews, saying "Here is the man" (19:5b): the soldiers, stripping Jesus of his false worldly royalty show that his true messianicity coincides with his being the man fulfilled according to God's plans, free to offer his life out of love on the cross.

41. See, for example, the episode of the paralytic (Mk 2:1–12).

42. See, for example, the debate between Jesus and the Jewish leaders in Jn 8:57–58.

43. I will return to the decisive importance of this below.

These elements and references of the evangelical tradition underline the unique origin, from God, of the mission and authority of Jesus, and also his unique personal identity as Son of the *Abbà*. A privileged locus that in some ways sums up the whole question is the parable of the "wicked tenants" (see Mk 12:1–9; Mt 21:33–45), where Jesus places his own identity on the same level as the son of the vineyard owner, while that of the prophets is placed simply in relationship to the servants of the owner.

The filial consciousness of Jesus—as has already been detailed—is manifested in his complete obedience and total dedication to the will of the Father and the completion of the mission that God had entrusted to him in favor of humanity. The crucial moment where this consciousness is represented is the episode of Gethsemane, where Jesus, aware of his freedom and the sacrifice of his life that awaits him, aligns his will with that of the Father ("not what I want, but what you want": see Mk 14:36; Mt 26:42; Lk 22:42). We are dealing here with two distinct identities, with two freedoms, that of God/*Abbà* and that of Jesus, which converge in Jesus' obedience to the plan of the Father. This, however, does not take anything from the dramatic nature and suffering of this decision, which will become fully clear once again in the moment of the cross and the forsakenness.

Jesus and the Spirit

In order to focus on the originality of the revelation of God/*Abbà* that is offered to us in Jesus, it is essential, as a third step, that we look at the presence and at the unprecedented and determining work of the Spirit in his messianic ministry. The Spirit, in fact, emerges from the Gospel witness as the gift (*cháris*) and power (*dýnamis*) of God and from God that form the filial identity of Jesus in his relation to the *Abbà* and which illuminate and guide his mission. In the synoptics, Jesus is presented as the messiah, the anointed one of YHWH, on whom the fullness of the Spirit that had been promised rests. This is the eschatological effusion of the Spirit both on the chosen one and on the messianic community. In the fourth Gospel, Jesus is contemplated, on the basis of the Paschal events, as the one from whom the "living water" of salvation and divine sonship flow.[44]

The Mission of Jesus as "Baptism in the Spirit"

The baptism in the Jordan, as I have already noted, is recognized in all Gospel traditions as the event of the personal and permanent descent of

44. On this topic, see Bordoni, "Lo Spirito nella esperienza carismatica di Gesù," in his *La cristologia nell'orizzonte dello Spirito*, 46–51. For an ample and detailed overview of the biblical aspect, see Max-Alain Chevallier, *Souffle de Dieu: Le Saint-Esprit dans le Nouveau Testament*, 2 vols. (Paris: Beauchesne, 1978–90).

the Spirit on Jesus of Nazareth. This is true, both in the perspective of the messianic investiture and mission brought about as a stable indwelling (see Jn 1:32–33) of the Spirit of YHWH on him, and in the perspective of the awareness on the part of the Baptist and of the first disciples of the fact that Jesus is by this fact the anointed one, the one sent by YHWH to announce the coming of his kingdom among human beings.

On the basis of the event, understood to be foundational for his vocation, of his messianic anointing and mission as narrated by the evangelists, the whole existence of Jesus is understood in the pre-Paschal tradition as a "baptism," that is, as the permanent and powerful presence of the Spirit on Jesus, the promised messiah, which drives him to immerse himself with ever more radical solidarity into the condition of human beings, to the point of the ignominious death on the cross. This death then becomes the unleashing source of the universal effusion, "without measure" of the Spirit (see Jl 3:1–2). In this way, reference to the baptism in the ministry of Jesus comes to designate both—in prophetic and symbolic form—the death on the cross and the eschatological effusion of the Spirit.

The ministry of Jesus, therefore, is recognized as a "baptism in the Spirit" (see Mk 1:8; Jn 1:33) because he, in the grace and power of the Spirit which descends on him and dwells in him, as the baptism in the Jordan attests, faithfully fulfills the plan of the Father to the point of the death on the cross so as to baptize in this way all peoples in the Spirit unleashed at Easter. Jesus' baptism in the Jordan attests that the Spirit that comes from the Father dwells in him. His death on the cross and resurrection are the eschatological event in which God/*Abbà*, for and in Jesus, is the eschatological effusion of his Spirit. The Spirit from the Father comes upon Jesus and dwells in him (at the baptism in the Jordan), and guides his ministry. The Spirit is then given to all people in superabundant and universal fullness by Jesus (the Easter events of the death and resurrection).

Before anything else, see the two *logía* of the synoptics which certainly come from the pre-Paschal tradition: "But Jesus said to them, 'You do not know what you are asking. Are you able to drink the cup that I drink, or be baptized with the baptism that I am baptized with?'" (Mk 10:38). "I came to bring fire to the earth, and how I wish it were already kindled! I have a baptism with which to be baptized, and what stress I am under until it is completed!" (Lk 12:49–50). In these *logía* Jesus' ministry is understood and presented—already in the self-consciousness of Jesus himself—as a "baptism in the Spirit" (Mk 1:8), fulfilled in the suffering obedience to the Father's plan ("the cup"), and from this the "fire" of the presence of the Spirit of YHWH among human beings will be lit. This theme recalls the promise of the eschatological baptism announced by Ezekiel (11:19).

The Ministry of Jesus in the Power of the Spirit

Even the scene of the inauguration of the messianic ministry of Jesus in the synagogue at Nazareth, narrated by the evangelist Luke (4:16–20), revolves around the theme of the messianic effusion of the Spirit on Jesus, with reference to Isaiah 61:1: "The Spirit of the Lord is upon me." In reality, in the Gospel of Luke the whole ministry of Jesus, from its very beginning, is understood and described as a mission lived out in the Spirit. *Kerygma*, exorcisms, healings, the call of the disciples and the constitution of the messianic community—all of these are, as we have seen, demonstrations of Jesus' *exousía*. All of these occur in the power and under the impulse of the Spirit which is given superabundantly by the Father to the Son.

Thus, for example, the Lukan version of the hymn of jubilation, of which I have spoken, explicates how it is precisely "in the Holy Spirit" (Lk 10:21) that Jesus lives his prayer, faith, and exultance in the Father. In fact, as Chevallier notes, "Jesus is presented by Luke as the man of the Breath *par excellence*, the only 'place' of the Breath during this period." All of this is eschatologically decisive for the history of salvation.[45]

Three *logía* of Jesus on the Spirit in the Synoptics

In the synoptic tradition we can isolate in particular three pre-Paschal *logía* in which the messianic self-consciousness of Jesus is attested and related to the eschatological presence on him of the Spirit in the event of the coming of the kingdom of God. First of all, the *logíon* recorded in Matthew 12:28 and parallels: "But if it is by the Spirit of God that I cast out demons, then the kingdom of God has come to you." Here Jesus forcefully emphasizes that the proclamation and inauguration of the kingdom of God which he is working through his *kérygma* and praxis come about through the working of the Spirit of YHWH. The presence of the Spirit is such, in its transforming and redeeming power, that the messianic signs indicate the coming and powerful presence of the kingdom among humankind.

Then we have the enigmatic *logíon* regarding blasphemy against the Holy Spirit in Mk 3:28–30 and parallels: "'Truly I tell you, people will be forgiven for their sins and whatever blasphemies they utter; but whoever blasphemes against the Holy Spirit can never have forgiveness, but is guilty of an eternal sin,' for they had said, 'He has an unclean spirit.'" The blasphemy against the Spirit is the willful failure to recognize the ministry of Jesus inasmuch as it is produced and manifested in the power of the

45. Chevallier, *Souffle de Dieu*, 1:221 (own trans.).

Spirit. To fail to recognize the origin of the identity of Jesus from God, and therefore the messianic character of his mission in virtue of the Spirit, means not recognizing the salvific presence and the eschatological action of YHWH himself in the midst of his people. It means, therefore, consciously obscuring the clear meaning, and attributing what Jesus is saying and doing in the power of the Holy Spirit to the action of evil.

Finally, the synoptic tradition (Mk 13:11 and parallels) attests to a promise made by Jesus regarding the gift of the Spirit to his disciples and witnesses in times of persecution: "When they bring you to trial and hand you over, do not worry beforehand about what you are to say; but say whatever is given you at that time, for it is not you who speak, but the Holy Spirit." This *logion* allows us to perceive an awareness in Jesus of being the one through whom the Spirit will be communicated to the disciples who will continue his work. This synthetic statement very probably constitutes the point of departure for what will be more fully developed in a post-Paschal horizon in the Gospel of John's so-called sayings of the Paraclete (to which I will return below).

Jesus the Source of "Living Water" in the Fourth Gospel

In the fourth Gospel, the meaning of the messianic mission of Jesus is also understood and expressed, synthetically, as "baptism in the Spirit" and is connected in a conscious and precise way to the Paschal event of Jesus. This is true starting from the witness of the Baptist about the identity and mission of Jesus: "I myself did not know him, but the one who sent me to baptize with water said to me, 'He on whom you see the Spirit descend and remain is the one who baptizes with the Holy Spirit'" (1:33). What is thereby stressed is not so much, as in the synoptics, the power of the Spirit in which Jesus speaks and works, but the fullness of the Spirit that will be poured out at this Easter of death and resurrection.

In chapters 4 and 7 of his Gospel, John explicitly connects the promise of the Spirit on the part of Jesus to the First Testament theme of "living water." The baptism in water of the Baptist is thus distinguished from the baptism in the Spirit of Jesus; and the baptism in the Spirit on the part of Jesus is expressed in its eschatological meaning as baptism in living water: the water that flows forth from the ever-gushing well that is God, the water that he offers to human beings through Jesus is life without end. This is symbolically recalled by Jesus in the conversation with the Samaritan woman in 4:10, 13–14:

Jesus answered her, "If you knew the gift of God, and who it is that is saying to you, 'Give me a drink,' you would have asked him, and he would have given you living water." … "Everyone who drinks of this water will be thirsty again, but those who drink of the water that I will give them will never be thirsty. The water that I will give will become in them a spring of water gushing up to eternal life."

In terms very similar to these, Jesus expresses himself at the Feast of Booths (Jn 7:37–39) which, in the Hebrew liturgy, is understood to be related to the eschatological gift of the living water springing forth from the Temple according to the vision of Ezekiel (see 47:1).

On the last day of the festival, the great day, while Jesus was standing there, he cried out, "Let anyone who is thirsty come to me, and let the one who believes in me drink. As the scripture has said, 'Out of the believer's heart shall flow rivers of living water.'" Now he said this about the Spirit, which believers in him were to receive; for as yet there was no Spirit, because Jesus was not yet glorified.

In order to understand the meaning of this text, it is important to acknowledge the challenge of its correct interpretation. Exegetes offer two readings: "If anyone is thirsty, come to me and drink; who gives me his adhesion—as that passage says—from his (i.e., the disciple's) heart"; "If anyone is thirsty, come to me, and let who adheres to me drink—as that passage says—from his (i.e., Christ's) heart." The second interpretation seems preferable, for three reasons: in the Johannine perspective the prophetic texts on water read in the liturgy of the Temple (Ezek 41:1; Zec 14:8) are related to Jesus the "new Temple" and not to the believer; the water of which Jesus speaks is identified with the water that will flow from his side on the cross (see 19:34), in the hour of the manifestation of his glory (7:39); and this reading is preferable because of the chiastic structure of the text: situation, thirst; imperative, drink; situation, adhesion.

The crucifixion of Jesus is related to the symbol of the Temple from whose side living water flows forth, a symbol of the Spirit. It is also found in another text of the Johannine tradition, the apocalypse: "Then the angel showed me the river of the water of life, bright as crystal, flowing from the throne of God and of the Lamb" (Rv 22:1; see 7:17, 21:6), where the Lamb referred to is the "Lamb standing as if it had been slaughtered" which stands for the crucified and risen one (Rv 5:6). In all of these cases the living water is the symbol of the Holy Spirit. Jesus is therefore presented in the fourth Gospel as the eschatological giver of living water/the Spirit which springs forth from the Father. All of this is made explicit in the Paschal scene narrated in John 19, and is developed in prophetic perspective in the sayings of the Paraclete.

The Novelty of Jesus' Experience of the Spirit

The apparent scarcity of explicit reference to the Spirit in the New Testament materials attributed to Jesus himself has led some to speak of a "pneumatic silence" almost mirroring the "messianic secret" in pre-Paschal Christology. But this, far from revealing an absence, tells us something rather significant for an understanding of the originality of Jesus' ministry. Chevallier writes: "In Jesus … preaching and action were, for faith, fully adequate witnesses that he was indeed the recipient of the breath [of the Spirit].… It was not because they witnessed pneumatic manifestations that the disciples recognized that Jesus was the Christ. Rather, because of what they heard and saw … they said both 'He is the Christ' and 'he has received the fullness of the Breath.'"[46]

Marcello Bordoni also points out that we have here something in the synoptic tradition that is faithful to the situation of Jesus' pre-Paschal existence but also

> an important datum that witnesses to the "semantic renewal" of the personal mystery of the Spirit revealed in Jesus due to his new experience of God as Father (*Abbà*), brought about precisely in the Holy Spirit. Jesus's silence/reserve with regard to the Spirit can be interpreted as a profound passage, a great turning point, that goes from the ancient charismatic experience to a new experience of the Spirit. Jesus shows … that he does not fit in with the model of the ancient charismatics, who were men of the Spirit, entirely subjected to Him. The relationship between Jesus and the Spirit is unique. We would say neither that the Christ of the gospels appears as a simple man subjected to the Holy Spirit, nor that the Holy Spirit appears as a functionary of the Christ. The novelty of the Christian revelation related to the Spirit consists in the fact that it relates not just to the Christ-Spirit relationship; it is defined in a trinitarian framework and, that is, in a dialogical relationship between Jesus and the Father.[47]

Bordoni's point should be borne in mind if we are to interpret a certain reading of the identity of the mission of Jesus that is today emphasized: Jesus as "man of the Spirit." This perspective, on the basis of the New Testament witness, correctly emphasizes the pneumatic quality of the ministry of Jesus, his obedience to the Father in constant openness to the presence and action of the Spirit on and in him. But this should not lead us to underestimate the originality of the *exousía* of Jesus which comes to him from the Father, and which he exercises as his own inasmuch as he is Son. It is precisely the quality and the trinitarian form of the identity and mission of Jesus—which are defined as such in relation to God/*Abbà* and the Spirit—that make his uniqueness evident.

46. Ibid., 234.
47. Bordoni, *La cristologia nell'orizzonte dello Spirito*, 49–50.

On the basis of the pre-Paschal testimony, the Spirit who manifests himself and acts in the messianic ministry of Jesus should be understood above all as the grace and the power coming from God, of the faithfulness of Jesus to the will of the Father, of the sovereign freedom and unconditional love which guide and illuminate his mission, to the offering of his life for his brothers which is completed in his death on the cross. In this perspective, Jesus of Nazareth presents himself on the scene of the history of Israel as provider and protagonist of the coming of YHWH into the midst of his people in that Spirit in virtue of which he lives his singular relation as Son with God/*Abbà* and operates his messianic ministry, and at the same time as the one who is destined to be the mediator of the eschatological gift of the Spirit, from God/*Abbà*, to the messianic community.

The Transfiguration

An event in the life of Jesus to which the Gospel tradition attaches particular significance is the episode of the transfiguration (Mk 8:2–8; Mt 17:1–13; Lk 9:28–36). This is positioned between the scene of the baptism, the beginning of his messianic ministry, and his agonized prayer in Gethsemane, the prelude to his crucifixion and death. Here too, as had been the case with the baptism, the light of Easter is projected backward. Nevertheless it is certainly valid to see synoptic narration as revelation of the Father and a real experience of Jesus, to which the apostles Peter, James, and John are eyewitnesses. As had happened in the baptism, here too the heavenly voice testifies that Jesus is the Son: "but now his filial reality becomes visible—so to speak—even in his humanity on the road toward the passion and the eternal transfiguration of the resurrection."[48]

A few words help to contextualize the event. In the synoptic narrations, the transfiguration follows the first announcement of the passion, after the confession of the messianicity of Jesus on the part of Simon Peter at Caesarea Philippi (see Mk 8:27–33 and parallels). It is almost like an anticipation of the destiny to which Jesus' *via dolorosa* will lead, and renewed confirmation on the part of the Father that the revelation of his will is to take the unprecedented form of Jesus' future suffering in Jerusalem. It is probable, further, that this moment of the ministry of Jesus is to be temporally located at the end of the Jewish Feast of Booths (*Sukkot*). As Jean Daniélou explains, the "booths" of the festival recall the protection that YHWH offered Israel in the desert, but also the anticipation of the tents in which the just will live in the kingdom to come.[49] The ref-

48. Rossé, *Il vangelo di Luca: Commento esegetico e teologico*, 339 (own trans.).

49. Jean Daniélou, *Bible et liturgie, la théologie biblique des sacrements et des fetes d'après les*

erence to a "high mountain" where the transfiguration takes place recalls the theophany of Sinai, where YHWH revealed himself and spoke with Moses and Elijah.

The event is embedded in the context of the nocturnal prayer (as in Lk 6:12 and 22:39), as is clear from Luke's account: "Now Peter and his companions were weighed down with sleep; but ... they had stayed awake" (9:32). The evangelist emphasizes the fact that it is precisely "while he was praying" (9:29, as in 3:21 following the baptism) that "the appearance [*eîdos*] of his face [*prósōpon*] changed."[50] Jesus' prayer is therefore the moment and place of transfiguration, the revelation of the Father in the face of the Son.

Jesus is in a state of prayer, and is spiritually transported in the *Abbà*. It is in this act that he "changes appearance" and is transfigured in glory. The glory is God himself in his splendor of light and holiness that shines out from him in the Spirit and transfigures whoever contemplates his face. The face of Jesus that thus is changed is therefore illuminated, invested, and transformed by the glory that radiates from the face of the Father. This point is decisive: the source of this glory is, of course, God, but the same glory shines here from the heart of Jesus. It is entirely directed toward the Father and thence engulfs all of his being. In other words, this glory is not simply something external and temporary (as with Moses on Sinai), but is the intimate and definitive reality: "light from light" one might say, using the expression from the symbol of Nicaea.[51]

It is this glory that the three apostles contemplate on the face of Christ, together with Moses and Elijah (the Law and the prophets). Mo-

Pères de l'Eglise (Paris: Cerf, 1951); translated into Italian as *Bibbia e liturgia: la teologia biblica dei sacramenti e delle feste secondo i Padri della Chiesa* (Milan: Vita e Pensiero, 1958), 451–59; see also Joseph Ratzinger, *Jesus of Nazareth* (New York: Doubleday, 2007).

50. Luke does not use the verb which Mark and Matthew use here: *meta-morphéo*, transform. Perhaps this was to avoid confusion with pagan metamorphosis?

51. As Ghislain Lafont notes, 2 Cor 3:7–4:6 offers perhaps the best comment on this episode of the transfiguration: "Now if the ministry of death, chiseled in letters on stone tablets, came in glory so that the people of Israel could not gaze at Moses's face because of the glory of his face, a glory now set aside, how much more will the ministry of the Spirit come in glory? ... And all of us, with unveiled faces, seeing the glory of the Lord as though reflected in a mirror, are being transformed into the same image from one degree of glory to another; for this comes from the Lord, the Spirit.... For it is the God who said, 'Let light shine out of darkness,' who has shone in our hearts to give the light of the knowledge of the glory of God in the face of Jesus Christ" (own trans.). We can also recall the prologue of John's Gospel here: "And the Word became flesh and lived among us, and we have seen his glory, the glory as of a father's only son, full of grace and truth" (1:14) and the dynamic of reciprocal glorification between the Father and the Son that is central to the Gospel of John, as we will see below. We should also mention, finally, 2 Pt 1:16–18: "For we did not follow cleverly devised myths when we made known to you the power and coming of our Lord Jesus Christ, but we had been eyewitnesses of his majesty. For he received honor and glory from God the Father when that voice was conveyed to him by the Majestic Glory, saying, 'This is my Son, my Beloved, with whom I am well pleased.' We ourselves heard this voice come from heaven, while we were with him on the holy mountain."

ses, remember, is the one who wished to see the glory of God, but was only permitted to see the hind parts (Ex 33:18, 22), and Elijah the one who was carried away on a chariot of fire toward the heavens. The presence of Moses and Elijah and Peter's reference to the "meeting tent," the place of the presence of God among human beings, emphasize the fact that the transfiguration of Jesus anticipates and manifests the fulfillment of the covenant that God had promised. Jesus speaks with Moses and Elijah of his exodus (*éxodos*) (Lk 9:31) which will be accomplished at Jerusalem. Thus it is clear that the theme of the Law and the prophets is the hope of Israel that is to be fulfilled in the Easter of Jesus.

For the apostles, it is the experience of the goodness that is beauty (*kalòn estín*, "it is beautiful," they exclaim). They foretaste their future dwelling in a new vital and pneumatic space, which is the space of the relationship between the Father and the Son. Their first reaction is to capture the presence of the glory, making three tents. They had failed to understand that there was only one tent "the greater and perfect tent not made with hands" (Heb 9:11), namely the body of Christ that was to be offered on the cross (see Heb 10:5). They will be able to participate in the glory that shines from the Father unto the Son only through the tent of his body offered in sacrifice and glorified in the resurrection.

This is the meaning of the cloud that enfolds them. It is a sign of the glory of God, as it was in the First Testament, in the exodus from Egypt and in the dedication of the Temple: "The revelation of God is revealed as it veils itself, and it veils itself as it reveals itself, just as his power is made manifest emptying itself and his love saves us by losing itself."[52] The glory of the cross is thus preannounced. A voice from the cloud, as in the baptism, proclaims the sonship of Jesus: "This is my Son, my Chosen; listen to him!" (Lk 9:35). The Father invites us to listen to the word of revelation and salvation which the Son will speak eschatologically in his name: it is the word of the cross and resurrection. The apostles see and listen. But in the end Jesus remains alone, determined and ready to face the destiny that awaits him.

Jesus' prayer is a space of transfiguration as reciprocal indwelling of the Father in the Son and of the Son in the Father in virtue of the Spirit. This prayer on Mount Tabor offers to the contemplation of the apostles the splendor of the truth and grace that it expresses. It also announces, however, the deepest and most paradoxical meaning, because it is directed toward Gethsemane and the cry of solitude of the cross. The path to glory passes through the exodus of the cross: the full and unconditional obedience of the Son to the will of the Father.

52. *Una comunità legge il vangelo di Luca* (Bologna: EDB, 1986), 1:347 (own trans.).

In the transfiguration, therefore, the unique quality of the relationship between Jesus and the Father comes into extraordinary light: communion which is mutual and mysterious "in-existence" of one in the other which is brought about in the free obedience of the Son to the will of the Father to the point of self-sacrifice. The manifestation of glory and the clouds indicate the making visible of the mystery, in the intimate unity of the Father and the Son (see Jn 17:22), which alludes to the Holy Spirit who, from the Father, illuminates and transfigures the flesh and the face of the Son. His final identity, nevertheless, remains veiled in the abyss of the divine life.

CHAPTER 14

The Paschal Event

Act of the Father, Son, and Holy Spirit

I now come to the culmination of the trinitarian reading of the ministry of Jesus proposed up to this point, and devote myself to the New Testament witness to the final outcome of his mission: the Easter events, the death and resurrection. On the basis of this, the entire and definitive theological truth of the entire Christ-event will be reread. This is not the place to analyze the reasons that brought about the intensification of the conflict between Jesus and the political-religious establishment of his time that stand behind his trial by the Jewish and Roman authorities and the condemnation to a humiliating death on the cross. It is sufficient to state, synthetically, that the rejection on the part of the leaders of Israel relates precisely to his witness and authority as the eschatological emissary as Son of the *Abbà*.

Jesus, in fact, according to the accounts handed down to us by the synoptics (see Mk 14:61–64 and parallels), in the course of the interrogation in the presence of the Sanhedrin, makes it quite clear that for the members of the supreme council of Israel his self-consciousness regarding the meaning of his mission, that of the Son of Man to whom YHWH had entrusted the eschatological inauguration of the kingdom, was both unequivocal and unacceptable. The high priest for this reason defines his claims as "blasphemy," which then becomes the formal reason for his condemnation.

The Johannine witness is in agreement and makes explicit the theological implication of the filial witness of Jesus as a declaration of his unique relationship with God/*Abbà*. Following the miracle at the pool at Bethsaida the evangelist explains, "For this reason the Jews were seeking all the more to kill him, because he was not only breaking the sabbath, but was also calling God his own Father, thereby making himself equal to God" (Jn 5:18), The Jews respond to Pilate who says that he cannot find Jesus guilty of any crime: "We have a law, and according to that law he ought to die because he has claimed to be the Son of God" (Jn 19:7).

Let us try, therefore, in the light of the foregoing, to go to the heart of what happens in the passion and death of Jesus: looking firstly at the meaning that he himself explicitly attributed to this decisive moment in his mission, in particular at the Last Supper that anticipates and interprets it (this is the point of view of the pre-Paschal Jesus) and then at the meaning of the revelatory event of the Easter of death and resurrection as it was interpreted by the post-Paschal community, faithful to the intention of Jesus and in the light of the appearances of the risen one and of the Pentecostal gift of the Spirit.

Jesus Faced with His Passion and Death

The biblical data show that Jesus is aware of the dramatic conclusion toward which the growing conflict with the Jewish authorities, due to the uniqueness of his mission and consequently the uniqueness of his filial identity, is leading. He freely hands himself over to the fulfillment of the mission that he receives from the *Abbà*. It is this fact, in the final analysis, that brings about the plot that will lead to his execution (see Mk 14:1–2; Mt 26:1–5; Lk 22:1–2; Jn 11:47, 49).

The destiny that awaits Jesus, his death, is then progressively integrated, in a fully conscious way, by Jesus into his messianic project. His death should not be understood as an accident or a mistake. Through his prayer and his actions in faithfulness to his mission, Jesus lives in full and transparent understanding of the Father's plan of salvation, in communion with which he works and acts. From the event of the confession of Caesarea onward, according to the synoptics, he announces to his disciples three times that the "the Son of Man must undergo great suffering, and be rejected by the elders, the chief priests, and the scribes, and be killed" (Mk 8:31; see also 9:31 and 10:33–34). He invites them to follow him on this path: "If any want to become my followers, let them deny themselves and take up their cross and follow me. For those who want to save their life will lose it, and those who lose their life for my sake, and for the sake of the gospel, will save it" (Mk 8:34–35 and parallels; see Jn 15:13). This death as supreme gift of self is therefore foreseen and chosen by Jesus as the fulcrum and seal of his mission in favor of humanity in obedience to the Father.

On several occasions, Jesus expresses the conviction that obedience to the will of God in the inauguration of his kingdom among humanity comes at the cost of faithfulness to the point of death (see Jn 10:17–18). "It is necessary" (*deî*) that that this happen, he affirms, evoking the divine passive of the First Testament. In the theological optics of revelation, this "need" does not mean submitting to an impersonal fate. It means rather the infallible carrying out on God's part of the design of salvation that the *Abbà* has gratuitously set out and which is now realized thanks to the Son's free obedience. The latter's fully aware journey toward death speaks of faithfulness to the plan of the Father and redemptive solidarity with human beings. Jesus lives this with particular reference to the biblical paradigm of the rejected and persecuted prophet (see Lk 13:32–33; Mt 23:37); he speaks of the chalice that he is called to drink in order to carry out the will of the Father (see Mk 10:38 and parallels); he tells the parable of the wicked vinedressers (Mk 12:1–9) as an eschatological interpretation of the history of Israel in its relationship with God. In this final case, it is clear that the chosen son is killed outside the vineyard, which stands for his rejection and exclusion from the people of the covenant. As it happens, he will be led outside the walls of Jerusalem, the holy city, and executed on unholy ground: Golgotha.

Further, the rejection that Jesus undergoes is not only integrated in his project, but he also lives it and announces it as the way through which God carries out his plan of salvation: "The stone that the builders rejected" precisely in this way "has become the cornerstone" (see Mt 21:42). Already in Deutero-Isaiah the redemptive and expiatory value of the mission of the servant sent by YHWH is foretold: through his sufferings and his death the servant would lead Israel to understand its sin and return to its Lord.[1] Jesus applies this figure to himself: "For the Son of Man came not to be served but to serve, and to give his life as a ransom for many" (Mk 10:45). With his passion and death he penetrates into the abyss of the mystery of iniquity, that is, the obstinate hardness of heart in rejecting God's plan, of dia-bolic action (separating and counterposing) of the "prince of this world," of fatal ignorance of the love of God on the part of human beings, to which he himself makes reference on the cross: "Father, forgive them; for they do not know what they are doing" (Lk 23:34). Jesus immerses himself in this mystery of iniquity and suffers the tragic consequences in order to illuminate and redeem, with the light and strength of obedience to the Father and of solidarity with human beings, their situation of shadow and the closure of sin.

It is therefore of decisive importance to understand how Jesus faces his death fully aware of the eschatological significance that this has assumed in the Father's plan. Paradoxically, it will be precisely his death—lived in this way—that will bring about the coming of the kingdom of

1. See Is 53:1–12: "Surely he has borne our infirmities and carried our diseases;.... But he was wounded for our transgressions, crushed for our iniquities; upon him was the punishment that made us whole,.... When you make his life an offering for sin, he shall see his offspring, and shall prolong his days; through him the will of the Lord shall prosper."

God. The "sign of Jonah" is therefore realized in him: "For just as Jonah was three days and three nights in the belly of the sea monster, so for three days and three nights the Son of Man will be in the heart of the earth" (Mt 12:38–40). It is precisely the salvific significance of his story that is outlined in the parable of the seed: "Very truly, I tell you, unless a grain of wheat falls into the earth and dies, it remains just a single grain; but if it dies, it bears much fruit. Those who love their life lose it, and those who hate their life in this world will keep it for eternal life" (Jn 12:24–25).

According to this logic, in the prophecies of the passion, there is always, at least implicitly, the hope of the resurrection. Jesus' hope, expressed in his self-entrustment to the Father in obedience to his will when faced with death, is witness to and announcement of the fulfillment of the beatitude proclaimed with respect to the poor and forgiveness offered to sinners. So too, the miracles of the resurrection carried out in the course of his ministry (the daughter of Jairus, Mk 5:21–24, 35–43 and parallels; the son of the widow of Nain, Lk 7:11–17; Lazarus, Jn 11:1–44) announce that the inauguration of the kingdom is effective even against death, the ultimate and definitive condemnation of humankind (see Mk 9:10). The resurrection of Jesus is the anticipation of the resurrection promised by God for the end of times.

The Paschal Meal, Interpretive Key of the New Covenant

In this context, the meaning that Jesus attributes to the Paschal meal is central. It is no accident that he concludes his personal story, which had begun on the banks of the lake in Galilee, in Jerusalem on the occasion of the most important feast for Israel. "According to Jewish expectation, the liberating Messiah was to manifest himself at Jerusalem on a night of the Paschal Feast. This is recalled in the ancient Aramaic paraphrase of Ex 12:42."[2] This is not the first time that the Gospels narrate a coming of Jesus for the Passover (see Lk 2:41–50; Jn 2:13–22; 6:1–14; 11:55). But the last Passover supper of Jesus (see Mk 14:22–24; Mt 26:26–28; Lk 22:19–20; 1 Cor 11:23–26), both in relation to his earlier history and in relation to what would take place afterward, takes on decisive value.

In the Paschal meal, in fact, Jesus anticipates and illustrates the definitive, permanent, salvific truth of his death. This is one of the strongest and clearest signs that tell us of Jesus' awareness of the eschatological meaning

2. Rinaldo Fabris, "Pasqua," in *Nuovo dizionario di teologia biblica*, ed. P. Rossano, G. Ravasi, A. Girlanda (Milan: Paoline, 1988), 1120 (own trans.). See also Heinz Schürmann, *Wie hat Jesus seinen Tod bestanden und verstanden?: eine methodische Besinnung* (Leipzig: St. Benno-Verlag, 1974).

of his death. The synoptics (Mk 14:22–25; Lk 22:15–20; Mt 26:26–29) and Paul (1 Cor 11:23–26) transmit the story in a stylized manner that recalls the way in which the memory of this event had come to be celebrated in the first Christian communities. John does not recount the event itself, but offers two illuminating references that explore its significance: the washing of the feet (Jn 13:1–20), signifying service that pushes itself to the gift of one's life which Jesus offers in the event of the cross; and the discourse on the bread of life (Jn 6:26–59), where Jesus presents himself as the bread that definitively gives the fullness of life to a travelling people, with reference to the episode of the manna in the desert. In the Paschal meal is concentrated the whole meaning of Jesus' mission. He illumines and enriches the interpretation of the event by linking it to the liberating and prophetic meaning of the exodus Passover. He himself offers the decisive interpretation of his own passion, death, and resurrection actualizing and eschatologically resignifying the memorial of the ancient exodus Passover in the light of the prophecy of the new covenant that is accomplished accordingly in him. In Jesus' self-consciousness, and in the witnesses of the apostolic faith, the Passover meal stands out clearly as the sign and act destined to transmit and perpetuate the fulfillment of the history of salvation in time.[3] In this sense, it unveils the richness of the salvific significance of the event that Jesus is about to live.

(1) From the soteriological point of view: Jesus identifies himself, first of all, with the Paschal lamb who, when sacrificed, gives its life for humanity, in the line of the suffering servant of YHWH (Is 52:13–53:12) who takes the sins of many on himself. (2) From the revelatory-theological point of view: his Passover is understood as an exodus from this world and return to the Father (see Jn 13:1), from whom he had come. It is precisely in the fulfillment of his will that the glorification of his name consists. (3) From the anthropological and ecclesiological point of view: the event constitutes both the passage of humans from slavery to sin to the freedom of the sons and daughters of God, in the pouring out of the Spirit "without measure" as the people of the new and definitive covenant. (4) From the eschatological point of view, finally: it expresses and proleptically anticipates the promise of the eschatological banquet thanks to Jesus, in communion with the Father and in the joy of the Holy Spirit.

All of this is expressed in the words over the bread and wine. The bread is the sign of the gift of life. The wine, which refers to the blood which is about to be spilled, is the sign of the eschatological communion between God and humanity. The atmosphere of the event preannounces the approach of the messianic joy that will be brought about through

3. See Mk 14:22–25; Lk 22:15–20; Mt 26:26–29; as well as Jn 13:1–20 and 1 Cor 11:23–26.

the sacrifice of the cross. In the light of the Last Supper, Jesus' Passover is therefore illuminated prophetically in its eschatological significance as decisive *kairós* of the coming of the kingdom of God that he announced. It revealed the very depths of the love of God/*Abbà* for humankind, indeed the God who is love (see 1 Jn 4:8, 16), and founds and illustrates the new commandment of love as the law of life of the people of God (see Jn 13:1–20:34).

Two Criteria of Interpretation

From the methodological point of view, we must keep two criteria in mind in order to ensure a correct and complete phenomenological and theological reading of the Paschal event in its relation to God as Trinity. First of all, we need to consider two overlapping points of view which, in point of fact, are indissolubly bound together in their telling of the Easter event. The first of these is the narration from the point of view of Jesus' self-consciousness, that is, his fulfillment of the mission that he received from the Father despite the opposition to this by the Jewish authorities. The second is the discernment of the theological meaning of the Paschal event in the light of the resurrection of Jesus, of his living presence at the heart of the apostolic community and the Pentecostal gift of the Holy Spirit. The first point of view, obviously, is prevalent especially in the Gospels. The second is more evident in the witness of Paul and in the apostolic writings, but also in the rereading of the event which—on the basis of the resurrection—informs the telling of the passion and death in the Gospels.

The second criterion concerns the trinitarian reading of the Paschal event. The telling of the Passover touches Jesus in the first place and thus must be read in a primarily Christological perspective. But the story of the passion, death, resurrection, and pouring out of the Spirit sees the Father and the Holy Spirit as co-agonists in intimate relationship with the Son made flesh who is the protagonist. Even if they remain in the background, while the figure of Christ is in the foreground, their presence and action are decisive compared with the many other actors involved: the Jewish leaders, the Roman authorities, the crowd, the apostles, the women, and—even if he is not clearly invoked—the "prince of this world."

The meaning of the event of Golgotha will remain unclear, or at best understood in a merely partial or distorted way, if one does not grasp the relationship that unfolds between Jesus, the Father, and the Spirit. For this reason, Easter is a trinitarian event because it "is the unique and essential relationship of Jesus to the Father and to the Spirit that gives a new and unique dimension to his 'being for us'" lived to the very end on the wood of the cross.[4] The presence and action of the Father, of Jesus, and of the Spirit should not be understood or expressed in an isolated manner, but in the reciprocal relation of one to the other. What is required, therefore, is that we realize in obedience to the deepest intention of the New Testament witness a dramatic and co-agonist reading of the Paschal event that permits us to draw out the fullness of the revelation of the trinitarian God's love which is realized in it.

In the synoptic accounts, but also in John and indirectly in the Pauline correspondence, Jesus' Passover is presented as the act of the Father, the Son, and the Holy Spirit: the culmination of the revelation of God/*Abbà* in Jesus and the supreme glorification of his name (see Jn 12:28) in the communication of his life to humanity through the eschatological pouring out of the Spirit. It is an act that involves first of all the Father, and should be understood in the context of the salvific plan of YHWH for the messiah, that is, the Son of Man; but also as an act of the Son, inasmuch as it is Jesus who freely offers himself to death in obedience to the Father, thus revealing "to the very end" his mercy, and it is, finally, the act of the Spirit, inasmuch as it is the Spirit who, coming from the Father, inspires and gives form to the free and full gift of himself on the part of Jesus, making of him, immolated and glorified, the personal principle of the eschatological effusion of forgiveness and total and definitive self-gift, from God, to humanity. Bearing in mind the keywords which, as we will see, express the co-agonistic and dramatic action of the three in the Paschal event, we can offer this general grid.

The Father	*The Son*		*The Holy Spirit*
love	freedom		consignment
giving	self-giving		making oneself gift
		passive	
silence	abandonment	↗ ↘	thirst
		active (= faith)	
resurrection	unfolded sonship		eschatological outpouring

FIGURE 2. The Paschal Event

4. Marcello Bordoni, *Gesù di Nazareth: Signore e Cristo*, vol. 2: *Gesù al fondamento della cristologia* (Perugia: Herder-Università Lateranense, 1982), 450–51 (own trans.).

The Paschal Event Act of the Father

Jesus' death on the cross represents, in the first place, a radical and decisive question mark placed at the end of his whole life and in particular on the revelation that he offered, in himself, of God as *Abbà*. The fact that he dies in this particular and tragic way would seem to bear witness to the failure of his mission before human beings and, even more, before God. Such a death seems to prove his messianic pretense and filial *exousía* empty. For the New Testament, Jesus' passion and death constitute the crucial trial that his whole mission goes through: this mission, as the episode of Gethsemane shows, immerses itself in the abyss of suffering, solitude, and death in naked and full conformity with the will of the Father.

The Fulfillment of the Plan of Love of the *Abbà*

Analyzing the pre-Paschal tradition, it becomes clear that Jesus interpreted and lived the destiny of passion and death imposed upon him by the Jewish authorities as obedience to the precise will of the Father: as obedience and fulfillment of his plan of salvation which through him was being offered to humanity. Of this I have already spoken. Even the witness of the Last Supper, as has been emphasized, certifies that it is precisely the offer of his life to the point of spilling his blood that represents, for Jesus, the hour and paradoxical form of the inauguration of the new covenant. The event of the suffering and death of Jesus are therefore to be understood within the context of the horizon of the gratuitous and unitary plan of salvation that YHWH is bringing about eschatologically through the messianic ministry of the Son.

It is not necessary, therefore, to interpret it as an act of vengeful justice or as the punitive anger of God: all of this is absent in the pre-Paschal witness. On the contrary, from the point of view of the *Abbà*, Jesus' death on the cross should be interpreted as the supreme demonstration of God's love and mercy, the expression of his will to be close to humanity in forgiveness and salvation, witnessed through the Son and pushed by him to the very extreme. It is also—in the mysterious and unquestionable horizon of his divine plan of salvation—the paradoxical instrument through which (i.e., through the Son) the new and definitive covenant will spring forth.

It is within this perspective that the post-Paschal interpretation of the apostolic church understands the death of Jesus, from the point of view of God-Father, as the offer that he makes of his Son in loving favor of human beings. In this perspective, the fourth Gospel states in the clearest way possible: "Indeed, God did not send the Son into the world to condemn the world, but in order that the world might be saved through him" (Jn 3:17). Paul too, overcome by the unheard of greatness of the gift that God made of Himself in the Son, exclaims: "He who did not withhold his own Son, but gave him up for all of us, will he not with him also give us everything else?" (Rom 8:32), wishing thus to show that if God gave that which is dearest to him, his Son, every other gift is included and infinitely overcome in this. The entire New Testament witness describes the death of Jesus as the eschatological offer (the almost technical verb used is *paradídōmi*) that the Father makes of the Son made flesh for the salvation of humanity.[5]

The Silence of the *Abbà*, Witness to His Fatherhood

Notwithstanding this, at first glance, the silence and concealment of the Father—the God so close as to be known as *Abbà*—in the culminating event of the ministry of Jesus certainly appears disconcerting. In point of fact, the *Abbà* does not intervene to save the Son. For this reason, those passing by the cross deride him whom to their eyes appears as a false messiah. They conclude that he is truly guilty of blasphemy, confirming his accusation and condemnation (Mk 14:61–64; 15:29–32 and parallels). In this way God does in fact abandon Jesus to his ignoble destiny, as the cry from the cross that Mark and Matthew attribute to Jesus suggests: "My God, my God, why have you forsaken me?" (see Mk 15:34; Mt 27:46). I will speak more of this below.

Yet, in the logic of the *kérygma* and praxis of Jesus, we must ask ourselves an important question: is not this the way that the "nonpaternalistic" paternity of the *Abbà* in relation to Jesus manifests itself? In point of fact, rather than protecting Jesus and freeing him from the trial, God shares in the passion and death in an inexpressible way. In this way he allows Jesus to fully and faithfully fulfill the mission that was entrusted to him. The silence and concealment of God, on the cross, his "abandonment" of Jesus to the atrocious trial of feeling himself forgotten, left alone, even rejected: these are paradoxically the truest sign of his being *Abbà* to the Son.

The Paternity of the *Abbà* in the Resurrection of the Son

Only once Jesus has tasted the very dregs of the chalice of suffering and forsakenness, in the extreme act of free obedience to the divine plan, does the Father intervene. First Jesus experiences death—the common and painful inheritance of a humanity that had distanced itself from God

5. See Wiard Popkes, *Christus traditus: eine Untersuchung zum Begriff der Dahingabe im Neuen Testament* (Zürich: Zwingli Verlag, 1967).

through sin—then God intervenes. The resurrection of Jesus is a cry of joy, exultation, and gratitude that explodes on Easter morning and illuminates the whole New Testament witness: "Jesus of Nazareth, who was crucified. He has been raised" (see Mk 16:6). This is the proof that God offers of the justice, truth, and eschatological finality of the mission of Jesus. It is the unequivocal seal (see Jn 6:27) that the *Abbà* places on the announcement and the actions of Jesus, on his existence and his faithfulness to the plan of salvation and love, which had led him to the abyss of forsakenness.

It is God the Father, according to the New Testament, who raised his Son, Jesus.[6] Precisely in this way he reveals himself in the most evident way as *Abbà*, the holy, all-powerful, and merciful God who "who gives life to the dead and calls into existence the things that do not exist" (Rom 4:17). He conquers death and sin with love and forgiveness, in the Son made flesh, bringing about the definitive life that transcends him and fulfills it.

In the inseparability of the two dimensions of death and resurrection, the Paschal event is therefore, first of all and essentially the place and culminating moment of the revelation of God announced by Jesus as *Abbà*. The fact that the eschatological seal of approval that the Father places on the mission and existence of Jesus is manifested in his resurrection constitutes the irruption of a novelty of a new life that has the taste of eternity—the taste that overcomes death and which Israel expected for the end of times—which in Jesus has now become reality in his humanity glorified by the Spirit, welcomed into the bosom of the Father and present and operative among human beings in the announcement of this word of salvation and in the sign of bread and wine.

The Paschal Event Act of the Son

Turning our attention now to Jesus, we can say that his messianic ministry and his existence constitute the eschatological confirmation of his identity and filial freedom in the definitive obedience of love to the Father.

The Death of Jesus, Act of the Son's Freedom

The death on the cross is, for Jesus, a free and conscious choice. It is true that he is captured, condemned to death, and murdered by human beings. It is also true, however, that all of this is in conformity with the divine plan of salvation and is, consequently, an act of obedience on the part of Jesus to God/*Abbà*. But it is Jesus himself who freely decides to give his

6. The resurrection of Jesus is described as the work of the Father in the kerygmatic speeches of the Acts of the Apostles (2:22–36; 3:12–26; 4:8–12; 5:29–32; 13:16–42) and in numerous other places in the New Testament (see, for example, 1 Thes 1:10; 1 Cor 6:14; 15:15; 2 Cor 4:14; Gal 1:1; Rom 4:24; 10:9; 1 Pt 1:21).

life in obedience to the will of the Father. As he himself declares in the fourth Gospel, "No one takes it from me, but I lay it down of my own accord" (Jn 10:18).

The choice to freely and consciously face the tragic destiny of death, as a consequence of the unprecedented announcement of the forgiving closeness of God to human beings in the Son—beginning with the poor and with sinners—a choice that is definitively assumed and expressed in the prayer at Gethsemane (see Mk 14:32–42 and parallels), is coherent with the messianic choice that Jesus makes from the very beginning of his ministry, and is in conformity with the will of the Father, as testified by the narrations of the baptism and the temptations, the predictions of the passion, the Paschal meal, and the prayer of Gethsemane.

Jesus' free decision is determined by his relationship of faithfulness and obedience in love for the Father and is expressed in his unconditional love for human beings (see Jn 13:1). Faithfulness to the Father, not only because he freely adheres to the Father's plan of salvation, but precisely because through this faithfulness he announces and gives witness to the coming of the kingdom even when he can already perceive that this faithfulness will cost him his life. Love for human beings, therefore, pushes him to risk his life in order to give witness to the mercy of the *Abbà*, to tell of the human vocation to be sons and daughters, and communicate to all the life that the Father gives him as Son. Jesus is condemned as a blasphemer and killed through the humiliating penalty of the cross, and thus his solidarity with mankind is pushed to the extreme as he identifies himself with the least fortunate of humanity, with those who are discarded and rejected. The experience of death on the cross is, therefore, for Jesus the limit experience of his being the Son, the limit experience of his freedom, his faithfulness and obedience of the Father, his solidarity and identification with human beings: "No one has greater love than this, to lay down one's life for one's friends" (Jn 15:13).

The Self-Entrustment to God of the Forsaken One

This limit experience is, in the Markan and Matthean tradition, expressed through the cry of dereliction or forsakenness that Jesus emits on the cross. This cry, in reality, gives us access to the deepest theological truth of his death as the crucified one.[7] First of all, the experience of the forsakenness should be read, following the logic of the New Testament witness, from two complementary points of view: that of the objective theologi-

7. Gérard Rossé, *Il grido di Gesù in croce: una panoramica esegetica e teologica* (Rome: Città Nuova, 1984); and, by the same author, *Maledetto l'appeso al legno, Lo scandalo della croce in Paolo e in Matteo* (Rome: Città Nuova, 2006), and "Il grido di Gesù in croce. Approccio biblico," *Sophia* 1, no. 1 (2008): 47–60.

cal meaning which the event itself makes clear and that of the subjective theological meaning with which it is lived by Jesus. Although these two points of view should not be separated, they can be distinguished so as to penetrate the full depth of the event.

We begin with the first meaning. Death on the cross is not just any kind of death: it is the fruit of the condemnation of Jesus as a blasphemer, as a false prophet, as a fake messiah. Such a death has more than simply sociological relevance, as in Greek and Roman cultures, as the death sentence of slaves and of the worst criminals; it also has, from the Jewish point of view, a theological connotation.[8] The one "hung on a tree" is guilty of the most serious crimes against the covenant community and as such has been expelled from it and cursed by God.

The understanding of the death on the cross as that of one cursed by God is witnessed to by the fact that Jesus was brought to justice "outside the walls of the city" (see Mt 27:32 and Heb 13:12–13), that is outside the visible sign of the covenant between YHWH and his people. Paul explicitly makes this theological connection between the crucifixion and its specifically religious meaning, based on the text from Deuteronomy cited above. Thus in 2 Corinthians 5:21 we read: "For our sake he made him to be sin who knew no sin, so that in him we might become the righteousness of God," and in Galatians 3:13 we read: "Christ redeemed us from the curse of the law by becoming a curse for us—for it is written, 'Cursed is everyone who hangs on a tree.'" The death of the crucified one constitutes to the eyes of those who condemned him, precisely because it is a death on the cross, the clear and incontrovertible proof of the failure of his mission and of God's rejection of him.

The cry of forsakenness in the Gospels of Mark and Matthew It is in this context that we should read the experience that Jesus himself makes of his own death in the light of his relationship with God/*Abbà*. As the Markan and Matthean accounts of the passion tell it, from Gethsemane onward, Jesus is plunged into the most total solitude. Abandoned and rejected by the crowds who had previously welcomed him with cries of "Hosanna!" and had followed him, denied by the apostles, Jesus finds himself deprived also of his relationship with the Father. The cry of forsakenness, where Jesus addresses the one that he had always invoked as *Abbà* and now calls simply as God (*Elì* in Matthew and *Eloì* in Mark mean "my God"). It is true that this is a quotation of Psalm 22, but—as von Balthasar and Moltmann note—"it is not Jesus for the Psalm, but the Psalm for Jesus."[9]

8. See the classic study by Martin Hengel, *Crucifixion* (Philadelphia: Fortress Press, 1977).

9. It is worth recalling the words of John Paul II in *Salvifici Doloris*: "When Christ says: 'My God, My God, why have you abandoned me?,' his words are not only an expression of that aban-

In other words, it is not enough to interpret the experience of Jesus simply in the light of Psalm 22, where we find expressed the classical biblical theme of the suffering of the righteous one. Instead, in the context of the Gospel accounts and more in general, of the meaning of his whole ministry, it is important to interpret the experience that Jesus lives in the light of his unique relationship with the *Abbà*. In this perspective, the cry of forsakenness attests that Jesus lives the tragic experience of the non-intervention of God in his favor. The solitude in which his disciples and friends leave him, the mockery of his enemies, the recognition of the most complete failure of his proclamation, all of these should be held together in our understanding of Jesus' understanding of the atrocious and meaningless absolute dereliction.

The cry of forsakenness is not, however, a cry of desperation. Anything but! It is rather an invocation, a prayer, the extreme witness of faithfulness and love for the Father that Jesus expresses from the depths of the trial and darkness into which he had sunk. The real experience of forsakenness (and that is the situation of dereliction in which the Father leaves him) cannot be separated from his complete self-entrustment to God/*Abbà*. These are two faces of the same medal (Chiara Lubich). The forsakenness, in other words, expresses the radical dimension of passivity (Jesus forsaken by the Father), but also an equally radical activity (Jesus abandons himself, i.e., he entrusts himself, to the Father). Joachim Gnilka affirms: "Jesus, abandoned by all men, needed to enter into this last forsakenness by God, so as to be able to remain fully faithful to God to the end. Even if he is forsaken by God, he addresses his prayer and his lament to God, so that he can be seen not to have abandoned God."[10]

Self-entrustment to the Father in Luke's account In the account of the passion according to Luke, it is precisely his extreme self-entrusting to the Father that comes into focus. From the very beginning of the crucifixion scene (see 23:33–49), Luke emphasizes the self-entrusting to the Father with which Jesus lives the events that are befalling him ("Father, forgive them; for they do not know what they are doing," 23:34), and then the cer-

donment which many times found expression in the Old Testament, especially in the Psalms and in particular in that Psalm 22 [21] from which come the words quoted. One can say that these words on abandonment are born at the level of that inseparable union of the Son with the Father, and are born because the Father 'laid on him the iniquity of us all.' They also foreshadow the words of Saint Paul: 'For our sake he made him to be sin who knew no sin.' Together with this horrible weight, encompassing the 'entire' evil of the turning away from God which is contained in sin, Christ, through the divine depth of his filial union with the Father, perceives in a humanly inexpressible way this suffering which is the separation, the rejection by the Father, the estrangement from God. But precisely through this suffering he accomplishes the Redemption, and can say as he breathes his last: 'It is finished'" (par. 18); Encyclical Letter, February 11, 1984, available at www.vatican.va.

10. Joachim Gnilka, *Marco*, trans. Gianni Poletti (Assisi: Cittadella, 1987), 890 (own trans.).

tain hope with which Jesus speaks to one of the criminals crucified alongside him: "Truly I tell you, today you will be with me in Paradise" (23:43). It is not by chance that the first of these words is a prayer of Jesus to the Father for his executioners: "Father, forgive them!" This word is almost a compendium of the "good news" that the Nazarene had been bringing to the world. Luke's version presents Jesus, crucified with two criminals, one on his right and one on his left, as one of the transgressors (see Is 53:12). And it is from this situation that he gives everyone the forgiveness from the Father. Thus, he is the one who perfectly fulfills the teaching of love of enemy that he had taught (Lk 6:27, 35), but he also brings about the mission that God had entrusted to him: to save those who had been lost. The first word of Jesus from the cross in Luke's account is, therefore, the invocation of forgiveness addressed to the Father. This underlines not just the greatness and heroism of Jesus' forgiveness of his executioners, but can also be considered to be a word of revelation. By forgiving his enemies Jesus reveals himself to be "Son of the Most High" who makes it rain and makes the sun rise on the righteous and unrighteous (see Mt 5:45).

The solemn word of promise that responds to the humble and trusting request of the repentant criminal—"Truly I tell you, today you will be with me in Paradise"—is the culmination of the Lukan story. The mockery comes to a close and a reversal is brought about. It is almost an anticipation of the resurrection. It is the revelation of a hope that is certain and available to everyone, in whatever condition of distance from the Father imaginable. It is a clear and concrete revelation of the last human personal relationship that Jesus lived with a human being during his earthly mission, and the revelation of the infinite mercy of God toward the lost one. The parable of the prodigal son and the merciful Father, which Jesus recounts in Luke 15, becomes reality in the dialogue between him and the criminal: "But we had to celebrate and rejoice, because this brother of yours was dead and has come to life; he was lost and has been found" (Lk 15:32).

For Luke, as for Mark and Matthew, Jesus dies after crying out in a great voice (23:46a), but the meaning of this cry is clearly that of self-entrustment: "Father, into your hands I commend my spirit" (23:46b). This word seems to be intended as an inclusion with the first saying attributed to Jesus as a child, addressed to Mary and Joseph, when he had been found in the Temple in the midst of the teachers: "Why were you searching for me? Did you not know that I must be in my Father's house?" (Lk 2:49). The life of Jesus, from the beginning to the end, is nothing other than a single act of filial obedience to the Father's plan of love spelled out in time. On the cross, he reaches the endpoint of the mission that had been entrusted to him. His exodus toward the Father is happening. The central event of salvation is reaching its culmination. The last word of Jesus, prior to dying, like the first one, is a word addressed to the Father: it is a prayer addressed to him, drawn from Psalm 30. It does not express only the sentiment of trusting self-abandonment that Jesus lives in the moment of his death, but it also reveals his attitude of full acceptance and conformity to the will of salvation of the Father. In this Psalm, the psalmist expresses total trust in God who will free his life from dangers and will protect him from death. Jesus, instead, expresses this same trust even in the face of death. Thus, he gives to his final breath the meaning of the definitive self-gift to the Father. He affirms the certainty in the resurrection, manifesting from the heights of the cross to the world his identity as Son in the highest and simplest way possible.

All of this takes place, for Luke, in the dramatic context of the passion, which had already been preannounced in the prayer on the Mount of Olives (22:41–44), but which doubtless assumes the serene and trusting inflection of self-entrusting to the Father that is not only a constant throughout his existence, but which remains uninterrupted and undisturbed even in the trial on the cross. In any case, if we did not have the witness of Mark and Matthew about the cry of forsakenness, we would find ourselves without the extreme and raw depth of Jesus' trial lived in relationship with the Father and overcome in his definitive self-entrustment to him. The cry of forsakenness is like an open wound which shows us the mystery of God/*Abbà* whom Jesus reveals.

"Jesus forsaken is faith" If we look closely, Luke's emphasis on self-entrustment helps us to interpret the abandonment of Jesus as found in Mark and Matthew as an intense experience of faith. Indeed, as Chiara Lubich affirms with lapidary concision, "Jesus Forsaken is faith" because he consigns himself (re-abandons himself) to the Father in the very moment in which he feels himself to be abandoned by him. Here we may quote Jacques Guillet:

> To sink thus into the dishuman world, to allow oneself to be stripped of every defense, to fall naked into the horror of sin, all of this is to live in total purity the only link that unites him to God, the filial bond. This bond must appear as the only thing holding him up. As long as it is possible to attribute strength and action to Jesus himself, he has not fully revealed who God is, who the Father is for the Son, and the Son for the Father. The only way he can fully reveal all of this is if he dies, forsaken by the Father, rejected by human beings in order to gather them in his forgiveness. This act has all of the characteristics of faith: total gift of oneself to another, total dependence regarding men and events, rejection of one's personal projects, welcoming the future that comes from the fulfillment of

the Father's will. But it also brings the most supreme grade of certainty and lights of faith: certainty of being in the hands of the Other, responding entirely to his love, being his joy.[11]

The event of the forsakenness, lived by Jesus as unconditional self-entrustment to the Father, unveils the trinitarian depths of the relationship between Father and Son. It is the definitive expression of Jesus' freedom, obedience, and faith—and therefore his sonship. These express from the abyssal depths of human experience the fact that the cross for Jesus is not just physical death, but, as Paul intuits, the experience of the one who has become "a curse for us" (see Gal 3:13), one who has been "made to be sin on our behalf" (see 2 Cor 5:21).

Jesus thus lives in faith the experience of the silence of God and the rejection of humanity, in faithfulness to the Father and love for his brothers and sisters. The forsakenness, therefore, both on the part of the Father and on the part of the Son represents the heart of the Paschal event: the event which Jesus lives in faith and which speaks of the ultimate correspondence of the Son to the love/truth of God/*Abbà*.

The Resurrection of Jesus, Epiphany of His Sonship

Jesus, therefore, in the event of the forsakenness, shows himself to truly be the one he is from the beginning: the Son. It is not by chance that the Gospel of Mark, almost as a seal on the revelation that occurs with the death of Jesus, reports the witness of the centurion (a pagan) who, seeing him die in this way, exclaims: "Truly this man was God's Son!" (15:39). Thus Mark closes the great inclusion with which his Gospel is framed: the first verse "The beginning of the good news of Jesus Christ, the Son of God" is fulfilled in the event of the crucifixion. The crucified and forsaken one is the revelation of God/*Abbà*.

The Letter to the Hebrews emphasizes that Jesus, "Although he was a Son, he learned obedience through what he suffered" (Heb 5:8). It is thanks to this abyssal experience of suffering and forsakenness lived in obedience to the Father up to the death on the cross that Jesus matures and brings about in his humanity the full and definitive unfolding of his being Son. The resurrection is therefore the eschatological witness of his unique identity as Son of the *Abbà* who has come in the flesh (see Jn 1:14) and who died on the cross for us. The apostolic tradition expresses this truth interpreting the event of the resurrection of Jesus in the light of the expression of the messianic Psalm: "You are my son; today I have begotten you" (Ps 2:7; see Heb 1:5; 5:5; Acts 13:33; Rom 1:4).

11. Jacques Guillet, *La fede di Gesù Cristo*, trans. Mimmi Cassola (Milan: Jaca Book, 1982), 174–75 (own trans.).

I still need to say something about the relationship of reciprocity between God/*Abbà* and Jesus in the resurrection itself. Is the resurrection exclusively the work of the Father? Or is it, and in what sense, work of the Son too? If we look at the New Testament witness, we encounter, especially in the fourth Gospel, the consciousness of the inseparable correlation between the action of the Father and the action of the Son, a correlation that is visible in supreme form in the Paschal event. The resurrection is certainly the work of the Father, who, seeing Jesus, recognizes the Son "generating" him as such in the flesh, through the Spirit. But it is also work of the Son.

Already in John 5:26 we read: "For just as the Father has life [*zoe*] in himself, so he has granted the Son also to have life in himself." The original and permanent source of life is the Father, but from the beginning (*en arche*) the Son/*Lógos* lives together with the Father because he also has life (see 1:4), which he receives from the Father. The Paschal event witnesses the dynamic of love (*agápe*) in which the life of God consists and translates it historically into the flesh of Jesus. This life has its origin in the Father, who pours it out in the Son and from him made flesh shares it in the Spirit with humanity: "For this reason the Father loves me, because I lay down my life in order to take it up again. No one takes it from me, but I lay it down of my own accord. I have power to lay it down, and I have power to take it up again. I have received this command from my Father" (10:17–18). This does not simply mean that the Son acts "as if" he gives life: the Son really offers it, to the very end, *eis télos*. And it is really he who takes it up again. This because the life that he received from the Father is *agápe*: one has something when one gives it completely. In doing this the Son obeys the Father, and indeed does what he saw the Father doing (see Jn 5:19, "Very truly, I tell you, the Son can do nothing on his own, but only what he sees the Father doing"). The Father, in fact, has life in himself, and gives it to the Son, so that also the Son has it in himself and communicates it. Here we gain a sense of the deepest secret of the relationship between God/*Abbà* and the Son. Note that this, already implied in the names of the Father and the Son, comes into full light in the unfolding of the Paschal event.

In the final analysis, the death/resurrection of Jesus is the undeniable witness to the Gospel law that Jesus proposed to his disciples: "For those who want to save their life will lose it, and those who lose their life for my sake, and for the sake of the gospel, will save it" (Mk 8:35 and parallels). The fruit of the resurrection, the common work of the Father and the Son made flesh, is therefore the constitution of the latter in the full and mature measure of his filial existence expressed in a transfigured humanity.

This transformation operated by the power and glory of the love of God reaches the most intimate fibers of Jesus' existence. This transfiguration, according to the unanimous witness of the New Testament, is the work of the Holy Spirit.

The Paschal Event Act of the Spirit

The presence and activity of the Spirit, which are undoubtedly determinative throughout the messianic ministry of Jesus are equally so in the Paschal event. Indeed, they constitute, just as do the work of the Father and the Son, an intrinsic and constitutive dimension.[12]

The Self-Gift of Jesus in the Spirit

The action of the Spirit is unanimously attested in the resurrection of Jesus. As the apostle Paul affirms in his Letter to the Romans, Jesus is "declared to be Son of God with power according to the spirit of holiness by resurrection from the dead" (see 1:3–4). These words should be understood in the sense that the eschatological effusion of the Spirit in the messiah, manifested from the baptism onward as the permanent and dynamic reality through the course of the whole of Jesus' messianic ministry, reaches its culminating point in the Paschal event. Recognizing and constituting Jesus definitively as the Son made flesh in his Passover of death and resurrection, the Father communicates his Spirit, that is, his own life, to him in fullness and superabundance, so much so that the most primitive rereading of the Jesus-event is marked out in the New Testament by the two moments: *katà sárka* (= according to the flesh, the pre-Paschal Jesus) and *katà pneûma* (= according to the Spirit, the post-Paschal Jesus). This does not mean separating, however, the two moments: the Spirit presides over the entire earthly story of Jesus, and the risen one does not abandon the flesh of the incarnation and the crucifixion, but transforms it.

The extreme gift that the Son makes of himself in the passion and death is itself the work of the Holy Spirit. Jesus, as the Letter to the Hebrews recognizes, offers himself as victim to the Father, on the cross, by virtue of an "eternal Spirit" (9:14). This affirmation suggests a pneumatological interpretation of the self-sacrificing and redemptive pro-existence of Jesus, in the sense that it is the Spirit who guides and illuminates the freedom of Jesus, conforming it to the will of the Father to the point of the supreme gift of self. The Spirit, in other words, acts in the Paschal

12. See François-Xavier Durrwell, *L'Esprit Saint de Dieu* (Paris: Cerf, 1987), and *L'Esprit du Père et du Fils* (Paris: Médiaspaul, 1989); Jean Kockerols, *L'Esprit à la Croix: la dernière onction de Jésus* (Brussels: Editions Lessius, 1999).

event as the living principle of that love which, springing forth from the Father, forms the freedom and sustains Jesus' decision in giving his life for the salvation of human beings.

The Thirst of the Spirit

If the presence of the Spirit is, so to speak, tangible in the resurrection of Jesus—the Father raising the Son in the power of the Spirit, the risen Son pouring out on human beings the fullness of the Spirit that he received—it is also true that the presence and action of the Spirit in the passion, forsakenness, and death are mysterious. If the Father is silent and does not intervene in favor of the Son, and if the Son does not feel the closeness and support of the Father, this means that the Spirit—in the supreme moment of the trial—almost holds back the light that he irradiates and the force that he emanates. Even the Spirit lives, therefore, a *kénosis* in love. Never as in that moment, in fact, does he actively intercede with "sighs too deep for words" (see Rom 8:26).

This fact, on the level of the New Testament witness, appears to be attested by the request of the dying crucified one in the fourth Gospel: "I am thirsty" (Jn 19:28). Here, as in the cry of forsakenness in Mark and Matthew, there is a reference to Psalm 22 (verse 15: "my mouth is dried up like a potsherd, and my tongue sticks to my jaws; you lay me in the dust of death"). In the broader context of Johannine theology, however, this request of the one who had claimed to be the one giving "living water" (see Jn 4:10–13; 7:37) to whoever is thirsty himself becomes symbol of an ever greater thirst. Jesus experiences this thirst at the culmination of his passion: the thirst of living water, which is the Spirit, which springs up in him from the Father, giving life to his existence as Son.

Thus, whereas the Gospels of Mark and Matthew show in the cry of forsakenness that the event of the cross—in the experience of rejection by humanity, tragic physical, psychological, and spiritual suffering—affects the relationship of communion between Jesus and the Father, the Gospel of John hints that in the experience of dying Jesus does not enjoy the comfort of that Spirit who, coming from the Father, filled his life and illuminated his ministry. We can say that Mark and Matthew point to the Christological dimension of the Paschal event, while the fourth Gospel points to the pneumatological dimension of that event.

Here we can intuit something of the paradox of love that links the event of the cross to the gift of the Spirit. Jesus experiences, in the abyss of his forsakenness, the absence of intimacy of the Father. This is like the drying up within himself of his filial identity, the bubbling-forth source of the Spirit. It is in this way that Jesus becomes the mediator of that living water, the gift of the Father, the water capable of slaking the thirst of humanity. Once again, the evangelical law of losing in order to gain comes into evidence: Jesus loses the Spirit in himself in identifying himself with a humanity that is so far from the Father that he no longer senses that joy that, in communion with the Father, is the gift and fruit of the Holy Spirit. But it is precisely in this way that he receives it anew and in fullness from the Father, and consequently communicates it in fullness to human beings.

In other words, as Paul makes clear, it is the crucified one, who by being treated as "sin" and "curse" shares with human beings his relationship of love with the Father, and makes them through the Spirit and in the only-begotten Son who is "firstborn within a large family" (Rom 8:29), sons of the *Abbà*: "you have received a spirit of adoption. When we cry, 'Abbà! Father!' it is that very Spirit bearing witness with our spirit that we are children of God" (Rom 8:15–16).

The Crucified/Risen One Source of the Spirit

The Spirit is present in the Paschal event, finally, because Jesus, having received the fullness of the Spirit from the Father, is himself the one who in the resurrection pours that Spirit out on humanity. The Spirit, thus, who had been promised by the prophets to the messianic community of the final times, is poured out by God/*Abbà* through the crucified and risen Son. This is made clear, in the first place, in the speech that, according to the Acts of the Apostles, Peter makes at Pentecost in the first announcement of the resurrection. The descent of the Holy Spirit is connected to the death of Jesus on the cross and comes about through his risen self: "This Jesus God raised up, and of that all of us are witnesses. Being therefore exalted at the right hand of God, and having received from the Father the promise of the Holy Spirit, he has poured out this that you both see and hear" (Acts 2:32–33).

In Paul and John too, in more mature theological reflection, it is clear that it is Jesus crucified, constituted Lord (*Kýrios*) in the resurrection, who is the eschatological giver of the Spirit. In particular, John interprets thus the exclamation of Jesus on the final day of the Feast of Booths: "and let the one who believes in me drink. As the scripture has said, 'Out of the believer's heart shall flow rivers of living water'" (7:38).[13] The fourth

13. The differing ways in which this affirmation can be punctuated leads to two possible interpretations, depending on whether the promise of "rivers of living water" are understood to flow from Jesus' heart or that of those who believe in him. In the light of the Paschal scene as it is narrated in the fourth Gospel, it is plausible to think that the original reference is to the crucified Jesus, from whose side flow "blood and water" (see Jn 19:34), but also, through participation in him, that of those believers who, receiving the living water of the Spirit of Christ, experience the inexhaustible and always new flowing of this water.

Gospel comments on the previous saying of Jesus: "as yet there was no Spirit, because Jesus was not yet glorified" (7:39). It is on the cross, therefore, that Jesus gives the promised Spirit: the water that flows from his side mixed with blood, just like the "final breath of his life, becomes a sign of that Spirit, principle of life and truth, that he had announced ... and which, in the hour of his 'death-exaltation' he sends to the messianic community" represented by Mary and John at the foot of the cross.[14]

The theological significance of Jesus' "giving up of the Spirit" It is important to note that the fourth Gospel, the most theological and contemplative of the Gospels, without for this reason being less historical or trustworthy, after the long journey of interpretation that begins with the Gospel of Mark, and passes through those of Matthew and Luke, should reach this penetrating reading of what may be the most hidden but doubtless the most decisive meaning of the moment of Jesus' death. Mark says that he "gave a loud cry and breathed his last" (*exépneusen*, 15:37), which records the simple physiological fact, even though this itself is full of meaning, so much so that the centurion, as the evangelist points out, "saw that in this way he breathed his last, he said, 'Truly this man was God's Son!'" (15:39). For his part, Matthew uses a more personal expression, saying that Jesus *aphêken tò pneûma*, *emisit spiritum*, "yielded up his spirit" (Mt 27:50).[15] Luke, at this point, emphasizes the faithful freedom of Jesus' extreme act, placing on his lips, "Father, into your hands I commend my spirit [*Páter, eis cheîrás sou paratíthemai tò pneûmá mou*]" (Lk 23:46). John here uses a verb which has almost technical value in the New Testament language, to say that the Father gives the Son to the world, and that the Son, Jesus, gives himself and his life for us: *paradídōmi*, to hand over or transmit. On the cross, Jesus *parédōken tò pneûma*, hands over the Spirit (Jn 19:30). The final breath exhaled by the crucified Jesus is, for John, the symbol of the breath of life that he had received from his Father and which he now, having spent his life in love, was transmitting to human beings.

The effusion of the Spirit and the new creation Jesus crucified and risen, then "gives [*dídōsin*] the Spirit without measure" (Jn 3:34) because the Father "out of the believer's heart [causes] rivers of living water" to flow (Jn 7:38). This is recalled in the telling of the fourth Gospel in the event of the risen Christ who breathes on the apostles in the upper room, telling them, "receive the Holy Spirit" (Jn 20:22). The evening of the first day after the sabbath, the risen Lord comes into the midst of the disciples,

14. Bordoni, *Gesù di Nazareth Signore e Cristo*, 2:508.
15. American Standard Version translation.

who had closed themselves in the upper room for fear of the Jews (see Jn 20:19). This is a new act of creation of man, who retrieves and completes that of Genesis, just as, immediately beforehand, the meeting of Jesus and Mary Magdalen in the garden where the body of Jesus had been laid in a tomb, recalls the meeting between the first man and first woman in the garden of Eden (see Jn 20:1). Jesus greets the disciples saying "peace," *shalóm*, and showing them his hands and pierced side, he breathes on them with the breath of life (literally he "breathes inside"), the breath with which his crucified flesh is filled and is overflowing. He spells out the meaning of this gesture, "receive the Holy Spirit," sending his disciples, as the Father had sent him, as witnesses and transmitters of the breath of life that already has the taste and substance of the eternal.

The Paschal Event, Trinitarian Event

Thus, according to the New Testament witness, the Paschal event, which is the fulfillment of Jesus' mission and the eschatological revelation of God in and through him, is the act of the Father, of the Son, and of the Holy Spirit. On the one hand, it is the act of each of the three. The Father, Son, and Holy Spirit—each in their own way—are freely and "personally" fully involved. On the other hand, it is the event that witnesses, precisely in this way, through their synergy, their being "one" in love for humanity. The distinction is emphasized by the fact that each one, in his own way, is the free subject of the gift of self (expressed by the verb *paradidomi*): the Father gives the Son, the Son in obedience gives himself, and giving himself in turn gives the Holy Spirit which the Father gives to him. The being-one is emphasized by the event of the giving of God in his self-production for our salvation through the Son in the Spirit, as revelation of the love of God in which he manifests Himself and communicates himself to humanity redeeming it from sin.

In the Paschal event God who is *agápe* (see 1 Jn 4:8, 16) manifests and communicates himself to history: *agápe* which has its source in and from the Father, which expresses itself and makes itself tangible in the Son made flesh, through whom it shares itself with human beings in the Holy Spirit. By means of the Son, who identifies himself with human beings to the point of forsakenness and death—the sign and fruit of sin—in the Spirit, this *agápe* consigns itself back to the Father, superabundantly giving itself in the heart of human beings and involving them, thanks to the response of their redeemed freedom, in the event of the welcome and universal communication of the *agápe* of the *Abbà*.

The unique relationship of sonship from and toward the Father in the

Spirit, which characterizes Jesus' existence and mission, reaches its maximum expression in the event of the cross. What distinction could be more clear than that of the Son who lives the forsakenness and dies on the cross? What communion could be more intense than that lived—in love and as love—by the Father, by the Son, and by the Holy Spirit in this event? This communion shines forth in the risen Christ, which irradiates the glory of the Father, pouring forth the fullness of the Spirit. In God's action, unity and distinction are therefore, so to speak, directly proportionate: they are the two faces of the self-revelation and self-communication of God to human beings in Jesus Christ through the Spirit.

Certainly, all of this is extremely profound and mysterious. The witness of the death and resurrection of Jesus, the fulfillment of his mission as Son of the *Abbà* on whom rests the Spirit, discloses the unseen face of the God which the first covenant had revealed as one and unique to be the communion of love of the Father, Son, and Holy Spirit. On this basis, we are now called to explore in faith three points: (1) What is the status of the filial existence of Jesus; in what sense can we say that he is truly Son of God? (2) What is the identity of the Spirit that God pours out in fullness on the Son in the resurrection, and through him on humanity? (3) What does it mean to say that the God of Jesus is the *Abbà* who sends the Son for the salvation of the world and through him, crucified and risen, communicates the Spirit "without measure"?

CHAPTER 15

The Trinitarian Faith of the Apostolic Community

In the light of the Paschal event, the faith of the apostolic church is, under the influence of the Holy Spirit (see Jn 16:13), introduced into the new divine life that Jesus Christ eschatologically communicated to humanity. The intellectual appropriation of this new life is developed especially in two complementary directions: (1) there is an ever greater and ever more precise understanding of the divine identity not only of God/*Abbà*, but also of the Son, the crucified and risen Son, and of the Holy Spirit, in the unique and concrete relation that each of these live in relation to the others; (2) there is a completely new understanding of the unity and unicity of the God of Israel who is the God/*Abbà* of Jesus in the Holy Spirit, in the light of the revolutionary novelty of the Christological event and its Paschal completion.

There is, therefore, a growth in understanding that is at once contemplative and sapiential: in the sense that alongside the formidable ontological questions raised by the affirmation of a God who is one and unique and is, at the same time, Father, Son, and Spirit, there is also the fact that the apostolic faith confesses and announces this mystery by grasping it in discipleship of Jesus crucified and risen, the exact form in which this mystery shines forth and offers itself. This process is sustained, doubtless, by the specific and unique light of the Spirit. For this reason, the writings of the New Testament are canonical, by which I mean normative as regards the revelation of the face of God in Jesus Christ. This is true not only with regard to the insuperable historical witness that they offer to the event, but also with regard to the particular and defining theological illumination of the truth that they offer. The speculative understanding of the mystery remains the task of subsequent theological and dogmatic reflection.

What the apostolic community experiences, beginning with the appearances of the risen Jesus that reconstitute that community, is being gratuitously inserted, in Christ and thanks to the gift of the Spirit, into the communion of the trinitarian life which in Christ Jesus becomes the historical experience of humanity. We are looking, thus, not so much at a theoretical conviction, as much as an existential and practical experience which of itself opens up to a new understanding of the mystery of God revealed in Jesus. The first Letter of John expresses this as follows (1 Jn 1:1–3):

> We declare to you what was from the beginning, what we have heard, what we have seen with our eyes, what we have looked at and touched with our hands, concerning the word of life—this life was revealed, and we have seen it and testify to it, and declare to you the eternal life that was with the Father and was revealed to us—we declare to you what we have seen and heard so that you also may have fellowship [*koinōnía*, communion] with us; and truly our fellowship is with the Father and with his Son Jesus Christ.

The Church, *koinōnía* of the Trinitarian Life

The Christian faith is not based on the witness of the finding of the empty tomb in which the body of Jesus was placed after the crucifixion (even if the texts which witness to this are of undoubted importance: see Mk 16:1–8; Mt 28:1–8; Lk 24:1–12; Jn 20:1–13), nor is it based on the eyewitness testimony to the event of the resurrection. It is based, rather, on the experience that apostles have with the risen Jesus. They encounter Jesus in a radically different state of existence than the one in which they previously knew him, though it is one in indissoluble continuity with the same Jesus. Thus, they can "recognize" him, even if such recognition depends on the grace of an openness and involvement in faith.

The Risen One's Appearances, the Advent of the Trinitarian God, and the Constitution of the Community of the New Covenant

A first nucleus of appearances is located in Jerusalem and occurs the day after the sabbath. Those involved are, firstly, women, then the apostles, then other disciples (see Jn 20:21–23; Mt 28:9–10; Lk 24:13–53; Jn 20, 24–29). Peter, both in the Gospel of Luke and in the first Letter to the Corinthians, plays a key role. In these writings the first appearance, not in a chronological sense, but in the sense that it is at the foundation of the apostolic witness, is to the prince of the apostles. His is the initiative of gathering together the messianic community that had been dispersed (see Lk 24:33–34; 1 Cor 15:5).

A second nucleus is that associated with Galilee, in the region where

Jesus had originally preached the coming of the kingdom. These are the appearances to the eleven who had returned there following Easter (see Mt 28:16–20; Mk 16:15–16; Jn 21:1–19). The conclusive moment is the appearance which culminates in the ascension of Jesus, when he, having promised the gift of the Spirit, "hides himself" from their eyes (Mk 16:19; Lk 24:50–53; Acts 1:3–14) and returns in glory to the Father.

Alongside these appearances, which can be considered decisive and foundational both of the faith of the apostles and for the reconstitution of the messianic community, the New Testament speaks of other appearances: that to James, that to more than five hundred of the brothers (1 Cor 15:6–8), and that to Paul. This final appearance is of particular importance because it is linked to the "revelation of the mystery hidden throughout the ages" (see Col 1:26), and that is the call to salvation of the pagans through the specific ministry toward them which had been conferred on Paul as apostle to the nations directly by the risen one.

We must ask what these appearances are. Looking at the New Testament, bearing in mind the precise literary genre in which the accounts of the appearances are written, we can conclude that the event of which these accounts speak is one in which Jesus takes the initiative. This fact is absolutely decisive, because it shows that the appearances are not to be explained as illusion, or the projection of the hopes or the subjective faith of the apostles. The verbs used always have the passive form (with the sense of the middle voice) that make Jesus the subject of the action: "Jesus was seen, he showed himself [*óphthē*]," in order to emphasize the initiative of Jesus (see 1 Cor 15:3–8; Lk 24:34; Acts 9:13, 17, 31; 26:16). Note that this is the same verb that the Greek translation of the First Testament uses to describe the theophanies of YHWH (see Gn 12:7; 17:1; 18:1; 26:2).

The recognition and response on the part of the apostles—and, in general, of whoever is involved—comes about thanks to the initiative of the risen one. Such recognition is not, however, something that can be taken for granted. It is neither automatic nor is it immediate. It passes, rather, through various phases: amazement and doubt, overcome by a manifestation of Jesus, a word, or a gesture (see Jn 20:11–18). The appearances are therefore to be understood as relational events, as the restoration and unexpected fulfillment of a relationship, with a specific dynamism of offer and response in continuity with the dialogical structure of the event of the kingdom in the preaching and praxis of Jesus.

In this perspective, Jesus privileges those who were witnesses to his pre-Calvary life (with the exception of Paul) and he seems to do this for two reasons. These reasons are clearly evident from the stories themselves: (1) because they are the ones who are open to being involved by that manifestation of Jesus, a manifestation that goes beyond the mere recognition of his identity, and extends to an understanding of the full and definitive meaning of his message and mission; and (2) because the continuity (within the discontinuity) between the Jesus prior to Easter and after is in this way made clear. These points are essential for the Christian faith, to the extent that it is founded on the indissoluble unity between *kérygma* of the kingdom that Jesus announces and the post-Paschal *kérygma* about the risen Jesus that the apostles make following these appearances (see Acts 1:21–22).

The experience that the apostles have of Jesus in the appearances is undoubtedly something new, because he—who already possesses the eschatological lordship that the Father has conferred on him—presents himself to them as the glorious Son of Man, the *Kýrios* who pours out the Spirit. For this reason, the event of the appearances implies a new and more radical involvement of faith. It is a faith that calls for a free response and brings about a cleaving to Christ as he who, in the Spirit, has reconciled men eschatologically to the Father, and inserted them as the community of the new alliance into the relationship of love that he himself lives with the Father. To use the category of the coming of the kingdom which Jesus himself had used at the beginning of his ministry, the appearances show that the coming of the kingdom takes place firstly in him, in his person as risen from the dead. Cleaving to the risen one is expressed in the faith that he is alive, present, and working in history, so as to witness to him with absolute faithfulness and remarkable conviction to the point of the gift of one's life (martyrdom).

With the appearances the apostles therefore regain the strength to relaunch and pursue the messianic project in which they had been involved in a new way, through faith in the mysterious but real victory of Jesus over humans' refusal to open themselves to the coming of God and over death itself. The appearances bring about the reconstitution of the messianic community, which immediately shows signs of formidable missionary and evangelizing dynamism, and where the apostles become witnesses to the global meaning and radical novelty of the event of Jesus, the crucified and risen one. The death of Jesus is thus not only integrated into his messianic project, but is understood as the path to the resurrection, and the place of the definitive unfolding of this same project.

The kingdom that Jesus preached consisted of the fatherhood of God who reconfigures relations among men, projecting reconciled existence in love toward its eschatological end. In the resurrection of Jesus, the crucified one, they participate in the radical actualizing, even if only in an initial way, of that event. On this basis there develops, on the one hand,

New Testament Christology (by which I mean the penetration in faith in the full meaning of the mystery of the theological identity and mission of Jesus) and, on the other hand, the reality of the church, which recognizes in Jesus the full and definitive Word of God addressed to the world.

The Crucified/Risen Lord as Principle of a New Creation

In the light of the appearances of the risen one, the understanding of the meaning of salvation and revelation stemming from Jesus' death on the cross is opened up to the faith of the apostolic church. What is it that happens through this light? Why is it precisely, in other words, from this light—the unexpected and decisive fruit—that the resurrection springs forth? It is not by chance that the apostle Paul, in order to express the deepest meaning of Paschal event, uses the expression *kainè ktísis*, new creation (see 2 Cor 5:17). The apostle seems to be suggesting that in his dying, Jesus pushed his self-giving to the Father to the extreme, to the point of "annihilating" himself. In this way, he offered his humanity, a humanity completely open to the Father's action, the virgin space within which the Father was able to unleash new creation in the power of the Holy Spirit. Such new creation means the renewal of the first creation from its very roots, redeeming it from sin and making it participate in the Spirit in the filial life of the Son made flesh who consigned himself entirely to the Father and, in himself, the whole of creation.

Thus God who in the first creation had called into existence the things which were not (see Rom 4:17), now, in Christ, is making them new through the incarnate Son, dead and risen, in the light and power of the Spirit. The "new creation" is therefore the breaking in of the *eschaton* into history, the bringing about of the announcement of the coming of the kingdom of God proclaimed by the Nazarene. Jesus crucified and risen is the personal space in which one freely enters in order to become a participant in the new creation. This is the meaning of the "dying" with Christ in order to "rise" with him (see Rom 6:3–6, 8; 2 Tm 2:11). In virtue of the faith it means welcoming the grace (*cháris*) of divine filiation in Christ, which is expressed in the baptism and Paschal meal and becomes a new style of existence in *agápe* which is reciprocal and aimed at everyone.

The Ecclesial *koinōnía* Edified by Baptism and Eucharist

The Acts of the Apostles tell of the practice in the earliest community of baptism "in the name of Jesus" (see, e.g., Acts 1:5; 2:38). This formula means receiving baptism as Christ ordered and, at the same time, taking part in his event of salvation, and thus entering into the church. A second formula, one which is not simply Christological but trinitarian, is found at the end of the Gospel of Matthew,[1] and gives witness to a later explication of the meaning of baptism, compatible with the first: baptism is participation in the event of salvation that is jointly the work of the Father, the Son, and the Holy Spirit. It is important to emphasize that there is only one name here, and this name alludes biblically to the one true God. "Go therefore and make disciples of all nations, baptizing them in the name of the Father and of the Son and of the Holy Spirit, and teaching them to obey everything that I have commanded you. And remember, I am with you always, to the end of the age (Mt 28:19–20). The faithfulness of the disciple to faith in Christ as well as the disciple's insertion into the *ekklesia* is manifested and realized, therefore, on the basis of the baptism in living water. In Paul, the symbolism of water is read as a participation, through the movement of immersion in the water and reemergence from the water, in the death and resurrection of Jesus (Rom 6). In the fourth Gospel, the baptismal water is a symbol of that living water, the eschatological gift of the Spirit which purifies the human heart and makes it capable of carrying out the will of the Father in the love that springs forth from Christ crucified and risen.

Further, in the apostolic witness, the risen Christ is presented as the spring and living center of the messianic community, which he convokes and assimilates to himself through the proclamation of the word of salvation and the memorial of the Last Supper. As the episode of the disciples on the road to Emmaus in the Gospel of Luke (24:13–35) illustrates, the risen one, after the period of the appearances remains present to the church through the word, the broken bread, and the fraternal union of the disciples that it brings about. He shows himself to be the interpretive key of the scriptures and of his own mission (see Lk 24:32). The "breaking of bread," in obedience to the command of the Last Supper, is a sign and effective instrument of his continuing presence in the midst of his disciples (see Lk 24:31, 35; Acts 2:42).

An analogous concept is expressed by Matthew, who presents the risen Christ as the full and continuing presence of the Emmanuel among his disciples (in the great inclusion of his Gospel: 1:23; 18:20; 28:18–20), and by Paul, with his idea of the body of Christ (see 1 Cor 12:12; Rom 12:4–5), born in a Eucharistic context. In a densely symbolic way, even the Gospel of John describes the coming of the risen Christ among his disciples, the first day after the sabbath (see 20:19–29): his side is open, which means that he is alive in the community of his disciples in the act of maximum

1. As Joachim Gnilka has pointed out, "baptism in the name of the Triune God, even though it is mentioned only here in the New Testament, should be considered as the form of baptism in use in the Matthean (and the Syrian communities, see *Didaché* 7,3)." *Il vangelo di Matteo* (Brescia: Paideia, 1991), 2:742 (own trans.).

love. The Paschal Christ, present in the church to the world, is therefore the making eternal in ever new ways of the supreme gift of the cross. The *kérygma* which is announced and the bread which is broken is the actualization of this presence and the transmission in the Spirit of his filial life to the messianic community.

Baptism and Eucharist are, in brief, effective signs of the building of the body of the risen Christ: the insertion of redeemed human beings into the new life communicated by the Father in the Paschal event of the Son through the pouring out of the Holy Spirit. Ecclesial *koinōnía* (see Eph 4:4–6; Gal 3:26–29; 1 Cor 12:12; Jn 17:20–23), the eschatological fruit of the Paschal gift announced by the apostolic *kerygma*, signified and realized in baptism and in the breaking of bread, and lived in relations of reciprocal *agápe* spread to all the disciples: all of this is the epiphany and the *traditio* of the Paschal event in the history of humanity.[2] This communion itself lives in a Paschal dynamic, synthesized in the "lose your life to regain it" commandment (see Lk 9:24; 17:33 and parallels) that, in the light of the Paschal event, is illuminated by the evangelist John as the revelation of the relationship of love between Son and Father, into which we are called in grace to participate (see Jn 10:17–18). This dynamic is expressed by Paul in the Christological hymn in the Letter to the Philippians, where the *kénosis* of Christ is presented as the paradigm of life to which the disciple must be conformed in the life of the ecclesial *koinōnía*.[3]

It is on the basis, on the one hand, of the Paschal event, which calls for the eschatological rereading of the message and the entire existence of Jesus of Nazareth and, on the other hand, of this rich experience of ecclesial life in the risen Christ through the Spirit that the church elaborates its witness and ever greater understanding of the action and trinitarian identity of God that reveals and communicates himself to the world in Jesus.

The Trinitarian Formulae and the Christological Hymns in the Pauline Letters

The authentic letters of Paul were written prior to the synoptic Gospels. Together with the other writings that make up the Pauline literature, they

2. On the trinitarian dynamic of Christian and ecclesial existence see also 1 Thes 4:6–8; Rom 5:1–5; 8:14–17; Eph 4.1; 1 Pt 1:1–12; Jude 20–21.

3. In the Paschal perspective of Christian life, even the negative which outside Christ appears only to be failure and rupture, when lived in the crucified-risen one is transformed into a way of meeting God in the transforming power of the Spirit, because all has been assumed and raised by him in his death and resurrection (see, for example, 2 Cor 1:8–10; 12:7–10; Rom 8:35–39). It is in this logic that the promise of the resurrection from the dead (as, for example, in 1 Cor 15) should be read, and the participation of the cosmos in the eschatological destiny of humanity (see Rom 8:18–23).

give evidence of a progressive and mature consciousness of the distinction and the strict synergy between Father, Son, and Holy Spirit in the event of salvation.

The Trinitarian Formulae

First of all, there are the trinitarian formulae[4] which name the Father, Son, and Holy Spirit distinctly and speak of their reciprocal relationship in the fulfillment of the mystery of salvation, and in the life and mission of the church. It is worth emphasizing that they attest to a trinitarian rhythm of the revelation and salvation of God which is actuated in Christ and transmitted in the Holy Spirit. Here are some of the more important passages: "But we must always give thanks to God for you, brothers and sisters beloved by the Lord, because God [*ho Theós*] chose you as the first fruits for salvation through sanctification by the Spirit and through belief in the truth. For this purpose he called you through our proclamation of the good news so that you may obtain the glory of our Lord Jesus Christ" (2 Thes 2:13–14). "Now there are varieties of gifts, but the same Spirit; and there are varieties of services, but the same Lord; and there are varieties of activities, but it is the same God who activates all of them in everyone" (1 Cor 12:4–6). "The grace of the Lord Jesus Christ, the love of God, and the communion of the Holy Spirit be with all of you" (2 Cor 13:13). "And because you are children, God has sent the Spirit of his Son into our hearts, crying, 'Abbà! Father!'" (Gal 4:6).

To these certainly Pauline texts, we can associate 1 Peter 1:1–2: "Peter, an apostle of Jesus Christ, To the exiles of the Dispersion in Pontus, Galatia, Cappadocia, Asia, and Bithynia, who have been chosen and destined by God the Father and sanctified by the Spirit to be obedient to Jesus Christ and to be sprinkled with his blood. May grace and peace be yours in abundance." See also Titus 3:4–7:

> But when the goodness and loving kindness of God our Savior appeared, he saved us, not because of any works of righteousness that we had done, but according to his mercy, through the water of rebirth and renewal by the Holy Spirit. This Spirit he poured out on us richly through Jesus Christ our Savior, so that, having been justified by his grace, we might become heirs according to the hope of eternal life.

Note that here we have formulae that can be characterized as functional, by which we mean that they give doxological confession to the action of the Father, Son, and Holy Spirit in the work of salvation (the economic

4. See Klaus Wengst and Martin Ritter, "Glaubensbekenntnis(se) IV–V," in *Theologische Realenzyklopädie* (Berlin: Walter de Gruyter, 1984), 13:392–412; Heinrich Schlier, "Gli inizi del credo cristologico," in *La storia della cristologia primitiva*, ed. Bernhard Welte (Brescia: Paideia, 1986), 15–70; Arthur W. Wainwright, *The Trinity in the New Testament* (London: SPCK, 1962).

Trinity, to use a modern expression). They do not aim primarily to speak of the identity and reciprocal relations in God (the immanent Trinity). The designation *ho Theós* (God) is reserved in a proper and original sense for the Father.[5] As noted above, however, what is most decisive is the trinitarian rhythm with which the soteriological event is described: salvation is imparted by the Father, through the Son in the Holy Spirit.

Witness to the Divine-Filial Identity of Jesus

The Pauline correspondence also demonstrates, however, a decisive and penetrating understanding of Jesus Christ as the Son of God in a sense that is more than simply functional and historical-salvific, but which is, to use a term from subsequent theology, properly ontological.

The theological meaning of the titles "Lord" and "Son of God" The identity of Jesus as divine son is affirmed with clarity and force through the titles *Kýrios* and *huiòs Theoû*. The Christological importance, according to Romano Penna, "appears evident and striking where it appears close to but distinct from the reference to 'God.'"[6] Thus, above all, in the following passage: "Yet for us there is one God, the Father, from whom are all things and for whom we exist, and one Lord, Jesus Christ, through whom are all things and through whom we exist" (1 Cor 8:6). The background to this confession is, undoubtedly, the Shema of Deuteronomy 6:4, which in the Septuagint translation reads: *Kýrios ho Theòs hymôn kýrios eîs estin*. Penna comments: "The enormous and scandalous Christian novelty consists in a kind of break with the ironclad Jewish monotheism, introducing an unprecedented distinction between the terms 'God' and 'Lord,' which in the Jewish context coincided perfectly."[7] In Paul, the first is attributed to the God whom Jesus revealed to be *Abbà* and the second to Jesus himself. In this way he is made equal to God.

This is taken further by the title of "Son of God" attributed to Jesus, a title that recurs fifteen times in the Pauline correspondence. Here the unique relation of sonship between Jesus and God is emphasized. Thus, God is now defined Christologically, in his being and action, as the "Father of our Lord Jesus Christ" (see Rom 15:6; 2 Cor 1:3, 11:31). Further, in the hymn of Philippians 2:5–11, to which I will return with reference to the incarnation, we find the description of a passage in reference to Jesus from the divine condition to the human condition: "who, though he was

5. On this see the classical treatment of Karl Rahner, "*Theós* in the New Testament," in *Theological Investigations* vol. 1: *God, Christ, Mary and Grace*, trans. Ernst Cornelius (New York: Crossroad, 1961), 79–148.

6. Penna, *I ritratti originali di Gesù il Cristo*, 2:185 (own trans.).

7. Ibid. (own trans.).

in the form of God [*morphé Theou*], did not regard equality with God as something to be exploited" (2:6) but in obedience he is brought to death on the cross. Then there is the further passage to the condition of exaltation, according to which God gives him the "name that is above every other name" (2:9), the name of *Kýrios* (see 2:11). Thus, the preexistence of Jesus in the condition of God[8] is affirmed, as well as his exaltation as *Kýrios* by his death and resurrection.

The protological identity of Jesus as foundation of his eschatological mission The ever-deepening understanding of the protological identity of Jesus comes about, already in Paul, by means of the First Testament category of wisdom (see, e.g., 1 Cor 2:6–8). In the light of the event of the resurrection, and with the interpretive assistance of this category, the subsequent Deutero-Pauline letters recognize in Jesus the one that prior to creation is with the Father, and through whom and in view of whom God brings about both creation and redemption. Thus, in Ephesians 1:3–14, and even more so in Colossians 1:13–19, a text upon which I will reflect at greater length.[9] "He [the Father] has rescued us from the power of darkness and transferred us into the kingdom of his beloved Son, in whom we have redemption, the forgiveness of sins. He is the image [*eikón*] of the invisible God, the firstborn [*prōtótokos*] of all creation" (Col 1:13–15). The term "image," in Greek *eikón*, recalls Wisdom (see Wis 7:26) as the image of God, as she is depicted in the wisdom texts. This text distinguishes the level of creation from that of the life of God which precedes it by using a specific term, *prōtótokos*, the firstborn, the first one to be generated. The generation of the Son is prior to creation.

It is worth noting, in confirmation of this, the difference that the text seems to suggest between generation and creation: "For in him all things in heaven and on earth were created, things visible and invisible, whether thrones or dominions or rulers or powers—all things have been created through him and for him (Col 1:16). Jesus Christ is described not just as the "first generated" but as the one "in whom" the creation occurs, himself being the space of life and truth. For this reason, as the Scholastics would put it, he is the "efficient cause" of creation, the one "by means of whom" the Father created, and also the "final cause," the one in view of whom everything was created. In him the *prótos* and the *éschatos* come together, because it is the same Christ who is the prototype of creation and the one in whom

8. The formulas of Jesus' mission on the part of the Father (see Gal 4:4; Rom 8:3) and those of donation (Rom 5:10 and 8:32) imply the preexistence of the Son who is the one who is sent and given by the Father.

9. See Penna, "La creazione in Cristo (Col 1, 15–20)," in his *I ritratti originali di Gesù il Cristo*, 2:229–36.

it is recapitulated.[10] "He himself is before all things, and in him all things hold together" (Col 1:17). Christ is the principle in which all things have life, existence and cohesion. Without him they would fall into the nothingness of dispersion and meaninglessness.[11] "He is the head of the body, the church; he is the beginning [*arché*], the firstborn [*prōtótokos*] from the dead, so that he might come to have first place in everything. For in him all the fullness [*plérōma*] of God was pleased to dwell" (Col 1:18–19).

If God is fullness[12] (and God is that by definition), he is everything which is: if God were missing even a minimal portion of being, he would no longer be God, because he cannot be missing anything. Now, God the Father makes the fullness of everything that he wishes to communicate of himself reside in the Son, without remainder. Jesus thus is not only the mediator of creation, but also of redemption, and he is that because he is the perfect image of the Father, the firstborn and fullness of life in God. Through his incarnation and resurrection, he becomes also the recapitulator of the universe (see Eph 1:10): the fullness of all that is.

The path that joins the creation that comes about in Christ with the redemption that is brought about in him and by means of him, such that all things converge in him and are recapitulated in him is synthesized in the pregnant affirmation according to which he is "God's mystery, that is, Christ himself, in whom are hidden all the treasures of wisdom and knowledge" (Col 2:2b–3). Jesus, in brief, personally gathers up in himself "the mystery of God": "as the son of a carpenter, as a friend of publicans and of sinners, as the crucified one, as the risen one and Lord, he reveals where lie hidden 'all of the treasures of wisdom and knowledge.'"[13]

The Prologue to the Letter to the Hebrews

Another very important text, which should be at least cited, is the prologue to the Letter to the Hebrews (1:1–4):

10. See Eph 1:10

11. As Paul explains in his wonderful speech at the Areopagus at Athens, it is already deeply part of the pre-Christian consciousness of God that in "Him we live, and move and have our being" (Acts 17:28). The experience of the resurrection of Jesus and the penetration of the mystery of his being "firstborn" and "recapitulator" of creation open up the horizon of our subsistence in him as Son of the Father. Existing for him is a gift of the Father and work of the Holy Spirit, as the divine "atmosphere" of life in God.

12. The word fullness (in Greek *plérōma*) is saturated with significance. On one hand, it means the fullness of divine life (as explicitly indicated in Col 2:9 and Eph 3:19); on the other hand, the presence of God who "fills" the earth (see Is 6:3; Jer 23:24; Ps 24:1; 50:12; 72:19; Wis 1:7; Sir 43:27). With his incarnation and resurrection, Jesus is shown to be the recapitulator of the whole divine world to which he belongs with his preexisting and glorified being, and of the whole created world, assumed in the incarnation and invested with his glory in the resurrection (see Col 1:19; Eph 1:23). But even the church, as Christ's body, is his fullness (see Eph 1:23). Engrafted in Christ, believers share in this same fullness: "you have come to fullness in him ..." (Col 2:10); "From his fullness we have all received, grace upon grace" (Jn 1:16).

13. Penna, *La creazione in Cristo (Col 1, 15–20)*, 2:242 (own trans.).

Long ago God spoke to our ancestors in many and various ways by the prophets, but in these last days he has spoken to us by a Son, whom he appointed heir of all things, through whom he also created the worlds. He is the reflection of God's glory and the exact imprint of God's very being, and he sustains all things by his powerful word. When he had made purification for sins, he sat down at the right hand of the Majesty on high, having become as much superior to angels as the name he has inherited is more excellent than theirs.

The author, in the light of the First Testament theology of the Word of God, reads the event of Jesus Christ as the advent of the unique and definitive Word of the Father. Jesus the Christ is this because he is the Son, the "reflection of God's glory," and that is God's splendor, and "imprint of God's very being," which means the exact and perfect reproduction of God, as a stamp impressed on sealing wax. He, therefore, though he is distinct from the Father, is to him equal in being and glory.[14]

The Identity of the Holy Spirit in Paul and Luke

In the Christological hymns of the Deutero-Pauline epistles, the preexistence of Jesus as Son is clearly set out, as the mediator of creation and redemption, and recapitulator of the universe. What can be said about the Holy Spirit?[15] Already at first glance, it is clear that the specific and innovative perspective that the New Testament offers as regards the revelation of the identity of the Spirit, beyond what is found in the First Testament, is shaped by two givens: (1) as I have already noted, the gift of the Spirit in the final times to the community of the new covenant is placed in indissoluble continuity with Christ, and in particular with Christ crucified and risen; (2) for this reason, the Holy Spirit acquires ever more clearly an identity that is distinct from that of the Father and the Son, even if it is intimately conjoined with them. It is worth noting that in the New Testament, the name "Holy Spirit," especially in the Lukan work, is reserved for the Spirit given at Pentecost, and in other words given to the Christological fullness of his gift and revelation, whereas we find formulae that place him in relation to the Father (Spirit of God or Spirit of the Father) and formulae that place him in relation to the Son (Spirit of Christ or Spirit of the Lord or Spirit of the Son).[16]

14. The First Testament theology of the "glory" of God should be borne in mind as a visible sign of his holiness and of his presence: it is Jesus here, the incarnate son, dead and risen, the manifestation of this glory as personal being distinct from him and one with him. The image of the seal is also used by John: "it is on him that God the Father has set his seal" (Jn 6:27).

15. See Yves Congar, *I Believe in the Holy Spirit*, trans. David Smith (New York: Crossroad, 2001); Chevallier, *Souffle de Dieu*.

16. "The Spirit of his Son" (Gal 4:6), "The Spirit of Christ (Rom 8:9), "The Spirit of Jesus Christ" (Phil 1:19), "The Spirit of the Lord" (2 Cor 3:17b).

Already in Paul,[17] who offers rich descriptions of the action of the Spirit as the principle of full and restored communion between God and man in Christ, some passages show an orientation, at least metaphorically, toward the meaning of personal identity of the divine *Pneûma* which "searches everything, even the depths of God" (1 Cor 2:10) and is "sent" (*exapostéllō*) into our hearts (see Gal 4:6). This personal character comes into even greater evidence in 1 Corinthians 12:11, where Paul describes the Spirit who distributes the gifts of grace "just as the Spirit chooses" (*kathòs boùletai*). Then there are the trinitarian formulae, which we have already encountered, in which the Spirit is presented in intimate connection with God (*ho Theós*, the Father) and with the Christ.

In the Book of Acts, the Holy Spirit is presented, finally, as the chief protagonist of the growth and conduct of the evangelizing mission of the church, not only as the force that spreads the good news, but often with all of the characteristics of a personal actor who guides and orients the history of the first community. Haya Prats writes:

> A remarkable development in the direction of a personalization of the Holy Spirit that goes beyond a merely literary personification can be discerned in the Acts of the Apostles. The author's repeated attribution of definite and important interventions in the history of salvation to the Holy Spirit would seem to indicate that the Spirit was regarded in practice as the subject of such attribution and therefore as in some way different from Yahweh, even though the problem of such a distinction is not posed as such.[18]

The Johannine Theo-logic

The writings of the Johannine tradition—in particular the fourth Gospel and the first Letter—are of decisive importance for the theological understanding of the revelation in Jesus Christ. The following significant elements at the least can be drawn from these: the identity of Jesus Christ as the *Lógos* (Word) and the only begotten Son of the Father made man, in whom the revelatory promise of the "I am" of YHWH is actualized eschatologically; the identity of the Holy Spirit as the other one sent by the Father, the Paraclete, who makes the work of the Son present and perfects it; and the dynamic of intimate and full unity between the Father

17. See Jean-Pierre Lémonon, "L'Esprit saint dans le corpus paulinien," in *Supplément au Dictionnaire de La Bible* (Paris: Latouzy and Ané, 1991), 11:192–327.

18. Gonzalo Haya-Prats, *L'Esprit force de l'Eglise: Sa nature et son activité d'après les Actes des Apôtres* (Paris: Éditions du Cerf, 1975), 82–90; quoted by Congar, *I Believe in the Holy Spirit*, 1:47. Beginning with the Pentecost account, it is said that the apostles "were filled with the Holy Spirit and began to speak in other languages, as the Spirit gave them ability" (Acts 2:4); then this formula is significant: "we are witnesses to these things, and so is the Holy Spirit" (Acts 5:32), while it is the Holy Spirit who is the real protagonist speaking to Philip (Acts 8:29) and snatching him away (Acts 8:39) in the episode of the Ethiopian minister's baptism.

and the Son, and of these with and in the Holy Spirit, which is extended as gift to human beings, described through the concept of mission and illustrated through the figure of the *dóxa* (glory) and of *agápe* (love), in which God himself is revealed and given to human beings in Christ Jesus through the Spirit.

The Son-*Lógos* in the Prologue

The only-begotten Son First of all, the fourth Gospel illustrates the relationship between Jesus and God as a relationship between the Father and the Son. These terms are used in their absolute forms, and are drawn from human experience. They had been used in the First Testament to express the relationship between God and Israel, though with only a metaphorical sense. They are used however in a completely new sense in relation to the event of Jesus. In John, "Son" is used twenty-three times to designate Jesus, and eighteen times in the absolute form: "the Son." A specifically Johannine Christological title is "only begotten" (in 1:14, 18; 3:16, 18, to which we can add 1 Jn 4:9), and it emphasizes the uniqueness of the relation of Sonship of Jesus with respect to the Father. To say that God is Father means, for John, to affirm that he is the originating principle and source of every life and every good; to say that Jesus Christ is the only-begotten Son means affirming that in him is the perfect reception of the life that is communicated to him fully by the Father, and which in turn is given back to him in the spirit of perfect obedience and unity.

An original meaning of Lógos The term *Lógos*, attributed to Christ in the prologue of the fourth Gospel, goes in the same direction. The Christ is the Word in whom the Father fully expresses himself and communicates himself to creation. In the theological perspective of the fourth Gospel, the affirmation according to which Jesus is the *Lógos* of God the Father, on the one hand, is in at least implicit reference to the Hellenistic thought, where *lógos* is used (from Heraclitus to the Stoics) to stand for the principle of unity and intelligibility of the cosmos as reflection and presence of the divine. In John, however, the First Testament reference to the Word of God and Wisdom of God is of decisive importance. We are thus in a context different than the Greek one, a context not determined by emanation and cosmology. The God here is living and personal, YHWH, who addresses his Word to the world, creating and ordering it in the light of his Wisdom.

The wisdom tradition had already offered, in the Pauline writings, a very useful and rich pre-comprehension, which was almost indispensable for the interpretation of the relation between the historical event of Jesus and the eternal contemplation of the plan of creation and salvation on the part of God and his Word. John, using the wisdom tradition, seems to recall, in an even more fundamental way, the theology of the word, *dābar*, the *lógos* of YHWH, both "in order to give to wisdom a universal character and its living nature of dialogue with all human beings," and because "the choice of the *Lógos* is more fitting in order to bring out the theme of the revelation that Jesus brings about God his Father and about the 'eternal' life of believers in him."[19]

The event of Jesus is clearly decisive for the fourth Gospel. The *Lógos* for the author simply is Jesus Christ. He does not read the Christological event simply in the light of the First Testament theology of Word and Wisdom, nor is he inspired in the first instance by the Greek category of *Lógos*. For him, instead, the event itself, that is, the story of the Nazarene and his destiny of death and resurrection, becomes the interpretive key that unifies and transcends the First Testament perspective of Word/Wisdom of God and, in the background, the Greek idea of the *Lógos*. It is sufficient to look at some of the most pregnant affirmations of verses 14 and 18 of the prologue: "In the beginning was the Word, and the Word was with God, and the Word was God. He was in the beginning with God. All things came into being through him, and without him not one thing came into being that has come into being" (Jn 1:1–3); "And the Word became flesh and lived among us, and we have seen his glory, the glory as of a father's only son, full of grace and truth" (Jn 1:14); "No one has ever seen God. It is God the only Son, who is close to the Father's heart, who has made him known" (Jn 1:18).

A triple novelty The originality of the Johannine conception of the *Lógos* is grasped once we look at the whole picture. The first and decisive novelty is the fact that *Lógos* takes on a human and personal face. Jesus is, in point of fact, the "*Lógos* (who) became flesh." The narrative that the prologue describes goes from the *Lógos*, who is oriented toward God and who himself is God, to his incarnation in Jesus Christ. It also works in the opposite direction, however, one that goes from Jesus Christ, recognized in faith as the eschatological revealer of the Father to the *Lógos* who is always oriented toward the Father. It is, therefore, in looking at Jesus that we can contemplate the eternal *Lógos* of the Father and, in him, the Father himself. In other words, the identity of the *Lógos* and his relationship with God can be recognized only by taking Jesus as starting point, and not vice versa. Thus, from the Christian point of view, it is impossible to have a precise and correct understanding of the identity of the *Lógos* apart from his incarnation in Jesus.

19. Xavier Léon-Dufour, *Lecture de l'évangile selon Jean* (Paris: Seuil, 1988), 1:61 (own trans.).

A second novelty is the distinction that is thus established, *en arche*, that is *in principio*, *in divinis*, between "the God" (*ho Theós*) or "the Father" (*ho Patér*), and *ho Lógos*, or the "Only Begotten God," *monogenès Theós* (in some versions, *monogenès hyiòs*, only-begotten Son). The *Lógos* therefore is distinct from God, but is not subordinated to him, because he himself is God. Accordingly, in the prologue we find: "In the beginning was the *Lógos*" (in the *arché*, that is prior to every temporal event), "and the *Lógos* was oriented toward (or with) God," and "the *Lógos* was God" (God, therefore, as "the" God, namely the Father; see Jn 1:1). In John's vision, which reflects the Paschal faith, Jesus is not less than the Father, even if he depends on Him totally ("the Father is greater than I," Jn 14:28).

The Johannine prologue thus authorizes that extraordinary religious and cultural revolution that becomes accessible in Jesus. In it we contemplate "the God" (*ho Theós*), with the article, and together with Him also "the *Lógos*," who is also God. He is not "the" God, but is also God. Thus is signaled a new penetration into the being of God which is unleashed from the Christological revelation. God is the subject and God is the predicate. No philosopher had ever dared to say as much! The concept of God speaks of the subject (the God) who speaks and of which we speak in response, but at the same time is the predicate: so that one can (and through the Jesus-event, one must) predicate God of distinct subjects (the God and the *Lógos*).

Already in the First Testament, we recognize two distinct levels in the name of God. Israel speaks of "its" God and other people understand that there is here a reference to God, because "God" is a concept that is common to all cultures. But there is also the name revealed by God to Moses (Ex 3:14). Israel affirms, therefore, that "The Lord (*Adonai*/YHWH), my God, is God (*Elohim*)," that God whom all peoples know. In some cases, an article is prefixed to God: "*Adonai* (YHWH) is the God (*ha Elohim*)," to say that he is the only God: that only he is God, and no one else is.

In John, the completely new hermeneutical context is that disclosed by Jesus in his Spirit. Thus, the affirmation "the God" does not intend to deny other gods, but to affirm that "another" (the *Lógos*) is God, though he is not "the" God. Thus, the article comes to distinguish, within the divine *koinōnía*, the one who is God in one way (the God, the Father) and the one who is God in another way (the *Lógos*, the Son). In the prologue of the Gospel of John, God comes to be also predicate. Now, the only predicate (that which determines the subject which is affirmed) that is suitable to use when speaking of God, is God himself! In the prologue, therefore, the predicate is not referred exclusively to the only one whom the First Testament revelation defined as "the God," and which becomes synonymous with the Father. In fact, although "the God" is God, so too is Jesus, the *Lógos* (and, as will be understood later, the Holy Spirit is God).

Now, the predicate expresses the being, the "substance" of God. Thus, the substance of God is predicable not only of the Father, but also of the Son (and of the Spirit). If, however, God is only one, I cannot predicate "being God" of more than one reality. It would be a contradiction. "Being God," predicated of distinct subjects—Father, Son, Holy Spirit—in virtue of the Christological revelation, cannot multiply the life of God or the being of God, as God is and remains one. There are not three Gods. In the prologue of the fourth Gospel, therefore, there is the basic seed, in contemplative theological language, of what the Council of Nicaea will affirm drawing also on the resources of philosophical language.

The third novelty is that the *Lógos* is "with" or oriented "toward" the Father (*pròs tòn Theón* in verse 1, and even more clearly in verse 18, *eis tòn kólpon toû patròs*). Between God and the *Lógos*, who are on the same plane, there is a relationship of distinction but also of reciprocity: because the *Lógos* is the Word, the expression of "the God" and inasmuch as he is both Son and only-begotten of the Father and for this reason oriented toward him. What we find expressed here, at the level of the divine life in itself, is the unique experience witnessed to of relation with God by Jesus of Nazareth. This relation is, on the one hand, receptive and obedient toward the Father and, on the other hand, a relationship of freedom and active donation toward him in the carrying out of the mission that he entrusted to him. Thus, in his pre-temporal existence, he, as only-begotten Son and *Lógos*, lives from all eternity this relationship of reciprocity with the Father.

Between Father and Son, there is therefore perfect unity and perfect distinction, as is explained on a historical-salvific level by the narration of the fourth Gospel. Unity: "The Father and I are one" (Jn 10:30; see also Jn 17:11, 21–22) because the Father *en arché* is not without the Son, nor is the Son without the Father. Distinction, because the Father is not the Son, nor is the Son the Father. God, therefore, is from the beginning, by which is meant "in himself"; he is not solitude, but dialogue, exchange, communion, reciprocal gift of self: "all that the Father has is mine" (Jn 16:15); "everything you have given me is from you" (Jn 17:7).

The prologue, in brief, suggests that "the God" in a unique and indivisible act of love, expresses himself in the *Lógos* as Father generating the Son and giving all things to the Son. The *Lógos*/Son receives himself and projects himself in love "very near to his Father's heart" (Jn 1:18), returning everything of himself to the Father.

The Lógos *and creation* The third verse, "All things came into being through him, and without him not one thing came into being," presupposes the existence of two levels. The first is that of the "beginning," which is the transcendence of God—God in himself—the distinction between "the God" and the *Lógos*, the Father and his only begotten. The second level is that of the creation of that which is other than God. The otherness here, it should be clear, is not the same as the otherness between God and the *Lógos*, but it is somehow embraced and comprehended within this first distinction. For this reason, it is affirmed not only that the *Lógos* "was in the beginning with God" (verse 2), but also, immediately after this, that "all things came into being through him, and without him [can also mean "outside him"] not one thing came into being" (verse 3). This lapidary affirmation brings us to understand that the self-expression of God in himself in the *Lógos* is the condition for the expression of God also "outside himself" (so to speak), in creation.

The Lógos/Sárx This distinction of the two levels—that of God and his *Lógos*, and that of creation—together with the relation between these, in virtue of the mediation of the *Lógos* in God's creative action, is aimed at an even more profound and unprecedented statement of the link between these. This is found at verse 14, the true high point of the prologue: *kaì ho lógos sàrx egéneto kaì eskénōsen en hymîn*. This is something new (as the *kaì* which introduces the phrase indicates), an unrepeatable and unique event (*egéneto*). Rudolf Schnackenburg writes that

> the phrase does not mean that "the Lógos transformed itself into flesh," because the following phrase ("and placed his tent in midst of us" [a literal translation of the Greek]), the Lógos remains the subject, and made his glory visible to believers in his flesh. Neither can the phrase mean that the Lógos simply appeared as if disguised in flesh, because that would not do justice to the force of the verb *gínesthai*.... With *egéneto* a change of the mode of being of the Lógos is expressed. First he was in glory with his Father (see 17:5–24), now he assumes the lowliness of an earthly and human existence. First he was "with God" (1:1b), now he plants his tent among human beings, and in a human figure, in the full reality of the *sárx*, to take up again, after his return to the Father, the glory of the heavenly mode of being.[20]

As Penna notes, the prologue highlights with the oxymoron *lógos/sárx* what is most disconcerting and unprecedented about the event. The *gínesthai sàrx* (the becoming flesh) of the *Lógos*—both conceptually and terminologically—offers a stable point of reference of Christian interpretation of the Christological event. *Sárkōsis*, *incarnatio*: thus Irenaeus of

20. Rudolf Schnackenberg, *Das Johannesevangelium* (Freiburg: Herder, 1965); Italian translation: *Il vangelo di Giovanni* (Brescia: Paideia, 1973), 1:337 (own trans.).

Lyons, probably for the first time, in the second century, defined the event of the coming of the *Lógos* into the midst of human beings in Jesus Christ. He does this in the light of verse 14 of the prologue.

It is sufficient for now to note that the expression *sárx*, without adjectives, in Johannine thought is more than a simple circumlocution for man, nor does it wish to indicate some dimension of man (for example, the material) to the detriment of others. It indicates rather the fragility of a mortal existence, linked to the earth (see Jn 3:6), weak and impermanent (see Jn 6:63).

The eschatological revelation of God Verse 14b expresses, finally, the fundamental consequence of the event of the incarnation of the *Lógos*: "and we have seen his glory, the glory as of a father's only son, full of grace and truth." In the incarnate *Lógos*, therefore, the glory of the only-begotten Son is revealed to humanity. This glory comes to him from the Father, the glory that, belonging to God, is given as such to the only-begotten in relationship with the Father. In this extraordinarily dense and beautiful statement the theological significance of the entire event of Jesus Christ is summed up. In him, according to the apostolic faith, we have contemplated (*theáō*, in the strong sense of seeing) the glory of the only-begotten one of the Father or, otherwise stated, the glory of the Father reflected in all of its splendor on the face of the Son who, for this very reason of his being Son, is rich, and full of "grace and truth" toward us.

All of this is summed up in another extraordinary and synthetic statement, in verse 18, at the end of the prologue: "No one has ever seen God. It is God the only Son, who is close to the Father's heart, who has made him known." Humanity's experience of desire and anticipation before the impenetrable mystery of God, which not even the revelation of Israel—to whom God had communicated his ineffable name—had satisfied, receives an unforeseen and overflowing response in the incarnation of the *Lógos*. Only he, who is the only-begotten God—God, that is, as the *Lógos* and Son forever oriented toward the heart of the Father—can reveal his face and give us life.

The Spirit in the "Paraclete Sayings"

Within the space opened up and illuminated by the relationship of reciprocal communion between the Father and the *Lógos*/Son in the fourth Gospel, the mission and identity of the Holy Spirit emerges into view.[21] This is the particular theme of the "speeches of the Paraclete" or "Paraclete

21. See Giuseppe Ferraro, *Lo Spirito Santo nel quarto vangelo* (Rome: Borla, 1981), and *Lo Spirito e Cristo nel vangelo di Giovanni* (Brescia: Paideia, 1984).

sayings" found in John 14–16. In these passages, five times Jesus promises the disciples the sending of "another Paraclete" (*allos paráklētos*) after his return to the Father. This name, which is unique to the Gospel of John and is found only there in the New Testament corpus, derives from the verb *para-kaleîn, ad-vocare*, which literally means to "call alongside" or to "call in assistance."

In these "sayings," Jesus illustrates in an illuminating and prophetic way the dynamic and objective of his mission in the first place in reference to the Father who sent him, but also in reference to the Spirit who continues and completes the mission of the Son. The first part of the third "saying" is of particular importance for the definition of the trinitarian dogma and for later debate on the *Filioque*; this dense formulation is worth quoting: "When the Advocate comes, whom I will send to you from the Father, the Spirit of truth who comes from the Father, he will testify on my behalf" (Jn 15:26). The Spirit is here evoked with decisively personal characteristics in the context of his relation to the Father, on the one hand, and to the Son, on the other. It is emphasized, in fact, that the Spirit comes forth from God the Father as from a source; this is the meaning of the verb *ekporeúomai* which is used here, for the first time in the New Testament, in order to express the relationship between the Father and the Holy Spirit. The Spirit is sent by the incarnate, crucified, and risen Son, and comes to the disciples as a person in order to "give witness" to the Son.

Thus, just as the Son is the *Lógos* who communicates the words of the Father, so too the Spirit interiorizes the words of the Christ, and indeed his very presence, in the hearts of the believers. He lives in them, thus giving witness to the Son, teaching, reminding (see 14:26), and guiding the disciples into all the truth (see 16:13). "He will glorify me, because he will take what is mine and declare it to you. All that the Father has is mine. For this reason I said that he will take what is mine and declare it to you" (Jn 16:14–15). The Spirit, *to pneûma*, which is of neutral gender in Greek—is "another." *Ho paráklētos* is masculine. John therefore describes him as *ekeînos*, "him," in the masculine. He, being distinct from the Son, like the Son and in indissoluble relationship with him is sent by the Father into the heart of the believers. As Chevallier points out, with the title Paraclete, John intends to emphasize the "active, personal and relational character of the Spirit."[22]

22. Even if that comes about according to Chevallier, within the predominantly functional framework of the Johannine pneumatology (*Souffle de Dieu*, 2:499; own trans.).

The "Being-One" of the Father, Son, and Holy Spirit

The fourth Gospel and the first Letter of John do not limit themselves to emphasizing the distinction between the three (Father, Son, and Holy Spirit) and their reciprocal relationships, but also give expression—a densely symbolic but also richly articulated expression—to their unity, that is, the ineffable mystery of their "being-one." What emerges is a unity that transcends the prior comprehension of the unity of God found in the First Testament, and the prior comprehension of the unity of God proper to Greek and Hellenistic thought. Particular attention is called for in order to grasp its specific originality.

The mission of the Son and of the Spirit The real unity and real distinction are expressed, first of all, using the language of mission. The Father sends the Son into the world, and after the Son and in relation to him, he also sends the Holy Spirit. Two verbs are drawn into service: *apostéllo* and *pémpō*. Two aspects of the use that the fourth Gospel makes of this central concept should be emphasized: first, that the mission to the world presupposes the coexistence, with the Father, of the Son and the Holy Spirit, who are both *parà toû Patrós*, with the Father, such that the Son returns to the Father, while the Spirit, living in the disciples, leads them to the Son. Second, that according to the *forma mentis* that had developed in Israel from the time of the revelation of the living God, mission implies the presence of the one who sends in the one sent in his name. This means that the one sent represents the sender in such a way as to make the latter present.[23] This is particularly true in the case of the Son and the Holy Spirit in relation to the Father, as we can see in the affirmation of Jesus where he says that everything that the Father has, he gives to the Son and the Spirit receives it in turn from the Son in order to communicate it to believers (Jn 16:14–15). From this perspective, there are two principal ways by which the Johannine tradition gives sapiential and contemplative expression to the novelty of the manifestation of the unity of God, on the basis of the mission, in the event of communication and communion between Father, Son, and Holy Spirit, realized in Jesus: *dóxa* (glory) and *agápe* (love).

Reciprocal glorification The theme of glory (*kābod, dóxa, claritas*), runs through the entire fourth Gospel. As we know from the First Testament,

23. In the First Testament, the one sent represents the one who sends as plenipotentiary spokesperson. Thus, for example, in *Mishna Berakoth* 5:5 we read: "The one sent by a man is just that man himself." The Aramaic word *shâliâh*, as St. Jerome understood, corresponds perfectly to the Greek *apostéllo*.

it represents the tangible evidence of the holiness of God and his salvific presence among human beings, which leads people to contact with the mystery of God in its self-expression. In the fourth Gospel, it is said that Jesus manifests the glory of God who is Father through the "signs" (*sēmeía*) that he works and through his entire earthly ministry,[24] and that the fullness of this manifestation occurs in the Paschal event of the death and resurrection (see Jn 17:1). It is for this reason that the apostolic witness can affirm with reference to Jesus: "we have seen his glory, the glory as of a father's only son, full of grace and truth" (Jn 1:14). On the other hand, Jesus, in the fourth Gospel, affirms that it is the Father who "glorifies" the Son, both in the sense that he manifests himself in him, manifesting him as his only-begotten Son through his works, and especially through his death and resurrection, and in the sense that the Father has from all eternity made the Son a participant in his own glory.

The fourth Gospel can therefore speak of a reciprocal glorification between the Father and the Son (in which the Father, as such, is certainly the principle and final end), and which has as its culmination the Paschal event. Before his passion, Jesus prays: "I glorified you on earth by finishing the work that you gave me to do. So now, Father, glorify me in your own presence with the glory that I had in your presence before the world existed" (Jn 17:4–5; see also 13:31–32; 17:24). It is in this reciprocal glorification that the Father and the Son are each for and in the other, and thus manifest their being one. To Philip who asks him, "Lord, show us the Father, and we will be satisfied," Jesus responds, "Whoever has seen me has seen the Father. How can you say, 'Show us the Father'? Do you not believe that I am in the Father and the Father is in me?" (Jn 14:8–10; see also 10:30).

The Paraclete too, the Spirit of truth, is an intimate and active participant in this reciprocal event of glorification. "He will glorify me, because he will take what is mine and declare it to you" (Jn 16:14). As he himself explains immediately afterward, everything that the Father has given to the Son, and everything that the Son has from the Father is in turn "taken" by the Spirit and announced to human beings (see 16:15). Indeed, the glory that the Father gives to the Son seems finally to be identified with the very gift of the Holy Spirit, wherever Jesus, in the culmination of the prayer of unity, affirms: "The glory that you have given me I have given them, so that they may be one, as we are one, I in them and you in me, that they may become completely one, so that the world may know that you have sent me" (Jn 17:22–23). Here "glory" is what makes the Father and the Son one, and through the gift that the Son makes to human be-

24. See Jn 2:11; 5:36; 10:58; 11:4, 40.

ings (the Spirit), it is what makes believers one with Christ and in him with the Father.

As one can understand from all of this, the theme of glory is central and uniquely profound in the fourth Gospel. The theme has the precise aim of expressing the "being-one" of God in the relationship of reciprocal communication of the divine life of the Father to the Son, and, through the Holy Spirit, to human beings. Glory, therefore, represents the eternal and reciprocal self-gift of the Father and the Son in the Holy Spirit, in which God shines forth in himself and to the world in the shining light of his being. Father, Son, and Holy Spirit are God inasmuch as they are participants in the same divine glory, and thus are one. They are, however, at the same time distinct as each of them is in their own way the destination of this infinite communication of glory that is God himself. All of this is contemplated and affirmed with a symbolic density that is offered to the experience of life and understanding of faith of the church.

The theme of glory is linked throughout the fourth Gospel with the theme of light, and again in 1 John 1:5: "God is light and in him there is no darkness at all." Then there is the designation of God as Spirit in John 4: "God is spirit, and those who worship him must worship in spirit and truth" (4:24). John is not seeking here to give a philosophical definition of God's being (in contrast, for example, with material reality), but rather to express the "quality of his life." Jacques Guillet writes: "God is Spirit and this means that He is at one and the same time omnipotence and total disposability … this means that in taking possession of His creatures He makes them exist in all their originality. … it is above all barriers and all retreats. It is to be eternally and at every moment a new, intact force of life and communion."[25]

In this sense, it is the Holy Spirit who pours forth from the cross of Jesus and who thus overcomes the abyss of separation between Father and Son in death and that between humankind and the Father; the Holy Spirit is the one who fully reveals the "quality" of the life of God as Spirit: free all-powerful love which is life that overcomes death, unity that overcomes separation. The reality of God as Spirit thus transcends the history of salvation and expresses the intimate and proper life of God as the one and unique God, the living one who overcomes every death and whose inexhaustible life is manifested precisely in the revelation that he makes of himself in the incarnate Son and in the Holy Spirit.

25. Jacques Guillet, "God," in *Dictionary of Biblical Theology*, ed. Xavier Léon-Dufour (London: Geoffrey Chapman, 1973), 211.

"God is agápe" The theme of *agápe*, finally, offers in a dense summary form the event of novelty which infinitely transcends the premise that founds its possibility: God's revelation to Israel. The New Testament attests to the fulfillment of this revelation in Jesus Christ. The merciful God of the First Testament shows himself and opens himself unveiling the secret of his holiness: he is love toward humanity, because he is love in himself. The name that God had revealed to Moses, YHWH, the God-with-us (see Ex 3:14), is made explicit with a new name that unveils in an unprecedented way its intimate and true content: God is *agápe* (1 Jn 4:8, 16).

The symbol of the divine *dóxa* which the Father shares with the Son, and which the Son gives back to the Father in the irradiating communion of the Holy Spirit, means that God communicates himself, and nothing other than himself, generating the Son and pouring out the Spirit. What *agápe* affirms therefore, in the light of the Paschal event, is the truth of God's being in a relationship of self-gift, reciprocity, and pouring out that makes the Father, the Son, and the Holy Spirit one in participation of his own life with human beings.

The first Letter of John (though some elements of this are already to be found in the Pauline literature) synthesizes the theological meaning of the event of Jesus Christ (from the incarnation to the Paschal event to the gift of the Spirit) in the revelation of God as *agápe*. The fourth chapter is decisive here. In it John affirms: "Anyone who does not love does not know God, because God is *agápe*. How did God show his *agápe* for us? He sent his one and only Son into the world. He sent him so we could receive life through him" (1 Jn 4:8–9). The famous "definition" of God as *agápe* is here grasped in its indissoluble relationship with the Christological event and with the fact that in him is revealed the Father. *Agápe*, in point of fact, is firstly the name of God's acting in the history of salvation culminating in Christ, who manifests the identity of God, and it is thus the name of God in himself. The theological meaning of the confession of faith, according to which "God is *agápe*" in other words, is determined by the relationship between the Father and the Son which freely includes their relationship toward the world in the Spirit.

The love of the Father (the love that is the Father), should first of all be recognized in the fact that he has an only Son, *monogenés*, who is the first object of his love. This means that "in an irremovable differentiation within himself, he is *lover and beloved*. In John's language, he is God the Father *and God the Son*."[26] In the first instance, therefore, the affirmation that "God is *agápe*" means this distinction, or—better—this unity in dis-

26. See Jüngel, *God as Mystery of the World*, 327; See also Augustine, *De Trinitate* VIII.10.14; VI.5.7.

tinction between the Father and the Son. Such divine and transcendent *agápe* is revealed in the sending on the part of the Father of the only-begotten Son into the world, for the world. The Son who is sent, then, is the expression of the *agápe* of the Father: God is the lover (Father) and beloved (Son), love who gives the beloved out of love for humanity.

The *agápe* of the Father, revealed in the Son, is made present to humanity by means of the Spirit: "By this we know that we abide in him [God] and he in us, because he has given us of his Spirit" (1 Jn 4:13). God, therefore, is the eternal act of *agápe* (Father, only-begotten Son and Holy Spirit) which communicates itself to humanity and freely involves human history in this self-communication in the faith that corresponds to it: "So we have known and believe the love that God has for us. God is love, and those who abide in love abide in God, and God abides in them" (1 Jn 4:16). In Christ, the revelation of God as *agápe* coincides with the fulfillment of the vocation of humanity to renew and fulfill its existence in love.

"So that they might be one as you and I" This *agápe*, which is God himself, is the unity of ones who are distinct—that is, of the Father and the Son, and of the disciples in them; it is expressed in an extraordinary synthesis in Jesus' prayer at the Last Supper, culminating in John 17. As was the case with the synoptics, the account of the Paschal meal offers the hermeneutical key that anticipates the meaning of the Paschal event of death and resurrection expressed in John's Gospel. Jesus' prayer to the Father, after having addressed his disciples during the Last Supper "speeches," throws intense light on the plan of love that the Father has entrusted to the Son and which the Son now, as his "hour" approaches, offers to his disciples, almost as a mirror of the will of the Father, the deepest and most intimate truth. Here are some passages from this prayer (Jn 17:3–6; 20–26):

And this is eternal life, that they may know [*ginóskosin*] you, the only true God, and Jesus Christ whom you have sent. I glorified you on earth by finishing the work that you gave me to do. So now, Father, glorify me in your own presence with the glory that I had in your presence before the world existed. I have made your name known to those whom you gave me from the world. They were yours, and you gave them to me, and they have kept your word.… I ask not only on behalf of these, but also on behalf of those who will believe in me through their word, that they may all be one. As you, Father, are in me and I am in you, may they also be in us [*hína pántes hèn ôsin, kathòs sú, páter, en emoì kagò en soí hína kaì autoì en hēmîn*], so that the world may believe that you have sent me. The glory that you have given me I have given them, so that they may be one, as [*kathòs*] we are one, I in them and you in me [*egò en autoîs kaì sù en emoí hína ôsin tete-*

leiōménoi eis hén], that they may become completely one, so that the world may know that you have sent me and have loved them even as you have loved me. Father, I desire that those also, whom you have given me, may be with me where I am, to see my glory, which you have given me because you loved me before the foundation of the world. Righteous Father, the world does not know you, but I know you; and these know that you have sent me. I made your name known to them, and I will make it known, so that the love with which you have loved me may be in them, and I in them.

The great theme of John 17 is the revelation of the name of the Father. In Jesus, the Father opens himself as the "being-one" in love of the Father and the Son, as the space of "eternal life" for those human beings who received the knowledge of the identity of the Father from the Son, and of his will which he communicates with his whole self by sending the Son into the world. Already in the previous chapters, this truth, in various ways and from various perspectives, had been hinted at and passed on to the disciples. We recall, for example, the metaphor of the vine and its branches (see Jn 15:5), in which Jesus presents himself as the one who gives life itself to the disciples, who have become one with him. Now, Jesus sums up the meaning and destiny of his mission in having communicated, through his words and works, and through himself, the name of the Father who is "the one true God." The First Testament promise contained in the name of God revealed to Moses on Mount Horeb has come about in Jesus. In him and through him, human beings now have definitive access to the very identity of God as the one who, by sending the Son, says in facts rather than simply in words that he wishes freely to share "eternal life" with them. This eternal life dwells in him and pours forth from him on all of those who recognize him, that is those who open themselves in faith in Jesus and receive the gift of God—the gift that he himself became for them in the Son through the Spirit.

The secret of "eternal life" that pours forth from the Father, and which is his very name, consists in this: Jesus prays that "as you, Father, are in me and I am in you, may they also be in us" (Jn 17:21). The "eternal life" that lies in the name of God is, therefore, the "being-one" of the Father and the Son, that is, the gift of the very life that the Father gives to the Son and that the Son lives and exercises as such, exclusively as gift, as the Son is always completely turned to the Father. This "being-one," which is the truth and fruit of the love of the Father for the Son, and, in response, of the Son toward the Father, is communicated by the Son to humanity by the very fact that he reveals to them the name of God so that they can know it.

Jesus, to use the words of Augustine, is the true and unique *mediator unitatis*: "I in them and you in me" (Jn 17:23). As Jesus is one with the Father, because the Father is one with him, so too, having become one with human beings, he makes them one, when they recognize him, as he and the Father are one. It is worth noting that Jesus produces the "being-one" through the reciprocal immanence of himself in the Father and of himself in the disciples. This is not just a fact that derives from his ontological identity, something that depends just on the fact that he is God as the Father is, and becomes a man as humans are. It is rather in the dynamic exercise of his being Son of the Father that becomes flesh: he is one with the Father as *Lógos*/Son, and is one with humans to the extent that he gives himself for them "to the very end" (Jn 13:1). In this way, he is not only the mediator of unity between the Father and human beings, but in virtue of this he is the mediator of unity among human beings themselves. The "being-one" of the disciples should not be understood in a purely vertical way, as something that happens when we are united to Jesus and through him brought into the unity that he lives with the Father. It is also to be understood in a horizontal sense, that is the "being one" of the disciples among themselves, with each other. Jesus is the model and path of this unity. Finally, the *agápe* of the Father for the Son and, through the Son, for the disciples (see Jn 17:23, 26), is the dynamism of life through which the gift of unity in Jesus is brought about, both with the Father and among brothers and sisters.

It is not by coincidence that when Jesus presents "his" new commandment in chapter 13, it is based on the precise will of the Father, the commandment of reciprocal *agápe*: "I give you a new commandment, that you love one another. Just as I have loved you, you also should love one another" (Jn 13:34). Just as the "being-one" of the Father and the Son implies the free reciprocity of their love, so should it be among the disciples: the "being-one" that is the fulfillment of reciprocity, the fruit which transcends and brings it to completion.[27] It is in this light that we should read the "as" (*kathós*) which Jesus uses to express the relationship which exists between the "being-one" which he lives with the Father and the "being-one" both with the Father and among themselves, that the disciples receive as a gift to live. It is an "as" which indicates not only similarity, but also the efficacious and participatory cause, in Jesus, of the unity of the disciples in the unity between the Father and the Son.

At least three points need to be made. First of all, this gift of "being-one" that Jesus makes and is in himself for humanity, is expressed also as the gift of *doxa*, the glory which the Son received from the Father (17:22).

27. As von Balthasar has noted, the centrality of the commandment of reciprocal love in the fourth Gospel is the specific correspondence, on the anthropological and ethical level, to God's revelation on the theological level. See "Nine Propositions on Christian Ethics," in Hans Urs von Balthasar, Heinz Schürmann, and Joseph Ratzinger, *Principles of Christian Morality*, trans. Graham Harrison (San Francisco, Calif.: Ignatius Press, 1986), 75–104.

As already noted, this seems to refer to the gift of life and irradiating holiness that beats in the heart of the Father, and from him, in the heart of the Son: the Holy Spirit. The Holy Spirit thus appears as the gift of God, the gift which is God himself, who has become, so to speak, "person," communicated to the other in his real otherness. This otherness which comes from God, being God, makes God the other, and makes him one with God, conserving him in his otherness. To the gift of such grace which produces unity, and which shines forth, in the second place, is bound up the witness of the truth of Jesus' mission and of the revelation of the name of the Father which is produced there. It could not be otherwise, for the revelation consists precisely in the self-communication of God's life, which is unitive love, and so in the unity of the disciples in Jesus the name of God which is revealed by him is made truly present. Thus, their unity is the eschatological *locus* in which God offers his name to the world: the Trinity that is love.

A final note. The heart and mind of Christ which vibrate as prayer to the *Abbà* are condensed in this extraordinary passage. There is an inexhaustible depth of light which reverberates with the infinity of God here, the truth of the mission and identity of Jesus: the Trinity, the life of God and human beings in and for him. It is this that will be unveiled as light that refracts into the colors of the rainbow, in the Paschal event of his death and resurrection. It is there, in that love carried to the very extreme, that the decisive word will be carried out: "When you have lifted up the Son of Man, then you will realize that I am" (Jn 8:28).

The Event of Jesus the Christ as a Trinitarian Event

It is important, finally, at the end of our examination of the New Testament, to emphasize that it almost gives us a comprehensive synthesis, in its witness to the eschatological self-communication of God to humanity, and places the whole Christ-event in a clear trinitarian frame. I will limit myself to a few brief comments on this.

The Trinitarian Rhythm of the Christ-Event and the Infancy Narratives

The New Testament, first of all, narrates the Paschal event of Jesus as the supreme and decisive *locus* of the revelation of the Father and of the gift of the Holy Spirit, for in this revelation the Father raises the Son in the power of the Spirit, and the glorified Son pours out the fullness of the Spirit on humanity. So the Gospel accounts of the infancy (see Mt 1:18–20; Lk 1:35)[28] illustrate the event of the incarnation of the Son as the work of the Father which comes about through the action of the Holy Spirit. As we recalled, the contemplation (in the Gospel of John) and the recounting (in the Gospels of Matthew and Luke) of the coming in flesh of the Word/Son of God represents the final stage of New Testament Christology, following the eschatological and protological stages. In the case of the infancy narratives, it is clear that these are theological readings of data that come from traditions that came to be formed around the figures of Joseph and Mary, the mother of Jesus.

What is clearly remarkable, from our point of view, is that in both of these accounts, and especially in the Lukan version, the rhythm is completely and only trinitarian in the dynamic horizon in which the event of the coming of God's Son in the flesh is interpreted. This is so much so that it can be assumed to flow from the intense light opened up by a faithful reading of the Paschal event, as its necessary premise: recognized in the very genesis of the Son of God who became man among human beings in Mary's womb. Thus we find in the account of the annunciation to Mary and the birth of Jesus, the distinct as well as unitarian action of the three characters discovered as Jesus' ministry unfolds, as this action comes from the Father's eternal plan and converges in its historical-salvific accomplishment. Each in his own proper way, but together and in unison, is recognized as cooperating at its culmination, in the Paschal event of the Son.

In the incarnation, the principal protagonists are the Father who gratuitously chooses Mary to generate in her womb, in the very heart of human history, the only-begotten and eternal Son. But this takes place in the power (*dýnamis*) of the Holy Spirit, who not only surrounds and graciously forms Mary's freedom, who makes the fully human choice to pronounce the decisive *fiat* to the realization of the Father's plan, but also prepares herself to welcome the generation in her flesh of the Son of God. The Son, in turn, is not simply the passive object of the Father's will, welcomed by Mary in the light and in the power of the Spirit, but himself consents in a mysterious and active way to the Father's design brought about by the Spirit thanks to Mary's *fiat*, thus manifesting from the beginning of his story, his identity and mission as Son. He is, in other words, the one who receives himself freely from the Father, and freely obeys this Father's plan of love in the joyous and total self-gift to the mission that

28. Matthew speaks of the *gennōmenon* of Jesus in Mary as being derived from the Holy Spirit (see Mt 1:18). In Luke, when Mary asks "how can this be?," the archangel Gabriel responds: "The Holy Spirit will come upon you, and the power of the Most High will overshadow you; therefore the child to be born will be holy; he will be called Son of God" (Lk 1:35).

the Father gives him. As the Letter to the Hebrews writes, placing these words on the Son's mouth: "See, God, I have come to do your will, O God" (Heb 10:7).

This tale, filled with theological light, thus witnesses to the awareness of the apostolic faith according to which the entire event of Jesus Christ is placed under the sign of the revelation of the Father and the work of the Spirit. The Father generates the Son in history, as man, in the power of the Spirit; the Son, in the death-resurrection, gives the Spirit and in the Spirit returns to the Father. Thus, we can set the whole complex trajectory schematically:

Father → Holy Spirit → Son/*Lógos* incarnate, crucified, and risen → Holy Spirit → Father

This trajectory interprets the history of salvation as the eternal communication of love among the three which is graciously shared with creation. The Father is the origin and goal, the Son/*Lógos* is the expression and the revelation of the love of the Father, and the Holy Spirit is the love communicated from the Father to the Son and from the Son to the Father, as their ineffable communion and opening and outpouring of this onto and into human history.

The Presence and Mission of Mary in the Coming of God-Trinity

While it is true that Jesus Christ is the event of the self-communication of God to history, and this involves the emptying of the Son in his incarnation as Son (see Phil 2), it is also true that all of this depends on the condition of the possibility of this event on the human side in Mary's *fiat*. This truth is already hinted at, almost in passing but with great theological significance, by the apostle Paul in his Letter to the Galatians: "when the fullness of time had come, God sent his Son, born of a woman" (Gal 4:4).

The incarnation and condescension of God in the Son thus finds echo in Mary, in her becoming the personal space of free and loving welcome of the Son of God in the flesh. It is this that is narrated in Luke's infancy narrative, especially in the scene of the annunciation (1:26–38). Mary is described there as the daughter of Zion and the womb of humanity that opens itself to welcome the love of God which becomes in her and from her, through the action of the Holy Spirit, flesh of humanity. The result of this is that the Marian dimension, understood personally, is an essential dimension on the human side of the trinitarian self-communication of God to the history of humanity. As such it precedes and gives shape to the ecclesial welcome of the gift of revelation. The cooperation of Mary in the event of the incarnation in the virginal conception should be extended to the whole of the Christ-event. If the human-divine maternity of Mary is, as I have stated, the condition of the possibility, on the human side, of the incarnation of the Son of God, the sharing of the fruits of this event with human beings cannot prescind her maternal cooperation.

This intrinsic dynamic of the Christ-event is intuited and expressed by the fourth Gospel. In this account, the first sign through which Jesus shows his glory to the disciples is at the wedding feast at Cana (Jn 2:1–12), and this occurs through the mediation of Jesus' mother. The presence of Mary at the foot of the cross and the substitution of the maternity that Jesus arranges with respect to Mary, between himself and the beloved disciple, figure of a new humanity (see Jn 19:25–27), certainly foreshadows Mary's active presence in the Paschal fulfillment of the incarnation of the Son. On her part, Mary, together with the Spirit poured out "without measure" by the crucified and risen one, shares in this way in the Paschal generation of sons in the Son.

In the Acts of the Apostles, furthermore, Mary is mentioned together with the apostles, some women, and the brothers of Jesus when they come together in the upper room to pray (Acts 1:12–14) while waiting for the gift of the Spirit that Jesus had promised (see Acts 1:7–8). The presence of Mary at the beginning of the church builds on her presence at the very beginning of Jesus' life (see Lk 1:26–38). In both cases, the one who brings about the birth of Jesus and the birth of the church is the Holy Spirit sent by the Father (Lk 1:35; Acts 2:4) in the presence of Mary. In a delicate and allusive way, the Lukan work thus wishes to emphasize that the pouring out of the Spirit through the messiah on all the people of the new covenant happens through the *fiat* and maternal intercession of the mother of God.

Thus already at the level of biblical witness, in a form that is normative for later experience and understanding of faith on the part of the church, Mary is contemplated in God's plan for her, and in her active response to it, at the heart of the self-communication of God the Trinity to the history of humanity. She appears as a created space which freely becomes the horizon of visibility and sharing of the holy mystery of the love of God with humanity—of the God, indeed, who is love.

The *génesis* and *kénosis* of God the Trinity in Jesus Christ

The New Testament also gives witness to a further step in the experience and understanding of the self-communication of God in Jesus when it illuminates the event of the incarnation in the light of the Paschal event. It is not only at the level of historical narration (the infancy accounts), but also at the level of theological contemplation (the prologue of the fourth Gospel). John describes the event of the *Lógos* who "comes into the world" (Jn 1:9), that he "became flesh and lived among us" (Jn 1:14). In this way it affirms, without further elaboration, a "coming" and a "becoming" of God (the Word that makes himself, who becomes flesh, that which he is not). Such expressions give witness to a fact which, at first sight, appears to contradict the immutability attributed to God by pre-Christian thought, but even a certain understanding of the absolute transcendence and sanctity of the First Testament God in reality invites us to contemplate the dynamic of self-gift as an expression of the being of God. The self-communication of God, his gratuitous self-gift, implies a going toward the other, indeed a "making oneself other" (the Son who makes himself man) which is certainly a "becoming," but this is a becoming which is not in contrast to his original being; rather it is unfolded and actuated in reference to humanity.

Paul in his Letter to the Philippians expresses himself in the same way, in a passage upon which rivers of ink have been spilled throughout the history of the church. "Christ Jesus, who, though he was in the form of God, did not regard equality with God as something to be exploited, but emptied [*ekénōsen*] himself, taking the form of a slave, being born in human likeness. And being found in human form, he humbled himself and became obedient to the point of death, even death on a cross" (Phil 2:5–8). Here the divine sonship of Jesus is presented in coordination with the free choice of the Son—who is and remains in the condition, which is his own, of equality with God—to empty himself of his divine prerogatives for the purpose of saving humanity, and becoming flesh in order to communicate his own divine sonship (see also 2 Cor 8:9). The first Letter of Peter goes so far as to say: "Christ, like that of a lamb without defect or blemish … was destined before the foundation of the world" (1 Pt 1:19–20). Here there is a further and stupefying insight into the total mystery of Christ. He, from all eternity, is predestined as lamb of sacrifice. This can be meant in the sense that his gift to humanity from the Father already included the real possibility of rejection and sin, and therefore of his death on the cross as a sign and supreme gesture of love. But it can also mean that the very life of God, as mutual and radical gift and exchange, lives a kind of "sacrifice" of joy and glory, in which the Son offers himself totally to the Father, and this offer always already includes the possibility of the sacrifice of himself for the salvation of creation, by means of him and in view of him according to the will of the Father.

The being and life of God are therefore witnessed to in the Son made flesh through a *génesis* and *kénosis*, which is to say a gift and a sacrifice of love that do not contradict but express in human form (marked by the creaturely state and the tragic exercise of freedom) the abyssal depths of the mystery of God's being as love. These are formidable insights into the life of God disclosed by the Christological revelation which cannot but have great impact on the trinitarian understanding of God.

The Eschatological Horizon of the Trinitarian Revelation

The Book of Revelation, finally, illuminates the essential eschatological tension of God's self-communication. This is begun and progressively realized in the history of the world and of Israel, and finally in Jesus, and orients in grace the final destiny of humankind to be fulfilled in the eternity of God.

The final book of the New Testament makes explicit mention of the Father, Son, and Holy Spirit not only for their roles in the drama which, after Jesus, moves with eschatological rapidity and even tragically toward its epilogue. It also mentions them in the approach to the definitive home and destiny of humanity. Thus, for example, in the vision of chapters 4 and 5, the Father is described as the "one seated on the throne," and the Son as the "Lamb that was slaughtered," and the Spirit through the symbolism of the "seven horns and seven eyes"—signs of the strength and knowledge of which the Lamb is filled.

Revelation further describes God as "Who is and who was and who is to come" (see Rv 1:4, 8; 4:8), as the "alpha and the omega," as the "beginning and end." Thus the divine name that was revealed to Moses (Ex 3:14) is unveiled in its full meaning, and the eschatological meaning of the ever more intense arrival of God, through Jesus Christ and in the power of the Spirit is emphasized. This coming is dramatically moving in history toward the fulfillment of the *parousia*.

In this definitive arrival, described as the descent of the new Jerusalem in the midst of human beings, the presence of God in the world will be unveiled and fully brought to completion. Thus "the city has no need of sun or moon to shine on it, for the glory of God is its light, and its lamp is the Lamb" (Rv 21:23). Then the "woman clothed with the sun" (Rv 12:1) will show to all, her panhuman and pancosmic vastness. The light of the risen one will orient all gazes toward the inaccessible glory of the Father, while "the river of the water of life, bright as crystal" will flow for eternal life from the throne of him and the Lamb (Rv 22:1).

Then, as Paul writes: God will be, through Christ and the Spirit, "all in all" (1 Cor 15:28). In the meantime, as the drama of history flows onward, "between the times" of the first and second and definitive coming of Christ "the Spirit and the bride say 'Come'" (Rv 22:17).

CHAPTER 16

Summary

From what we have seen thus far, the New Testament offers not simply the deepest novelty regarding the face of God that the event of Jesus Christ presents us with, but also the extreme wealth and depth of his message. We should not, of course, deny the continuity with the First Testament, nor the essential and marvelous coherence of the revelation of God that is witnessed to by the New Testament. But the novelty and inexhaustible wealth of what is said and hinted at are, nevertheless, always greater. A new horizon of life and thought is thus opened up for the history of humanity. How true are the words of the apostle John, who writes: "In this is love, not that we loved God but that he loved us" (1 Jn 4:10). God, the mystery toward which the deepest aspirations and hopes of the human heart are concentrated, is, in the extraordinary experience of Israel, revealed as the "I am" which stands in front of humanity and creation, with infinite power and infinite mercy, and with the obstinate will to live together with human beings and free them integrally and definitively.

In Jesus, the "I am" is revealed—in an unexpected and surprising, but also liberating and inviting, way—as a "We are": "The Father and I are one" (Jn 10:30). And this is made fully manifest in the event of the death and resurrection: "When you have lifted up the Son of Man, then you will realize that I am" (Jn 8:28). This is where the extraordinary novelty of the Christological revelation lies, the originality of Christian monotheism: the being "one" of God which is unfolded in the "we" of the Father, of the Son, and of the Holy Spirit. This "being one" offers itself to be known and shared in grace, by the human being in the cross and resurrection of Jesus. This is an undeniable truth: we wish to be rigorously faithful to the message of Jesus Christ and to the New Testament witness.

The experience and understanding of this event by the apostles and the earliest church is that of participating by grace in this event. In other words, it is first being introduced by Jesus of Nazareth, and then fully by the Paschal Christ, into the relationship of love of the Son with the Father in the Holy Spirit: "You have received a spirit of adoption. When we cry,

'Abbà! Father!' it is that very Spirit bearing witness with our spirit that we are children of God" (Rom 8:15–16). The revelation of God—Father, Son, and Holy Spirit—is the experience of freedom and participation in "eternal life" for those who adhere to Jesus. This experience has the seal of undeniability as well. Knowing the God of Jesus is participating in the same relationship that he has with his Father in the Holy Spirit. Did he not pray to the Father "that they may all be one. As you, Father, are in me and I am in you, may they also be in us" (Jn 17:21)? The Trinity, before being a doctrine, is an experience of life, a gift of Jesus through his Spirit, an anthropological truth and a theological truth.

The remarkable fact remains of the surprising novelty of the image of God that is thus given to experience and thought. One can contemplate God on the basis of the revelation that he makes of himself in Jesus, in a new way, without losing any of that holiness or unicity of YHWH as witnessed by the First Testament, but which is understood ever more deeply in the novelty and truth that Jesus brings to the world. This is the challenge which the church will have to face, in contact with the culture of its time: becoming aware of the gift of grace testified by its faith and its life. The journey will necessarily be long and difficult. It will also be engrossing. It will be certain, because the revelation of Jesus—fixed in the New Testament and communicated in baptism and in the Eucharist—represents the certain criterion of truth and the inexhaustible source for deeper understanding, while the Holy Spirit introduces and guides us "into all the truth" (Jn 16:13).

Thus begins the adventure of the church, and also that of the cultures in which the message of Jesus will be cast as a seed that brings about new life. For both life and thought a new phase begins, the exploration of a horizon previously unknown, stupefying and inviting, a life and a thought which invest meaning in all of the dimensions of personal and social life. In what follows, however, I will touch upon those matters which are specifically linked to the understanding of the mystery of God the Trinity.

PART 4

THE WAY

God the Trinity in the Way of History

> I am the Alpha and the Omega . . . who is and who was and who is to come, the Almighty.
>
> —Revelation 1:8

CHAPTER 17

The Theological Understanding of God-Trinity

We have seen the novelty and wealth of the New Testament witness to the self-communication of God in Jesus the Christ. It is a "novelty" both in relation to the First Testament and in relation to the philosophy and the religiosity of the Hellenistic world. The Asian religions are not yet in the picture: it is only today that there is real contact with them. It is "wealth" because of the density and variety of the formulas in which the faith in God the Father, Son, and Holy Spirit is expressed.

As has been emphasized, the New Testament witness is normative for the successive experience and understanding of the Christian face of God, for it is the direct and immediate transmission and interpretation of the event of Jesus witnessed to by the apostolic church in the breath of the Spirit. It thus represents, for the centuries following, an indispensable and insuperable access to the Jesus-event. It is and remains absolutely essential. One must always continue to make reference to it, attentive to the Spirit, in order to deepen and make fruitful its inexhaustible truth-content. This is because the Son/Word, in which God/*Abbà* expresses himself, became incarnate in the history of Jesus of Nazareth and in this way communicated the fullness of his self-revelation.

This is clearly stated in the Letter to the Hebrews: "Long ago God spoke to our ancestors in many and various ways by the prophets, but in these last days he has spoken to us by a Son, whom he appointed heir of all things, through whom he also created the worlds" (Heb 1:1–2; see also *DV*, no. 4). It is expressed, perhaps even more vividly, in the fourth Gospel: "No one has ever seen God. It is God the only Son, who is close to the Father's heart, who has made him known" (Jn 1:18). Certain methodological clarifications flow from this, and should be mentioned here, so that we can better understand how the transmission, interpretation and assimilation in human life and thought of the mystery of God the Trinity come about in the history of the church, and as a consequence in civilization.

From Economy to *theo-logía*

First of all: salvation history is the necessary point of departure for *theo-logía*, the faith's understanding of the mystery of God. Let us recall here something that has already been mentioned, but which may now be more completely understood; this is a theological principle that the Church Fathers knew well, and which was formulated in the following terms: *theología*, the contemplation of the mystery of God in Godself, is necessarily based on *oikonomía*, that is, God's plan of salvation carried out in history through the incarnation of the Son and the gift of the Spirit. This same principle—as we have seen in part 1, above—has been proposed again by contemporary theology through Karl Rahner's formulation: "the economic Trinity is the immanent Trinity."[1]

The Itinerary of the Experience and Understanding of God the Trinity Offered by the Holy Spirit

There is, however, another sense in which the history of salvation is the place of the knowledge of the mystery of God. Following the coming of Jesus, following his death and resurrection and the gift of the Spirit, a process of vital intellectual penetration of the mystery of God revealed in Christ gets underway in the experience of the church. The definitiveness of the revelation that had occurred in him implies both that the Holy Spirit—as the Gospel of John writes—guides and directs the church toward "all the truth" (see Jn 16:13).

This means that the history of the church—and, in a more general sense, human history itself—to the extent that it is penetrated completely by and enwrapped in the Holy Spirit, and despite human resistance and distortion, represents the human and cosmic space providentially prepared and guided by the Spirit himself, within which the inexhaustible wealth of the Jesus-event can be fully appreciated. It follows that the ever-greater understanding of the mystery of God the Trinity is produced within the space of a polarity. On the one hand, there is the normative reference to the eschatological revelation of Jesus Christ which was given in the New Testament. On the other hand, there is the docility to the impulses of the Spirit and the discernment of the signs of the times which continually encourage Christian thought to penetrate more deeply the treasure of this mystery in order to illuminate personal and social life with it.

Dei Verbum describes in a precise and articulate way how this process comes about (no. 8):

1. See part 1 above.

> This tradition which comes from the Apostles develops in the Church with the help of the Holy Spirit. For there is a growth in the understanding of the realities and the words which have been handed down. This happens through the contemplation and study made by believers, who treasure these things in their hearts (see Lk 2:19, 51)[2] through a penetrating understanding of the spiritual realities which they experience, and through the preaching of those who have received through Episcopal succession the sure gift of truth. For as the centuries succeed one another, the Church constantly moves forward toward the fullness of divine truth until the words of God reach their complete fulfillment in her.... Thus God, who spoke of old, uninterruptedly converses with the bride of His beloved Son; and the Holy Spirit, through whom the living voice of the Gospel resounds in the Church, and through her, in the world, leads unto all truth those who believe and makes the word of Christ dwell abundantly in them (see Col. 3:16).[3]

From this text, it is clear that the progressive penetration of the mystery of God the Trinity involves the whole life of the church, and that therefore it is not just an intellectual question, but a vital and global question, touching both the personal and communitarian level. This progressive penetration has the whole history of humanity as its theater. It also finds in the Holy Spirit its main protagonist, thanks both to the continuous assistance that the Spirit offers to the church (in particular through the dynamism of tradition, the role of the magisterium, and the gift of special charisms), and thanks also to the always new impulses of grace and light that the Spirit gives on a cultural and social level.

Inside Human History

The progress in understanding the mystery of God takes place, therefore, in strict interaction with the history of humanity. This is true, on the one hand, in the sense that it responds to the challenges and situations of the cultures that the announcement of the revelation encounters as it spreads. Thus, there can be distorted or reductive interpretations that can emerge as those cultures seek ways to express the truths of the faith in their own languages. The heresies, for example, that are encountered in the first centuries of the Christian epoch, played a paradoxically important role in the first centuries of the Christian age because it was in order to clarify and defend the truth of revelation that the church was obliged to formulate the dogmas. On the other hand, such progress also depends on the reception, purification, and engagement with the preoccupations and needs of various cultures and the incessant historical development of thought, in

2. The reference to Lk 2:19, 51 should be noted. Here Mary's attitude indicates the model and form of faithful understanding of the Word.

3. See also *DV*, no. 12, and the document of the International Theological Commission, "The Interpretation of Dogmas."

which, despite the ever-present dangers, the Holy Spirit is ever at work.

This has at least two consequences. First of all, as Vatican II emphasizes, it means that there is a *mutua relatio* between the life of the church and the history of the world into which the life of the church is inserted. *Gaudium et Spes* is quoted by *Novo Millennio Ineunte*: "Even as she engages in an active and watchful discernment aimed at understanding the 'genuine signs of the presence or the purpose of God,' the Church acknowledges that she has not only given, but has also 'received from the history and from the development of the human race'" (no. 56; see *GS*, nos. 40–44). In the second place, it means that the meeting between revelation and different cultures, in that process which is defined as inculturation,[4] through the discernment of the "truths of faith" and "moans of the Spirit" which are generously spread in human traditions, constitutes an important stimulus to deeper understanding and explication of revelation itself. Pietro Rossano points out in this regard that the understanding and expression of the wealth of Christian revelation—to the extent that this is possible within history itself—comes about when revelation is welcomed by the various cultures in which human creativity expresses itself.[5]

The Criteria of Apostolicity and Catholicity and the Meaning of Dogmas

In this perspective, it is important to emphasize that the growth in understanding and expression of the mystery of God should be tested and

4. This process, as J. Ratzinger explains, should not be understood simply as a transplantation of the naked and pure truth of revelation into different cultures, but rather as the meeting between a culture already formed by revelation, present in scripture and church tradition, and various cultures with which that culture comes into contact. Thus, it is more precise to speak of a continuous event of "inculturation." See Joseph Ratzinger, "Fede, religione e cultura," in his *Verità Fede Tolleranza: Il cristianesimo e le religioni del mondo* (Siena: Cantagalli, 2003), 57–82, esp. 60–68.

5. See Pietro Rossano, *Il problema teologico delle religioni* (Catania: Paoline, 1975), 44. In this same perspective, John Paul II affirms in *Novo Millennio Ineunte*: "This missionary duty, moreover, does not prevent us from approaching dialogue with an attitude of profound willingness to listen. We know in fact that, in the presence of the mystery of grace, infinitely full of possibilities and implications for human life and history, the Church herself will never cease putting questions, trusting in the help of the Paraclete, the Spirit of truth (cf. Jn 14:17), whose task it is to guide her 'into all the truth' (Jn 16:13). This is a fundamental principle not only for the endless theological investigation of Christian truth, but also for Christian dialogue with other philosophies, cultures and religions. In the common experience of humanity, for all its contradictions, the Spirit of God, who 'blows where he wills' (Jn 3:8), not infrequently reveals signs of his presence which help Christ's followers to understand more deeply the message which they bear. Was it not with this humble and trust-filled openness that the Second Vatican Council sought to read 'the signs of the times'? Even as she engages in an active and watchful discernment aimed at understanding the 'genuine signs of the presence or the purpose of God,' the Church acknowledges that she has not only given, but has also 'received from the history and from the development of the human race.' This attitude of openness, combined with careful discernment, was adopted by the Council also in relation to other religions. It is our task to follow with great fidelity the Council's teaching and the path which it has traced" (par. 56).

verified using two fundamental criteria: the criterion of the apostolicity of the faith, by which I mean conformity of the experience and understanding of the trinitarian mystery to what is testified to and transmitted by the New Testament and the tradition, and the criterion of the catholicity of ecclesial life, by which I refer to the reception on the part of the one church, which means concretely on the part of the many individual church communities in communion among themselves and with their visible sign of their unity which is the church of Rome.[6]

Essential points in this development are the Christological and trinitarian dogmas of the first centuries. In these, the self-consciousness of the church, with the help of the Holy Spirit and in expression of the church's apostolicity and catholicity, expressed some fundamental interpretive keys of the event of Jesus Christ. These should be considered as firm and irreversible points in the understanding of the mystery of God who became present to history in revelation. These, on the other hand, require a correct interpretation and, rather than thinking of them as the definitive end points of a development, they should be considered as a secure and indispensable starting point for further reflection. In this sense, the dogmas, far from being—as sometimes is superficially assumed—external limitations imposed on the free search for the truth, are rather precious and irreplaceable points of reference, almost like springboards for a correct understanding of the mystery and for ever new investigation. Indeed, the great Eastern Orthodox theologian of the last century, Sergius Bulgakov, to whom I will return, defined them as "salvation and condition of freedom" for human thought.

Working Hypothesis

On the basis of these methodological premises, we can synthetically delineate a framework of two great epochs in which the development of the understanding of the mystery of God took place in the history of the church, framed with a prologue and with a relaunch of new perspectives in the twentieth century. This overview will bear in mind not just the intellectual and dogmatic developments, but also the existential and charismatic developments witnessed to by the whole Christian people, with particular reference to the experience of saints and mystics as well as to the contribution of philosophical and scientific thought, not to mention that of various cultures.

6. See my chapter 3 above. Obviously, this communion, which has never been completely interrupted in the course of history, because it is founded on God's faithfulness to the church of Christ, and efficaciously marked by the faith in him attested to by the apostolic doctrine and by baptism, allows for various degrees of actuation, as the Second Vatican Council states in *Lumen Gentium* and *Unitatis Redintegratio*.

The Pre-Nicene Prologue

The pre-Nicene period represents the prologue. This period goes from the time of the New Testament until 325, the year of the first Ecumenical Council of Nicaea. In this initial section of the history of Christianity, we can speak of a luminous communion with the mystery of God revealed in Jesus which is expressed at all levels in the life of the church, up to the supreme witness of martyrdom, with some timid but precious beginnings of exploration in faithfulness to the data of revelation and in dialogue with the surrounding culture. Quite quickly, however, a crisis emerges, which was crucial for the orthodox faith, which led to the dogmatic definitions of the first councils.

The Fathers and the Middle Ages: *Trinitas in Excelsis*

Following this prologue, what stands out is the long and decisive epoch of theological understanding reflecting on and elaborating the trinitarian mystery on the basis of the first Council of Nicaea. This period includes the patristic and Scholastic eras, and has its secure foundation in the dogmas of the first centuries (Nicaea I in 325, Constantinople I in 381, Ephesus in 431, and Chalcedon in 451). These assume and transcend the ontological categories elaborated by Greek philosophy in the light of revelation in order to establish the equal divinity of the Son and the Holy Spirit with the Father and the divine-humanity of Jesus Christ, true God and true man, thanks to the language of the unity of the divine *ousía* or *substantia* and the threeness in it of the *hypostáses* or *personae* of the Father, Son, and Holy Spirit. The theological intuitions of the Church Fathers and the *summae* of the medieval doctors represent extraordinarily important acquisitions for Christian faith. They penetrate the mystery of God and illuminate the transcendent and inexhaustible truth of his inner life: unity and distinction of the three persons as the principle, form, and destiny of creation.

The Modern Period: The Trinity in History and from the Cross

With the modern period and the anthropocentric turn that characterizes it, a second epoch begins. The Trinity, which to that point was confessed and contemplated in its perfect and inexhaustible transcendence, is once again placed in relationship, not just existentially (as it had always been) but also theoretically with the history of humankind. It is true, on the one hand, that we can say that the process of secularization that marked the West brought about a kind of "exile of the Trinity" (Bruno Forte) so that it is relegated in splendid isolation *in excelsis*, both on the part of academic theology, and in another way by a culture that has emancipated itself from the faith. But, on the other hand, it is also possible and necessary to speak of the growth of awareness already in the High Middle Ages (with Joachim of Fiore, St. Bonaventure, and St. Thomas) and then in the theology of Luther, the Carmelite and Ignatian mystical traditions, and in modern philosophy (it is enough to think of German Idealism), casting intensely significant links of life and understanding between the trinitarian mystery of God and the history of humanity in a new way.

The Twentieth Century and the Announcement of a New Season

The need to reestablish the relationship between the Trinity and the history of humanity and the impact that this vision of God has on the understanding of the conception of humanity, society, and the cosmos constitute the presupposition of a new experience and understanding of the revelation of the mystery of God the Trinity as the decisive horizon of illumination of human destiny. The twentieth century represents, from this point of view, a providential rebirth of interest for the trinitarian doctrine which is progressively investing all areas of knowledge and action. This is a challenge that still awaits us in large part.

CHAPTER 18

The Pre-Nicene Period

The Trinity Lived and Confessed by the Church

As anticipated, in the period of the history of the church immediately following the apostolic era, the mystery of God revealed in Jesus Christ is lived and confessed as a gratuitous and extraordinary gift received in revelation and welcomed in faith. This experience is lived in joyful but peaceful amazement. Indeed, in these first centuries, "the Church itself, as communion, expresses the true and salvific profession of faith in the Trinity."[1] As the first Letter of John affirms, this is nothing other than the *koinōnía* with and in Jesus Christ and, through him, with the Father, a communion into which all human beings are gratuitously called to participate in the Holy Spirit (see 1 Jn 1:1–4).

The Witness of Liturgy and Martyrs

All of this is tangible in the liturgy, in the first place in the celebration of baptism and the Eucharist, which are events that found and constitute the life of the ecclesial community. In these, thanks to the profession of the symbol of faith, faith in the Trinity is explicitly affirmed[2] such that the circularity of *lex orandi* and *lex credendi* is to be seen from the very beginning. Thus, for example, this is evident in the witness of St. Justin at the beginning of the second century.[3] In this same spirit, Hip-

1. Anton Weber, Silvano Cola, and Giovanni D'Alessandro, "La Chiesa dei Padri e dei grandi concili," in Università Popolare Mariana, *Il Dio di Gesù Cristo*, 151 (own trans.).

2. It is enough to refer to: Adalbert Hammann, "La Trinità nella liturgia e nella vita cristiana," in *Mysterium Salutis*, vol. 3: *La storia della salvezza prima di Cristo*, ed. Johannes Feiner and Magnus Löhrer (Brescia: Queriniana, 1969), 169–85; John Norman Davidson Kelly, *Early Christian Creeds* (London: Routledge, 1982).

3. This is how he describes, respectively, the baptismal and Eucharistic liturgy celebrated by the first Christian communities under the sign of the trinitarian faith: "(Those that must be baptized) are brought by us where there is water, and are regenerated in the same manner in which we were ourselves regenerated. For, in the name of God, the Father and Lord of the universe, and of our Saviour Jesus Christ, and of the Holy Spirit, they then receive the washing with water" (*First Apology*, 61). "We bless the Maker of all through His Son Jesus Christ, and through the Holy

polytus of Rome, at the beginning of the third century, clearly states the meaning and breadth of the originally trinitarian dynamic of Christian prayer, addressed to the Father through Christ in the Holy Spirit—thus is expressed that the whole existence of the believer and of the church is lived in a trinitarian rhythm. The trinitarian faith is further testified, to the point of the spilling of the blood of martyrs. Thus, for example, St. Polycarp of Smyrna who, around the year 155, concluded his earthly life with a beautiful profession of faith in the Trinity:

> I bless you because you have considered me worthy of this day and hour, that I might receive a place among the number of the martyrs in the cup of your Christ, to the resurrection to eternal life, both of soul and of body, in the incorruptibility of the Holy Spirit.... For this reason, indeed for all things, I praise you, I bless you, I glorify you, through the eternal and heavenly High Priest, Jesus Christ, your beloved Son, through whom to you with him and the Holy Spirit be glory both now and for the ages to come. Amen.[4]

The unity of the church, nourished and guaranteed by the communion of the presbyters and believers with the bishop, is intuited and sung by another apostolic father and martyr of the beginning of the second century, St. Ignatius of Antioch, reflecting the trinitarian communion of the Father, Son, and Spirit in time. For this, the unity among believers, he emphasizes, is indispensable if we are to confess the true unity of God himself.[5]

The Dawn of Trinitarian Theology

Quite quickly the need becomes apparent to reflect more deeply on the theoretical and practical meaning[6] of the face of God: Father, Son, and Holy Spirit, as revealed in Jesus. There are basically two apologetically

Ghost.... bread and wine and water are brought, and the president in like manner offers prayers and thanksgivings, according to his ability, and the people assent, saying Amen" (ibid., 67); available at newadvent.org.

4. *Martyrdom of Polycarp*, no. 14, in *The Apostolic Fathers*, trans. J. B. Lightfoot and J. R. Harmer, ed. Michael W. Holmes, 2nd ed. (Grand Rapids, Mich.: Baker Book House, 1989), 141.

5. "I congratulate you who are united with him [your bishop], as the church is with Jesus Christ and as Jesus Christ is with the Father, that all things might be harmonious in unity" (*Letter to the Ephesians*, no. 5), in *The Apostolic Fathers*, 87–88.

6. See George Prestige, *God in Patristic Thought* (London: William Heinemann, 1936); Basil Studer, *Dio salvatore nei Padri della Chiesa: Trinità-cristologia soteriologia* (Rome: Borla, 1986), 38–52. See also the imposing and well-documented essay on the history of trinitarian dogma, *Le Dieu du salut: La tradition, la règle de foi et les Symboles: L'Économie du salut: Le développement des dogmes trinitaire et christologique*, ed. B. Sesboüé and J. Wolinski, Histoires des dogmes (Paris: Desclée, 1994), and recently, Michel Fédou's precise study, *La Voie du Christ: Genèse de la christologie dans le contexte religieux de l'Antiquité du II siècle au début du IV siècle* (Paris: Cerf, 2006). This work puts into evidence the wealth and value of the theological proposals of the pre-Nicene period; as such these cannot and should not be simplistically evaluated in the framework of the subsequent orthodox dogma formulated in the fourth-century councils.

inspired reasons that brought this need to the fore. The first of these, more internal to the life of the church, comes from the need to correctly express and defend the originality of the apostolic faith professed in the New Testament when faced with deviations and improper interpretations which quickly emerged within the ecclesial community. The second is related to the first, and comes from the desire to present and illustrate this mystery, so new and intellectually impermeable, in the most adequate manner in the religious and philosophical culture of that time. These two motives converge in the need to penetrate even more deeply, in life and with thought, into the truth of the faith. In this context, the first writings of Christian "theologians" begin to appear.

Irenaeus of Lyons against the Gnostics

The first of these is undoubtedly Irenaeus of Lyons, who died around the year 202.[7] In his *Adversus haereses*, he defends and explains the orthodox faith against the Gnostic speculations which attempt, through an imaginative syncretism of doctrines from various sources, to penetrate the mystery of God prescinding from the faith of the church and the truth of the real incarnation of Jesus Christ, the Word of God. Based on a faithful reading of scripture, Irenaeus illustrates the contents of the faith describing salvation history attested by scripture in profound and convinced communion with the apostolic church.

In his theology, the Christological revelation, with its essential presuppositions in the First Testament, is given a thoroughgoing trinitarian interpretation. This is done in an entirely original way in conformity with a logic of thought which roots itself in the heart of revelation, especially in the Pauline and the Johannine literature, and without making use of the categories of Hellenistic philosophy. Jesus Christ is witnessed to and understood as the center and recapitulation of the entirety of history. He is the Word of God who comes out of the heart of the Father, even as he remains in perfect unity with him, to give us the Holy Spirit and gather us all together in the heart of the Father, from whence he had come and toward which he returns.[8] Thus, the Father and Son and Holy Spirit operate together in the history of salvation of humanity, as they had in the cre-

7. Among studies of his thought, see the following: Réal Tremblay, *La manifestation et la vision de Dieu selon saint Irénée de Lyon* (Münster: Aschendorff, 1978); a helpful overall look at his trinitarian theology is offered by Bart Benats, *Il ritmo trinitario della verità: La teologia di Ireneo di Lione* (Rome: Città Nuova, 2006), or, in brief, Benats, "La fede secondo Ireneo di Lione," in *La fede: Evento e promessa*, ed. P. Coda and C. Hennecke (Rome: Città Nuova, 2000), 167–86.

8. "We—who were but lately created ... have received, according to the ministration of the Word, who is perfect in all things, as the mighty Word, and very man, who ... has also poured out the Spirit of the Father for the union and communion of God and man, imparting indeed God to men by means of the Spirit" (*Adversus haereses* V.1.1); available at newadvent.org.

ation of humankind, with the Son and the Spirit almost like the "hands" with which the Father brought about and shaped his work: "there is one only God, the Creator—He who is above every Principality, and Power ... He is Father, He is God, He the Founder, He the Maker, He the Creator, who made those things by Himself, that is, through His Word and His Wisdom."[9] The understanding of the trinitarian mystery is therefore entirely located in a historical-salvific perspective. A famous passage affirms: "the glory of God is a living man; and the life of man consists in beholding God."[10] The vision of God makes itself available according to the trinitarian rhythm (from the Holy Spirit to the incarnate Word to the Father) which corresponds to the trinitarian rhythm through which God created and saved humanity (from the Father by means of the Word in the Spirit which is given):

> because those who ... bear the Spirit of God are led to the Word, that is the Son, and the Son welcomes them and presents them to the Father and the Father makes them incorruptible. Thus, without the Spirit it is not possible to see the Word of God and no one without the Son can approach the Father, for the knowledge of the Son of God comes about by means of the Holy Spirit.[11]

This is the order, the rhythm, the movement with which the human, created and modeled in the image and likeness of the uncreated God becomes that which he is called to be: the Father decides and orders, the Son executes and forms, the Spirit nourishes and gives growth, and the human gradually progresses toward his destiny.[12]

Tertullian and the Invention of Trinitarian Language

Another theologian of the pre-Nicene period, this time a Latin speaker, whose teaching will be decisive for the subsequent development and consolidation of trinitarian theology, is Tertullian, who died around the year 230. He is well aware of the need that "God be believed in, in a new way,"[13] if we are to be faithful to the revelation of Jesus Christ. For this reason, beyond the correct exposition of the trinitarian faith in the controversy with the monarchian heresy, about which I will speak immediately below, Tertullian is the first to use certain expressions that were to become standard in the Latin language to express the mystery of

9. Ibid., II.20.9: here Wisdom means Holy Spirit.

10. Ibid., IV.20.7.

11. *Demonstratio apostolica* 5.

12. *Adversus haereses* IV.38.3.

13. *Adversus praxean* 31 (PL 2:196B). On the theology of Tertullian, before anything else, see Jean Daniélou, *Le origini del cristianesimo latino: Storia delle dottrine cristiane prima di Nicea*, trans. I. Ribeiro and T. Cavazzuti (Bologna: EDB, 1991); besides the classic study by Joseph Moingt, *Théologie trinitaire de Tertullien*, 4 vols. (Paris: Aubier, 1966–69).

the Trinity. The first of these is *Trinitas*, to say the new face of the God who is one and three together, and then *persona* to say the distinct reality of the three, and *substantia* to speak of their unity and equality of nature.

In Dialogue with Hellenistic Philosophy: The School of Alexandria

While Irenaeus develops his trinitarian reflections in polemical engagement with Gnosticism, the school of Alexandria commits itself with decision to dialogue with Hellenistic philosophy. This dialogue, in practice, constitutes the principal task of the maturing Christian thought of the early centuries. The first question that emerged for Christian faith in this dialogue was related to the Greek *lógos*.[14] The confrontation was not so much between the faith and pagan religion (even though the so-called mystery religions would play an important role in this context), but rather with the great tradition of Greek philosophy (Socrates, Plato, Aristotle, the Stoics, etc., up to and including the various versions of Platonism). This is so clearly the case that quite a few Church Fathers see the meeting between the Hebrew revelation (culminating in Christ) and Greek philosophy as a kind of providential event, part of the divine plan of salvation.

In the Egyptian city of Alexandria, the cultural center of the ancient world in the first centuries of the Christian age, there is a confluence of the tradition of Greek thought, the cross-pollination of Hebrew and Greek thought in the work of Philo of Alexandria (25/20 BCE–40 CE) and, especially starting from the end of the second century, the still youthful Christian religion. In the third century, the greatest and most ingenious heir to the Greek philosophical tradition, Plotinus (205–70), representing both the culmination and the swan song of that tradition, taught in Alexandria.

The philosophical conception of God with which the Christian faith came into dialogue was, in this rich and varied cultural tapestry, characterized by two fundamental concepts: (1) the concept of the One, beyond everything, and as such ineffable. This vision is already to be found in basic form in Plato's dialogues *Parmenides* and *Sophist*, and in the so-called unwritten doctrines, and was taken up and developed by Plotinus. (2) The concept of the mediating realities between the ineffable One and the visible world. This is of a lower level with regard to the first principle and yet gives the cosmos an imprinting of the intelligibility and beauty of God. In particular among these, there is the *Lógos* and the *Psyché* (world soul).

14. See Joseph Ratzinger, *Introduction to Christianity*, trans. J. R. Foster (San Francisco, Calif.: Ignatius Press, 2004), 137–43.

This framework certainly offered points of support for Christian thought, both in relation to the transcendence of God (the One), and for the notion of the *Lógos* which is present in the fourth Gospel, even if there it is derived more from a biblical source than from philosophical writings. The Christian vision of the *Lógos* and *Pneûma* are not so very distant from Plotinus. Furthermore the Jewish writer, Philo, had already attempted a synthesis between the Jewish and Greek perspectives, emphasizing on the one hand the absolute transcendence of the biblical God and, on the other hand, also his presence to creation through Wisdom and the Spirit.

What was so new about the Christian vision was, in any case, remarkable. The revelation of a God who is Father, personal love, and who is also the *Lógos* who is the Son of God who truly became flesh (see Jn 1:14), while remaining always really "one" with the Father (Jn 10:30) was especially unusual. The school of Alexandria was characterized precisely by its commitment to protect and express the novelty of the New Testament revelation, entering into dialogue with Hellenistic philosophy and trying to illustrate in clear language the transcendent truth of the mystery revealed by Christ.

Clement of Alexandria and Origen

Already in Clement of Alexandria (150–211/15), who is considered the founder of the school of Alexandria, we find witness to this tension.

> This discourse respecting God is most difficult to handle. For since the first principle of everything is difficult to find out, the absolutely first and oldest principle, which is the cause of all other things being and having been, is difficult to exhibit.... And if we name it, we do not do so properly, terming it either the One, or the Good, or Mind, or Absolute Being, or Father, or God, or Creator or Lord.... It remains that we understand, then, the Unknown, by divine grace, and by the word alone that proceeds from Him.[15]

In this text, the influence of the conception of God as the One of Platonism is clear. God is necessarily ineffable as is the need to aim our gaze at Jesus as the *Lógos* who comes down to earth to reveal him.

This is the general picture that is inherited and developed by the theological genius of Origen (185–253), especially in his *Peri Archôn* (*On First Principles*).[16] He, as Pope Benedict XVI affirmed, "gathered up the legacy of Clement of Alexandria ... and launched it for the future in a way so

15. *Stromata* 4, 5, 12, 81.

16. See Henri Crouzel, *Origène* (Paris: Lethielleux, 1985); and Manlio Simonetti, "Note sulla teologia trinitaria di Origene," in *Vetera Christianorum* (Bari: Istituto di Letteratura Cristiana Antica, 1971), 8:283; Michel Fédou, *La sagesse et le monde: Le Christ d'Origène* (Paris: Desclée, 1994).

innovative that he impressed an irreversible turning point on the development of Christian thought."[17] Origen particularly illustrates the mystery of God as pure Spirit, in which the only begotten Son is the Wisdom (*sophía*) in which and through which the world was created.

In this way, Origen clearly affirms the eternal generation of the Son distinct from the act of creation. Nevertheless his thought continues to show some oscillation, at least on a terminological level, between the assertion of the divinity of the Son (generated *ab aeterno* by the Father and of the same substance) and the inclination to subordinate the Word (*deúteros Theós*) and the Holy Spirit as intermediaries between God (*ho Theós*) and creation. It will be by emphasizing this subordinationist tendency that Arius will develop his thought, dangerously misunderstanding the Origenist teaching.

Two Irrelevant Solutions

It is precisely the objective difficulty of expressing in concepts and language faithful to the biblical data that brings about, between the second and third centuries, certain mistaken and distorted interpretations of the event of Jesus Christ and the mystery of God revealed in him. These basically all arise from the scandal that the truth of faith according to which the Son of God became flesh and died on the cross is something unthinkable both for the Hellenistic *forma mentis* and the Jewish orthodoxy of the time. This profession of faith clashes with a conception of God who is essentially one, transcendent, immutable, ineffable, and completely separated from the sphere of multiplicity and becoming. It is here that the church faces the vital need to bring together in the understanding of faith the idea of God as unique and one that had been inherited from the Jewish faith and which had somehow reached Greek philosophy, with the New Testament witness of full and true communion with and in him of the Son and the Holy Spirit.

Simplifying somewhat, we can summarize these interpretations, which in the light of the later definitions of dogmatic orthodoxy will be regarded as heresies, in two major categories: monarchianism and subordinationism. Both of these attempt to resolve the same basic problem, respectively affirming: that there is only one God, and the Son and Holy Spirit are not really distinct from that God; and that the Son and the Holy Spirit are distinct, but for this very reason they are not God in the full sense. Beyond their objective historical meaning, these tendencies express in a paradigmatic way opposite errors to which, even in the course

17. General Audience of April 25, 2007; available at www.vatican.va.

of later centuries, until today, the understanding and expression of the trinitarian mystery will be constantly exposed.

Monarchianism

Monarchianism (from the Greek *mónos*, "only one," and *arché*, "principle")[18] emphasizes that God—that is, the Father, following the New Testament usage—is the only principle. Monarchianism expresses itself in two different forms. (1) Dynamic monarchianism comes from the Greek *dýnamis*, "force." The main proponents of this view are Theodotus of Byzantium (second century) and Paul of Samosata (third century). They held that the *Lógos* and the *Pneûma* are simple "forces" or "divine energies" that flow forth from the one principle (God) and which came to dwell in the man Jesus (according to some in the baptism, or to others in the resurrection), in such a way as to "adopt" him as son and give him power to fulfill the function of messiah and savior (thus we speak of adoptionism). In this conception, there is no recognition of the real distinction between the Father and the Son, and consequently, the divine sonship of Jesus. The same is true in an even stronger way with the Holy Spirit.

(2) Modalist monarchianism was principally proposed by Noetus (second century), Praxeas (unknown person of the second century), and Sabellius, from whom derives the name Sabellianism (second and third centuries). This position holds that the Father, the Son, and the Spirit are three different modes or aspects that the one God assumes to reveal himself and to save humankind. God in Godself remains absolutely one. This position is also designated as patripassianism, as it affirms that it is the Father, the One God, who is incarnate and who suffers in the Son on the cross.

Subordinationism

Subordinationism, in contrast, holds that the Son and the Spirit, although they are really distinct from the Father, are ontologically subordinated to Him.[19] They are at a lower level in the hierarchy of being, while only the Father is fully and absolutely God, as YHWH in the First Testament, and, in a different way, as the One is conceived in Greek thought. In the pre-Nicene period, a certain subordinationism—at least linguistically—is common to Christian thought, also because one generally looks at the Son and the Holy Spirit in an economic perspective. Origen is an example of this. Such subordinationism betrays the truth of the faith only when

18. This expression comes from Tertullian, *Adv. Prax.* 3.2; 10.1.

19. See Santiago del Cura Elena, "Subordinacionismo," in *Diccionario Teológico: El Dios Cristiano*, ed. X. Pikaza and N. Silanés (Salamanca: Secretariado Trinitario, 1992), 1311–17.

it formally affirms that Jesus is not on the same ontological level of the Father, but that he is among created beings. This was to happen in the teaching of the presbyter Arius of Alexandria in the fourth century. He interprets and carries to heterodox extreme certain of Origen's expressions and goes so far as to affirm that Jesus is the first creature that God created in view of the rest of creation, that there was a time when he was not, and that therefore he is not of the same substance of the Father.[20]

The Need for a Third Way

As will become clear, these interpretations alter the truth and integrity of the Christological revelation about the trinitarian face of God as it is witnessed to by the New Testament and transmitted by the church's tradition, remaining prisoner to conceptions of God proper to the Greek world, and also to a certain rigid interpretation of the Hebrew faith (as in heterodox Judeo-Christianity). They demonstrate, on the one hand, the difficulty of expressing the novelty of the Christian truth about God in the understanding of faith and, on the other hand, the need for a profound reworking, in the light of the revelation in Christ, of the ways of understanding the being of God proper to the Hellenistic culture, with which Christianity came into contact in its first centuries. It was to respond to these heresies that the first councils of the history of the church were convened.

Worthy of attention in this context is the letter of Bishop Dionysius of Rome to Bishop Dionysius of Alexandria (ca. 260), of which a fragment survives, in which the author deals with the opposite errors of the tri-theists, of Sabellian modalists, and of those who reduce the Son/Word to creaturely status, even if the first and highest. Even though the language that he uses reflects doubt, it is clear that Dionysius witnesses to the church's firm faithfulness to the apostolic faith. In the light of this faithfulness, there is no hesitation or uncertainty with regard to his responses to the interpretations that are being proposed:

It is quite appropriate now for me to speak against those who are tearing apart, destroying, and annihilating the most venerable proclamation of God's Church, the <divine> Monarchy [*monarchía*], by making three powers [*treîs dynámeis*], divided subsistences [*hypostáseis*] and three gods. For I have learned that there are some among you who, in preaching and teaching God's Word, are of this way of thinking. They are, so to speak, diametrically opposed to the opinion of Sabellius, who blasphemes in saying that the Son is the Father, and vice versa. But

20. Fragments of his thought have reached us in the *Thalia (Banchetto)* and two letters to Eusebius of Nicomedia and to Alexander: see Maurice Geerard, *Ab Athanasio ad Chrysostomum*, in *Clavis patrum Graecorum* (Turnhout: Brepols, 1974), 2:2025–42.

they, in a certain manner, proclaim three gods by dividing the sacred unity into three hypostases, completely divided and estranged from one another. In fact, it is necessary that the divine Word be united to the God of all, and the Holy Spirit must dwell in God and inhere in him. Therefore, it is absolutely necessary that the divine Trinity [*Theían Triáda*] be brought together and united in one, as in a summit, namely, the God of all, the Almighty. The doctrine of that foolish Marcion, which cuts and divides the Monarchy [*monarchía*] into three principles [*treîs archàs*], is a diabolical teaching that belongs neither to the true disciples of Christ nor to those who enjoy the teachings of the Savior. These disciples know for certain that the Trinity is proclaimed by the divine Scriptures and that neither the Old nor the New Testament proclaims three gods.

Nor is anyone less worthy of blame who maintains that the Son is a creature [*poíēma*] and who thinks that the Lord was made like any of those things that were really made, even though the divine Word testifies to his suitable and appropriate generation [*génnēsin*], but not as though he were something formed and created. And it is not any blasphemy, but the greatest of blasphemies to say that the Lord is some type of thing fashioned by hands. For if the Son was made, then there was a time when he was not; but he always was in the Father, as he himself says [Jn 14:10]. If Christ is Word, wisdom, and power—which, as you know, the sacred Scriptures say he is [Jn 1:14; 1 Cor 1:24]—these happen to be powers of God; and if the Son was made, then there was a time when these powers did not exist, and there would have been a time when God was without them, which is completely absurd.[21]

21. DH 112–13. This letter, which was not written before the end of the year 260, expressly takes a position against the tri-theists and monarchians.

CHAPTER 19

From Nicaea to the *Filioque*

Trinitas in Excelsis

The Council of Nicaea (325) plants a fundamental pillar, on the basis of which the first, majestic arch of trinitarian theology in the history of Christianity is built. This coincides historically with the progressive construction and cultural and social expression of the Christian civilization of Western and Eastern Europe (the Latin and Byzantine Middle Ages). The faith in *Deus Trinitas* is the living and beating heart of this construction. It is a millennium of life and thought that we can consider, notwithstanding the breadth and internal variety, *ad modum unius*: because there is a common focus on the contemplation of the *Trinitas in excelsis*, the Trinity in the highest heavens, of which the earthly city, the *christianitas* and the entire cosmos, which is its stage, must be a provisional image awaiting final fulfillment.

This epoch is decisive for the dogmatic fixing of the trinitarian language, in the councils of the fourth and fifth centuries, and in the theology of the Church Fathers, but also in the subsequent, extraordinary commitment to speculative study of the trinitarian truth. I will focus more attention on the West, without ignoring the luminous contributions of Eastern Christianity, and in particular on the development in the understanding of God as Trinity that is represented in an exemplary fashion by Augustine of Hippo, Thomas Aquinas, and Bonaventure of Bagnoregio.

The Christological and Trinitarian Councils of the Fourth and Fifth Centuries[1]

Let us begin our descriptive journey of this first daring archway designed by trinitarian theology, dwelling on the trinitarian councils of Nicaea I and Constantinople I of the fourth century. In these the trinitarian faith

1. With regard to the patristic period in general, in addition to the texts already mentioned, see Leo Scheffczyk, "Dichiarazioni del magistero e storia del dogma della Trinità," in *Mysterium*

of the church comes to be defined with precision, expressed in the symbol of the faith that will be named "Nicene-Constantinopolitan," starting precisely from these councils. I will then say something more briefly about the Christological Council of Chalcedon in 451, together with its preparation in the Council of Ephesus in 431 and its necessary completion in the second and third Councils of Constantinople in 553 and 680, insofar as the definition of the identity of Jesus Christ, true God and true man, has a decisive significance in the understanding of the trinitarian truth.

In a second moment I will take up again the witness and the principal themes of the trinitarian theology that prepared the councils and developed from them. Considering its paradigmatic significance in illustrating the penetration into the newness of the *Deus Trinitas* with reference to the philosophical ambiance of classical thought, and at the same time its determining influence on the configuration of the experience and thought of the Trinity above all in the West, I shall reserve a more ample space for the exposition of Augustine's *De Trinitate*.

The First Council of Nicaea

The context The council was convened in 325 by the Emperor Constantine in order to respond to the Arian question. Besides the letter that the bishops gathered in synod wrote to the church of Alexandria in Egypt, we possess direct testimony of two witnesses of the Council: that of Eusebius of Caesarea (260/64–339/40) and that of Athanasius (ca. 295–373) who participated in the Council as a deacon to then succeed Bishop Alexander in the see of Alexandria and take on the role of intrepid defender of the Nicene faith.[2] The Council formulated a profession of faith appropriately reworking the baptismal symbol of the church of Caesarea as its basis.

The profession of faith The symbol of Nicaea is comprised of three articles concerning respectively: God the Father [1], the Son [2], and the Holy Spirit [3]. The most elaborated article is the Christological one, distinguished in turn in two parts, the first concerning God in himself [2a], and therefore the eternal generation of the Son by the Father and the participation of the Son in creation, and the second concerning the economy

Salutis, vol. 3: *La storia della salvezza prima di Cristo*, ed. Johannes Feiner e Magnus Löhrer (Brescia: Queriniana, 1969), 187–278; Aloys Grillmeier, *Christ in Christian Tradition: From the Apostolic Age to Chalcedon (451)* (London: A. R. Mowbray and Co., 1975); Ignazio Ortiz de Urbina, *Storia dei concili ecumenici*, vol. 1: *Nicaea e Costantinopoli* (Vatican City: Libreria Editrice Vaticana, 1994); Antonio Orbe, *La teologia dei secoli II e III: Il confronto della grande Chiesa con lo gnosticismo*, 2 vols. (Casale Monferrato: Piemme, 1995). For a rapid but rigorous historical framing of the first two Ecumenical Councils, see Hubert Jedin, *Breve storia dei Concili: I ventuno Concili ecumenici nel quadro della storia della Chiesa* (Brescia: Herder-Morcelliana, 1978).

2. On this topic, see Enrico Cattaneo's introduction to Athanasius's Italian edition, *Il credo di Nicaea* (Rome: Città Nuova, 2001), 5–49.

of salvation [2b] (incarnation, death/resurrection, ascension, last judgment). It concludes with the condemnation of the heresy of Arius [4].

> We believe
> [1] In *one God*, the Father Almighty,
> Creator of all things visible and invisible;
> [2] and in *one Lord* Jesus Christ
> the Son of God
> [2a] the Only-Begotten *generated* [*gennēthénta*] from the Father,
> that is, *from the substance* [*ek tês ousías*] *of the Father*,
> God from God, light from light, true God from true God;
> *generated not made* [*gennēthénta ou poiēthénta*],
> *consubstantial* [*homooúsion*] with the Father, through whom all things were made, those in heaven and those on earth,
> [2b] *who* for us men and for our salvation
> came down and became flesh, was made man, suffered, and rose again on the third day, (and) ascended into heaven and will come to judge the living and the dead;
> [3] *and in the Holy Spirit.*
> [4] However, those who say: "there was a time when he was not" and "Before he was born he was not" and that he was made from nothing or who say that the Son of God may be of a different subsistence [*hypostáseōs*] or essence [*ousías*], or may be created or subject to change and alteration, <such persons> the Catholic Church anathematizes.[3]

The content The decisive term used in affirming the identity of the divinity between the Father and the Son is *homooúsios*. In Greek philosophy *ousía* designates the being of a reality: that is to say, what makes it such and makes it subsist in itself. To affirm that Jesus Christ is "from the substance of the Father" (*ek tês ousías toû Patrós*) and therefore "consubstantial with the Father" (*homooúsios tô Patrí*) means to underline that he participates truly in the same divine being of the Father and therefore he is God just as the Father. Therefore, it is nothing more than the witness contained in the scriptures. What is new is the assumption of a technical term from Greek philosophy in order to affirm, with undeniable clarity also in philosophical language, the truth expressed in biblical terms in the faith of the church.

The same idea, in polemics with Arius, is expressed by taking up the language of generation (*génnēsis*) witnessed (implicitly and explicitly) by the New Testament in order to express the relationship between the Son, Jesus Christ, and the Father, thus making precise that Jesus is "generated not created." In that way a clear distinction is highlighted between the

3. *Symbolum Nicaenum*, in DH 125–26; the Italian translation is mine and is meant to be as faithful as possible to the original, with some of the key expressions in italics.

level of created things that come from God by means of the free act of creation, and the Son who comes from the Father by eternal generation. It follows that Jesus Christ is "God from God." This is the truth affirmed by the profession of faith in harmony with biblical revelation. The symbolism of light (*phôs ek phōtós*) is very significant: it is enough to remember the fact that in Neoplatonism the most pure and ineffable light is the light of the One alone, after which there begins the inevitable process of its degradation to the point of its eclipse in absolute darkness.

The formula of Nicaea does not enter into the merit of an explication of what is meant by, and how one is to understand, the reality of a unique and identical substance of the Father and of the Son. The introduction of the term *ousía*, when examined in depth, could mean that the Son comes *from* the same substance as the Father, as if there were one *ousía* alone with two manifestations (modalism). On the other hand, one could think on the contrary that there are two different *ousíai*, one in the Father and one in the Son (di-theism). Both interpretations are certainly to be excluded as deadly misunderstandings of the truth that the Nicene symbol of faith is meant to profess: the Son, Jesus, is God *as* the Father is. The intention of the Council, therefore, is simply to deny the denial of Arius by affirming positively the true divinity of Christ in fidelity to the scriptural data. The value of the dogmatic affirmation is in each case its decisive significance for the faith of the church and for subsequent Christian theology.

The meaning The first question on which it is necessary to stop for a moment with the purpose of highlighting the theological significance of the profession of Nicene faith concerns the introduction of philosophical language. It is Athanasius who explains the reason for this fact. The leaders of the party of Arius, and in particular of the position championed by Eusebius of Caesarea,

> maintained that the expression "from God" was common to us and to the Lógos of God, and that in this (the Christ) did not differ in any way from us; [for this reason] the Fathers ... were forced to say more clearly what "from God" meant, and they wrote that the Son came from "the substance" [*ek tês ousías*] of God, so that it would not be thought the expression "from God" was common and identical for the Son and created things, but it expressed the faith that only the Lógos was from "the Father," while all other things were created.[4]

The term *homooúsios* performed a similar function; it was deployed with the intention of unmasking the term *hómoios* (similar). The bishops, Athanasius explained, "were forced to summarize the thought of the

4. Athanasius of Alexandria, *The Nicene Creed*, 19.1–2.

Scriptures ... to express it more clearly and to write that the Son is 'consubstantial [*homooúsios*] with the Father.' In that fashion they affirmed that the Son is not only 'like' [*hómoios*], but identical [*tautón*] because of that resemblance [which comes to him from his being] from the Father."[5] It is therefore a more than legitimate fact. The confession of the truth of revelation attested by scripture throughout history triggers the process of the understanding of the faith which has to come about in the most rigorous fidelity to the tradition of the *deposit of faith*, but at the same time in a commitment to its actualizing interpretation in relation to the questions of the time and the categories elaborated by the culture in whose context the faith is lived.[6]

Utilizing the term *ousía*, theology does not bring about an unjustified Hellenization of the faith. It rather initiates a process of radical semantic transformation of Greek philosophical categories: opening them toward new meanings in the effort to express at the intellectual level the originality of Christological revelation. This opens up, it is true, the possibility of making a merely metaphysical concern prevail over the contemplative and grateful reception of the event of revelation. In fact, theology progressively tended to move the history of salvation out of view during the following centuries.

But the meaning of the Nicene Creed is essentially that of clearly reaffirming the ontological foundation and soteriological import of faith in Jesus Christ as the only-begotten Son of God become man for us and for our salvation. As Athanasius explains, "Man could not be divinized by remaining united to a creature, if the Son were not true God."[7] The affirmation of the divinity of Jesus Christ is therefore the necessary ontological foundation (the immanent Trinity) of the real saving efficacy of the redemption brought about in him for our benefit (the economic Trinity).

The First Council of Constantinople

The context The reefs of the subordination of the Son to the Father were overcome, even if the reefs of the subordination of the Holy Spirit remained after the Council of Nicaea. As we know, in the New Testament it is only in the fourth Gospel that the divine identity and the "personal"

5. Ibid., 20.3.

6. What St. Athanasius narrates in the *Life of St. Anthony* is noteworthy in this regard. Interrogated about the question debated at Nicaea, the great patriarch of eremitism had confessed without a shadow of doubt the grave error contained in Arius's doctrine and he confirmed the orthodoxy of the church's faith (see no. 69).

7. St. Athanasius, *Orationes adversus Arianos* 69–70, in *Patrologiae Cursus Completus, Series Graeca*, ed. J.-P. Migne (Paris, 1857–66) [hereafter "PG"], 26:293A, 296A; and his four *Epistole a Serapione* (written around 359 and 360). Also see Charles Kannengiesser, *Le Verbe de Dieu selon saint Athanase d'Alexandrie* (Paris: Desclée, 1999).

distinction of the Holy Spirit are explicitly affirmed, but in terminology more clearly nuanced than that of the Son become flesh. For this reason and while not entering fully into the merit of the pneumatological question, in the exercise of the understanding of faith done by the church in the first centuries there was sometimes the temptation to prefer a "binary" scheme in the understanding of God, privileging the Father and the Son.

It was only about the middle of the fourth century that some arrived at the explicit conviction, in analogy with and sometimes as a consequence of the subordinationism of the Son, of the subordination of the Holy Spirit understood as the simple "energy" or "power" of God present in Christ in an eminent manner and given to humanity for their sanctification. This was the position of Eunomius (after 393) and of the "Pneumatomachians" (adversaries of the divinity of the Holy Spirit), inappropriately called as well "Macedonians" (from Macedonius, bishop of Constantinople, 370 CE). While Athanasius was the torchbearer of the dogmatic formulation of Nicaea, the Cappadocian fathers (Basil the Great, Gregory of Nyssa, and Gregory Nazianzen) were the torchbearers of the orthodox position sanctioned by the first Council of Constantinople convened in 381 by Emperor Theodosius.

Athanasius had already expressed himself on the question in his letters to Bishop Serapion of Thumis (362). But it was Basil who addressed the question in his celebrated treatise, *On the Holy Spirit*. The theological argument which he illustrates in order to affirm the divinity of the Holy Spirit beyond every equivocation is of a soteriological character in this case as well. He argues that if the Holy Spirit truly makes us participants in the divine nature (see 2 Pt 1:4), and that means he makes us sons in the Son (see Gal 4:6; Rom 8:15), it follows that it is necessary to conclude that the Holy Spirit is of divine nature just as the Father and the Son are.[8] In order to render this affirmation clear and free of every ambiguity, Basil utilizes, beside the traditional doxology, "glory be to the Father through the Son in the Holy Spirit," a doxology he derives from the baptismal liturgy celebrated in obedience to the command of the risen Jesus (see Mt 28:18–20): "glory be to the Father with the Son and with the

8. Basil writes in "Letter 159" (PG 32:621): "The creature is a slave; but the Spirit sets free. The creature needs life; the Spirit is the Giver of life. The creature requires teaching. It is the Spirit that teaches. The creature is sanctified; it is the Spirit that sanctifies. Whether you name angels, archangels, or all the heavenly powers, they receive their sanctification through the Spirit, but the Spirit Himself has His holiness by nature, not received by favor, but essentially His; whence He has received the distinctive name of Holy. What then is by nature holy, as the Father is by nature holy, and the Son by nature" (available at newadvent.org). Athanasius had written earlier: "If the Holy Spirit were a creature, being in him would not bring us any share in God; we would simply be united with a creature and estranged, not having any share in it" (*A Serapione* 1.24; PG 26:585C). See also Bernard Sesboüé, *Saint Basile et la Trinité: un acte théologique au IV siècle: Le rôle de Basile de Césarée dans l'élaboration de la doctrine et du langage trinitaires* (Paris: Desclée, 1998).

Holy Spirit," with the purpose of underlining the equality of the three in that fashion.[9]

The profession of faith In the Nicene Creed, following the clear affirmation of the divinity of the Son, one professes in summary, "and (we believe) in the Holy Spirit." The Constantinopolitan Creed enlarges and specifies a previous profession of faith, above all with respect to this third article. Some have suggested that it refers to the baptismal creed that Bishop Epiphanius of Costanza had recommended in his book *Ancoratus* and that had come from the church of Jerusalem. Today this contention/thesis is considered to have too little foundation, while the hypothesis gains ground that the point of departure was the ancient Roman creed, integrated with the formula of Nicaea and sent by Pope Damasus to the Synod of Antioch of 379.

In any case, the sequence on the Holy Spirit as developed by the profession of faith of the first Council of Constantinople is presented as a dense recapitulation of the pneumatology of Basil, then already deceased, but whose position found echo in the two most prestigious theologians of the council, Gregory Nazianzen, who presided over the council for a time, and Gregory of Nyssa who actively participated in it. Still it would take the later Council of Chalcedon to associate the Constantinopolitan Creed with that of Nicaea. We believe:[10]

[1] in one God, the Father Almighty, creator *of heaven and earth*, of all things visible and invisible. [2] And in one Lord Jesus Christ, *the only begotten* Son of God, generated from the Father *before all ages* [that is, from the substance of the Father] [God from God], light from light, true God from true God; begotten, not made, consubstantial with the Father, through whom all things were made [in heaven and on earth]; for us men and for our salvation he came down *from heaven* and became flesh *from [ek] the Holy Spirit and the Virgin Mary* and was made man. For our sake, too, *he was crucified under Pontius Pilate*, died, *and was buried*. On the third day he rose again, *according to the Scriptures*; He ascended into heaven *and is seated at the right hand of the Father; and he will come again*

9. Basil's stupendous treatise written around 374 or 375 is meant to respond to such a question: "Lately when praying with the people, and using the full doxology to God the Father in both forms, at one time *with the Son together with the Holy Ghost,* and at another *through the Son in the Holy Ghost*" (1.3). And he explains, "The preposition *in* states the truth rather relatively to ourselves; while *with* proclaims the fellowship of the Spirit with God. Wherefore we use both words, by the one expressing the dignity of the Spirit; by the other announcing the grace that is with us. Thus we ascribe glory to God both *in* the Spirit, and *with* the Spirit; and herein it is not our word that we use, but we follow the teaching of the Lord as we might a fixed rule, and transfer His word to things connected and closely related, and of which the conjunction in the mysteries is necessary. We have deemed ourselves under a necessary obligation to combine in our confession of the faith Him who is numbered with Them at Baptism" (27:68; available at newadvent.org).

10. Original affirmations with respect to Nicaea appear in italics. The Nicaean affirmations that were not adopted by Constantinople appear instead in brackets.

in glory to judge the living and the dead; *to his kingdom there will be no end.* [3] And in the Holy Spirit [*eis tò pneûma tò hágion*] *(who is) the Lord* [*to Kýrion*] *and Giver of life, who proceeds* [*ekporeuómenon*] *from the Father* [*ek toù Patrós*]; *who together with the Father and the Son is worshiped and glorified, who has spoken through the prophets. In One, Holy, Catholic and Apostolic Church. We acknowledge one baptism for the forgiveness of sins. We await the resurrection of the dead and the life of the world to come. Amen.*[11]

The content and the meaning In the Constantinopolitan Creed, biblical and liturgical language clearly prevail in reference to the Holy Spirit in fidelity to scripture and the baptismal creed from which it sets out. This is true, evidently, with respect to the ineffability and dynamism typical of the presence and the action of the Holy Spirit in the experience of salvation and also, in all probability, in order not to destroy prejudicially the bridges with the pneumatomachians, thereby following the *ante litteram* "ecumenical" attitude of Basil.

Above all, one ought to note the attribution to the Holy Spirit of the title "the Lord" (*tò Kýrion*),[12] which the Greek translation of the Pentateuch reserves to YHWH and the New Testament refers to Jesus Christ risen: and this in order to underline the fact that the Spirit is God as the Father is and the Son is. The same concept is invoked by affirming that the Holy Spirit is worthy of the same adoration and the same glorification (*sýn*, with, introduced by Basil) that are attributed to the Father and the Son. The qualification of the Spirit as "the giver of life" (*Zōopoiôn*) is also important, that is, as the giver of life, certainly the divine life, given through Jesus Christ to humanity, but even earlier, of the life graciously granted by God to the whole of creation. At the same time, the reference to his speaking "by means of the prophets," attributes to him the activity of preparation and, at the same time, of illustration of the event of Jesus Christ.

Finally, in order to express the relationship between the Father and the Spirit, and in that way distinguish it from the relationship between the Father and the Son, the profession of faith uses the verb "to proceed as from a spring," "to go forth" (*ekporeuómai*), according to the indication proposed by Gregory Nazianzen taken from John 15:26.[13] However, they substituted the preposition *parà*, itself present in the Johannine text, with *ek*, in a desired parallelism with Nicaea. And the verb *ekporeúetai*, in the present, is replaced by *ekporeuómenon*, the past participle that alludes to the eternal procession.[14] Nothing is said, however, about the relation-

11. *Symbolum Constantinopolitanum*, in DH 150.
12. The neutral, *tò Kýrion*, is explained with the neutral apposition, *tò Pneûma*.
13. Gregory Nazianzen, *Theological Oration* 31.8–9.
14. Thus Yves Congar, *Je crois en l'Esprit Saint* (Paris: Cerf, 1980), 3:79n1. The same verb is

ship between the Son and the Spirit; and as we will see, it was precisely beginning from this silence that the distinctive reflections of Eastern and Western theology developed, which are the origin of the heated polemics on the *Filioque*. Finally, it is worth noting that the profession of faith in the church, in baptism, in the resurrection from the dead, and in eternal life combine to complete the article of faith concerning the Holy Spirit to underline that the church is the place "where the Spirit flourishes" (Irenaeus) and which grants to humanity the divine life of Christ even to its consummation in the kingdom of heaven.

In Synthesis

The first Councils of Nicaea and Constantinople define in clear and definitive fashion that the Father, the Son, and the Holy Spirit are God, and therefore of the same substance.[15] They specify also, and with a terminology of biblical origin, the relationship of origin between the Father and the Son (*génnēsis*) and between the Father and the Holy Spirit (*ekpóreusis*). The mystery of God is therefore professed and contemplated in its transcendent truth (with reference to the immanent Trinity) beginning with its revelation in the economy of salvation (economic Trinity). On the foundation of this first and decisive dogmatic definition it will be necessary to penetrate and express correctly the inexhaustible meaning of this truth. This will be done both in the East and the West with an interpretation which is the fruit of different spiritual sensibilities and different theological perspectives.

The Councils of Ephesus, Chalcedon, and Constantinople II

With the affirmation of the full divinity and true humanity of Jesus Christ in the first Council of Nicaea and its reaffirmation in the first Council of Constantinople a tension soon became manifest between two theological approaches deployed in the understanding of the relation, in him, between his "two natures," the divine and the human. Almost as if to underline that from this moment on, the question is transferred from the level of understanding of the Trinity *in God* to that of the understanding of the humanity of Jesus in relation to the event of the incarnation of

used in Rv 22:1 to speak of "the river of the water of life, bright as crystal, flowing from the throne of God and of the Lamb [*ekporeuómenon ek thrónou toû Theoû kaì toû Arníou*]."

15. Although Constantinople I does not use *homoousía* (in Latin, *cumsubstantialitas*) to affirm the divinity of the Holy Spirit, such language is used in the profession of faith found in the letter (*Tome of Damasus*) sent in 382 by the bishop of Rome, Pope Damasus, to Paulinus, bishop of Antioch: "Anathematizamus eos, qui cum tota libertate proclamant eum [Spiritum Sanctum] cum Patre et Filio unius potestatis non esse atque substantiae" (DH 135).

the *Lógos*/Son of God. This is an evident symptom of the arduous task, needing rigorous clarification, not only to accept and express the meaning of the trinitarian "logic" that governs the being of God, but also the relationship between divinity and humanity in Jesus.

Alexandrian and Antiochian Christology: Lógos-sárx *and* Lógos-ánthropos The theology of these centuries travels on two roads, in fact. The first, prevailing in Alexandria, is expressed in the scheme *Lógos-sárx* (*Lógos*-flesh), the second, prevailing in Antioch, by the scheme *Lógos-ánthropos* (*Lógos*-man). The first taught that in Jesus the true subject is the *Lógos* and the flesh is that which the *Lógos* has assumed, while the second placed the emphasis on the integrity of the humanity taken on by the *Lógos*. The two perspectives are certainly pertinent: but taking the two visions to extreme consequences without taking into account the other viewpoint leads in fact to putting the equilibrium of the Christological faith in jeopardy: with monophysitism, on the one hand, by which the human in Jesus is absorbed by the divine; and with Nestorianism, on the other side, by which the man-Jesus is other than the *Lógos*/Son of God.

Within the scope of the first model, Apollinaris of Laodicea (310–90) formulates a theory on the divine-human unity in Christ that ends in heresy because by affirming "one nature alone [*mía physis*] composed of impassible divinity and of vulnerable flesh,"[16] he concluded it was necessary that the human body be animated *fully* by the *Lógos* which in Jesus takes the place of the rational human soul. This position, already condemned in the first Council of Constantinople, risks docetism (Jesus "appears" to be man but deep down, he really is not); denying the assumption of the rational human soul on the part of the *Lógos* puts at risk the salvation of the total person according to the well-known principle, "Only that which is assumed by God is saved."[17]

The *Lógos-ánthropos* Christology of Antioch, propounded by Bishops Diodorus of Tarsus (d. ca. 394) and Theodore of Mopsuestia (ca. 350–428), contained the claim instead of a moral or conjunctive union of the two natures (*dúo phýseis*) in the person (*prósōpon*) of Jesus Christ as the result of the union between the *Lógos* and the humanity: "The Son is united because of the perfect conjunction [*synápheia*] of the natures operated by the divine will."[18] This is a solution which shows itself to be too weak, and, through the ambiguity of the use of the concepts of nature (*phýsis*) and person (*prósōpon*), risks separating the humanity and divinity in Christ.

16. Apollinaris of Laodicea, *Ep. ad Dion.* 6.
17. Gregory Nazianzen, *Ep.* 101.7 and 32.
18. Theodore of Mopsuestia, *Hom. cat.* 3.10; see also *De incarn.* 8 and 11.

The Council of Ephesus: Mary Defined as Theotókos Nestorius (ca. 381–ca. 451), patriarch of Constantinople, pushed the *Lógos-ánthropos* model to the extreme when he refused to attribute to Mary the title *Theotókos* (Mother of God) in favor of the simple title of *Christotókos* (Mother of Christ) in 428. In that way he also rejected the principle of the *communicatio idiomatum* (the communication of attributes) typical of the school of Alexandria that affirms the possibility of the exchange of the attributes of the divinity and the humanity in Jesus Christ in virtue of the oneness of his person. The Council of Ephesus (431), thanks above all to the action of Cyril of Alexandria (370/80–444), condemns Nestorius on this point, affirming that Mary is truly *Theotókos* (Mother of God) because she is the mother of Jesus, that is, because Jesus joins in his *hypóstasis* the divinity of God and the humanity of man. But the theological debate continued.

The distinction of the two natures, typical of Antiochian thinking and certainly acceptable to the Alexandrian school, came to be absolutized when Nestorius tried to show the independence and integrity of both natures in relation to the other, claiming in fact that in their coexistence each of them would have a *prósōpon* (in the sense of individuality) and a *hypóstasis* (subsistence) in virtue of which it really exists. He then attempted to explain in some way the union in terms of the *prósōpon* of Christ: a position that truly seems to introduce a third element. But the accusations soon became reciprocal. According to Nestorius, the Alexandrian Christology compromises the integrity of Christ in claiming only one nature (*mía phýsis*). This is the case even if Cyril defends his position by explaining that the distinction of the two natures is not to be lost in the "hypostatic union," but that these continue to subsist in a relation of unity analogous to what subsists between soul and body.

The dogma of Chalcedon and its meaning The Alexandrian theory of "only one nature" (monophysitism) was taken to the extreme by Eutyches (ca. 378–454) who claimed the unity of nature only after the union understood as the fusion or assimilation of the humanity by the divinity. In that way Christ is no longer ultimately consubstantial with humanity. The monophysite doctrine of Eutyches was condemned at the Council of Chalcedon (451) which affirmed the unity of the person of Jesus Christ "in the two natures" and not "from the two natures."

The Council of Chalcedon took up the formula proposed by John of Antioch in 433 which tried to reconcile the bishops of Antiochian sensibility and recover the language of the distinction of the two natures in Christ. This would be recognized as the "formula of union": Jesus is true God and true man, "consubstantial with the Father in divinity, and consubstantial with us in humanity." Chalcedon thus affirms the uniqueness of the person of Jesus Christ in two natures, teaching that:

There is one and the same Son, our Lord Jesus Christ, perfect in his divinity and perfect in his humanity, true God and true man, [composed] of a rational soul and of a body ... one and the same [*kai ton auton*] Christ the only-begotten Lord, to be recognized in two natures, without confusion, unchanging, undivided, inseparable [*asynchýtōs, atréptōs, adiairétōs, achōrístōs*], the difference of the natures not being reduced on account of their union, but the properties of each nature having actually been safeguarded and together forming one only person and hypóstasis; he is not divided or separated in two persons, but is the one and same Son, Only begotten, God the Word and Lord Jesus Christ.[19]

Then it affirms that, following the incarnation, one of the persons of the Trinity, the Son/*Lógos*, has become the Lord Jesus Christ. The sixth Ecumenical Council, Constantinople III (680–81), will reiterate the relationship of unity and distinction of the two natures in Christ:

He has two natures that are resplendent in his one hypóstasis [*dúo autoû tàs phýseis en tê miâ autoû dialampoúsas hýpostásei*] in which, during the whole economy of his earthly life, he worked wonders and suffered sorrows not in appearance but really. The difference of the natures in this one hypostasis is recognized by the fact that each nature, without difference or confusion, moved and operated in harmony with its being in communion [*koinōnía*] with the other. In that way we proclaim two natural wills and activities [*dúo physikà thelématá te kaì energeías*] that work together for the salvation of the human race.[20]

The dogma of Chalcedon is meant to ultimately protect and express the paradoxical identity of the Word become flesh. He is "one and the same [*héna kaì tòn autòn*] ... perfect in divinity and perfect in humanity, truly God and truly man ... consubstantial [*homooúsion*] with the Father according to divinity and consubstantial [*homooúsion*] with us in humanity."

In that way we have a new equilibrium with regard to humanity and that which the first Council of Nicaea defined with regard to the divinity of Christ. The identity in distinction of the divinity and at the same time of the humanity of the incarnate *Lógos* is affirmed by means of the conceptual instrument of the double natures (*en dúo phýsesin*) which are united in one person (*eis èn prósōpon*) and in one *hypóstasis* alone (*mían hypóstasin*). The unity/identity of the incarnate *Lógos* is therefore recognized at the level of the *person*, in which the otherness of the two natures is not suppressed but conserved (and expressed). From the bitter debate finally emerging at Chalcedon one sees that saving the originality of the Christological event brought with it the need to formulate its truth in adequate ontological

19. DH 301–2.
20. DH 558.

language, a language that would express the transcendence of the (personal) identity of the *Lógos* become flesh, Jesus Christ, with respect to his being, together and indissolubly, true God and true man. It is that which was subsequently defined as *unio hypostatica*, union according to *hypóstasis*.

The development of the Chalcedonian perspective That this was the line on which the dogma of Chalcedon was correctly interpreted is clear from the fact that the second and third Councils of Constantinople (553 and 680) unpack it in this direction. In fact the first speaks of the union of the *Lógos* with humanity "according to synthesis" (*katà sýnthesin*) or "according to *hypóstasis*" (*kath'hýpostasin*): so that Jesus Christ is defined as *Unus de Trinitate* (*eis tês hagías triádos*). The second was convened to affirm, on the line of Chalcedon, that in Christ there are "two natural wills and two natural operations [*dúo physikàs thelésis étoi thelématha kaì dúo physikàs energeías*], without division, without change, without separation or confusion. The two natural wills are not in contrast with each other ... but his human will follows, without opposition or reluctance, or better, is subject to his divine and omnipotent will."[21] The same comes to be affirmed with respect to the two activities or centers of operation in Christ.[22] The motivation for this Christological refinement is once again soteriological; without a human will and action, Jesus Christ would not have been able to welcome the Father's saving plan in free obedience as true man, and at the same time he would not be consubstantial with us so as to able to redeem humanity.

One may therefore conclude that "in Jesus, the Word became, in view of the incarnation, a humanized (divine) person, that is, he has lived in an authentically human manner his individual and social existence; he has lived his being as person in the human world of becoming."[23] St. Thomas Aquinas affirms the fact for all in the *Quaestio disputata De Unione Verbi Incarnati*: "The Word became flesh, that is, man; almost as if the Word should personally be man" (a. 1). Now conversely, this also opens a glimpse into the ontological comprehension of how human persons grafted into Christ can live from that fullness of life that is given to them from God by means of the Word in the Spirit; they become, as said in the noted affirmation of the first Letter of Peter, "*theías koinōnoì phýseōs*, participants of the divine nature" (2 Pt 1:4). In this case as well, the vocation of the person is that of transcending by grace the human nature within which it was originally given to itself.

The "trinitarian formula" of Constantinople II Although the concept of the unity and Trinity of God as sanctioned by the councils of the fourth

21. DH 556.

22. See DH 557.

23. Marcello Bordoni, *Gesù di Nazareth: Signore e Cristo: Saggio di cristologia sistematica*, vol. 3: *Il Cristo annunciato dalla Chiesa* (Rome: Herder-PUL, 1986), 848 (own trans.).

century was universally shared, there still remained a problem of linguistic clarification between East and West. How could the Latin fathers translate the Greek concepts into their language without losing their meaning or creating misunderstandings? The Greek *hypóstasis*, for example, indicating the distinct reality of Father, Son, and Holy Spirit was rendered in Latin by "substance," the very term with which *ousía* was also translated. The Latins meanwhile used the term *persona* to express the distinct reality of the three, which in Greek was translated by *prósōpon*, which had a weaker meaning alluding to the metaphor of the "mask." This is where the misunderstandings arose: the translation of the Greek *hypóstasis* into Latin by *substantia* gave room for the misunderstanding of tri-theism, just as the translation of the Latin *persona* into Greek by *prósōpon* gave room to the misunderstanding of modalism.

On the basis of the precise use of the terms *hypóstasis* and *ousía* (person and substance or nature) in the Christological dogma of Chalcedon (in Christ there is only one *person* or *hypóstasis* in two *natures*) as well, the problem would be clarified definitively by the second Council of Constantinople in 553, which stated:[24]

> Whoever does not confess that the Father, the Son and the Holy Spirit have only one nature [*phýsis*] or substance [*ousía*], only one virtue and power, since they are a consubstantial Trinity [*homooúsios*], one only divinity to be adored in three hypostaseis or persons [*prósōpa*], let him be anathema. One in fact is God the Father from whom are all things; one the Lord Jesus Christ by whom are all things; one the Holy Spirit in whom are all things.[25]

The Trinitarian Theology of the Cappadocian Fathers

In the East the understanding in faith of the trinitarian mystery was sought in the first instance by the Cappadocian fathers, who, as already mentioned, were able to give a substantial contribution to the dogmatic formulation of Constantinople I. Having revisited the history of the dogmas of the first centuries, it is therefore important to return to the fathers' decisive contribution. The perspective within which they move seems characterized by two complementary contributions.[26] First, in a

24. This council was convoked to resolve the so-called question of the three chapters by Emperor Justinian and Pope Vigilio.

25. See the first canon of the Second Council of Constantinople in DH 421.

26. The pertinence of their theological method is sharpened when compared with the misleading theses advanced by Eunomius. In fact, the latter bears witness to the Neoplatonic tradition in the second half of the fourth century (Jean Daniélou); he is the last representative of the Arian conception (R. P. Vaggione); he sustains that God (the Father) is completely other with respect to the world, producing an intermediary (the *Lógos*) to create the world. And together with these

forthright perspective of faith and adoration contemplating the mystery of God, they affirm that the essence of God, his most profound nature, his intimate mystery, remain unfathomable in their infinity and therefore they are ineffable; second, thanks to a wise utilization and resignification of the categories forged by the philosophical contributions of Greek culture (Aristotelianism, Platonism, Stoicism), they seek with audacity to express, also at the intellectual level, the transcendent truth of the mystery of the three divine Persons beginning with their action in the history of salvation. In other words, according to a terminology that would become classical in the tradition of the church, the Cappadocians give life to a theology characterized by a wise dialectic between the positive moment of the affirmation of the truth of God revealed in Christ by means of the resources of human reason (*kataphatic* or positive theology), and the negative moment of silence and the recognition of the ineffable transcendence of the mystery (*apophatic* or negative theology).

Basil the Great: The Distinction between *ousía* and *hypóstasis*

The contribution of Basil the Great (330–79) is most important; we already spoke of him with regard to the Holy Spirit. He committed himself to find and to forge the conceptual expressions capable of expressing at the same time the distinct identity of each of the three and their substantial unity. This is the source, in particular, of the appropriate hermeneutic that Basil offers, respectively, of the term *hypóstasis* which means substance in singular fashion, and the term *ousía*, which means substance in a common and undetermined mode.

> *Ousía* has the same relation to *hypóstasis* as the common has to the particular. Every one of us both shares in existence by the common term of essence [*ousía*] and by his own properties is such an one and such an one. In the same manner, in the matter in question, the term *ousía* is common ... while *hypóstasis* is contemplated in the special property of Fatherhood, Sonship, or the power to sanctify.[27]

Gregory Nazianzen: *ousía* and the Distinctive Characters of the *hypostáseis*

In his own way, Gregory Nazianzen (329–90), called "the Theologian," affirms with intensely mystical accents the indivisible unity of the Trinity

positions, he asserts that the term *agennétōs* (= not generated) is God's own name revealing his substance. In this way, he captures the otherness of God with a certain use of reason (so much so that Gregory of Nyssa accuses him of being *technológos*, someone that uses the *lógos* as a mere rational technique) dissolving the truth of trinitarian revelation.

27. Basil, *Letters* 214; available at newadvent.org.

while he attempts at the same time in every way to express the distinctive characteristics of each of the three by underlining the antinomian and indestructible complementarity of these two points of view.[28]

No sooner do I conceive of the One than I am illumined by the Splendor of the Three; no sooner do I distinguish Them than I am carried back to the One. When I think of any One of the Three I think of Him as the Whole, and my eyes are filled, and the greater part of what I am thinking of escapes me. I cannot grasp the greatness of That One so as to attribute a greater greatness to the Rest. When I contemplate the Three together, I see but one torch, and cannot divide or measure out the Undivided Light.[29]

The One sets in motion because of its perfection. The Two is "valicato" because he is beyond every opposition. Perfection is reached in the Three who first overcome the composition of the Two. In that way the divinity does not remain restricted, nor is it indefinitely communicated.[30]

To us there is One God, for the Godhead is One, and all that proceeds from Him is referred to One, though we believe in Three Persons. For one is not more and another less God; nor is One before and another after; nor are They divided in will or parted in power; nor can you find here any of the qualities of divisible things; but the Godhead is, to speak concisely, undivided in separate Persons; and there is one mingling of Light, as it were of three suns joined to each other. When then we look at the Godhead, or the First Cause, or the Monarchia, that which we conceive is One; but when we look at the Persons in Whom the Godhead dwells, and at Those Who timelessly and with equal glory have their Being from the First Cause—there are Three Whom we worship.[31]

In the divine *hypostáses* there is therefore perfect identity of nature with the exception of their relationships of origin (*skésis*): for this reason it is precisely the modality of their reciprocal rapport, as the rapport of origin of the one from the other, which defines them as such as divine hypostases:

The Proper Name of the Unoriginate is Father, and that of the unoriginately Begotten is Son, and that of the unbegottenly Proceeding or going forth is The Holy Ghost.[32] The Father is Father, and is Unoriginate, for He is of no one; the Son is Son, and is not unoriginate, for He is of the Father. But if you take the word Origin in a temporal sense, He too is Unoriginate, for He is the Maker of Time, and is not subject to Time. The Holy Ghost is truly Spirit, coming forth from the Father indeed, but not after the manner of the Son, for it is not by Generation but by Procession (since I must coin a word for the sake of clearness); for neither did the Father cease to be Unbegotten because of His begetting something, nor

28. In the collection of his forty-five orations of a theological nature, *Theological Orations* 27–31 are the most interesting with regard to trinitarian theology.

29. *Orations* 40:41; available at newadvent.org.

30. Ibid., 23:8.

31. Ibid., 31:14.

32. Ibid., 30:19.

the Son to be begotten because He is of the Unbegotten (how could that be?), nor is the Spirit changed into Father or Son because He proceeds, or because He is God—though the ungodly do not believe it.[33]

Gregory of Nyssa: Essence and Persons

The Trinity is at the center of the theology of Gregory of Nyssa (335–ca. 394), who sets himself the task of developing Basil's intuitions in order to respond to the error of Eunomius in particular.[34] Like the two other Cappadocians, he bases his understanding of the trinitarian mystery on the solid ground of biblical and liturgical testimony, and digs for the theological significance of the rhythm of life and prayer handed on in these and by these two kinds of testimony: *ek Patrós, di'huioû, en pneúmati*. He underlines the fact that in the very name of Christ the mystery of his person as well as that of the one and triune God is declared: "In this name the mystery of the Trinity is confessed. In this name we are taught He who anoints, He who is anointed and That with which he is anointed. In fact, if anyone of these is omitted, the name of Christ has no foundation."[35]

In order to describe the divine Persons, Gregory moves from their *kínēsis* (movement, acting) as it is unpacked in the *oikonomía*, then ascending from there to the immanent dynamic of their eternal life. In this life he distinguishes "what it is" (*tí esti*), that is, the divine *essence* that remains absolutely ineffable, from the "how it is" (*pôs esti*) that says the mode of being of the Father, the Son, and the Holy Spirit. Such a mode of being is specified by the succession of relation (*sketikè akolouthía*) of the three, which Gregory expresses with the precise language that is subsequently taken up by the dogmatic and theological tradition: "In fact, one and the same is the Person [*prósōpon*], that of the Father, from whom the Son is generated [*gennâtai*] and the Holy Spirit proceeds [*ekporeûetai*]."[36]

The trinitarian immanence, therefore, is dynamically illuminated in terms of relation (*skésis*) and of mutual indwelling as the reciprocal gift of the divine glory; the human is also called to participate in this through his reason, by means of the incarnate Son and the Holy Spirit:

Do you see the circulation of the glory by means of the same cyclic movements [*tèn egkýklion tês dóxēs dià tón homoíōn periphorán*]? The Son is glorified by the Spirit: the Father is glorified by the [*hypó*] Son. And reciprocally, the Son has the glory from [*pará*] the Father and the Only-begotten becomes the glory of

33. Ibid., 39:12.

34. In many of his works he deals with the mystery of the Trinity, the real beating heart of his bold theology: see Giulio Maspero, *La Trinità e l'uomo* (Rome: Città Nuova, 2004), and by the same author, the beautiful article dedicated to the Trinity in *Gregorio di Nissa: Dizionario* (Rome: Città Nuova, 2007), 538–55.

35. *In inscriptiones Psalmorum*, in *Gregorii Nysseni Opera*, 6:119.20–33.

36. *Ad Graecos*, in *Opera* 3.1:25.4–6.

the Spirit. In fact, in what would the Father be glorified if not in the true glory of the Only-begotten? And in his turn, in what would the Son be glorified if not in the greatness of the Spirit? Thus also reason by inserting itself in this circular movement [*anakykloúmenos*] gives glory to the Son by means [*diá*] of the Spirit and to the Father by means [*diá*] of the Son.[37]

In this perspective, Gregory comes to illustrate in penetrating fashion the distinctive property of the Holy Spirit with respect to the Father and the Son: it "does not consist in being in a non-generated [*agennétōs*] mode, nor in only-begotten [*monogenôs*] mode, but being in a mode in such a way as to be a whole [*eînai dè hólos*]."[38]

The mode by which the Holy Spirit is the one God is constituted, as G. Maspero underlines, "by bringing to unity, closing the circle of glory, as the bond of the Father and the Son."[39] Therefore when Jesus prays to the Father that his followers may share in the very life of God, he cannot but refer to the Holy Spirit as that glory that he has given to his own that they may be one as he and the Father are one:

It is better to quote textually the very divine words of the Gospel: "That they all be one thing. As you, Father, are in me and I in you, may they also be one in us" (Jn 17:21). And the bond of this unity is the glory [*tò dè syndetikón tês henótētos taútēs hē dóxa estín*]. But no prudent person could deny the fact that the Holy Spirit should be called glory if he considers the words of the Lord. In fact, he says, "The glory that you have given me I have given them" (Jn 17:22). He truly gives, in fact, such glory to the disciples, saying to them, "Receive the Holy Spirit" (Jn 20:22). Having embraced human nature, he received this glory which he had always possessed before the world existed (Jn 17:5). And because this human nature was glorified by the Spirit, the communication of the glory of the Spirit happens to all that belongs to the same nature, beginning with the disciples. For this reason he says, "And the glory that you have given me I have given to them, that they may be one even as we are one, I in them and you in me, that they may become perfectly one" (Jn 17:22–23).[40]

Augustine's Trinitarian Theology

If the Cappadocian fathers set the scene for the shape of Eastern Christianity's trinitarian theology, St. Augustine (354–430) sets the scene for trinitarian theology in the Western church. In his *De Trinitate* he continues the preceding developments and makes a decisive leap forward with his particular spiritual and speculative genius in an original way. He does this by setting the lines on the chessboard for all the various options that

37. *Adversus Macedonianos, De Spiritu Sancto*, in *Opera* 3.1:109.7–15.
38. *Contra Eunomium*, in *Opera* 1:108.7–13.
39. Maspero, *Trinità*, 552 (own trans.).
40. Gregory of Nyssa, *In Canticum canticorum*, in *Opera* 6:467.2–17 (own trans.).

trinitarian theology will later take. On the other hand, it was Augustine himself who energetically formulated the theological method later canonized by St. Anselm of Canterbury in the axiom *fides quarens intellectum* (faith seeking understanding), which meant employing all intellect's resources to penetrate and express the truth of revelation.

De Trinitate's Historical and Theological Impact

The impact of *De Trinitate* can be seen first of all from the time in which it emerges within the history of trinitarian theology. It is the first systematic reflection on the central truth of faith after the first Councils of Nicaea and Constantinople.[41] The long and troubled drafting of the book occurred with various interruptions between 399 and 421.[42] Secondly, its importance is brought into evidence by its extraordinary reception and the inspiration it has given, especially to Western spirituality and theology. Certainly without *De Trinitate* these would not have been what they are. But more generally it has had an effect on the common destiny of all of Christianity in the first two millennia of its history, as is shown by some of the keenest contemporary interpreters of Orthodoxy, for example Sergius Bulgakov.[43]

So it is not out of place to speak of *De Trinitate*'s charismatic quality insofar as it was sparked off by an impulse of the Spirit to fulfill a specific service to the church, to understand and illustrate the trinitarian faith. This does not mean setting aside its unavoidable historical and theoretical context, along with its limits and internal complexities. Rather it means seeking to penetrate its deep inspiration, its lasting contribution,

41. At the beginning of his work, in fact, Augustine says to be aware of *omnes quos legere potui qui ante me scripserunt de Trinitate*, that is, "all [the authors] whom I could read who had written on the Trinity before me." It is a matter above all of Latin writers, but Augustine also knew the most important Christian Greek-language writers. Among the Latins, he certainly read Tertullian; Ambrose of Milan, under whose guidance he participated in the baptismal catechesis of Lent in 387; Marius Victorinus, rhetor and Neoplatonic philosopher, converted in his old age to Christianity, opponent of the Arians, is mentioned by Augustine in the *Confessions*; Hilary of Poitiers is explicitly remembered (*De Trinitate* VI.10.11), and during his exile in Phrygia after 350, he had written a *De Trinitate* in twelve books. On Hilary, see Luis F. Ladaria, *La cristología de Hilario de Poitiers* (Rome: Editrice Pontificia Università Gregoriana, 1989). Among the Greeks, Augustine probably knew Didymus the Blind, the last great teacher of the school of Alexandria; Gregory Nazianzen's *Five Theological Orations* delivered at Constantinople in 380, and Basil the Great's two dogmatic writings, *Against Eunomius* and *On the Holy Spirit* (before 379).

42. Augustine writes in the prologue: "I was a young man when I began these books on the Trinity which the one true God is, and I am now an old man as I publish them [*De Trinitate quae Deus summus et verus est libros iuvenis inchoavi, senex edidi*]." So the *De Trinitate* accompanies almost all of Augustine's theological journey.

43. Sergius Bulgakov takes up an original position in *The Comforter*, trans. Boris Jakim (Grand Rapids, Mich.: Eerdmans, 2004), 42, with respect to the criticism the Orthodox tradition has often made of Augustine's trinitarian theology: "Augustine makes a true discovery in the trinitarian and pneumatological theology: He is the first to express the idea, wholly foreign to Eastern theology, of the Holy Trinity as Love."

the promise toward which it directs its gaze. This means starting out from Augustine's experience, in other words focusing on his theology's source and its spiritual and mystical orientation.[44]

The Augustinian Journey toward God

Behind all the speculative efforts of Augustine's theological understanding, as G. Lafont well notes, before everything there is

> the luminous discovery of the transcendent reality of God in the interiority of the soul seeking wisdom. The human person prepares for this discovery through a process of self-recollection characterized by the ascending dialectic of Plotinus and Plato, tracing back from the realities outside the senses, then to the memory, then to the person him/herself, seeking to understand him/herself through this activity. But the experience of God is granted from On High: it is perceived as an "illumination," emanating from a light higher than the soul, but received within the soul's interiority.[45]

It is a journey marked by the two moments of *rede in te ipsum* (return into yourself) and of *transcende te ipsum* (go beyond yourself): the discovery of one's own interiority and, at its depth, rather, beyond that, of God. But here is the vibrant account of his first encounter with God offered by Augustine in *Confessions* VII.[46]

> Warned by these writings[47] that I must return to myself, I entered under your guidance the innermost places of my being; but only because you had become my helper (Ps 29:11) [*Et inde admonitus redire ad memet ipsum intravi in intima mea duce te et potui, quoniam factus es adjutor meus*] was I able to do so. I entered, then, and with the vision of my spirit, such as it was, I saw the incommutable light [*lucem incommutabilem*] far above my spiritual ken, transcending my mind: not this common light which every carnal eye can see, nor any light of the same order but greater, as though this common light were shining much more powerfully, far

44. This is emphasized by one of the greatest Augustine experts of our time, the Augustinian father Agostino Trapè: "even in his theological penetration, which was exceptionally deep and reliable, mystical experience had a predominant influence." *Agostino: L'uomo, il pastore, il mistico* (Rome: Città Nuova, 2001), 358 (own trans.). Von Balthasar also considers him among the great spirits that received a gift from God for the benefit of the church, the charism to illuminate and illustrate Christian truth: "Great charisms like those of Augustine, Francis and Ignatius can be granted glances into the center of revelation by the Spirit, glances that enrich the Church in completely unexpected yet ever-relevant ways." *Teologica III: Lo Spirito della Verità* (Milan: Jaca Book, 1992), 22 (own trans.). See also the studies by Goulven Madec, *Le Dieu d'Augustin* (Paris: Cerf, 2000); *La Patria e la Via: Cristo nella vita e nel pensiero di S. Agostino* (Rome: Borla, 1993); *Saint Augustin* (Paris: Desclée, 1989); *La meditation trinitaire d'Augustin* (Paris: Association Communio, 1999), 79–102.

45. Lafont, *Peut-on connaître Dieu en Jésus Christ?*, 74–75 (own trans.).

46. Augustine, *Confessions* VII.10.16, ed. John E. Rotelle, trans. Maria Boulding, in *The Works of Saint Augustine* I/1 (Hyde Park, N.Y.: New City Press, 1997), 172–73. I have added some of the original Latin expressions in brackets and notes of explanation.

47. This concerns the Neoplatonic writings which Augustine said, shortly before, that he had come across. In Plotinus's *Enneads*, for example, the way of interiority up to the point of self-transcendence toward the One is found: 4.3.1.8–12; 5.1.1.30–33; 12.12–50; 5.3.4–5.

more brightly, and so extensively as to fill the universe. The light I saw was not this common light at all, but something different, utterly different, from all these things. Nor was it higher than my mind in the sense that oil floats on water or the sky is above the earth; it was exalted because this very light made me, and I was below it because by it I was made.... you are my God, (Ps 42:2),[48] and for you I sigh day and night (Ps 1:2; Jer 9:1). As I first began to know you [*et cum te primum cognovi*],[49] you lifted me up and showed me that while that which I might see exists indeed [*ut viderem esse, quod viderem*] so that I could see what is, what you were enabling me to see,[50] I was not yet capable of seeing it [*et nondum me esse, qui viderem*].[51] Your rays beamed intensely upon me, beating back my feeble gaze, and I trembled with love and dread.[52] I knew myself to be far away from you in a region of unlikeness[53] [*Et reverberasti infirmitatem aspectus mei radians in me vehementer, et contremui amore et horrore: et inveni longe me esse a te in regione dissimilitudinis*], and I seemed to hear your voice from on high: "I am the food of the mature; grow then, and you will eat me. You will not change me into yourself like bodily food: you will be changed into me."[54] ... Then from afar you cried to me, "I am who am" [*Ego sum qui sum*].[55] I heard it as one hears a word in the heart, and no possibility of doubt remained to me; I could more easily have doubted that I was alive than that truth exists, truth that is seen and understood through the things that are made.[56]

In Augustine's experience, God is the unchanging light of truth grasped by the eye of the soul beyond itself. It is God himself, the light, who guides and draws the soul in search toward himself. Augustine, in telling

48. This is the passage, typical of Augustine's approach, of his account of prayerful dialogue with God.

49. This reference to the "first time" Augustine knew God brings out that he is dealing with a specific event, a lived experience.

50. This clear and strong expression is often mistranslated or indeed even betrayed in the translation. Augustine wants to emphasize that God, "lifted him up," to see that he is—in the strong ontological sense—that very being, God himself, that he is thus able to see. The light Augustine speaks of is the light of the being of God as he who fully and truly is, as he says immediately after this.

51. He wants to say that in the same act by which God lifts him up to see that immutable light that he is, Augustine becomes aware in that very light that he is not of himself capable of seeing what he in fact does see. In other words, Augustine is speaking of a completely gratuitous grace which anticipates the vision, that he will then have to attain, with the help of that same grace by means of the asceticism of the *purgatio mentis* (purification of mind) and of *caritas* (charity); he will reach its definitive fullness in the *visio beata* (beatific vision).

52. "I trembled with love and fear [*Contremui amore et horrore*]": this is a strong and precise description of the experience of God, that in some way recalls the spiritual and emotional impact of the *fascinosum et tremendum* (fascinating and tremendous) described by Rudolf Otto in his *The Idea of the Holy*, trans. John W. Harvey (London: Oxford University Press, 1923).

53. The expression is taken from Plotinus's *Enneads*. See Lk 15:13: *in regione dissimilitudinis* seems to echo the prodigal son's leaving his father's house for a far country *regionem longinquam*. Ultimately it has a pregnant ontological and spiritual meaning; it is the place of the one living far from God, as a creature, and even more as a sinner.

54. The reference to being nourished on God with a food that transforms the one receiving it into the one that was received evidently brings to mind the Eucharist, and therefore Christ. It is a premonition of what Augustine subsequently lives.

55. Recalling the revelation of the name of God, YHWH, in Ex 3:14.

56. See Rom 1:20. Augustine is drawing the obvious parallel between the God revealed in the Exodus and the God known through creation. Also see *Confessions* VII.11.17.

of this experience, recognizes in this light the God who revealed himself to Moses, the invisible and eternal creator of changeable and temporal things. Because God is transcendent and ineffable, God's light completely exceeds the capacity of the soul. And the soul cannot contain the light it has received: it stays blinded by its dazzling intensity, wounded, overcome, and enlivened by it, yet it experiences the inability to keep present and continuous the experience it has received. Once having touched God, the soul wants to remain immersed in him forever. But the illumination lasts only for the moment of ecstasy.[57] Thus the soul is provoked to ascetic purification and to the intellectual quest. In fact, contemplation (*visio*) of God is the act that invades the soul's fine tip, where each human is one. And to arrive at that point and dwell there, "the soul has to be purified so it becomes able to see that Light within, and adhere to it, once it has seen it."[58]

In this journey he has undertaken Augustine discovers and adheres with all his soul to Jesus.[59] The moment of conversion, as he describes it himself in *Confessions* VIII, comes about when, irresistibly attracted by then by a life of complete dedication to God and experiencing his misery and incapacity to make this step, he is urged by the sound of a song to open the New Testament to read the first verse that caught his eye:

I snatched it up, opened it and read in silence the passage on which my eyes first lighted: *Not in dissipation and drunkenness, nor in debauchery and lewdness, nor in arguing and jealousy; but put on the Lord Jesus Christ, and make no provision for*

57. Returning to the experience I have mentioned, Augustine writes that the soul "attained to *That Which Is*, in the flash of one tremulous glance. Then indeed did I perceive your invisible reality through created things (see Rom 1:20) but to keep my gaze there was beyond my strength. I was forced back through weakness and returned to my familiar surroundings, bearing with me only a loving memory, one that yearned for something of which I had caught the fragrance, but could not yet feast upon" *Confessions* VII.17.23 (177–78).

58. *De doctrina christiana* I.10.10 (Rome: Città Nuova, 1992). Augustine in his *De quantitate animae* describes the soul's seven activities: to animate the body, feel by means of the senses, reason and attain science and art, struggle against the vices, consolidate itself in the good, enter into light, and dwell in the reign of light. The first three of these activities belong to our natural humanity and are shared by all, good and bad; our journey toward virtue begins with the fourth and terminates with the sixth, arriving at perfection in the seventh, in contemplation of God.

59. "Something like this (the contemplation of that Light) would be impossible for us if Wisdom himself had not deigned to lower himself to the level of our inferiority.... Thus being himself the homeland, he wanted to make a way for us to the homeland too" (*De doctrina christiana* I.11.11). As we know, Augustine had a Christian mother, Monica, who educated him in the faith since when he was little. But he quickly strayed from the Catholic church without getting baptized. His mother continued to follow him closely, imploring God with tears and sacrifices for the conversion of her beloved son. In his long and tortuous quest, he even found himself confronted with the great works that brought him close to contemplation of the truth, like Cicero's *Hortensius* and later, the Neoplatonic writings. But he confesses, "Only one consideration checked me in my ardent enthusiasm: that the name of Christ did not occur there. Through your mercy, Lord, my tender little heart had drunk in that name,... with my mother's milk, and in my deepest heart I still held on to it. No writing from which that name was missing, even if learned, of literary elegance and truthful, could ever captivate me completely" *Confessions* III.4.8 (80).

the flesh or the gratification of your desires (Rom 13:13–14). I had no wish to read further, nor was there need. No sooner had I reached the end of the verse than the light of certainty flooded my heart and all dark shades of doubt fled away.... for you had converted me to yourself.[60]

For Augustine, then, Jesus is the master of wisdom who heals us from sin and guides us toward the Light. Even more, he is the very Wisdom of God having come in the flesh to make himself our way toward the Father. He is the meeting point, the mediator, between the creator and the creature, holy God and me a sinner, because he is true God and true man: "Accordingly I looked for a way to gain the strength I needed to enjoy you, but I did not find it until I embraced the mediator between God and humankind, the man Christ Jesus, who also is God, supreme over all things and blessed for ever [*donec amplecterer mediatorem Dei et hominum, hominem Christum Jesum, qui est super omnia Deus benedictus in saecula*]."[61]

So, in Augustine's experience the starting point is contemplation of God as light, truth, being. Knowledge of God the Trinity comes from adhering to Christ in the faith of the church, which teaches precisely that God, through Jesus Christ, is revealed as Father, Son, and Holy Spirit, leading humanity to salvation. So when Augustine arrives at faith, he feels impelled to bring into unity, even intellectually, the experiential and philosophical data that have come his way (God is the ineffable light that illuminates the soul of the one seeking wisdom), with the doctrine of faith and the experience of salvation offered him through Christ in the church. These elements tell him that God, the God you have found and that Christ fully reveals to you, guiding you toward him, is Trinity: Father, Son, and Holy Spirit.

The specific tonality of the Augustinian experience as a way of interiority, in the love of wisdom, toward God who is light, has to affect his theological approach to the mystery of the Trinity. Just as that theological approach must also be affected by his increasing awareness of two central dimensions of the Christian life offered him in the experience of the faith: charity, and the church as body of Christ and the whole Christ. In fact, Augustine understands that what is new and perfect in Jesus' message is contained in the commandment of love: God, the light, revealed himself in Jesus as charity (see 1 Jn 4:8, 16).[62] At the same time, as a result, he is

60. *Confessions* VIII.11.29–30 (207–8).

61. Ibid., VII.18.24 (178).

62. In *De doctrina christiana*, for example, he writes: "this is the sum of all that has been said: that we understand that the fullness and the end of the Law and of all the divine scriptures is love" (I.35.39). "Nevertheless, whoever thinks they have understood the divine Scriptures or any part of them, if through that understanding they are not able to build this double charity of God and of their neighbor, they have not yet understood" (I.36.40). Augustine was prepared for this by his

fascinated by the Pauline doctrine of the church, the body of Christ; that is why Christians become members of Christ, and through and in him, of each other, as a result of baptism and the Eucharist.[63]

Through the interweaving of these two main passageways, of interiority and of the unity of the body of Christ, Augustine forges his rich spiritual doctrine. Thanks to his *Rule*,[64] he thus becomes one of the great inspirations of the common life in the West, along with constituting a rich thread of Christian spirituality for all times. This is also the source of the two paths Augustine figures out to illustrate the truth of the Trinity starting from its dwelling in the human person redeemed by Christ: that of the interior experience of the spirit and that of the experience of mutual love to the point of unity.

Theological Method

Augustine's *method* in *De Trinitate* is articulated in three distinct moments, which are not juxtaposed nor do they simply follow one another; rather they are organically arranged. The *regula fidei* (rule of faith) or *fides catholica* (Catholic faith) is his starting point in the first four books—complete and faithful acceptance of the creed as professed by the church. There follows the exposition and analysis of the revelation of the face of God the Trinity as attested by scripture—First and New Testament. In fact, scripture is the origin and norm of the church's tradition but Augustine approaches it through the tradition, in that living channel within which scripture has taken shape and is authentically interpreted.

The second moment, in Books V–VIII, is the speculative analysis, the *intelligentia fidei* (understanding of the faith). Having gathered together the scriptural data illuminated by the *regula fidei* (rule of faith), he begins to "make sense" of them, illustrating the connections, the perspectives, the horizons of truth implied in what is affirmed by the rule of faith. Such an analysis is traced out thanks to two instruments: the logical-dialectic analysis of names and concepts, speaking of God, what kinds of names

great openness to the ideal of friendship, a topic often mentioned in his writings, which he sees completed and transfigured on another level, that of the grace of Christ, of mutual charity.

63. "The Church is the body (of Christ)—as the apostles' teaching suggests—and is even called his spouse. So he binds his body, of many members with different tasks, by the bond of unity and charity, sign of its health" (I.16.15).

64. This is a compendium of principles and norms drawn up by Augustine about 397 for the community of lay brothers of the monastery he founded at Hippo in 391 and then extended to the women's monastery, guided for many years by Augustine's sister. His *Rule* is the oldest monastic rule in the West, adopted throughout the centuries by about five hundred institutions. We read in the first chapter: "The main purpose for you having come together is to live harmoniously in your house, intent upon God in oneness of mind and heart [*Primum, propter quod in unum estis congregate, ut unanimes habitetis in domo et sit vobis anima una et cor unum in Deum*]"; available at augustinians.net.

does scripture use? Substantial or relative ones? Proper names, or metaphors or analogies? Thus Augustine produces a very refined analysis of the language of revelation. He also seeks out the true and specific metaphysical basis, in other words clarifying in what sense the scriptural concepts express God's being. An adequate metaphysics is needed to reply to this kind of question. This is why Augustine opens the way toward a radical rethinking of classical metaphysics.

Finally there is the moment where the first two steps lead back toward contemplation. The mystery of God remains ever transcendent; it is always and anew the object of prayerful confession and praise. This existential and contemplative constant becomes explicit especially from Book VIII on, where Augustine engages in seeking and showing the concrete locus where it is possible "to meet" God the Trinity. This is the moment of *experientia fidei* (the experience of faith) in Books VIII–XIV, of living and spiritual contact with the mystery of the Trinity.[65]

There are two central themes, among many others, in the Augustinian journey which have been consistently drawn upon in the later history of theology. The first is expressed in the discovery of the language of relation in speaking of God. It is at the heart of the *De Trinitate*'s second part, developed in Books V–VII, where Augustine proceeds from presenting the dogmatic and biblical data of the doctrine of the faith to the understanding of the faith, according to which "Father and Son and Holy Spirit in the inseparable equality of one substance present a divine unity; and therefore there are not three gods but one God."[66] On the other hand, the second theme determines the unfolding of the third part of the work, in Books IX–XIV. It is a matter of analyzing the image of God the Trinity which is in the human person, considered in the person's spirit. The connection and juncture between the two themes is found in Book VIII,

65. This reference to the contemplative dimension of Augustine's trinitarian theology requires a more general clarification. In VII.4.7, he expresses the awareness of the transcendence of the mystery in relation to knowledge with this fine formula: "God is thought more truly than expressed, and is, truly more than what is thought [*Verius cogitator Deus quam dicitur, et verius est quam cogitator*]." So Augustine makes a distinction always to be kept in mind when his writings are being read, among these three levels: saying, thinking, and being. Being is more than thinking: that is, being is more true in the Scholastic sense of the transcendental, where "more true" means to have greater ontological density. Being is more than thinking it; thinking it is more than saying it. There is a transcendence of the being of God in relation to the thinking that we may have of it, and there is a transcendence of thought in relation to speaking of him. This brings out the otherness and inexhaustibility of the divine mystery, that in itself can never be exhaustively captured; it really is thought, and it really is expressed, but God always remains beyond that. The God of revelation is the God who is always greater than what we can think and say of him. This has to be emphasized, as it is often said that Latin theology lacks the apophatic dimension which instead characterizes Eastern theology. Now it is undoubtedly true that Western theology is more kataphatic in many respects, but not completely so, as the dimension of divine transcendence is always respected. For Augustine, the mystery of God is the transcendent horizon from which one starts and toward which one tends in doxology.

66. *De Trinitate* I.4.7.

where Augustine, crowning as it were the first seven books, has an insight about the life of God as love.

The Doctrine of the Relations

I will begin with the first theme. On the firm basis given to theological understanding by the *fides Catholica*, Augustine begins with the affirmation of "the inseparable equality of one substance."[67] Starting from a metaphysical exegesis of Exodus 3:14 where God reveals his name to Moses,[68] his philosophical and intellectual framework has no difficulty saying: "There is only one unchangeable substance or essence, that is God, to whom it applies in the strongest and most exact sense, this being from which essence derives its name."[69] But this does not mean, as it is sometimes written, that the personal identity of Father, Son, and Holy Spirit is only then just cut out in a second moment, from within the "impersonal" space of the one divine substance.[70] In fact, Augustine simultaneously affirms the unity of the essence and the distinction of the three, and this latter particularly strongly on the basis of the incontestable witness of scripture. Thus, already in Book I:

> Father and Son and Holy Spirit ... are not three gods but one God; although indeed the Father has begotten the Son, and therefore he who is the Father is not the Son; and the Son is begotten by the Father, and therefore he who is the Son is not the Father; and the Holy Spirit is neither the Father nor the Son, but only the Spirit of the Father and of the Son, himself coequal to the Father and the Son, and belonging to the threefold unity.[71]

67. Ibid.

68. Augustine goes back several times to the name of God revealed to Moses in Ex 3:14 (see for example, *De Trinitate* V.2.3; VI.5.10). He recalls the Latin translation of the original Hebrew *hejeh asher hejeh* (literally: *I am who I am*) as *Ego sum qui sum*, and he interprets this name philosophically in the sense that in it God affirms himself to be being. While not excluding this meaning, we know that the Hebrew formula is really richer, also evoking God's personality, the closeness of his relationship with humans, openness to the future, and so on. Still, Augustine's translation/exegesis—which the Scholastics will adopt—is fundamental because it shows how for Augustine, what Greek philosophy says coincides with revelation: God is being. Even though Augustine uses the terms "substance" or "essence" regarding God according to the context, this is why he decisively prefers "essence," not only because God is a substance completely other than created substances (he is unchangeable, eternal, without accidents), but also because *essentia*, in his way of thinking, is derived from *esse* (existence, being), as sapiential (wisdom) is derived from *sapere* (to know). That is why God is essence in the sense that he is being itself: the one who is being in himself.

69. *De Trinitate* V.2.3.

70. This is the accusation the Eastern theologians make against Augustine, especially following the polemics regarding the *Filioque*. However, it does not seem completely justified. Rather, it is evident that the approach chosen by Augustine, adopted by the Latins after him, is different from the one favored by the Greeks (beginning with the Cappadocians), but both approaches are plausible, as we will see below. On this issue, which we will discuss later, see the classic studies by Theodore de Régnon, *Études de théologie positive sur la Sainte Trinité* (Paris: Retaux, 1892); Walter Kasper, *Der Gott Jesu Christi* (Mainz: Grünewald, 1982); and Gisbert Greshake, *Der dreieine Gott: Eine trinitarische Theologie* (Freiburg: Herder, 1997), 60–171, translated into Italian as *Il Dio Unitrino: Teologia trinitaria* (Brescia: Queriniana, 2000), 59–189.

71. *De Trinitate* I.4.7.

The emphasis on the "not" of otherness and distinction in the co-original equality and unity could not be more explicit and marked. And right away he overcomes not only a rigid conception of Hebrew monotheism, but also the conception of the One beyond any possible categorization of otherness from Plato's *Parmenides*[72] and from Plotinus's Neoplatonism.[73] Augustine is passing beyond the point of no return, to the new reality manifested by revelation. But if the otherness (of the Father, of the Son, and of the Holy Spirit) is real in God, and if unity is just as real, how can they both be held and understood together? Augustine takes on this formidable question in Book V.

Coming to contemplate the Trinity in itself, he intends to offer an illustration of the being of God one and three at this point, even while aware that he is unequal to the enormous task to which he feels called. Thus he makes the traditional Aristotelian doctrine his own, which held that in changeable things, substance and accidents have to be clearly distinguished. Substance is what a reality is in itself, while the accidents "refer to something that can be lost by some change of the thing it modifies."[74] Now it is obvious that not only is God that unchangeable substance, "or perhaps a better word would be being,"[75] but also that "there

72. In Plato's *Parmenides* 139b–c, he states the absolute unity of the One as follows: "one shall not be identical to another nor to itself, neither does the other part differ from itself nor from the other.... By being in some way different from itself it would be different from the One and so it would not be One.... By then being identical to another it would be that other and no longer itself; as a result it would not be what it is, that is One, but would differ from the One.... Therefore, insofar as it is One, it will not in fact be different" (own trans.).

73. This is how Plotinus describes the ineffability of the One beyond any kind of otherness: "Thus we are always brought back to the One. Every particular thing has a One of its own to which it may be traced; the All has its One, its Prior but not yet the Absolute One; through this we reach that Absolute One, where all such reference comes to an end. Now when we reach a One—the stationary Principle—in the tree, in the animal, in Soul, in the All—we have in every case the most powerful, the precious element: when we come to the One in the Authentically Existent Beings—their Principle and source and potentiality—shall we lose confidence and suspect it of being—nothing? Certainly this Absolute is none of the things of which it is the source—its nature is that nothing can be affirmed of it—not existence, not essence, not life—since it is That which transcends all these" (*Enneads* III.8.10); "The Primal touches nothing, but is the center round which those other Beings lie in repose and in movement. For Movement is aiming, and the Primal aims at nothing; what could the Summit aspire to?" (III.9.9); "so in a light diffused afar from one light shining within itself, the diffused is vestige, the source is the true light; but Intellectual-Principle, the diffused and image light, is not different in kind from its prior; and it is not a thing of chance but every point is reason and cause" (VI.8.18).

74. *De Trinitate* V.4.5. As is known, in the *Categories*, Aristotle sets out nine accidents along with substance: "The terms ... express, case by case, either a substance, or a quantity, or a quality, or a relation, or a place, or a time, or the being in one situation, or a having, or an action, or a passion" (*Categories* 1b25). Relation is defined by Aristotle as that "whose essence consists in standing in a certain connection to something" (8a33). Because of this, "relation is among all [the categories] the one that can least be identified with a determinate nature or with a substance," indeed it "is identified neither with a substance nor with a real being" (*Metaphysics* XIV.1088a20–25). In a word, for Aristotle, not only is relation not a substance but an accident, but among the accidents it is the furthest from substantial being.

75. *De Trinitate* V.2.3. And this is because "thus only that which not only does not but also absolutely cannot change deserves without qualification to be said really and truly to be" (ibid.).

is nothing accidental in God because there is nothing in him that can be changed or lost."[76]

But now, suddenly, Augustine makes the decisive step forward: starting from revelation to grasp that while in God, "there is nothing that has an accidental meaning," still in him, "not everything that is said of him is said according to the substance."[77] In fact, he explains, "some things are said with reference to something else, like Father with reference to Son and Son with reference to Father, which is not accident, because the one is always Father and the other always Son."[78] On the other hand, "although being Father is different from being Son, there is no difference of substance, because they are not called these things substance-wise but relationship-wise; and yet this relationship is not accident, because it is not changeable."[79] This is how Augustine makes sense of the noncontradictory dimension of the Christian doctrine on God, testified by scripture and formulated by dogma. God is being and as such is one: but at the same time revelation points out he is Father and Son and Holy Spirit, each one as the one being, but each in a different way (*diversus est Pater esse et Filius esse*) through the reciprocal relation of each to the other (*ad invicem atque ad alterum*). This is how he succeeds in bringing together the two realities he acknowledges—one from philosophy, but also Mosaic revelation, the other from New Testament revelation. The two realities are connected in such a way that the unity of the divine being (which has to do with the level of substance) is not shattered by the otherness of the Father, Son, and Holy Spirit. This expresses the relation of one to the other, where that relation is not accidental, because the Father is always Father, the Son always Son, and the Holy Spirit always Holy Spirit.

The solution is inspired by, and adheres to, the New Testament data, inasmuch as it is based on the analysis of the language of the relations of fatherhood, sonship, and gift (the Holy Spirit)[80] used by revelation to express the being of the one true God who, in Jesus, opens out the mystery of his unity and Trinity. In conclusion, the distinction can be predicated of the one God *secundum relativum*, according to relation. A radical transformation of the metaphysical context Augustine inherited and with which he grapples, follows from this, at least in his intention.[81]

76. V.4.5.

77. V.5.6.

78. Ibid.

79. Ibid.

80. Augustine explains (V.11.12) that if the concept of relation is itself implicit in the name of the Father (that expresses relation to the Son) and of the Son (that expresses relation to the Father), it is not initially obvious regarding the Holy Spirit. But upon reflection on the fact that scripture calls the Holy Spirit "the gift of God" (see Acts 8:20; Jn 4:10), we can easily grasp that he is the gift both of the Father and of the Son, rather "a kind of inexpressible communion or fellowship of Father and Son." And precisely because of this he too is relation in the highest sense.

81. See what Joseph Ratzinger has said about this in his *Introduction to Christianity*.

God is not simply the substance, or better, absolute *essence*, the one being that denies in himself any otherness and distinction, precisely because he is one. But he is the being-one who expresses his unity in the reciprocal relations of the three who are distinct: the Father, the Son, and the Holy Spirit, each one being the one true God.

Still, one question remains open, or better, resurfaces from within Augustine's proposed solution: exactly what modality of being is that of the *secundum relativum*? In fact, the epithets designating Father, Son, and Holy Spirit are not predicated according to the substance, nor can they be predicated as accidents. Is *secundum relativum* therefore a *tertium quid*? Augustine implicitly replies, "yes," even if it is then very difficult, perhaps indeed impossible, to express what is being discussed here. So, referring to the language already used by some Latin Christian writers,[82] he can conclude: "Yet when you ask 'Three what?' human speech labors under a great dearth of words. So we say three persons, not in order to say that precisely, but in order not to be reduced to silence."[83] The bishop of Hippo admits with humility and sincerity therefore that he cannot penetrate further into the thick of the mystery of God revealed in Christ, which he had tried to explore with understanding, adhering to the faith and calling on help from above.

The "Locus" of the Trinity: Reciprocal Love and Human Interiority

But Augustine does not give up and takes up another path, as we can already see from the beginning of Book VIII: "What we are asking, though, is from what likeness or comparison of things known to us we are able to believe, so that we may love the as yet unknown God."[84] Even though he is transcendent and ineffable, God is truly the creator of the universe, where his "vestiges" are disseminated, especially the human being whom he created "in his image and likeness" (see Gn 1:26). Without any doubt now, love is the highest reality we can find in human experience, what is most noble and perfect. This does not only characterize the relation that God has lived and continues to live with respect to humanity according to revelation, but it is also the true relation humans are called to live, by grace, with respect to God and the neighbor: "Thus it is that in this ques-

82. *De Trinitate* V.8.10. The language used by the Latin writers who distinguish *substantia* (substance) that is one, from *personae* (persons) who are three, is clearer for Augustine than the Greek distinction, which remains obscure for him: between *ousía* (substance, which designates the one being of God) and *hypóstasis* (subsistence, which designates the distinct being of the Father, Son, and Holy Spirit). See also VII.4.8.

83. V.9.10.

84. VIII.5.8.

tion we are occupied with about the trinity and about knowing God, the only thing we really have to see is what true love is; well in fact, simply what love is."[85]

Before anything else, the New Testament, and St. John's first Letter in a particularly luminous way, reaches the point of saying, "God is love, and those who abide in love abide in God" (1 Jn 4:16). Thus Augustine exclaims: "Why should we go running round the heights of the heavens and the depths of the earth looking for him who is with us if only we should wish to be with him?"[86] It is enough for each one to look at the love with which he or she loves their neighbor. In fact, what is that love by which we love our brother or sister? Is it not God's gift? Is it not the presence in us of God himself who is love? "He can already have God better known to him than his brother, certainly better known because more present, better known because more inward to him, better known because more sure. Embrace love which is God, and embrace God with love."[87] When I love my brother or sister in reality I am experiencing a love that is in me, and yet does not come from me. So by loving I know that love that makes me able to love. By loving I know God as the love that makes me able to love and who, dwelling in me, is greater than my heart (see 1 Jn 3:20): *intimior intimo meo, superior summo meo* (more within me than myself, higher than the highest point in myself). God is love in fact, and so I know him in some way when I love, when I love him and when, in him, I love my neighbor. Scripture tells me this, along with my experience of the Christian life.

And yet, I still have not reached the Trinity with this. Augustine makes this objection himself: "Yes I can see charity, and to the best of my ability grasp it with my mind, and I believe the scripture when it says that *God is charity and whoever abides in charity abides in God* (1 Jn 4:16). But when I see it, I don't see any trinity in it."[88] And he replies: "Oh but you do see a trinity if you see charity. I will just remind you of a few things, and so help you if I can to see that you see it."[89] In fact, in love, "there are three, lover and what is being loved, and love. It still remains to rise from

85. VIII.7.10.

86. VIII.7.11: "Utquid imus et currimus in sublimia caelorum et ima terrarum quaerentes eum qui est apud nos, si nos esse velimus apud eum?"

87. VIII.8.12: "Iam potest notiorem Deum habere quam fratrem; plane notiorem, quia presentiorem; notiorem, quia interiorem; notiorem, quia certiorem. Amplectere dilectionem Deum, et dilectione amplectere Deum."

88. Ibid.: "At enim caritatem video, et quantum possum eam mente conspicio, et credo Scripturae dicenti: 'Quoniam Deus caritas est, et qui manet in caritate in Deo manet' (1 Jn 4:8, 16). Sed cum illam video, non in ea video Trinitatem."

89. Ibid.: "Immo vero vides Trinitatem, si caritatem vides. Sed commonebo, si potero, ut videre te videas." We should note the force of that *videre*: for Augustine it is the living contemplation of God the Trinity.

here and investigate these things on a higher plane as far as it is granted man to do."[90] This is a moment of light for Augustine: love is something that is triune in itself, requiring the one who loves, the one who is loved and their reciprocal love. It is a matter of taking a leap toward the heavens, toward God who is love—such a love that he allows himself to be glimpsed in the secret of his own being, one and three. Augustine has grasped that he had found *the locus* in which to look, the direction toward which contemplation's glance should be directed. And yet, he recognizes at the same time that he needs to hold back, at least for a while: "But here let us rest our effort for a little, not supposing that it has already found us what we are looking for, but as if finding a place where something has to be looked for. It has not yet been found, but we have found where to look."[91]

Beginning from Book IX up to the beginning of Book XV, Augustine no longer gazes directly on high, toward God, but focuses on the image of God the Trinity imprinted on each of us, and especially on what most resembles God in us, our spirit.[92] Thus the master marks out the way of interiority to reach contemplation of God. He first does this by incomparably illustrating how the spirit, created in God's image and likeness, becomes the dwelling place of the Trinity by grace. His lesson will last for centuries by inspiring mystics with the ineffable experience of God the Trinity's indwelling in the soul: theologians with his description of the Trinity in terms of analogy with the human spirit (God the Father who knows in the Word and loves in the Holy Spirit); and philosophers with his analysis of the metaphysical depth of human interiority.

But what happened to the other way, that of love, of mutual love to the point of consummation in unity, of the "trinity," in other words of the lover, the loved and the love that merges them into one? Augustine answers this question himself at the end of his journey, in Book XV:

If we try to recall where it was in these books that a trinity first began to appear to our understanding, it will occur to us that it was in the eighth book.... But when we came to charity, which is called God in holy scripture, the glimmerings of a trinity

90. *De Trinitate* VIII.10.14: "tria sunt: amans, et quod amatur, et amor. Restat etiam hinc ascendere, et superius ista quaerere, quantum homini datur."

91. Ibid.: "paululum requiescat intentio, non ut se iam existimet invenisse quod quaerit, sed sicut solet inveniri locus, ubi quaerendum est aliquid. Nondum illud inventum est, sed iam inventum est ubi quaeratur."

92. And in the human spirit he recognizes a human trinity, as is well known: that of its being, its knowledge with which it knows, and its love with which it loves. They are one and three. True, it is a pale reflection of the Trinity, a simple analogy. But it demonstrates how the mark of the Trinity is imprinted on each human being, created in God's image and likeness. Then when the human spirit welcomes God in itself, God who gives himself by grace, and this human spirit knows and loves him, then the image (the human spirit) participates in the one of which it is the image (God). It gradually grows in his likeness—like a mirror pierced and brightened by the light illuminating it—to the fullness of the vision of, and union with, God in the kingdom of heaven (see XIV.12.15; 18.24).

began to appear, namely lover and what is loved and love. However, that inexpressible light beat back our gaze, and somehow convinced us that the weakness of our mind could not yet be attuned to it. So to relax our concentration we turned ourselves back in reflection, between the beginning and the completion of our search, to what could be called the more familiar consideration of our own mind insofar as it has been made to imagine God. And from then on we lingered over the creature which we ourselves are from the ninth to the fourteenth book in order to behold if we could the invisible things of God by understanding them through those that have been made. So here we are, after exercising our understanding as much as was necessary, and perhaps more than was necessary in these lower things, wishing and not being able to raise ourselves to a sight of that supreme trinity which is God.[93]

Augustine's reply includes the *pathos* of an illumination[94] and almost a regret that he was not able to follow it.[95] Why? Because it was not the

93. XV.6.10: "Si enim recolamus ubi nostro intellectui coeperit in his libris Trinitas apparere, octavus occurrit ... ubi ventum est ad caritatem, quae in sancta Scriptura Deus dicta est, eluxit paululum Trinitas, id est amans, et quod amatur, et amor. Sed quia lux ineffabilis nostrum reverberabat obtutum, et ei nondum posse, obtemperari nostrae mentis quodam modo convincebatur infirmitas, ad ipsius nostrae mentis, secundum quam factus est homo 'ad imaginem Dei,' velut familiariorem considerationem, reficienda, laborantis intentionis causa, inter coeptum dispositumque reflexímus; et inde in creatura, quod nos sumus, ut invisibilia Dei, per ea quae facta sunt, conspicere intellecta possemus, immorati sumus a nono usque ad quartum decimum librum."

94. In itself, this is a genuine illumination, in other words an almost ecstatic drawing from the mystery of God, who in the very act of his giving himself to be known, shows and confirms his ineffable transcendence. I think this can be shown by comparing this passage, where Augustine narrates the insight that he records in Book VIII, and the account of his insight about the mystery of God offered in *Confessions* VII.10.23. Both narrations are intense and vivid, revealing the originality and depth of the lived experience, expressed in a mystically flavored language which is really similar in both cases. As we have seen in *Confessions*, Augustine speaks of that first experience of the knowledge of God (*cum te primum cognovi*) where the unchanging light (*Lux incommutabilis*) that cried out to him from afar, *Ego sum qui sum* ("I am who am")—in obvious reference to God's revelation to Moses in Ex 3:14—is offered to the *visio* (mystical sight) of his mind: "And you repulsed the weakness of my gaze powerfully dazzling me, so that I trembled in love and awe: and I found myself far from you in the region of unlikeness [*Et reverberasti infirmitatem aspectus mei radians in me vehementer, et contremui amore et horror: et inveni longe me esse a te in regione dissimilitudinius*]." The language effectively describes the powerful radiation of the light that is God; its reverberation affects the soul's weak eye, provoking love and awe at the same time, making the human person aware of the immense distance separating him/her from God, which only God's love can traverse. In Book XV of *De Trinitate*, Augustine uses similar language again, indeed identical at times—he speaks of *lux ineffabilis* (ineffable light), of its *reverberare* and of the *infirmitas nostrae mentis* (the weakness of our mind) to describe the insight, no longer into that *Lux incommutabilis* (unchanging light) crying out, "I am who am," but of the Trinity that began to *eluxit paululum* (to dawn upon us a little), when he arrived at the *caritas* that in scripture is called God. But in this case as well, the reverberation of this (new) light is so forceful that Augustine recognizes that the moment has not yet come when he can fix his gaze on it. We can draw at least two things from this comparison: (1) that for Augustine, the insight about *caritas* (and about God's charity) as *locus* for the contemplation of God the Trinity is the fruit of a grace and insight at least equal to the earlier knowledge of God testified in *Confessions*. It thus constitutes the highest point reached in the journey to respond to the desire which gave rise to it, and which feeds *De Trinitate*: "I have sought you, and have desired to see by my mind what I believed [*quaesivi te, et desideravi intellectu videre quod credidi*]" (*De Trinitate* XV.28.51). (2) That the way of charity, that is, the knowledge of God through the experience and analogy of charity as interpersonal reciprocal relationship, is not excluded in principle by Augustine. He merely holds that the moment has not yet come to penetrate the mystery, to the point of leaving the definite impression that the other way, of the mind's interiority, is more a partial solution, valid but temporary, than a definitive choice.

95. As the following phrase suggests: "So here we are, after exercising our understanding as

moment, nor had Augustine been touched by the grace of the Spirit allowing him to embark on and journey along this way. I think that H. U. von Balthasar is right when he identifies the reason for this hesitation in the fact that Augustine did not yet have the necessary conceptual tools available to continue:

> We must therefore ask in what ways the charisms of the founders of the great religious orders achieved philosophical expression. The charismatic *indifferentia* has rarely been immediately reflected in its philosophical counterpart.... Not the least reason for this was the fact that intersubjectivity, upon which the ethics of the Gospel is based, failed to find an adequate philosophical foundation in the classical period, and even today has yet to become the principal theme of Christian philosophy. Accordingly, it is a largely Neoplatonic (and therefore undialogical) metaphysics which provides the conceptual underpinning for the Augustinian theology of *caritas*.[96]

I do not fully share this judgment, which seems to me too drastic and rough.[97] I would rather say that the times were not yet ripe in spite of Augustine's ingenious insight, which was the fruit of a gift from on high.

The Opening to the Future: God's Being Is Love

In reality, Augustine briefly takes up in the last part of Book XV, dedicated to the Holy Spirit, what he had said in Book VI: "Deus substantia et Deus caritas [est],"[98] by reaffirming the identity, yet to be penetrated, of being and love in God. The discourse on charity in 1 John is once again the reference point, the pneumatological aspect of which is now articulated. What in fact makes possible the reciprocal indwelling of God in us and of us in God? John answers as follows: "By this we know that we abide in him and he in us, because he has given us of his own Spirit" (1 Jn 4:13). Augustine concludes:

much as was necessary, and perhaps more than was necessary in these lower things, wishing and not being able to raise ourselves to a sight of that supreme trinity which is God [*Et ecce iam quantum necesse fuerat, aut forte plus quam necesse fuerat, exercitata in inferioribus intelligentia, ad summam Trinitatem, quae Deus est, conspiciendum nos erigere volumus, nec valemus*]" (*De Trinitate* XV.6.10).

96. Hans Urs von Balthasar, *The Glory of the Lord: A Theological Aesthetics*, vol. 5: *The Realm of Metaphysics in the Modern Age*, trans. Oliver Davies, Andrew Louth, Brian McNeil, John Saward, and Rowan Williams, ed. Brian McNeil and John Riches (San Francisco, Calif.: Ignatius Press, 1991), 23.

97. It would be enough to reread, along with the Augustinian remarks already quoted, the essays of Maurice Nédoncelle, "L'intersubjectivité humaine est-elle pour Saint Augustin un image de la Trinité?," in *Augustinus Magister* (Paris: Etudes augustiniennes, 1954), 1:595–602; and of Jean-Baptiste Du Roy, "L'expérience de l'amour et l'intelligence de la foi trinitaire selon saint Augustin," *Recherches augustiniennes* 2 (1962): 415–45.

98. *De Trinitate* VI.5.7: "What is meant is that while in that supremely simple nature substance is not one thing and charity another, but substance is charity and charity is substance, whether in the Father or in the Son or in the Holy Spirit, yet all the same the Holy Spirit is distinctively named charity [*Ut scilicet in illa simplici summaque natura, non sit ailiud substantia et aliud caritas; sed substantia ipsa sit caritas, et caritas ipsa sit substantia, sive in Patre, sive in Filio, sive in Spiritu Sancto, et tamen proprie Spiritus Sanctus caritas nuncupetur*]" (XV.17.29).

So it is the Holy Spirit of which he has given us that makes us abide in God and him in us. But this is precisely what love does. He then is the gift of God who is love.... So it is God the Holy Spirit proceeding from God who fires man to the love of God and neighbor when he has been given to him, and he himself is love (Jn 15:26; Rom 5:5).[99]

The apostle Paul confirms this after all: "God's love has been poured into our hearts through the Holy Spirit, that has been given to us" (Rom 5:5). This then is the theological reason that mutual love according to Jesus' new commandment, is the specific locus of the knowledge of God the Trinity because the grace of the Holy Spirit which shares divine life with us becomes effective in mutual love. Through the Holy Spirit, this grace makes us one in Christ as the Father and the Son are one in the Holy Spirit. In fact, the Holy Spirit "is not just the Father's alone nor the Son's alone, but the Spirit of them both, and thus he suggests to us the common charity by which the Father and the Son love each other."[100] Wherever reciprocal love in Christ is implemented therefore—the experience of the Spirit, the reciprocal love of Father and Son—is realized there. And the theological locus precisely for the knowledge of God the Trinity can be recognized there. As the human spirit fully becomes the image of the Trinity when God dwells in it, similarly the relationship of communion among human beings becomes image of the Trinity when the Spirit dwells there.

But we are at the conclusion of *De Trinitate* and Augustine is advanced in years by this point. All that remains for him to say is: "So now let us bring this book to a close at last with a prayer in preference to an argument."[101] The prayer is the one for unity, translated into the words of the great doctor: "So when we do attain to you, there will be an end to these many things which we say and do not attain, and you will remain one, yet all in all, and we shall say one thing praising you in unison, even ourselves being also made one in you."[102]

99. XV.17.31: "Sanctus itaque Spiritus de quo dedit nobis facit nos in Deo manere, et ipsum in nobis. Hoc autem facit dilectio. Ipse est igitur Deus dilectio.... Spiritus Sanctus qui procedit ex Deo, cum datus fuerit homini, accendit eum in dilectionem Dei et proximi, et ipse dilectio est."

100. XV.17.27: "nec Patris est solius, nec Filii solius, sed amborum; et ideo commune, qua invicem se diligunt Pater et Filius, nobis insinuat caritatem."

101. XV.27.50: "Librum itaque istum iam tandem aliquando precatione melius quam disputatione concludam."

102. XV.28.51: "Cum ergo pervenerimus ad te, cessabunt 'multa' ista quae 'dicimus et non pervenimus'; et manebis unus 'omnia in omnibus'; et sine fine dicemus unum laudantes te in unum, et in te facti etiam nos unum."

Eastern and Western Trinitarian Theology and the Question of the *Filioque*

The Christological and trinitarian dogmas of the fourth and fifth centuries, together with the ingenious theological studies by the Cappadocians and Augustine, constitute a secure patrimony on which the subsequent speculation is based. This includes the less creative late patristic period and early Middle Ages as well as that apex of Christian theology which drew from the medieval *christianitas* in the twelfth and thirteenth centuries.

But the Cappadocians and Augustine, as can be glimpsed from what has been said so far regarding their doctrine, express the different sensitivities of the East and the West in trinitarian theology. It is not only a matter of different terminology smoothed over by the Second Council of Constantinople in 553, but at a deeper level, they emphasize different theological perspectives and spiritual intuitions. To be clear, there is nothing so diverse as to make one or the other tradition deviate from orthodoxy. It becomes difficult to recognize their unity when the differences are raised and juxtaposed, though trinitarian unity can never mean uniformity.

This becomes painfully evident in the polemics regarding the *Filioque*, such that the doctrine on the Holy Spirit, who is the bond of communion in God and between God and human beings, can actually become the occasion for separation among Christ's disciples. In any case, the heated debate regarding this issue offers the possibility to further clarify ideas, as occurred with the heresies of the first centuries, even if it means bearing fruit only in times closer to our own.

Two Different Models for Trinitarian Theology

The *Filioque* is undoubtedly the trinitarian theme of interest toward the end of the patristic period and the beginning of the Middle Ages, at least from the standpoint of the theological diatribe between East and West. To understand the genesis of the controversy about the procession of the Holy Spirit, or more precisely, about the Son's role in it, it is necessary first of all to recall that the first Council of Constantinople took no position in this regard. It simply and unequivocally affirmed the Holy Spirit's divinity. Utilizing the verb employed in the fourth Gospel, it determined that he is *ekporeuménōn*, in other words, springing forth as from a fountain, from the Father. But it did not say anything about the relationship between the Son and the Holy Spirit. In fact, it established a close correspondence between the relationship of generation (*génnēsis*) between the

Father and the Son on one hand, and that of springing forth (*ekpóreusis*) between the Father and the Holy Spirit. The council wanted to confirm that both the Son and the Spirit receive their divinity from the Father and therefore, like the Father from whom they come, they themselves are both God, the one and only true God. Starting from this definite dogmatic datum, both the Eastern and Western trinitarian theologies come to develop different perspectives with different sensitivities. I will now try to summarize the different approaches that they gradually take on, well aware of a certain simplification in doing so.

The primacy of economy and/or of ontology? Remaining more closely linked to the economy of revelation, Eastern theology starts from the persons whose actions unfold in the history of salvation. The one God is the Father who shares divinity with the Son and together shares the same divinity with the Holy Spirit by means (*diá*) of the Son. In this way the emphasis is on the Father's *monarchía* and the *táxis* (orderly procession) of the Son and the Holy Spirit from him. Western theology strives instead to penetrate the mystery of the trinitarian being *ad intra*, beginning especially with St. Augustine. It starts from the one divine essence which is actualized through the relationships of origin in the three Persons: the Father generates the Son and the Holy Spirit proceeds from the reciprocal love between the Father and the Son. It could be said that the Eastern point of view is primarily that of the one God in three persons, whereas the Western perspective is that of the three persons in the one God.

Linear and/or circular framework? The contemplation of the trinitarian mystery that is typical of Eastern theology can be represented linearly:

$$F \longrightarrow S \longrightarrow HS$$

The Western theological understanding of the trinitarian mystery is instead expressed by a triangle (or circle):

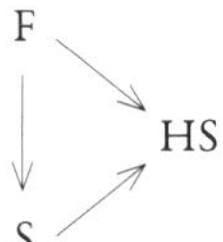

It is evident from the Eastern perspective that the Spirit springs forth (*ekporeúetai*) from the Father through (*diá*) the Son. In the Western view, the Spirit proceeds from the Father and from the Son (*Filioque*) even though the Father remains the source (*a Patre principaliter*, as the

Latin fathers say) because the Son receives divinity from the Father, and consequently, the capacity to spirate the Spirit as well.

The Holy Spirit: the extreme and/or the intimate interior of God? Following the linear framework, the Eastern Church Fathers emphasize that the Holy Spirit is the outermost expression of God, the overflowing of the Father's and the Son's life of love in creation and history. They focus at the same time on the distinction of the persons according to the *táxis* of divine life revealed in salvation history. Furthermore, along the line of the Cappadocians and then the tradition of Dionysius the Areopagite, the "negative" (*apofasi*) approach is preferred to decisively safeguard the transcendence of the mystery.[103]

The circular approach of Western theology places the emphasis instead on the Holy Spirit as God's intimate interior, the bond of love between the Father and the Son. Preference is given to the unity and the equi-divinity of the three. The resources of reason are increasingly utilized, especially with the advent of Scholastic theology, to penetrate the mystery.

Rublev's Trinity and/or Masaccio's Trinity? The classic pictorial image illustrating the Eastern point of view is Andrej Rublev's (ca. 1360–1430) icon of the Trinity. I will say more about this later. The three divine Persons are depicted in it as the three mysterious characters that appeared to Abraham at the oaks of Mamre (Gn 18:1). In the West, the Father is portrayed either upright in his majesty or enthroned, sustaining the Son's cross, while the Spirit hovers between them in the form of a dove. This is how it is depicted for example in Masaccio's (1401–ca. 1428) Trinity in the Santa Maria Novella Church in Florence, where the distinguishing characteristics of the three are more prominent from the Christocentric perspective of the redemption.[104]

The Augustinian crossroads St. Augustine's trinitarian theology is decisive for the formulation of the doctrine of the *Filioque* in the West. He explains with great clarity in *De Trinitate* in fact how it is to be understood that the Father is the principal cause of the eternal procession of the Holy Spirit, while the Son actively participates in this at the same time as well:

103. See John Meyendorff, *Byzantine Theology: Historical Trends and Doctrinal Themes* (New York: Fordham University Press, 1974); Yannis Spiteris, "La dottrina trinitaria nella Teologia ortodossa. Autori e prospettive," in *La Trinità in contesto*, ed. Angelo Amato (Rome: LAS, 1994), 45–69.

104. The Father is represented in the form of "one that was ancient of days" in Daniel's vision, the Son in the moment—considered the iconic apex by John and Paul—of the elevation of the cross, the Holy Spirit in the form of a dove recalled by the synoptics.

Therefore anyone who can understand the generation of the Son from the Father as timeless should also understand the procession of the Holy Spirit from them both [*ab utroque*] as timeless. And anyone who can understand that when the Son said, "As the Father has life in himself, so he has given the Son to have life in himself" (Jn 5:26) ... should also understand that just as the Father has it in himself that the Holy Spirit should proceed from him (cf. Jn 15:26), so he gave to the Son that the Holy Spirit should proceed from him too, and in both cases timelessly; and thus that to say that the Holy Spirit proceeding from the Son is something which the Son has from the Father. If the Son has everything that he has from the Father, he clearly has from the Father that the Holy Spirit should proceed from him.[105]

Ultimately, the Holy Spirit proceeds from the Father and from the Son because he is the gift of the reciprocal love of both of them, their communion:

So the Holy Spirit is a kind of inexpressible communion or fellowship of Father and Son, and perhaps he is given this name just because the same name can be applied to the Father and the Son. He is properly called what they are called in common, seeing that both Father and Son are holy and both Father and Son are spirit. So to signify the communion of them both by a name which applies to them both, the gift of both is called the Holy Spirit. And this three is one only God, good great, eternal, omnipotent; his own unity, godhead, greatness, goodness, eternity, omnipotence.[106]

Genesis and the Terms of the Dispute concerning the *Filioque*[107]

While expressing different theological and spiritual sensitivities, each with its own merits and limitations, the two perspectives are not contradictory, but possible together and complementary. In fact, the church was still breathing in harmony with its "two lungs," when the doctrine of the procession of the Holy Spirit from the Father and from the Son

105. *De Trinitate* XV.26.47: "Qui potest intellegere sine tempore generationem Filii de Patre, intellegat sine tempore processionem Spiritus Sancti de utroque. Et qui potest intellegere in eo quod ait Filius: *Sicut habet Pater vitam in semetipso, sic dedit Filio vitam habere in semetipso* ... intellegat sicut habet Pater in semetipso ut et de illo procedat Spiritus Sanctus, sic dedisse Filio ut de illo procedat idem Spiritus Sanctus, et utrumque sine tempore; atque ita dictum Spiritum Sanctum de Patre procedere, ut intellegatur, quod etiam procedit de Filio, de Patre esse Filio. Si enim quidquid habet, de Patre habet Filius; de Patre habet utique ut et de illo procedat Spiritus Sanctus."

106. V.11.12: "Ergo Spiritus Sanctus ineffabilis est quaedam Patris Filiique communio, et ideo fortasse sic appellatur, quia Patri et Filio potest eadem appellatio convenire. Nam hoc ipse proprie dicitur quod illi communiter quia et Pater spiritus et Filius spiritus, et Pater sanctus, et Filius sanctus. Ut ergo ex nomine quod utrique convenit utriusque communio significetur, vocatur *donum* amborum Spiritus Sanctus. Et haec Trinitas unus Deus, solus, bonus, magnus, aeternus, omnipotens; ipse sibi unitas, deitas, magnitudo, bonitas, aeternitas, omnipotentia."

107. See in this regard, Yves Congar's work, *I Believe in the Holy Spirit*; and the description of the history of dogma offered by Bulgakov in *The Comforter*.

began to loom in Western theology. This can be seen in Hilary of Poitiers, Ambrose of Milan, Augustine, and the councils of Toledo. In the East in the seventh century, Maximus the Confessor was still able to appreciate the Latin position theologically, only making the suggestion that "what is peculiar to it [the *Filioque*] be expressed in a way that avoids the obscurity which could ensue from it."[108]

Unfortunately two traditions became so distant from one another that their respective languages also became alien, due to the cultural distance between the East and the West which was felt increasingly through the centuries, the political issues (relationships between the Carolingian West and the Byzantine Empire) and ecclesiastical issues (relationships between the *prima sedes* of Rome and Constantinople, the new Rome) which overlapped, the liturgical, spiritual, and theological differentiation, and finally, the difficulty in communicating across two shores of the Mediterranean, which grew increasingly acute with the expansion of Islam.

In addition, a significant linguistic issue was cause for many misunderstandings, not unlike what had occurred previously with the terms *hypóstasis* and *persona*. To describe the relationship between the Spirit and the Father along the lines of the first Council of Constantinople the Greeks used the Johannine verb *ekporeúomai*, which means precisely "to flow from the source," "to gush forth," "to proceed from the origin," and which as such can only be used with respect to the Father because he alone is the non-originated origin in the Trinity. In a language which was philosophically poorer and less precise, the Latins translated this term with the verb *procedere* (in Greek *proiénai* or *prochórein*), which simply meant to "come forth," and which could therefore be used with regard to the origin of the Holy Spirit both with respect to the Father as well as with respect to the Son. Even though it was not connected with a council, this formula (*procedere a Patre Filioque*) was plausible in the Latin language for the Latin fathers as a consequence, but it became unacceptable in the Greek language for the Greek fathers.[109]

The formula was already present in the Pseudo-Athanasian Creed *Quicumque*,[110] and it was sanctioned at the third Council of Toledo in 589 and from there it spread to Gaul and Northern Italy.[111] The *Filioque*

108. PG 91:136 (own trans., based on Jean Miguel-Garrigues's "Procession et ekporèse du Saint Esprit. Discernement de la tradition et réception oecumeénique," *Istina* 17 [1972]: 363–64); see Congar, *Je crois en l'Esprit Saint*, 3:84–85.

109. See Bruno Forte, *The Trinity as History: Saga of the Christian God*, trans. Paul Rotondi (New York: Alba House, 1989): here in reference to the original *Trinità come storia: Saggio sul Dio cristiano* (Cinisello Balsamo: Ed. Paoline, 1985), 125–27.

110. It most likely surfaced from the work of an unknown author between 430 and 500 precisely in the Arles region in southern France. It is affirmed: "Spiritus Sanctus e Patre et Filio, non factus nec creatus nec genitus, sed procedens" (DH 75).

111. DH 470 (see also 485, 527, 568).

was asserted in reality in order to emphasize the Son's divine nature in a milieu of Arianism which was still flourishing in the West, without putting the Father's monarchy into question. Because of Charlemagne's influence, and as a result of the polemics with Byzantium, a unilateral decision was taken to add it to the Nicene-Constantinopolitan Creed.[112] Pope Leo III, who consecrated Charlemagne as emperor in 800, authorized it, but he did not want it to be introduced into the Roman liturgy for prudential considerations. This came about only with Benedict VIII in 1014.

The controversy exploded with Photius. His election as patriarch of Constantinople in 858 was clearly meant as a rebuke to Rome. In 867, Photius denounced both the unilateral interpolation to the creed as well as the content of the *Filioque*. He accused the Latins of maintaining that there are two principles in God and in doing so, destroying the unity of the Trinity. In his *The Mystagogy of the Holy Spirit*, he affirmed instead that the Holy Spirit proceeds "from the Father alone" (*ek mónou toû Patrós*). As time passed, this formula was often considered by the Orthodox church to be the binding interpretation of the Nicene-Constantinopolitan dogma. Although the specific meaning of the verb *ekporeúō* is maintained, it runs the risk nevertheless of altering the linear and dynamic framework of the Greek tradition by adopting something like the following framework:

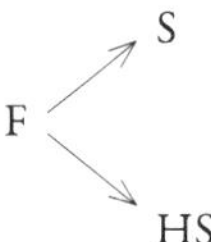

It was still possible to settle the controversy nonetheless after ups and downs. The situation degenerated two centuries later for reasons that were ultimately not theological. Cardinal Humbert of Silva Candida, the pontifical legate to Constantinople, anathematized Patriarch Michele Cerulario, reproaching him for having "removed" the *Filioque* from the creed. Michele Cerulario's counter-anathema soon followed, noting in his protest that the Greeks had been excommunicated precisely because they had not wanted to alter the creed. This was in 1054. The reciprocal excommunications were annulled only in 1965 after the historical encounter in Jerusalem between the Roman Pope Paul VI and Patriarch Athenagoras I of Con-

112. Starting with the Council of Ephesus (431) in fact, up until the final Ecumenical Council of Nicaea II (787), the prohibition was confirmed against adding any kind of modification to what the creed dictated; the addition occurred in the West in the Council of Aquileia-Friuli in 796 (Mansi XIII, 836D) and in Aachen in 809 (Mansi XIV, 17).

stantinople, making it possible to open a new phase in the dialogue. Both sides now agree moreover that there were not the necessary conditions from a purely theological standpoint to constitute a real schism in 1054.

The *Filioque* from the Medieval Councils to the Failed Attempts for Union

After the communion was broken, the councils held in the West explicitly proclaimed the *Filioque* as an article of faith. The Lateran Council affirmed in 1215: "Sine ulla diminitione Filius nascendo substantiam Patris accepit, et ita Pater et Filius habent eandem substantiam: et sic eadem res est Pater et Filius, nec non et Spiritus Sanctus ab utroque procedens."[113] The second Council of Lyons accentuated the Latin position in 1274 by defining the spiration of the Holy Spirit by the Father and by the Son "tamquam ex uno prinicipio," a formulation that was even more difficult for the Greeks to understand: "Fideli ac devota professione fatemur, quod Spiritus Sanctus aeternaliter ex Patre et Filio, non tamquam ex duobus principiis, sed tamquam ex uno principio, non duabus spirationibus, sed unica spiratione procedit."[114] Furthermore, the efforts for union initiated after 1054, always ended in failure not only because of the growing theological distance, but also because of the historical situations in which they were carried out, that is, Byzantium's political difficulties and the unilateral imposition of the *Filioque* by Rome.

Above all, the attempt pursued by the Council of Ferrara-Florence (1439–45) did not lead to a good outcome. Under the pressure of political events (the Turks were about to conquer Byzantium) a "formula for union" was sanctioned affirming on the one hand that the two sentences (the *per Filium* of the East and the *Filioque* of the West) are not mutually exclusive, but on the other hand that the *Filioque* constitutes the authentic interpretation of the Greek sentence as well.[115] Byzantium did not accept

113. DH 805.

114. DH 850.

115. See the text of the bull of union with the Greeks *Laetentur caeli* (July 6, 1439) of the Council of Florence: "In the name of the Holy Trinity, Father, Son and Holy Spirit, we define, with the approval of this holy universal Council of Florence, that the following truth of faith shall be believed, accepted and professed by all Christians and thus shall all profess it: that the Holy Spirit is eternally from the Father and the Son, and has his essence and his subsistent being from the Father together with the Son, and proceeds from both eternally as from one principle [*tamquam ab uno principio*] and a single spiration. We declare that when holy doctors and fathers say that the Holy Spirit proceeds from the Father through the Son, this bears the sense that thereby also the Son should be signified, according to the Greeks indeed as cause, and according to the Latins as principle of the subsistence of the Holy Spirit, just like the Father. And since the Father gave to his only-begotten Son in begetting him everything the Father has, except to be the Father, so the Son has eternally from the Father, by whom he was eternally begotten, this also, namely that the Holy Spirit proceeds from the Son. We define also that the explanation of those words *Filioque* was

the compromise. In any case, Pope Benedict XIV confirmed in 1742 and again in 1755 that the formula for the creed without the *Filioque* could be used in the liturgy of the churches of the Greek rite united with Rome.

Current Perspectives for Reconciliation

Theological dialogue has taken some decisive and noteworthy steps within the last few decades pursuant to the new ecumenical atmosphere established for the Catholic church following the Second Vatican Council. The Catholic side serenely affirms that agreement is possible and desirable in a framework of complementarity, provided extreme positions like that of Photius are avoided. The Orthodox position is more diversified.

There are those who, like V. Lossky, affirm that the *Filioque* is still unacceptable because it is the basis of all the flaws of Catholic theology and ecclesiology: "Christomonism," meaning exaggerated Christocentrism at the expense of the Holy Spirit; the tendency toward rationalism forgetful of the noetic value of the sapiential mystical life; and, as a consequence, on the ecclesiological level, the Roman primacy understood and exercised juridically and absolutely, at the expense of synodal *koinōnía*.[116] Other theologians, like S. Bulgakov, are more conciliatory. They are inclined to see two different theological opinions in the two formulas; they seek a common interpretation that does not elide them, but transcends both.

In the wake of Bulgakov, P. Evdokimov in particular affirmed that if the *Filioque* were to be justified from the scriptural point of view on the basis of the correspondence between the temporal missions (for which the Holy Spirit was poured forth by the Father and by the crucified and risen Son in the history of salvation) and the eternal processions, a certain reciprocity between the Son and the Holy Spirit would have to be emphasized, always on the basis of scripture. As the Nicene-Constantinopolitan Creed repeats with reference to Luke and Matthew, the Son is generated in the flesh "by Mary" and "by the Holy Spirit," who then visibly descends upon him at his baptism. That suggests a really trinitarian understanding of the relationship among the divine Persons; this would balance out the *Filioque* (the Holy Spirit proceeding from the Father and from the Son) with the *Spirituque* (the Son who is generated by the Father in the Holy Spirit).[117] Moreover, this perspective fits well with the general renewal of theology beginning in the twentieth century.

licitly and reasonably added to the creed for the sake of declaring the truth and from imminent need" (DH 1300–1302).

116. See Vladimir Lossky, *The Mystical Theology of the Eastern Church* (Crestwood, N.Y.: St. Vladimir's Seminary Press, 2002); Piergiuseppe Bernardi, *Trinità e rivelazione: Le due economie in V. Losskij* (Rome: Città Nuova, 2004).

117. Paul Evdokimov, *L'Esprit Saint dans la tradition orthodoxe* (Paris: Cerf, 1969).

A solid point of reference, in the Catholic church, is represented by the document published on September 8, 1995, by the Pontifical Council for the Unity of Christians: "The Greek and Latin Tradition Regarding the Procession of the Holy Spirit."[118] It offers four criteria for a correct hermeneutic of the Latin *Filioque* as a perspective that is complementary to the Greek *dià Hyión*. (1) Recognition of the "conciliar and ecumenical, normative and irrevocable value" of the creed professed by the second Ecumenical Council; the linguistic and theological distinction between the Greek *ekpóreusis* and the Latin *processio*, recognizing that "the Father alone is the principle without principle of the two other persons of the Trinity, the sole source [*pegé*] of the Son and of the Holy Spirit," (3) the interpretation of the Latin formulation of the procession of the Holy Spirit from the Father and from the Son "tamquam ex uno principio"[119] not in the sense of the divine essence's supra-personal unicity, but in the sense of the origin from the Father in his relationship with the Son; and (4) the reciprocity of the Holy Spirit with respect to the Son in the trinitarian life and in salvation history, acknowledging the original and active role of the Holy Spirit.

With this in mind, Catholics renouncing the *Filioque* in an ecumenical context could be considered as a concrete possibility on one hand, as an act of charity and humility, acknowledging a historical wrong inflicted upon the ecclesial principle of *consensus* (this has already become a praxis during ecumenical liturgical celebrations). In addition, an acknowledgment by the Orthodox of the theological legitimacy of the *Filioque* could be considered on the other hand in the light of what has been definitively clarified by now.

Greek *perichoresis* and Latin *circumincessio*/*circuminsessio*

Upon the closing of the patristic period something new and important from the lexical and conceptual standpoint was appearing. It was represented by the discovery of a particular new expression in trinitarian discourse, used especially in recent times, to describe what characterizes the relationships among the three divine Persons. The word is *perichoresis*. Let us briefly examine its origin, its development, and its significance.

118. In EV/19, nos. 2966–92; English translation in the Bulletin of the Pontifical Council for Promoting Christian Unity, *Information Service* 89 (1995): II/III, 88–92; see Lukas Vischer (ed.), *La théologie du Saint-Esprit dans le dialogue entre l'Orient et l'Occident* (Paris: Le Centurion, 1981); Maria Helene Gamillscheg, *Die Kontroverse um das Filioque: Möglichkeiten einer Problemlösung auf Grund der Forschungen und Gespräche der letzen hundert Jahren* (Würzburg: Augustinus Verlag, 1996); J. M. Garrigues, "À la suite de la clarification romaine sur le *Filioque*," *Nouvelle Revue Théologique* 119, no. 3 (1997): 321–34; Bernd Oberdorfer, *Filioque: Geschichte und Theologie eines ökumenischen Problems* (Göttingen: Vandenhoeck and Ruprecht, 2001).

119. See the statement of the Council of Lyons (1274) at DH 850.

The Doctrine of John of Damascus

St. John of Damascus (first half of the eighth century) had a genius for synthesizing the preceding patristic doctrine. He is the first one to utilize the term *perichóresis*[120] in Christology and trinitarian theology to express both union without confusion of the divine and human natures in Christ[121] as well as the relationship of mutual indwelling of the three divine Persons.[122]

Dealing with the Trinity, he draws from the Johannine texts in which Jesus suggests this reality: "The Father and I are one" (Jn 10:30); "The Father is in me and I am in the Father" (Jn 10:38; see 14:9–11; 17:21). Taking some cues from Irenaeus of Lyons and Gregory Nazianzen, he emphasizes:

> The subsistences dwell and are established firmly in one another. For they are inseparable and cannot part from one another, but keep to their separate courses within one another, without coalescing or mingling, but cleaving to each other. For the Son is in the Father and the Spirit: and the Spirit in the Father and the Son: and the Father in the Son and the Spirit, but there is no coalescence or commingling or confusion. And there is one and the same motion: for there is one impulse and one motion of the three subsistences, which is not to be observed in any created nature.[123]

The Latin Precedents: Hilary of Poitiers and Augustine of Hippo

The concept of the mutual indwelling of the divine Persons is also present in the Latin fathers before this term was used. For example, Hilary of Poitiers dedicates the third of his twelve books on the Trinity to this, affirming among other things: "what is in the Father is also in the Son ... one [is derived] from the other and both are one thing.... They are reciprocally in one another [*in se invicem*]."[124] For his part, Augustine picks up this concept in *De Trinitate*: "in the supreme triad one is as much as three are together, and two are not more than one, and in themselves they are infinite. So they are each in each all in each, and each in all and all in all,

120. The noun *perichóresis* is derived from the verbs *peri-chōreíō*, "dancing around" and *peri-chōréō*, "going around," and it was probably coined by the philosopher Anaxagoras (ca. 500–428 BC) to express the presence together and the dynamic interaction of the natural elements operated by the spiritual principle (*noûs*) which dwells and acts in them (see Diels-Kranz B59, fr. 12). Historians then utilized it both to express the blending (*krâsis*) among distinct bodies that nevertheless maintain their properties and to express the interpenetration of body and soul.

121. Gregory Nazianzen uses it in this Christological sense (*Ep.* 101.6).

122. We find it in this context in *De Trinitate* X (see PG 77:1144B) by Pseudo-Cyril.

123. John of Damascus, *De fide orthodoxa* XIV, in the *Nicene and Post-Nicene Fathers (Second Series)*, ed. Philip Schaff (London: T and T Clark, 1980), 9:17.

124. *De Trinitate* III.24.

and all are one [*ita et singula sunt in singulis et omnia in singulis et singula in omnibus et omnia in omnibus et nica omnia*]."[125]

Medieval Scholasticism

Proceeding along this line, medieval Scholasticism utilizes the Latin terms *circumincessio* and *circuminsessio* to translate the Greek *perichóresis*, meaning the same concept but with different nuances. *Circuminsessio* (from *circum* = around, and *insidere* = to be seated, or to stay above or within), in a more static way, is like mutual presence and inhabitation, while *circumincessio* (from *circum*, and *incedere* = to advance), is in a more dynamic way, like mutual effusion and interpenetration.

St. Bonaventure uses the term *circumincessio* explicitly, affirming that "the authorities and reasoned arguments demonstrate that a highest and perfect *circumincessio* reigns among the divine Persons," inasmuch as "one is in the other and vice versa," and that "this is understood in a really perfect sense only in God because this circumincessio in being posits distinction and unity simultaneously; in God alone is there the highest unity with distinction, so that it is possible to make this distinction without mixture and this unity without separation."[126] Even though he does not use the expression, St. Thomas amply addresses the question, "Whether the Son is in the Father, and conversely?" and he responds that "There are three points of consideration as regards the Father and the Son; the essence, the relation, and the origin; and according to each the Son and the Father are in each other."[127] Both Bonaventure and Thomas also confirm that created analogies cannot be used to express this mutual indwelling; nor can the eight possibilities of "being in" known from Aristotle.

The Theological Significance

Apart from the different emphasis given to *perichóresis* by the Greek tradition and then followed by the Bonaventurian line (which starts from the persons) on one hand, and the Latin tradition of *circuminsessio* (generally centered on the unity of the essence) on the other, it should be said with regard to this concept that it is extremely important to exclude any possibility of tri-theism or of modalism given that the three persons are one, "unconfused and undivided." As we shall see below moreover, Aquinas tries to synthesize the two classical interpretations of trinitarian life (the Greek and the Latin), basing the mutual indwelling on the unity of the essence, as well as on the relations and on the rapports of origin.

125. *De Trinitate* VI.10.12; see IX.5.8.
126. *In Sent.* I, d. 19, q. 4.
127. *ST* I, q. 42, a. 5.

Referring to a formulation by Fulgentius of Ruspe (467–533)[128] and to St. Anselm,[129] it is the Council of Florence (1442) that describes the mutual indwelling of the three in these terms:

> These three persons are one God alone, not three gods, since there is only one substance, one essence, one nature, one divinity, one immensity, one eternity of the three, and all the things are one thing alone where they are not opposed to one another in relationship. Through this unity the Father is completely in the Son, completely in the Holy Spirit; the Son is completely in the Father, completely in the Holy Spirit; the Holy Spirit is completely in the Father, completely in the Son.[130]

As we see below, the concept of *perichóresis* is widely taken up and studied in the second half of the twentieth century to express in personalistic terms the dynamic, inclusive, and effusive unity contained within the love of the three divine Persons in both their *ad intra* life and their *ad extra* missions.

128. *De Fide ad Petrum seu de regula fidei* 1.4.
129. *De processione Spiritus Sancti* 1.
130. DH 1330–31.

CHAPTER 20

Medieval Scholasticism

As has already become evident in the topics treated above, medieval Scholasticism recovers the patristic tradition, especially the Latin part,[1] which it studies with a vigorous speculative examination, further developing it in all its potential. Thomas's refined and balanced speculation can undoubtedly be considered the climax of this great epoch. But we cannot forget Scotus Eriugena's (ninth century) reflection elaborated during the Carolingian period, with his brilliant synthesis of Neoplatonic philosophy and the theology of the Greek fathers; nor Richard of St. Victor's resumption of Augustine's unfinished work on love; nor Bonaventure of Bagnoregio's grandiose Christocentric and trinitarian fresco along with Duns Scotus's speculative penetration, both following in the footsteps of Francis of Assisi.

The true longstanding master of the knowledge of God during the Middle Ages and beyond, both in the East and the West, was Dionysius the Areopagite, of whom I shall say something later on. Decisive progress was made in this regard during the Middle Ages in spite of his strong prohibition against using the intellect to fathom the mystery of the Trinity, and in spite of his authority. One could almost say that the Trinity wanted to reveal itself more, which meant that Jesus, the way, the truth, and the life (see Jn 14:6) had to enter more intimately into the hearts and minds of men and women. A response to that can be found moreover in the renewal of the monastic tradition associated with St. Benedict, the widespread success enjoyed by the Augustinian rule and its theology in the school of St. Victor of Paris for example, and the Holy Spirit's two great, innovative gifts to medieval Christianity: the Dominican and Franciscan charisms.

1. We cannot exclude other influences, for example, in Thomas Aquinas there are numerous references to the Areopagite and John of Damascus.

Richard of St. Victor's Recovery of Augustine's *via caritatis*

Although he was not so well known or appreciated, at least until a few decades ago, Richard of St. Victor is very original and profound, and probably best represents the twelfth-century Victorine school of Paris in many respects. His theological thought, which is rich and penetrating, blossomed in the midst of the fervent contemplative and academic environment of St. Victor's Abbey. It represents an ideal reconciliation between the opposed tendencies of Abelard's dialectic (ca. 1079–ca. 1142) and Bernard of Clairvaux's mysticism (1090–1135) that enlivened the first half of the century.

Fides quaerens intellectum

Regarding his work on the Trinity, Richard knew the Church Fathers very well; he was especially inspired by Augustine. But he wanted to follow through on the demands of *fides quaerens intellectum* strongly confirmed by St. Anselm (1033–1109) as the meaning and method for theology. In this, Richard's approach manifested the spirit animating Scholasticism in the best possible way and with great balance. To the extent that it is possible from this perspective, he sought to understand the *rationes necessariae* that illuminate for the intellect the mystery of the Trinity transmitted by the faith, by wisely combining rigorous speculation and a refined mystical intuition fostered by the intense community life of the Victorines. Using a typical medieval style, he describes the objective of his work in this way:

> I have read about my God that he is one and triune, one in substance but three in person. All these things I have read, but whence all this should be proven, I do not remember having read.... Authorities abound in all these matters, but not equally arguments; in all these things experience is lacking and arguments are rare. Therefore I suppose that I shall have done no little thing, as I said above, if I shall be able to assist learned minds in this occupation even a little. Even if it should not be granted to me to satisfy them.[2]

The Intuition of *condilectus*

Richard brilliantly begins with the Johannine definition of God as charity, recovered from Augustine. He shows that God cannot be other than full and pure love, in the light of a rich phenomenology of love in human experience. For this to be the case, there must be a plurality of persons in him:

2. *De Trinitate* I.5, in *On the Trinity: Book One*, trans. Jonathan Couser; available at pvspade.com/Logic/docs/StVictor.pdf.

The fullness and perfection of all goodness reside in the highest and completely perfect good. On the other hand, where the fullness of goodness is found, the true and highest charity cannot be missing. Now no one says that they possess charity in the true sense of the word because of the fact that they love themselves exclusively; for love to be charity therefore it must be addressed to another. Consequently, wherever a multiplicity of persons is absent, there is no room for charity.[3]

Richard does not stop at this point, however. He wonders why there are precisely three Persons in the Trinity. Would two not suffice in order for God to be love?

The highest charity must be absolutely perfect; and to be supremely perfect, it must be so great that it could not be greater. At the same time, it must have such a quality that it could not be better. In fact, as the peak of greatness cannot be absent in supreme charity, similarly there must also be the culmination of excellence. Well it seems that the maximum of excellence is this in authentic charity: to want that another is loved as we ourselves are loved. Effectively, nothing is more precious nor admirable in ardent, mutual love than the desire that another comes to be loved in the same way by the one that is the most loved and by whom one is most loved. Therefore, the proof of perfect charity consists in the desire that the love of which one is an object be shared.... As can be seen then, the perfection of charity requires the Trinity of persons; without this in fact, (charity) cannot subsist in the fullness of its totality.[4]

Condilectus is undoubtedly a profound intuition. After what St. Augustine had barely opened up in Book VIII of *De Trinitate*, this is the first time that the interrupted path of charity as intersubjective experience is once again considered to express the *locus* where God the Trinity can be known. One can only add that if Richard had reflected more on the specific Christological and Paschal meaning of *agápe* in the New Testament, for example, in 1 John, in addition to the phenomena of love, it would have been possible to go further ahead precisely by taking salvation history as a starting point. Either way, Richard reaches this illuminating conclusion, although it was ignored for quite a few centuries:

Therefore it is necessary and without any doubt that being and love coincide in sovereign simplicity; that is why one's own person is identified with one's own love in each of the three. Consequently, the fact that there are several persons in one divinity alone means nothing other than this: a plurality possesses just one delight alone, the highest one; rather, to say it better, a plurality is (this delight), according to different properties.[5]

3. Ibid., III.2, translated from the Italian translation by Mario Spinelli (Rome: Città Nuova, 1990), 127–28.

4. Ibid., II.11.137–38.

5. Ibid., V.20.205.

A New Concept of Person

On a final note, Richard offers a noteworthy attempt to understand the meaning of the word "person" applied to God. He is convinced first of all of the value of this term, even while specifying that its meaning had not yet been fully understood:

This is precisely what I will say—what I think and firmly believe and without hesitation; that is that in the sublime and very eminent mystery of the Trinity the term "person" was absolutely not adopted without divine inspiration and without the teaching of the Holy Spirit.... We can certainly acknowledge as well that the one applying the term "person" for the first time to the divine reality did it out of necessity to be able to respond in some way to those asking in what sense there were three in the Trinity; in fact it was not possible to answer that it is a case of three gods. In spite of that, the Holy Spirit guiding their hearts, knows well in what way and with what precise meaning (the term) was to be utilized by them who had used it only because they had no choice. If we are sincerely convinced of that, let us make every effort to know not so much with what meaning (this word) was initially used by people, nor for what reason it was subsequently used with reference to divine reality, but with what true meaning it was inspired by the Spirit of truth to those utilizing it and with what meaning it entered into the universal usage of the Latin Church.[6]

Placing himself in the wake of the Latin tradition, Richard knows very well that there is a huge difficulty in applying the notion of person to the triad in God, at least in the sense expressed by Severinus Boethius as a "rationalis naturae individua substantia":[7] because viewed in this way it would lead to tri-theism. This already posed a difficulty for St. Augustine.

Richard changes the point of departure. In reality, person means a "someone" about whom two elements must be defined: (1) "what it is" (nature) and (2) "where it comes from" (its origin). The person, therefore, is *ex-istentia*: that is someone who is in himself (expressed as *sistere)* coming from (*ex*). In God, the nature of the three is the same (divinity), while the origin is different. The plurality of persons as *ex-istentiae* refers not to the nature of God (which would be tri-theism), but to the origin which specifies each one of the three in a unique way that cannot be communicated to the other two. Consequently, the term "person" can be applied to each one of the three in the Trinity if this means "an incommunicable existence of the divine nature."[8] This clears the way for an understanding of the divine tri-personality from a metaphysical perspective as well; the meaning of person becomes fully tied to that of origin, that is, as relationship-from.

6. Ibid., IV. I.156–57.
7. *Contra Eut.* III.1–6.
8. *De Trinitate* IV.22.175.

Thomas Aquinas: The Trinity

St. Thomas Aquinas (1225–74) is undoubtedly the most mature fruit of the trinitarian theology of the medieval Christian West, although not the only nor the definitive one. He also demonstrated a remarkable sensitivity to the Eastern tradition. He knowingly welcomed the gift and the task expressed by the charism of St. Dominic of Guzman (ca. 1175–1221) with ingenious creativity. It is summarized in the motto: *contemplari et contemplata aliis tradere*, which means to contemplate God and creation in him, so as to transmit this light as a guide to everyone's existence. Precisely for this reason characterized by a charism, Thomas courageously overcame the silence of the apophatic tradition of Dionysius the Areopagite and developed the doctrine of St. Augustine in a profound way. One could say that the great doctor took over from where Augustine left off penetrating with *intelligentia fidei* the mystery of the Trinity.[9]

The Inheritance from Dionysius the Areopagite and Maximus the Confessor

A word is necessary at this point on Dionysius's contribution. He constitutes the unsurpassed climax of the apophatic tradition of Eastern theology. The most recent studies suggest that he was "a Syriac Christian who followed the lessons of Proclus and Damascius in the late fifth and early sixth century in Athens."[10] This is another reason that Neoplatonic influence, particularly Plotinian Neoplatonism which reached Proclus and Damascius through Porphyry, is much more pronounced in Dionysius than in the Greek fathers such as Clement of Alexandria, Origen, and the Cappadocians who preceded him.

A significant example of this lies in the fact that Dionysius adopts the exegesis of Plato's *Parmenides* proposed by Proclus. The first hypothesis of the dialogue regards the "One that is One," marked by a series of negations. The exegesis refers this first hypothesis to the *moné*, the utter transcendence and ineffability of the One. The second hypothesis regards "the One that is" or "being-one" and it is marked as well by a series of ne-

9. I will limit my references to the following particularly penetrating works from the endless bibliography concerning the angelic doctor's trinitarian theology: Lafont, *Peut-on connaître Dieu en Jésus Christ?*, 107–67; Hans Christian Schmidbaur, *Personarum Trinitas: Die trinitarsiche Gotteslehre des heiligen Thomas von Aquin* (St. Ottilien: EOS Verlag, 1995); Gilles Emery, *The Trinitarian Theology of Saint Thomas Aquinas*, trans. Francesca Aran Murphy (New York: Oxford University Press, 2007).

10. Salvatore Lilla, *Dionigi l'Areopagita e il platonismo cristiano* (Brescia: Morcelliana, 2005), 162 (own trans.). Among the more significant recent interpretations of the significance of Neoplatonism with respect to the Dionysian synthesis, see Werner Beierwaltes, Pierre Hadot, and Giovanni Reale.

gations parallel to the negations of the first. The exegesis refers this second hypothesis to the *próodos*, the procession of all beings from the One. In the first case, the verb of being serves a purely logical function whereas in the second it has a precisely ontological function.

Books attributed to him are *De divinis nominibus* and the *Theologia mystica*, in which God is described as the mysterious and ineffable source of all that is. To reach God it is necessary to renounce all thought and extinguish the word. This is so much so that beginning with Dionysius mysticism becomes synonymous with the culminating, unspeakable experience of God, guarded by silence and therefore incommunicable. In addition, he is considered a great authority because of his identification with the Dionysius who became Paul's disciple after his discourse at the Areopagus of Athens (see Acts 17:23–34).

Here is how he describes the ascent toward God, modeled on Moses ascending Mount Sinai:

> But then he (Moses) breaks free of them, away from what sees and is seen,[11] and he plunges into the truly mysterious darkness of unknowing. Here, renouncing all that the mind may conceive, wrapped entirely in the intangible and the invisible, he belongs completely to him who is beyond everything. Here, being neither oneself nor someone else, one is supremely united to the completely unknown by an inactivity of all knowledge, and knows beyond the mind by knowing nothing.[12]

Dionysius introduces the illustration of the trinitarian mystery in *De divinis nominibus* within this speculative context. The absolute and ineffable One of the Neoplatonic interpretation of the first hypothesis of *Parmenides* expresses well, while also safeguarding, the transcendence of the God of Christian revelation. But according to Christian revelation, the One expresses itself in three equal and distinct hypostases. To illustrate this truth Dionysius resorts to two concepts close to the heart of Neoplatonism and used earlier by the Cappadocians: that of *énōsis* (unity) and that of *diákrisis* (from *dià-krínō*, I discern, I distinguish through, i.e., within). He affirms in this way that in the *énōsis* of the *moné* a *diákrisis* is manifested nevertheless which is not that of the multiplicity characteristic of the *próodos*, but precisely what is ineffable of the three distinct hypostases in God himself, the Father, the Son, and the Holy Spirit.[13] And to designate the three hypostases, he uses the metaphor of the fountain (*pegé*) for the Father, well known to the Cappadocian fathers, and for the

11. *The things seen* and those *that see* are respectively beings which can be sensed and beings gifted with reason and intelligence (see PG 4:421A).

12. Dionysius the Areopagite, *Theologia mystica* I.3, 1001A. The relationship between the human being and God in the super-intellectual (nebulous) state is indicated with words that say union and contact, like adhere (literally, "being in"), belonging and being united.

13. *De divinis nominibus* II.3.

Son and the Spirit, those of the "buds," the "flowers," the "supra-essential lights," typical of Proclus.

The truth of the *Deus Trinitas*, acquired through revelation and about which it is possible and necessary to assert that it subsists in three hypostases, can only be expressed in symbolic language ultimately for Dionysius, as it is unspeakable in ontological language, remaining enshrouded in the ineffable mystery of the first principle: "Or, again, we learn from the sacred scriptures that the Father is the originating source[14] of the Godhead and that the Son and the Spirit are, so to speak, divine offshoots, the flowering and transcendent lights[15] of the divinity. But we can neither say nor understand how this could be so."[16] This prohibition to inquire and speak about the mystery of the divine fecundity that expresses the trinitarian processions, to the extent that it is possible to do so using the human intellect and language visited by grace, is consistently confirmed on the level of the doctrine of the spiritual and intellectual ascetical practice necessary to reach the One. This is so much so that we need to definitely note that "although in some passages pseudo-Dionysius recognizes Jesus's role in the process of approaching the first principle, we also have to note objectively that in him this role seems notably reduced with respect to what is noted in Clement, Origen and Gregory of Nyssa."[17]

A further comment is necessary with regard to the rich theology of Maximus the Confessor (579–662). In fact, he proposes an extraordinary synthesis that recovers and rereads Origen and the Cappadocian fathers within a Christocentric context opened up by the study of the Chalcedonian dogma. Read in a trinitarian key, his teaching on creation and divinization is theologically suggestive. Within his one eternal *Lógos*, the Father contemplates the multiple *logoi* of things that were created through Christ (the *Lógos* incarnate) and formed through the gift of the

14. The Father is defined as the divine font (*Divinità fontale / pēgaîa Theótēs*) because he is the first principle. This expression is rare, however. The Father is defined as the source (*pēgé*) of divinity more frequently.

15. This is an expression originally taken from Dionysius. See S. Lilla, "Terminologia trinitaria nello Pseudo-Dionigi l'Areopagita: Suoi antecedenti e sua influenza sugli autori successivi," *Augustinianum* 13 (1973): 609–23.

16. Dionysius the Areopagite, *De divinis nominibus* II, 645C; own trans. from the Italian translation by P. Scazzoso in Dionysius, *Tutte le opere* (Milan: Rusconi, 1981). I include the Latin version of the passage, for which see the Marietti edition, ed. C. Pera (Turin: 1950), which took up the text by John Saracen (twelfth century) that Thomas utilized: Rursus quod Pater quidem est fontana Deitas, Filius autem et Spiritus Sanctus deigenae Deitatis, si ita oportet dicere, pullulationes divinae naturae et sicut flores et supersubstantialia lumina a sanctis eloquiis accepimus. Quomodo autem haec sunt neque dicere neque cogitare est possibile.

17. Salvatore Lilla, *Dionigi l'Areopagita e il platonismo cristiano*, 185 (own trans.). See Pantelis Kalaitzidis, "Theologia. Discours sur Dieu et science théologique chez Denys l'Aréopagite et Thomas d'Aquin," in *Denys l'Aréopagite et sa postérité en Orient ed en Occident*, ed. Ysabel de Andia (Paris: Études Augustiniennes, 1996), 457–87; Ysabel de Andia, "La théologie trinitaire de Denys l'Aréopagite," *Studia Patristica* 32 (1997): 278–301.

Spirit who bring them back into the unity of the Father's bosom through the gratuitous and free process of divinization. Maximus paves the way for the speculative theology of Thomas Aquinas in some way, even if it is only indirect.

The Charismatic Inspiration and the Writings of Thomas

In order to grasp the theological inspiration of Thomas it is helpful to go back to one of his famous sermons, "Exiit qui seminat," preached probably in February 1270 in Paris.[18] In that sermon, Thomas identifies the concept of the theological ministry which guides him and also elaborates on the original meaning of the vocation to which he intends to respond: *contemplari et contemplata aliis tradere.*

What attracts the attention of Thomas and is the key to his interpretation of the pericope in Luke 8:4–15 is the movement of *exire*: "A sower went out to sow" (8:5). "Who is the sower?" asks Aquinas; "It must be," he answers, "first of all the Holy Trinity ... the Father sowed from heaven peace, the Son truth, and the Holy Spirit charity." However, by appropriation (as one would say using the terminology of that school) the sower is Christ, and on the other hand, Christ is also the seed, as he is the Word of God (see 8:8). From here, with a daring interpretation, Thomas sees—in the *exire* of the Word from "the secret bosom of the Father" in the incarnation-event—the model and dynamics of the mission of the preacher. If the Word became incarnate to show us the Father and to become the way to the Father, it is clear that the preacher, in exercising his ministry, will need to follow the way on which the Word journeyed: first, in order to contemplate the mystery of God and then to share with humanity the fruit of such contemplation.

Obviously, there is an essential difference between the Word who goes out from the Father to reveal God and the preacher who is called to go out to sow among the people the Word. The Word actually goes out from the Father only once and comes into the world. From where and how does the preacher need to go out? Thomas describes three exits: the first two, actually, are required by his condition of human being and sinner, and are necessary to help him "enter" that place—the contemplation of the Father—from which, later, in following Christ, he will be called to "go out" and preach. Let us consider the three exits more in detail.

The first one "is the exit from a state of guilt, because it is not allowed to the preacher to preach to others what he in the first place does not

18. See the Latin text, "Exiit qui seminat," in Thomas Käppeli, *Una raccolta di prediche attribuite a S. Tommaso*, in *Archivium Fratrum Praedicatorum* 13 (1943): 75–88. On this sermon, see the article by Jean Pierre Torrell, "Le semeur est sorti pour semer. L'image du Christ prêcheur chez frère Thomas d'Aquin," *La vie spirituelle* 147 (1993): 657–70.

do." However, for the preacher, another exit is needed: the exit "from the world." What is it exactly? Thomas sees it as symbolically represented by Abraham's experience of faith. The Lord talks about this exit to the biblical patriarch, prophetically, when inviting him to "leave all that is earthly and can be loved" to go to a land God will show him. In actuality, it is only Jesus who manifests "the way of the evangelical counsels" as the way to perfection to those who already observe the precepts of the Law: "If you wish to be perfect, go, sell your possessions ..." (Mt 19:20). What is therefore the "land" toward which we need to start walking, following God's call and leaving behind everything else? It is the *terra visionis sive contemplationis*, answers Thomas; *quae est status religionis*. Here it is clear that Aquinas illustrates the understanding of religious life developed in light of the Dominican charism. Exiting from the world, by adhering to the evangelical counsels, is therefore interpreted by him as the necessary condition to "enter" into the land of contemplation.

This is nothing new with respect to the centuries-old tradition of the church. Since ancient times, actually, those who wished to devote themselves to Christ with undivided heart left the world, giving life to the various forms of eremitical and cenobitic life. But St. Dominic's charism brings about a novelty. The one who goes out from the world in order to contemplate God—once the contemplation of the divine mysteries *in sinu Patris* is achieved in communion with Christ, following the example of the Word who went out from the Father to come into the world—also needs to go out "from the secrets of contemplation to the audience to whom he needs to preach." It is telling that Thomas establishes such a close connection between contemplation and preaching. The preacher is called to live with maximum intensity the union with God described in the Song of Songs and at the same time to offer everyone what he has experienced.

What Aquinas actually lays out in the sermon is also something he explores in depth from a doctrinal perspective in the *Summa Theologiae*. In IIa-IIae, after having treated the charismatic graces (qq. 171–78), Thomas focuses on the various forms of life (qq. 179–82) and on the various states of perfection (qq. 183–89). He draws a distinction between active and contemplative life (q. 179), describes them separately (qq. 180–81) and finally compares them (q. 182). He states that, "absolutely speaking, contemplative life is superior to active life" (q. 182, a. 1) as supported by the words of the Lord: "Mary has chosen the better part, which will not be taken from her" (Lk 10:42). However, much like Augustine, Thomas remarks that "sometimes a man is called away from the contemplative life to the works of the active life on account of some necessity of the present life, yet not so as to be compelled to forsake contemplation altogether." This happens "because charity demands it of us" and does not interrupt contemplative life, but rather brings about a communication of its fruits.[19] Thus we read in another sermon by Thomas, entitled *Puer Jesus*:

> Human beings need to acquire wisdom by sharing it with others. Therefore in Wis 7:13 we read, "I learned without guile and impart without grudging." Anyone can experience that no one can grow as well in knowledge as when sharing with others what he or she knows. Furthermore, it is a duty for human beings to answer others if they know the answer. Prov 22:21 says, "To show you what is right and true so that you may give a true answer to those who sent you." Christ answered and, "All who heard him were amazed at his understanding and his answers" (Lk 2:47).[20]

Once the inspiration of all of Thomas's theological works is clarified, it is not pointless to be introduced to the study of his trinitarian theology—which he considered since the beginning of his teaching career as "the fruit [*fructus*] and fulfillment [*finis*] of our entire lives"—by providing a brief overview of his writings.[21] Thomas examines the trinitarian mystery in various places, albeit from different and complementary perspectives. First of all, Thomas does so in his commentaries on scripture (especially relevant is *In Johannem*);[22] secondly, in the *Scriptum super Sententiis* written in his youth, where he comments on the well-known text by Peter Lombard (ca. 1100–1160) and unifies the creative and salvific perspectives employing the Neoplatonic pattern of *circulatio* (creatures "go out" from God and to God "return"); finally, in the more systematic vision of the *Summa Theologiae*. While in the earlier writings, in a more historical-salvific perspective what is more emphasized is what has been defined as the "trinitarian personalism" of Thomas, that is, the emphasis on the identity and role of the divine Persons,[23] in the more systematic perspective of the *Summa* a more ontological perspective is emphasized, which sheds light on the infinite tri-personal dynamism of the divine *Esse*.[24]

I will examine in depth this last perspective, without neglecting the first one and referring to part 1 of our journey with respect to my examination (especially of *essentia* and *distinctio Personarum*) because that

19. *ST* II-II, q. 182, a. 1, ad 3 (1936–37).

20. Thomas Aquinas, "Puer Jesus," in *I sermoni (Sermones) e Le due lezioni inaugurali (Principia)*, ed. C. Pandolfi and G. M. Carbone (Bologna: Ed. Studio Domenicano, 2003), 108–23, at 119 (own trans.).

21. *In Sent.* I, d. 2, q. 1, a. 5 (own trans.).

22. On this, also Riccardo Ferri, comparing this with St. Augustine, *Gesù e la verità: Agostino e Tommaso interpreti del vangelo di Giovanni* (Rome: Città Nuova, 2007).

23. See Francesco Marinelli, *Personalismo trinitario nella storia della salvezza: Rapporti tra la SS.ma Trinità e le opere "ad extra" nello "Scriptum super Sententiis" di San Tommaso* (Rome / Paris: PUL / Vrin, 1969).

24. See Lafont, *Structures et méthode dans la "Somme théologique" de Saint Thomas d'Aquin*.

had the greatest influence on Catholic doctrine in subsequent centuries. However, it is first necessary to say a word on the relevant epistemological innovation which Thomas introduces in the concept and exercise of theological intelligence.

Overcoming Neoplatonism, the Metaphysics of Aristotle, and the Transcendental *aliud*

Thomas soon became aware of the difficulty inherent in Dionysius's Christian Neoplatonism. The principle of an absolute and ineffable One, which preserves the transcendence of the mystery of God, entails that the trinitarian distinction, though asserted clearly on the basis of scripture and church tradition, cannot be illustrated on the level of *intelligentia fidei*. Why? Because the absoluteness and ineffability of the One constitute the unarguable metaphysical presupposition which causes—as a necessary theological consequence—an *under-determination of the noetic meaning* of the Christ-event, as related to the revelation of the triune God which happened in him, in its ontological relevance.

For this reason, Thomas, without giving up the Dionysian claim of the transcendence of the One, draws from Augustine in the commitment to continue the task of contemplating in Christ the mystery of the Trinity in order to be able, in turn, to share it with others.[25] This presupposes and fosters an adequate ontology, as Augustine intuited and began to do in Book V of *De Trinitate*. Within this context, it is easier to appreciate the strategic role, in Thomas, of Aristotle's philosophy. To value Aristotle's metaphysics means essentially for Thomas two things: first, breaking with the predominant Platonic henology as the only and exclusive philosophical current available for Christian theology within the intelligence of the faith. Secondly, it means finding and employing a more rigorous conceptual tool to illustrate the trinitarian truth. This tool is more rigorous because it is more consistent with the ontological constitution of reality than the Platonic-Stoic eclectic stance of Augustine.

The Platonic/Neoplatonic perspective, actually, in itself tends to claim the exteriority of otherness, and therefore of multiplicity, compared to the One who, as such, being identical (to himself) and not-other (with respect to himself and in himself) is and remains absolute and ineffable. The Neoplatonism of Dionysius and every Christian Neoplatonism remains marked by this metaphysical framework. Embracing the truth of the Trinity from revelation solves the tension thus created between the absoluteness of the One and its trinitarian expression, safeguarding the

25. Here lies the deeper meaning achieved by the Christological position gained by Thomas Aquinas compared to Augustine, as compellingly argued by Riccardo Ferri (*Gesù è la verità*).

ineffability of the One and at the same time stating that God is triune, as defined in the *doctrina fidei*, albeit without offering a rationale. Thomas goes beyond this situation of *impasse* by using Aristotle as his preferred witness (whom Thomas calls *philosophus*, the philosopher *par excellence*). Thomas employs Aristotle for a theological interpretation of reality along with a stronger commitment to being lead by revelation in Jesus Christ into an understanding of the trinitarian mystery.

The essential result of this operation, as brilliantly demonstrated by G. Ventimiglia, is summarized in the statement, "the *Ipsum esse subsistens* (of Thomas) is capable of embracing not only unity and identity but also inner division and multiplicity."[26] The reversal of perspective is indicated by the fact that he does not talk as Dionysius did, about the "One who is one" while being triune; but without being able to explain it, he talks rather about the being who is one while being triune: because being is expressed in the Trinity.

The claim, which we find in Augustine's *De Trinitate*, that in order to tell the truth revealed by the Trinity one needs to say that Father, Son, and Holy Spirit are each *diversus* from the other, becomes a more specific claim that this is understandable because the *aliud* and the *diversum* are transcendentals of the *esse*—just like the *unum, bonum, verum*—thanks to the careful hermeneutics of Aristotelian metaphysics, immersed in the light of Christological revelation. The fact is, argues Thomas in *De Ente et Essentia*, that "esse est diversum in diversis."[27] This means that "while things that have only one gender are not distinct in virtue of that gender but of something else [*idem in alio*], things which share the *esse*, on the contrary are not distinct in virtue of something else but of the same being which, therefore, is *diversum in diversis* or, which is the same, *aliud in alio et alio*."[28] In this way, the revelation of the God who is one in being while being at the same time triune in the Persons is not merely an expressible and nonexplorable truth of faith. It becomes knowable through revelation and intelligible and expressible through the *intelligentia fidei*. On the one hand, the trinitarian revelation expresses *in divinis* the ontology of the *ipsum esse* and, on the other, sheds light in fullness, beginning from the *esse*, on the ontology of created being. God is the beginning and the end by definition, and therefore the *analogatum princeps*, of each created being, precisely because God is the *ipsum esse per se subsistens*.

In Thomas, contemplation and participation in the life of God remain, in line with Dionysius, ultimately apophatic, at least *in statu viae*,

26. Giovanni Ventimiglia, *Differenza e contraddizione: Il problema dell'essere in Tommaso d'Aquino: esse, diversum, contradictio* (Milan: Vita e Pensiero, 1997), 163 (own trans.).

27. *De Ent.* V.

28. Ventimiglia, *Differenza e contraddizione*, 151.

both in terms of the supra-rational contact with the One and triune God, which takes place only by grace, and in terms of establishing God's essence by negation. Having said this, continuing Augustine's commitment of *intelligentia fidei*, and using Aristotle's ontological ratio, Thomas states fearlessly that one can and has to penetrate with one's intelligence the perfections of God in light of the effects of God's creative causality and revelation. First of all, starting from revelation, one can and must contemplate and communicate the mystery of divine Trinity as the decisive light which is light for the whole of being. This mystery will be knowable "face to face" in the *visio beata*.

Thus, a new equilibrium is achieved between contemplation, intelligence of faith, and metaphysical rationality. Human reason's ability to think gives strength to the intelligence of faith which penetrates the contemplated truth and communicates it. However, this can happen because God has truly communicated Godself to humanity in Christ, thus affirming the essence of each creature (being *capax Dei*) and bringing to fruition the intrinsic dynamism of freedom and intelligence by introducing human beings into the ontological depths of the truth. From here stem the essential perspectives of Thomas's interpretation of the Trinity as supreme light of the intelligence of being.

The *esse per se subsistens* and Creation

First off, Thomas centers his reflection on the vision of God as the *ipsum esse per se subsistens*. His argument rests on Aristotle's metaphysics but also and most of all on God's revelation of God's name to Moses ("Ego sum qui sum"), as Thomas explicitly states.[29] While for Aristotle the first and essential meaning of being is substance (*ousía*), in virtue of which a thing is what it is and consists of itself, for Thomas the first and essential meaning of being is the *actus essendi*, the act of being in virtue of which something subsists. In the discovery and systematic exercise of this intuition at the theological and metaphysical level,[30] the philosophical elaboration of the biblical concept of the name of God is evident, with *Ego sum qui sum* linked to the related concept of *creation ex nihilo sui et subjecti*, according to which the created realities owe their subsistence exclusively and completely to God.

In its proper sense, therefore, *being* pertains only to God. God is the *ipsum esse per se subsistens*, while all creatures have their being from God only by participation. Thus the clear distinction between the being of

29. See *ST* I, q. 13, a. 11; *In Sent.* I, d. 8, q. 1, a. 3.

30. On this topic during the twentieth century, the writings of E. Gilson, J. Maritain, and C. Fabro are essential.

God and the being of creatures is established. At the same time, the possibility is opened up, at the level of knowledge, of saying something true also about God in virtue of the principle of analogy. Created beings have ontologically within themselves the mark of their creator, so that from them one can understand something about God. Even if the modality of being which is typical of the *ipsum esse per se subsistens* is such that it goes beyond that of the created beings and its splendor, its fullness and simplicity remain infinitely beyond the possibility of perception and understanding of our reasoning. From here stems the absolutely apophatic outcome achieved by human knowledge of the mystery of God through the sole use of our human natural ability to know. Only the freely given light of revelation can break through this darkness and offer human beings the actual possibility of entering a little, already in this life, through faith and in anticipation of the "vision," into the very heart of God's own being.

Psychological Analogy and Processions

Concerning the content of revelation, Thomas, like Augustine, solidly rests his *intelligentia fidei* on the doctrine handed down by the church, affirmed by the councils, explained by the Church Fathers, and stemming from scripture: God who reveals Godself in Jesus Christ is Trinity: Father, Son, and Holy Spirit. The decisive point at which Thomas goes back to past tradition, especially from Augustine, and summarizes and explores it in depth, is the psychological interpretation, which starts from the analogy with the act of cognition and will in the human mind to illustrate the dynamics of the Trinity. Thanks to this analogy, Thomas aims at supporting theologically the light of truth offered to intelligence by revelation mediated by *doctrina fidei*.

The substantial step ahead taken by Thomas is this: while in Augustine, thanks to the psychological analogy, the focus was primarily on the trinitarian structure and dynamics of the human spirit (according to the movement of *memoria, intellectus, voluntas*) as *imago Trinitatis*, Thomas enters into the very mystery of divine processions thanks to a trinitarian ontology of God as absolute Spirit. He writes:

> In evidence whereof we must observe that procession exists in God, only according to an action which does not tend to anything external, but remains in the agent itself. Such action in an intellectual nature is that of the intellect, and of the will. The procession of the Word is by way of an intelligible operation. The operation of the will within ourselves involves also another procession, that of love, whereby the object loved is in the lover; as, by the conception of the word, the object spoken of or understood is in the intelligent agent. Hence, besides the

procession of the Word in God, there exists in Him another procession called the procession of love.[31]

Persons as *relationes subsistentes*

Thomas picks up Augustine's journey of *intelligentia fidei* where the latter had left it. Thomas brilliantly brings together two languages received from tradition: the Augustinian language of relationships and the language influenced by Greek philosophy (canonized in the dogmas) of the hypostases or persons (see *ST* Ia, qq. 28–44). The divine person is defined by Thomas as *relatio subsistens*, a "subsistent relation."[32] "Relationship designates the determining element which distinguishes the person, while subsistent designates the absolute ontological position of the person."[33] This means that, in the divine Persons, the subsistent identity coincides with the relationship, the being-in-itself (*esse-in*) coincides with being-for and in the other (*esse-ad*).

Thomas shows that he appropriated and metaphysically explored in-depth the concept of person as *existentia* elaborated by Richard of St. Victor. This will become a classic definition and remains one of the highlights of Western trinitarian doctrine. The consequence, decisive for later development of Western culture, is going from a concept of person as absolute (as "individual substance of rational nature," as Boethius would say) to a definition which entails a relationship, at least when it concerns trinitarian life.

Furthermore, linking back to John Damascene, but centering on the concept of person as *relatio subsistens*, Thomas explains that, in God, unity is dual: "That of divine nature and that of Love, who is the Holy Spirit."[34] In other words, the unity of God is both on the stage of being but also of the life of the Persons: essential and perichoretic (or dynamic-personal) unity. This is a synthesis of the two perspectives, Eastern and Western.

Trinity and Creation

Thomas elaborates upon the relationship between the mystery of the Trinity and of creation with great insight.[35] The latter is understood as

31. *ST* I, q. 27, a. 3.

32. *ST* I, q. 29, a. 4.

33. Lafont, *Peut-on connaître Dieu en Jésus Christ?*, 124 (own trans.); A. Krempel, *La doctrine de la relation chez Saint Thomas: Exposé historique et systematique* (Paris: Vrin, 1952).

34. *In Johannem* 17, 26.

35. See for example, Gilfredo Marengo, *Trinità e creazione: Indagine sulla teologia di Tommaso d'Aquino* (Rome: Città Nuova, 1990); Gilles Emery, *La Trinité créatrice: Trinité et création dans les commentaires aux "Sentences" de Thomas d'Aquin et de ses precurseurs Albert le Grand et Bonaventure* (Paris: Vrin, 1995).

the continuation of trinitarian processions: the generation of the Son and procession of the Spirit are *ratio* and *causa* of creation. Thomas had already stated this in the *Commentary on the Sentences of Peter Lombard* and in the *Summa Theologiae*. He further explains: "As therefore we say that a tree flowers by its flower, so do we say that the Father, by the Word or the Son, speaks Himself, and His creatures; and that the Father and the Son love each other and us, by the Holy Ghost, or by Love proceeding."[36] Creation, therefore, is situated by Thomas at the heart of trinitarian life, in the intimate loving relationships of the three Persons. Not only that: the trinitarian interiorization of creation is brought to fulfillment by the mystery of the incarnation of the Word and the gift of the Holy Spirit. Therefore, as Christians, "we need to replicate the unity which exists in God. Therefore, it is not enough that we all have, through grace, the same divine life, which makes us participate in divine nature; we need to be united with God and among us through love in the personal Love who is the Holy Spirit."[37]

Through grace, which is *participata similitudo naturae divinae* (participated similitude of God's nature)[38] we become one in being (i.e., we receive the same divine nature); through love we become one in the *perichoresis*, that is, in the reciprocity of our being one in Christ for and with others, just as it is in God. Reciprocal love, therefore, is for Thomas the realization of the trinitarian existence of Christians, or rather, as recently demonstrated, this principle is somehow the secret which inspired the great *Summa*.[39]

A Contemplation Which Lights Up the Desire and the Waiting

Thomas Aquinas, prompted by Dominic's charism, bravely goes beyond Dionysius's boundaries and skillfully develops in depth the doctrine of Augustine. It is as if, as I noted earlier, the great doctor takes up the theme of *intelligentia fidei* from the point where Augustine left it in *De Trinitate* and through it he enters with fearless trust into the redeemed and strengthened resources of grace in the mystery of God the Trinity. Both the intimate life of God and the relationship between God and creation are to be understood and lived out in a trinitarian way.

This is an extraordinary contemplation which is mainly the result of

36. *ST* I, q. 37, a. 2.

37. *In Johannem* 17, 26.

38. See Marcelo Sanchez Sorondo, *La gracia como participación de la naturaleza divina segun santo Tomas de Aquino* (Salamanca: Universitas Pontificias Buenos Aires, 1979).

39. See Wojciech Janusiewicz, *La sapienza è amicizia: Nella "Summa Theologiae" di Tommaso d'Aquino* (Rome: Città Nuova, 2012).

exercising intelligence illuminated by faith and nourished by the Eucharist (about which Thomas sings passionately), rather than vital and shared experience of the Trinity. Thomas has "entered beyond the gate," which Augustine and Dionysius had not deemed possible, but he has done so through a daring and humble leap of his intelligence. The existential aspect, though healed and transfigured by grace, is still on the outer side. Thomas was aware of this. He, like Augustine, was waiting for something to happen. This is revealed by the sudden and definitive silence at the end of his life.

According to an account shared by Reginald, Thomas's secretary and confessor, on December 6, 1273, while celebrating Mass in the chapel of St. Nicholas in the Church of St. Dominic Major in Naples, Thomas experienced a deep change ("Fuit mira mutatione commotus"). "After that Mass, he did not write nor did he dictate anything; he put down the tools for writing the third part of the *Summa*."[40] Reginald did not understand what was going on and insisted that his Magister continue to dictate: "Father, why did you stop writing such great work which you began to give glory to God and light to the world? Fr. Thomas replied: Reginald, I cannot … I cannot because everything I have written seems like straw to me compared to what I have seen and has been revealed to me."[41] After a few days spent in the castle of Maenza, Thomas asked to be brought to the Cistercian abbey in Fossanova to die in a religious place. Here he lay ill for about a month, cared for by the monks, to whom he allegedly dictated a brief commentary to the Song of Songs. This information, not supported by other sources, reflects the intense dialogue of faith and love that Thomas had with God in the last days of his life. The Eucharist revealed to him the bosom of the Father but he did not know how to find the words to share what he had seen.

This is the advent, in Thomas's thought, of the crucified and risen flesh of Christ. This not to say that up to this point the Eucharist was not part of Thomas's thinking as his inspiration, his content, as the *humus* of his thought. On the contrary. But, perhaps it had not been radically present as the form of his thinking. This may help give a glimpse of the event which intervenes in the midst of the massive composition of Thomas's thought. Thomas did not write any more, not because it was useless or impossible to communicate what he had contemplated, but because the realities which were revealed to him—through the communion with the glorified flesh of Christ received in the Eucharist—were so great and light-filled that he was not able to find adequate and proper words to express them.

40. *Processus* 79, 376.
41. Ibid.

Francis of Assisi and Trinitarian Christocentrism in the Franciscan Tradition

If Thomas excels in the rational analysis of the trinitarian mystery, his contemporary Bonaventure (1217–74), enamored in typical Franciscan fashion with creation as a reflection of the glory of the creator, offers an extraordinary theological synthesis transfigured by the light of trinitarian revelation. So much that it was even said: "A trinitarian theology as explicit as in Bonaventure has never been developed by any theologian in history."[42] Bonaventure recognizes explicitly the source of his theological inspiration:

> Francis beheld in fair things Him Who is the most fair and, through the traces of Himself, that He had imprinted on His creatures.... For by the impulse of his unexampled devotion he tasted that fountain of goodness that streameth forth, as in rivulets, in every created thing, and he perceived as it were an heavenly harmony in the concord of the virtues and actions granted unto them by God, and did sweetly exhort them to praise the Lord.[43]

Francis and the Way of the Crucified One

In order to provide a proper context for the trinitarian theology of Bonaventure, I need to devote a few words to Francis of Assisi (1182–1226) on the significance of his charism for the understanding of the Trinity.[44] I think we can say, in a very synthetic way, that the Holy Spirit showed Francis the "way" to enter the bosom of the Father: the crucified one. All of his life, starting from the time of his conversion, was devoted to following Jesus, or rather to wanting to be as much as possible like him in everything, soul and body. Consider, for example, the intense contemplation of Jesus' incarnation, passion, and death which Francis experienced, to the point of being called *alter Christus*.

A decisive event on this journey took place when Francis received the stigmata at Mount La Verna (September 1224). St. Bonaventure, in the *Legend maior*, tells us how it happened. Francis realized that Jesus, if he had opened the Gospel, would have revealed "what would be most pleasing unto God in him and about him."[45] "As in the threefold opening of the Book, the Lord's Passion was each time discovered, Francis, full of

42. Hanspeter Heinz, "Un esempio tra tutti: San Bonaventura," in Università Popolare Mariana, *Il Dio di Gesù Cristo*, 180 (own trans.).

43. St. Bonaventure, *Legenda maior*, 9.1; *The Life of Saint Francis of Assisi*, trans. E. Gurney Salter (London: Aeterna Press, 2015).

44. See Eduard Prenga, *Il Crocifisso via alla Trinità: L'esperienza di Francesco d'Assisi nella teologia di Bonaventura* (Rome: Città Nuova, 2010).

45. St. Bonaventure, *Legenda maior* XIII.2.

the Spirit of God, verily understood that, like as he had imitated Christ in the deeds of his life, so it behooved him to be made like unto Him in the trials and sufferings of His Passion before that he should depart from this world."[46] Francis immerses himself in prayer, all inflamed with love. "By seraphic glow of longing he had been uplifted toward God, and by his sweet compassion had been transformed into the likeness of Him Who of His exceeding love endured to be crucified."[47] An echo of this is preserved in the prayer attributed to Francis and known as *Absorbeat*: "May the power of your love, Lord Christ, fiery and sweet as honey, so absorb our hearts as to withdraw them from all that is under heaven. Grant that we may be ready to die for love of your love, as you died for love of our love."

At that point, the crucified Jesus appeared to Francis, the mystery of God's fiery love for humanity: the crucified one shows himself to Francis fastened to a luminous fiery seraph. In Francis's body the same wounds appear as in the crucified one: "The true love of Christ had transformed His lover into the same image."[48] The stigmata, which Francis from this point on carried in his body, are the visible sign that he has become one with the crucified Jesus and already in this life has entered with him into the bosom of the Father. He entered in God through the crucified one, with all of himself. Now, remaining in the flesh, he sees his brothers and sisters and the world, which he already loved so much, with new eyes. Consider the "Canticle of Brother Sun." To his contemporaries, Francis appeared as a man who had already gone through death and had been glorified.

Francis, living in God, in virtue of being one with the crucified Christ, lived at the same time in the world, loving everyone intensely and in every circumstance. Love, through the crucified one, brought him to the Father. The Father, in making him another Jesus, son in the Son, gives him new eyes and a new heart to see and love his brothers and sisters and all creatures.[49]

The Trinitarian Christocentrism of Bonaventure

The echo of this extraordinary experience and the awareness of its novelty and effects—spiritual, theological, and cultural—is alive especially at the beginning of the Franciscan movement. They find a most acute expression in the theological genius of Bonaventure.

46. Ibid.

47. Ibid., XIII.3.

48. Ibid., XIII.5.

49. See Noel Muscat, *The Life of St. Francis in the Light of St. Bonaventure's Theology on the "Verbum Crucifixum"* (Rome: Pontificium Athenaeum Antonianum, 1989).

The novelty of Francis's experience as the key to theo-logy St. Francis is the first, as far as we know, to have received the stigmata, and he did so within the specific spiritual context described earlier. The following can be considered a non-negotiable point: the crucified one, from here on, is inscribed in the history of the Christian experience and understanding of God the Trinity. Talking about the theology of St. Bonaventure recently Benedict XVI highlighted something quite relevant:

> Until that moment, the idea that the Fathers of the Church were the absolute summit of theology predominated, all successive generations could only be their disciples. St. Bonaventure also recognized the Fathers as teachers forever, but the phenomenon of St. Francis assured him that the riches of Christ's word are inexhaustible and that new light could also appear to the new generations. The oneness of Christ also guarantees newness and renewal in all the periods of history.[50]

Christ as universal "medium" If we look for the key idea of the theological synthesis proposed by Bonaventure, we can easily find it in the concept of Christ as universal and final mediator. This concept is typical of St. Paul's Christology, which Bonaventure preferred and studied in depth, reading and interpreting it in light of the charismatic experience of Francis, culminating in a certain way on Mount Alverno. Christ, recapitulator of creation and of salvation history, the Christ who makes the believer similar to himself to the point that Paul says, "It is no longer I who live, but it is Christ who lives in me" (Gal 2:20), the crucified Christ, wisdom and power of God; all Paul's Christocentrism is embraced and expressed by Bonaventure in such a unique way, consistent with the inspiration of Francis and the theological sensibility of his times.

Bonaventure's trinitarian theology, remarked K. Hemmerle,[51] is none other than the theorization of his lived experience of walking in the footsteps of Christ as Francis had done. For Bonaventure, as for Paul, Augustine, and Francis, in Christ, who is the way to the Father, the human movement of living (he is life) and the movement of thinking (he is truth) are intertwined and fulfilled. Bonaventure's insight is that by living and thinking in Christ, the Christian theologian places the start of his or her own thinking and living in the very heart of reality and truth: "We need to begin from the medium (the center) which is Christ. He is the mediator between God and human beings and is at the center of everything.... Therefore, one needs to begin from Him if one wants to achieve

50. Benedict XVI, "General Audience," March 10, 2010; available at www.vatican.va.

51. Klaus Hemmerle, *Theologie als Nachfolge: Bonaventura – ein Weg für heute* (Freiburg: Herder, 1975); see Luc Mathieu, *La Trinité créatrice d'après Saint Bonaventure* (Paris: Editions Franciscaines, 1992).

Christian wisdom."[52] The beginning is the center! This is possible because, created in the uncreated Word and redeemed in the incarnate Word, we live in history carrying within our hearts the vital light and dynamism of the inspired Word, that is, of the glorified Christ who makes us like him in the Spirit. Christ, therefore, is the *medium*, the universal center. "The Word expresses the Father and the things which are created through Him, and especially leads us to the Father who puts everything together in unity."[53]

Christ is first of all the medium and, *ab aeterno*, in the Trinity, between the Father and the Holy Spirit. He is also in the going out of creatures from the hands of God as "model" in whose image everything is created and in the creatures' returning to the Trinity, toward which he becomes the way through the cross. In the uncreated Word "all things are spoken."[54] God is like an artist who conceives and carries out in the Word a project of love of unparalleled beauty. "If we consider the *production*, we shall see that the work of art proceeds from the artificer according to a similitude existing in his mind.... The artist, moreover, produces an exterior work bearing the closest possible resemblance to the interior exemplar, and if it were in his power to produce an effect which would know and love him, this he would assuredly do."[55] Creation is a work of art which has its eternal model in Christ; its purpose is a loving dialogue with the divine artist. But sin denaturalized human love, making human beings withdraw into themselves and far from God. Thus, "as creatures went forth from God by the Word of God, so for a perfect return, it was necessary that the Mediator *between God and man* be not only God but also man so that He might lead men back to God."[56]

Human beings, who, in the Word, had been placed at the center of the love lived in and by the Trinity and who by their free choice decided to distance themselves from it, are brought back by the incarnate and crucified Word, at the price of his life, to the original center God had always thought about for human beings. Through the effusion of the Spirit, the glorified Word is interiorized into the heart of each human being, where he grows and develops until he achieves perfection and brings us with himself and in himself to the Father. This happens especially through charity and its most relevant expression, the cross, the annihilation of self with the crucified Christ: "It is necessary that human beings die for this

52. *Collationes in Hexaemeron* I.10 (own trans.).

53. Ibid., II.17.

54. *Itinerarium mentis in Deum* VI.2.

55. *De reductione artium ad theologiam* 12; trans. Emma Thérèse Healy (St. Bonaventure, N.Y.: The Franciscan Institute of Saint Bonaventure University, 1955), 33.

56. Ibid., 23 (41).

love,"[57] for God in Christ, because there is no other way to access the Trinity "but through the most burning love of the Crucified."[58]

Anticipating a new state of revelation In his *Itinerarium mentis in Deum*, inspired by the event of Francis's stigmata understood as sanctifying grace which made him similar to Jesus, Bonaventure incisively synthesizes what Francis's experience offered to the Christian understanding of God the Trinity as follows: "Nemo intrat recte in Deum nisi per Crucifixum." The apex of his spiritual and theological journey is therefore *transire* with Christ through the mystery of love and suffering of the cross to finally enter into the bosom of the Father. However, Francis remains *unicum*, a gift and sign of God pointing toward the future. Francis alone is the icon of humanity/the church identified with the crucified one so that in it life may flow from the Father and in the Holy Spirit and immerse the risen body of Jesus to create "new heavens and a new earth" (Rv 21:1).

Bonaventure, like Thomas, feels that the philosophical and theological approach to God in the form it has been carried out up to that point is inadequate. He has the insight that Francis was like "an anticipation of [a] new state of revelation."[59] He reaches the point of wishing, with an almost prophetic statement:

> Believe me, there comes a time in which "the gold and silver vessels" (Ex 3:22, 12:36), that is, the arguments will no longer have value and there will be no defense of faith by ratio but only by auctoritas. To show this, our Redeemer in his temptation did not defend himself with rational arguments but only with authority, though he certainly knew very well the rational defense. Thus, he indicated what his mystical body was going to do in His upcoming suffering.[60]

Duns Scotus and Nicholas of Cusa: God as Freedom and Cipher of the Universe

This wonderful Christological "synthesis of Christian wisdom in function of mystical asceticism," as Bougerol defined the theology of Bonaventure, was always jealously kept by the Franciscan school, which renewed it through the centuries. Shortly after Bonaventure, John Duns Scotus (1266–1308), the Subtle Doctor, revisited it daringly with an interpretive approach which became mainstream in the following centuries. Scotus sees everything from God. Because God is infinite being, God opened in

57. *Collationes in Hexaemeron* II.31.

58. *Itinerarium mentis in Deum*, prol., 3; trans. Zachary Hayes (St. Bonaventure, N.Y.: Franciscan Institute Publications, 2002), 37.

59. Joseph Ratzinger, *The Theology of History in St. Bonaventure* (Chicago: Franciscan Herald Press, 1989), 70.

60. St. Bonaventure, *Hexaemeron* XVII.28 (own trans.).

front of Godself the infinite sea of possibilities; but because God is love, he orders all his actions (creation and re-creation) toward a goal which is to share the love God intimately is with what is other-than-Godself. Christ therefore becomes at the same time the instrument and goal of this salvific plan.

Following the Christocentric intuition of Bonaventure, and inspired mostly by St. Paul in understanding the primacy of Christ as recapitulator of the universe, Duns Scotus starts from the incarnation as the center of humanity's and the world's destiny of love to ideally reimagine the divine plan of salvation in its essential components.

> Firstly, God loves Himself; secondly, God loves Himself through others who are other than God [creatures] and this is pure love; thirdly, God wants to be loved by another who can love Him supremely, talking about the love of someone outside of himself. Fourthly, God foresaw the union of that nature which is to love Him supremely, even if no one had sinned [incarnation]; finally, in a fifth stage, God saw the mediator [Jesus] who came to suffer and redeem his people [redemption].[61]

Within this context, we find the insight about the divine *convenientia* of Mary's immaculate conception which will remain through the centuries a luminous point in the Franciscan school up to the definition of the dogma by Pope Pius IX (1854). An original perspective, worthy of attention, explained with intended courage by Duns Scotus is that regarding the theme of freedom related to God. For Scotus, freedom should not be predicated only concerning the relationship between God and creation, so that creation is understood as the fruit of absolute freedom, but also in the relationships among the divine Persons. The very act of generation of the Word and the breath of the Spirit has the mark of freedom because it is an expression of love. This is one of the most insightful intuitions and in a way foretells the season and struggles of modernity by presenting to theology a question that up to this day is largely untreated.

Bonaventure's influence goes beyond Franciscan authors. In the fifteenth century, a creative and acute scholar, Nicholas of Cusa,[62] drew also from the concept of *medium* elaborated by Bonaventure and the concept of infinite applied to God by Duns Scotus to elaborate one of the highest philosophies in the Renaissance. He combined these two concepts with the understanding of apophaticism in the Eastern fathers and especially in Dionysius as well as the Neoplatonic tradition revisited in light of the early stages of modernity. For Nicholas of Cusa, Christ is the center of

61. *Reportata parisiensia* l.3 (own trans.).

62. Nicholas of Cusa (1401–64) was bishop of Brixen and a cardinal. His major work is *De docta ignorantia*. In his brilliant philosophical-theological synthesis are hinted the most relevant insights of the Renaissance and even some which will be later developed in modern thought.

convergence of the infinite and the finite: the absolute being who, remaining such, "contracts" into human nature. But the sound of these words already tells us that we have moved on to another era in history.

Byzantine Theology: Simeon the New Theologian and Gregory Palamas

Before moving on to modernity, a question arises spontaneously, after my previous mention of Dionysius and Maximus the Confessor: what is going on in Eastern theology after the great synthesis of John of Damascus? The answer is not difficult: Eastern Christian theology remained faithful to the letter and the spirit of the Greek fathers, with an increasing emphasis on the pneumatological dimension and an in-depth elaboration of the idea of "divinization," through the Holy Spirit, of human beings who thanks to baptism and the Eucharist are inserted into Christ.

One needs to remember St. Simeon (949–1022), one of the greatest Christian mystics, called "new theologian" because "he had and communicated a new experience of God" (Yves Congar). Before St. Simeon, the Eastern tradition gave the title of theologian only to St. John the Evangelist and St. Gregory Nazianzen. The journey Simeon suggests—first of life, then of knowledge of God, which, for Simeon are one and the same—is simple and luminous: going with Christ through his passion and death to arrive at his resurrection. The agent and protagonist for this is the Spirit, which brings us into union with the Father.

More specifically, to achieve union with God, one needs to focus and pray in "silence" (*hēsychía*). This is the privileged life of *hesychasm*, an ascetic and mystic method which, through the invocation of the name of Jesus, makes the mind descend into the heart, from which the presence of the risen Jesus irradiates onto the whole being of the individual. Being a mysticism of the resurrection and the Holy Spirit which deifies, Simeon's mysticism is also a mysticism of light: the light which transfigured Jesus on Mount Tabor.

> God is light, and his contemplation is similar to a light.... He [Simeon] asks, "My God, is it You?" And He answers and says: "Yes, I am He, God, who for your sake became man; and behold, I have made you, as you see, and shall make you god." ... Since this light above him became like the sun shining in the afternoon, he realized he was in the center of the light and all filled with joy and tears.... He saw the light unite amazingly to his flesh and penetrate little by little his body ... and make him all fire and light.[63]

63. Quoted in Paul Evdokimov, *La connaissance de Dieu selon la tradition orientale* (Lyons: Edition Xavier Mappus, 1967); Italian translation: *La conoscenza di Dia secondo la tradizione*

It (the light) shines on us ...: speaks, acts, lives and vivifies, transforms into light all those on whom it shines. God is light and those God makes worthy of seeing God see God as light; those who received God, received God as light.... Receiving the grace one receives divine light and God.... Repentance is the gate that leads from the region of darkness to that of light.... Light is the Father, Light is the Son, Light is the Holy Spirit. The three are one Light outside of time, indivisible, without confusion, eternal, uncreated ... invisible ... a Light no one could see before being purified....

For those who became children of the light and children of the future day, for those who walk always in the light, the day of the Lord will never come, because they are always with God and in God.[64]

Because of this, a "baptism of the Spirit" is necessary to render effective the sacramental baptism.

And I would also say that the door is the Son: "I am the door" (Jn 10:7, 9) and that the key of the door is the Holy Spirit: "Receive the Holy Spirit. If you forgive the sins of any, they are forgiven; if you retain the sins of any, they are retained" (Jn 20:22–23). What is more, the house is the Father: "In my Father's house are many rooms" (Jn 14:2). Pay great attention, then, to the spiritual meaning of the word. If the key does not open—for "to him the gatekeeper opens" (Jn 10:3)—then the door will not be open; but if the door is not open, no one will enter the Father's house. Christ himself said: "No one comes to the Father, but by me" (Jn 14:6). Now that it is the Holy Spirit who first opens our spirit (see Lk 24:45) and teaches us about the Father and the Son, is what he himself has said.[65]

If the Holy Spirit is called the key, then it is above all through and in him that our spirit is enlightened and that we are purified, illuminated by the light of knowledge, baptized from on high, born anew (see Jn 3:3, 5) and made children of God. Paul himself said: "The Spirit himself intercedes for us with sighs too deep for words" (Rom 8:26) and "God has sent the Spirit of his Son into our hearts, crying *Abbà*! Father!" (Gal 4:6). It is therefore he who shows us the door and that door is light.[66]

It is St. Gregory Palamas (1296–1359), a monk on Mount Athos and later archbishop of Thessalonica, who defended the hesychasts from the accusations of not respecting God as transcendent and impossible to be comprehended. He does so by establishing a distinction (already known to the Greek fathers) between the essence of God, which remains inaccessible, and his "energies" or "operations" through which God communicates

orientale (Rome: Paoline, 1983), 2:67–68 (own trans. from the Italian). See Simeon the New Theologian, *Eth.* 5, in *On the Mystical Life: Ethical Discourses*, vol. 2: *On Virtue and Christian Life*, trans. Alexander Golitzin (Crestwood, N.Y.: St. Vladimir's Seminary Press, 1996), 54.

64. *Sermone* 57, 2.4, ed. russa del Monte Athos, II, 37. Translated from Marisa Cerini, "La riflessione su Dio nelle Chiese d'Oriente," in *Il Dio di Gesù Cristo*, 197–212 (Rome: Città Nuova, 1982).

65. *Catech.* XXXIII, in Sources Chrétiennes 113 (255), quoted in Congar, *I Believe in the Holy Spirit*, 1:97.

66. Ibid.

Godself outside of Godself, divinizing the creatures, a doctrine approved by various synods in Constantinople in the fourteenth century.

Palamas intends to affirm both the divinity of God, which is and remains beyond everything and unknowable in itself, and the real divinization of human beings in Christ. The suggested solution is on a contemplative level. This is why it will not be well understood by the Latin fathers. It is essential to have the intuition, as Congar remarks, that the uncreated energies are what is irradiated into the world by the unknowable being of God. Scripture, in this interpretation, talks about this through images such as "glory," "light," and "power" of God. This is precisely the light which transfigures Christ on Mount Tabor. This is not an impersonal irradiation which subsists in itself: "energy is like the expression of the Trinity of which it translates *ad extra* the mysterious otherness in unity," a "procession of nature" of God which emanates from the Father, through the Son in the Spirit and manifests the *perichóresis* of the divine Persons who "enter into each other so they possess but one energy."[67] What the doctrine of the divine energies seems to suggest is that, if God is one and as such subsisting in the three divine Persons, it is possible that God's own self is absolutely incommunicable (as God) but at the same time he truly communicates to creatures participation in God's own life.

67. Olivier Clément, *Byzance et le Christianisme* (Paris: Presses Universitaires de France, 1964), 46 (own trans.).

CHAPTER 21

The Modern Epoch

The Trinity Starting with the Cross and History

Ghislain Lafont is undoubtedly correct when he emphasizes that the trajectory of understanding and study of trinitarian revelation has involved two major stages in the history of Christianity: one signified by the Greek word *homoousios*, referring to consubstantiality with the Father of the incarnate Son (who is true God and true man) and of the Holy Spirit who was poured forth at Pentecost; the other signified by *kénosis*, in other words the abyss of annihilation lived by Jesus through the incarnation and death on the cross, with the paradoxical outcome that this death revealed the intimate mystery of God's life, namely, and this is the point, God's total self-sacrificing love. At the same time, we recognize that there are limits and exceptions to this hypothesis about the reading of historical development of dogma.

The Turning Point of Modernity and Its Triple Expression

When we take a panoramic view of this historical development extending from Nicaea and the Church Fathers (especially the Cappadocians and Augustine) to the medieval synthesis of Thomas and Bonaventure in the West, this interpretation is confirmed. The task that occupied the best minds and the spiritual resources of these great disciples of Jesus and theologians of the living God, was that of thinking the mystery of the Trinity *in divinis* to use Thomas's words, that is, from on high, the "immanent" Trinity. The starting point, salvation history, the "economic" Trinity, was certainly never overlooked: this was the source of that trinitarian faith requiring the thinking and implementation of an authentic semantic revolution in the understanding of God's being (it is sufficient to recall the Cappadocians, Augustine, and Thomas).

It is also true however that salvation history risks staying a bit too much in the background in this way (except for Bonaventure's synthesis), and rather detached from the concrete history of men and women. If this is not evident in the theologians of whom I have spoken, most of whom are mystics and saints, then at least it can be seen in the common sentiment of the Christian people. So once this speculative patrimony was acquired, which is fundamentally and enduringly important for the intellectual clarification of trinitarian revelation on the ontological level, something new was needed—a return to the freshness and appealing novelty of existence that emerges from the Christological event and which is entrusted to us in the New Testament. And as a consequence, a study which could more intimately connect trinitarian revelation with the experience of the person and human history was needed as well.

One might have noticed in the centuries reviewed to this point, moreover, that it is only due to the charism of St. Francis that the centrality of the Paschal event has come to light as the culmination of trinitarian revelation. What attracted the attention of theologians beginning with the dogma of Chalcedon in fact, was the incarnation of the Son of God, the salvific mystery, more than the cross. The soteriological aspect (the death on the cross as redemption for sin) is what was emphasized in the Paschal event more than the revelatory and trinitarian aspects, especially in the Latin tradition. So the event of modernity represents a turning point, a transition, even on the level of the illumination of the face of God as revealed in Jesus, as with all the other aspects of human experience. Our day may be reaching its sunset to pass the baton to a new epoch, something further ahead; it is still difficult to decipher its genesis, its characteristics, and its global significance in a balanced way.

But let us narrow the view to our theme, namely, that of God and the trinitarian God revealed in Christ. We might ask what are the lines of development that can be discerned in this journey? In my opinion, we can note at least three moments or principal directions (because it is not always a matter of successive events which can be distinguished).

The Theological Shakeup of Joachim of Fiore and Luther

We witness a strong shakeup of traditional (Scholastic) trinitarian theology first of all with both Joachim of Fiore (who anticipated at least some aspects of modernity) and Luther. Each of these started from different points and took different directions. Theology in the strict academic sense does not have much that is new to offer after that, being content instead to report and systematize what has already been said, without denying that some of these later works were of remarkable value. One speaks of a "second Scholasticism" and of its successive repropositions especially regarding St. Thomas in Catholicism after the Council of Trent. The vital centrality and the intellectual vitality of the trinitarian image of God emigrates therefore in two directions (and these are the two other directions of modernity), on one hand to the experience of the mystics and on the other to philosophical speculation.

The Flourishing of Trinitarian Mysticism

It is precisely this characteristic of modernity that interests us. In contrast with the patristic and Scholastic eras when both theology and spiritual experience were united, although in different ways, they became distinct and separate after the Middle Ages. Theologians became more abstract and distant from ecclesial life while mystics like Catherine of Siena, St. Teresa of Avila, and St. John of the Cross transmitted an experience of the triune God, an intuition pregnant with a rich theological doctrine. They were recognized as doctors of the church for this. From this point there has also been recognition of a precisely theological competence of the great Christian mystics according to that *scientia amoris* described by Pope John Paul II, even if only in times closer to us.[1]

The Trinity in Philosophy

For its own part, philosophical thought also became autonomous to the extent of separating from the faith and its theological expression. This resulted on the one hand with philosophy having less and less contact with the novelty of Christianity and thus moving gradually to a purely theistic vision (affirming God as absolute, knowable through reason but prescinding from revelation), then to a deistic position (a vague affirmation of the existence of a transcendent, distant God),[2] then to agnosticism and finally to atheism. By way of the German Idealism of Fichte, Schelling, and Hegel, on the other hand, there is a great attempt to incorporate the trinitarian discourse on God into philosophy. Although their overall attempt was aborted, it was undoubtedly promising and rich with suggestions that would be reconsidered later within a theological context by subsequent Christian thought. It is necessary to wait for our times, with some significant foreshadowings from the nineteenth century, to recognize the emergence of something new and constructive in both fields of theology

1. See *Novo Millennio Ineunte*, par. 42; and on this topic, François-Marie Léthel, "Verità e amore di Cristo nella teologia dei santi: L'orientamento teologico della Lettera Apostolica 'Novo Millennio Ineunte,'" *PATH* 1, no. 2 (2002): 281–314.

2. For the meaning of "theism" and "deism" see what I wrote for the *Dizionario del Cristianesimo*, 2:1059–60 and 1:319–21.

and philosophy.[3] But let us take things in order trying to retrace some of the most significant steps in this history, albeit briefly.

Joachim of Fiore and Luther: History and the Cross

It may seem risky to juxtapose two personalities and theologians so closely who are as different, even in time, as Joachim of Fiore and Luther. The plausibility of such a juxtaposition lies in the fact that both emblematically refer to the two great themes that constitute the novelty of the modern era with respect to the theological understanding of the trinitarian God. Indeed, perhaps no others have had such a determining and pervasive influence on the further development of Western thought, and not only on a theological level. In the case of Luther, this is evident in evangelical theology but also in the philosophical thought from this paradigm, as documented by K. Barth and E. Jüngel.[4] Henri de Lubac has demonstrated the same in the case of Joachim of Fiore with his documented historical fresco.[5]

The Trinity and History in the Thought of Joachim of Fiore

The great contribution to theology made by the twelfth-century theologian and abbot from Calabria, Joachim of Fiore,[6] a thinker undoubtedly ahead of his time, was his effort to consider "the Trinity historically and history in a trinitarian way" (B. Forte). His reflections showed the immaturity of being among the first works on the subject, however, presenting more than a little ambiguity to a discerning reader, at least with respect to the reception he met. The originality of Joachim's thought ultimately lies in wanting to reintroduce the great biblical and Christian category of salvation history in the light of the trinitarian mystery. It was not only a reaction against a certain absence of pneumatology within Western theological reflection, but also against the absence of reflection on history

3. See part 1 in this volume.

4. See Karl Barth, *Protestant Theology in the 19th Century: Its Background and History* (Grand Rapids, Mich: Eerdmans, 2002) and Jüngel, *God as the Mystery of the World.*

5. Henri de Lubac, *La postérité spirituelle de Joachim de Fiore*, vol. 1: *De Joachim a Schelling* and vol. 2: *De Saint Simon à nos jours* (Namur: Culture et vérité, 1979–80).

6. On the original "trinitarian" interpretation of salvation history by the Calabrian abbot, Joachim of Fiore (1135–1202), and its varied impact, see Henry Mottu, *La manifestation de l'Esprit selon Joachim de Fiore: Herméneutique et théologie de l'histoire d'après le Traité sur les Quatres Evangiles* (Paris: Neuchâtel Delachaux, 1977); Congar, "Joachim of Fiore and the Fate of Joachimism," in *I Believe in the Holy Spirit*, 1:126–37; Bruno Forte, "La Trinità e la storia. G. da F.," in his *Sui sentieri dell'Uno* (Cinisello Balsamo: Paoline, 1992), 105–21.

typical of philosophies adopted by Scholastic thought stemming from Greek, Platonic, and Aristotelian roots.

Without wanting to diminish the centrality and irreplaceability of the Christological event, Joachim associates a first "stage" of world history with the Father or the law, a second stage with the Son or grace, and a third stage with the Holy Spirit or freedom and love.[7] The Trinity and history are organically joined together again in this way so that in its own becoming, history becomes the *locus* of trinitarian revelation, while the Trinity becomes the key to understand the origin, the horizon, and the end of history.

His writings run the risk in any case of separating the age of the Spirit from that of the Son with all the theoretical and practical consequences that this involves. And some subsequent reductive interpretations of Joachim's work focused on this. As Bonaventure subsequently showed nevertheless, it is to Joachim's credit to have recognized Christ at the center of history and to have highlighted the Spirit's fundamental role in this journey toward "the fullness of Truth" (see Jn 16:13), in which human history consists after Christ.

Luther's Theology of the Cross

The turning point impressed by Luther[8] on Christian theology focuses instead substantially on placing the doctrine of justification of the human sinner by grace alone at the center of Christian discourse, as the only way to ultimately safeguard God's being God. By definition in fact, God is the *absconditus* and therefore he absolutely cannot be known through human reason alone, which is limited, fallible, and furthermore radically corrupted by sin. It is only possible to know him thanks to his free and gratuitous revelation of Godself through the incarnation, passion, and death on the cross of his Son, Jesus Christ. With this as a starting point, the expression "theology of the cross" came into full light in a technical sense, to then be rediscovered by contemporary theology thanks especially to Luther's

7. Something similar appears in the Church Fathers. For example, as Gregory Nazianzen said: "The Old Testament proclaimed the Father openly, and the Son more obscurely. The New manifested the Son, and suggested the Deity of the Spirit. Now the Spirit Himself dwells among us, and supplies us with a clearer demonstration of Himself. For it was not safe, when the Godhead of the Father was not yet acknowledged, plainly to proclaim the Son; nor when that of the Son was not yet received to burden us further... with the Holy Ghost;... but that by gradual additions, and, as David says, Goings up, and advances and progress from glory to glory." *Fifth Theological Discourse*, 31.26; available at newadvent.org.

8. On the *theologia crucis* see: Walther von Löwenich, *Luthers Theologia Crucis* (Witten: Kaiser, 1954); Bruno Gherardini, *Theologia crucis: L'eredità di Lutero nell'evoluzione teologica della Riforma* (Alba: Paoline, 1978); Giuseppe Marco Salvati, *Teologia trinitaria della croce* (Turin: LDC, 1987); Hubertus Blaumeiser, *Martin Luthers Kreuzestheologie: Schüssel zu seiner Deutung von Mensch und Wirklichkeit* (Paderborn: Bonifatius, 1995).

polemical use of it. In the famous *conclusiones* (in particular, nos. 19 and 20) of his Heidelberg Disputation (1518), he affirmed in a systematic and peremptory manner: "19. Non ille digne Theologus dicitur, qui 'invisibilia Dei' 'per ea quae facta sunt, intellecta conspicit.' 20. Sed qui visibilia et posteriora Dei per passiones et crucem conspecta intelligit."[9] With a certain simplification reflecting polemical intentions therefore, Luther pits a "theology of glory" completely intent on penetrating God's invisible perfections through the signs present in creation, against a "theology of the cross" intent instead on discovering God's true face where it is shown in a culminating and paradoxical way for human knowledge in the cross of Christ.

Although the Lutheran rediscovery of the centrality of the cross is important in the form itself of theological knowledge and in its exercise, it is necessary to stress that throughout the great Christian theological tradition, there has always been a lively awareness that it is necessary to pass through the "folly of preaching" to reach God. In other words, we cannot come to the knowledge of glory except by way of the cross. The classical text that expresses this unsurpassable peculiarity of theological knowledge—to which Luther himself refers systematically—is the first Letter of Paul to the Corinthians where the apostle affirms: "For I decided to know nothing among you except Jesus Christ, and him crucified" (1 Cor 2:2), indicating that it is precisely in him, Jesus crucified, a scandal to the Jews and folly to the pagans "but to those who are the called ... the power of God and the wisdom of God" (1 Cor 1:24). In this passage, the apostle not only puts the wisdom of the cross in opposition to purely human wisdom which renders the cross of Christ something vain, but he also underlines that the true *gnosis* of God is found only through the cross of Christ.

The same concept expressed by his own theology, can be found again in the fourth Gospel where the *Lógos* incarnate is made fully manifest during the hour of exaltation, the hour when his crucifixion and his glory become inseparable. Recalling the paradigmatic figure of Job, von Balthasar notes the paradox of God's wisdom who had become flesh and who turns to the Father and dramatically cries out "Why?" (see Mk 15:34) at the culmination of his existence. Referring to the spiritual lesson of Francis of Assisi and his mystical identification with Christ crucified already in the medieval tradition, Bonaventure affirmed that "ad Deum nemo intrat recte nisi per Crucifixum," as mentioned

9. "19. That person does not deserve to be called a theologian who looks upon the invisible things of God as though they were clearly perceptible in those things which have actually happened, 20. He deserves to be called a theologian, however, who comprehends the visible and manifest things of God seen through suffering and the cross" (own trans.).

earlier.[10] Paraphrasing the Aristotelian syllogism he ardently added: "Maior proposito fuit ab aeterno, sed assumptio in cruce; conclusivo vero in resurrectione ... haec est logica nostra, ut simus similes Deo."[11] What characterizes Luther's theology is having put the cross at the center as way (and consequently, method) to reach knowledge of the God revealed in Christ; he deserves credit for this. At the same time, he does not go very far in substantively connecting the theology of the cross and trinitarian theology. The premises are now in place however, as E. Jüngel notes.[12]

The Trinity in the Interior Experience of the Mystics

After the medieval synthesis and Luther's impetus, the mystical life in these centuries has certainly been the privileged place in which the Christian trinitarian experience continues to be luminously present, opening extraordinary paths for study, even if theology has not borne fruit of great originality in the modern period.

The Speculative Mysticism of Northern Europe

Already toward the end of the Middle Ages, we note the witness of the Flemish and Rhenish mysticism with J. Ruysbroeck (1293–1381), Meister Eckhart (1260–1327), and G. Tauler (1300–1361), but this is in a more speculative and philosophical key. Their mysticism is profoundly trinitarian, but when it comes to translating it into more reflected thought, it stumbles with the difficulty of not being able to fully express the novelty of the trinitarian mystery through the currently available metaphysical categories because of their strong speculative propensity.

The need is felt in these authors in other words to go beyond St. Thomas's thought to also express the trinitarian mystery that they lived and contemplated on a speculative level. The absence of an adequate epistemology and ontology, however, often provoked real short-circuits in their thinking on a linguistic and conceptual level. This did not always allow them to safeguard the novelty and truth of the trinitarian mystery. In particular, the distinction among the three divine Persons at times seems to be absorbed into an abyssal unity (*Abgrund*) that almost cancels them out. This shows the precise need to think of the unity of God's being more radically, beginning with the distinction among the persons, and to come to know God beyond simple conceptual representations with an immediacy that

10. *Itinerarium mentis in Deum*, prol., 3.
11. *Collationes in Hexaemeron* 28 and 30.
12. See Jüngel, *God as the Mystery of the World*.

allows speaking it and living it already in history. It is a task that seems to be reemerging strongly today in contemporary theological consciousness. It is enough to cite as an example the following text by Ruysbroeck, which describes the aim of his mystical search:

> Every spirit becomes a burning piece of charcoal which God has lit with the fire of his infinite love. All of us together are an inflamed brazier with the Father, Son and Holy Spirit that cannot be extinguished. In the same way, the same divine Persons are snatched up into a unity of their essence, that is in the subsistence of the divine Persons. Therein we are all one and return to being un-created in our eternal image.[13]

Italian and Spanish Mysticism

The mysticism of the Italian and the Spanish (Carmelite) mystics was certainly more experiential and more respectful of the distinction of the divine Persons. It undoubtedly represented a culmination of Western trinitarian contemplation. If within the Flemish and Rhenish mysticism a speculative emphasis prevailed, a personalistic and spousal characteristic dominates within the Italian and Spanish tradition instead.

Catherine of Siena and the reemergence of the Augustinian tradition For example, St. Catherine of Siena (1347–80), one of the "Mantellate" of St. Dominic, recovers the Augustinian tradition and the teaching of Thomas Aquinas to illustrate how the soul is made in the image and likeness of God:

> And this you did, eternal Trinity, willing that we should share all that you are, high eternal Trinity! You, eternal Father, gave us memory to hold your gift and share your power. You gave us understanding so that, seeing your goodness, we might share the wisdom of your only-begotten Son. And you gave us free will to love what our understanding sees and knows of your truth, and so share the mercy of your Holy Spirit.[14]

What Catherine affirms in the following interpretation she offers of the biblical text is very interesting also because of its strong, intrasubjective coloring: "I told you that two are not without three, nor three without two, and so it is.... These two cannot be gathered together in my name without three—that is, without the gathering of the three powers of the soul: memory, understanding, and will.... When these three powers of the soul are gathered together, I am in their midst by grace."[15]

13. Quoted in *I mistici del nord* (Rome: Studium, 1981), 122 (own trans.).

14. Catherine of Siena, *The Dialogue*, trans. Suzanne Noffke (New York: Paulist Press, 1980), 49; also see Paul Hirtz, *Das Geschöpf der Liebe – Menschsein in der Spiritualität der Caterina von Siena: Ein Beitrag zur "Theologie der Heiligen"* (Trier: Paulinus Verlag, 1988).

15. Catherine of Siena, *The Dialogue*, 107–8.

Carmelite mysticism: the "interior castle" of Teresa of Avila I will dedicate a little more attention to the Carmelite mystics Teresa of Avila (1515–82) and John of the Cross (1542–91) because of their extraordinary and unprecedented experience of God the Trinity. Moreover, like Catherine of Siena before them, Teresa and John are both doctors of the church, which means that the church recognizes that their doctrine has something precious and important for Christian faith and life. Both of them underlined that the way to God is through self-annihilation (the *nada, nada, nada* of John of the Cross) lived in union with Jesus crucified by way of baptism, faith, and the Eucharist. Having reached and laid bare the center of the soul in such annihilation, this becomes the "negative pole" which is united in love (the Holy Spirit) to God, "the positive pole" (Chiara Lubich's exemplification). In this way the life of the Trinity flows between God and the soul, which is illuminated and which becomes the dwelling place of the Trinity.

Let us listen to Teresa's testimony. She describes the clear understanding that she acquires through a direct experience of the trinitarian mystery in these words:

To us ignorant people it appears that all three Persons of the Blessed Trinity are—as represented in paintings—in one Person, as when three faces are painted on one body.[16] And thus we are so scared away that it seems the mystery is impossible and that no one should dare think about it. For the intellect feels hindered and fears lest it might have doubts about this truth, and it thereby loses something very beneficial. What was represented to me were three distinct Persons, for we can behold and speak to each one. Afterward I reflected that only the Son took human flesh, through which this truth of the Trinity was seen. These Persons love, communicate with, and know each other.... In all three Persons there is no more than one will, one power, and one dominion, in such a way that one cannot do anything without the others. But no matter how many creatures there are, there is only one Creator. Could the Son create an ant without the Father? No, for it is all one power, and the same goes for the Holy Spirit; thus there is only one all-powerful God and all three Persons are one Majesty.[17]

The soul is created to become an "interior castle" where the Trinity comes to dwell, according to the metaphor made famous by Teresa.

It is that we consider our soul to be like a castle made entirely out of a diamond or of very clear crystal, in which there are many rooms, just as in heaven there are many dwelling places. For in reflecting upon it carefully, we realize that the soul of the just person is nothing else but a paradise where the Lord says He finds

16. St. Teresa refers to a representation of the Trinity which was well known in her culture.

17. Teresa of Avila, *Spiritual Testimonies*, chap. 29, nos. 2–3, in *The Collected Works of St. Teresa of Avila*, trans. Kieran Kavanaugh and Otilio Rodriguez (Washington, D.C.: ICS Publications, 1976), 1:400–401.

His delight.... I do not find anything comparable to the magnificent beauty of a soul and its marvelous capacity. Indeed, our intellects, however keen, can hardly comprehend it, just as they cannot comprehend God; but He Himself says that He created us in His own image and likeness.[18]

So Teresa's testimony appears in this light like a charismatic exegesis, and almost the incarnation of Jesus' word: "Those who love me will keep my word, and my Father will love them, and we will come to them and make our home with them" (Jn 14:23). Teresa recounts:

When the soul is brought into that dwelling place,[19] the Most Blessed Trinity, all three Persons, through an intellectual vision, is revealed to it through a certain representation of the truth. First there comes an enkindling in the spirit in the manner of a cloud of magnificent splendor; and these Persons are distinct, and through an admirable knowledge the soul understands as a most profound truth that all three Persons are one substance and one power and one knowledge and one God alone. It knows in such a way that what we hold by faith, it understands, we can say, through sight—although the sight is not with the bodily eyes nor with the eyes of the soul, because we are not dealing with an imaginative vision. Here all three Persons communicate themselves to it, speak to it, and explain those words of the Lord in the Gospel: that He and the Father and the Holy Spirit will come to dwell with the soul that loves Him and keeps His commandments.[20]

It seemed to me there came the thought of how a sponge absorbs and is saturated with water, so, I thought, was my soul which was overflowing with that divinity and in a certain way rejoicing within itself and possessing the three Persons. I also heard the words: "Don't try to hold Me within yourself, but try to hold yourself within Me." It seemed to me that from within my soul—where I saw these three Persons present—these persons were communicating themselves to all creation without fail, nor did they fail to be with me.[21]

My soul began to enkindle, and it seemed to me I knew clearly in an intellectual vision that the entire Blessed Trinity was present.... And so it seemed that all three Persons were represented distinctly in my soul and that they spoke to me.... I understood those words the Lord spoke, that the three divine Persons would be with the soul in grace (Jn 14:23).[22]

Carmelite mysticism: John of the Cross, the doctor of nothing Also John of the Cross, the doctor of nothing (*nada*), describes the trinitarian experience of the divinization of the soul with perfect and surprising faith-

18. Teresa of Avila, *The Interior Castle* 1.1.1, in *The Collected Works of St. Teresa of Avila*, vol. 2, trans. Kieran Kavanaugh and Otilio Rodriguez (Washington, D.C.: ICS Publications, 1980), 283.

19. Here Teresa is referring to the beginning of the seventh mansion of the *Interior Castle,* that constitutes the last stage on her journey toward the full communion with the Trinity, culminating in the perfect spousal union with Christ.

20. Teresa of Avila, *The Interior Castle* 7.1.6; in *Collected Works*, 2:430.

21. Teresa of Avila, *Spiritual Testimonies*, chap. 14, in *Collected Works*, 1:392–93.

22. Ibid., chap. 13, in *Collected Works*, 1:391.

fulness to the biblical texts in a reflection that represents one of the peaks of Christian mysticism. Passing through the annihilation of the self with Christ on the cross, fully conformed to Christ, he reaches the point of participation in the dynamic of the trinitarian life. He is enabled in him to spirate the Holy Spirit to the Father as a result.

In the transformation which the soul possesses in this life, the same spiration [*aspiración*] passes from God to the soul and from the soul to God with notable frequency and blissful love, although not in the open and manifest degree proper to the next life. Such I believe was St. Paul's meaning when he said: *Since you are sons of God, God sent the Spirit of His Son into your hearts, calling to the Father* [Gal 4:6]. This is true of the Blessed in the next life and of the perfect in this life according to the ways described.

One should not think it impossible that the soul be capable of so sublime an activity as this breathing [*aspire*] in God, through participation as God breathes [*aspira*] in her. For, granted that God favors her by union with the Most Blessed Trinity, in which she becomes deiform and God through participation, how could it be incredible that she also understand, know, and love—or better that this be done in her—in the Trinity, together with it, as does the Trinity itself! Yet God accomplishes this in the soul through communication and participation. This is transformation in the three Persons in power and wisdom and love, and thus the soul is like God through this transformation. He created her in His image and likeness that she might attain such resemblance.

No knowledge or power can describe how this happens, unless by explaining how the Son of God attained and merited such a high state for us, the power to be sons of God, as St. John says (Jn 1:12). Thus the Son asked of the Father in St. John's Gospel: *Father, I desire that where I am those You have given Me may also be with Me, that they may see the glory You have given Me* (Jn 17:24), that is, that they may perform in us by participation the same work that I do by nature, that is, breathe [*aspirar*] the Holy Spirit. And He adds: *I do not ask, Father, only for those present, but for those also who will believe in Me through their doctrine: that all of them may be one as You, Father, in Me and I in You, that thus they be one as We are one. The glory which You have given Me I have given them that they may be one as We are one, I in them and You in Me; that they may be perfect in one; that the world may know that You have sent Me and loved them as You have loved Me* (Jn 17:20–23). The Father loves them by communicating to them the same love He communicates to the Son, though not naturally as to the Son, but, as we said, through union and transformation of love. It should not be thought that the Son desires here to ask the Father that the saints be one with Him essentially and naturally as the Son is with the Father, but that they may be so through the union of love, just as the Father and the Son are one in essential unity of love.[23]

In his *Ascent of Mount Carmel* moreover, John of the Cross is the first mystic in Christian history to place the cry of Jesus forsaken (see Mk 15:34;

23. John of the Cross, *The Spiritual Canticle*, Stanza 39, nos. 4–5, in *Collected Works*, 558–59.

Mt 27:46), *expressis verbis*, at the center of his meditation on the journey of the soul to union with God. This expresses the salient point of the savior's work for him. It means that "to love God is to be stripped of everything that is not God." So the soul has to empty itself of everything, even itself, so as to be completely full of God.

This is what Jesus lived in the abandonment. Jesus did not only suffer the abandonment as something passive but also as something active. By not intervening, God the Father allowed him as a man as well, to empty himself to that point, so that he might fill himself with God in this way. The doctor of *nada* writes:

At the moment of His death He was certainly annihilated in His soul, without any consolation or relief, since the Father left Him that way in innermost aridity in the lower part. He was thereby compelled to cry out: *My God, My God, why have You forsaken me?* (Mt 27:46) ... And by it He accomplished the most marvelous work.... That is, He brought about the reconciliation and union of the human race with God through grace ... for He was forsaken by His Father at that time so as to pay the debt fully and bring man to union with God. David says of Him: *Ad nihilum redactus sum et nescivi* (*I was brought to nothing and did not understand*, Ps 72:22).[24]

John of the Cross explains, "The true love of God," is not to seek "ourselves in God" (in other words, "gifts and divine consolations" for oneself), but "God in ourselves" (that is, to make of oneself an empty chalice that welcomes God's presence without bias or obstacle).[25] The abandonment is recognized therefore as the peak of the Father's and the Son's love, entirely for humanity's benefit. And for human beings it becomes in Jesus who lives it the communication of the soul to God who is the Trinity, an infinite abyss of love.

The novelty of Christian mysticism in modernity: Ignatius of Loyola St. Augustine's lesson is recovered by Teresa of Avila and John of the Cross, but with something additional: while for Augustine the Trinity was seen, so to speak, mainly as being reflected in the soul, for them the Trinity is contemplated as *living* in the soul itself, so that it participates in the life of the living God, *in God*. There is also a deeper explication with respect to the experience lived by Francis, the soul's participation in the life of the Trinity. Yet, thinking precisely of Francis, one spontaneously recalls that in him there was the promise of a transfiguration in God, not only of the soul but also of the body and all of creation through Jesus crucified.

Aside from this, if the doctrine of the doctors of Carmel represents

24. John of the Cross, *The Ascent of Mount Carmel* II, chap. 7, in *Collected Works*, 124–25.
25. See ibid.

in a certain sense the fulfillment of the Augustinian intuition that the Trinity dwells within, and if it also experientially confirms the *regula fidei* of the church and of the *intelligentia fidei* in its development from Augustine to Thomas Aquinas, then what about Augustine's other intuition, that of reciprocal love as the *locus* from which the flight takes off to contemplate the Trinity?

Against this background of the Carmelite mystics, we should also recall the trinitarian vision of Ignatius of Loyola (1491–1556) which was granted to him at Manresa; Paul of the Cross (1694–1755) with his abyssal mysticism of conforming to the crucified one; Louis Marie Grignion de Montfort (1673–1716) with the mystery of Mary embedded within his trinitarian vision. Closer to us is the witness of Thérèse of Lisieux (1873–97), the Carmelite with her paradoxical experience of the "little way" and her trial of faith, as "sitting at the table" with those who do not know nor feel God's presence (for which she would be declared a doctor of the church), and another Carmelite, Elizabeth of the Trinity (1880–1906) with her mysticism centered on the indwelling of the Trinity.

It is especially important to underline how the mysticism of Ignatius of Loyola has played a decisive role in theology and in Catholic culture through the centuries of modernity. We speak in fact of a Christocentrism in which being conformed to Christ becomes the road to building his reign in history *ad maiorem Dei gloriam*. And all of this is in the light and the dynamic of a radically trinitarian spirituality. It is not by accident that some of the great protagonists of trinitarian renewal in the twentieth century are Jesuits like Rahner and de Lubac, while von Balthasar understood that his mission as a renewed expression of St. Ignatius's charism was indissolubly linked to that of Adrienne von Speyr at the beginning of his theological ministry as a Jesuit.

One could object that this extraordinary line of trinitarian mysticism that develops from the sixteenth century to the dawn of the twentieth century is out of date in this modern era which is entirely oriented toward the horizon of history and the human subject. Would it not belong in the previous era therefore, which we associated with a "Trinity in the highest heavens"? The answer is not difficult because this mysticism is really decisively modern, not only because it starts precisely with that experience of the subject (the soul in mystical language) which constitutes the interest and the starting point for the modern way of understanding (from Descartes on). But it is also modern because it is always a matter of a mysticism of communion with God the Trinity in different ways which passes through the experience of *kénosis* and the cross. While the cross of Christ was for Luther a theological requirement (but not only this), for the Catholic mystics of these centuries it is an experience lived by the soul, which opens a priceless and infinite horizon of trinitarian love.

Russian Mysticism: From Sergius of Radonezh to Seraphim of Sarov

Also in Russia, where Byzantine orthodoxy transmigrated, initially enculturated in the tenth century beginning with the baptism of St. Vladimir of Kiev, the Russian prince, we witness the initial stages of a spirituality with a strong trinitarian imprint as the centuries pass. This is especially true of St. Sergius of Radonezh, the charismatic restorer of the Christian life in this great nation. He transmitted a limpid and deep experience of the trinitarian God to his monks, and through them to the people. In the words of P. Evdokimov:

> St. Sergius of Radonezh, 1313–1392, left no theological treatise, but his whole life was dedicated to the Holy Trinity. This divine mystery was the object of his endless contemplation; it flowed into him and turned him into incarnated peace, a peace which very visibly radiated from him for everyone. He dedicated his church to the Holy Trinity, and in his immediate circle of monks, as well as in the political arena, he tried to reproduce a unity that was the image of the Trinity. We can even say that he assembled the whole of contemporary Russia around his church and God's Name so that men "through the contemplation of the Holy Trinity would be able to conquer the divisive hatred of the world." In the memory of the Russian people, St. Sergius remains their heavenly protector. He gives them strength and is the very expression of the trinitarian mystery, of its Light and of its Unity.[26]

From him we have this stupendous page of contemplation:

> God the Father. God the Son. God the Holy Spirit.
> Immense the Father. Immense the Son. Immense the Holy Spirit.
> One the Father, one the Son, one the Holy Spirit.
> Within the Trinity indivisible each divine Person
> is the Potency, the Wisdom, the Love.
> Each Person
> is the divinity, unique and immense.
> He is all Immensity, all Unity that transcends all.
> The Holy Spirit is:
> The Gift that from the abyss spreads
> And penetrates all
> And of Himself, undivided and one, he fills all things,
> And all is transformed into light.
> No man, no creature

26. See Paul Evdokimov, *The Art of the Icon: a Theology of Beauty*, trans. Steven Bigham (Redondo Beach, Calif.: Oakwood Publications, 1990), 244–45.

Nothing of heaven or on the earth adores you more;
Nobody knows you or admires you:
Nobody serves you, or loves you more.
Illuminated by the Spirit,
Baptized by fire
Whoever you are
Virgin, monk, priest, lay person
You are the throne of God:
You are the dwelling place, the instrument,
You are the light of the Divine.
You are God; You are God. God. God.
God in the Father, God in the Son, God in the Holy Spirit.
You are God: God. God. God.[27]

Andrej Rublev was a disciple of St. Sergius. He was commissioned to paint an icon of the Trinity for the church at the monastery founded by St. Sergius. As I have already mentioned, this very celebrated icon was inspired by the theophany of Abraham's three visitors as narrated in the Book of Genesis. It is universally recognized as the most evocative depiction of the Trinity that has ever come to light. It epitomizes the spirituality of the Russian Orthodox church in an intense way. The Trinity is represented in it as the indescribable mystery of communion of the three that contemplates in the intimacy of their love, the reality of creation and the Paschal sacrifice of the lamb represented by the chalice that lies on the table at the center of the icon.

The revered mystic, St. Seraphim of Sarov (1759–1833), would transmit a very profound new experience of the mystery of God through the gift of the Spirit some centuries later. It was almost a renewal of the motifs that had become central to the Byzantine tradition, beginning especially with St. Simeon the New Theologian. This experience is described in the famous account of the conversation between Seraphim and Motovilov:

The same Holy Spirit comes to dwell in our souls, and this settling of the Almighty in us, this presence of his Trinity-Unity in our soul, is only granted to us through the acquisition of the Holy Spirit within the measure of our strength. He is the one preparing the throne for the Presence of the Creator God in our souls and bodies, in accordance with the divine saying, "I will live with them … and I will be their God, and they will be my people." … I said to him, "Father here you keep talking about the acquisition of the grace of the Holy Spirit, and you tell me that the goal of the Christian life consists in that; but how is it possible to see Him? Good works are visible, but how is it possible to see the Holy Spirit? How can I know if He is in me or not?" The holy staretz answered, "The grace of the Holy Spirit is the light that illuminates the human being. Quite a few times the

27. Quoted in Daniel Ange, *Dalla Trinità all'Eucaristia: L'icona della Trinità di Rublev* (Milan: Ancora, 1984), 84 (own trans. from the Italian).

Lord manifested the Holy Spirit's action in the persons that He sanctified and illuminated with great outpourings of His Person in front of many witnesses. Remember Moses ... the Lord's transfiguration on Mount Tabor ..." I asked Father Seraphim, "How could I recognize if the Holy Spirit's grace is in me?"

It is very simple, Friend of God," he answered ... and holding onto my shoulders, he added, "We are both inside of the divine Spirit now, little Father. Why don't you look at me?" I answered, "I cannot look at you, Father, because light is flashing out of your eyes; your face has become brighter than the sun and this hurts my eyes." And Seraphim said to me, "Thank God for the ineffable grace he has given you ... Did you see? I did not even make the sign of the cross, but I only prayed to God inside in my thought and heart, 'Lord, grant him the grace to see what you give your servants when you deign to come in all your glory ...' And the Lord immediately granted poor Seraphim's request. And how can we not render him thanks for that?"[28]

The Trinity and Modern Philosophy

There seems to be little that is new in the study of the trinitarian mystery in theology from the seventeenth to the nineteenth century, as I said above, even if there are many questions left open by medieval theology. The novelties ripen among harsh quarrels and many ambiguities in the philosophical arena instead, with some reference to the speculative mysticism of northern Europe. These novelties end up dissolving the identity itself of the mystery of the Trinity however, because they are unhinged from the living context of ecclesial faith and the dogmatic tradition, as we will see.

I have already spoken of the transition from theism to deism where the faith in the living God of salvation history gradually fades away. Nothing would seem to be more remote to modern philosophy in this way than the incomprehensible dogma of the Trinity. Immanuel Kant is the one who makes the succinct affirmation toward the end of the eighteenth century that seems to forever rid reasonable exercise of rational study of the Trinity:

The doctrine of the Trinity, taken literally, has *no practical relevance at all*, even if we think we understand it; and it is even more clearly irrelevant if we realize that it transcends all our concepts. Whether we are to worship three or ten persons in the Divinity makes no difference: the pupil will implicitly accept one as readily as the other because he has no concept at all of a number of persons in one God (hypostases), and still more so because this distinction can make no difference in his rules of conduct.[29]

28. Quoted by Thomas Spidlik in *I grandi mistici russi* (Rome: Città Nuova, 1987), 174–75 (own trans.).

29. Immanuel Kant, *The Conflict of the Faculties*, trans. Mary J. Gregor (New York: Abaris Books, 1979), 65–67.

Things suddenly changed with disconcerting rapidity with German Idealism however. This undoubtedly represents a great epoch in which the Trinity is once again at the center of speculation. Fichte, Schelling, and Hegel recognized the Christian dogma of the Trinity as the highest "object of thought" offered to the exercise of understanding, although in different and even sometimes opposed ways.

The Failed Promise of Hegel

We need to say something about Hegel (1770–1831) first of all.[30] This is not only because he had a wide and profound influence on subsequent thought but also because he tried to systematically place trinitarian discourse at the center of his thought. This trinitarian focus was derived from his early Lutheran formation with the decisive influences of Meister Eckhart's writing and J. Boehme's somewhat esoteric mysticism. Hegel reached the point of affirming that the cross of Christ is the true cardinal point around which the history of the world rotates and that whoever does not know that God is triune has understood nothing of Christianity.

A double novelty: nonbeing as the key in the transition from substance to the subject The true novelty of Hegelian thought resides in how he connected Luther's theology of the cross with trinitarian theology in a profound and organic way, as E. Jüngel acutely underlined. It is imperative to qualify in this regard that he connected what he meant by both of these. It is in this connection that the great Hegelian "promise" lay, as K. Barth defined it. That is, the comprehension of the dynamism of the tri-personal being of God beginning with the *kénosis* of the incarnation, of the cross and death of Jesus Christ—precisely that "qualitative leap" and change in perspective that traditional dogma needed.

The promise was unfulfilled unfortunately, both because Hegel did not fully listen to the content of scripture and dogma (when he indeed betrayed his failure to even know them with precision and relevance), and because he used categories of thought often rooted in a non-Christian matrix, trying to force the novelty of revelation within them. He failed to confront these categories with revelation, to rethink and render them adequate vehicles for the content of faith, as the great theology of the Church Fathers and the Scholastics had done. These categories are reduced in the end to that of subject (*Subjekt*) or Spirit (*Geist*) and to that of "negativ-

30. Let me refer to my *Il negativo e la Trinitá: ipotesi su Hegel: Indagine storico-sistematica sulla "Denkform" hegeliana alla luce dell'ermeneutica del cristianesimo: Un contributo al dibattito contemporaneo sul Cristo crocifisso come rivelazione del Dio trinitario nella storia* (Rome: Città Nuova, 2007). Also see Emilio Brito, *La Christologie de Hegel: Verbum Crucis* (Paris: Beauchesne, 1983), and *Dieu et l'être d'aprés Thomas d'Aquin et Hegel* (Paris: Presses Universitaires de France, 1991).

ity." Hegel wants to rethink the identity of the absolute as movement to achieve the full, conscious realization of itself with the first two, also in light of the modern "discovery" of the subject as self-consciousness (from Descartes to Kant). Inspired by what he defines as the "speculative Good Friday" in his systematic essay *Glauben und Wissen* (*Faith and Knowledge*), Hegel wants to rethink the latter (the negative) as the necessity for the absolute to come to itself, to dialectically pass through an antithetical moment of alienation as manifestation of itself.

These concepts were evidently inspired by Christianity, as Hegel himself recognized moreover, defining Christianity as "the religion of modern times." But it is also evident that rationalism influenced this thought. Faith ends up being totally absorbed into reason (*Vernunft*) in fact, and God is absorbed into the self-consciousness that humanity has (or is) of it as a consequence. Hegel expressed the key to understanding his intuition and his system which derives from it in these words in the well-known *Vorrede* (preface) to his most brilliant work, the *Phenomenology of Spirit* (1807):

> In my view, ... everything turns on grasping and expressing the True, not only as *Substance*, but equally as *Subject*.... The living Substance is being which is in truth *Subject*, or, what is the same, is in truth actual only in so far as it is the movement of positing itself, or is the mediation of its self-othering with itself. This Substance is, as Subject, pure, *simple negativity*, and is for this very reason the bifurcation of the simple; it is the doubling which sets up opposition, and then again the negation of this indifferent diversity and of its anti-thesis [the immediate simplicity]. Only this self-*restoring* sameness, or this reflection in otherness within itself—not an *original* or *immediate* unity as such—is the True.... Thus the life of God and divine cognition may well be spoken of as a disporting of Love with itself; but this idea sinks into mere edification, and even insipidity, if it lacks the seriousness, the suffering, the patience, and the labor of the negative. *In itself*, that life is indeed one of untroubled equality and unity with itself, for which otherness and alienation, and the overcoming of alienation, are not serious matters.[31]

Already in the *Phenomenology of Spirit* therefore, but more explicitly in his *Lectures on the Philosophy of Religion*, toward the end of his philosophical career, Hegel sees Christianity as the "absolute" religion, fully unveiled: that is as the historic *locus*, in Jesus Christ, in which the absolute manifests (becomes) what it is.

The inevitable issue and the fatal misunderstanding Is it too easy to fundamentally criticize Hegel by asking where the distinction between God

31. Georg Wilhelm Friedrich Hegel, *Phenomenology of the Spirit*, trans. A. V. Miller (Oxford: Clarendon Press, 1977), 9–10.

and history has gone, or where is the distinction among the persons in the one absolute subject? The reversal of the Hegelian system into atheist anthropocentrism in which history itself becomes the absolute because God is "realized" in it without a residue eventually developed the ambiguity hidden at the heart of Hegelianism, beginning with L. Feuerbach and J. Strauss.

However, in spite of all this, what impetus came to trinitarian theology from Hegel? There was certainly a remarkable influence as seen from the numerous attempts by evangelical, Anglican, and even Orthodox (nineteenth-century Russian) scholars at so-called theologies of *kénosis*, always running the risk of falling victim to Hegel's charm unfortunately. W. Pannenberg noted this with a good dose of optimism, but also with an undeniable truth deep down:

> By way of the profound idea that a person's being exists through his or her dedication to another person, Hegel understood the unity of the Trinity as a unity that is realized only through the process of reciprocal donation. For him the unity of God was so intense and of such an energy, that it was reached not by diminishing the triple personalities but by an acute accentuation of the idea of personality.[32]

It must be recognized in my opinion regarding this affirmation by Pannenberg that it is true that Hegel at least partially sensed the kenotic dimension of the divine person as explaining the intrinsic relatedness with the others, but it must also be noted at least that the following indispensable fixed points of trinitarian doctrine are still problematical in his doctrine: (1) the real distinction of the persons: does not *kénosis* of the person mean for Hegel in fact that the person is alienated in the otherness without a residue? (2) The real trinitarian dimension of the divine being, guaranteed by that "third asymmetrical" between Father and Son which is the Spirit: the latter, in Hegel, not only lacks a clear personal constitution, but, if it has one, it appears like the all-encompassing "synthesis" of Father and Son cancelling them out in itself; (3) what the theological tradition ultimately apophatically expresses and defends thanks to the concept of *perichóresis* of the divine Persons, is neither expressed nor safeguarded by Hegelian speculation, leading to the monologism of the one and only self-evolving subject.

The Revelation of *Deus Trinitas* and Freedom in Schelling

An alternative hermeneutic to Hegel's Christian God is that proposed by F. W. J. Schelling (1775–1854) in his *Philosophie der Offenbarung*, published posthumously in 1861. The central content of revelation for the

32. Wolfhart Pannenberg, *Cristologia: Lineamenti fondamentali*, trans. Gianni Poletti (Brescia: Morcelliana, 1974), 230–31 (own trans.).

"positive philosophy" of the late Schelling is in fact the Christological event, whereby creation is freely restored by him and brought to fulfillment in God. But to fully understand this event it is necessary to connect it to the background of the historical process of religion that preceded him. Rather, it is necessary to discern the meaning of creation and ultimately of the relationship existing between God and the world which implies understanding who God is and why God freely decided to create.

Schelling thus felt authorized to propose a Christological and trinitarian hermeneutics that did not coincide with traditional dogma because this started from a preconception of divine ontology and of creation prior to revelation itself (even if some kind of particular influence by revelation should not be excluded). He affirmed: "The fundamental content of Christianity is Christ himself, not what he says but who he is and what he did. Christianity is not immediately a doctrine; it is a reality, an objectivity."[33] Christology is at the center therefore of the section which specifically focuses on the event of revelation, covered in lectures XXIV–XXXVII of the *Philosophie der Offenbarung*. Schelling distinguishes three unsatisfactory approaches in this regard: (1) the Scholastic one, which is abstract and doctrinal; (2) the historical one, which functions in a certain sense as an external observer without discerning the meaning and the esoteric trend of the events; (3) the mystical one in the sense of "accidental illumination influenced by sentiment."[34] The philosophy of revelation should instead be in relationship with that higher viewpoint which grasps the ontology of freedom as truthful content of the event of revelation. Schelling explains: "Christianity must never ask how it should be interpreted from the perspective of philosophy but vice-versa: What type of philosophy is required to contain and understand Christianity as well?"[35]

So Schelling's Christology rotates around Philippians 2:6–8, that "magnificent passage that reveals the deepest mystery." Based on the parallelism between the first and second Adam, well known in the hymn's exegesis, the *Ur-mensch* (Adam) wants to rule over created being in a false way, independently of the Father. Jesus Christ becomes master of the being detached from the Father by becoming incarnate, freely making it his own and restoring it to the Father. His is the extreme act of freedom that responds to God's freedom, overcoming the temptation to establish the "kingdom of this world" for himself alone.[36] In this way, Schelling concludes, "Christ is already implicitly in paganism, although not as

33. *Lessons* IX (own trans.).
34. Ibid., XXV.
35. Ibid. (own trans.).
36. See ibid.

Christ. Christ is already as Christ in the First Testament, but still only understood as someone who has yet to come. Christ reveals himself also as Christ in the New Testament."[37]

In a word, Jesus Christ is the subject, the content, and, if we want, the objective of revelation, to the extent that he fulfills creation as Son of the Father in the *homoousía* of the Spirit. He reveals himself; he reveals humanity to humanity and in the human person he reveals creation to creation. But he does not reveal the Father, who remains unknowable and beyond us, who remains the presence/absence of all time.

As the great interpreters of the rediscovery of the originality of Schelling's philosophy have opportunely observed in the last few decades (from X. Tillette to K. Hemmerle and W. Kasper, from L. Pareyson to M. Cacciari and F. Tomatis),[38] if we find ourselves in front of the stimulating horizon of an ontology of freedom that is meant to be rooted in the Christological event, it is also necessary to remark that the radically trinitarian form of such an ontology still remains to be fathomed ultimately. There is rather the danger of distorting the original meaning of God's being by starting with a biased interpretation.

37. Ibid., XXVII (own trans.).

38. See Xavier Tillette, *Schelling: une philosophie en devenir*, 2 vols. (Paris: Vrin, 1970), *Attualità di Schelling*, ed. N. De Sanctis (Milan: Mursia, 1974), and *L'absolu et la philosophie: essais sur Schelling* (Paris: Presses Universitaires de France, 1987); Klaus Hemmerle, *Gott und das Denken nach Schellings Spätphilosophie* (Freiburg: Herder, 1968); Walter Kasper, *Absolute in History: the Philosophy and Theology of History in Schelling's Late Philosophy* (New York: Paulist Press, 2018); Luigi Pareyson, *Schelling: Presentazione e Antologia* (Geneva: Marietti, 1975) and *Estetica dell'idealismo tedesco*, vol. 3: *Goethe e Schelling*, ed. M. Ravera (Milan: Mursia, 2003); Massimo Cacciari, *Dell'inizio* (Milan: Adelphi, 1990); Francesco Tomatis, *Kenosis del Logos: Ragione e rivelazione nell'ultimo Schelling* (Rome: Città Nuova, 1994).

CHAPTER 22

The Rediscovery of God the Trinity in the Twentieth Century

Twentieth-century theology begins with Karl Rahner's rather sour observation that we already know: there is the basis for the impression that for many Christians "despite their professed faith in the Trinity, when it comes to their religious practice they are almost only 'monotheists.'" Twentieth-century theology was decisively, freshly immersed in biblical, liturgical, patristic, and mystical expressions of the Christian faith starting from this situation. It became engaged in rediscovering the originality of trinitarian monotheism and its repercussions on all dimensions of theology and existence. So much so, beginning with the 1960s (and also coinciding with the Second Vatican Council), the twentieth century is decisively characterized by a great return of the Trinity in Christian awareness on both the existential and theological levels.

It is a matter of a movement that was and is of interest to all the Christian confessions. This engendered an attitude of listening and reciprocal dialogue with respect to each other. It also makes mutual enrichment possible offering a reliable meeting point on the dogmatic level, for the great commitment to the full recomposition of ecclesial unity. So even though the themes and also the more original results that this renewed theological reflection brought into focus are really close in these different theological areas, I will say a brief word on each of these traditions, or better, on some one of their main representatives.

Reformation Theology

Karl Barth and the Lordship of God the Trinity

One cannot speak of twentieth-century theology in general, and of trinitarian theology in particular, without first thinking of Karl Barth (1886–1968). It is not by accident that I already mentioned him at the onset of this work. In fact, he is the initiator and protagonist of evangelical theology's reaction against the dissolution of Christian identity into an evanescent theism characterizing "liberal theology" in the second half of the nineteenth and early twentieth centuries. "Dialectical theology" is the term for this reaction, which is aimed at restoring otherness as the name suggests, rather, restoring the infinite "qualitative difference" between God and the world.

With a resumption of the central themes of Luther's "theology of the cross," but also of Calvin's theological perspective (Barth belonged to the Reformed church) and the paradoxical philosophy of Søren Kierkegaard, he forcefully affirms that God is known to us as God, in other words as Lord (the YHWH of the First Testament, the *Kýrios* of the Septuagint and of the New Testament), only if and to the extent that God makes Godself known. This happens in the revelation of Godself culminating in Jesus Christ thanks to the indisputable and gratuitous gift of grace. There is no way for man or woman to rise to God therefore; rather it is God alone who breaks through and descends into our history. For this reason, theology is born from the revelation of God which is in the trinitarian rhythm of the trinitarian God. Christian dogma therefore begins with the doctrine of the Trinity.

> It is the point at which it is fundamentally decided whether the truly important expression "God," important in every aspect, is used in Church proclamation in the manner appropriate to its object which is its norm. It is the doctrine of the Trinity which fundamentally distinguishes the Christian doctrine of God as Christian—it is it, therefore, also, which marks off the Christian concept of revelation as Christian, in face of all other possible doctrines of God and concepts of revelation.[1]

Revelation essentially consists of the unique divine subject's (the Hegelian influence is evident) movement of self-communication by way of his "three distinct modes of being" (*drei Seinsweisen*) from this perspective. Barth preferred this designation in place of the classic one of "persons," because this latter term—given its semantic development in the modern era suggesting an autonomous and self-conscious subject—ends up leading to tri-theism in his opinion. The Christian God is therefore the one Lord alone as revealer, revelation, and revealed: "It is God who reveals Himself in a like manner as the Father in His self-veiling and holiness, as He does as the Son in His self-unveiling and mercy, and as the Spirit in His self-impartation and love."[2]

And in this way—within the light of the event of revelation—the

1. Karl Barth, *Church Dogmatics*, vol. 1, part 1: *The Doctrine of the Word of God*, trans. G. T. Thomson (Edinburgh: T and T Clark, 1949), 346.

2. Ibid., 438.

unity of the one subject is reconciled with his three "ways" of revealing himself which correspond (and are identical) to the same being-God:

The name of Father, Son and Spirit means that God is the one God in a threefold repetition; and that in such a way, that this repetition itself is grounded in His Godhead; hence in such a way that it signifies no alteration in His Godhead; but also in such a way that only in this repetition is He the one God; in such a way that His Godhead stands or falls with the fact that in this repetition He is God; but also precisely for the reason that in each repetition He is the one God.[3]

It is to Barth's indisputable credit that he reemphasized God's lordship, his being-God. What can be disputed, or at least needs to be further studied and clarified instead are (1) the excessive opposition between "natural" knowledge of God (and religious experiences apart from the Bible) and revelation, (2) the thesis regarding the oneness of the divine subject of revelation, and (3) the rejection of the concept of person (does it in fact safeguard the real distinction among the three in this way?). In other words, does it suffice to reaffirm God's divinity in order to penetrate into faith in his Trinity, or should further steps be taken instead, precisely in the direction of the centrality of the incarnation and the cross which characterize Barth's dogmatic project?

The Rediscovery of the Crucified God

Some of the more significant postwar theologians from the Reformation move right in this direction. The tragic experience of the Second World War together with more careful engagement with the challenge of atheism (dismissed too abruptly by Barth) leave their mark on subsequent trinitarian reflection.

The ecclesial ontology of Dietrich Bonhoeffer Dietrich Bonhoeffer's (1906–45)[4] human and intellectual experience is enough to exemplify this. He died in a concentration camp, having launched his precious effort, even if only in the embryonic stage, to think of God in a Christological key starting with his "absence" in the world. Having lived in the first half of the twentieth century, Bonhoeffer was undoubtedly one of the most influential Protestant theologians on the postwar world. He incar-

3. Ibid., 402. Barth repeats here a concept taken from St. Anselm of Canterbury: "quotiescunque repetatur aeternitas in aeternitate, non est nisi una et eadem aeternitas" (*Ep. de incarn.* 15).

4. Among his principal works, now collected in *D. Bonhoeffer Werke: Kritische Ausgabe* (Munich: Kaiser, 1986–): *Sanctorum Communio* (1930), *Akt und Sein* (1931), *Ethik* (1949), and *Widerstand und Ergebung* (1951). On his thought, see Nicola Ciola, *La crisi del teocentrismo trinitario nel Novecento teologico: il tema nel contesto emblematico della secolarizzazione* (Rome: Dehoniane, 1993); Alberto Gallas, *Anthropos Téleios: L'itinerario di Bonhoeffer nel conflitto tra cristianesimo e modernità* (Brescia: Queriniana, 1995); Nynfa Bosco, *Bonhoeffer: Un'etica cristiana della responsabilità per laici e credenti* (Naples: ESI, 1995).

nated the struggle and the promise of a new beginning in the vicissitudes of his thought and existence. The singular form of theological knowledge that he constantly sought is held in dynamic tension between "the question what Christianity really is, or indeed who Christ really is, for us today"[5] and the intuition that in the words and gestures handed down to us by the faith, we are offered "something quite new and revolutionary, though we cannot as yet grasp or express it."[6]

In truth, all of this is already clearly evident in his early work, *Akt und Sein* (1930),[7] which demonstrates an extraordinary perception of the stakes in the confrontation with E. Troeltsch's religious sociology, Barth's theology of God's word, and Catholic theology's traditional proposal, but also with the possibility opened up by Heidegger's ontology. In this work, he proposes an epistemology of faith which is both ecclesial and Christ-centered. It is worthwhile lingering on this work therefore because it truly constitutes an original proposal of ontology of freedom and of (trinitarian) reciprocity in Christ even though it does not deal with the Trinity explicitly.

The question that he tackles with unrelenting rigor is that which theology sees as imposed by Kant and idealism, but which ultimately goes to the heart of the originality and possibility of thought of the Christological event, namely, how to define the rapport between God's being and the act capable of grasping it. In other words, it is a matter of understanding (*verstehen*) and not simply explaining (*erklären*) if and how God can be known as God and, consequently, what that implies for humanity's being-human. Bonhoeffer goes back to three philosophical answers to the question: a transcendental one, an idealist one, and an ontological one (borrowing from Heidegger's *Sein und Zeit* and from Przywara's *Drei Richtungen der Phänomenologie*). All three, although distinct from one another on the basis of ultimate choices, are not able to provide a definitive satisfactory response. The failure lies in not having comprehended that the rapport between God's being and the human act is only given in and as liberty: human liberty and originally God's liberty. The fact is that in the actual event of the revelation of God as received in faith, the existential structure of *Dasein* is involved and transformed.[8] And therefore it is not possible to anticipate with respect to revelation human self-understanding and pre-understanding (as Bultmann would like). On the

5. Dietrich Bonhoeffer, letter dated April 30, 1944, in his *Letters and Papers from Prison*, ed. Eberhard Bethge (New York: Macmillan, 1972), 279.

6. Bonhoeffer, *Thoughts on the Day of the Baptism of Dietrich Wilhelm Rüdiger Bethge*, in his *Letters and Papers from Prison*, 300.

7. *Act and Being*, trans. Bernard Noble (New York: Harper and Row, 1961).

8. Ibid.

other hand, it is also not possible to think of revelation as a pure object of self-donation that remains independent of the event in which it is offered (Barth).

This shows the need for theology to be adequately located in (*zwischen*, in-between) the dynamic place of the encounter between God's freedom and human freedom, so that it can respond to the provocation, making it possible for the event of revelation to offer its own specific doctrine of knowledge (*Erkenntnislehre)*. Pursuing such a possibility, Bonhoeffer depicts two solutions: the first, an actualist approach, which conceives of the human-divine relationship as an actuality of pure faith in order to safeguard God's freedom as subject on one hand and a person's free choice on the other. The second solution uses an ontological approach which attempts to give historical continuity both to revelation and to faith, but it risks confining them within doctrine, within psychological experience, within the institution. Both of them are guilty of the sin of abstraction and presumption to the extent that they fail locate themselves in depth in the *novum* of the event of revelation and in the *zwischen* that opens up between God and the human person. And they sin in addition because of individualism, to the extent that a human being is only considered singly in front of God, set apart from history and the community.

Bonhoeffer's solution is meant to be both Christological and ecclesiological instead because the event of God's revelation happens for me today in and by way of the *Christus präsens* (Christ present) which is the *Christus als Gemeinde existierend* (Christ existing as community). The fact is if God links himself to humanity in Christ, Christ links himself to humanity in the church. This certainly means that the preached word and the celebration of the sacraments constitute the trans-subjective guarantee of the continuity and the "extra" of the event of revelation. But it inevitably means together with this that revelation takes human existence as historical reality and as social relationship implemented in freedom only in the community and as a historical and lived community, with the drawback that the church relapses into being an institution and the revelatory event into a reified object.

The human correlate of God's revelatory event in Christ is not so much an individual and ultimately ahistorical act of faith therefore, but a "new sphere" of knowledge and praxis in which humankind is/becomes free in history; it is the sphere of existence in social relationship. Christ existing in and as community is therefore the unique form of God's revelation (*Offenbarungsgestalt*) within history, in both the existential and historical sense described in this way.

Bonhoeffer's acquired point of view continued to mold his research and the intentionality of his theology when the almost unstoppable rise of Nazism forced a radical *metanoia* on him of Christian thought and action in the world. Bonhoeffer's concept was then filtered through a radical *theologia crucis*, in which he identified the crucified Christ abandoned by the Father with the form of ecclesial existence in the world and for the world, which Christ had already definitively reconciled with God. In this kenotic pro-existence all of the dual categories—God-world, private-public, interior-exterior, penultimate-ultimate—are reinterpreted in a Christological context in the perspective sanctioned by the dogma of Chalcedon.

Bonhoeffer's message has to be understood from the point of view of his situation in time and not seen as a banal compromise, as some of his subsequent interpreters have been tempted to do.[9] It was consigned to theology and the church of the future from the *lager*. His message speaks of fidelity to "the discipline of the arcane," in which the life of Christ is passed on to history; it speaks of witness to a "non-religious Christianity" to be lived in the worldliness of the adult world.[10] This is what he wrote from prison:

> And we cannot be honest unless we recognize that we have to live in the world *etsi Deus non daretur*. And this is just what we do recognize—before God! God himself compels us to recognize it. So our coming of age leads us to a true recognition of our situation before God. God would have us know that we must live as men who manage our lives without him. The God who is with us is the God who forsakes us (Mark 15:34). The God who lets us live in the world without the working hypothesis of God is the God before whom we stand continually. Before God and with God we live without God.[11]

The theological lesson of the death of God The theology of "the death of God" itself is a short-lived flowering with a good dose of superficiality, ultimately. It started with a philosophical-theological mixture blending and misrepresenting the cues offered by Bonhoeffer with Hegel's, Nietzsche's,

9. The reference is to Hanfried Müller's Marxist reading, *Von der Kirche zur Welt: Ein Beitrag zu der Beziehung des Wortes Gottes auf die Societas in Dietrich Bonhoeffers theologischer Entwicklung* (Hamburg-Bergstedt: H. Reiche, 1961); and to that of the radical theologians and the death of God: John A. T. Robinson, *Honest to God* (London: Westminster Press, 1963); Paul van Buren, *The Secular Meaning of the Gospel* (London: Macmillan, 1966); Harvey Cox, *Secular City* (New York: Macmillan, 1966); Thomas J. J. Altizer and William Hamilton, *Radical Theology and the Death of God* (New York: Bobbs-Merrill, 1966); Thomas J. J. Altizer, *The Gospel of Christian Atheism* (London: Westminster Press, 1966); William Hamilton, *The New Essence of Christianity* (London: Association Press, 1966).

10. In this regard, and worthy of interest, is the theology of secularization which was launched with Friedrich Gogarten's (1887–1968) reflection; it deserves credit for seriously raising the question of the relationship between modernity and Christian faith. Among his works: *Verhängnis und Hoffnung der Neuzeit: die Säkularisierung als theologisches Problem* (Stuttgart: Vorwerk, 1953); *Jesus Christus Wende der Welt* (Tübingen: J. B. Mohr, 1966).

11. Bonhoeffer, *Letters and Papers from Prison*, 360.

and Heidegger's reflections on the "death of God." It teaches something important to twentieth-century theology nevertheless. L. Serenthà remarked on it pertinently: "With this affirmation (of the death of God) there is effectively a nostalgia of a fundamental revealed truth ... and the truth is that the life of God, as revealed, includes a moment of death, self-giving, a loss of self. It expresses the intimate life of God, as Trinity consisting of God giving Godself as the Father, Son and Holy Spirit give to each other."[12]

The Crucified God *of Moltmann* Jürgen Moltmann's possibly most original work, *The Crucified God* (original German publication in 1972),[13] was based on his earlier work on the eschatological theology of Christian hope. It should be understood in the cultural and theological framework delineated above and in the light of the Lutheran tradition, but it also explicitly stemmed from the New Testament *theologia crucis*.

This work is a systematic attempt to read the trinitarian newness of the Christian God and its repercussions on the history of humankind, beginning with the passion and death of Christ crucified and forsaken by God. Moltmann writes:

What occurs between Jesus and the Father in Jesus' abandonment or dedication on the cross? The Father "abandons" his "own" Son and rejects him. The One whose Kingdom Jesus had announced as "imminent" becomes the God that abandons. The Son dies being cursed by the Father. He is the abandoned God. The Son suffers the death of abandonment. The Father instead suffers the Son's death in the suffering of his love. After announcing the Father's law of grace, the Son suffers his abandonment. The Father suffers the abandonment of the Son that he had chosen and loved.

If the Father acts upon his own Son by abandoning him and the Son suffers this abandonment by the Father, then this death on the cross occurs between the Father and the Son. It is to be found in the same divine being, between the Father and the Son; it totally separates the Son from the Father through the curse. Since the Son sacrifices himself as well however and accepts the cup of abandonment in the Garden of Gethsemane, as we can deduce by connecting Rom 8:32 with Gal. 2:20, both of them act and suffer in this sacrifice, and the cross joins the Son and the Father in the full communion of that willing which is called love. 1 Jn 4:16 testifies that this love is the being of God himself; "God is Love" and so in the communion of willing which is accomplished in the sacrifice, we find a substantial communion of existences. On the cross, Jesus and the Father are separated in the most radical way because of the death as a curse; as a result of the dedication instead they are joined in the most intimate way. From this event

12. Luigi Serenthà, "Dio," in *Dizionario Teologico Interdisciplinare* (Turin: Marietti, 1977), 1:699 (own trans.).

13. In particular by Moltmann, see *Der gekreuzigte Gott* and *Trinität und Reich Gottes*.

occurring between the Father and Son, gifting itself is unleashed, the Spirit that welcomes those that have been abandoned, that justifies the ungodly and gives life to the dead. The God that abandons and the God that is abandoned are one thing alone in the Spirit of dedication. The Spirit proceeds from the Father and from the Son because he is unleashed by Jesus' being neglected.[14]

It is to Moltmann's credit that he very rigorously drew attention back to the center of trinitarian theological discourse (and Christian discourse, indisputably), to the material to be treated in theology. This can be seen in the numerous works following *The Crucified God* branching its many dimensions into anthropology, theology of creation, ecclesiology etc. The remaining limits consist of a certain dialectical and conflictual one-sided reading of the Paschal event and an incomplete processing and criticism of the Hegelian lesson from a purely dogmatic angle. In a word, we find ourselves facing a failure in Moltmann's work to study the ontological dimension, even running the risk of ultimately confusing the immanent Trinity with the economic Trinity.

God as the Mystery of the World *by Eberhard Jüngel* Eberhard Jüngel meant to offer a rigorous ontological study of the relationship between the economic Trinity and the immanent Trinity within the context of his own theological tradition and the culture of modernity, especially in his important work, *God as the Mystery of the World* (third German edition published in 1977).[15] In fact, he moves from an incisive and tight discussion with the modern affirmation (philosophical and theological) about "the death of God," bringing out its Christian origin, and simultaneously the incompatibility between its meaning and authentic ecclesial faith. He penetrates from here into the theological-trinitarian dynamic primarily along the main path of the biblical concept of *agápe* by focusing his thesis on the Paschal event of the crucified one as *vestigium Trinitatis*.

14. Jürgen Moltmann, "Prospettive dell'odierna teologia della croce," in *Sulla teologia della croce*, trans. D. Pezzetta (Brescia: Queriniana, 1974), 42–46 (own trans. from the Italian). This is an essay in which Moltmann clarifies, in dialogue with his critics, the position expressed in *The Crucified God.*

15. Among his works are *Paulus und Jesus: Eine Untersuchung zur Präziesierung der Frage nach der Ursprung der Christologie* (Tübingen: J. B. Mohr, 1962); *Gottes Sein ist im Werden: Verantwortliche Rede vom Sein Gottes bei K. Barth: Eine Paraphrase* (Tübingen: J. B. Mohr, 1965); *Tod* (Berlin-Stuttgart: Kreuz Verlag, 1971); *Gott als Geheimnis der Welt*; *Entsprechungen: Gott - Wahrheit - Mensch: Theologische Erörrterungen* (Munich: Kaiser, 1980). On his thought, see Angelo Bertuletti, "Per una fondazione del sapere teologico. Saggio su 'Dio mistero del mondo' di. Jüngel," *Teologia* 61, no. 3 (1983): 247–64; Engelbert Paulus, *Liebe - Das Geheiminis der Welt: Formale und Materiale Aspekte der Theologie E. Jüngels* (Würzburg: Echte, 1990); Juan A. Martinez Camino, *Recibir la libertad: Dos propuestas de fundamentación de la teología en la modernidad: W. Pannenberg y E. Jüngel* (Madrid: Universidad Pontificia Comillas, 1992); Alessandra Cislaghi, *Interruzione e corrispondenza: Il pensiero teologico di E. Jüngel* (Brescia: Queriniana, 1994); Paolo Gamberini, *Nei legami del vangelo: L'analogia nel pensiero di E. Jüngel* (Rome: Gregorian University Press-Morcelliana, 1994).

The New Testament confession according to which "God is love" (1 Jn 4:8, 16) is to be understood in fact beginning with Jesus Christ's death and resurrection. This confession absolutely cannot be turned around into, "love is God," as L. Feuerbach wanted to do, without the dissolution of the Christian faith.

God is love.... God is not only *in* love just as two people who love each other are *in* love. God is not only a loving I and a beloved Thou. God is rather the radiant event of love itself.... he is that event in that he, as the one who loves and who separates himself from his beloved, not only loves himself but (in the midst of such great self-relatedness still more selfless) loves another one and *thus* is and remains himself. God has himself only in that he gives himself away. But, in giving himself away, he has himself. That is how he *is*. His self-having is the event, is the history of giving himself away and thus is the end of all mere self-having. As this *history*, he is God, and in fact, this *history of love* is "God himself."[16]

The God of Jesus Christ should therefore be understood as an event of *agápe*, that is as God's freely coming to Godself, of Godself and in Godself, in his coming to the world at the same time—by way of the incarnation and the cross—to save and bring it, gratuitously (from God's side) and freely (from the human side) into Godself. G. Lafont synthesizes Jüngel's reflection with great precision in these terms: "God is he who comes (and who speaks) on his own initiative, freely (the Father), he to whom he comes (the crucified Son), he who comes as God even into death itself (the Spirit). This divine dynamic takes place *for us*, that is to say that it is impossible to think God without an 'overflowing' of his Being toward nothingness and sin."[17] In this sense, the trinitarian God is the "Mystery of the world," whose presence, beginning with his withdrawal from the world, leaves room for humanity to freely accept his offer of adoption. Although Jüngel's reflection is very suggestive and profound, it leaves open the problem of the distinction between God in himself and his coming into creation and history. And this is not a minor thing.

Once again the need to study the ontology of the mystery of salvation becomes evident. In other words, how should we understand the rapport between God the Trinity and the world (creation, incarnation, and the Paschal mystery), and how should we understand the dynamic interior life of the Trinity? This undoubtedly implies a "becoming" but in a way that does not prove to be in contradiction with God's being God, but rather as a presupposition for his *génesis* and his *kénosis* in salvation history.

16. Jüngel, *God as the Mystery of the World*, 327–28.

17. Ghislain Lafont, *God, Time and Being*, trans. Leonard Maluf (Petersham, Mass.: Saint Bede's Publications, 1992), 273.

Catholic Theology: Trinitarian Ontology and the *Mysterium Paschale*

Catholic theology moves from the need to safeguard the Augustinian and Thomistic distinction between God's transcendent being and God's real self-communication in salvation history, while at the same time showing the newness that this self-communication entails in the experience and understanding of the ontology of creation. It is in line with a creative renewal of Aquinas's theological vision, based on the principle of the analogy of being.

The Trinitarian *teo-onto-logia* of Antonio Rosmini

In this context, it is necessary to mention *in primis* the mighty speculative project of Antonio Rosmini (1797–1855), which was ahead of its time. We shall ponder his works first of all because of their relevance in recovering the lesson of the Augustinian and Thomistic tradition which was reread in the light of some issues advanced by modernity. Rosmini clearly recognized the need to come to grips with those issues. At first glance, the way in which the abbot from Rovereto deals with the understanding of the trinitarian mystery may appear on one hand to be a simple development of the Thomistic framework of *ipsum esse per se subsistens*. On the other hand, it could appear to be a revival of that psychological interpretation of the trinitarian mystery which was prevalent in the Latin tradition beginning with Augustine. As a third alternative, it could also appear to be an audacious attempt to review everything in the light of absolute subjectivity, an evident echo of the tradition and translation of "substance in subject" found in Hegel's *Phenomenology of Spirit*. After thoroughly analyzing his overall daring project of theological reform, however, it turns out in reality that his originality lay in the quest for an innovative reconciliation of these different approaches while remaining faithful to the structure of truth of revelation.

Subjecting the psychological analogy to ontological rigor In the first place, Rosmini resumes and elaborates the Augustinian-Thomistic line of thought of God as "Pure Act," the being of which can be interpreted starting with the psychological analogy of the created person. The fact is that "the divine essence is not really distinct from each person, meaning that it could not be if there are not the persons; nor is it simultaneously identical in the three persons and so it would be absurd to conceal it in one or two and not in the other or others."[18] He continues: "The only way we can form the concept of God the Father is to conceive him as an infinite *act* of intelligence, which as an absolute and totally first act is simultaneously *subject*. This infinite act of intelligence is *pure being*."[19]

Secondly, "this absolute act of totally complete intelligence, which at the same time is subject, has its own self as object, absolute being."[20] Thus in God "another person subsists who repeats the origin from the first. This second person has the same essence as the first who is being absolute subject, but in another way, that is, in an objective way in itself, manifest in itself, understood in itself, having in itself the life and subjectivity of the first."[21] However—this brings us to the third person—"this principle does not hold and stop its act in the object generated as person; but it continues in this and with this, and proceeds finalizing itself."[22]

In fact, God "does not produce the person-object as simply intelligible but He produces it together as infinitely lovable, loved and loving," and therefore as "the same subject, but in a third way, which is that of being loved in itself in act; and being loved in itself means subsistent loving act. Hence there is necessarily a third person, equal and co-eternal to the first two who with one act of satisfaction spirate him."[23] From this it is possible to conclude:

The efficient, intellective act which is absolute being, God, is one and constitutes three persons. These persons are distinguished from each other solely through processions and relationships, and the processions are the intellective act. This act of absolute, divine essence has a principle and two terms. Consequently, if the act is considered as *principle* in relationship with the first term, it is and is called "Father," and the first term is called "Son." If the second term is considered in relationship with the act in so far as the act is identical in the Father and Son, it is not called by a proper name but by a common and appropriate name "Holy Spirit." But if the act alone is considered, without any attention to the relation-

18. Antonio Rosmini, *L'Introduzione del Vangelo secondo Giovanni commentata*, ed. Ia, 1887, Lesson XLVII, ed. Samuele Francesco Tadini, Opere di Antonio Rosmini 41 (Rome: Istituto di Studi Filosofici – Centro Internazionale di Studi Rosminiani – Città Nuova Editrice, 2009), 194 (3:132; own trans.).

19. Rosmini, *Theosophy*, trans. Denis Cleary and Terence Watson (Durham: Rosmini House, 2007), no. 1257 (3:97–98).

20. Ibid., no. 1258 (3:98).

21. Ibid. (3:98–99).

22. Ibid., no. 1259 (3:99).

23. Ibid. (3:100). A study would be interesting in this regard to demonstrate how Rosmini manages in this framework to brilliantly overcome the polemic of the *Filioque* in the Latin and Greek traditions. For example, he writes in *L'Introduzione del vangelo secondo Giovanni*: "the Father spirates the Holy Spirit through the Word [this recalls the Greek *diá*].... But the Holy Spirit proceeds not only from the Father through the Word, but also from the Father and from the Word [*Filioque*] with one spiration alone." Lesson XLVII, 195 (3:134; own trans.).

ships and therefore abstractly, it is called divine essence, which is distinguished only mentally from the persons.[24]

It is to be noted how Rosmini succeeds with extreme vigor and speculative dexterity in this way, to illustrate the formal reason why the truth of the unity and trinity of the divine being has its intrinsic evidence beyond the accommodating but contradictory solutions presented by modalism and/or tri-theism. In fact, the intellectual and volitional act of being which is the one God is realized as such only in the three distinct subsistences. And here is the clearly identified and displayed reason regarding the Word (an analogous argument should be made with regard to the Holy Spirit):

> Indeed, if the intellective act has itself in fact as object, and this object remained simply a term and final point of the intellection without subsisting with its own personal subsistence, the intellection would not be infinite and totally perfect; the divine essence, which is the understood entity, would not be fully understood because, even though the intelligent divine essence subsists, the understood entity would not subsist. Consequently, the understood entity, as understood, would not be the divine essence but a likeness of idea.[25]

Rosmini completes the line of reasoning that unfolds from Augustine to Thomas in this way, by explaining the sense in which the one intellectual and volitional act of being, which is God, has to formally subsist as such in three distinct persons.

On the other side, Rosmini avoids the reef of tri-theism precisely because he firmly holds onto the reality of God's being-one, showing that if it is to be "abstractly" understood in the framework of the oneness of the essence, however, it is to be interpreted "concretely" in the infinite actuality of the absolute subject because it is the act of being realizing itself intellectually and volitionally. In terms of terminology and content, this position is at least partially new with regard to the tradition. With respect to the concepts of (divine) essence and (divine) persons, Rosmini introduces that of (divine) subject in fact, which is the act of the divine essence, being itself one in the Trinity of its personal subsistences.[26]

The complementary perspective of the ontology of dedication A second perspective, complementary to the preceding one, concerns absolute being as "self-communicating." This means that the divine nature is such that "it necessarily encompasses the concept of an eternal *giving* of itself

24. Ibid.

25. Ibid., no. 1310 (3:164).

26. See ibid., trans. Terence Watson (Durham: Rosmini House, 2007), no. 1031 (2:347): "We must first note that essence in absolute being and fully determined by its very infinity is naturally a real, living and intelligent subject."

through those two ways known by the consecrated words, generation and spiration."[27] Rosmini not only anticipates the modern focus of this perspective in this way, a perspective which, on deeper analysis, springs from the heart of revelation and therefore from the constitution itself of the absolute being,[28] but he offers a way to deepen the understanding of it without irretrievably destroying the ontological tradition. But he renews it by bringing out the virtues that immunize it from the stinging criticism of the so-called Heideggerian *onto-teo-logia*.

In what sense, therefore, is the divine nature in itself such that "it necessarily encompasses the concept of an eternal giving-of-itself," according to Rosmini? He explains in the sense that the first Person of the Trinity gives and has always given everything to the second. In other words: "the first person himself is this act of giving. Hence the first person would not be, if he did not give and had not always given everything to the second."[29] It reminds us of Thomas's affirmation that "relatio in Deo est substantia eius."[30] It follows that

> the act of the source principle of the divine Trinity is an act that always tends into another and into another, and has from eternity always attained and, of itself, emanated this other and other.... Consequently, in this constitution of the divine Trinity, in the operation of the principle, we can logically but not in reality distinguish two characteristics or conditions: 1. a giving of everything to others, and 2. a retaining of everything, that is, a putting of everything in act in itself, so that the divine essence, which is in the principle and is communicated, is put in act through the same act through which the divine persons, really distinct from each other, are put in act. The result is therefore that the principle's giving of its total self to its object and to the beloved object is the act by which the principle is constituted in its final and infinite perfection. The principle and its perfection are therefore constituted by the fact that the terms are something different from the principle. The principle would neither be, nor understand itself, nor be perfect, if it did not, of itself, produce the terms that as terms are different from it. On the other hand, the act of producing the terms is the principle itself, producing them in itself and as something different from itself.[31]

It becomes clear in this way that the psychological perspective and the perspective of interpersonal otherness are not mutually exclusive in interpreting God's trinitarian being. Rather they entail one another on the secure foundation of an ontology which by definition is true and proper

27. Ibid., no. 1383 (3:281).

28. "In its [Christianity's] heart a striking philosophy is hidden which brightens and pleases intellects because of its divine origin and because it leads to God again." Antonio Rosmini, *Epistolario completo*, letter to M. Parma on January 30, 1831 (3:611; own trans.).

29. Rosmini, *Theosophy*, no. 1320 (3:184). The theme reoccurs in the section dedicated to the topic of inobjectivation; see ibid., section 3, chap. 1, a. 4.

30. Thomas Aquinas, *De pot.*, q. 8, a. 1, ad 8.

31. Rosmini, *Theosophy*, no. 1383 (3:282).

teo-onto-logia to paraphrase the Rosminian concept of theo-sophy, not *onto-teo-logia*.

Karl Rahner, from the *Grundaxiom* to the Renewal of Ontology

As noted above, Karl Rahner (1904–84)[32] formulates that fundamental principle of trinitarian theology in the second half of the twentieth century affirming the identity of the immanent and economic Trinity, while trying to safeguard the distinction between the two. Having already examined the genesis of the *Grundaxiom* and the questions it raises, it is useful at this point in our journey to make the perspectives explicit which shaped his trinitarian theology and the vast reception it encountered in Catholic and non-Catholic theology especially after the Second Vatican Council, even if this reception was ambiguous at times.

The question regarding access to the one-triune God As I have already demonstrated, the *Grundaxiom* is meant to respond to the first and basic methodological question concerning access to the truth of the one-triune God. Rahner points out that trinitarian revelation is the supreme fulfillment of God's self-communication to history, thanks to the *Grundaxiom*. God communicates as Trinity because God really only self-communicates in this way, which means that God himself is trinitarian self-communication of Godself to Godself in Godself in his divine immanence. This means that from the point of view of the recipient of God's self-communication *ad extra*, namely humanity, the trinitarian truth of God's being is the condition by which it is possible to have real communion with God on one hand; creation and redemption are freely and gratuitously designed for this. On the other hand, this truth only becomes accessible through the experience of God's self-communication in the threefold way that it effectively comes about: "The Father, the Word, and the Spirit

32. Among his many works (the *Säntichle* is projected to consist of thirty-two volumes); *Geist in Welt: Zur Metaphysik der endlichen Erkenntnis bei Thomas von Aquin* (Innsbruck: Rauch, 1939), reworked under the care of J. B. Metz (Munich: Kösel, 1957); Italian translation, *Spirito nel mondo* (Milan: Vita e Pensiero, 1989). See also *Hörer des Wortes: Zur Grundlegung einer Religionsphilosohie* (1941), reworked under the care of J. B. Metz (Munich: Kösel, 1963; reprinted in Freiburg i.B: Herder, 1971); the principal collection of Rahner's theological writings is comprised of the *Schriften zur Theologie*, 14 vols. (Einsiedeln: Benzinger, 1954–79); and the powerful concluding work of summary, *Grundkurs des Glaubens: Einführung in den Begriff des Christentums* (Freiburg i.B: Herde, 1976). For an introduction to his thought: Herbert Vorgrimler, *Karl Rahner: His Life, Thought and Works*, trans. Edward Quinn (Glen Rock, N.J.: Paulist Press, 1966); Karl-Heinz Weger, *Karl Rahner: An Introduction to his Theology*, trans. David Smith (New York: Seabury Press, 1980); Klaus Fischer, *Der Mensch als Geheimnis: Die Anthropologie K. Rahners* (Freiburg i.B.: Herder, 1974); Friedemann Greiner, *Die Menschlichkeit der Offenbarung: Die transzendentale Grundlegung der Theologie bei Karl Rahner* (Munich: Kaiser, 1978); Bernd J. Hilberath, *Karl Rahner: Gottgeheimnis Mensch* (Mainz: Grünewald, 1995).

(however deficient all these words may and must be) point to a true distinction, to a double mediation within this self-communication."[33]

Rahner underlines the need to always return again to "the originating experience" of salvation history therefore. We have the experience in faith of the Spirit as God, of the Son as God of the Father as God in the grace of this originating experience.[34] It should be noted in addition however that it is a matter of an eminently individual access for Rahner deep down; each man and woman is considered in his or her solitude in front of God. This undoubtedly fits with one fundamental dimension of the experience of revelation. There would be the need to widen our horizon to include the concrete, structural communitarian situation of human existence. This finds a new and more radical form of expression moreover precisely in virtue of God's self-communication as Trinity.

Rahner himself proposed some avenues to be pursued again and expressed in different contexts in this regard. I will limit myself to two examples. The first is the essay *Über die Einheit von nächsten-und Gottsliebe*[35] in which he speaks of "that mystical and intimate experience of God," "lived within the deep, individual interior of the human person, precisely where he/she is . . . a unique human being who is responsible for him/herself alone . . . only the one that loves his/her neighbor can have this."[36] The second avenue recalls the apostolic community's communitarian experience of the Spirit at Pentecost which is the archetypal ecclesial experience of God the Trinity. This is why Rahner is led to affirm: "I think that the element of spiritual fraternal communion, of a spirituality lived together, can play a more determining role in a spirituality of the future, and that this path must be slowly but decisively followed."[37]

The divine* táxis *and the need for a formal trinitarian perspective The question regarding the shared access to the *Deus Trinitas* in itself leads to a second question. In continuity with the theological tradition, Rahner reiterates the existence of a trinitarian *táxis* not only on the level of God's free and gratuitous self-communication to the spiritual creature,[38] but also on the level of the immanent Trinity, where he writes, "these 'distinct

33. Rahner, *The Trinity*, 37.

34. See ibid., 488.

35. "The 'Commandment' of Love in Relation to the Other Commandments," in *Theological Investigations*, vol. 5: *Later Writings*, trans. Karl-H. Kruger (London / New York: Darton, Longman and Todd / The Seabury Press, 1966), 439–59.

36. Karl Rahner, *Im Gesprach*, ed. P. Imhof and H. Biallowons (Munich: Kösel Verlag, 1982), 2:41–45; translated as "Dialogo con Slavko Kessler," in *Dimensioni politiche del cristianesimo*, trans. Martina Radig (Rome: Città Nuova), 69 (own trans. from the Italian).

37. Karl Rahner, "Elementi di spiritualità nella Chiesa del futuro," in *Problemi e prospettive di spiritualità*, ed. T. Goffi and B. Secondin (Brescia: Queriniana, 1983), 440–41 (own trans.).

38. Rahner, *The Trinity*, 83.

manners of subsisting' should be seen as relative and standing in a determined *táxis* to each other (Father, Son and Holy Spirit)."[39] In his opinion, then, there is a need to rediscover and illustrate the original meaning of *táxis* as expressed in the New Testament and formalized by dogma, not only by overcoming every residual shadow of subordination but also by determining the positive content of the principle of otherness *in divinis*[40] in its constitutive dynamic of personal relations which are reciprocal and cannot be exchanged, in a framework that is not simply dialogical but trinitarian.

The need for an ontology forged from the event of Jesus Christ But the question of the trinitarian *táxis ad intra* and *ad extra* presses in turn for further reflection. Augustine, Aquinas, and Rahner himself know well that trinitarian revelation imposes on the *intelligentia fidei* a determination of God's being in which the *esse in* and the *esse ad* are not only not in opposition to one another, but they mutually explain each other according to the logic of the trinitarian *agápe*. The question is another in reality. The medieval Christian elaboration of metaphysics, certainly in continuity with Greek philosophy, but also within the new horizon opened up by revelation, offered an understanding of being that harmoniously articulates the rapport between uncreated being and created being thanks to the principle of analogy. And for what concerns uncreated being, it also delineated a penetrating illustration of the rapport between subsistence and relation. The *Grundaxiom* invites us to take a further step forward. From the moment that he introduces the reflection on the notion of relationship *in divinis*, Rahner is in fact illustrating this methodological criteria: "Hence really to understand the concept of 'relation' as used here (at least at first), we must not consult any general ontology, but return to the more primitive statement ... about our experience of the 'economic' Trinity."[41]

The examination of the question, which Rahner himself recognizes, moves in reality then more in the framework of logic than the more specifically ontological framework in the theological tradition. What is intriguing is that precisely this affirmation by Rahner pushes the advancement of the question of what would be called trinitarian ontology (as termed by K. Hemmerle).[42] If it is true that the notion of relation, within its trinitarian formality, should be inferred starting with the eco-

39. Ibid., 112.

40. See Hans Urs von Balthasar, *Theo-drama: Theological Dramatic Theory*, vol. 5: *The Last Act*, trans. Graham Harrison (San Francisco, Calif.: Ignatius Press, 1998), 81–85.

41. Rahner, *The Trinity*, 69.

42. See Klaus Hemmerle, *Thesen zu einer trinitarischen Ontologie* (Einsiedeln: Johannes Verlag, 1976); translated into Italian as *Tesi di ontologia trinitaria* (Rome: Città Nuova, 1996).

nomic Trinity, then it must be forged by looking at the relationship that the Word incarnate, Jesus, lives with the Father in the Spirit, in the face of, with, and for humanity.

This is possible because human nature is the real symbol of the *Lógos*[43] from the beginning, as Rahner explains, in such a way that "what Jesus is and does as man reveals the Logos himself; it is the [*Dasein*] the Logos as our salvation amidst us."[44] The ontology of God's being as Trinity becomes accessible—in the lights and shadows of faith in front of the mystery of *Deus semper maior*—in the figure of the Word incarnate, including his crucifixion and resurrection, of course, thanks to God's full communication of himself in the Holy Spirit.

There is a need then to consider the ontological implications of the event of the incarnation—in classical dogmatic language, the mystery of the hypostatic union. As noted in this regard, Rahner has offered a penetrating attempt to reread and study this especially in the context of his Christology. I will restrict myself to recalling the explanation of the meaning of the incarnation which Rahner offers, not by chance, in his article on the Trinity in *Mysterium Salutis*. He introduces a broad justificatory reflection on it in "the Incarnation as an 'instance' of a more comprehensive reality."[45] It is a matter of illustrating the relationship of identity in fact between the immanent *Lógos* and the economic *Lógos,* Jesus Christ. Rahner expresses it like this:

> Since our problem concerns not the formal subject of the Logos in the abstract, but the concrete incarnate Logos, this sameness is the one about which Ephesus and Chalcedon both say that it is unconfused, unseparated, hence not the sameness of a lifeless identity in which there is nothing to distinguish because from the start everything is identically the same, but the sameness in which one and the same Logos is himself in the human reality not because something foreign (human nature) has been joined to him in a merely additive way, but because the Logos posits this other reality as his way of positing and expressing himself. In the case of mere addition this "joining" could no longer be thought as a real one. We would simply have a case where two realities are thought of as juxtaposed. In fact, the difference should be conceived as an inner modality of the unity. Thus within the Trinity and "outside" it an immediate sameness not mediated by something really different should be considered not as the highest form, but rather as a negation of authentic sameness.[46]

It suffices to call attention back to how Rahner tries here to define "the difference as an inner modality of the unity," and how at the same time

43. Rahner, *The Trinity*, 33.
44. Ibid.
45. Ibid., 25–33.
46. Ibid., 33n30.

he specifies that this is analogically valid both "within the Trinity as well as *ad extra*." It is interesting how the event of the incarnation is in accordance with a formality referring back to the intra-trinitarian relations. And this is not simply in the obvious sense that even though the event of the incarnation directly involves the *Lógos* alone hypostatically, that at the same time it reflects the synergetic operation of the Father and Holy Spirit; but rather in the sense that the relationship of hypostatic unity of the *Lógos*, with its unsurpassable distinction between the divine and human natures, is interpreted according to a trinitarian logic.

Rahner does not further develop this position, already outlined in his previous *Schriften zur Theologie* and reproposed in his subsequent work, *Grundkurs des Glaubens*. There is no doubt that this constitutes the last condition of possibility for trinitarian ontology in any case. It is necessary to take into account in this regard (as Rahner himself does explicitly, by radically distancing himself from any interpretation of his thought in a merely Hegelian sense) both the Chalcedonian *asynchýtōs* as intrinsic moment of the *union hypostatica*,[47] as well as the fact that if the human nature in Christ is the same as it is in us, it is nevertheless a self-expression of the *Lógos* in him, while it is not for us.[48]

From the incarnation to the Easter event The only adequate place to relevantly establish the explication of such an ontology, on the other hand, is not a consideration before the incarnation but rather an *a posteriori* consideration of the concrete form exhibited by the incarnation in the Pascha of the death and resurrection of the incarnate *Lógos* and the Spirit's Pentecostal gift as the ultimate event of the trinitarian self-communication. Rahner clearly affirms this:

> Man's absolute dependence on the self-bestowing mystery of God becomes an historical event, realized in fact in the death achieved there as such, and otherwise impossible. That man's transcendence toward God in his immediacy is really finally achieved through God himself and carries the person away beyond all detailed and provisional classifications: this is the substance of the Christian revelation that became an event in the cross of Jesus and was made evident there. And for that reason the cross is the completion of Christian revelation.[49]

47. See Rahner, "Current Problems in Christology," in *Theological Investigations*, vol. 1: *God, Christ, Mary and Grace*, trans. Cornelius Ernst (London / New York: Darton, Longman and Todd / The Seabury Press, 1974), 149–200, at 179.

48. Rahner, "On the Theology of the Incarnation," in *Theological Investigations*, vol. 4: *More Recent Writings*, trans. Kevin Smyth (London / New York: Darton, Longman and Todd / The Seabury Press, 1974), 105–20, at 115–16.

49. Rahner, "The Death of Jesus and the Closure of Revelation," in *Theological Investigations*, vol. 28: *God and Revelation*, trans. Edward Quinn (London / New York: Darton, Longman and Todd / The Seabury Press, 1983), 132–42, at 141.

> The real miracle of Christ's death resides precisely in this: death which in itself can only be experienced as the advent of emptiness, as the impasse of sin, ... and which "in itself" could be suffered, even by Christ himself, only as such a state of abandonment by God, now, through being embraced by the obedient "yes" of the Son, and while losing nothing of the horror of the divine abandonment that belongs to it, is transformed into something completely different, into the advent of God in the midst of that empty loneliness.[50]

Finally, this "finds its fulfillment and becomes historically perceptible only through the resurrection."[51]

Hans Urs von Balthasar: God and Man in the Trinitarian Light of Christ's *Pascha*

The encyclopedic work of Hans Urs von Balthasar (1905–88)[52] is more original (at first glance, at least) and harmonized with trinitarian thought. It unfolds by focusing on Jesus Christ's Paschal event for access to the understanding of *Deus Trinitas*. He develops that Christocentric and trinitarian intuition that is expressed in a kind of synthesis in his *Mysterium Paschale* and in the fifteen volumes that comprise *The Glory of the Lord*, *Theo-drama*, and *Theo-logic*, displaying an incredible knowledge of the entire Christian intellectual tradition and of the gamut of Western culture in general. It is a contribution to the collective renovation of Catholic dogmatics from the perspective of salvation history as developed in *Mysterium Salutis*.

The original inspiration and the central intentionality Although it is not easy, we can find von Balthasar's central trinitarian inspiration expressed in a few words in some way in these affirmations that move from the mystery of the *kénosis* in the incarnation of the Word and his death on the cross to interpret from this point the Christian image of God, and in him, of man:

50. Rahner, *On the Theology of Death*, 2nd ed. (New York: Herder and Herder, 1967), 70.

51. Karl Rahner and Wilhelm Thsing, *Christologie Systematisch und exegetisch* (Freiburg i.B.: Herder, 1972); translated into Italian as *Cristologia: Prospettiva sistematica ed esegetica* (Brescia: Morcelliana, 1974), 56 (own trans.).

52. From the vast work on his theology, I will limit myself to indicating Georges de Schrijver, *Le merveilleux accord de l'homme et de Dieu: Étude de l'analogie de l'être chez Hans Urs von Balthasar* (Leuven: Leuven University Press, 1983); Vincent Holzer, *Le Dieu Trinité dans l'histoire: Le différend théologique Balthasar – Rahner* (Paris: Cerf, 1995); Jörge Disse, *Metaphysik der Singularität: Eine Hinführung am Leitfaden der Philosophie H.U. von Balthasars* (Vienna: Passagen Verlag, 1996); Rudolf Zwank, *Geschlechteranthroplogie in theologischer Perspektive? Zur Phänomenologie des Geschlechtlichen in Hans Urs von Balthasars 'Theodramatik'* (Frankfurt a.M.: Lang, 1996); Mario Imperatori, *H.U. von Balthasar: una teologia drammatica della storia: Per un discernimento dialogico della modernità* (Milan: Glossa, 2001); Neri, *La testimonianza in H.U. von Balthasar: Evento originario di Dio e mediazione storica della fede*; Ide Pascal, *Pour une théo-logique du don: Le don dans la "trilogie" de Hans Urs von Balthasar* (Paris: Institut Catholique de Paris, 2009).

What is at stake, at least in a perspective of depth, is an altogether decisive turnabout in the way of seeing God. God is not, in the first place, "absolute power," but "absolute love," and his sovereignty manifests itself not in holding on to what is its own but in its abandonment.... The exteriorization of God (in the Incarnation) has its ontic condition of possibility in the eternal exteriorization of God—that is, in his tripersonal self-gift. With that departure point, the created person, too, should no longer be described chiefly as subsisting in itself, but more profoundly (supposing that person to be actually created in God's image and likeness) as a returning (*reflexio completa*) from exteriority to oneself and an "emergence from oneself as an interiority that gives itself in self-expression." The concepts of "poverty" and "riches" became dialectical. This does not mean, however, that God's essence becomes itself (univocally) "kenotic," such that a single concept could include both the divine foundation of the possibility of kenosis, and the kenosis itself. It is from here that many of the mistakes of the more modern kenoticists take their rise. What it *does* mean ... is that the divine "power" is so ordered that it can make room for a possible self-exteriorization, like that found in the Incarnation and the Cross, and can maintain this exteriorization even to the utmost point. As between the form of God and the form of a servant there reigns, in the identity of the Person involved, an analogy of natures—according to the principle maior dissimilitudo in tanta similitudine (DS 806).[53]

I will restrict myself here to delineating the intention and form of von Balthasar's theological project in a quick synthesis in the light of the event of the triune God, as we will avowedly be occupied with his model to illuminate the rapport between unity and trinity in God in part 5 of this book. Aside from his criticism of Rahner's model,[54] it is beyond doubt in fact that he shared Rahner's commitment to overturn the Neoscholastic perspective, rejecting that isolation of theology from human knowledge as the inevitable outcome of a theology that draws the categories of its conversation from a conception of divine absoluteness; for this reason it appears to be disconnected from humanity's historically determined vicissitudes.

The trinitarian "form" of Christological revelation As von Balthasar systematically expresses himself in his book *Love Alone Is Credible*, God's revelation cannot undergo any "cosmological" or "anthropological reduction" in truth. It cannot stay trapped within any kind of *a priori* that prejudices the free and unpredictable nature of God's freedom and man's,

53. Von Balthasar, *Mysterium Paschale: The Mystery of Easter*, 28–29. The original inspiration expressed in this passage owes much—as is well known—to Adrienne von Speyr's (1902–67) mystical intuition of the Christian faith: von Balthasar and von Speyr always saw their works as two inseparable dimensions of the same ecclesial mission.

54. Von Balthasar, *The Moment of Christian Witness*, trans. Richard Beckley (San Francisco, Calif.: Ignatius Press, 1994).

in other words.[55] The evidence and the intelligibility of the form (*Gestalt*) of revelation cannot be sought outside of the concrete happening of the Christological event. That total dependency on the other-than-self is fulfilled in fact only in the relationship between Christ's freedom and his historical rendering of himself in obedience to the Father's design. This relationship represents the unique condition by which it is possible to comprehend the Christological event in its dimension as a manifestation (*Erscheinung*) of the trinitarian foundation.[56] This represents the only way to affirm the truth that God's transcendence is not foreign with respect to human history according to von Balthasar. It is likewise the only way to theologically renew classical ontology. Coming to the recognition that it has to be for-an-other, the free dynamism of human consciousness requires an unimaginable event which effectively demonstrates that this has been possible. This occurs in the Christological event, in which Christ's identity is shown to be in the form of complete dedication to fulfillment of the Father's will. With his freedom being in perfect correspondence with the Father (which is the coincidence of his being-in-himself and his being-for-the-other) in this way, the act is accomplished in which the foundation's self-showing, self-giving, and self-expressing take place in unity. On these bases, von Balthasar can construct his theology articulating an aesthetic (*pulchrum*) moment of God's manifestation in history together with the dramatic (*bonum*) moment of the action in the encounter and clash between God's freedom and human freedom, together with the ontological (*verum*) moment exhibiting God's truth and the world. The three sections of his monumental *Trilogy* correspond to the three transcendentals in this way, where the intention is to show that the theo-Christological revelation alone guarantees the unity in act of the transcendentals of being.

This unity therefore takes the form of the action (drama) of the redemption, where what makes it possible to bestow unity on the respectively aesthetic, ethical, and ontological moment is the dialogical profile of revelation itself, namely the graceful inclusion of anthropological freedom in the same event of revelation. Von Balthasar's undertaking in the *Trilogy* can be conducted back in this way to the problem of anthropological correspondence (*Entsprechung*) to Christological revelation. Apparently this can only be taught starting from a connotation of God's self-manifesting form in a dramatic key, as this alone calls human freedom into question primarily.

55. Von Balthasar, *Love Alone Is Credible*, trans. D. C. Schindler (San Francisco, Calif.: Ignatius Press, 2004).

56. Von Balthasar, *Epilogue*, trans. Edward T. Oakes (San Francisco, Calif.: Ignatius Press, 2004).

Admirabile commercium *and* analogia libertas So von Balthasar's project seems objectively centered on the mutual articulation of the ontological question of the unity of the transcendentals and the correspondence between God and man in revelation. The work unfolds materially, culminating in the soteriological doctrine of vicarious substitution (*Stellvertretung*), because the fact that the definitive divine appearance (*Erscheinung*) coincides with the perfect human correspondence to God in the dramatic action of the cross is what is energetically put into evidence in that context. The central category that von Balthasar uses to express this conviction is *admirabile commercium*—that mysterious "exchange of roles" where the manifestation of God's glory in the disfigured face of the crucified one conforms the human person to the divine will, not only because humanity directly shares in the redemption carried out by God in Christ's freedom in virtue of the hypostatic union, but above all because a freedom finalized in the form of Christ and therefore correspondent is given to human beings on the cross through the Spirit. In this way, the theme of *admirabile commercium* present in the *Theo-Drama* is the arrival point in which the most mature clarification of the category of correspondence converges. This correspondence is understood as the code explaining the Balthasarian route to revisit the problems with *analogia entis*.[57]

After having rejected the idealist and Barthian notions of the God/human relationship, accused of anthropocentrism and theomonism respectively, Balthasar reaches the point of clarifying the problems with the *analogia entis* in terms of an *analogia libertatis*, thanks to the recovery of patristic and Scholastic thought in the light of the revival offered by Erich Przywara (1889–1972) in particular. This *analogia libertatis* reconfigures the relationship of correspondence between the theological and anthropological in terms of liberty. In *Theo-Drama*, it flows from within the soteriological perspective of the *admirabile commercium* where the sovereign beauty of God's glory is made manifest in the event of Christ's total abandonment to the Father's will. It follows as a consequence that the form of beauty revealed in Christ "cannot be appreciated beginning with the norms of aesthetic philosophy alone.... The expressive form of beauty manifested here in Glory, is completely subordinated to the dramatic action of a crucified love which goes all the way down to the most dissimilar region of dereliction and death in a way that is beyond our comprehension."[58] The form of this "previously unimaginable" divine action is the trinitarian-Eucharistic one, because Christ experienced unity with the Father at the same time as the moment of darkness when he felt

57. De Schrijver, *Le merveilleux accord de l'homme et de Dieu*, 282–96.
58. Ibid., 255–56 (own trans.).

furthest from God. This was realistically anticipated in the Passover meal where the most sinful negation of God which he willingly assumed becomes thanksgiving, namely a moment of eternal love between the Father and the Son in the Holy Spirit: "Thus God the Father, in the Holy Spirit, creates the Son's Eucharist. Only the Eucharist really completes the Incarnation.... In the Eucharist of his surrendered Son, God concludes his new and eternal covenant with mankind, committing himself to it utterly and with no reservation."[59]

Aspects of the intramundane drama which absolutely could not be understood to belong to God's life, namely sin, was transfigured in the Eucharist through Christ's filial obedience, and given back in a form corresponding to the Trinity's original and free relationship of love. Von Balthasar grounds each aspect of the world drama within the theological *a priori* of intra-trinitarian freedom because it is a category that refers to a practical form in which what precisely cannot belong to God paradoxically becomes an expression (*Ausdruck*) and representation (*Darstellung*) of the self-manifestation of divine love. The divine manifestation includes in itself the form of human correspondence to God's self-manifesting action because in Christ's action of freedom everything that belongs intrinsically to finite freedom, even sin, is gratuitously assumed as an expression of the original trinitarian love.

Gift and/or reciprocity? It is no little thing, but if a remark is needed concerning von Balthasar's project it lies in the central question of "reciprocity" or better yet, "trinitization" as a dynamic belonging precisely to God's being, to say it in a more suggestive than exhaustive word. According to John's first Letter, this is *agápe* (see 1 Jn 4:8, 16). Rather simplifying things, but only to make the observation more clear and provocative, the interpretation of love as gift freely offered to freedom risks ending up prisoner to a monadic reading in reality in von Balthasar in spite of his clamorous intentions. In other words, it is a reading focused on "each one" (both in God and in man), about whom the rhythm and the strain for reception, self-possession, and donation are brought out, but it ends up not being centered enough on the reciprocity and the trinitarian co-originality of the Father, of the Son (and of the sons and daughters in him), and of the Holy Spirit as love.

The challenge that certain critics have made to von Balthasar's trinitarian project, perhaps a bit excessively, is that God's unity is presented as a simple unification, therefore suggesting the primacy of multiplicity over

59. Hans Urs von Balthasar, *Theo-Drama: Theological Dramatic Theory*, vol. 4: *The Action*, trans. Graham Harrison (San Francisco, Calif.: Ignatius Press, 1994), 348–49.

oneness ultimately. This indicates a real difficulty. It is the fact that the Balthasarian interpretation of love as free dedication, as the gift of oneself (received, possessed, and offered) is undoubtedly an expression of *agápe*, but it is not the "whole" thing, which is to love, to be loved, and to be one in love in reciprocal freedom and inexhaustible openness. It is what Augustine intuited deep down and as I previously remarked, what Antonio Rosmini is best able to express, engrafting his study on the reliable and indispensable trunk of Thomas Aquinas's work.

The Second Vatican Council: *Ecclesia de Trinitate*

The rereading of God's trinitarian being, starting with salvation history and culminating in the Paschal event marks the theological work of Rahner and von Balthasar, though with different emphases. It also characterizes the best contemporary reinterpretations of *De Trinitate*—that by W. Kasper in Germany and that by B. Forte in Italy. In tune with this prevailing direction, Catholic theology has been characterized by a renewed ecclesiological and anthropological reflection in the light of the trinitarian mystery in the twofold sense of an understanding of the church and of humanity starting from the Trinity and, vice versa, a penetration of God's mystery starting from ecclesial and personological experience.

Ecclesia de Trinitate is a determining perspective in fact for *Lumen Gentium*. In its origin, in its form of life and in its aim, the church is seen as "a people made one with the unity of the Father, the Son and the Holy Spirit" (no. 4, using St. Cyprian's expression). This has been implemented historically by the church as a limpid Christological-trinitarian understanding of revelation in *Dei Verbum*. The church is understood in this context as a sacrament of union with God and of the unity of all humankind (see no. 1) in Christ. On the other hand, while the anthropological vision outlined in *Gaudium et Spes* is decisively Christological in that it pivots on Jesus Christ as the new Adam who "by the revelation of the mystery of the Father and His love, fully reveals man to man himself and makes his supreme calling clear" (no. 22), it is also just as decisively determined and disclosed in a trinitarian horizon:

> Indeed, the Lord Jesus, when He prayed to the Father, "that all may be one ... as we are one" (Jn 17:21–22) opened up vistas closed to human reason, for He implied a certain likeness between the union of the divine Persons, and the unity of God's sons in truth and charity. This likeness reveals that man, who is the only creature on earth which God willed for itself, cannot fully find himself except through a sincere gift of himself (see Lk 17:33).[60]

60. *GS*, no. 24. I take the liberty to refer to two contributions I offered on this topic: "L'uomo nel mistero di Cristo e della Trinità: L'antropologia della 'Gaudium et spes,'" in *Lateranum* 54,

It becomes evident with a careful reading that these themes are significant and fecund, allowing authors like H. Mühlen to reflect on the existential and operative meaning of the trinitarian mystery from a pneumatological perspective considering that "we can 'know' (and donate) the mystery of the Trinity only in the measure that we in our turn try to implement the divine self-donation manifested upon the cross."[61] Theologians like J. Ratzinger[62] are also enabled to bring out a central category and an original modality for living the Christian faith in the structure of the "pro" (being-for, relationship). In the trinitarian concept of God in fact, Ratzinger writes:

> Therein lies concealed a revolution in man's view of the world: the sole dominion of thinking in terms of substance is ended; relation is discovered as an equally valid primordial mode of reality. It becomes possible to surmount what we call today "objectifying thought"; a new plane of being comes into view. It is probably true to say that the task imposed on philosophy as a result of these facts is far from being completed—so much does modern thought depend on the possibilities thus disclosed, without which it would be inconceivable.[63]

Orthodox Theology: Trinitarian Logic, *kénosis*, and Sophiology

Orthodox theology has participated in the renewal of contemporary trinitarian theology as well, in an original way. In fact, it did not conclude its contribution with the Byzantine era (where we last encountered it) but has continued its life, not without difficulty. It found a fertile spiritual and cultural soil especially in Russian lands, as Sergius of Radonezh and Seraphim of Sarov testified. Russian thought has flourished in an exceptional way after a long maturation process during the course of the nineteenth and early twentieth century. Then it made its way to the St. Sergius Institute in France after the October Revolution. It has grown hand-in-hand in a certain way with the appearance of a current in Greece and the United States which has been more faithful to the patristic and Byzantine legacy.

---

no. 1 (1988): 164–94; and "Antropologia teologica e agire umano nel mondo nella 'Gaudium et Spes,'" in *Lateranum* 55, no. 1 (1989): 176 207.

61. "Esperienza sociale dello Spirito come risposta a una teologia unilaterale," in *La Riscoperta dello Spirito Santo*, ed. Claus Heitmann and Heribert Mühlen (Milan: Jaca Book, 1977), 287–308 (own trans. from the Italian).

62. See among his works, *Introduction to Christianity*, trans. J. R. Foster (San Francisco, Calif.: Ignatius Press, 2004); *Principles of Catholic Theology: Building Stones for a Fundamental Theology* (San Francisco, Calif.: Ignatius Press, 1989); *The Nature and Mission of Theology: Approaches to Understanding Its Role in the Light of Present Controversy* (San Francisco, Calif.: Ignatius Press, 1995).

63. Ratzinger, *Introduction to Christianity*, 184.

Without wanting to undervalue the contributions of other great but more traditional twentieth-century Orthodox theologians such as V. Lossky, P. Evdokimov, and D. Staniloae, for example, the most original work is certainly that of Sergius Bulgakov (1871–1944). It was so original that it drew opposition because the innovation was within the heart of Orthodoxy itself. It was not by chance that Bulgakov was defined as "the most important monument of Orthodox theology after the fall of Byzantium" (C. Andronikov). This mighty work would not have been possible however without the contribution of two other brilliant Russian thinkers: V. Soloviev and P. Florensky.

The Sophiology of Vladimir Soloviev

Vladimir Soloviev's (1853–1900)[64] launching from the intuition of a refoundation of Christianity based on wisdom[65] capable of integrating the positive results of philosophy and modern science, while transcending their limits and neutralizing their errors in the light of the great tradition of the church of the East, is particularly striking in his polyphonic work. Soloviev's approach reaches beyond the separation between philosophy and theology for this reason. He proposes an "integral knowledge" that is expressed fundamentally in a free "theosophy" in which revelation and reason are transfigured into a sort of mystical intuition of God's trinitarian pleroma which is revealed and realized within the universal history of humanity, thanks to the theandric event of Christ.

With some naivety in fact, Soloviev makes wide use of the epistemic and conceptual tools put at his disposal by German Idealism, especially Schelling's. Nor does he worry about drawing from esoteric and kabbalistic sources. But everything is put at the service of rediscovering and shaping the authentic "form" of thinking and living in Christ. This is demonstrated by the sure ecclesial and ecumenical inspiration that increasingly comes to characterize his reflection and his action. Even more, it characterizes the apocalyptic reserve that becomes decisive for the authentically Christian interpretation of the meaning and destiny of history toward the end of his life.

64. Among his works, of interest to my study are: *La crisi della filosofia occidentale* (1874); *I principi filosofici del sapere integrale* (1877); *Lectures on Divine Humanity* (1877–81), ed. Boris Jakim (Hudson, N.Y.: Lindisfarne, 1995); *La critica dei principi astratti* (1877–80); *La Russia e la Chiesa universale* (1888); *Tre dialoghi* (1900). On his thought, see M. George, *Mystische und Religiöse Erfahrung bei V. Solov'ëv* (Göttingen: Vandenhoeck and Ruprecht, 1988); Nynfa Bosco, *Vladimir: Ripensare il cristianesimo* (Turin: Rosenberg and Sellier, 1999); see also H. U. von Balthasar, "Soloviev," in his *The Glory of the Lord: A Theological Aesthetics*, vol. 3: *Studies in Theological Style: Lay Styles*, trans. Andrew Louth, John Saward, Martin Simon, and Rowan Williams, ed. John Riches (San Francisco, Calif.: Ignatius Press, 1986), 279–352.

65. He first used the term "sophiology" to characterize this actual true *Weltanschaauung* that then impacted the theology of thinkers from the "silver age."

The Trinitarian Ontology of Pavel Florensky

Soloviev's work could not go unnoticed in Russia at the end of the century. It became the reference point for that young intelligentsia which had been attracted by positivism and Marxism earlier. This group was rediscovering the way toward the heritage of the Orthodox faith. Pavel Florensky (1882–1943)[66] is undoubtedly the most acute and original thinker among them all in this unusual period of renewal. It was not by mistake that he was described as "a Russian Leonardo De Vinci" as a result of his encyclopedic interests and studies.

The trinitarian law of truth Following Soloviev's path, Florensky recovers the lessons of German Idealism by going on to discover its Platonic roots. And what is even more decisive, he wants to refurbish the light and the strength themselves emanating from the truth of Christ, the Word incarnate, through the testimony of the divine liturgy and the Church Fathers. Within the framework of the Christological *homooúsia*, he strives to overcome in this way the split tormenting the modern consciousness between subject and object, intelligible and empirical, transcendent and immanent.

Quite cognizant of the limits and the dangers connected with Soloviev's theosophy, Florensky conceives in his masterpiece, *The Pillar and Ground of the Truth*, the ambitious project of gathering from within the trinitarian revelation manifested by Christ, the divine-human logic of the knowledge of truth which alone is capable of overcoming the disastrous errors of Hegel's totalitarian dialectic and the obtuse materialism of scientistic ideology. He understands in this way in an extraordinarily intense and lucid manner the need to conceive the rule for theological knowledge in correspondence with the central event of revelation which is the unfolding of the mystery of the Trinity in history.

His intuition begins with the question about the trinitarian being of the subject of the truth: "Truth is the contemplation of Oneself through Another in a Third: Father, Son, and Spirit.... The Subject of the Truth is a relationship of the Three, but this is a relationship that is a substance, a relationship-substance.... the *ousía* of the Truth is the Infinite act of

66. Among his writings that have been translated: *The Pillar and Ground of the Truth*, trans. Boris Jakim (Princeton, N.J.: Princeton University Press, 1997); *Iconostasis*, trans. Olga Andrejev and Donald Sheehan (Crestwood, N.Y.: St. Vladimir's Seminary Press, 1996); *Beyond Vision: Essays on the Perception of Art*, ed. Nicoletta Misler and trans. Wendy R. Salmond (London: Reaktion Books, 2002); *Early Religious Writings, 1903–1909*, trans. Boris Jakim (Grand Rapids, Mich.: Eerdmans, 2017). On his writings, see Natalino Valentini, *La sapienza dell'amore: Teologia della bellezza e linguaggio della verità* (Bologna: EDB, 1997); Lubomir Žak, *Verità come ethos* (Rome: Città Nuova, 1998).

Three in Unity."[67] From this it is possible to found a new formulation of the law of identity using an ontological key: "Instead of an empty, dead, formal self-identity A=A, in virtue of which A should selfishly, self-assertively, egotistically exclude every not-A, we get a real self-identity of A, full of content and life, a self-identity that eternally rejects itself and that eternally receives itself in its self-rejection."[68] We are dealing with an intuition that becomes intensely luminous within an anthropological perspective even if it was little developed by Florensky in reference to God the Trinity. This is the case not only where he portrays the dynamism of the reciprocal donation-*kénosis* as constitutive of the rapport among created persons, recovering the Hegelian concept of negative in a manner that respects trinitarian revelation (nonbeing understood as a condition of the possibility of the immanent trinitarian structure of being); but also and above all where such dynamism is described as participation in the event itself of trinitarian love. This is conveyed in the following masterful passage:

> The love of the lover, by transforming his I into the I of the beloved, into Thou, gives to the beloved Thou the power to know the I of the lover in God and to love this I in God. The beloved then becomes the lover and rises above the law of identity. And in God the beloved identifies himself with the object of his love. He transfers his I into the first I through a third I, and so on.... Rising above the bounds of its nature, I goes out of temporal-spatial limitedness and enters into Eternity. There the whole process of the interrelation of the lovers is a single act, in which an infinite series of individual moments of love is synthesized. This single, eternal, and infinite act is the consubstantiality of the lovers in God, where I is one and the same as the other I, but also different.[69]

The need for a Christological reinterpretation of Platonism A question regarding Florensky's thought is still open however. It concerns the congruency and virtuality of Platonic thought as it relates to the expression of Christian revelation's newness and originality. According to the incisive and striking Johannine description, "And the Word became flesh" (Jn 1:14), the fact is that the Christological event and its ontological impact in the understanding of created being are formidable. This understanding of created being is impacted both in its constitutive relationship to God and in its intrinsic trinitarian "rhythm" in God's image and likeness and through participation by grace in God, one and three. God's "weight" and "light" (*kabòd* in Hebrew, *dòxa* in Greek, *claritas* in Latin) are communicated from heaven to earth in the Word incarnate and

67. Florensky, *The Pillar and Ground of the Truth*, 37.
68. Ibid., 36.
69. Ibid., 68.

through the gift of the Holy Spirit. The "two worlds," to use Florensky's words, certainly remain, but they are also hypostatically united while staying distinct in the Word incarnate; they are also united by means of him through the Holy Spirit in those who become "Eîs en Christō" (one in Christ, see Gal 3:28).

Florensky is obviously aware of all this. From the perspective of the Christological *homoousías*, his primary intent is precisely to overcome the "Kantian" dualism that torments modern awareness of reality. I wonder however if the Platonic system that he so enthusiastically embraces without reservation from his youth is enough to express and indeed is fully reconcilable with the *novum* represented by the event of the incarnation, as Florensky seems to think? Is it still possible to speak of "two worlds" in that way, precisely in a Platonic way? And is it still necessary to pick out a "boundary" between them?

For example, it is not by chance that Florensky precisely identifies the "boundary" of the "two worlds" in the notion of "Sophia," which he inherited from Soloviev and thought back to its origin. He links this asserted identification to the traditional doctrine of "the divine ideas" clearly coming from Plato. It is a concept that has undoubtedly been forgotten by modernity, even in theology, but which played a central role instead in the thought of the Church Fathers and Scholastics. It can and perhaps must be reconsidered but in a radically new form therefore, as A. Rosmini and S. Bulgakov for example attempted to do, but not by simply following a Platonic approach; rather they used a more radically Christological and trinitarian one.

Florensky's proposed trinitarian logic—his effort to articulate a connection between theodicy, or the human ascent to God or the metaphysics of trinitarian love, and anthropodicy, or God's descent to man or the concrete metaphysics of action—as with his subsequent outline of a symbolic epistemology, each represent a luminous and prophetic attempt in each case to reaffirm the dignity and fecundity of the knowledge of faith and the truth of the Trinity. It is his principal objective, beyond the crisis of modernity.

The Innovative Systematic Proposal of Sergius Bulgakov

Along with the Eastern theological tradition and an excellent knowledge of modern thought, the three principal and typically Russian sources inspiring Bulgakov's theology[70] are enumerated as follows: (1) A. Chomja-

70. Among his works translated into English: *Unfading Light: Contemplations and Speculations*, trans. Thomas Allan Smith (Grand Rapids, Mich.: Eerdmans, 2012); *The Lamb of God*, trans. Boris Jakim (Grand Rapids, Mich.: Eerdmans, 2008); *The Comforter*, trans. Boris Jakim

kov's trinitarian doctrine inspired by ecclesiology and N. Fedorov's trinitarian doctrine inspired by social anthropology (with his famous "the Trinity is our social program"); (2) Metropolitan Filarete of Moscow's kenotic inspiration and A. Bucharev (who emphasizes the centrality of the biblical theme of the Lamb "sacrificed before the founding of the world"); and finally, (3) V. Soloviev's sophiological perspective and P. Florensky's ontological intuitions.

An intersubjective perspective derived from revelation The essay "Chapters on Trinity"[71] together with the shorter article "Hypostasis and Hypostatizedness"[72] represent a pivotal moment in which the former philosophical-religious intuitions marking Bulgakov's getting over his earlier flirtation with Marxism are rigorously brought back to the Slavic-Orthodox tradition. The pair of words, spirit/love, is central in this text; they are key concepts to express the being of the one-triune God and the lens through which to read the dynamic of the trinitarian *perichoresis*. Bulgakov indicates the need to leave behind any form of intra-trinitarian causality to recover the deepest substance of the dogma, where the one-triune are antinomically thought together, describing an absolute which is not dead egoism but a vital and an original relation of love within Itself. This is antithetical to the Western tradition, which has the concept of procession as its starting point to think of the Persons' relationship.

In fact, the starting point of this study is a close comparison with the modern concept of the "I," which Bulgakov ingeniously opens out beyond the straits of atomistic solipsism into its concrete correlation with the you and with the he/she in the living communion of the we. Already being "a living miracle that hovers above the abyss, wings of the soul, touch of the Spirit, seal of the Divine," in itself, such a correlation finds its unshakeable base only in the revelation of the holy, consubstantial Trinity. In this way, trinitarian doctrine is decisively freed from any materialistic presupposition. It is illuminated within an intersubjective perspective that is drawn from revelation to interpret the constitution of the human I. It is not applied to God beginning from the anthropological experience. The dis-

(Grand Rapids, Mich.: Eerdmans, 2004); *The Bride of the Lamb*, trans. Boris Jakim (Grand Rapids, Mich.: Eerdmans, 2002). On his theological thought, see Leon Alexander Zander, *Bog i mir* (Paris: YMCA Press, 1948); Piero Coda, *Sergej Bulgakov* (Brescia: Morcelliana, 2003) and *L'altro di Dio: Rivelazione e kenosi in Sergej Bulgakov* (Rome: Città Nuova, 1998); Graziano Lingua, *Kénosis di Dio e santità della materia: La sofiologia di S. N. Bulgakov* (Naples: ESI, 2000); Arvydas Ramonas, *L'attesa del Regno: Eschaton e apocalisse in Sergei Bulgakov* (Rome: PUL-Mursia, 2001).

71. *Glavy o troichnosti*, in *Trudy Pravoslavnogo Bogoslovskogo Instituta v Parizhe* 1.2; trans. Graziano Lingua as *Capitoli sulla trinitarietà*, in Coda, *Sergej Bulgakov*, 67–171.

72. "Ipostas'i ipostasnost,'" in *Sbornik statej, posvajaš enniych Petru Berngardovi u Struve, Collection in Honor of P. B. Struve* (Prague, 1925); trans. A. B. Gallaher and I. Kutkova in *St. Vladimir's Theological Quarterly*, 49, no. 1–2 (2005): 5–46.

cussion develops from this point into a derivation of an ontology of love, as Bulgakov defines it, together with an ontology of freedom, freeing the understanding of God from any bond of necessity. This anticipates lines of thought that will only come to the light many years later and in other philosophical and theological contexts.[73]

The originality and unity of a great theological project Together with the great influx of ideas that accumulated while he gradually approached the faith, these intuitions bear witness to a lively contact not only with scripture but also with the patristic tradition, Eastern and Western,[74] with Scholasticism and Catholic theology in general, as well as with the best Protestant writings at the turn of the twentieth century. His own teaching demand and participation in numerous theological and ecumenical encounters[75] moreover, favored the study of Orthodoxy and a simultaneously sympathetic and critical comparison of the other Christian traditions. Even if Bulgakov would always be unique, he approached the historical-critical method in exegesis and in the analysis of the development of dogma, but with great freedom. He turned to the Church Fathers, but without that enthusiasm for archaicism characterizing other authors. He accepted church dogma not as some untouchable endpoint, but rather as a creative point of departure. He remained faithful to his original experiences and the illuminating intuitions of his youth above all because of an intimate spiritual consistency before the intellectual dimension. As P. C. Bori has noted, it was precisely these experiences and intuitions in fact that "constituted the most intimately creative and dynamic nucleus of Bulgakov's personality, unforeseeably determining its inventiveness and reactivity in front of the present."[76] All of this explains the simultaneous vastness and interior unity of his theological reflection on one hand; on the other hand, it explains the misunderstanding that he would meet in the world of Russian Orthodoxy itself, especially on account of the difficulties of recognizing the continuity of his thought and more daring intuitions with the earlier tradition.

73. This calls to mind the already mentioned Klaus Hemmerle and his *Theses of Trinitarian Ontology*.

74. In 1932, Bulgakov wrote a volume on *The Orthodox Church*, a kind of catechetical exposition of the Orthodox church's teaching, intentionally distinct from his more personal theological interpretations (Crestwood, N.Y.: St. Vladimir's Seminary Press, 1988).

75. In 1927 he attended the first congress of the World Council of Churches at Lausanne, "Faith and Constitution," and in 1937, he attended the second in London, "Life and Action." He offered his contribution to the Orthodox-Anglican fellowship encounters, besides the informal reunions among Orthodox, Catholics, and Evangelicals organized by Berdyaev. Bulgakov and Florovsky were among the first to participate. Jacques Maritain, G. Marcel, L. Laberthonnire, and E. Gilson were among the second, while M. Boegner and W. Monod were among the last.

76. Pier Cesare Bori, "Introduzione," in *Il prezzo del progresso: saggi 1897–1913*, trans. P. C. Bori (Casale Monferrato: Marietti, 1984), lix (own trans.).

The vastness and unity of his theological work would arouse admiration everywhere, to the point of comparisons between Bulgakov and St. Thomas Aquinas on account of the systematicity and universality of his thought.[77] This can be seen in the great trilogy[78] entitled *O Bogotchelovtchestve* in Russian and *La Sagesse divine et la Théanthropie* in French, a title approved by him because it further specifies the design of the overall project, substantially concluding ten years of work (the 1930s): *Agnets Bozhyi (L'Agneau de Dieu)* which develops the Christology, *Uteshitel' (Le Paraclet)*,[79] which delineates the pneumatology and the trinitarian doctrine, and *Nevesta Agntsa (L'Epouse de l'Agneau)*.[80] This last publication's subtitle is translated into English as *Creation, Man, the Church and its Fulfillment*. As the inspiring core and the keystone to this vast and articulate triptych is the doctrine of Sophia, Bulgakov would recognize the need to publish a "summary of sophiology," first appearing in English under the title *The Wisdom of God*.[81]

Divine Sophia and created Sophia The fact is that each of the three divine Persons in the life of the Trinity hypostasizes the divine nature in Bulgakov's vision, but each in a different way. This means that each divine Person realizes the divine nature in a distinctive way; God is the one and only divine subject that actualizes in Godself (his *ousía*) in three distinct correlative modes of subsistence. This is the main point of Bulgakov's reflection: the divine *ousía* is precisely Sophia, God's wisdom-glory, to the extent that it is actualized in the hypostasis of the Son and the Holy Spirit. One cannot properly speak of Sophia with regard to the Father, because in him "the divine Sophia dwells primordially as *ousía*, as the hidden depth of his nature."[82] It is the Son and the Spirit instead that hypostatically reveal the divine *ousía*; therefore they hypostasize it to the extent that it is Sophia, that is, *ousía* revealed. The Son, or *Lógos*, hypostasizes Sophia as the organic and multiple unity of divine thought, God's *plérōma*,

77. His style is quite different from that of Soloviev and Florensky, the two Russians inspiring him. His is more imaginative and impressionistic, so as to even appear esoteric at times.

78. There are actually two trilogies, a greater and a lesser. The greater is composed of *The Lamb of God* (1933) on Christology, *The Comforter* (1936) on the Holy Spirit, and *The Bride of the Lamb* (published posthumously, 1945) on ecclesiology and eschatology. The lesser is composed of *The Burning Bush* (1927) on Mary, *The Friend of the Bridegroom* (1927) on John the Baptist, and *Jacob's Ladder* (1929) on angels.

79. Aubier translated the Russian text (reaching completion in 1934 and publication in 1936) into French in 1945; the English translation appeared in 2004 (Eerdmans).

80. Russian text (completed in 1938) was published by YMCA Press in Paris in 1945; the French translation at l'Age d'Homme in Paris in 1945; the English translation appeared in 2004 (Eerdmans).

81. New York and London, 1937; the French translation, already mentioned, was based on the original unpublished Russian text.

82. *La Sagesse de Dieu*, 29 (own trans.).

the uni-totality of the revelation of God's nature that remains hidden in the Father instead as an infinite wellspring, while the Holy Spirit reveals *ousía* as "glory," because the Spirit vivifies the Son's revelation, clothing it in beauty.

In this vision, Sophia is nothing other than God's nature as revealed in the Son and in the Spirit on an intra-trinitarian level as *polypoíkilos sophía toû Theoû*, a multiformed wisdom of God (see Eph 3:10), irradiation of God's glory, infinite fullness of his being which is revealed originally and eternally in the intra-trinitarian life.[83] Because God is love, it happens in creation that God freely decides to not hold on to what is most distinctively his, namely, his same self-revelation (the divine Sophia). Therefore he gives it an existence in itself (created Sophia), so that it can give itself to God in turn in a free act of love.[84] In this sense, creation is the not-God, brought into being by God as God's other, as a free projection of Godself "outside" of Godself so that it would become God (by participation), returning to him, but remaining distinct from God.

A kenotic-perichoretic interpretation of the formula "God is love" In this light, Bulgakov offers a very original *kenotic-perichoretic* interpretation of the Johannine formula "God is Love." In fact, it "means not only that love is proper to God, for He is loving, but that He Himself is love, that love is His very being. Here we have a definition that is not descriptive but ontological in character."[85] This is the starting point to penetrate the mystery of the Trinity. Precisely what is love in fact? Here is the definition Bulgakov offers by way of two "axioms": (1) "there is no love without sacrifice"; (2) "there is no love without joy and bliss; and in general there is no bliss other than love." Of the two the second is "supreme, because final," as the result of the first. "Being tragic, love is also the overcoming of tragedy;

83. Bulgakov multiplies the metaphors (almost all of them common to the great Christian tradition: Western and Eastern, patristic and Scholastic) to express this intra-trinitarian conception of Sophia. So it is "the *fullness* of the absolute white light that cannot be decomposed into lines of the color spectrum but that contains them (the kataphatic element)" (*The Lamb of God*, 101); "the All as unity and unity as All, *All-Unity*" (ibid., 102); "the Pleroma, the Divine world, existent in God and for God, eternal and uncreated, in which God lives in the Holy Trinity" (ibid., 103); "the real and fully realized divine Idea ... actualized as Beauty" (ibid., 104); "the 'body of God' in its integrity, as the self-revelation of God and the glory" (*The Bride of the Lamb*, 80). To be noted, as an example, this sounds similar to the concept of *ars divina* typical of St. Bonaventure's theology.

84. According to Bulgakov, creation is "that self-determination by which the hypostatic God, eternally possessing this divine world as His own nature, *releases* it from the depths of hypostatic being into *self-being*, makes it the cosmos in the true sense, *creates* the world 'out of nothing,' that is, out of Himself, out of His own divine content" (*The Bride of the Lamb*, 48). "But 'in creating the world,' in giving it self-being, God does not take away from it the divine force of its being. Rather, he posits the world outside Himself, as it were, releases it from Himself into divinely extra-divine and even non-divine being" (ibid., 50). See Alojz Litva, "La "Sophie" dans la création selon la doctrine de S. Boulgakov," in *Orientalia Christiana Periodica* 16 (1950): 39–74.

85. *The Comforter*, 61.

and the *power* of love consists precisely in this overcoming. Love is a concrete antinomy: sacrifice and the finding of oneself through sacrifice."[86]

God's life is expressed in the rapport of the three divine hypostases, as revealed in the incarnation and death on the cross of the Word made man; this life is traversed therefore by that *kénosis* which is an emptying of self out of love and which is continuously and perfectly overcome by infinite beatitude by its intrinsic logic. One cannot properly speak of God's sacrifice and suffering as a consequence, but of perfect love. By developing the theme of the *kénosis* of love with respect to the single divine hypostases, Bulgakov expresses it in these terms. First, with respect to the Father,

> Fatherhood is precisely the form of love in which the loving one desires to have himself not in himself but outside himself, in order to give his own to this other I, but an I identified with him, in order to manifest his own in spiritual begetting: in the Son, who is the living image of the Father.... This begetting power is the ecstasy of a going out of oneself, of a kind of self-emptying, which at the same time is self-actualization through this begetting.[87]

Second, with respect to the Son: "Sonhood is already *eternal kenosis*.... The Son's love is the sacrificial, self-renouncing humility of the Lamb of God, 'foreordained before the foundation of the world' (1 Pt 1:20)."[88] Finally, the Holy Spirit "is the mutual love of the Father and the Son and the joy of this love; it is the accomplished self-revelation of Divinity in its nature.... He establishes the mutuality of the Father and the Son."[89]

It is certainly new to speak of *kénosis* with respect to the Father. As can be inferred from Bulgakov's overall concept however, this in no way implies any form of patripassianism. What is also new is how he emphasizes the Holy Spirit's *kénosis*, both in the life of the Trinity and in the process of the divinization of created persons:

> The Holy Spirit Himself is hypostatic love. It is not only by Him and in Him that the other hypostases love, but He Himself loves. He Himself is love, comprising the whole path of love: sacrificial self-renunciation, the sacrificialness of love, and its bliss. His sacrificial self-renunciation consists in hypostatic self-annulment: unlike the Father and the Son, He Himself by His hypostasis does not reveal and is not revealed. He is only Their revelation, the Holy Spirit, who "searcheth ... the deep things of God" (1 Cor 2:10).... He is a transparent medium, imperceptible in His transparence. He does not exist *for Himself*, because He is entirely in the others, in the Father and the Son; and His own being is a nonbeing, as it were. But in this sacrificial self-dying is realized the bliss of love, the self-comforting of the Comforter, Self-joy, Self-beauty, Self-loving, the peak of love. Thus, in the

86. Ibid., 66.
87. *The Lamb of God*, 98.
88. Ibid., 99.
89. Ibid., 100.

Love that is the Holy Trinity the Third hypostasis is Love itself, hypostatically actualizing in itself the entire fullness of love.[90]

Because God is Love, if this infinite dynamism of love is realized eternally in him, it happens as anticipated that God freely decides to not possess as his own what is most his own, namely, his same self-revelation, his nature. Therefore God gives creation an autonomous existence (at least relatively) so that in its turn, it can donate what is its own to God himself in a free act of love. Creation is therefore "that self-determination by which the hypostatic God, eternally possessing this divine world [Sophia] as His own nature, *releases* it from the depths of hypostatic being into *self-being*, makes it the cosmos in the true sense, *creates* the world 'out of nothing,' that is, out of Himself, out of His own divine content."[91]

The act of creation is an expression of free and infinite love, therefore, because it is the supreme *kénosis* with which the Trinity, being itself, poses the infinite wealth of its capacity to share, as other than itself. As the Psalms chant, therefore, "the heavens and the earth, all of creation, narrate the Glory of God," not in a metaphorical but in an ontological sense, because creation is the wisdom-glory of God reflected in nonbeing that becomes being by God's free will. Even these rapid comments alone make it evident that we are faced with a powerful and daring synthesis, besides being decisively innovative and original. It is still a synthesis fecund with suggestions and contributions in all the fields of theology illuminated by the centrality of the trinitarian mystery in spite of some lack of moderation and some possible misunderstandings.

Chiara Lubich's Trinitarian Mystical Theology of the "Exterior Castle"

The trinitarian renewal traversing theology finds an intense and original parallel in the twentieth century as well, as I already noted with regard to the modern epoch. Or better, it experiences a providential synergy with spirituality and the mystical life. I shall limit myself to saying something about Chiara Lubich's (1920–2008) mystical theology of unity, not only because it is trinitarian from top to bottom, but also because it better attests to the significant passage in the second half of the century, from the primacy of interiority as the "place" where the Trinity dwells,[92] to the discovery of the interpersonal relationship as a harnessing of an interior

90. *The Comforter*, 67.

91. *The Bride of the Lamb*, 48.

92. Elisabeth of the Trinity, of the Carmelite tradition, who lived at the turn of the twentieth century, is a luminous witness to this life of interior indwelling of the Trinity.

dimension widened to embrace otherness in the experience of reciprocal love lived in Christ. This undoubtedly entails relevant consequences for the trinitarian illumination of ecclesial and social praxis in their different explications. It is useful to enter into the topic in a suitable way however, trying first of all to at least briefly reconstruct the golden thread of the journey that has brought us to this point.

Christian Mysticism and the Trinity: The Golden Thread of a Journey

Christian mysticism is expressed and actualized through the personal experience of the encounter with Jesus Christ, and in and through him, with the Father by virtue of the Holy Spirit. This implies Christ's living and actual presence in history; he reaches each man and woman of every time and place in his definitive reality as risen. This presence is mediated by the Word, the sacrament, and the new humanity that it forms. Christian mysticism is nourished on the Word, the Eucharist, and *agápe* precisely for this reason. For only in this way does the encounter with the risen Christ take place. He introduces persons in turn into the rapport that he lives with the Father, as a gratuitous gift in virtue of the outpouring of his Spirit.

The manifestation of the risen Christ to men and women is at the origin therefore (not only the historical and chronological origin, but also the ontological and existential origin) of Christian mysticism. His "apparitions" as recounted toward the end of the Gospels are the seal of the veracity and the vitality of the event of Jesus Christ and of faith in him. Not only are they a significant and foundational fact constitutive of Christian faith, but they express the paradigm of the new rule for the experience of God the Father. It now becomes possible to realize this experience in the Spirit, once the event of Jesus Christ has occurred in history. Luke's account of the disciples of Emmaus (see Lk 24:13–25), whose hearts were burning within them and whose minds were illuminated as Christ walked in their midst illustrating scripture's meaning and breaking bread with them in the end, illustrates the *locus* in an unequivocal form. It is starting from this *locus* that the experience of God is born and develops in its original Christian profile. This obviously suggests an attentive and determined study, beyond what was contemplated until now, of the foundational accounts of the New Testament through which the disciples and the apostolic community handed down their experience of the encounter with the risen Christ.

It is obvious that the requirements intrinsic to the faith for inculturation, in other words witness and dialogue with respect to other cultural contexts, entailed the opportunity for a further, almost endless study of this extraordinary and unexhausted heritage with the passage of time and the chronological (not ontological) distancing from the original event, together with the danger of some contamination. From the point of view of the experience of God, one could interpret the unfolding Christian journey through the centuries as the progressive conscious emergence and flowering of unforeseen originality that is preserved and offered in the experience of God the Trinity, rendered possible by way of the crucified and risen Christ.

An express understanding and affirmation that the humanity of Jesus the Christ remains essential for progress on the journey was reached only with time, hesitation and fatigue. This was not by chance. One example among others suffices to show that this understanding is more than just pedagogically essential for access to God, as if it were supposed to be "surpassed" at a certain point. Because the event of the incarnation is irreversible as such, so it is that only through the crucifixion and resurrection of the Son incarnate, crucified, risen, and glorified in the Spirit beside the Father that the depths of the Father's abyss have become accessible to man in virtue of the movement of the same Spirit. The clear and explicit testimony to this truth, which in itself is intrinsic to the experience of the Christian faith, constitutes an acquisition which is of maximum importance. Indeed, it is described by Teresa of Avila in her meditation about the mystical experience she had lived.

The originality of Christian mysticism is gradually explicated along another line, however. It can be recovered in some of the fundamental steps of the course that I have offered in these pages. To use a suggestive image taken from the writings of Chiara Lubich, it regards the passage from the mysticism of the "interior castle" to that of the "exterior castle." Let it be clear: this does not mean replacement or removal, but broadening and bringing to perfection, growth, and maturation according to the limpid logic exhibited in itself by the development of the reception and tradition of Christological faith.

It is not difficult in reality to recognize the unwinding of a precious golden thread which connects the experience of God in its deep and mystical reality in the Christian West, through an unfolding which begins with St. Augustine, passes through Teresa of Avila, and reaches our present age. What is this about? One fact stands out among the others; it is worth studying. After having illustrated the *intelligentia* of the *doctrina fidei* concerning the trinitarian face of God, Augustine asks in Book VIII of his *De Trinitate* where it is possible to "touch" this God in our experience with the fine tip of the soul, as I have previously noted. In other words, how is it possible to reach the trinitarian God revealed by Jesus Christ? Augustine turns to the interior dimension of the human spirit, and with an amazing, detailed examination of the depths and rhythm of the graced spirit, he sees the living imprint of the trinitarian *relatio* that distinguishes the Father, Son, and Holy Spirit in their ineffable unity, realizing itself in the dynamic unfolding of memory, intellect, and will.

This teaching is decisive for the history of Christian mysticism. In fact it constitutes the experiential production and intellectual explication of Jesus' words which are also a promise: "Those who love me will keep my word, and my Father will love them, and we will come to them and make our home with them" (Jn 14:23). Edith Stein, St. Teresa Benedicta of the Cross, drew from Teresa of Avila's mystical theology with extraordinary speculative skill in the heart of the twentieth century.[93] Such theology is a mature illustration of this authentically trinitarian mystical journey in which the soul becomes an "interior castle" through grace. The Trinity comes to dwell in this "interior castle," bringing the radical intentionality of its faculties to gratuitous fulfillment.

Before taking this way, however, Augustine intuited another possible approach, affirming in Book VIII of *De Trinitate* again that he had contemplated for a moment the *locus* of the trinitarian vision (*visio Trinitatis*) in reciprocal love, Christ's new commandment—"as I have loved you, you also should love one another" (Jn 13:34)—the place for the most intense experience of communion with God the Trinity while still here on earth. But he confesses with realism that he was not up to undertaking this task because of the intensity of the light assailing his weak eyes. Augustine could not hide his nostalgia and almost his disappointment nevertheless for the failed enterprise in Book XV toward the conclusion of *De Trinitate*.

I think that the times were not yet spiritually and culturally ripe, in fact. It was first necessary for the church to sound the depths of the "interior castle" after the unceasing and always new visits by the Word made flesh and by the Spirit of love. Only after having passed through a type of epochal and collective dark night reflected in the thousand faces of the twentieth century, only in much more recent times, does humanity seem ready to try the beauty and the thirst for that experience of God in our midst that Chiara Lubich defined as the "exterior castle": "as you, Father, are in me and I am in you, may they also be in us" (Jn 17:21). An unprecedented potential for Christian mysticism becomes explicit without a doubt; it had been more or less neglected until now. And once again,

93. See the lucid and original research in Alejandro Bertolini, *Empatia y trinidad en Edith Stein: Fenomenologia, teologia y ontologia en clave relacional* (Salamanca: Ed. Secretariado Trinitario, 2013). Among other things, he documents the opening in Stein to further study of the mysticism and ontology discussed here.

the *experientia* and *intelligentia fidei* are called to express the best of themselves in this regard. All this will lead to remarkable gains not only in the existential dimension, but also in the cultural one.

A Turning Point in Faith?: Two Biblical Icons

The New Testament is undoubtedly the principal and indispensable source of contemporary spiritual and mystical renewal as illustrated by the unbroken tradition of the life of the church through the centuries. But the confrontation with contemporary culture, especially Western culture, deeply marked by the phenomenon which the Second Vatican Council refers to as the "absence" and the "death of God" (see *GS*, nos. 19–21) has played an important role, directly and indirectly, in this regard. It is unsettling especially because it has been established in these dimensions and with these characteristics precisely in the fertile ground where the seeds of the Gospel had been sown historically. It is a fact that challenges not only Christian thought but also the life of the church itself and the church's global way of perceiving and incarnating the faith.[94]

Such a situation is decisively confronted in a unique way today with the transmission and the paths of rebirth of the experience and understanding of the faith, which are oriented to overcoming the typically modern distance between mysticism and theology. E. Biser has noted in this regard that "a spiritual turning point has been reached that opens new possibilities to announce the Christian message."[95] The characteristics of this turning point are expressed in paradigmatic form by two biblical icons, according to Biser.

The first is that of the crucified Christ who cries out the abandonment from the cross. K. M. Woschitz emphasizes that a "panorama of cry" is the panorama of our time: "The cry—suffocated often enough—becomes the visible illustration there where literature, philosophy and modern psychology, as with Karl Jaspers and Carl Gustav Jung in particular, concentrate on the person of Job and see in him the representative of their problematical framework."[96] This cry is not only echoed in Christ's cry on the cross, but it finds its paradoxical response there as well: "He, who in his abandonment was not supposed to be consoled by any visible aid, but only by turning to God, gave those who could not be helped in any other way what no one but he could give—himself!"[97]

94. See Giuseppe Maria Zanghì, *Notte della cultura europea: Agonia della terra del tramonto?* (Rome: Città Nuova, 2007).

95. Eugen Biser, *Svolta della fede: Una prospettiva di speranza*, trans. M. Albertino (Brescia: Morcelliana, 1989), 113 (own trans. from the Italian).

96. Ibid., 112. See Gianluca Zurra's lucid analysis, *"I nostri sensi illumina". Coscienza, affetti e intelligenza spirituale* (Rome: Città Nuova, 2009).

97. Ibid., 65.

The second biblical icon is that of the disciples on the road to Emmaus. They discover the presence of the risen one in their midst thanks to the burning of their heart while listening to the Word and breaking the Eucharistic bread as the living Christ penetrates their existence and introduces it into a new horizon of meaning. As Biser writes, this indicates that the faith "becomes perceptible where the preachers make an effort to translate the written testimony into an actual living language. It occurs where the words: 'where two or three are gathered in my name, I am there among them' (Mt. 18:20) are implemented in the conscience of the Christian community."[98] Taking up the later Rahner's image of "a wintertime of the Church," Biser concludes that in reality "life is preparing for a reawakening under the snow-covered fields,"[99] and this provokes a reinterpretation of faith's destiny in adulthood, which Nietzsche gave in his time. Nietzsche spoke of a faith that had become dogma and then was transformed into morality only to evaporate in the end.

Biser emphasizes instead that Christian faith is about to enter into a new stage of its existence because of the breath of the Spirit. As he notes, "only a faith deepened from the mystical point of view can reach humanity in its current identity crisis and in its existential crisis."[100] It is a faith that has a future therefore because "in the measure in which it has learned to 'go out from itself,' it has acquired a capacity for empathy never reached before, but it also acquired an unprecedented candor to express and declare itself."[101] In this way, today's great task ultimately becomes that of engagement, with the two poles constituting Christological and trinitarian faith not only theologically but also on the existential and practical levels. These two poles are Jesus' Paschal mystery culminating in the abandonment and, through this mystery, the incorporation into the newness of the trinitarian life of *agápe* as life of unity and freedom among men and women in God.

The Locus of the Experience of God: The Bosom of the Father

The terrain has been abundantly prepared in the twentieth century. This includes the rediscovery of the centrality of the Word of God and of the Eucharist, as well as the church as communion, the need to overcome an individualistic concept of man in favor of a personalist and dialogical one, the tragic experience of the night of God especially in the Second World

98. Ibid., 74.
99. Ibid., 124.
100. Ibid., 35.
101. Ibid., 155.

War and in the cultural and social atmosphere of nihilism, with the intuition that the face of the crucified one is hidden in this night (Thérèse of Lisieux, Dietrich Bonhoeffer, Simone Weil, Edith Stein, and many others). The experience of the trinitarian God received and transmitted by Chiara Lubich however, is a gratuitous and unforeseen expression of a gift from on high, able to eventually manifest its fruitfulness thanks precisely to what had been prepared in its surroundings, as always happens in the way of the Spirit.

I will take into consideration the experience of light lived by Chiara herself in the summer of 1949 together with Igino Giordani and her first companions; I will confine myself to some records that underline the distinctiveness of this trinitarian contemplation, as it bears in itself an original understanding of God and of creation in him.[102] To begin, here is the summary of Chiara's own account of the opening of this experience dating back to July 16, 1949, but which reflects her spiritual journey that had already begun on December 7, 1943 (the date of her consecration to God).[103]

In love with Saint Catherine of Siena, Foco[104] had always sought a virgin he could follow in his life. And he had the impression now of having found her among us. So one day he proposed making a vow of obedience to me, thinking that he would be obeying God in this way.... I did not understand either the reason for obedience nor this unity involving only two in that moment.... I had the impression at the same time that Foco might be moved by a grace which should not be wasted however.

And so I said the following to him, more or less: "Perhaps, what you feel is truly from God..." And I added, "you know my life; I am nothing. I want to live as Jesus Forsaken who completely annihilated himself in fact. You are also nothing because you live in the same way. OK, tomorrow we will go to the church and when Jesus in the Eucharist comes into my heart, as into an empty chalice, I will say: 'On the nothingness of myself, make a pact of unity with the Jesus in the Eucharist in the heart of Foco. And, Jesus, do in such a way that the link coming out between us is the one that you know.'" Then, I added: "And, you Foco, do

102. To illustrate this, see Gérard Rossé in particular, "Il 'carisma dell'unità' alla luce dell'esperienza mistica di Chiara Lubich," *Nuova Umanità* 22, no. 127 (2000): 21–34, in addition to the indications which can be drawn from Chiara Lubich, *La dottrina spirituale*, ed. Michel Vandeleene (Rome: Città Nuova, 2009), with a wealth of precise bibliographical indications. In English, see Lubich, *Essential Writings, Spirituality, Dialogue, Culture*, trans. Tom Masters and Callan Slipper (Hyde Park, N.Y.: New City Press, 2007).

103. See Bernhard Callebaut, *Tradition, charisme et prophétie dans le mouvement international des Focolari: Analyse sociologique* (Bruyères-le Châtel: Nouvelle Cité, 2010); Florence Gillet, *Chiara Lubich: Fondatrice des Focolari* (Bruyères-le Châtel: Nouvelle Cité, 2009) and *La scelta di Gesù Abbandonato, nella prospettiva teologica di Chiara Lubich* (Roma: Città Nuova, 2009); Chiara Lubich, *Lettere dei primi tempi (1943–1949): Alle origini di una nuova spiritualità*, ed. F. Gillet and G. D'Alessandro (Rome: Città Nuova, 2010).

104. This was Igino Giordani's (1894–1980) "new" name, used internally within the Focolare Movement. Chiara Lubich considered him to be one of the cofounders of the Focolare.

likewise." We did it and then we left the church. Foco had to go to the sacristy to give a talk to the friars. I felt an inner urge to return to the church. I went in and stayed in front of the tabernacle. And I was about to pray to Jesus in the Eucharist there, to say to him, "Jesus." But I was unable. In fact, that Jesus who was in the tabernacle, was also here in me; it was I as well, identified with Him. Therefore, I could not call myself. And I felt the word "Father" come spontaneously from my mouth there. And I found myself in the bosom of the Father in that moment.[105]

A fascinating "journey" developed beginning with this "pact of unity" between a young woman who offered her life in consecration to God and a married man involved in the world of culture and politics. It was a journey of contemplation (which was also participation) of (in) the life of God the Trinity, and of creation in him. I will now try to establish some distinguishing characteristics of this event.

A New Experience and Understanding of the Trinity

We can intuit first of all upon looking at the original "pact" made by Chiara with Igino Giordani in obedience to an inner prompting of the Holy Spirit that it constitutes an unforeseen and gratuitous realization of St. Augustine's discovery in Book VIII of his *De Trinitate* in a certain sense: the "place" where God lets himself be known is reciprocal love consumed in unity through the Eucharist which introduces us, made one in Jesus, into the bosom of the Father. The way to the bosom of the Father in particular is thus rediscovered in Jesus forsaken, lived in the nothingness of love for self and for the other. For Chiara in fact, Jesus forsaken is the crucified one in the culmination of his love in front of the Father and for humanity. I would say that he is the crucified one seen "from God," from the Trinity. He conforms to the Trinity not only in the relationship with the Father but also in the relationship with the brothers and sisters.

The "interior castle" is completed in the "exterior castle"; God the Trinity dwells not only "in" each one of us, but also "among" us, informing the flesh of history and the created world with himself by way of our loving relations, and therefore by way of our physical nature and the social dimension that it makes possible.[106] Dwelling with perseverance in this *locus* in this way, it becomes an experience of also welcoming the "mind of Christ" (see 1 Cor 2:16), in other words a new *intelligentia fidei*, to know God and creation in a new way from and within God the Trinity. Chiara Lubich makes the meaning and implications of this experience

105. Unpublished text, quoted in Rossé, "Il 'carisma dell'unità' alla luce dell'esperienza mistica di Chiara Lubich," 22 (own trans.).

106. Chiara Lubich underlines that "our being one was such that it not only made us an image of the Trinity, not only united with the Trinity, but it made us, by participation, Trinity" (unpublished text; own trans.).

explicit immediately after the event opened up by the 1949 pact of unity, and then little by little over subsequent years in the space opened up by the panorama of life and light produced as a result of the rich current of spirituality and praxis drawing from it.

Trinitarian Life with the Neighbor: Sharing the God in Me with the God in My Brother or Sister

Consider, for example, the following text from 1949:

The doctrine of the Church is like a tree blossoming and growing throughout the centuries. Our Ideal gives a new flourishing to it: as the crowning cover of the tree with a new mantle of flowers. It seems—and it is—that all of the tree tends toward this blossoming, which is both in function of it and because of it.... God who is in me, who has shaped my soul, who lives there as Trinity (with the saints and the angels), is also in the heart of my brother and sisters.

Thus it is not enough that I love him only in me. If I do, my love there is still something personal and ... potentially self-centered: I love God in me, and not God in God, while perfection is: God in God (that is unity and Trinity).

Therefore, my cell, as the souls intimate with God would say, and my heaven,[107] as we would say, is within me and, just as it is within me, it is in the soul of my brothers and sisters. And just as I love him in me, recollecting myself in this heaven—when I am alone—I love him in my brother or sister when he or she is close to me.

And so I no longer love only silence, but also the word (expressed and tacit): the communication between God in me with God in my brother or sister. And if these two heavens meet, a single Trinity comes to be, where the two are like Father and Son and among them is the Holy Spirit....

But we need to know how to lose God within us for God in our brothers and sisters. And this can be done by whoever knows and loves Jesus crucified and forsaken.[108]

The awareness is evident in these lines of one's own experience being grafted into the centuries-old tree of the ecclesial tradition on one hand; on the other hand, there is the note of originality produced by the Holy Spirit's action in this experience. Rooted in the Gospel and in particular in Jesus' prayer to the Father in John 17, this originality is grasped in a trinitarian way in the communication of the God in oneself with the God in the brother or sister.

The communication of God to God in God—the Trinity—comes to be perceived and lived in the identification with Christ as communication

107. [Translator's note: there is a subtle play on the original Italian words, cell (*cella*) and heaven (*Cielo*).]

108. Text published in part in *Nuova Umanità* 24, no. 143 (2002): 586–87. Most of this meditation was translated into English and published in *Essential Writings*, 33–34.

of God in oneself with God in the other, and vice-versa. The communication of God in God is achieved by way of our humanity assumed into Christ where the reciprocity of love is given, as in God the Trinity. This love is the openness and welcoming, the dedication and offering in relationship with the other. The "on earth as in heaven" is implemented in other words in the prolepsis of eschatological time inaugurated by Jesus. It should also be noted that this communication comes to be intuited as the perfection of the Gospel. It is not only a matter of simply not seeking oneself in God, in other words the fulfillment of oneself in him, but seeking God in oneself—as understood in the classical mystical theology of the "interior castle"—in other words, welcoming the presence of God in Jesus into the emptiness of oneself. It means taking a further step which is to seek God in God. For Chiara, this means loving God in oneself as one loves God in the other, in such a way that there is the communication of God in God between the two when reciprocity is given: because God is unity and Trinity.

Jesus Forsaken as the Way to Union with God, Unity with the Brothers and Sisters

This is where the Gospel intuition is picked up; Jesus forsaken is the only true way to the Father's bosom. Chiara's crucified one is certainly the same as that of Francis and John of the Cross, but he is revealed in his interior "trinitarian" wound, the one in which the loving relationship with the Father is realized and the relationship with brothers and sisters (and this is what is new) is realized as well. We could try to make this intuition more explicit in these terms.[109] Objectively speaking, Jesus forsaken is gift that descends from on high through the ministerial and sacramental mediation of the Church; he is the way by which God gave and continues to give himself as God to humankind. Subjectively speaking at the same time, Jesus forsaken is a gift existentially welcomed and adopted by humanity, the model and the way to live in front of and with the others on the basis of that gift which is God's life among men and women. Did not Jesus pray to the Father: "As you Father are in me and I am in you, may they also be in us" (Jn 17:21)?

So if John of the Cross teaches that the way to communicate with God is to be empty of everything, like Jesus in his abandonment, Chiara reaffirms this, emphasizing that precisely with this, Jesus forsaken is the

109. For a deeper understanding, see Anna Pelli, *L'abbandono di Gesù e il mistero di Dio uno e trino: Un'interpretazione teologica del nuovo orizzonte di comprensione aperto da Chiara Lubich* (Rome: Città Nuova, 1995); Stefan Tobler, *Jesu Gottverlassenheit als Heilsereignis in der Spiritualität Chiara Lubichs* (Berlin: Walter de Gruyter, 2003).

way to find God again in the relationship with the brothers and sisters. As she wrote in 1950:

St. John of the Cross was not able to go further.[110] His soul reached the best disposition so that God would fill it. With his dark night of the soul in fact, he was the negative pole that, united with God, the positive pole, he made the Light shine or spring forth in himself.

We are also [called to be] negative and positive poles among brothers and sisters.... When these poles are in contact they radiate the Light of Jesus between them and therefore in both of them. In this way, we bring the Reign of God *on earth*. In fact, God is among us and by way of us this current of love (which is the current of trinitarian Love) passes through the world into all the members of the Mystical Body, illuminating everything.[111]

Jesus forsaken is intuited and advanced therefore as the existential law of God's life which is love, Trinity, poured out on earth. What is new should be grasped precisely in this: to have "discovered" in him the key to receiving that love which is God's life incorporated into human flesh: rather, God himself among human beings.

It is a kind of "Copernican revolution" of the Christian experience of God which is accomplished not in the clamor of ideas, projects, and actions but first and foremost in the heart and the eye of the soul. Jesus forsaken becomes the model not only for union with God but for loving and thinking, for doing and action as well. Mysticism is "democratized" to become part of human history in this way:

This is the great attraction
of modern times:
to penetrate to the highest contemplation
while mingling with everyone,
one person alongside others,
I would say even more:
to lose oneself in the crowd
in order to fill it with the divine,
like a piece of bread
dipped in wine.
I would say even more:
made sharers in God's plans
for humanity,
to embroider patterns of light on the crowd,
and at the same time to share with our neighbor
shame, hunger, troubles, brief joys.

110. Chiara added a comment: "I would say that this 'not able' means that God had brought him to this point but no further."

111. Unpublished (own trans.).

Because the attraction
of our times, as of all times,
is the highest conceivable expression
of the human and the divine,
Jesus and Mary:
the Word of God, a carpenter's son;
the seat of Wisdom, a mother at home.[112]

The *itinerarium mentis in Deum* does not turn its back on the world, but penetrates it and recognizes Jesus forsaken in its darkest wounds. God is already there, hidden or even rejected in it. He is already there because Jesus has infinitely multiplied the presence in his abandonment. And he is right there where God is not (from a human point of view). This presence should be reawakened everywhere; rather, it should be resuscitated. It must be recognized and loved to the point that each person is reawakened to love in turn because of the loving gaze that reaches him or her. And love flows between two, among many, and spreads out in concentric circles without excluding anyone any longer; and it builds works of truth and freedom, of justice and peace.

The Trinitarian Understanding of Jesus' Abandonment

As the path introducing and permitting people to dwell in the Father's bosom, the experience of being identified with Jesus forsaken becomes the focus of a penetrating *intelligentia fidei* of the mystery itself of Jesus' abandonment. On one hand it is in harmony with the trinitarian interpretation of Jesus' Paschal event that marks twentieth-century theology especially from the 1960s onward; it exhibits some significant original elements[113] on the other hand, precisely from the fire of the mystical experience nourishing it.

Chiara's mystical and theological intuition about Jesus forsaken is therefore undoubtedly profoundly rooted in the church's tradition, but it also moves in harmony with the sensibilities of contemporary philosophy and theology. This last characteristic is even more interesting because it is a matter of an intuition which is not the fruit of theological study but of a charismatic experience. Von Balthasar explains that there are charisms which have the light from God to open up a new look at the center of revelation. In that regard, Chiara could say that the charism of unity is "the revelation of Jesus Forsaken."

This intuition is expressed and lived from 1943 onward, when the

112. Lubich, *Essential Writings*, 169.

113. See Fulvio Gamba and Bernhard Körner, "Das Kreuzesereignis in der Theologie Hans Urs von Balthasars und in der spirituellen Erfahrung Chiara Lubichs," *Freiburger Zeitshrift für Theologie und Philosophie* 55, no. 2 (2008): 418–33.

topic of Jesus forsaken was still very marginal in theological reflection and spiritual experience, if not unknown, as someone said to Chiara.[114] In those same years nevertheless, in the wake of Teresa of Avila's mystical journey, Edith Stein, Simone Weil, and Dietrich Bonhoeffer rediscover, as if it were the first time in two thousand years of Christianity, that when everything is collapsing and the abyss of the night of God is experienced, that tragic abandonment is precisely where Jesus reveals God's face.

Yet Chiara's intuition not only demonstrates something new with respect to the earlier tradition, but also an originality distinguishing her from the contemporary panorama. In particular, it concerns the comprehension of the mystery of the abandonment as a trinitarian event, indeed, as the door giving access to the deepest mystery of the life of God the Trinity. It is enough to quote the following interpretation regarding the mystery of the abandonment, where she connects the revelatory trinitarian dimension (Jesus forsaken as "explanation" of the trinitarian life) and the soteriological dimension (Jesus forsaken as redeemer of humanity). Chiara wrote this in 1971:

> As a completely unfolded, opened flower after giving his own blood, his own natural death, Jesus also gives ... his own spiritual death, his own divine death, by giving God. He even empties himself of God; he gives God. And he does that in the moment of his abandonment.
>
> It is a real abandonment for Jesus' humanity because God leaves him in this condition without intervening. It is an unreal abandonment since he is God; God is One and cannot be divided. If anything he can be distinguished, but this is no longer suffering; it is love. And that is what may have happened with respect to Christ's divinity in that moment in the bosom of the Holy Trinity....
>
> So perhaps that abandonment was a new operation like what undoubtedly happened in the incarnation when the Trinity decreed that the Word should become flesh, or in the resurrection when the Father's power raised him.
>
> Upon seeing Jesus obedient to the point of being ready to regenerate his children, to give a "new creation" back to him (2 Cor. 5:17) ... the Father saw him so similar to Himself, identical to Himself, almost another Father, that He distinguished him from Himself.
>
> A new gasp of joy in God-Love Who is always new. A cry of infinite suffering in Christ's humanity: "My God, my God, why have you abandoned me?"[115]

The background to this piece is the theological truth of the hypostatic union: the Word, the second Person of the Trinity, really and fully assumed human nature. It follows that it is the person of the Word made flesh that lives the abandonment. This makes it possible to contemplate

114. See Bernhard Callebaut, "Lettura sociologica di una novità: Gesù abbandonato nella proposta di Chiara Lubich," *Sophia* 2, no. 1 (2010): 102–15.

115. Chiara Lubich, *Jesus Crucified and Forsaken*, December 6, 1971 (own trans.).

a divine and a human dimension in it, distinguishing without separating these two dimensions.

Because the abandonment is lived by the Word made flesh first of all, this opens wide the mystery of God's being as trinitarian love. As Chiara affirms in another place: "Three ... form the Trinity, yet they are one because love is and is not at the same time. Even when love is not, it is because it is love. In fact, if I renounce a particular possession of mine and *give it away* (I deprive myself of it—it is not) out of love, *I have love*—therefore it is."[116] Jesus forsaken, who is the Word (and therefore, the revelation of the Father) made flesh, reveals that God's being is love, because precisely by "losing" union with the Father out of love, a unity that makes him God, he is fully himself, God the Son, love. Jesus lives the law propounded to his disciples in the abandonment therefore. "Those who lose their life for my sake, and for the sake of the gospel, will save it" (Mk 8:35; see Jn 10:17–18). It is understood as a consequence that the Word as God, fully lived the movement of his trinitarian distinction from the Father in history in love and as love in the abandonment.

As regards the human dimension of the abandonment, it must be affirmed that Jesus, as true man, really suffered and experienced the anguish of death associated with the historical human condition marked by sin. According to St. Paul's expression, he became "sin" for us. But he redeemed humanity's sin in this way, being God and living in solidarity with the human condition out of love. In line with the Eastern tradition of the church which speaks of redemption but also of deification ("God became man in Christ, so that man could participate in the divine life in him"), Chiara sees the effective cause of the deification of humanity in the abandonment. She explains that Jesus suffers the abandonment in fact, because he deprives himself of his divine condition to give it to human beings. Only by "emptying" himself of God—as St. Paul makes us glimpse in the hymn of the Letter to the Philippians—can he really give himself to human beings entirely. Through the abandonment lived out of love therefore, Jesus is fully restored with his humanity to the splendor of his divine state (the resurrection and ascension to the bosom of the Father), and all human beings can become "son in the Son" together with him and in him.

Chiara points to the presence of the Holy Spirit in the event of the abandonment, as recalled by the Gospel of John (Jn 19:30: "Jesus bowed his head and gave up his Spirit"):

116. Quoted in Judith Povilus, *United in His Name: Jesus in Our Midst in the Experience and Thought of Chiara Lubich* (New York: New City Press, 1991), 66.

though it is not yet affirmed by others, we can perhaps think that this particular pain of Jesus, His being forsaken, has a special relationship with the Holy Spirit. And this for the simple reason that when we give something away we have to feel its loss. On the cross Jesus felt, at that tremendous moment, His detachment from the Father. But who bonded Him and still bonds Him to the Father in a personal communion, if not the Holy Spirit Himself? . . . And so it is possible to think that in the abandonment is the "sign of the breath of love from which the Divine Spirit proceeds."[117]

In short, we find in these affirmations a way marked out to understand the abandonment as a trinitarian event. Chiara writes:

The Three within the Trinity are One because of their mutual indwelling. But to be One it is necessary that each of the Three be really nothing, a huge nothingness, a divine nothingness just as their being One. We need to penetrate this state of their being nothing, their total inexistence. It remains, undoubtedly, a mystery as to how in the Trinity, the Word is nothing and at the same time is the Son. The same goes for the Father and the Holy Spirit. Certainly it is God who is Love that has the capacity to make Godself nothing. Therefore, it is Jesus Forsaken, who is Love completely explained, that can throw light on this mystery. I think that it is as if each of the divine Persons, in making themselves nothing, clothes themselves with Jesus Forsaken because Jesus Forsaken is precisely God clothed with nothingness. He, therefore, can explain the reality of the One-God, even though immediately afterward all is once again surrounded in mystery.[118]

The Unity and Trinity of God in the Paschal Light of the "Not" of Love

A deep and original understanding of what it means for God to be love and for the divine Persons to be "subsistent relations" is disclosed in Jesus forsaken. Chiara expresses herself using mystical language to translate its content onto the level of theological explication in the following dense text:

The Father generates the Son out of love; he "loses himself" in him, he lives in him. In a certain sense he makes himself "non-being" out of love and in so doing he is, he is Father. The Son, who is the echo of the Father, returns to the Father out of love, he "loses himself" in him, he lives in him. In a certain sense he makes himself "non-being" out of love and in so doing he is; he is Son. The Holy Spirit who is the love that circulates between the Father and the Son, their bond of unity, also in a certain sense makes himself "non-being" out of love and thus is: he is the Holy Spirit.[119]

If we think of the Son in the Father, then we have to think of the Son as

117. Chiara Lubich, *Unity and Jesus Forsaken* (New York: New City Press, 1985), 75–76.
118. Unpublished (own trans.).
119. Lubich, *Essential Writings*, 205.

nothing (nothingness of Love) to be able to think of God-One. If we think of the Father in the Son, we have to think of the Father as nothing (nothingness of Love) to be able to think of God-One.

They are three Persons in the Holy Trinity, and yet they are One because Love is not and is at the same time. The Father is distinct from the Son and from the Spirit, even though He contains the Son and the Spirit within Himself. The same for the Spirit who contains the Father and the Son within Himself, and for the Son who contains the Father and Holy Spirit within himself. By not being, in other words, each one is completely because He is Love, because He is in the others perchoretically, in an eternal self-giving in the divine Persons' relationship.

In the light of the Trinity unfolding in Jesus forsaken, God who is Being, reveals himself in his depths as guardian of non-being, as Self-gift if it could be expressed this way; certainly not the non-being which denies Being, but the non-being that reveals Being as Love.

This is the dynamism of the intra-trinitarian life, that is manifested as an unconditional reciprocal gift of Godself in a mutual nothingness of love that is total and eternal communion.[120]

Trinitarian Reflections within History

This experience of love that has Jesus forsaken as its measure and the original Christian lifestyle it forms are the source of the originality of this culture of solidly Christian inspiration. But precisely for this reason, it is opened wide to a 360-degree horizon on all fronts, characterizing the patient but progressive social production inspired by Chiara's intuition. It is enough to think of the perspective that Jesus forsaken makes possible with respect to modernity and the "night of God" that marks it so radically. We are not asked to end up being imprisoned, but to take it seriously and make it a path for a new presence of God to humanity on the measure of Jesus forsaken. In Chiara's words, he is the "God of our times."[121]

Or one could think of dialogue between the faith in Christ and the great religious traditions of the East, still to be explored; I am thinking of the Buddhism of *nirvana* and *sunyata*.[122] Jesus forsaken seems to stand out as the demanding but indispensable way to a hope that we can barely imagine, and that might surprise us as the existential and intellectual

120. Published in part in Chiara Lubich, "Spiritualità dell'unità e vita trinitaria. Lezione per la laurea *honoris causa* in teologia," *Nuova Umanità* 26, no. 151 (2004): 15. For more about the theological meaning of the trinitarian perspective of this text, and more specifically about its reference to the "nonbeing" of love, see my "Alcune riflessioni sul conoscere teologico nella prospettiva del carisma dell'unità," *Nuova Umanità* 21, no. 122 (1999): 191–206, esp. 200–205, and the articles contained in the monographic issue of *Nuova Umanità* 22, no. 132 (2000), *Theology and the Charism of Unity* (own trans.).

121. See in particular Zangh, *Gesù Abbandonato maestro di pensiero*.

122. See Roberto Catalano, *Spiritualità di comunione e dialogo interreligioso: L'esperienza di Chiara Lubich e del Movimento dei Focolari* (Rome: Città Nuova, 2010).

method for the encounter, and as the "eye" focused on the event of God's communication to humanity and among human beings in God.[123]

The mystics in the Christian tradition sometimes describe the eternal Word as the eye through which God looks upon and knows the world. In a dazzling passage from her mystical writings of 1949, Chiara notes: "Jesus Forsaken is the pupil of God's eye on the world, an infinite emptiness through which God sees us, the window of God opened up to the world and the window of humanity through which it sees God."[124] We know God to the extent that God first knows us, in that knowledge that creates and recreates us. And from revelation, God knows us in Jesus, his Word made flesh who even suffers the abandonment on the cross for us. In him, God reaches the heart and soul of each and every one with his love made flesh and blood. Nothing and no one can stay outside of what is both the universal and personal horizon of his glance. God the Trinity knows us as we are in Jesus forsaken, making real on a promise that illuminates and transforms us with his immeasurable love. And in reply, we can also know him for who he is, in God's unsettling and limitless love.

123. See Chiara Lubich's magisterial address given in Castelgandolfo on June 23, 2003, for an honorary degree in theology offered by the University of Trnava, Slovakia: "Spiritualità dell'unità e vita trinitaria," *Nuova Umanità* 26, no. 151 (2004): 11–20.

124. Published later in Chiara Lubich, *Gesù abbandonato* (Rome: Città Nuova, 2016), 60–61; see also Katarzyna Waiutyńska, "Pupilla dell'Occhio di Dio: Qualche spunto sul linguaggio metaforico dell'esperienza spirituale di Chiara Lubich," *Nuova Umanità* 41, no. 236 (2019): 132.

PART 5

ON EARTH AS IT IS IN HEAVEN

Unity and Trinity of God and in God

> That they may all be one. As you, Father, are in me and I am in you, may they also be in us.
>
> —John 17:21

In the fifth and final part of my inquiry I will try to study, in synthetic fashion, the meaning of the language used by the tradition in the formulation and interpretation of the truth revealed by God the Trinity. According to that language, forged by dogma and illustrated by theological speculation, God is one in substance or nature, and triune in persons. I will then try to examine the problems which this language encounters in the context of modern and contemporary culture, calling forth a renewed ontological understanding and a relevant linguistic expression of the originality of revelation. But first it seems good to outline, in a sort of synthesis of the preceding sections, the "state of the question" that trinitarian theology faces today setting out from the gains acquired in the spontaneous ecclesial consciousness of the twentieth century and from the questions that remain open.

Beginning with a renewed listening to the logic of revelation there will follow three lines of research which, keeping in mind the relevant data acquired with accuracy from the dogmatic and theological tradition, will suggest a reinterpretation and a further penetration in relation to the understanding of revelation which today is inspired by the incessant action of the Spirit who "will guide you into all the truth" (Jn 16:13). This is a matter of integrating the concept of the person as subsistent relation with that of reciprocity in a formally trinitarian sense; it involves the articulation in trinitarian language of the already acquired concept of relative nonbeing in relation to that dynamic concept with a Paschal origin and form, of relational nonbeing; and, finally, it involves the rereading of the proposal advanced in modernity of an ontology of freedom in an explicitly and intrinsically trinitarian horizon. All this clearly takes, with force and genuineness, Christian theological discourse to its decisive "place" of institution, existential experience and intellectual resolution.

CHAPTER 23

Perspectives and Questions regarding the Trinity in Twentieth-Century Theology

The twentieth century has been a decisively trinitarian century both for theology and for Christian spirituality. Not since the era which studied the intense debates and conflicts leading to the dogmas of the first Ecumenical Councils, the great patristic syntheses of Augustine for the Latins and of Maximus the Confessor for the Greeks, the superb cathedrals of the *intellectus fidei* (understanding of faith) of Thomas and Bonaventure in the Middle Ages, had theology shone so intensely with trinitarian light, with rare exceptions such as Antonio Rosmini and Matthias Scheeben in the nineteenth century. In modernity the Trinity lives in mysticism and is thought about in philosophy, while theology is devoted to the precious inheritance from the past and the apologetical engagement with new challenges.

The three principal theologians of the twentieth century—one each for the three principal ecclesial traditions—Barth for the Reformation, Bulgakov for Orthodoxy, von Balthasar for Catholicism—are trinitarian from head to toe in their theologizing, or at least wish to be such. There is in them the determined intention to present the originality of Christian revelation, its incandescent and irreducible focal point, in creative fidelity to two thousand years of theological tradition, while at the same time welcoming, with seriousness and openness of spirit, the challenges and the languages of mysticism and modern philosophy.

But the match remains completely open. Without taking anything away from their merits (what would trinitarian theology be today without them?), we must recognize that theology is flanked by two sharp thorns. On the one hand, the crisis of metaphysical language, be it that of being or that of the subject, in the final analysis, still imbues the impressive reflection of these exceptional twentieth-century witnesses of twentieth-century theology. On the other hand, there is the epochal *novum* of the encounter in the West (but with gradually more extensive reflections) with nihilism, and in the Far East (but with much more pervasiveness) with the religious traditions and thinking that say God, being, and man in languages different from the Greek *lógos* and the Hebrew-Christian *pistis*.

The question arises, whither should we look? I believe, in fidelity to the route traced until now by the Spirit and his specific and unprecedented impulses in our days, that we should look forward with courage. Without forgetting what stands behind us and supports us, there is no doubt, but it is no longer able to satisfy our quest. And to look ahead it is necessary to look yet again at the origin, at the center, at the *ephapax*, the once-for-all, of Jesus Christ. It is a fact that he is for theology what the first day after the sabbath was for Mary Magdalen: he is recognized only when one turns toward him who calls by name, and in that fashion finding him before the eyes of the mind and of the heart, present without however being able to hold on to him: because he withdraws, there remains the task of keeping alive and burning the desire and the awaiting of his free and unforeseeable coming (see Jn 20:11–18).

With this responsorial and desiring freedom, in itself essential for theology as for every authentic discipline of thought, we are able to seek to welcome and to speak the Trinity—the God who has already come but in order to come always anew in our life and in our thinking—setting out from certain disputed questions (*quaestiones disputatae*). These can appear fragmentary, but they are able to recapitulate in a certain fashion the journey traveled until now, and are able to bear witness to the sincerity and the labor of the *fides quaerens intellectum* (faith seeking understanding).

The Access to the Trinity

The first question: what is the way to the Trinity, the way, the method (*methodos*)? I interrogate myself as a theologian and insofar as I am a theologian. It could seem that I should have the answer nicely packaged: faith. But what is faith? In reality, the access to the Trinity is the "test case" of faith; because faith is the way to Christ and Christ is the way to the Trinity. In saying that, I wish to say two things.

First of all, I cannot speak of the Trinity, in the Christian sense of the term, while leaving out Christ: both Hebrew and Muslim monotheism, for example, are neither able nor desirous to speak of the Trinity precisely because, though they accept the revelations of the same God of Abraham and at the same time recognize respectively the expectation of the messiah and the prophetical identity of Jesus, they still do not recognize him, Jesus of Nazareth, as the Son of God, or better, God the Son become flesh. This is the key point.

But then—this is the question *sine qua non*—does the truth of the Son who is God correspond to the consciousness of Jesus Christ? "The Father and I are one [*hén*]" (Jn 10:30). This affirmation of Jesus in the fourth Gospel summarizes the consciousness and the experience of Jesus, witnessed as it is in the Gospel narratives by the exceeding novelty of his *exousía*, his singular authority, together with his radical dedication to the will of the Father in favor of men, all of which culminates in the paradox of the crucifixion, the resurrection, and the outpouring of the Spirit. Between God (the Father) and Jesus there is always a distinction: this means otherness (I and the Father) and plurality (we are). And simultaneously there is unity: the Johannine *hén* (one) expresses it in a form which could not be neater nor more peremptory.

It is precisely this existential tension—in that it unfolds in dramatic fashion—that makes sense of the whole of the drama of Jesus: from the baptism in the Jordan to the baptism of the cross and the abandonment. The cipher of distinction, the key to the manifestation and the enactment of being-one are the same: the freedom of Jesus. Vocation, decision, and temptation, all the way from the sojourn in the desert until the prayer in Gethsemane, bear witness to it. Even to the hour of feeling separated from God, which he cried out in the abandonment and traversed in the faith of the unity with him.

From this, one sees the second aspect I intend to underline by saying that the Trinity is the test case of the faith: I cannot gain access to the Trinity as the truth touched by the soul and tasted in the Spirit, a truth always greater and always beyond, except in the faith of Jesus in the Father who reveals the event of faith in him as the Son of the *Abbà* in whom I live when he lives in me. This is the unique and free access to the Father. I have not said, let it be noted, that I cannot in some way think about it, the Trinity: this is certainly possible and fruitful, at least up to a point, even outside explicit faith that unfolds in Christ. Rather, I said that I cannot experience it: the experience which communicates, in the Spirit, Jesus himself, recognized as the Son, and which germinates growth in understanding in the faith of him as the way to the Father. It is important to be quite clear that the faith of Christ not only activates but also transcends the explicit and professed faith in Christ.

Two affirmations of Jesus in the fourth Gospel, formulated during the discourses of the Last Supper, express all of this in concise form. The first does so in the form of the knowledge of faith, the second in the form of the gift of grace: "On that day (the day of the lifting up on the cross and simultaneously in the resurrection) you will know [*theōrîte*] that I am in the Father and you in me and I in you" (Jn 14:20); "Father, I desire [the verb is strong and precise: *thélō*] that those also, whom you have given me, may be with me where I am, to see [*theōrôsin*] my glory which you have given me; because you loved me before the foundation of the world" (Jn 17:24).

The same relationship of freedom in being one, which Jesus lives with the Father, acquiring it as man, and doing so to the very limit and once for all in his handing himself over upon the cross, is lived through faith in the relationship between Jesus and those whom the Father has given him, and, in Jesus, is lived by them with the Father. The "where" of Jesus consists in being-one in the Father and the where of the disciples consists in their being-one in Christ and through him in the Father. Faith is therefore participation in the same event that Jesus expresses with the words, "I and the Father are one." And therefore it is grace and it is freedom; it is vocation, decision, temptation, dedication, unity.

And this both expresses and presupposes the actual presence of the risen Jesus Christ, not just the contemporariness of faith, but the contemporariness elicited by faith. "Where two or three are gathered in my name, I am there among them" (Mt 18:20). "This is my body that is for you … this cup is the new covenant in my blood. Do this, as often as you drink it, *eis tèn emen anámnēsis*" (1 Cor 11:24–25); in that "remembrance of me," we could translate, "which is the event of life." In the final analysis, the Trinity is the key moment of the Christian faith, because it expresses what the faith itself is: its being given and its being, its act and its truth.

The Trinity: Anthropological and/or Theological Truth?

The second question: if this—the faith of Christ in the Father and the faith in Christ of the disciples—is the access, is the Trinity only anthropological truth or also, and originally, theological? In other words, is the Trinity the name of God (the name revealed by Christ according to his word, "Father, I made your name known to them, and I will make it known," Jn 17:26), or is it simply the name of our relationship with God, or better, of God with us? Is God shown (and freely expressing himself) as Trinity only in creation and in revelation, and therefore is God Trinity in a provisional manner for us; or is God Trinity in Godself, always and forever?

Finally and ultimately we ask ourselves if in faith it is possible to speak and to speak meaningfully about the in-oneself of God; or whether God is beyond our reach and beyond his trinitarian manifestation. In a still more radical manner we ask ourselves whether we are called to even overcome the Trinity in order to reach the *ab-solutus* (absolute)—and that is as disconnected from every relation and indifferent to every relation—of him who precisely is by his essence the absolute. Theology, mysticism, and philosophy have taken up different positions with respect to the crucial question: it is enough to remember the intense stage-by-stage struggle between revelation and apophaticism, between the affirmative way and the negative way, in Dionysius, Eriugena, Eckhart, Nicholas of Cusa, Schelling, and so on.

The Christian *tradition* seems to me to offer in the dogmatic and mystical strand two relevant fundamental criteria, which beginning with Irenaeus of Lyons in the second century and lasting until today, though in the legitimate plurality of its expressive forms, have been recognized as being faithful to the event of Jesus Christ. The first has to do with what cannot be transcended—not only noetically but in being itself—of the relation with God, and in God as a *personal relation*, and therefore as free, between the Father and the Son (and we in him) in the Holy Spirit. That means that theologically there is not a before or an after or a bottom or an abyss from which the Trinity originates and toward which the Trinity is drawn. God reveals and communicates himself just as he is. Trinitarian faith has a realistic significance. "The act of the believer," Thomas Aquinas says summarily, "does not terminate in a proposition, but in a thing."[1]

The second criterion is of Christological character and the Council of Chalcedon (451) expresses it: Jesus Christ is true God and true man, consubstantial (*homooúsios*) with God in divinity and consubstantial (*homooúsios*) with us in humanity, without separation and without confusion. In the final analysis, even if on another plane, it is a question of the same dynamic of alterity in unity of which I have already spoken in relation to the rapport between Father and Son. The prologue of the fourth Gospel expresses the fact with a rich sequence of affirmations which will be decisive in illuminating the journey, studded with obstacles, to Chalcedon. In the first verse, one reads, as we have seen: "In the beginning was the Word, and the Word was with God, and the Word was God" (Jn 1:1); and later, "And the Word became flesh and pitched his tent among us, and we have seen his glory, the glory as of a father's only son" (Jn 1:14); and further, "No one has ever seen God: [and here two different readings] it is God the only Son [or better, "the only begotten God"] who is in the bosom of the Father, who has made him known" (Jn 1:18). The distinction and unity between God (the Father or "the" God in the language of the New Testament) and Jesus, in other words, refers back to and expresses the original distinction and unity between God and the *Lógos*. It is from here that trinitarian theology unfolds.

1. *ST* II-II, q. 1, a. 2, ad 2: "Actus autem credentis non terminatur ad enuntiabile, sed ad rem."

The Trinitarian Dynamic of Faith and the Challenge of a New Ontology

In this way we are confronted by the third question which can be articulated in two questions. First of all, does the perspective expressed in the prologue of the fourth Gospel correspond to the consciousness and message of Jesus, and to his event which takes place in the crucifixion and resurrection? Or is it the fruit of an unwarranted Hellenization or Gnosticization, as the charge is made against Christian theology?

And now for the second question: how much has the great construction of trinitarian metaphysics—which, especially in the West, represented the determined speculative direction of theology from Augustine to Thomas and Rosmini, and whereby the philosophy of modernity abandoned the language of being in order to take up that of the subject and of liberty, respectively in Hegel and Schelling—expressed and/or how much has it betrayed the original event of revelation in Jesus Christ?

With regard to the first question, I answer that access to what St. Paul calls *tà báthē toû Theoû*, "the depths of God," is constitutive of the very event of faith (1 Cor 2:10). It is worth rereading the intense and, in my opinion, decisive Pauline passage (1 Cor 2:9–16):

> It is written, "What no eye has seen, nor ear heard, nor the human heart conceived, what God has prepared for those who love him"—these things God has revealed to us through the Spirit; for the Spirit searches everything, even the depths of God. For what human being knows what is truly human except the human spirit that is within? So also no one comprehends what is truly God's except the Spirit of God. Now we have received not the spirit of the world, but the Spirit that is from God, so that we may understand the gifts bestowed on us by God. And we speak of these things in words not taught by human wisdom but taught by the Spirit, interpreting spiritual things to those who are spiritual. Those who are unspiritual do not receive the gifts of God's Spirit, for they are foolishness to them, and they are unable to understand them because they are spiritually discerned. Those who are spiritual discern all things, and they are themselves subject to no one else's scrutiny. "For who has known the mind of the Lord so as to instruct him?" But we have the mind of Christ.

What makes possible, indeed actual, the access to the depth of the mystery of God, not with arrogant and vain Gnostic presumption, but in the trusting and courageous welcoming of the gift of the wisdom and discernment of the Spirit, is the free participation in the *noûs* of Christ by means of the Holy Spirit. If God had not expressed himself "outside Himself," humanly—in his very Word which had always, *en arché*, expressed him fully "in Himself"—in Christ, we would not be able to know his depth.

Christ is the Word that God says about himself to us: Word spoken in human language, in the mind and flesh of Christ, but for what he is in himself, Word of God.

It is in this perspective, then, that the prologue of the fourth Gospel, with mystical and narrative language, temporally dislocates the *arché* in which God speaks his Word—which is his very self as expressed—and which is the origin, the life, and the form of all that God says and does beyond himself (in creation); and which is the precise and unforeseen event (for us, but willed by God) of the Word who becomes flesh in the fullness of time, in Jesus Christ, in order to reveal the face of the Father and fulfill the design of creation. Intrinsic and even essential to the logic of Christological faith is the distinction between the Word who is God in himself and the Word who becomes flesh, who is the very Word of God, the Word who is God, but in another form of being—human flesh—without this contradicting its original condition of being: the abiding in the *arché*, beginning with God. It is essential to be absolutely clear that it is only the Word become flesh, Jesus Christ, who guides and introduces, by means of the grace of the Holy Spirit, into the inexhaustible abysses of the mystery of God revealed by the Word who is God.

Nicaea and Chalcedon wish to defend this truth whatever the cost, against the danger (Arius) of reabsorbing the Word who has become flesh: either in the beyond, in the one without distinction who precisely as such and when it speaks the Word, is not able to say Itself to the end/fully, but only its simple and weakened reflection; or on this side, in the flesh of the man Jesus as inhabited and externally assumed as the provisional symbol of the Word of God spoken to us. To do this the dogma uses the Greek language of *ousía*, the one substance, and of *prósopa* or *hypostáseis*, the distinct persons. Of course one does this by reworking from within such categories which the scriptures do not know, but running the risk at the same time of presupposing, at least in part, an already given and known ontology of the divine for the *pneumatikós* ("spiritual") language, in order to say God who is revealed in Christ and who gives us God as communicated in his Spirit.

I would reply therefore in these terms to the second question mentioned above: the great trinitarian metaphysics, both classical and modern, to what extent has it expressed and/or to what extent has it betrayed the trinitarian event revealed in Christ? Classical metaphysics, in obedience to the originality of the event, has given new meaning to Greek metaphysics, speaking, for example in Augustine's thought, of that relation which in God is not predicated as an accident (*De Trinitate* V); and more ardently, with St. Thomas, of the relation which in God is identical with the essence (*ST* I, q. 29, a. 4). But it has done so while leaving too much in the background, even as far as forgetting that place of revelation which in Jesus speaks the truth of his filial relation with the Father: the freedom of love pushed all the way to the experience of abandonment by the Father.

Modern trinitarian metaphysics, by contrast, has with Hegel positioned the ontological significance of the *verbum crucis* (Word of the cross) at the center, but has sacrificed on the altar of speculative thought both the distinction between the Word who is God and the Word who becomes flesh and, in definitive fashion, the otherness between the Father and the Son and between God and creation; and, in the case of Schelling, even if it intuited the absolute transcendence of freedom over nature and over the revelation of God, it still placed that transcendence in original antecedence with respect to the space disclosed by the free event of God, as tri-Personal love, in the history of humanity.

Trinitarian Ontology Springing Forth from the "Bowels of Revelation"

A fourth question now arises. In my opinion it is a decisive question for today's theology: how to contemplate the being-one of God, the one God, the being-God of God, beginning from the revelation of Jesus Christ and from being-in-Christ? On the one hand, certainly one may not simply premise a *De Deo Uno* already completed in itself to the trinitarian revelation, as was attempted by a certain trinitarian metaphysics in classical theology, at least in the West; nor reduce apophatically the *De Deo Trino* to an absolutely unspeakable *De Deo Uno*, as a certain Christian mysticism was tempted to do with the risk of prevailing with an approach of a true, but pre-Christian mysticism. Likewise, today a certain agnosticism is tempted to account for neither the intentionality of the intelligence nor the realism of faith: because God shows himself for who he really is in trinitarian revelation.

On the other hand, however, the being-one of God is not to be understood as only "unification," the result that is manifested at their summit at Easter by the relations of the three, which much of the trinitarian personalism of the twentieth century was tempted to do in reaction to preceding models and being carried away by the fascination of the Trinity as thought by means of the philosophy of the subject and freedom: it would be too little because in that way the unity and the transcendence of the being of God is neither guaranteed nor expressed.

In other words, one cannot presuppose a definitive ontology or "me-ontology" of the being-one of God to the eschatological revelation of God in Jesus Christ, even as there clearly exists a human knowledge of the mystery of God prior to that revealed in Christ, and even if the mystery of God remains inexhaustible and always in the beyond. However, beginning with the revelation in Christ and within this revelation, starting out, that is—and using the language of Rosmini—from "the bowels of revelation," there is need of a *pneumatikós* language that would express the being-one of God as simultaneously source and end of the relations of love that are the three divine Persons. That being-one would have to be, as revealed, also freely shared with creation, and in that way known in the mystery, thanks to the gift of the Spirit. Does not the New Testament view the being one in Christ (see Gal 3:28) which, at the end of time, is called to the eschatological reality of "God as all in all" (1 Cor 15:28)?

Creation in the Logic of Incarnation, Incarnation in the Logic of the Trinity

There is a fifth question which at this moment it is sufficient merely to remember. If God is, and he is one in the Trinity of the Father, the Son, and the Holy Spirit, what (ontological) meaning do creation and incarnation have? Do they not plunge as such (if God is the one) into the unfathomable "region of dissimilarity" (Augustine)? In Christological perspective we must remember the fact that it is not creation that constitutes the sense-horizon of the incarnation, but rather the incarnation that determines in itself the meaning of creation. The New Testament has clearly intuited, when in the Letter to the Ephesians it says that in God, the Father of our Lord Jesus Christ, we have been chosen in Jesus Christ (not simply in the Word!): "before the foundation of the world ... He destined us for adoption as his children through Jesus Christ" (Eph 1:4–5). On the basis of the charism of Francis of Assisi and the mysticism of Bonaventure, Duns Scotus has gone further than Augustine or Thomas.

The question remains, however: how should we understand the *sárx eghéneto* of the prologue of John (Jn 1:14), the *kénosis* (emptying) of the Letter to the Philippians? In the trinitarian context just now disclosed one may and one ought to say that the incarnation of the Son, but as read to the point of the death of the abandoned one, illuminates the meaning and the destiny of the event of creation which breaks forth from the heart of God himself in an act of infinite liberty.

God, the Father, freely says himself, nothing less than himself, in himself—this is the theological truth of the Trinity. If he had said anything less, we would fall back into either a degrading emanation or into creation as a provisional, or ultimately illusory, placement by someone other than God. But God, who is freedom, says himself not only in himself (the Word), but also beyond himself. The language cannot be other than figurative. This means not only that God places someone other than himself, who is really such, and thereby subsistent and free (it is that which we call creation), but it also means that he proposes to invite this other in full freedom, to also become Word of God just as the Word of God is in God (it is what we call incarnation).

This design (the *mystérion* of Paul) is revealed and realized in the death of Christ abandoned on the cross, where the Word, if I may say so, is reduced totally to being man, a man: so that in his human freedom he receives and entrusts everything to the Father, even in the darkness of the abandonment, and also in death, as his Word: other than God (he is man), but as the free expression of God (he is the Word). The cry of abandonment, the cry of the birth of the new creation, declares that the Word become flesh has become fully the other of God; the cry of Easter morning—"He is risen, he is not here!" (Mk 16:6)—declares that the other of God, the man Jesus in whom the Son has said himself to the end in the world, has been received in God as Word in the Word.

Therefore the Easter of Jesus Christ is an eschatological event: because the internality and the externality of God coincide in a point, that is, in an act by means of which God and creation are already one, remaining distinct (because there would otherwise not be freedom either for God or for the creature) and in the outpouring of the Spirit "without measure" guiding and shaping freedom toward conformity with Christ and recapitulation in him; the final times (qualitatively) commence in which we are all called to become one in Christ just as Christ is one with the Father (see Jn 17), "that God may be all in all" (1 Cor 15:28). This does not remove, but actually heightens, and decisively, the risk and the drama of the history of freedom (see the Book of Revelation).

From the Vision "as in a mirror" to the Vision "face to face"

We have returned in this way to the point of departure: access in faith to the Trinity. Being grace and freedom, this access of faith is completely one with *agápe*. It was not for nothing that Paul summed up Christian existence in the pregnant formula of *pístis di'agápēs energouménē*, "the faith working through *agápe*" (Gal 5:6). While waiting for the *parousia*, Christian faith experiences and knows already the life of the Trinity—the absolute in the relative—when it relives Christ in itself, allowing itself to be guided by his Spirit. Time then becomes the transparence of the eternal, the particular of the universal.

Matthew expresses it in this fashion: "as you did it to one of the least of these who are members of my family, you did it to me" (Mt 25:40); whoever touches man touches the Word. And John expresses it thus: "No one has ever seen God; if we love one another, God lives in us and his *agápe* is perfected in us" (1 Jn 4:12). "*Vides Trinitatem, si caritatem vides*: you see the Trinity if you see charity"—this is the intuition of Augustine. In the final analysis, faith in the Trinity professes this hope: "For now we see in a mirror, dimly, but then we will see face to face [*prósopon pros prósopon*]. Now I know only in part; then I will know fully, even as I have been fully known" (1 Cor 13:12).

CHAPTER 24

The Ontology of Nature and of the Person

Setting out from the sketch of the state of the question just traced, I will now try to study, from a theoretical perspective, the core of the *quaestiones disputatae*: disputed questions which the twentieth century has left us. This is the limited but precise objective I will consider below. Over the centuries, theological speculation has forged the language of the unity of divine substance (*ousía, phýsis*) and the distinction of the Persons (*prósōpa, hypostáseis*) with the purpose of rendering intelligible the mystery of God revealed in Christ. It was a matter of making sense on the one hand of the oneness of God and, on the other hand, of the distinction and communion—setting out from the revelation of Jesus—of the Father, the Son, and the Holy Spirit. As we have seen, this language has been taken up and authoritatively specified by dogma. I will try to gather its central significance in order to draw out its relevance and the possibilities of reusing and deepening it.

The Language of Substance/Nature

Ousía derives from the verb *eînai*, "to be" / "being," and it denotes what being is as such, translated into Latin as essence or substance; *phýsis* derives from the verb *phúein*, to generate, cause. It indicates the individuating and dynamic principle of the thing itself as translated by the Latin *natura*. These concepts have been mediated by the Greek philosophical tradition and their introduction into the realm of theology has been wholly unproblematic, at least in appearance, on the basis of an almost obvious presupposition of identification between the God of biblical tradition and the supreme being/substance of Greek philosophy. The Septuagint has contributed more than a little by translating the self-revelation of the name of God, YHWH, witnessed by the Book of Exodus (see in particular Ex 3:14) into the Greek language as *egó eimi ho ón*, "I am being."

In reality, the use of the philosophy of being, of substance, and of nature with reference to God could not, in the end, resist unchanged the impact of the Christological revelation which imposed its own rethinking and re-expression. Already in Augustine, for example, we find the affirmation according to which, though there are not accidents in God, revelation invites us to think that not everything in God is predicated according to substance, but also according to relation: for the names of Father, Son, and Holy Spirit say precisely relation, not in accidental form, but permanent form.

Thomas, for his part, rethinks the Aristotelian concept of substance introducing the concept of *actus essendi*: the act of being, the act by which something is, distinguishing in that fashion between essence and *actus essendi*, the act of being, or *esse*, being in the proper sense. With regard to God, Thomas thus excludes speaking of God as substance and affirms that in him there is identity between *essentia* (essence) and *esse* (being). With modernity and with Hegel, and precisely with a rereading of a "speculative Good Friday" one arrives in fact at proposing the substitution of the concept of substance (read, actually, from the perspective of Spinoza) with that of subject or spirit. Heidegger formulates a radical critique of classical metaphysics (and its usage in theology) as deformed, according to him, by ontotheology: such that God ends up being thought of simply as the supreme being, forgetting that which he defines as the "ontological difference." To this it should be added, on a specifically theological level, the emergence in the twentieth century of central themes such as *agápe* and *kénosis* with their specific relevance in relation to the semantics of the divine being.

The Language of the *Hypóstasis*/Person

Much more controversial from the very beginning is the debate around the concept of person which was forged in a properly theological context. The analysis of its emergence and development offers two important lessons on the methodological level. Above all, it shows a structural hermeneutical circle between its theological meaning and its anthropological meaning in "a circular movement" where anthropology and theology are mutually intertwined.[1] One could say that the concept of person represents not only a significant example of the analogical statute of being but even constitutes its very emblematic instance. "Person" says in fact what is proper to the being of God as revealed in Christ and, at the same

1. Virgilio Melchiorre, "Per un'ermeneutica della persona," in *Persona e personalismi*, ed. A. Pavan and A. Milano (Naples: Ed. Dehoniane, 1987), 289–307.

time, what is proper to human being as created in "the image and likeness of God." In fact, St. Thomas can say, "The name person as referring to the thing signified is both earlier and more truly applied to God than to creatures, so that it is in the latter analogically; but as applying to the manner/mode of signification and of imposition of a name is more appropriate to creatures."[2]

The second lesson unfolds in consequence from the first. Exactly insofar as it is made precise in an analogical movement which rises from below (from human experience) to what is above (the mystery of God that is revealed), and in a corresponding descent from above to what is below (to illumine the vocation of human beings in the light of the mystery of God), the notion of person can only be clarified by a historical and hermeneutical process of an always greater and almost indefinite deepening. The reason for this above all else is in the analogical understanding of being and, consequently, of the person, which intersects with and is definitively marked by Christological revelation. With von Balthasar one ought to affirm the person of Christ as the principal analogy from which there begins, and toward which there converges, the movement from below upward and, earlier (in an ontological sense), from above downward, as previously mentioned.[3]

This means, finally, to stress the fact that the notion of person, in both a theological and anthropological sense, may not be presupposed as given *a priori* and once for all, but rather that there is growth in the understanding of its meaning. This is true to the point that the notion may not be characterized as a concept deriving from a definition, but rather as an open metaphor marked by a continuous "transfer of meaning."[4] It is enough to remember in rapid succession the journey which such a

2. *In Sent.* I, d. 25, q. 1, a. 2: "quantum ad rem significatam per prius est in Deo quam in creaturis; sed quantum ad modum significandi est e converso"; see also *ST* I, q. 29, a. 3, ad 2, and *In Joan.* I, 30: "quamvis hoc nomen persona non conveniat Deo quantum ad id a quo impositum est nomen, tamn quantum ad id ad quod significandum imponitur, maxime Deo convenit." See Melchiorre, *Per un'ermeneutica della persona*, 293. Jean Galot emphasized in this regard: "The principle of analogy, accepted in the domain of nature, is equally applicable in order of persons. If man has been created in the image and likeness of God, then his person as well as his nature bear a reflection of what exists in God. So we cannot claim that the human person must be defined in completely different terms from the divine person. According to the fundamental analogy, if, in God, what constitutes person is relation, then we must expect that relation likewise formally constitutes the human person.... True, this intellectual exercise follows the analogy by an upward process. We raise our sights from man to God. Now, on the contrary, we are proceeding in the opposite direction. From what is said about the divine persons in Trinitarian doctrine we come back down to the level of the human person." *The Person of Christ. Covenant between God and Man: A Theological Insight*, trans. M. Angeline Bouchard (Chicago: Franciscan Herald Press, 1984), 29–30.

3. Von Balthasar, *Theo-Drama*, 3:220–30.

4. Melchiorre, *Per un'ermeneutica della persona*, 289; and, in a wider context, Paul Ricoeur, *The Rule of Metaphor: Multi-Disciplinary Studies of the Creation of Meaning in Language*, trans. Robert Czerny (Toronto: University of Toronto Press, 1977), esp. 257–313; and Jüngel, *God as the Mystery of the World*.

notion has known in the three environments where it was both forged and applied: the trinitarian, the Christological, and the anthropological. One must also remember the fact that its significance and resulting use have been developed with a certain autonomy in each of them, even if also with important interactions.

The Ancient Epoch

In trinitarian doctrine It is in trinitarian doctrine that the concepts of *prósōpon* and *hypóstasis* (in Greek) and *persona* (in Latin) appear in the area of theology.[5] The semantic history of these three terms is instructive: *prósōpon* ("that which is before the eyes") designates the individual in his standing before others as a face,[6] a figure, and, in the language of tragedy, a mask, as is witnessed by the ample use made of it by the Septuagint, thereby translating the Hebrew *panîm*, face. *Hypóstasis*, in the philosophical language originating with Aristotle means that which "lies beneath," that which is existing of itself. *Persona*, in the philosophy influenced by Stoicism, indicates the single individual, and thus also in everyday language and in that of law, with reference to its social role.

The result is, even at the dictionary level, that the concept of person implies and expresses a tension between being in oneself and for oneself and being for the other. This tension is expressed in Greek in the relation between *hypóstasis* and *prósōpon*, but it is implicit in the Latin *persona*. In any case, the use of the two Greek terms in theology is not without ambiguity. While *prósopon* when used in reference to the three of the Trinity can be equivocated in modalistic fashion as if these were provisional "modes" or "masks" of the manifestation of the one God; *hypóstasis*, by means of its contiguity with *ousía*, could lead to the equivocation of tri-theism, as if the Father, Son, and Holy Spirit were three distinct substances. The Latin term *persona* was simpler and more concrete, but it could also lead to misunderstandings in both senses depending on the meanings toward which it tended. The authentic and pertinent meaning was therefore to be drawn from revelation and should itself clearly connote the use of a preexisting term.

In that fashion one determines that *hypóstasis* in Greek and *persona* in Latin—which in the end are seen as equivalent—express the distinct subsistence of the Father, Son, and Holy Spirit who are and remain one on the plane of substance (*ousía*) or nature (*phýsis*). The usage of the

5. See the accurate historical/systematic presentations by Andrea Milano, *Persona in teologia. Alle origini del significato di persona nel cristianesimo antico* (Naples: Ed. Dehoniane, 1984); and by Greshake, *Der dreieine Gott*.

6. It is the use we find for example in Paul, "Now we see as in a mirror, dimly, but then we will see face-to-face [*prósōpon prós prósōpon*]" (1 Cor 13:12).

two terms shows that the otherness implied by means of them *in divinis* "should not only be understood as the difference of names or of forms which, after properly fulfilling their function, are dissolved totally in God."[7] Person, in God, indicates that which is *per se* distinct and other, without breaking or damaging the unity of the being of God, but rather expressing by itself its truth.

Still in the realm of the Trinity, by the necessity of showing how the distinction is not to be understood as a breaking of the unity or the multiplicity of substance, the notion of person is clarified still further, and always more decisively, in the perspective of relation that Father, Son, and Holy Spirit live by, or better are, the one with respect to the other. This is true for the Cappadocians and Augustine and all the way to the definition of Thomas according to whom the divine person is subsistent relation (*relatio*) or subsistent relationship (*relativum*): where "relation designates the individuating element that distinguishes the person, and as subsisting designates the absolute ontological position of the person."[8] Even the concept of *perichoresis* in Greek, *circuminsessio/circumincessio* in Latin, by evoking the dynamic mutual indwelling of the three divine Persons in each other, calls for an essential unity in the order of mutual exchange in which each divine Person is fully himself in relation to the others.

In Christology In Christology the concept of person indicates instead, and directly, the function of stating the one identity of Jesus Christ, in the twofold of his two natures, divine and human, that subsist precisely in him in the uniqueness of his person as Word incarnate. This is so in the perspective of the dogmatic affirmation of Chalcedon (451) and in post-Chalcedonian development. In this case the aspect of relationality remains in the background.

In anthropology In the realm of anthropology, finally, there is the affirmation in Latin theology of the concept of person proposed by Severinus Boethius: "the individual substance of rational nature." In this case the accent is placed on the substantial individuality, with reference to relation not being omitted: because the rational nature of the human being is intelligent and free which therefore indicates openness and relation to the other. Of course, whereas in Thomas the very concept of the person is qualified as a subsisting relation at the trinitarian level, the interpersonal relationship remains almost completely implicit at the anthropological level.[9]

7. Basil Studer, "Der Person-Begriff in der fruhen kirchlichamtlichen Trinitaetslehre," *Theologie und Philosophie* 57 (1982): 168 (own trans.).

8. Lafont, *Peut-on connaitre Dieu en Jesus Christ?*, 124 (own trans.).

9. Richard of St. Victor proposed an integration in this sense, as mentioned earlier. Devel-

The Modern Era

Man as subject In modern philosophy we witness a development which in a certain way follows the inverse direction of the direction outlined up to now: what gains our attention in the first instance is the anthropological interest. Accordingly, the classical theological and philosophical concept of the person increasingly gives way to the philosophical concept of the subject which is also derived in its origin from Aristotelian metaphysical analysis.

On the one hand, the concept of *ousía*, translated in Latin as *substantia*, is speculatively clarified and distinguished to mean both essence (that which a being is) and subsistence, in Greek *hypóstasis* (the being which is in itself). The distinction was developed in a trinitarian ambiance in order to express the unity of the being of God and the threefoldness of personal subsistence (in that sense subsistence is equivalent to the concept of person, even if it tends toward defining its ontological constituent, that by which the person is such).

On the other hand, the concept of subject has its own history. Translating the Greek *hupokeimenon*, that which stands beneath, that which carries in itself the accidents, the subject in Aristotelian and Scholastic metaphysics has a general meaning indicating any kind of an individual existing being. In modern philosophy, however, it acquires instead a more restricted meaning in harmony with the anthropological change; the subject is, almost by definition, the psychological subject, the soul, man.

The concept of subject thus comes progressively to be characterized by four connotations, even if in a form that is not organic and coherent. These are as follows: consciousness and self-consciousness (from Descartes to Kant and to idealism); freedom; historicity (the being-there: the *Da-sein* of Heidegger, the being here and now of the subject); and intersubjectivity (the subject is such only in the presence of another subject). This is so even if the prevailing accent remains that of self-conscious individuality, an accent which, if absolutized and closed against any reference toward transcendence and otherness in general, cannot but bring about subjectivism and so immanentism and solipsism.

The consciousness of Christ In this context there emerged in the twentieth century *the question of the consciousness* (at the psychological level) *or of the I* (at the ontological level) of Christ: is it possible to speak of a

---

oping his reflection in a trinitarian framework, he proposes a definition of person in these terms: "Persona divina est divinae naturae incomunicabilis existentia." The decisive term is *ex-sistere*: *sistere* indicating the way of being and the *ex* indicating where from, the relationship that defines the person as such, his/her incommunicable singularity.

human consciousness of Jesus Christ? May we speak of a real growth in that consciousness? And how is one to connect his awareness as truly a man with the I of the Word, the second Person of the Trinity?

Is God a subject? The theme of consciousness and that of the I are then turned to God. The question is raised about whom should one or more consciousnesses be predicated? In other words, do the notions of awareness and the I attain the level of the divine nature or the level of the Persons? The theme of freedom also acquires in this context a fresh interest in both the Christological and trinitarian realm. How should we understand in fact the human and filial freedom of Jesus? And how should we speak of the freedom not only of God (with respect to creation) but also in God (in the relations among the three divine Persons)?

New Horizons

Modern philosophical development seems therefore to turn a deep furrow between trinitarian theology—which continues to use the classical metaphysical language of substance and persons in relation to God—and philosophical anthropology which interprets the human being in terms of subjectivity, consciousness, freedom, historicity, and intersubjectivity. There are even efforts to apply to God himself the concept of subjectivity, both in the sphere of philosophy (thus Fichte and Hegel), as also in the field of theology (thus Rosmini, Bulgakov, and Barth) and to think the freedom of God or, better, God as freedom in relation to creation and history (from Schelling to Pareyson). But there emerges also the question raised by Rahner as to whether the concept of person, tinged by now with the definition of self-consciousness, is still applicable to the trinitarian God in order to express the truth expressed by the dogma.

At the same time, during the twentieth century, the dialogical and personalistic philosophies of alterity, along with the emergence of the theme of the sexual difference, push for the integration of the positive conquests of modern thought, liberating them from their subjectivist and immanentistic derivation, in the theological and philosophical anthropology of Christian inspiration. At the same time concentration on the Paschal event brings about the emergence in an original fashion of the dynamic of gift, of *kénosis* (in the light of the Pauline hymn of Phil 2) and of reciprocity as constitutive expressions of the being-Person of Jesus, and, in the light of the trinitarian revelation which is realized eschatologically in him, of the divine Persons. This has obvious repercussions also on the anthropological level.

CHAPTER 25

Toward the Recovery of the Ontology of Unity and the Trinity

The journey traced out to this point shows how the need and the possibility to study the identity of the person in the fields of Christology, the Trinity, and anthropology is being proposed again today against a renewed horizon. As a result, at the same time this journey has illustrated how the trinitarian question *par excellence* can and must be studied with its important consequences for the interpretation and the exercise of the human relation with God and of human beings with each other—namely, how should the unity and the Trinity of God and in God be understood? L. Ladaria has noted: "Unity is not a datum preliminary to Christian revelation, but with it unity receives a new and much more profound sense. There is no Unity without Trinity, and vice versa. The divine unity that Christianity affirms is the *Unitas in Trinitate*, while it is not possible to understand the Trinity without keeping in mind the divine Unity, *Trinitas in Unitate*."[1] Let us summarize rapidly as in an ideal form the principal lines of solution proposed over the centuries. By distinguishing the solutions offered in Western theology and in Eastern theology, then reproposing the efforts at re-elaboration of the twentieth century, to arrive finally at the task which is put before contemporary theology.

1. Ladaria, *The Living and True God*, 31. It should be noted that in this way, the question is posed in renewed terms about the specific form of monotheism which is trinitarian monotheism. It is disclosed from within theological discourse, but at the same time, as I emphasized in part 1, it draws wider attention because of some phenomena emerging in this last stretch of time: comparison with Jewish and Islamic monotheism on one hand, and the challenge to, or even the criticism of, any form of monotheism as if it were not fully humanistic, or even worse, as if it were even considered anti-humanistic.

The Classical Solutions: Latin Theology and Greek Theology

In Western Theology

In the manualistic system, the unity of God is guaranteed, as has been said, by metaphysical discourse on the being of God as *per se* one, confirmed and corroborated by First Testament revelation that precedes and in a certain sense provides the foundation of discourse about the Trinity of the Persons. This presentation is meant to take up the approach of speculative theology on the Trinity which in the Western tradition was stressed, beginning with St. Augustine, and then was definitively elaborated by St. Thomas: setting out from the unity of the divine essence to show how, of itself, it would be activated in the Trinity of the Persons, known by means of revelation.

In reality and as we have been able to see when closely following the actual course of the Western theological tradition, the positions of Augustine and Thomas are much more nuanced and, at the same time, rich in possibilities, still largely unfathomed. Even though they are not linked in Augustine, the theme of *relatio in divinis* may not be definitively placed in its true place without taking into account the interpretive key of *caritas* perceived even as the explanatory sense of the divine being: *esse*. In Thomas there follows from our examination that discourse on the being of God as essentially one receives, in fact and by right, its content in the light of Christian revelation, and so from the mission *ad extra* of the Son and the Holy Spirit. The speculation of Rosmini runs in that very direction.

In Eastern Theology

The way followed by Eastern tradition is different. In it precedence is given to the concreteness of the hypostases, each one of which hypostatizes according to its property the divine *ousía* which of itself remains shrouded in its transcendent ineffability. In that way the unity of God is expressed hypostatically in the Father who is the principle (*arché*), the fountain (*pegé*), the root (*ríza*) from which divine life flows in the Son and in the Holy Spirit, and at the same time the end and the goal (*télos*) to which everything is led back and in which everything is recapitulated.

The Crisis of the Twentieth Century and the New Proposals

In the trinitarian theology of the twentieth century the crisis of metaphysics and the abandonment of the *De Deo Uno*[2] have relegated the reality of the unity of God to the margins, to the level of theoretical study if nothing else. Thus it has been in the theology of the West; for in that of the East—if one excludes the original proposals of the religious philosophers and the theologians of Russia—the traditional system has remained, although it has been more or less profoundly rethought. The protagonists of the trinitarian renewal of the twentieth century, however, did not avoid the question which is vital for the understanding of the trinitarian mystery. But they proposed solutions that are necessary to evaluate carefully in their results and in the questions they raise or in any case leave open. We can describe them with reference to the two stages of renewal as expounded earlier,[3] that which is expressed in the Rahnerian *Grundaxiom* and that which is concentrated in the rediscovery of the Paschal event.

The Horizon of Subjectivity

With regard to the first it is symptomatic to note how both Barth and Rahner, by placing at the center of theology the principle of revelation understood in a rather formal sense, even if radically determined in Christocentric perspective, arrive at a conclusion converging in many respects. God for them is the absolute mystery (*Deus absconditus*) who is revealed (*Deus revelatus*), and therefore he is the subject of the free and gratuitous revelation of himself.

With this, even if for different reasons, the principle of unity is no longer understood in terms of the category of divine being or substance, but in terms of the divine subjectivity which is one and is expressed, according to the terminology drawn into use by both, in three distinct modes of being (*Seinsweise*, thus Barth) or of subsistence (*Subsistenzweise*, thus Rahner).[4] In that fashion they intend to remain faithful to the event of

2. As L. Ladaria notes, the work of J. M. Rovira Belloso is brought to mind as one of the few recent essays that maintain the classical subdivision: *Tratado de Dios uno y trino* (Salamanca: Secretariado Trinitario, 1993). G. L. Müller first deals with the creator God as the God of Israel and Father of Jesus and then illustrates the Christology and pneumatology in his *Katholische Dogmatik. Für Studium und Praxis der Theologie* (Freiburg i.B.: Herder, 1996). For a rapid review of some recent analyses, see Ladaria, *The Living and the True God*, 41–45.

3. See part 1.

4. See Barth, *Kirchliche Dogmatik*, I/1: *Die Lehre vom Wort Gottes*; Rahner, "Il Dio Trino come fondamento originario e trascendente della storia della salvezza," in *Mysterium Salutis* III, Italian translation (Brescia: Queriniana, 1969), 401–507.

revelation and overcome the substantialistic drift of manualist theology, thus honoring the modern turn toward subjectivity.[5]

As has been carefully noted, the limit of such a proposal, which in Rahner is intended indeed to obviate the incipient tri-theism caused by the modern understanding of the concept of person as applied to the trinitarian being of God, is a certain modalism.[6] This becomes evident, for example, from the critique of the concept of person in trinitarian theology which Barth and Rahner consider to be inadequate and even misleading because of the evolution of meaning it has undergone during the course of modernity; Rahner explicitly excludes it from the dialogical lexicon expressing the rapport among the three of the Trinity. In the final analysis the impression is that of a God who, truly recognized in his mystery and absolute lordship, still runs the risk of presenting himself simply as "the condition of possibility of human subjectivity,"[7] and ultimately as the infinite analogate of the same.[8] In short, this is a unity that is considered too little from a biblical and trinitarian standpoint.

The Horizon of Communion

This is so true that in the second stage of trinitarian renewal of the twentieth century, which was marked in its beginning by the rediscovery of

5. What Hegel incisively affirmed is brought to mind with regard to the passage from a conception of God's being in terms of substance to an intuition of it as subject: "everything depends on understanding and expressing what is true not as *substance*, but just as decisively as *subject*" (*Phenomenology*, §60); "that the substance is essentially subject, in other words, expressed in that representation that enunciates the Absolute as *Spirit* [*Geist*], a very elevated concept belonging to the modern age and its religion" (*Phenomenology*, §19). In this regard see my *Il negativo e la Trinità*. See also Wolfhart Pannenberg, "Die Subjektivität Gottes und die Trinitätslehre," in *Grundfragen systematischer Theologie. Gesammelte Aufsätze* (Göttingen: Vandenhoeck and Ruprecht, 1980), 2:96–111; Ewald Vienken, "Einheit in Person – Person in Einheit. J. E. von Kuhns konkreter Monotheismus," in *Der Dreieine Gott und die eine Menschheit, für Bischof K. Hemmerle* (Freiburg i.B.: Herder, 1989), 85–101.

6. Thus for example, Kasper, *The God of Jesus Christ*, 300–303. With regard to the Hegelian *Denkform* and its impact on the trinitarian understanding of God, I take the liberty to refer to my *Il negativo e la Trinità*; in addition, the work of Michael Schulz, *Sein und Trinität: Systematische Erörterungen zur Religionsphilosophie G.W.F. Hegels im ontologiegeschichtlichen Rückblick auf J. Duns Scotus und I. Kant und die Hegel-Rezeption in der Seinsauslegung und Trinitätstheologie bei W. Pannenberg, E. Jüngel, K. Rahner un H.U. von Balthasar* (St. Ottilien: EOS Verlag, 1997).

7. Kasper, *The God of Jesus Christ*, 401. Nicola Ciola pertinently brought out that the trinitarian deficit for which Barth and Rahner are criticized stems from different motivations: "the 'seduction' of idealism plays a role in Barth, but connected with a hypostatized conception of the Word; in Rahner, the 'trinitarian defect' of his thought may be due to a lack of clarity in the relationship between the transcendent and history, but even more because of the lack of the hermeneutical circle with the trinitarian history of God in Jesus Christ." "Monoteismo cristiano come monoteismo trinitario," *Lateranum* 55 (1989): 250n56 (own trans.).

8. "While recognizing that the concept of person in modern times insists on the idea of the subject, of individuality, etc., Barth and Rahner not only did not reject it, but once they had received it, they applied it, not to the three persons in traditional language, but to God Himself as absolute subject. If this subject is the starting point, it is clear that it becomes difficult afterward to speak of three persons" (Ladaria, *The Living and True God*, 324).

the centrality of the Paschal mystery, the category of the subject in its usage *in divinis* was put aside. The dynamic of the reciprocal love of the three divine Persons was put into relief. The unity, let it be stressed, is not simply that of the one divine essence (because it is really given only in the relation among the Persons); nor is it even the unity of the one unique divine subject (because it would not take into account the dialogicality of the love lived by the divine Persons at Easter); it is rather the unity of the trinitarian "we." This approach finds various modulations according to the authors:[9] thus, for example, H. Mühlen speaks of an "*a priori We*";[10] J. Moltmann of unification (*unitedness* and also *unification*) or of "perichoretic unity";[11] E. Jüngel of "the radiant event of love itself" and "history of love,"[12] a language that has been taken up by B. Forte.[13]

Taking into account the preceding proposals, and having put them through an attentive analysis that weighs their positive aspects and their limits, G. Greshake arrived at the formulation of this summary thesis: "the one Christian God is communion, he realizes his being in the dialogue of love of the three Persons."[14] And this is how he expresses it:

The unity of God is a relational unity of love, more original and superior to every understanding, in which the three divine persons communicate reciprocally the one divine life and, in such an exchange, are distinguished and at the same time are manifested as one thing in the highest possible degree. Unity of relation, of love, and not unity of substance or of the collective: this is the new Christian idea of unity which shines out in the revelation of the one-triune God.[15]

9. In addition to the specific sections dedicated to a review of these positions by G. Greshake and L. Ladaria, see John O'Donnell, "The Trinity as Divine Community," *Gregorianum* 69 (1988): 5–34; Bernd J. Hilberath, *Der dreieinige Gott und die Gemeinschaft der Menschen* (Mainz: Matthias-Grünewald, 1990).

10. Heribert Mühlen, *Der Heilige Geist als Person: In der Trinität bei der Inkarnation und im Gnadebund: Ich-Du-Wir* (Münster: Aschendorff, 1963), and *Una mystica persona: die Kirche als das Mysteriu der Identität des Heiligen Geistes in Christus und den Christen: eine Person in vielen Personen* (München: F. Schöning, 1964), a thesis that the author was defining over several years. For a rigorous reexamination of the question of personhood in Mühlen's theology, see Alessandro Clemenzia, *Nella Trinità come Chiesa: In dialogo con Heribert Mühlen* (Rome: Città Nuova, 2012). The author persuasively demonstrates how in reality the personological category of the "We" is used in two ways by Mühlen: on one hand indicating "a priori," the intrinsic communional intentionality of the divine nature; and at the same time, on the other hand, being a property of the Holy Spirit as the reciprocating event of the I-you relationship between the Father and the Son which fulfills the trinitarian life and transmits it to humanity in the church as *Una mystica Persona*.

11. See Moltmann, *Trinität und Reich Gottes*, summarized in his "L'unità invitante del Dio uno e trino," *Concilium*, no. 1 (1985): 75–87; see also his *In der Geschichte des dreieinigen Gottes. Beiträge zur trinitarischen Theologie* (Munich: Kaiser Verlag, 1991).

12. Jüngel, *God as the Mystery of the World*, 327–28.

13. Bruno Forte, *The Trinity as History: Saga of the Christian God*, trans. Paul Rotondi (New York: Alba House, 1989), 145: "The unity of the paschal event is the unity of the event of love which loves (the Father), which is loved (the Son), and which unites in freedom (the Spirit: see 1 Jn 4:7–16)."

14. Greshake, *Der dreieine Gott*, 182.

15. Gisbert Greshake, *An den drei-einen Gott glauben: Ein Schluessel zum Verstehen* (Freiburg

Toward a Re-engagement with the Question

But even these last proposals, while deliberately taking into account, and much more than the classical positions do, the originality of the event of Jesus Christ witnessed to in the New Testament, and while explicitly committing themselves to avoiding that the accentuation of the personal *agapic* dynamism should decline into a sort of naïve tri-theism, are not completely satisfactory. Is it sufficient to say—we ought in fact to ask—that the being-one of God is communion? Is there not thereby the danger of equivocating unity with the addition, even if completely within the unity, of three realities already given in themselves as distinct? W. Pannenberg, for example, in the first volume of his *Systematic Theology* incisively underlines:

> The unity of Father, Son and Spirit certainly finds expression in the relations of salvation history.... But this joint working of the persons and their mutual perichoresis must also be seen as an expression of the unity of the divine essence. The unity of the divine essence is a theme of its own in this regard.... It must also show whether ... we can think of the divine essence as the epitome of the personal relations among Father, Son, and Spirit.[16]

The questions directed toward the perichoretic or communional perspective in the understanding of the trinitarian unity in order to bring out its insufficiency, and the possible avenues of solution subsequently proposed move in different directions.

In the Perspective of the Tradition of the West

The first approach, indicated for example by G. Lafont, holds the necessity of the recovery of the notion of being in the sense of *ousía* in order to mention the unity and unicity of God. Lafont writes:

> We need in fact the concept of the one, in no way multiplied and expressed in a direct manner, analogous of course, but not metaphorical, because here we are dealing with absolute monotheism.... The dynamism is in the hypostatic exchange; only a static concept, that of *ousía* precisely, can show us that which is exchanged and that which, in the exchange, constitutes each person as person. In this precise point, I cannot see how we can avoid having recourse, quite simply, to the being of God, which St. Thomas declares at the same time to be absolutely simple (and therefore beyond every determination) and perfect (and therefore comprehensive, and beyond, every determination).[17]

i.B.: Herder, 1998), translated into Italian by Paul Renner as *Il Dio unitrino: Teologia trinitaria* (Brescia: Queriniana, 1999), 29 (own trans.).

16. Wolfhart Pannenberg, *Systematic Theology*, vol. 1, trans. Geoffrey W. Bromiley (Grand Rapids, Mich.: Eerdmans, 1991), 334.

17. Translation from a letter addressed to me dated July 21, 1999; see also Lafont, *God, Time*

In the Perspective of the Tradition of the East

A second direction is that of a recovery of the perspective of Eastern theology in the sense of the unity (formal and recapitulatory) of the three in the Father. Thus, for example, John Zizioulas links the vision of the communional being of the divine Persons with that of the Father, precisely as the fountain and recapitulator of the three,[18] while in the Catholic field A. Staglianò, basing himself on certain insights offered by K. Rahner and W. Kasper, arrives at this formulation: "God is Father, Son and Spirit, *but in the Father God is one*."[19]

In the Perspective of a Critical Hearing of Modernity

Another direction is that indicated by E. Salmann. Having brilliantly accounted for the fact that "the divine nature or essence has almost disappeared from the scene," as the disappearance of the "ablative" from the exercise of trinitarian theology demonstrates, and having discussed critically the efforts to replace it in some of the ways previously recalled, he translated the concept of divine nature into that of "shared divine consciousness" which obviously "does not exist in itself, but only insofar as it is communicated and fully shared by and in the persons." It may only be described, according to Salmann, as "the clear self-rapport of God with Himself in Himself," which "acts in such a way that He sees and understands everything and by means of Himself, in His own consciousness."[20]

---

and Being. L. Oeing-Hanoff positioned himself along this line years earlier, taking a position concerning the concept of "perichoretic unity" proposed by Jürgen Moltmann; see Oeing-Hanoff, "Die Wesensidentität der göttlichen Personen ist Grund ihrer Perichorese, nicht ist umgekehrt die Einheit Gottes Resultat der Perichorese der göttlchen Personen," in *Trinität. Aktuelle Perspektiven der Theologie*, ed. W. Breuning (Freiburg i.B.: Herder, 1984), 143–82, at 159–60.

18. John Zizioulas, *Being as Communion* (New York: St. Vladimir's Seminary Press, 2000): "Among the Greek Fathers the unity of God, the one God, and the ontological 'principle' or 'cause' of the being and life of God does not consist in the one substance of God but in the *hypostasis*, that is, *the person of the father*.... If God exists because the Father exists, that is, He who out of love freely begets the Son and brings forth the Spirit. Thus God as person—as the hypostasis of the Father—makes the one divine substance to be that which it is: the one God" (40–41).

19. Antonio Staglianò, "Le sfide dei monoteismi per il ripensamento della dottrina trinitaria: prospettive sistematiche," *Vivarium* 6, no. 1 (1998): 49–77 (own trans.), which develops the themes already presented (with reference not only to the Eastern tradition, but also to the indications advanced in this regard by Rahner and Kasper) in the previously mentioned volume, *The Living and True God*. Ladaria, in fact, decisively affirms: "I do not agree with the opinion that tends to identify the one God with the Father. There are clear conclusions that can be derived from the article written by K. Rahner, "*Theos* in the New Testament," in *Theological Investigations* (New York: Seabury, 1961), 1:79–148, on the fact that in the New Testament God refers to the Father and that God is the God of the Old Testament. Hence, we do not follow the idea that whatever must be said about God is simply said about the Father. The Father is such only in his relationship with the Son and the Holy Spirit, and the three of them make up the one God." *The Living and True God*, 43n45.

20. Elmar Salmann, "La natura scordata: Un futile elogio dell'ablativo," in *Abitando la Trinità*, 27–43 (own trans.). For a broader formulation of the issue, see what Salmann already wrote in *Neuzeit und Offenbarung. Studien zur trinitarischen Analogik des Christentums* (Rome: Pont.

In that way the classical theme of the divine *ousía* is rethought in modern terms of consciousness, but avoiding falling into the Hegelian trap of a tendentially monological subjectivity in which the proposals of Barth and Rahner still appear to be employed in many respects. But the question arises if it is possible in this way to express the original vitality and concreteness of the relationships among the Father, the Son, and the Holy Spirit as salvation history presents them to us: expressions of God, *agápe*. On the other hand, is not the concept of "shared consciousness" still simply collective?

The Approach of Hans Urs von Balthasar

Von Balthasar traces out a different perspective. He is certainly the person who more than everyone else has been engaged in rethinking and reproposing the classical language of the unity and trinity of God. He illustrates the divine essence as coinciding with the event of the reciprocal interpersonal donation.[21] To my mind this is the most fruitful approach. It invites a focusing of attention on the being of God as *agápe* and, therefore, as co-original coincidence of unity and distinction realizing themselves in the dynamism of the reciprocal trinitarian giving of Father, Son, and Holy Spirit: a giving that is simultaneously expropriation and appropriation, emptying and filling, sacrifice and joy.

In reality von Balthasar does not offer a systematic treatment of the question but, considering it essential and urgent, deals with it with clarity in more than one context and on more than one occasion. He claims in fact that it is necessary to go beyond the classical treatment that gives precedence to the discourse on the essence over that of the Trinity,[22] but at the same time he evaluates the concept of "perichoretic unity" to be insufficient.[23] The perspective he proposes moves in the direction of the essence of God "in hypostatic unity" which he defines as "substantial love."[24] He explains: "Since each Person, existing as one element in the stream of processions, is per se identical with God's essence or being, there is no question of the latter being regarded as a fourth thing, aloof from the busy to-and-fro of what passes between the Persons: no, it must be identical with it."[25] On the other hand, as I have already noted earlier,

Ateneo Sant'Anselmo, 1986), esp. 271–315 and 355–88. Recently the proposal was reexamined in his "Presenza e critica. Sulle affinità elettive tra filosofia e mistica," in *Filosofia e mistica*, ed. A. Molinaro and E. Salmann, 29–60 (Rome: Pont. Ateneo Sant'Anselmo, 1997), esp. 44.

21. See Massimo Serretti, *Il mistero della eterna generazione del Figlio attraverso l'opera di H.U. von Balthasar* (Rome: PUL-Mursia, 1998), esp. 39–66.

22. Hans Urs von Balthasar, *Theo-Logic*, vol. 2: *Truth of God*, trans. Adrian J. Walker (San Francisco, Calif.: Ignatius Press, 2004), 138.

23. With explicit reference to Moltmann, see von Balthasar, *Theo-logic*, 3:157n2.

24. Ibid., 2:154.

25. Von Balthasar, *Theo-Drama*, 5:66.

in spite of the objective reference to the tri-Personal dynamic of the divine love, in von Balthasar there does not appear with sufficient force and clarity the trinitarian reciprocity that is attested by the New Testament testimony to the divine action in Jesus Christ.

In Summary

Taking into account, then, the perspective outlined by von Balthasar and attempting to integrate it further with the acquisitions gained positively from the other perspectives, one could show the following "solid points" that ought to be affirmed at the same time: the being of God, which is revealed to us in Jesus, is *agápe* (which therefore expresses the nature of God in traditional terms). This means that God is the original coincidence of indissoluble unity and real distinction and otherness: Father, Son, and Holy Spirit (the three divine Persons). Such coincidence is activated ordinarily (according to the *táxis* of the divine Persons) and in trinitarian fashion (in the perichoretic relationship of Father, Son, and Holy Spirit), in the event of their reciprocal giving revealed and shared in the Passover of death/resurrection of Jesus who pours out the fullness of the Spirit, an event in which each Person is himself (a divine Person who is the one God) in being for, with and in the others (the *perichoresis* as the event of the one God). What emerges with the summary proposed up to now, beginning with the questions raised by contemporary theology, is that ultimately the theme of the unity and unicity of the trinitarian God has returned to the center of attention and at the same time its explanation is anything but agreed upon. It rather invites a renewed ontological hermeneutic of the revealed data and their dogmatic expression.

CHAPTER 26

The Unity and Trinity of God in the Logic of Revelation

Thus far we have seen the *status quaestionis*, which pivots around the following question: how is it possible to think about the unity of God in the light of Christological-trinitarian revelation which culminates in the Easter event? Or, in other words, what defines Christian monotheism as such, in the originality of its event, as trinitarian monotheism with respect to the other forms of monotheism? In order to reply it seems above all essential to trace out in relevant form—beginning with Christological revelation—certain basic lines of a methodological character which, taking into account instances and acquisitions yielded by the journey followed until now, permit the formation of a theological response to the question in an appropriate form.

On the Biblical Meaning of the Unicity and Unity of God

Above all, it is necessary to reflect more fully on the work I have done until now, already at the semantic level, on the term "monotheism" and on the connection and distinction between the concepts of the unicity and the unity of God as referred to him. It is important in fact to remember that the concept of monotheism was created, in its current meaning, fairly recently and precisely in its opposition to "polytheism" with the purpose of qualifying, on the level of the sciences of religion, those religious experiences and traditions which arrive at the affirmation of only one God over against the inconsistent plurality of the many and false gods.[1]

The notion of monotheism is therefore rather generic and negative to the point, as I noted above, that it is specified either in reference to the other religions that are based on the faith of Abraham (and then one

1. See for an example, how Birkheuser frames the treatment under the title "Monoteismo" in the *Nuovo Dizionario delle Religioni*, ed. H. Waldenfels (Cinisello Balsamo: San Paolo, 1993).

speaks of Abrahamic monotheism or revelation) or with reference to the revelation of Jesus Christ (and then one speaks of Christian or trinitarian monotheism). This means that it is not correct simply to compare the Trinity with monotheism: it is necessary to specify at once the *kind* of monotheism in question, identifying precisely the Trinity itself as the specifically Christological figure of monotheism.

As to the use of the concepts of unicity and unity with respect to the semantics of monotheism, it is necessary to dwell on their real significance which is diverse at least in part. This is true both under the historical-salvific profile and the theoretical profile (this second profile was clearly present in the manualist treatment of the *De Deo Uno*).[2] In fact, from the point of view of the history of salvation it was first the unicity of God that was revealed and welcomed in faith: as a result, Israel professed to have only one God, YHWH, recognized as "the" God, excluding the false gods; and as a consequence then his being is revealed in itself as one and only one.

The concept of unicity, therefore, *per se* indicates at once the exclusivity of God which is revealed so that only God (YHWH) is God; while the concept of unity is meant to indicate the very being of God, his "nature," to use the terminology of the theological tradition. But unity also is not to be understood only in its metaphysical meaning previous, so to speak, to revelation (by which the unity of God is the foundation of his unicity), but at the same time according to that original form that is proposed by revelation.

Relational, Inclusive, and Effusive Unity

This means—and this is a second consideration—that to live in faith and to think in its relevant intelligibility the Christological and trinitarian meaning of Christian monotheism, it is necessary to be faithful to the logic unfolded by revelation. Revealed monotheism is not a datum of faith acquired once for all from the beginning: rather it is an event that unfolds in time.[3] God is known for who he is in the very act of his being

2. See Manaranche, *Il monoteismo cristiano*, 183–90.

3. In accordance with what I presented in part 1 regarding the significance of the name revealed by God himself, YHWH, the International Theological Commission writes: "The monotheism of the Old Testament has it origins in a supernatural revelation and therefore retains an intrinsic relation to—indeed, demands—the Trinitarian revelation" (ITC, "Theology, Christology, Anthropology," 1.B, 3); and F. Ladaria comments: "In a certain sense the revelation of the fullness of the divine 'common' essence and the revelation of God as Father, as Son, and as Holy Spirit almost run parallel. Or better yet, both revelations make up a unity, grow at the same time and the same understanding, because they constitute the *sole* self-revelation of God who is one, Father, Son, and Holy Spirit. We must think, consequently, that there exists a progressive manifestation of the one and only one God in the history of salvation of the old and the new testament" (*The Living and True God*, 404–5).

revealed to humanity as the living God, he who sets up a covenant with his people (notice at once the revelation of the name of God to Moses). The exceptional Christological newness resides in the fact that in the fullness of time the "I am" pronounced by God in the First Testament is manifested, from its center, in the "I am" of Jesus Christ who thereby may say, "The Father and I are one" (Jn 10:30). In this affirmation, which in the light of Easter sums up the meaning of the entire Christological event, "When you have lifted up the Son of Man, then you will realize that I am" (Jn 8:28), Jesus does not simply reaffirm the monotheism of the Fathers as in fact he did referring to the *Shema Israel* (see Mk 10:18; 12:29–32). Rather, he introduces us into the very life of God.

That involves two things indissolubly linked to each other: on the one hand, that Jesus, and Jesus crucified and risen, comes to define the face of God whose being unique and one cannot be understood anymore without or outside of the distinction in the unity between Jesus and the Father in the Holy Spirit. On the other hand we are freely introduced by the gift of the Spirit who arouses faith as a response of our freedom to contemplate, nay to participate truly—in our relationship with the Father and with one another—in the same relationship of love that Jesus lives with the Father in the Holy Spirit. As St. Paul says: "And because you are children, God has sent the Spirit of his Son into our hearts, crying, 'Abba! Father!'" (Gal 4:6). In the final analysis, this is the purpose of the coming of the Son of God into the world: "to gather into one [*eis hén*] the dispersed children of God" (Jn 11:52). For that reason Jesus prays to the Father at the Last Supper, "As you, Father, are in me and I am in you, may they also be one [*hén*] in us, so that the world may believe that you have sent me" (Jn 17:21).

This reality, which is basic in Christian faith, has a fundamental methodological consequence for the theology of the unity and the trinity of God: and that is that it cannot be understood from outside God but only lived and contemplated from within our participation as church in the divine filiation of the Son/*Lógos* which is given to us gratuitously in Jesus Christ by means of the gift of the Holy Spirit. The unity of God, insofar as it is trinitarian, is not simply *exclusive*: in the sense that it affirms the absolute sovereignty of God, though also that, of course; but it is *inclusive*, or better still *effusive*, in the sense that it opens and shares the same mystery by means of the revelation of Jesus Christ, as the only-begotten Son, and the gift of the Holy Spirit, as the Spirit of divine filiation for creatures. This happens without God ceasing thereby to be the one true God and without the Son and the Holy Spirit multiplying the being of the one God or causing confusion between the divinity of God and the creatureliness of human beings.

The fact is that, thanks to Jesus Christ, the Son of God become flesh, we are able to access ontologically and existentially the unity and Trinity of God, which remains indeed a mystery transcending us infinitely as God transcends creation, not placing us in front of it but being introduced there as the body and spouse of Christ by means of the gift of the Holy Spirit. In that sense, the Christian religion, as John Paul II wrote in *Tertio Millennio Adveniente*, is "the religion of '*dwelling in the heart of God*'" (par. 8). The theological truth of the unity and the Trinity is at the same time anthropological truth: it is the truth of God who is love and as such creates us in order to become in him participants in his very life.

The Double Language of the Unity of/in God

If this is the logic of revelation, how does one understand then the unity and the Trinity of God beginning with the event of Jesus Christ, or rather with our being-in-Christ? From what has been said, it is clear that one may not presuppose a definitive ontology of the being one of God within trinitarian revelation, even if, anthropologically speaking, a preliminary human perception of the mystery of God does occur prior to being fully revealed in Christ.[4] However, beginning with revelation and within revelation it is necessary to develop coherently an ontology that would express the being-one of God as the principle and the realization, the *alpha* and *omega*, at the same time of the relations of love that constitute and that manifest in the history of salvation the three divine Persons. A unity in distinction, which, precisely inasmuch as it is revealed, is at the same time freely participated in by creation.

The New Testament in fact speaks of a being one in Christ (Gal 3:28) which, at the end of time, will flow into the eschatological reality so that "God may be all in all" (1 Cor 15:28). Obviously, in order to fulfill this task, indispensable as it is for an authentic Christian theology of the triune God, it is necessary to take into account the analogical character of

4. It is enough to recall what the First Vatican Council teaches in this regard in the dogmatic constitution, *Dei Filius*, in conformity with the biblical and theological tradition. As I noted earlier, it does not only affirm: "Sancta catholica apostolica Romana Ecclesia credit et confitetur, unum esse Deum verum et vivum ... qui cum sit una singularis, simplex omnino et incommutabilis substantia spiritualis, praedicandus est re et essentia a mundo distinctus" (DH 3001), but also: "Eadem sancta mater Ecclesia tenet et docet, Deum, rerum omnium principium et finem, naturali humanae rationis lumine e rebus creatis certo cognosci posse" (DH 3004; see also 3026). In this sense, the ITC emphasized that "Christian Theism does not exclude natural Theism, but on the contrary presupposes it in its own way. For Christian Theism takes its origin from God revealing himself according to a most free intention of his will; while natural Theism pertains intrinsically to human reason, as the First Vatican Council teaches" ("Theology, Christology, Anthropology," 1.B, 2); even though both the concept of "theism" as well as the adjective "natural" pose some problems. J. B. Metz called attention to all of this, emphasizing that the conception of revelation offered by *Dei Verbum* should be more organically linked with that proposed by Vatican I in *Dei Filius*.

language along with the fact that what we must understand over time to be able to reach a provisional though realistic comprehension happens simultaneously in God in the act of eternity. With this in mind, we should express the unity and the trinity of God by interweaving the two languages or perspectives used by tradition ("redoublement du langage" as G. Lafont has defined it): the language of being (being one expressed *essentialiter*) and that of the Persons (being one expressed *personaliter*), but shaping both more than has been done in the tradition whether in the West or the East, whether classical or modern, in the newness disclosed by the Christological event of God who is *agápe*.

On the one hand, and for its own sake, it is necessary to affirm that God is one in the original being and personal subsistence of the three divine Persons, inasmuch as he is the act or the tri-Personal event of the Father who loves the Son generating him in the Spirit, of the Son who is generated by the Father who loves him again by re-donating himself in the Spirit, and the Holy Spirit who proceeds from their reciprocal love and who re-donates himself to them in such a manner that God would not exist if the Persons did not exist. He is only in the Persons, and in all three simultaneously in such a manner that each one of them is God, the one true God.[5]

5. The proposed utilization of the concepts of act and event here is meant to re-express in a dynamic and personalistic form what is static and prepersonal as essence. It is enough to think for example of the Thomistic *actus essendi*. I am aware however that it would be necessary to also be able to express the subjective-conscious dimension of the one God without falling into the dangers indicated earlier. Therefore, the relationship between God as one subject and the three Persons, must be studied further. This was attempted by A. Rosmini and S. Bulgakov, for example (see in this regard what I wrote in *L'altro di Dio*, 90–98, where G. Lafont's pertinent proposal was reviewed). B. Lonergan also dealt with the issue, simultaneously affirming the unity of the divine consciousness and the ontological and psychological circumincession of the divine persons; see G. B. Sala's presentation and evaluation of his claims in *"Persona" e "Natura" nell'itinerario speculativo di B. J. F. Lonergan s.j. (1904–1984)* (Milan: Glossa, 1998), esp. 260–82. See also what F. Bourassa, J.-H. Nicolas, and L. Ladaria succinctly write in this regard, referring to B. Lonergan in Ladaria, *The Living and True God*, 325–31. In any case, it seems to me that the prospect presented above can find confirmation in the work of two of the most ingenious theologians that attempted to rethink this: A. Rosmini and P. Florensky. As the former writes: "the divine *essence* which is in the principle and is communicated, is put in act through the same act through which the divine persons, really distinct from each other, are put in act.... The principle and its perfection are therefore constituted by the fact that the terms are something different from the principle. The principle would neither be, nor understand itself, nor be perfect, if it did not, of itself, produce the terms that as terms are different from it" (*Theosophy* 43:282). Pavel Florensky, for his part, expresses it this way: "Truth is the contemplation of Oneself through Another in a Third: Father, Son, and Spirit. Such is the metaphysical definition of the 'essence' (*ousía*) of the self-proving Subject, which is, as is evident, a substantial relationship.... the *ousia* of the Truth is the Infinite act of Three in Unity" (*The Pillar and Ground of the Truth*, 37). The concept of event is utilized by von Balthasar with respect to the immanent Trinity when he writes: "What happens in the Trinity is, however, far more than a motionless order or sequence, for expressions such as 'beget,' 'give birth,' 'proceed' and 'breathe forth' refer to eternal acts in which God genuinely 'takes place.' We must resolve to see these two apparently contradictory concepts as a unity: eternal or absolute Being—and 'happening'" (*Theo-Drama*, 5:67).

On the other hand, and for its own sake, it is necessary to state at the same time that God is one because of and in the relations of love of the three divine Persons precisely by reason of the fact that each of them, in the manner appropriate to each, is given fully to the others and is received from them in return, to the point that all of them "are consumed," so to speak, in one, being the one God: "I and the Father are one." The divine Persons are each themselves inasmuch as they give themselves fully to the others: they are themselves inasmuch as they are for and in the other two who give each back to themselves.

This is the theological meaning of the faith of the church in the God revealed in Jesus Christ as simultaneously one and triune. To say it once again with St. Gregory Nazianzen, "I have only begun to think of the unity and here I am immersed in the splendor of the Trinity: I have only begun to think of the Trinity and it is the unity that lays hold of me" (*Orationes* 40–41, in PG 36:471). The pulsating and radiating heart of the event in which the one God is disclosed in the three, and the three are consumed in the one, is the *agápe* of which the crucified and risen Christ is the eschatological manifestation in the history of salvation, *agápe* which is given to us in the gift of the Holy Spirit and which introduces us gratuitously and freely into the infinite dynamism of this life.

CHAPTER 27

The Unity and the Trinity of God in the Rhythm of a Trinitarian Ontology

Having attempted to delineate the lines that describe the horizon disclosed concretely by the revelation culminating in Jesus Christ, of the unity and the Trinity of God, I will now attempt to delineate the distinctive traits of an ontology measured by this event and on this event. With regard to such an ontology, in truth, the theological tradition and its critical reuse in our times have offered points that are solid and to be retained. From them we may not prescind. However, it is a matter of taking up, with mature and conscious hermeneutics, this precise language as handed on by the tradition, drawing from its intrinsic meaning the explication of some directions proposed to our theological understanding by ecclesial self-consciousness and by contemporary, modern thinking. These, it seems, can be synthesized in three fundamental themes: reciprocity, nonbeing, freedom.[1]

The Horizon of Trinitarian Ontology

The whole journey we have followed makes evident the strict connection between philosophical discourse on being (ontology) and theological discourse about God. The convergence between the conception of God as substance and Greek philosophy's first being, and the revelation of God as "he who is" in the Book of Exodus, which has characterized the first centuries of Christian theology and the synthesis of Scholasticism has provided the sure foundation for a progressive manifestation of the newness implied by Christological revelation, not only for the image of God embraced in faith but also for its theological and philosophical understanding.

1. Something of what I will try to say here was offered in a nutshell as the task of trinitarian theology in the preface to the Spanish edition of my *Evento pasquale. Trinità e storia.*

A Decisive Task for Thought

Already in his *Introduction to Christianity* (1968), Joseph Ratzinger, when dealing with the dogmatic understanding of the Trinity and referring vigorously to St. Augustine and to the question of the predication *in divinis* of substance and relation, affirmed that here

> lies concealed a revolution in man's view of the world: the sole dominion of thinking in terms of substance is ended; relation is discovered as an equally valid primordial mode of reality. It becomes possible to surmount what we call today "objectifying thought"; a new plane of being comes into view. It is probably true to say that the task imposed on philosophy as a result of these facts is far from being completed—so much does modern thought depend on the possibilities thus disclosed, without which it would be inconceivable.[2]

Three observations: the vigorous underlining of the novelty in the picture of being as offered by trinitarian revelation; connected with the emergence of a new thinking (not "objectivizing" but "personalistic"); and the arduous and fascinating task that remains to be done and that is demanded by modern thought itself, apparently so distant from Christian faith.

According to Ratzinger, among many others sharing this position, the hope is that "This will perhaps make it clear how the doctrine of the Trinity, when properly understood, can become the reference point of theology that anchors all other lines of Christian thought."[3] For his part, John Paul II has written in *Fides et Ratio* (par. 93):

> The very heart of theological enquiry will thus be the contemplation of the mystery of the Triune God. The approach to this mystery begins with reflection upon the mystery of the Incarnation of the Son of God: his coming as man, his going to his Passion and Death, a mystery issuing into his glorious Resurrection and Ascension to the right hand of the Father, whence he would send the Spirit of truth to bring his Church to birth and give her growth. From this vantage-point, the prime commitment of theology is seen to be the understanding of God's *kenosis*, a grand and mysterious truth for the human mind, which finds it inconceivable that suffering and death can express a love which gives itself and seeks nothing in return.

The indication is clear and precise. The mystery of God may only be contemplated beginning with the event of the incarnation which finds its summit in the Passover of the death and resurrection of Jesus Christ. The Paschal event is the key to accessing the mystery of God. This is in harmony with what contemporary theology, as I have shown, has decisive-

2. Ratzinger, *Introduction to Christianity*, 184.
3. Ibid., 188.

ly highlighted by placing methodically at the center of its reflection the "fundamental axiom" of Rahner. However, the affirmation of John Paul II is not satisfied with this determination, as fundamental as it may be, but it urges our thinking by saying that to penetrate into the mystery of God in himself, as revealed to us in Christ crucified and risen, "the understanding of the *kenosis* of God" is necessary.

The invitation is not only to contemplate in faith the abyss of love that is made visible and tangible in the Paschal event, but to also penetrate its meaning with a view to the understanding of the being of God and, in its light, of created being. It is John Paul II himself who made explicit this issue both when he invited theologians to pay "particular attention to the philosophical implications of the Word of God," and to "reflect in their work all the speculative and practical breadth of the science of theology" (*Fides et Ratio*, par. 105); as also when he exhorted them to "to propose anew the problem of being—and this in harmony with the demands and insights of the entire philosophical tradition, including philosophy of more recent times, without lapsing into sterile repetition of antiquated formulas" (par. 97).

It is significant that Benedict XVI, in the social encyclical *Caritas in Veritate*, emphasizes the significance of the cultural understanding which derives intrinsically from faith in God the Trinity (par. 54):

> The theme of development can be identified with the inclusion-in-relation of all individuals and peoples within the one community of the human family, built in solidarity on the basis of the fundamental values of justice and peace. This perspective is illuminated in a striking way by the relationship between the Persons of the Trinity within the one divine Substance. The Trinity is absolute unity insofar as the three divine Persons are pure relationality. The reciprocal transparency among the divine Persons is total and the bond between each of them complete, since they constitute a unique and absolute unity. God desires to incorporate us into this reality of communion as well: "that they may be one even as we are one" (Jn 17:22). The Church is a sign and instrument of this unity. Relationships between human beings throughout history cannot but be enriched by reference to this divine model. In particular, *in the light of the revealed mystery of the Trinity*, we understand that true openness does not mean loss of individual identity but profound interpenetration.

In the frame designed by the revelation of God in Jesus there is manifested in that fashion—looking at God the Trinity of love in whose "image and likeness" humanity is created and re-created—"a metaphysical interpretation of the humanum in which relationality is an essential element" (par. 55). This demands the reawakening of an "anthropological and ethical spirit" capable of orienting globalization "towards the humanizing goal of solidarity" (par. 42). In the concrete dimension of doctrinal and practical politics and economics, this implies the utilization of that anthropology of relation, in other words, of gift and gratuity (par. 34), of reciprocity and fraternity (pars. 9, 38, 57), which is the interior grammar and the value verification of every authentic and constructive political and economic activity.

On the Concept of Trinitarian Ontology

The concept of trinitarian ontology is actually rather recent. In its essence already the Church Fathers—for example, St. Augustine in his *De Trinitate*—observed in creation the imprint of the creator who, being Trinity as Christ reveals, cannot but impart a trinitarian imprint. Nonetheless, a trinitarian ontology in a specific sense has been spoken of only in recent decades. It has in fact risen to importance mostly thanks to the brief treatise by Klaus Hemmerle, published in 1976, which carries the programmatic title of *Theses for a Trinitarian Ontology*. In this work the author provides an organic and programmatic form to a series of intuitions which were circulating for some time in some circles of Catholic philosophy and theology—it is enough to think of von Balthasar, to whom the *Theses* are dedicated, but one should not forget T. Haecker, C. Kaliba, and E. Przywara. Nor should one forget the more classical perspective of the "metaphysics of charity" going back to A. Rosmini, as well as the more Christological idea of the "ontology of gift" (P. A. Sequeri) which with their peculiar accents move along similar lines.

But what is the specific meaning of trinitarian ontology? Does it not risk confusing philosophy, to whose discourse ontology belongs, with theology, which has every reason to speak of the Trinity? Does it not risk, in other words—as Heidegger wrote in *Phenomenology and Theology* (1927)—to speak of a "fiery iron"? In reality, the first objective of a trinitarian ontology is that of overcoming the abstract separation between philosophy and theology according to the rigid model prevailing with Neoscholasticism in order to activate a fecund reciprocity between the two that would avoid at the same time every compromising confusion.

The truth ultimately is that trinitarian ontology is meant to study seriously that model of relation between the human and the divine which is sanctioned by the dogma of Chalcedon which in order to express the divine and human natures of the one Person of the Christ, the Word become flesh, affirms that this takes place "without separation" and "without confusion." Hemmerle stresses that "in the relationship of exchange between philosophy and theology there is entailed even today, a *chance* to recover ontology again."[4] But such a chance implies an awareness of the

4. Hemmerle, *Tesi di ontologia trinitaria*, 29 (own trans.).

complex relationship between Greek philosophy and Hebrew-Christian revelation in the course of the formation of Western culture.

On the Relationship between Revelation and Ontology

The term *ontology*, the bearer of a long history that begins in the West with the dawn of Greek philosophy and reaches as far as Heidegger and beyond, points to something extremely simple and decisive at the same time: the knowledge of the *lógos* of beingness, of meaning, of the truth of that which is. It has nothing to do with knowing anything in particular, with one genus of reality rather than another: rather it has to do with the very horizon within which every knowing is activated.

This reality in front of me *is*; I myself *am*; you *are*: in their own way, each of these realities *is*, is an existing being is something which is. But what is being and being a being, what are the truth, the light, the meaning offered to you by that which is? That is the question to which ontology is meant to reply which without doubt reaches a rigorous and organic expression within the horizon of the Greek understanding of being in the philosophies in spite of being so diverse from one another in Parmenides, Plato, Aristotle, and Plotinus, interacting in depth as they do with mathematics, biology, and physics, in accordance of course with the typically Greek meaning of each of these terms. This horizon encounters Christianity giving rise to the reflection of the Church Fathers and the Scholastics. With the Hebrew faith and then with Christianity one witnesses the irruption of something decisively new on the horizon of the thought elaborated by the Western tradition: revelation. It is an event, a reality: "Actus fidei non terminatur ad enutiabile, sed ad rem."[5]

It is enough to mention two intuitions which interact with the classical ontological horizon. The first is that of creation, which points up otherness between God and creation, the imprint of the divine truth (*lógos*) in creation, the relation of personal freedom between God and humanity. The second is the incarnation, which of itself constitutes an event of ontological illumination, as the prologue of John illustrates: "In the beginning was the *Lógos* … and the *Lógos* was God" (Jn 1:1), showing otherness and relation in God, and "the *Lógos* became flesh" (Jn 1:14), showing the "becoming" of God and "new" relation, in the Word become flesh, between God, man, and the world. It is in this context that the horizon of interpretation of being disclosed by Christian revelation becomes progressively visible. It is enough to recall the figures of Augustine, Thomas, Rosmini,

5. *ST* II-II, q. 1, a. 2, ad 2.

and Bulgakov whom we have revisited in the course of our journey and who could represent respectively the patristic age, the medieval, the modern, and the contemporary.

It is therefore evident that the trinitarian horizon has been operative in the course of these two thousand years of history, not only in theology but also, at least in an indirect form, in philosophy and even in the sciences, remaining often constrained within a tendentially cosmological ontology, first (in the ancient era) or subsequently anthropological (in the modern era), both in the final analysis reductive. Indeed, one may say with Hemmerle that this follows closely a judgment already expressed by von Balthasar, that "in the symbiosis of the specifically Christian with ontology, the first, almost inadvertently, continued being a kind of guest in the multiple projects and philosophical systems of heterogeneous orientation."[6]

To become aware of this means effectively that the moment has come in which to disclose *explicitly* that horizon of interpretation of reality that derives from the revelation of God the Trinity. And this, evidently, should be without any absolutist or deductivist pretense, but taking into account the perspectives of interpretation of the real offered by the history of thought, and not least by the natural and human contemporary sciences, where the paradigm of relationality becomes central under different profiles. It would be naïve and misleading, for example, to think that while classical metaphysics concentrates on the concept of substance, trinitarian ontology would abandon substance in order to give the primacy to relation. It is the issue rather to make the dynamic of relation enter—and not of any relation, but the one in trinitarian rhythm—into the determination of being in itself, as, for instance, St. Augustine began to do in Book V of *De Trinitate*.

According to Hemmerle: "Everything is done and realizes its most proper essence by conquering its own proper relationality, its own self-transcendence, its own self-possession in the ambience of self-gift, the capacity of turning to the other and being-for the other, in a trinitarian perspective according to which the self-giving of God gives God."[7] From this comes the central thesis:

> From the moment that God is triune, and as such has his history in our history, our fundamental situation as human beings, our thinking and our being, even all being, experience a change, a conversion. Such a change is superior to every measure of "traditional" thinking about God, about oneself, about the world,

6. Hemmerle, *Tesi di ontologia trinitaria*, 37 (own trans.).
7. Ibid., 66–67.

about being. The pure and simple re-reading of ontological pre-comprehension, traditionally characteristic of the faith, does not reach as far as taking up what is revealed and communicated to being and the intellect of man. The need for a "new ontology," for a "trinitarian ontology," is the direct consequence of this faith.[8]

By means of its very configuration, therefore, trinitarian ontology is not so much meant to offer a system nor a table of codified and definitive categories so much as the disclosure of a plausible horizon of interpretation in itself open and dialogical. It is possible to indicate two perspectives, the one relative to the object, the other to the subject of knowledge.

A Double Perspective, Subjective and Objective

The first perspective: Christian revelation discloses the horizon of being as *agápe*, and that is as the free, gratuitous, reciprocal, and effusive gift of self. This is the *novum* of Hebrew revelation which reaches an unexpected fulfillment in Christ. It is expressed by the incarnation of the Son of God, his death on the cross and resurrection, the being of God as Trinity, creation, salvation, etc. We should ask ourselves, what does it mean, within such a horizon, to think about being and to know the different dimensions of the realities investigated by different sciences? Is there not here an illumination as decisive as it is discreet for the exercise of every field of knowledge and the relation among them? Trinitarian-ness means: relation, reciprocity, self-transcendence toward the other (one plus one does not make two), transcendence of self and the other toward the *novum* that reciprocity discloses, the dwelling of the one in the other without cancelling the self or cancelling the other. In a word, trinitarian ontology discloses the possibility of reading the analogically trinitarian grammar in and by which reality is written and lived at its various levels.

The second perspective concerns the subject and the form of knowing: if the meaning of being consists in the giving of self, knowing is the gathering of the self-giving of being in the giving of self in its turn. Only in the giving of myself am I able to grasp the meaning of being in its self-giving to me and by means of me. The horizon of trinitarian ontology, in other words, becomes event there where knowing allows the event that gives itself, to live in itself, and it lives from it.

It is an epistemological axiom well known to classical philosophy: the soul becomes in some way all things, which the New Testament expresses in accordance with the trinitarian logic of *agápe*: "everyone who loves is born of God and knows God. Whoever does not love does not know

8. Ibid., 48.

God, for God is love" (see 1 Jn 4:7–8). Only a knowing that embraces the rhythm from which being lives, participating in it, becomes itself in communion with the being that it embraces.

In summary, one could express by means of this succinct thesis the intuition that inspires the various efforts which are employed today in the direction of a trinitarian ontology: the giving of self to the end (*eis télos*), to the Father and to others, of the incarnate Son/*Lógos* on the cross and in the abandonment, going as far as the experience of death, and the receiving of self in return from the Father by means of the eschatological outpouring of the Holy Spirit in the resurrection; this is the expression in the flesh of the man of the *agápe* who is God, in the reciprocal and perichoretic gift of self of the three divine Persons which gratuitously involves, in the free correspondence of faith with this gift, the created persons who, in Christ, respond to the Father's gift by means of the Holy Spirit in the reciprocal giving of each one to the others.

A consequence of this stated thesis is that the radical meaning of a trinitarian ontology is revealed in Jesus Christ's mediation opening up in the Spirit the experience and understanding of God's mystery as the tri-Personal event of *agápe*, as the eschatological place for the experience and understanding of the mystery of humanity and creation. It is this mandatory Christological centering that unites and distinguishes, "without separation" and "without confusion," the ontology of the divine with the ontology of the creature in the theandric *perichoresis* of being "one in Christ Jesus" (Gal 3:28) in virtue of the Holy Spirit.

On the Christological Place of a Trinitarian Ontology of the Person

If it is true that from the point of view of the understanding of revelation, the definition of the human person cannot be provided apart from the transcendence of God, it is equally true that the originality of Christianity is in the event of Jesus Christ as the personal place in which one finds united, in distinction, the "divine nature" and "human nature"—to say it with classical language—such that the transcendence of God is offered in its original form, and that is trinitarian, in the event of Jesus Christ, true God and true man.

The transcendence of God with respect to history being true, it is equally true therefore that the self-transcendence (through grace and in freedom) of human persons toward him cannot happen except by the mediation of the event of Christ in history. Contemporary theological thinking has thus made the gain according to which the person can be correctly defined only from within a Christological horizon. In that way it is possible not only to recover the ontological achievements of the patristic-medieval tradition and the positive elements provided by the modern philosophy of intersubjectivity, but to open them toward a new profundity in which the connection between the trinitarian dynamic of the divine Persons and the connection, in Christ, of and among created persons is not only one of analogy, but of mutual interiority, rendered freely available by the incarnation of the Son of God and by the Paschal gift of the Spirit.

At least three acquisitions stem from this. Above all, from the theological point of view, not only should it be said (with the Scholastic speculation of Thomas and Duns Scotus) that the incarnate person of the Son of God constitutes the singular and exemplary case in which human nature is fully "personated"; but also that, in the gift of grace, the human individual attains full personal being in Christ: realizing distinction and identity in the gratuitous participation in Christ's being-person and finding access through him to the complete relation of sonship with respect to the Father in the Spirit.

In the second place, it should also be said that the decisive agapic rapport between created persons is fully realized in Christ; as the Letter to the Ephesians says, so "that he might create in himself one new humanity in place of the two" (2:15; see Gal 3:28). The presence of the risen Christ among those who believe in his name (see Mt 18:20) and who are inserted into him by faith and the sacraments, cannot be grasped as only a moral or intentional presence, but as ontological presence. Not only is the relationship with God in Christ constitutive of the definition of the human person but also the relation with the other in-Christ so that, as Zizioulas writes, one ought to speak of the person as "ecclesial" being and hypostasis.

Finally, it ought to be said that in Christ the intersubjective relation is realized in the perichoretic logic of the gift of self to the other and of the reception in oneself of the other in the space of newness and openness of the Holy Spirit: according to the Paschal dynamic of death-resurrection, and that is the gift-of-self that opens up to the full self-possession of self in the freedom of the relationship with the other and the divine other. This leads to the intuition that the human person can be understood and exercised in the perspective of a "trinitarian" ontology under at least three profiles: that of the interiority of his spirit (St. Augustine); that of being son in the Son, according to the trinitarian "rhythm" of being received (from the Father), being formed (in Christ), and self-giving (in the Spirit), on which see Hemmerle; and that of the intersubjective relation between the created persons which has its paradigmatic expression in the relation man-woman, created "in the image and likeness of God" and which occurs in the interiority of the trinitarian divine life in accordance with the prayer of Christ to the Father: "The glory which you have given to me I have given to them so that they may be one as we are one" (Jn 17:22).

The trinitarian structure and dynamic of human intersubjectivity in Christ occurs in fact in the gratuitous and effusive reciprocity (see Jn 15:12) which is not the simple "face to face" of the two, but occurs in the receiving "space" opened "between" them, thus bringing about that indefinitely open relation which not only touches the other with whom one enters directly into a relationship but the "each-one-without-a-face" (to say it with P. Ricoeur) that I reach through the mediation of structures and institutions.

There follows from this an undeniable *conditio sine qua non* for the exercise of a trinitarian ontology of the person. Saying it with the words of Jacques Maritain, it is a condition that touches theological epistemology under its existential profile. In order to "enter" also intellectually into this Paschal and perichoretic dynamic it is necessary in fact to thematize and practice, with critical awareness, but also with virginal ingenuity, the original space/place of the experience and the thought of God the Trinity which Jesus announced and of which he renders persons participants in his Spirit.

From Subsistent Relation to Trinitarian Reciprocity

As we have ascertained from the history of dogma and of trinitarian theology, the use of the concept of hypostasis/person with reference to Father, Son, and Holy Spirit has answered the unavoidable issue posed by revelation of affirming in the unity of the one and true God the real distinction and otherness of the three. After this was affirmed with incontestable clarity, it was necessary at the same time to describe the real relation between the divine Persons pertinently in such fashion as to thus express dynamically the movement of their full unity in their real trinity.

The Relation among the Divine Persons

In the final analysis there are two lines followed by the patristic and Scholastic tradition. On the one hand, and in obedience to the witness of the New Testament and the ecclesial experience of the liturgy and the spiritual life, this relationship has been expressed by following the rigorous order of the divine *táxis*: Father, Son, and Holy Spirit, and identifying the relationship among the hypostases/persons according to the immanent logic of the processions (corresponding to the economic logic of the missions): designating, with biblical language, generation (*génesis*) as the relationship between the Father and Son, and source (*ekpóreusis*) as the relationship between the Father and the Holy Spirit.

The question of the *Filioque*, in reality, and beyond its historical aspects, introduces an ulterior (and complementary) point of view. This is made evident in the trinitarian thought of Augustine and Thomas: where the former, for example, speaks of the Holy Spirit as *Donum amborum*, and the latter, while he attributes to the Holy Spirit the relation of *passive spiration* with respect to the Father and the Son, attributes to both of these the relation of *active spiration*. In that way the linear pattern of the *táxis* of the procession from the Father as from a first principle is crossed not only by the reciprocity of activity (Father) and passivity (the generation of the Son and the spiration of the Spirit), but also by that (active and passive together) reciprocity between Father and Son which terminates in the spiration of the Spirit. By triggering this process the Holy Spirit is also recognized as an activity. And this applies in the first place in relationship to the act of generation of the Son by the Father (as the event of the incarnation shows). Thus the *novum* introduced, with theological relevance, by the *Filioque* should still encounter a corresponding *Spirituque* (P. Evdokimov).

Psychological Analogy and Interpersonal Analogy

In any case the ontological analogy, which begins with Augustine and reaches its mature proposal in Thomas and its decisive explication in Rosmini, prevails in Western theology, being founded, at the anthropological level, on an intrasubjective base (the spirit of the single person) that cannot but confirm the movement in the direction of the *táxis* affirmed by the tradition: the Father knows himself in the Word and loves himself in the Spirit, with these being, as real objects of the double paternal intentionality (intelligence and will), each in turn a subject like the Father. In this context it is certainly possible to grasp why it is precisely the extraordinary antinomian definition of the divine Person as *subsistent relation* by Thomas Aquinas that sets up the summit toward which ontological language pushes to the limit of its capacity in order to express together the real and distinct subsistence as well as the full and undivided unity. "In God," opines Aquinas without leaving any room for appeal, "if you take away relation nothing remains."[9] But this extraordinary metaphysical concept, drawn from "the heart of revelation," must be necessarily integrated into the logic of the *táxis* of the processions and the psychological analogy for the purpose of providing content to the concept of subsistent

9. Aquinas, *In Sent.* I, d. 26, a. 2, co. (own trans.).

relation with reference to the Father, Son, and Holy Spirit, determining precisely and following the same logic, the qualities of the three in the concrete reality of their reciprocal relations. It is precisely the intersubjective dynamic (and no longer only or preeminently intrasubjective) of *agápe* as reciprocal self-gift, as intuited by Augustine and recovered by Richard of St. Victor, which seems to provide precious opportunities in this regard: providing concrete content for *relatio subsistens* attributed to the three divine Persons by Aquinas, and avoiding the difficulty implicit in the integration of this discourse within the logic of the psychological analogy which, at least in its human point of support, fails fatally to account in personalistic terms for the real otherness of the terms of its intentionality.

The Agapic Dynamic of Reciprocity

It seems that this line of interpretation is the one primarily suggested, and without a possibility of alternative, by the witness of New Testament revelation. This is so because Jesus Christ, the Son/*Lógos*, precisely in the personal otherness of his human existence, lives the relation of self-gift to the *Abbà* in the Spirit; and because, and not accidentally, the new commandment, which in the Gospel of John synthesizes the new law promulgated by him, is the law of reciprocal love (see Jn 13:34). Perhaps above all Rosmini in the nineteenth century and Bulgakov in the twentieth century, at the theological level, and Chiara Lubich at the mystical level, are those who have more and better centered their thinking and/or experience of the Trinity (and of the trinitarian life among human beings) in the agapic dynamic of reciprocity.

On the other hand, the dialogical thinking of the twentieth century, as von Balthasar has clearly noted, seems to have offered to the theological intelligence the most persuasive and pertinent anthropological grammar to think and live the rhythm of trinitarian revelation according to the form of an ontology that is itself trinitarian.[10] The dynamic and the category of agapic reciprocity, therefore, are recognized today as necessary for integration of the mature, transmitted language of the theological tradition in connection with the unity and Trinity of/in God. Reciprocity, in fact, stresses the fact that the other is constitutive of the I, in the ontological sense above all, according to which the relation which the other is/lives with regard to me, in response to the relation which I am/live with the other, is neither accidental nor peripheral to the dynamic constitution of my very identity.

10. Hans Urs von Balthasar, *Love Alone Is Credible*, trans. D. C. Schindler (San Francisco, Calif.: Ignatius Press, 2004).

A Reciprocating and Trinitarian Reciprocity

Obviously this perspective needs to be attentively weighed and evaluated as soon as it is posited as necessary to illustrate the divine life. We are only at the beginning, in reality, of the demanding work of its pertinent and fruitful deployment. It is the case in fact of distinguishing the different modalities of relation involved in the relationship of reciprocity: in God, of humanity with God, and of human beings with one another, keeping in mind however that, according to the logic of revelation, it is always Christ who is the *medium* of this multiple network of relations. On the other hand, limiting our work for the purposes of this essay to life *in divinis*, if it is evident that one cannot not speak of reciprocity in relation to the rapport of Father and Son, and of each of the three with each of the others (because the Father would not be Father without the Son, in that the Son, recognizing the Father, restores so to speak the Father to his true being, which is to be Father; and so on), it is equally evident that this reciprocity be integrated into the indispensable discourse about the *táxis* and the sequence of the processions. Therefore it is not a matter of a flat, leveling reciprocity, in which the terms of the relation are interchangeable, but of a reciprocity constitutively articulated and asymmetrical: in which, therefore, what is reciprocal and therefore formally identical is the *agápe* (which is the being of God) lived according to the threefoldness of its form of execution (that of the Father, the Son, and of the Holy Spirit).

Nor should the dynamic or category of reciprocity be equivocated in the sense of a simply dialogical or binary logic. In trinitarian terms, in fact, reciprocity presupposes and always requires a *tertium*: not only as "in the middle" or as the "between" (*zwischen*) of the relation or as its fruit, but (integrating these two meanings, both being pertinent) as the intentional term intrinsic to the very relation of reciprocity. If this finds its normative and paradigmatic explication in the relation between Father and Son (and the sons in the Son), it finds in the Holy Spirit its condition of possibility and its result, always proposing again and again the dynamism of the reciprocal relation between the Father and the Son (and the sons in the Son).

The intuition of the *condilectus* (shared love) of Richard of St. Victor should be taken up again and appropriately explored at the level of anthropological analogy. That it is necessary to be two in the experience of love is evident: otherwise there would not be love in the absence of that object by which it is love. A jump of intelligence is perhaps required to see that in love there needs to be more than two, and not only in the (Augustinian) sense by which the relation of love between the lover and the beloved is necessarily given (and vice versa: reciprocally), but in the sense that there be a *tertium* as the intentional object of the love of the lovers. In reality, what is there in fact that is deeper and truer in the experience of love? Love wills gratuitously the good of the other: it does not appropriate the other, it wills his/her good, and that is that the other be fully him/herself. Now, what is the good which is the greatest and truest for the other? It is that he/she experience what love is, and that is that in turn he/she wants what is good for another. It is not only that he/she wills my good: certainly this because love is such when it is reciprocal. But the reciprocity is true when it is open and effusive. Reciprocity is such when it is effusively reciprocating: in other words, it is intended to multiply infinitely the very dynamism by which it is reciprocity.

The Positive Nonbeing of Love

The category of reciprocity, understood in the trinitarian sense, offers room for adequate illumination to discover the positive and actual indispensable value of "nonbeing" in trinitarian language. The first author to have vigorously underlined, with theological pertinence, the necessity of a close and rigorous employment of the "ressources de la negativite" in order to express the truth of God the Trinity was G. Lafont in his *Peut-on connaitre Dieu en Jesus Christ?* Only a little while after him, it was G. Zangh, following Chiara Lubich's intuition about Jesus forsaken, who illustrated in an incisive and programmatic fashion this same issue on the level of a trinitarian ontology. But let us proceed with order: which concept of nonbeing is being properly dealt with here?

The Greeks: Absolute Nonbeing and Relative Nonbeing

The classical metaphysical tradition is aware, as noted, of two understandings and two different contexts of usage of the concept of nonbeing already at the time of Plato: the *absolute*, by which it is stated that something simply does not exist; and the *relative*, by which it is stated that one thing is not the other. Obviously this discourse in the Greek vision of the cosmos does not touch the divine, which absolutely is or, better still, is absolutely beyond being, the one being which is of itself ineffable in that it excludes every otherness from itself.

Augustine: The Predication of Nonbeing "in Divinis"

But it is precisely in that new space of the knowledge of God opened by Christian revelation that the necessity of the use of the language of nonbeing to describe the figure of God the Trinity takes off. As we have noticed, it was Augustine who, in order to affirm logically and ontologically, in the rigor of theological discourse, the real distinction and otherness of the three in the one divine essence, clearly stated that the one is not the other, each one however being the one true God.[11] The relative nonbeing—this is what is new in Christian discourse about God—is valid therefore (even with its peculiar formality) also *in divinis*, and not only on the level of finite and created things.

From the Relative Nonbeing to the Relational Nonbeing

But here is the question which is asked logically at this point: does this relative nonbeing express only in the absolute mode the distinct subsistence of the three, or does it also express something of their rapport? In other words, does the relative nonbeing not open consequently to the intuition, based on the event of revelation, of a relational nonbeing? In truth, this intuition advances progressively, and with great difficulty, only with modernity. It requires in fact three givens in order to make itself explicit with pertinence: the gaining of a grounded theological presupposition, the rediscovery of a central datum of revelation, and a specific and challenging cultural context like the modern one.

The necessary theological presupposition is that of the concept of a divine Person as subsisting relation formulated with crystal-clear clarity by Thomas Aquinas. It is only by beginning with this concept in fact, but as located within the trinitarian reciprocity of the rapport among the divine Persons, that it becomes possible (and necessary) to speak of a relational nonbeing, and therefore eminently positive, in order to express the being, in relation to the other, of the three divine Persons. But for this to happen, for access to such language on the horizon of reciprocity, it is necessary to rediscover and to utilize a central datum of Christological revelation: the fact, namely, that God as he is eschatologically communicated to man in the Passover of Jesus Christ is *agápe* (see 1 Jn 4:8, 16), that is, as gratuitous and complete self-gift in the expropriation of self (*kénosis*; see Phil 2:7). This is probably the most precious gain, as I have noted, in contemporary Christology and theology.

Finally, one should not underestimate the modern context of the absence and death of God, even if it is necessary to make a careful discernment on account of its intrinsic ambiguity. The fact is that modernity, for the first time in the history of human civilization, touches upon the experience of nonbeing (the *nihil*) which advances in the trajectory of nihilism: both as the unprecedented experience of God in history and as the equally

11. See what I wrote in "*Quaestio de alteritate in divinis*: Agostino Tommaso Hegel," *Lateranum* 46, no. 3 (2000): 509–28.

unprecedented experience of that negative nonbeing that is the fruit of the liberty that refuses to make the gift of self in response to the gift of God.

This vehement and often tragic discovery of nonbeing, also in its negative and even destructive weight, has become possible in fact only with the event of Jesus Christ—and this is the point on which the theology and the culture that are of Christian inspiration ought attentively to reflect. Previously it was not possible. The reason is that it was Jesus himself who in the event of his death and resurrection descended into the abyss of the negative nonbeing. And it is only with him that it becomes possible to close oneself to God's love, to the point of experiencing the meaninglessness of one's very being.

It is no accident therefore that thinkers such as Hegel have intuited in the dramatic space of modernity, together with the fatal misunderstandings which I have mentioned earlier, that nonbeing is not of itself the alternative and external dimension of being, but the very motor of its internal movement. This becomes theologically pertinent only there where the Christological event is read, in the light of faith, as the free act of the gift of self of the incarnate Son/*Lógos* who out of love descends into the abyss of the negative nonbeing of the closure to God and to the brothers and sisters: by living out the tragic consequences, nay the very situation of negative nonbeing, in the perfect positivity of that love which is the gift-of-self. Nonbeing (losing life) in order to be (refinding it).

The semantics therefore of the positive or relational nonbeing is that which expresses the intrinsic dynamic of the Christological event, revealing, in the language of analogy, that the being of God as *agápe* is traversed and vivified by the reciprocal nonbeing out of love, and as love of each of the divine Persons in relation to the others. It is that which, using other languages, is already expressed by the theosophy of Rosmini in the nineteenth century and, above all, by the theologies of Bulgakov and von Balthasar in the twentieth century, as also by the trinitarian mysticism of Chiara Lubich. In the words of von Balthasar:

> We must try to grasp the fact that where absolute Being is concerned, Being that has possession of itself, "divine self-possession expresses itself in perfect self-giving and reciprocal surrender; furthermore the creature's own existence, over which it has not control, is drawn into this movement" (A. Brunner).... In giving himself, the Father does not give something (or even everything) that he has but all that he is ... passes over, without remainder, to the begotten Son.... This total self-giving, to which the Son and the Spirit respond by an equal self-giving, is a kind of "death," a first, radical "kenosis," as one might say. It is a kind of "super-death."[12]

12. Von Balthasar, *Theo-Drama*, 5:82–84.

In this text it is possible to show two affirmations: the analogical elevation of the concept of *kénosis* and of death (with the typical reference to the excellence of Dionysian flavor: "super-death"); and the discovery that we find ourselves before a limit concept in the expression of the ontology of the divine: after the Augustinian concept of relation, the Thomistic concept of subsistent relation, and the Rosminian concept of the act of giving all/retaining all.

As to the pertinence of the first assertion, opinions are divided (for example, on the one side S. Bulgakov, and on the other G. Lafont) and in any case much linguistic and conceptual prudence is necessary in order to correctly distinguish and express the different levels and meanings of the Christological event with reference both to its anthropological and its theological-trinitarian dimension. As to the second assertion, one may say that if God is the being that is *agápe*, God is the infinite and reciprocal self-gift of the Father, the Son, and the Holy Spirit. Thus, to express the very profound dynamic of such a gift—as revealed by Christ crucified/risen who pours out the Holy Spirit "without measure"—it may be said with pertinence that the Father, the Son, the Holy Spirit, each in their own way, give themselves to the point of consuming themselves, and thus being/becoming fully themselves (being and becoming, understood not according to a Greek ontology but according to the ontology disclosed by revelation, coincide in God).

As to God, beginning with revelation one may and ought therefore say that he is, and that he is *agápe*. As to the Father, the Son, and the Holy Spirit, one may and should say, insofar as they subsist as relation, and that is in giving themselves fully in reciprocity, that they are (themselves) only insofar as they are not (in themselves, independently of the others), but give themselves totally and thus receive themselves in return (see Jn 10:17–19). This is precisely what is proper to the divine Persons who are God. Of themselves, created persons are not able to live fully the nonbeing of love precisely because they are created: and that is that they receive being from God and do not have the possibility to deprive themselves of it ontologically. At most it is possible for them to give themselves intentionally (at the level, that is, of the act of knowledge and of love), but not as far as giving up their own being as being. This means that in the creature, being and *agápe* do not coincide: only God in fact "is" *agápe*. Only death constitutes the commendation, into the hands of God, of the whole being of the creature.

But the crucified and risen Christ, by communicating the Holy Spirit, brings about that "new creation" which is the fulfillment to which the created person is destined by grace. He is the Son who became man and lives the trinitarian rapport of love, in his humanity, as the gift of self even unto death, with the Father through the Holy Spirit. This is so true that his humanity, because united personally to the Word, can experience (in the abandonment and in the death accepted and lived out of love) that vertiginous self-annihilation as the love by which it is fully inserted with the resurrection into the trinitarian life. Therefore, it is only in Christ, received and lived through grace by freedom, that the created person can participate sacramentally in the reality of filial *agápe*. It was not for nothing that St. Paul speaks of a "dying" and a "rising" with Christ (see Rom 6:4–5).

Creation has its root in this trinitarian "nonbeing," this infinite "nonbeing" of love of which only God is capable. The *ex nihilo* of creation must therefore be understood as *nihil amoris*: in harmony with the progressive comprehension of the event of creation which begins with revelation but with that unexpected *novum* disclosed by the event of a God who becomes flesh and dies on the cross. Nothingness thus assumes paradoxically a rich and full meaning. It does not only say, in the negative, that nothing preexisted creation but God; it also says, in the positive, that the act of creation by God is an act of pure love, an act with which he himself makes himself nothing, with respect to creation, so that creation might be. In order that the other than himself (and not only the other *in* himself: the Son/Word and the Holy Spirit) be, God freely prepared in the very core of his being, which is *agápe*, the existence-space for such another desired by his love. This is his true and infinite omnipotence.

The *nihil* of creation is therefore, when viewed from the angle of creation, the absolute gratuitousness of its own coming to be; and, seen from God's side, it is the love with which God, without alienation from himself, expropriates that which is most proper to him, being itself, in order to make a gift of it gratuitously to the other than himself. The *ex nihilo* of the act of creation is the fullness with which God communicates himself, and nothing less, to that which is not himself. This is the source of the wealth of potential that germinates from the nothingness of creation, as the history of the universe shows, inasmuch as it is nothing other than the created image, extended in space and time, of that nothing/all of the love which in God the Trinity is the Word/Son of the Father, his eternal wisdom: nothing because he receives his being from the love of the Father; all because the infinite fullness of the Father is fully reflected and expressed in him. To say, as the New Testament does, that everything has been created through the Word means to say also that creation, being nothing because receiving everything from God, is itself thereby called to receive the all of God in that God there pours out, by means of the Word incarnate who pours out the Spirit "without measure" (see Jn 3:34), his very own fullness (see Col 2:9; Eph 3:19). This is true to the point that the eschatological goal of the becoming of the created universe is intuited by the apostle Paul as the free and gratuitous existence of God in all created things: *ína ê ho Theòs* [*tà*] *pánta en pâsin*, "that God may be all in all" (1 Cor 15:28).

Just as the "not" of the distinction and the "making oneself nothing" in reciprocal love express the unity and the trinity of God who is *agápe*, so too the *ex nihilo* of creation expresses the distinction and the relation of love between God and creation: without separation and without confusion. And it tells the story of unity and multiplicity with which creation itself, at its diverse levels of being and development, is interwoven in space and time. The nothingness of love is the trinitarian grammar with which the book of creation is written.

The Trinity as the Place of Freedom

The ontological category of relational or positive nonbeing, illuminated in the horizon of trinitarian reciprocity, cannot but send one back ultimately to the great issue of freedom, modern on the one hand and ancient as the gospel of Jesus Christ, on the other.

The Provocation of the Ontology of Freedom

It is true that there is no reality so much at the center of modern and contemporary philosophical reflection as freedom, and that contemporary theology (from von Balthasar to Jüngel and Moltmann) is more than engaged on this front, and precisely in a trinitarian key. And still the situation is that we are far from a real, innovative, and enduring understanding, such as the times require and of which the event of the self-communication of God in Christ is pregnant. It is evident in fact that both the widespread ancient substantialist horizon and the widespread modern subjectivist horizon are not capable of guaranteeing to the full and expressing the extreme measure of liberty (of God and man) which Jesus Christ testifies. Only the space of intersubjectivity as reciprocity among people, lived and thought out according to the act of freedom of Christ (who freely offers his life, losing it and only thus reacquiring it; see Jn 10:17), is able to permit, thanks to the gift of the Spirit without measure (see Jn 3:34) which he brings about in his Paschal gift, an experience and an understanding of freedom in the light of the ontology of the Trinity.

In his ontology of freedom, Luigi Pareyson has outlined in clear and compelling terms the unavoidable challenge to which philosophy and theology are called to respond today. It is a matter, he affirms, of "thinking out being itself as liberty."[13] On the one hand, by giving a positive outcome to that "philosophy of liberty" which constitutes modern philosophy's great impulse, interrupted and often misrepresented; and, on the other hand, and precisely with the aim of a positive result of such an undertaking, by reproposing in an original and rigorous form the relation between theoretical speculation and Christian experience, by means of the fact that "the idea of hinging everything on liberty, of making everything depend on it, giving it central position, elevating it to be the origin and the source, cannot be other than Christian." The Pareysonian provocation to confront with decision and serenity the *tolmeros lógos* (the courageous discourse) of God's freedom as the event/advent of his very own self-origination, in effect cannot but encounter and challenge Christian theology in the most profound dimension of its constitution. What is at stake is the very figure of God as thought by theology. What does it entail about the freedom of God, and even of the experience of God as freedom granted by revelation?

Apart from the minority and definitively marginal current of divine voluntarism, to which Pareyson refers in his last treatises and which emerged with the demise of the Middle Ages, I would hazard the thesis—to be verified critically but evident for example in S. Bulgakov—that the theme, without doubt in Hebrew and Christian revelation, of the freedom of God has been, indeed, vigorously expounded and investigated, but principally, if not exclusively, with reference to the relation between God as the creator and savior and the world as the object precisely of his free and gratuitous decision to create and to redeem. Even the current of divine voluntarism, it is clear, moves within this horizon. The very affirmation of God's absolute and unchallengeable free will in relation to the other cannot but draw the fascinated and amazed attention toward the vertiginous and unfathomable abyss of the self-making of God as God. This is what Schelling attempts in his *Philosophy of Mythology and Revelation*.

13. Luigi Pareyson, "Il nulla e la libertà come inizio," in his *Ontologia della libertà*, 457 (own trans.). C. Ciancio offers an original development of Pareyson's ontology of freedom in the recent publication, *Libertà e dono dell'essere* (Genoa: Marietti, 2009). Worth mentioning in Ciancio's essay are, on one hand, the historical and theoretical contextualization of the ontology of freedom in the development over time of Western philosophical and theological thought, which objectively constitutes an appreciable integration of Pareyson's perspective; on the other hand, it is a theoretical penetration of the "freedom-being relationship." With this theoretical perspective, an effort is made to think of freedom "as constitutively defined by the relationship of otherness, without at the same time dissipating the significance of unity," inasmuch as otherness is thought of "before anything else as being (being is posited by freedom as a condition for its self-manifestation) and then as a plurality of existing freedoms" (153). However, this work does not value the clearly speculative appeal that the revelation of God as Trinity can put in play, which I am trying to manifest in this study.

There is in truth an exception that must be carefully evaluated. It is Duns Scotus who is the first and only author of weight and recognition speaking not only of God's freedom with respect to creation but also speaking of freedom *in* God. In his manner of seeing things, even if there is a certain terminological and conceptual oscillation, the very act of the generation of the Son by the Father, for example, is an act of freedom. But, I repeat, the doctrine of Scotus in the specific perspective that interests us here must be carefully studied.

In any case, the speculative constitution of Scholastic theology of Thomistic origin, which prevailed in the Catholic world beginning with the sixteenth century, was strictly connected to a metaphysics of being as unchangeable, apathetic, and necessary substance.[14] It succeeded only in proposing the question of the freedom of God in relation to creation, but not the daring question of the freedom of God in himself, or better of God as freedom. A glaring symptom of such a speculative structure lies for example in the affirmation, taken for granted in much theological parlance, according to which, while one may and one should speak of God's liberty with respect to creation,[15] one cannot and ought not do so for God in himself, for in God freedom coincides with perfect harmony with his essence in conformity with a reductive interpretation of the Scholastic definition by which God is the *ipsum esse per se subsistens*.[16] In all of this, what happens to the gratuitous and free event of revelation that definitively opens the view onto the dynamism of the infinite and paradoxical freedom which God himself is? I refer to the freedom of the Son, Jesus Christ, which is activated as such in adhering to the will of the Father, from the *kénosis* of the incarnation to that consummated on the cross and in the abandonment; and in the freedom of the Spirit who "blows where it chooses" (see Jn 3:8). The freedoms of the Son and of the Spirit point and orient toward the infinite freedom of love and mercy of the Father. All this is not only constitutive, but actually determinative, of the most proper and original quality of Christian experience.

Such is the centripetal force, however, of the tendentially substantial

14. In particular, I refer to a certain line of thought which unfortunately became preponderant, inspired by the Scholastic tradition in Catholic theology, but certainly not among masters like Augustine, Thomas, and Rosmini. For them, instead, the progressive assumption of the provocation that comes to ontology from Christological revelation is evident.

15. See Jesús A. Lopez Casuso, "Nota sobre la 'necesidad' de Dios frente a su 'obra libre,'" *Est Trin* 7 (1973): 441–50.

16. It is symptomatic that the ITC recently dealt with the question of the relationship between the immanent Trinity and the economic Trinity, affirming in its document, "Theology, Christology, Anthropology," that "the distinction must be maintained between the immanent Trinity, where liberty and necessity are the same thing in the eternal essence of God, and the Trinity of the economy of salvation, where God exercises his liberty absolutely, with no suggestion of his being forced to it" (I.C.2, 2); available at www.vatican.va.

metaphysical constitution of classical theology that when one moves from the historic-salvific Trinity to the immanent Trinity, to use the language of Karl Rahner, the trinitarian relations are expressed in terms of the most rigorous necessity, becoming identical with the most original divine freedom in its ultimate meaning. This does not take into account above all the clear precision announced by Thomas Aquinas according to whom God is *supra ordinem necessarii et contingentis sicut est supra totum esse creaturae*, "above the order of the necessary and the contingent just as he is above the whole being of the creature."[17] Besides, the theology of the twentieth century which had strongly struggled for emancipation from the guardianship of an objectivistic metaphysic by placing at the center of its understanding Christological revelation, the abyss of the abandonment and the event of the relations of love of the three divine Persons, in reality did not succeed in making consistent and definitive steps forward in the direction of a convincing ontology of freedom.[18]

This is true to the point where the sharp criticism that Massimo Cacciari has lodged in his *Dell'Inizio* seems to be generally on the mark: if not always under the profile of hermeneutical correctness in the analysis of the theses of the individual authors, much more in terms of the form of the trending speculative configuration which remains dominant.[19] Thus, there is one guiding thread running through the interpretation of trinitarian theology from Augustine to Hegel to the theologies of the cross of the twentieth century (Barth, Moltmann, Jüngel).

The Trinity Is Freedom

The fact is that because liberty is without doubt that which specifies the unique dignity of the human person in the created world, it cannot but be *in* God, as principle and archetype. Obviously the passage from creation to God, also and above all in relation to the understanding of freedom, has to be done keeping in mind the methodological criterion of analogy: *maior dissimilitudo in similitudine*. In this analogical movement it is also necessary to keep in mind the classical distinction at the anthropological level between *libertas minor* as self-determination in the possibility of choosing between that which is good and that which is bad, and *libertas maior* as self-determination in the choice of the good. In God where

17. Aquinas, *De Malo*, q. 16, a. 7, ad 15.

18. Leonardo Paris persuasively grasped this need in the theological and philosophical fields (starting from a tight comparison with the neurosciences), *Sulla libertà. Prospettive di teologia trinitaria tra neuroscienze e filosofia* (Rome: Città Nuova, 2012). Useful elements can undoubtedly be found in E. Jüngel, in the dimension of a definitive liberation of God's intelligence from any form of Neoplatonism beginning with Christological revelation, and in H. U. von Balthasar, from the perspective that seems the most pertinent and fruitful—the trinitarian one.

19. Cacciari, *Dell'Inizio*.

the *libertas maior* may fairly be applied, that which specifies the act of self-determination *sic et simpliciter* has also to find root as the dimension intrinsic to the choice of the good.

But analogy for the theological reason expressed above must be Christologically centered and therefore determination of freedom in God should be measured from top to bottom on the freedom of Christ and decisively on his self-expression "to the end" in the Paschal event. This is what I have tried to show in the section dedicated to it in our journey through this book. In the Paschal event in fact the freedom of Jesus finds its definitive space for dramatic expression in relation to the Father in favor of humanity and by means of the Spirit. This introduces us theologically onto the level of divine immanence and in a space of illumination, formally trinitarian, of freedom of/in God. From here, always by way of Christological mediation, it will then be possible to move down in order to an ontological interpretation of freedom on the anthropological level.

In the Paschal "hour" the freedom of Christ, pushed even to the abyss of the abandonment, expresses itself fully for what it is: the revelation of the free choice of love for the Father: "For this reason the Father loves me, because I lay down my life in order to take it up again. No one takes it from me, but I lay it down of my own accord. I have power [*exousía*] to lay it down, and I have power to take it up again. I have received this command from my Father" (Jn 10:17–18). It is thus, and only thus, that Christ can say with fullness and finality "whoever has seen me has seen the Father" (Jn 14:9). Such freedom may not be absorbed and dissolved in any necessary being nor in any necessary self-development of the same. But let us focus on the significance of freedom *in divinis*. As the Christological event requires normatively, the essence of freedom of/in God is to be found in the immanent space of the Trinity. In other words, it is to be determined as that property identifying divine being (and, by participation, human being) inasmuch as it regards the divine Person in subsisting as relation in virtue of the trinitarian reciprocity with the other divine Persons.

In other words—and here I must distinguish my position from the ontology of freedom of Pareyson—freedom is not to be placed before being, but rather harvested as its essential expression where being (in the light of the trinitarian revelation of the Passover of Christ) is identified with *agápe*. In fact, God is by being love or, reciprocally, by loving he is: in the sense that the event of his being (*actus*) is given in love—and that is in loving, in being loved and in being one and distinct in this reciprocal love. If being is because it is love, the love which is God is of itself Trinity: and that trinitarian reciprocity in which each person is not (in and of himself) if not in relation (with and to the others). This involves freedom as an act of fully giving oneself, and that is as relation in act. Freedom in God, therefore, neither precedes nor posits being, but being the being of love, it is the very act by which each one of the divine Persons, in the trinitarian *táxis* that distinguishes each from the others,[20] is himself in the giving to the others who in turn return him to himself.

Driving our understanding of faith in this direction, in fidelity to the logic of revelation, it is possible to intuit how, in the Trinity, freedom could not be defined ontologically as an absolute greatness but, as everything in God, relational. Therefore, if it means the gratuitous and full gift of self to the other, it also means, correlatively, the integrity of subsistent being as experienced by every person through the reception of the self in the other, the restitution of self in self by the other, and the ever-renewed gift of self to and for the other. The freedom of love and in love, in other words, is for each of the divine Persons at the same time the principle of his own inalienable act of donation received by the other and the result of the act of donation by the other with regard to himself in the third. It is also for this theological reason, and that is proceeding from this perspective, that one can intuit how each of the divine Persons is God, the one true God, and at the same time is such only with the others and never without them. If this perspective is theologically plausible, it is necessary at this point to outline such logic, with respect to the trinitarian *táxis* and its perichoretic movement, with specific reference to each of the persons.

The Being of God as the Event of Freedom in Love

In fidelity to the Christological revelation of the Trinity, one may interpret the original (and eternal) event of God, as Father, as the first and immaculate awe experienced by God with respect to his own being which is love: awe which, for the very fact of the novelty and inexhaustible joy that originates from it, which is for itself and simultaneously it is desire for the other to exist: the one in front of me, the beloved. It is precisely as the double account of Genesis narrates on the level of creation: there where it is narrated that man and woman are created co-originally, and the wonder of the man-Adam at being placed in being, which resounds as candid, unexpected and full only when he is placed before the woman-Eve.

20. When I use "co-original" in these pages, I do not mean to deny the trinitarian principle of patristic and Scholastic theology according to which the name of *arché* (principle) is to be attributed to the Father alone in the *táxis* (the order) of the Persons of the Trinity; rather I am referring to biblical language, particularly Johannine, according to which the Father, the *Lógos*, and the Holy Spirit are in the *arché* which is God. In this sense, I think it is not only correct but necessary to speak of a co-originating of the three divine Persons in the unity of the Trinity. On the other hand, the principle of co-origination is decisively important for a pertinent elaboration of the trinitarian ontology (as I tried to show since writing *Evento Pasquale: Trinità e Storia*, 178–84).

Thus, according to trinitarian symbolism, and in respect for the greater dissimilarity in so much similarity, it occurs originally in God. In the act of freedom in which God originally, and beginning from himself, "becomes,"[21] by willing it, *Abbà*, Father: by giving all that he possesses and is to that other than himself who comes into being in the very act in which God/*Abbà*, freely consenting to his being, which is love, chooses that the other may also be. In this original act of love/liberty there is consummated the primordial and archetypal "drama" of the history of God: that in which is manifest the setting within which the drama of the history of mankind and of the God become man, will also take place.

This is a drama, a risk, more dizzying and decisive than any other, because the act in which God recognizes himself as and desires to be Father in the total and full gift of himself to the Son (who as such, i.e., total and full, has freely to be: because if this were not the case, it would not be the original act of that freedom which, as freedom, is fully possessed only in full self-giving) not only takes place on the edge of the abyss of nothingness, but it crosses it intrepidly: it is the original *kénosis*. The Father, willing the other, the Son, gives him all he himself is, and hands this over to him without residue. He annihilates himself in that handing over. If this were not the case, the liberty of God/*Abbà* would be neither true freedom nor true relationship with the other. It would be an original and immobile turning to stone in that necessity and identity that coincide with the implosion of the self in the self: emptiness, nothingness.

If this were not the case, the liberty of the Son—*Lógos* and *Eikón* of the Father, according to the language of the New Testament—would not be true freedom. In fact, following through our account of the event in which the Son is made and at the same time—and indissolubly—makes himself the Son, we are able to intuit his original wonder echoing that equal and, if possible, still more original wonder of the Father. It is the stupor of finding oneself a gratuitous participant in the original miracle of being "God from God, light from light," according to the creed of Nicaea (and we could add, freedom from freedom). From here the sudden transmutation of the event of his coming to be, in freedom, from the Father, in a similar act of freedom, in which he chooses with gratitude his original being-Son and, with it, returns himself, in love-freedom, to the Father, restoring in that fashion and at the same time the Father to his free being Father by means of his free choice of his being the only-begotten Son. In that way, the original and abyssal risk of the Father, his crossing over the nonbeing of himself so that the Son could be, and be freedom, finds an

21. It is evident that the "becoming" of which I speak here is identical with being, and it is coextensive with it, precisely because we are dealing with God's being as love which is freedom.

echo and reply and restitution, both free and gratuitous, in the risk of the Son who, recognizing his beginning from nonbeing out of love that the Father does so that he might be, annihilates himself freely in turn, crossing over himself the abyss of his nonbeing and in that way refinding himself before and in the Father as who he is: the Son.

Among contemporary theologians it is Hans Urs von Balthasar who perhaps has most intuited the necessity of a similar approach, even if it seems to me he has not gone all the way. Nonetheless, he uses this language in *Theo-Drama*[22] to describe, already on the level of the immanent Trinity, "the principle of the positivity of the other: it is absolutely good that the other exists":

> The ideal of a mere unity without "the Other" (Plotinus's *hén*, but also the *Mónos Theós* of Judaism and Islam) cannot do justice to the Christian affirmation that God is love. Such a unity would be self-sufficient and could not be communicated; "otherness" would be a mere declension from it. But where God is defined as love, he must be in essence perfect self-giving, which can only elicit from the Beloved, in return an equally perfect movement of thanksgiving, service and self-giving. Absolute self-giving of this kind cannot exist in the creaturely realm, since man has no control over his existence and, hence, over his "I," and "we cannot give away that over which we have no control" (Brunner, 24). We must try to grasp the fact that where absolute Being is concerned, Being that has possession of itself, "divine self-possession expresses itself in perfect self-giving and reciprocal surrender; furthermore the creature's own existence, over which it has no control, is drawn into this movement" (Brunner, 25). This self-giving cannot be motivated by anything other than itself; hence it is a boundless love where freedom and necessity coincide and where identity and otherness are one: identity, since the Lover gives all that he is and nothing else, and otherness, since otherwise the Lover would love only himself. Yet, even where it is a case of total reciprocal self-giving, this distinction cannot be ultimate: without disappearing, it must transcend itself in a new identity of love given and received, which the lovers themselves are bound to regard as the miracle, ever new, of their mutual love. Thus in God there must be "an eternal amazement at, and affirmation of, this reciprocal otherness that accompanies the oneness" (Brunner, 42) and "an eternal newness characterizing perfect, supratemporal constancy" (Brunner, 45).[23]

The account of the original event/advent of God in God does not end here in fact. The event of the co-original relation in reciprocal freedom of the Father and the Son, precisely because it is an event of inexhaustible and creative freedom, does not terminate with them, with neither of the two, nor with their rapport as something abstract or substantialistic. The

22. Pursuant to August Brunner's, *Dreifaltigkeit. Personale Zugänge zum Geheimnis* (Einsiedeln: Johannes Verlag, 1976).

23. Von Balthasar, *Theo-Drama*, 5:82–83. Page references in parenthesis are to Brunner's *Dreifaltigkeit* as quoted by von Balthasar.

lived relation in freedom by the Father toward the Son, and by the Son toward the Father, is fascination inebriated by joy, of each before the gratuitous act of freedom of the other: *it is the fascination of joy resulting from the emergence of love as the event of freedom*—initial (of the Father) and responsorial (of the Son)—*in which the being God of God as love becomes an event of freedom.* It is the amazement of joy for the victory of being over nonbeing. Just as for the Father amazement of being is converted into the free choice of love by which the other is; and just as for the Son the amazement of being is converted into the decision to receive and redonate oneself in love to the Father; in that way the amazement of the free reciprocity of love of the Father and the Son is the discovery that they in that fashion make of the freedom of love as the living essence and truth of being which they are as God. Such a discovery is expressed in the free co-origination of the Spirit, the Spirit of freedom and love, on the part of the Father and the Son.

This Holy Spirit, being the revelation and glorification (*dóxa*) in God of the love and the freedom that God the Father and the Son are jointly, cannot be conceived as mere passivity (as simply "proceeding" from the Father and the Son—the Western *Filioque*—or from the Father by means of the Son, the Eastern *diá huión*). Being, in fact, *en arché* with the Father and the Son, and also being co-original with the Father and the Son in the timeless event and ever-arriving of the origination of God from God as God, the Holy Spirit is also freedom in God himself: being, so to say, the becoming event of the freedom and the love which God himself is. This permits, in this moment in which the original history *in divinis* has apparently completed itself, the rereading and complete renewal of the entire account, deepening further its meaning in the perspective of a trinitarian ontology of freedom.

The trinitarian truth of the co-originality of the Father, the Son, and the Holy Spirit, as well as the meaning of the freedom that the origination of the Spirit acquires in the proposed narrative, results in the fact that the presence and action of the Spirit in the original event of God's being God as Trinity may be convincingly interpreted as the movement of the novelty and inexhaustibility of God in God. It is precisely the Spirit of freedom, aroused by the reciprocal amazement in which the Father and the Son recognize in their reciprocity the gratuitous and excellent emergence of the freedom of love, which in its turn calls forth in its depth the freedom of the Father to arouse the original act of freedom in which he becomes himself—Father—originating the Son; and at the same time arousing from within the freedom of the Son so that he might receive himself ever anew as the fruit of the freedom of the Father, projecting everything toward the Father and granting him to be Father in this fashion, he himself becoming with this the Son.

The event of freedom and love, therefore, is continuously renewed in God and, if possible, it is enriched and grows. The trinitarian truth of the co-origination of the Father, the Son, and the Holy Spirit, suggests that if the Spirit is the sure fruit of the recognition of the Father and the Son and therefore comes "after" them, yet; he is also contemporary with them. Just as the Father would not be Father without the Son, so the Father could not posit the originating act of love/liberty, which he himself is when generating the Son/*Lógos*, without that Spirit who is the unforced breath of the freedom of love. And the very same may be said of the Son/*Lógos* in the manner appropriate to him. At this point one could continue the account with reference both to creation as an act of freedom, on the part of God and at the same time though differently on the part of humanity, as well as to the event of the incarnation and abandonment of the Son made flesh, in the light of the risen one and of the Spirit poured out "without measure." This would inevitably project our view toward the fulfilled *eschaton*. But this would open our narrative specifically toward anthropology, cosmology, and eschatology.

CHAPTER 28

A Truth Witnessed in Charity, the Locus of the Trinity

With all of this it will perhaps be said, have we not gone so far from the ground that we have lost ourselves in the contemplation of the ineffable? What about the challenge that comes to us from the other monotheisms and, in another direction, from the pluralist sensibility of postmodernity and the allergy toward monotheistic personalism on the part of Eastern religions? I think that a patient and convincing reply to these problems, in themselves not in the least secondary, ought to be sought precisely by following the logic of the revelation of God, one and triune.

"That they may all be one. As you, Father, are in me and I am in you, may they also be in us" (Jn 17:21): this is how Jesus prayed. God, and his being one and triune, are not an abstract theorem: they are the expectation promised to every freedom and at the same time the grace given in faith because they are the root and the horizon of the history of the world. They cannot be explained from outside: not to the person who, not recognizing in faith the revelation of the filial identity of Jesus Christ, has not yet gained conscious access to the Trinity as occurs in Hebrew and Islamic monotheism; nor to the person who, for the same reason, does not perceive in the unity of the trinitarian God the guarantee of freedom and at the same time the transcendence of personal identity in an authentic communion as happens in Far Eastern traditions and, in other ways, in the serious critique of monotheism as exclusively understood.

As Jesus asked the Father, it is necessary to make of one's own existence, given to Christ in love for the brothers and sisters, the locus in which the unity of the Father, the Son, and the Holy Spirit takes on form and visibility in history by means of participation in the event of Jesus: "You see the Trinity," says St. Augustine, "if you see charity."[1] The human person, created in the image and likeness of God (see Gn 1:26), is himself or herself in the gift of self. This comes into clear light in the life and Pass-

1. *De Trinitate* VIII.8.12.

over of Jesus: "those who lose their life in this world will keep it for eternal life" (see Jn 12:25). To live in Christ thanks to the gift of the Spirit in faith and baptism to the point of full unity with him as the fruit of the Eucharist means being made a participant in the life of the Trinity not only as individuals but in reciprocal rapports. For this reason, as *Gaudium et Spes* indicates, the Lord Jesus when he prays to the Father "that they may all be one. As you, Father, are in me and I am in you" (Jn 17:21), opening horizons closed to human reason, has taught us a certain similarity between the unity of the divine Persons and the union of the sons of God in truth and charity: "This likeness reveals that man ... cannot fully find himself except through a sincere gift of himself" (no. 24).

Wherever a rapport of reciprocal openness and reciprocal love is established, also with the faithful of the other religions and with whoever is sincerely open to the truth, it is possible to open a pathway, existential and cognitional at the same time, to the mystery of the unique and true God, in whom we are all already introduced by the grace of Christ and the gift of the Holy Spirit. John Paul II said: "The fruit of dialogue is union between people and union of people with God.... By dialogue we let God be present in our midst; for as we open ourselves in dialogue to one another, we also open ourselves to God."[2] This consideration leads me to a provisional conclusion of our journey by speaking a word that reconnects to the New Testament wellspring of understanding of the Trinity. It is only meant to be a further provocation to think together beginning from the "place" in which the event of Jesus Christ introduces us always anew by grace into the personal and at the same time communitarian following of him.[3]

What could the apostle Paul ever have wished to suggest in that passage in the first Letter to the Corinthians (1 Cor 2:9–16), to which I have referred many times, where he witnesses with certainty that it is already possible and definitively real to have the *noûs* of Christ himself dwell in our very thinking? And this is the understanding in which the depths of the mystery are no longer relegated to an inaccessible distance in indifference or in nostalgia. But they are offered to be known and explained in their historical impact. Saying them does not capture nor denaturalize them, but rather takes delight in them as something true and substantial in the lively exchange that is always new and always different. Could this be that thinking and knowing *pneumatikà en lógois pneumatikoîse* (1 Cor 2:13) the realities of the Spirit in spiritual words and concepts of

2. John Paul II, "Address in Madras to Exponents of Non-Christian Religions," February 5, 1986; available at www.vatican.va.

3. A testimony that this path can be taken is found in *Dio-Trinità tra filosofi e teologi* (eds. Coda and Donà).

which Paul himself says we have ultimately become heirs in the *Lógos* become flesh?

These words of Paul are demanding. Just as it is only the human spirit, he argues, that is able to know what truly passes through the human heart and mind, so it is only the Spirit of God who "can scrutinize the profundities of God." God in fact dwells irremediably separated in the "cloud of unknowing" for whoever is other than he. Unless he—and this is what is unprecedented in the *lógos* of Jesus, in the *Lógos* which is Jesus himself—gives and donates his very Spirit to such a person. This happens in the crucified flesh of Jesus, who, in his death lived as *agápe*, "gave up his Spirit" (see Jn 19:30). It is precisely through this handing over, Paul concludes, that "we have the *noûs* of Christ."

The "cloud of unknowing," therefore, is ripped open even if the mystery remains and shows itself to be inexhaustible. The "cloud of unknowing," however, is definitively ripped open: as happened with the veil of the Temple of Jerusalem in the very act of the *Lógos* become flesh dying abandoned. From the recesses of the Holy of Holies the presence of God runs toward the tents of human beings: because already the crucified *Lógos* has pitched his tent among them—among the least, the marginalized, and the rejected. On Calvary there is already the extension of the world, because with all and with each person Jesus has "become one" (see 1 Cor 9:19–22) in order to open us, in himself, toward one another in the space of that *agápe* which is the sign and fruit of the resurrection.

All of us, none excluded, are therefore in God and God is in us. But this gift—*cháris*, grace—is not realized, meaning it has not become a historically lived reality in our thinking as well, until the form of the crucified *Lógos* becomes the form of our contemplation of God where he is now: in the "in our midst" which we access every time in a new way, the one going toward the other and thus really welcoming one another in dialogue. And this means venturing to the end in a speaking and listening composed of reciprocity without residue and conditions. It is there that we touch and welcome, together, the *Lógos* who in the Spirit becomes *our* flesh. The truth of the *Deus Trinitas*—Father, Son/*Lógos*, and Holy Spirit—occurs (measuring and directing) in the truth that is being made of our being and our thinking.

I think this *place of thinking* is that which ought to be welcomed and constructed decisively and patiently. Dialoguing, in fact, will not alienate us any more by scattering voices without them ever returning an echo of themselves. We become closer in fact: not to make us similar, no, but to make us listen and discern more distinctly the word which each one says as the different and multiple echoes of the inexhaustibly rich Word, which is pronounced by the silence in the breath of the Spirit and which we all touch in speaking. This is the Word which, in the fullness of time, was made flesh and was crucified. This was not in order to remain an *unicum* but to indicate the way precisely of a dialogue which is made completely one with the pilgrimage of history in which it breaks the bread of sharing and the wine of consolation with everyone—in an exodus from self toward the unexplored land in which we recognize the dwelling of the divine other, and, in him, our dwelling place.

Therefore it is no pacifying reply that is to be sought. Rather it is the disarmed sharing of the most acute and even lacerating question in which the "why?" of the abandoned Jesus is renewed; the ultimate and definitive word in which the crucified *Lógos* expresses himself, offering himself to the *Abbà* in the Spirit. One may therefore contemplate God through Jesus in his abandonment, in the flesh of human beings and in the midst of human beings. This is what Chiara Lubich has written with an intensely mystical language: "The wound of the abandonment is the pupil of the eye of God on the world; an infinite emptiness by means of which God looks at us; it is the window of God thrown open on the world and the window of humanity by means of which God is seen." God looks at the world by means of Jesus in his abandonment: when he recapitulates in himself humanity—every expectation, every sigh, every desire, every defeat, every sin, every death. And the Father sees everything in that fashion, in himself wrapped in the Holy Spirit by his love, shot through with his love, gathered by his love. He, Jesus in his abandonment, is the pupil, an infinite void, great as God who in that makes himself "nothingness of love": an emptiness which is the expression of love and in that way brings everyone in direct contact with God in whatever situation they may be. And each one with the other. He is the window of God thrown open upon the world, but precisely for that reason he is the window thrown open to humanity, the contemplation of God among men and women in the pained concreteness of life.

The contradiction, in its multiple expressions, is not resolved and reconciled: it is plunged into *agápe*. It is entrusted. It finds a reply, if ever, in that Spirit who, coming from the Father, vivifies it from within, in the dialogue which happens responsibly among us. In that way it makes that radical question "arise"—radical because it cries out from the root of our being which is irremediably wounded by the presence of the other and the divine other. It makes it "arise" new and satisfied, but in the inexhaustible movement of the desire that searches, thanks to the ever renewed event of *agápe*.

The journey therefore of thinking God the Trinity through dialogue can find its place again through grace, there where it finds its truth in itself, because it already lives and searches elsewhere. The challenge is that of moving, but without abandoning this place: the one in which that ontology opens and grows—that living/thinking of being that we indwell in love—in which God and humanity meet in trinitarian fashion in the encounter among human beings by means of the Spirit of Jesus.

Epilogue

that God may be all in all.

1 Corinthians 15:28

We have to recognize at the conclusion of our journey that a good number of questions are still open along with the many points I have mentioned. Besides and beyond the evident limits of my reading, it is necessary to renew the awareness, itself always witnessed anew by the experience of faith, that our knowledge of God remains veiled by the provisional, the fragmentary, and the awaited. This is so even if the difference between the understanding of the faith and the vision "face to face" is of degree and not of essence, thanks to the revelation of/in Jesus. And yet, how much the amazement of opening our view of God in God will be ever new, exceeding every measure! The hope is that it will be intuited, following the history of revelation witnessed by the First and New Testament and by the journey of the church and of humanity "into all the truth" (Jn 16:13), that the trinitarian face of God is the heart of the Christian faith, the extraordinary originality which specifies and directs it, transfiguring all the dimensions of existence, the cosmos, and of history with its light.

In reality, God the Trinity is the living and infinite horizon within which the truth and the vocation of creation are disclosed. This truth arises from the depths of the life of God: there where the Father, in an eternal and infinite act of love, contemplates the unending and fascinating riches of his being which is love in an other than himself, the Son/Word, and out of love shares being on its own. Creation, therefore, is born from the bowels of love of the living God: it is the work of the Father, realized in the Son in virtue of that inexhaustible breath of life which is the Holy Spirit.

For this reason, the purpose of creation is to become a partaker of the life of God in order to be, through grace, a second God, a created God.

This happens by means of the human person who is called in himself to receive creation giving it language. This happens by means of Jesus Christ, the Word/Son become flesh, the redeemer and the one who recapitulates creation. It is necessary to pass through him; it is necessary to fill ourselves, in the Spirit, with the same fullness which has been given to him by the Father in order to be one in God. Only when he, the Christ, will have become "all in all" (Col 3:11), thanks to the work of the Holy Spirit who excavates in our being in order to create there the space necessary to receive the being of God, the Father who also lives in him will be forever "all in all" (1 Cor 15:28).

The Father is completely in the Son; the Son become man is completely in whoever welcomes him; and thus, by means of the Son, the Father becomes all in all, bringing to fulfillment the prayer of Jesus: "that they may all be one. As you, Father, are in me and I am in you, may they also be in us" (Jn 17:21), thanks to the Holy Spirit. And as the Father is Father by giving himself to the Son, so he is God, the infinite one, by giving himself really, totally, by means of the Son and the Spirit, to his creatures. As the mystics bear witness, the only (!) distinction that will remain in the fulfillment of the times, between God and creatures made God in God, is that God is God because he is God (by his being), while creatures are such by the gift (the grace) of God, responsibly and creatively made their own by the freedom of human beings. But this, the only true and inexhaustible aspiration of man, happens because God is Trinity, he is love: he is himself by being the other. Looking at Jesus and in Jesus we are therefore called to preach not only the God of the three, but of all created reality inasmuch as it participates in the mystery of God, being made distinct from him. At the end of time there will remain only God in God: uncreated and created. The ultimate truth of everything is to be itself in reference to God, indeed to be itself distinctly from God, but insofar as it is expression of God. The vocation of all created reality is to become Eucharist: the real presence of God distinct from God.

Thus the end, the *éschaton*, the *omega* of creation (as its principle, the *próton*, the *alpha*) is trinitarian: it is the calling of creation to become the spouse of the lamb. It is being one with Christ, but also distinct from him in a relation of love that can find no relevant analogy other than that of the Trinity. Mary is mother of Jesus, *Theótokos*. A creature, by the infinite power of the love of God in the Holy Spirit becomes mother of her creator. It is the perfect exchange of positions of which only the love of God is capable. His joy is to give all he is to the other than himself, making the person free and not absorbing the person in himself. God wishes that the human being should take up his/her position beside God, not forgetting the origin of this gift, but with infinite gratitude.

This represents for creation the fascinating call, in Christ, to become one in its free multiplicity: Christ being all in everything, everything will reflect and will have in itself the whole, in a unique and unrepeatable way with respect to every other thing. Everything will announce something of the love which is God, in such wise that this something will become in the end a visible and tangible expression of the being of God. For this reason, in the fullness of time, God becomes man in Jesus; Jesus communicates the Spirit to humanity; human beings freely are called to say their yes to God, receiving in themselves the fullness of the gift that God makes of himself. In that way all of nature participates in this reality and is filled with God. First it was only an echo and a ray of God: in the consummation of history, thanks to the incarnation and the Pasch of Jesus as well as the mediation of the freedom of human persons, but in effusive reciprocity of love, God becomes all in all. The cosmos itself, therefore, awaits "with eager longing" the "revealing of the children of God" and groans and suffers as in the pangs of a gigantic birth (see Rom 8:19, 22): a participation stretched out in time to the birth of Christ on the wood of the cross, there where he generated a new humanity together with "new heavens and new earth."

This will be creation, therefore, at the end of time in the glory of God, already personified in that "woman clothed with the sun" and evoked by the Book of Revelation (see Rv 12:1–17): "a woman the measure of the cosmos, the measure of the whole work of creation," Mary (according to John Paul II). In her, humanity already contemplates the advent of the trinitarian *eschaton* and is called to discover there and to build actively, in love that is mutual and toward all, its definitive identity. In that way, the final word of the profession of faith in God who is Trinity coincides with the institution of the place of the experience and the understanding of God who is revealed as love in Jesus: "we have known and believe the love that God has for us. God is Love; and those who abide in love abide in God and God abides in them" (1 Jn 4:16). Already now, and forever.

BIBLIOGRAPHY

Trinitarian Theology Study Guides

Auer, Johann. *Gott: Der Eine und Dreieine*. Regensburg: Pustet Verlag, 1978.

Belloso, J. M. Rovira. *Tratado de Dios uno y trino*. Salamanca: Secretariado Trinitario, 1993.

Bertuletti, Angelo. *Dio, il mistero dell'unico*. Brescia: Queriniana, 2014.

Bobrinskoy, Boris. *The Mystery of the Trinity: Trinitarian Experience and Vision in the Biblical and Patristic Tradition*. Translated by A. P. Gythiel. Crestwood, N.Y.: St. Vladimir's Seminary Press, 1999.

Brunner, Emil. *The Christian Doctrine of God*. Translated by O. Wyon. London: Lutterworth Press, 1949.

Ciola, Nicola. *Teologia trinitaria: Storia – Metodo – Prospettive*. Bologna: Ed. Dehoniane, 1996.

Coffey, David. *Deus Trinitas: The Doctrine of the Triune God*. New York: Oxford University Press, 1999.

Courth, Franz. *Der Gott der dreifaltigen Liebe*. Paderborn: Bonifatius Verlag, 1993.

Cozzi, Alberto. *Manuale di dottrina trinitaria*. Brescia: Queriniana, 2009.

Duquoc, Christian. *Dieu différent: Essai sur la symbolique trinitaire*. Paris: Ed. du Cerf, 1978.

Emery, Gilles. *The Trinity: An Introduction to Catholic Doctrine on the Triune God*. Translated by Matthew Levering. Washington, D.C.: The Catholic University of America Press, 2012.

Forte, Bruno. *The Trinity as History: Saga of the Christian God*. Translated by Paul Rotondi. New York: Alba House, 1989.

Fortman, Edmund J. *The Triune God: A Historical Study of the Doctrine of the Trinity*. London: Hutchinson and Co., 1972.

Greshake, Gisbert. *Der dreieine Gott: Eine trinitarische Theologie*. Freiburg i.B.: Herder, 1997.

Hill, William J. *The Three-Personed God: The Trinity as a Mystery of Salvation*. Washington, D.C.: The Catholic University of America Press, 1982.

Hunt, Anne. *Trinity: Nexus of the Mysteries of Christian Faith*. Maryknoll, N.Y.: Orbis Books, 2005.

Kasper, Walter. *The God of Jesus Christ*. Translated by Matthew J. O'Connell. New York: T and T Clark, 2012.

LaCugna, Catherine M. *God For Us: The Trinity and Christian Life*. San Francisco, Calif.: Harper, 1991.

Ladaria, Luis F. *The Living and True God: The Mystery of the Trinity*. Edited by Rafael Luciani. Translated by Maria Isabel Reyna and Liam Kelly. Miami, Fla.: Convivium Press, 2010.

Laurentin, René. *Trattato sulla Trinità. Principio, modello e termine di ogni amore. Testamento Spirituale.* Rome: Edizioni ART, 2009.

Mateo-Seco, Lucas F., and Giulio Maspero. *Il mistero di Dio uno e trino: Manuale di Teologia Trinitaria.* Rome: Edusc, 2014.

Nigro, Carmelo. *Dio più grande del nostro cuore: Il mistero di Dio nella storia della salvezza, verso una sintesi teologica.* Rome: Città Nuova, 1974.

O'Collins, Gerald. *The Tripersonal God: Understanding and Interpreting the Trinity.* London: Geoffrey Chapman, 1999.

Rahner, Karl. *The Trinity.* Translated by Joseph Donceel. New York: Crossroad, 1997.

Staglianò, Antonio. *Il mistero del Dio vivente: Per una teologia dell'Assoluto trinitario.* Bologna: Dehoniane, 1996.

Torrence, Thomas F. *The Christian Doctrine of God: One Being Three Persons.* Edinburgh: T and T Clark, 1996.

The Revelation of God in the Old Testament

Albertz, Rainer. *Religionsgeschichte Israels in alttestamentlicher Zeit.* 2 vols. Göttingen: Vandenhoeck and Ruprecht, 1996–97.

Beauchamp, Paul. *L'un et l'autre Testament*, vol. 1: *Essai de lecture.* Paris: Seuil, 1976.

———. *L'un et l'autre Testament*, vol. 2: *Accomplir les Écritures.* Paris: Seuil, 1990.

———. *La loi de Dieu: d'une montagne à l'autre.* Paris: Seuil, 1999.

Cazelles, Henri. *La Bible et son Dieu.* Paris: Desclée, 1989.

Crüsemann, Frank. *The Torah: Theology and Social History of Old Testament Law.* Translated by Allan W. Mahnke. Minneapolis, Minn.: Fortress Press, 1996.

Dal Bo, F. *La Legge e il volto di Dio: La Rivelazione sul Sinai nella letteratura ebraica e cristiana.* Florence: Giuntina, 2004.

Deissler, Alfons. "L'autorivelazione di Dio nell'Antico Testamento." In *Mysterium Salutis: Nuovo corso di dogmatica come teologia della storia della salvezza*, vol. 3: *La storia della salvezza prima di Cristo*, edited by Johannes Feiner and Magnus Löhrer, 285–344. Brescia: Queriniana, 1969.

Diesel, Anja Angela. *«Ich bin Jahwe»: Der Aufstieg der Ich-bin-Jahwe Aussage zum Schüsselwort des alttestamentlichen Monotheismus.* Neukirchen-Vluyn: Neukirchener Verlag, 2006.

Eichrodt, Walther. *Theology of the Old Testament.* 2 vols. Translated by J. A. Baker. Philadelphia: Westminster Press, 1961–67.

Jacob, Edmond. *Theology of the Old Testament.* Translated by Arthur W. Heathcote and Philip J. Allcoc. Second edition. London: Hodder and Stoughton, 1961.

Jeremias, Jörg. *Theophanie: Die Geschichte einer alttestamentlichen Gattung.* Neukirchen-Vluyn: Neukirchener Verlag, 1977.

Lohfink, Norbert, E. Zenger, G. Braulik, and J. Scharbert. *Gott, der einzig: Zur Entstehung des Monotheismus in Israel.* Freiburg: Herder, 1985.

Loretz, Oswald. *Des Gottes Einzigkeit: Ein altorientalisches Argumentationsmodell zum "Schma Jisrael."* Darmstadt: Wissenschaftliche Buchgesellschaft, 1997.

McKenzie, John L. *A Theology of the Old Testament.* Eugene, Ore.: Wipf and Stock, 2009.

Noth, Martin. *The History of Israel.* Second edition. New York: Harper and Row, 1960.

Pontifical Biblical Commission. *The Jewish People and their Sacred Scriptures in the Christian Bible.* May 24, 2001. Available at www.vatican.va.

Rendtorff, Rolf. *The Canonical Hebrew Bible: A Theology of the Old Testament.* Translated by David E. Orton. Blandford Forum: Deo Publishing, 2011.

Rossé, Gérard. "La rivelazione di Dio nell'Antico Testamento: il periodo post-esilico." In Università Popolare Mariana, *Il Dio di Gesù Cristo.* Rome: Città Nuova, 1982.

Schulte, R. "La preparazione della rivelazione trinitaria." In *Mysterium Salutis: Nuovo corso di dogmatica come teologia della storia della salvezza*, vol. 3: *La storia della salvezza prima di Cristo*, edited by Johannes Feiner and Magnus Löhrer, 61–110. Brescia: Queriniana, 1969.

Soggin J. Albert. *A History of Israel: from the Beginnings to the Bar Kochba Revolt, AD 135.* Translated by John Bowden. London: SCM, 1984.

Van Imschoot, Paul. *Théologie de l'Ancien Testament.* 2 vols. Tournai: Desclée, 1954–56.

Von Rad, Gerhard. *Old Testament Theology.* 2 vols. Translated by D. M. G. Stalker. San Francisco, Calif.: Harper and Row, 1962–65.

Vriezen, Theodorus Christian. *An Outline of Old Testament Theology.* Newton, Mass.: C. T. Branford, 1958.

Zimmerli, Walther. *I am Yahweh.* Edited by Walter Brueggemann. Translated by Douglas W. Stott. Atlanta: John Knox Press, 1982.

Zimmermann, Heinrich. "Das Absolute 'egò eimì' als Neutestamentliche Offenabrungsformel." *Biblische Zeitschrift* 4 (1960): 54–69.

The Revelation of God in the New Testament

Beauchamp, Paul, et al. *Monothéisme et Trinité.* Brussels: Facultés universitaires Saint-Louis, 1991.

Bordoni, Marcello. *La cristologia nell'orizzonte dello Spirito.* Brescia: Queriniana, 1995.

———. *Gesù di Nazareth: Signore e Cristo. Saggio di cristologia sistematica.* 3 vols. Bologna: EDB, 2018.

Brague, Rémi. *Il Dio dei cristiani: L'Unico Dio?* Milan: Raffaele Cortina, 2009.

Brown, Raymond E. *The Death of the Messiah: from Gethsemane to the Grave. A Commentary of the Passion Narratives in the Four Gospels.* 2 vols. New York: Doubleday, 1994.

Chevallier, Max-Alain. *Souffle de Dieu: Le Saint-Esprit dans le Nouveau Testament.* 2 vols. Paris: Beauchesne, 1978–90.

Duquoc, Christian. *Jésus, homme libre.* Paris: Cerf, 1973.

Durrwell, François-Xavier. *The Resurrection: A Biblical Study.* Translated by Rosemary Sheed. London: Sheed and Ward, 1986.

———. *Le Père. Dieu en son mystère.* Paris: Cerf, 1987.

———. *L'Esprit du Père et du Fils.* Paris: Médiaspaul, 1989.

———. *Holy Spirit of God: an Essay in Biblical Theology.* Translated by Scott Hahn and Benedict Davies. Cincinnati, Ohio: St. Anthony Messenger Press, Servant Books, 2006.

Fabris, Rinaldo. *Gesù di Nazareth.* Assisi: Cittadella, 1983.

Ferraro, Giuseppe. *Lo Spirito e Cristo nel vangelo di Giovanni.* Brescia: Paideia, 1984.

Forte, Bruno. *Gesù di Nazareth, storia di Dio, Dio della storia.* Rome: Edizioni Paoline, 1981.

Haya-Prats, Gonzalo. *Empowered Believers: The Holy Spirit in the Book of Acts.* Translated by Paul Elbert. Eugene, Ore.: Cascade Books, 2011.

Hengel, Martin. *Crucifixion.* Translated by John Bowden. Philadelphia: Fortress Press, 1977.

Jeremias, Joachim. *Abbà*. Göttingen: Vandenhoeck and Ruprecht, 1966.

———. *The Parables of Jesus*. Translated by S. H. Hook. Revised third edition. London: SCM Press, 1972.

Kasper, Walter. *Jesus the Christ*. Translated by V. Green. New York: Paulist Press, 1976.

Kockerols, Jean. *L'Esprit à la Croix: la dernière onction de Jésus*. Brussels: Editions Lessius, 1999.

Labbé, Yves. *Essai sur le monothéisme trinitaire*. Paris: Cerf, 1987.

Léon-Dufour, Xavier. *Life and Death in the New Testament: The Teachings of Jesus and Paul*. Translated by Terrence Prendergast. San Francisco, Calif.: Harper and Row, 1986.

Lupieri, Edmondo. *Giovanni Battista fra storia e leggenda*. Brescia: Paideia, 1988.

———. *Giovanni Battista nelle tradizioni sinottiche*. Brescia: Paideia, 1988.

Manaranche, André. *Le monothéisme chrétien*. Paris: Cerf, 1985.

Merklein, Helmut. *Jesu Botschaft von der Gottesherrschaft*. Stuttgart: Verlag Katholisches Bibelwerk, 1983.

Penna, Romano. *I ritratti originali di Gesù Cristo: Inizi e sviluppi della cristologia neotestamentaria*. 2 vols. Cinisello Balsamo: San Paolo, 1996–99.

———. *Paul the Apostle: A Theological and Exegetical Study*. 2 vols. Translated by Thomas P. Wahl. Collegeville, Minn.: Liturgical Press, 1996.

Popkes, Wiard. *Christus traditus: eine Untersuchung zum Begriff der Dahingabe im Neuen Testament*. Zürich: Zwingli Verlag, 1967.

Rahner, Karl. "*Theós* in the New Testament." In *Theological Investigations*, vol. 1: *God, Christ, Mary and Grace,* translated by Ernst Cornelius, 79–148. New York: Crossroad, 1961.

Ratzinger, Joseph. *Jesus of Nazareth*. 3 vols. New York / San Francisco, Calif.: Doubleday / Ignatius Press, 2007–12.

Rossé, Gérard. *Il grido di Gesù in croce: Una panoramica esegetica e teologica*. Rome: Città Nuova, 1984.

———. *Maledetto l'appeso al legno: Lo scandalo della croce in Paolo e in Matteo*. Rome: Città Nuova, 2006.

———. "Il grido di Gesù in croce: Approccio biblico." *Sophia* 1, no. 1 (2008): 47–60.

Sacchi, Paolo. *Gesù e la sua gente*. Cinisello Balsamo: San Paolo, 2003.

Schnackenburg, Rudolf. *God's Rule and Kingdom*. Translated by John Murray. Second edition. London: Burns and Oates, 1968.

Schoonenberg, Piet. *The Christ: A Study of the God-man Relationship in the Whole of Creation and in Jesus Christ*. Translated by Della Couling. New York: Herder and Herder, 1971.

Schürmann, Heinz. *Das hermeneutische Hauptproblem der Verkündigung Jesu*. Freiburg: Herder, 1964.

———. *Praying with Christ: the "Our Father" for Today*. Translated by W. M. Ducey. New York: Herder and Herder, 1964.

———. *Wie hat Jesus seinen Tod bestanden und verstanden?: eine methodische Besinnung*. Leipzig: St. Benno-Verlag, 1974.

———. *Jesu ureigener Tod: Exegetische Bessinnungen und Ausblick*. Freiburg: Herder, 1975.

———. *La tradizione dei detti di Gesù*. Italian Translation by F. Montagnini. Brescia: Paideia, 1980.

———. *Jesu: Gestalt und Geheimnis. Gesammelte Beiträge*. Edited by Klaus Scholtissek. Paderborn: Bonifatius, 1994.

Van Iersel, Bastiaan. *The Bible on the Living God*. Translated by H. J. Vaughan. Del Pere, Wis.: St. Norbert Abbey Press, 1965.

Vermes, Géza. *Jesus the Jew: A Historian's Reading of the Gospels*. London: SCM Press, 2001.

Wainwright, Arthur W. *The Trinity in the New Testament*. London: SPCK, 1962.

Classics of the Theological and Mystical Tradition (in chronological order)

Irenaeus of Lyons. *Against the Heresies*. Translated by Dominic J. Unger. Ancient Christian Writers 55. New York: The Newman Press, 1992.

Tertullian. *Against Praxeas*. Translated by A. Souter. New York: MacMillan, 1919.

Origen. *Commentary on the Gospel of John*. Translated by Ronald Heine. 2 vols. Fathers of the Church 80 and 89. Washington, D.C.: The Catholic University of America Press, 1989 and 2006.

———. *On First Principles*. Translated by G. W. Butterworth. Notre Dame, Ind.: Ave Maria Press, 2013.

Athanasius. *The Orations of St. Athanasius against the Arians, According to the Benedictine Text: With an Account of His Life* by William Bright. Eugene, Ore.: Wipf and Stock, 2005.

———. *Letters to Serapion on the Holy Spirit*. In Athanasius the Great and Didymus the Blind, *Works on the Spirit*, translated by Mark Del Cogliano, Andrew Radde-Gallwitz, and Lewis Ayres. New York: St. Vladimir's Seminary Press, 2013.

Hilary of Poitiers. *The Trinity*. Translated by Stephen McKenna. Fathers of the Church 25. Washington, D.C.: The Catholic University of America Press, 1954.

Gregory of Nyssa. *To Ablabius*. In *Collection*. London: Aeterna Press, 2016.

Gregory of Nazianzus. *Theological Orations*. In *On God and Christ: The Five Theological Orations and Two Letters to Cledonius*, translated by Frederick Williams and Lionel Wickham. New York: St. Vladimir's Seminary Press, 2002.

Basil of Caesarea. *Against Eunomius*. Translated by Mark Del Cogliano and Andrew Radde-Gallwitz. Fathers of the Church 122. Washington, D.C.: The Catholic University of America Press, 2011.

———. *On the Holy Spirit*. Translated by Stephen M. Hildebrand. New York: St. Vladimir's Seminary Press, 2011.

Augustine of Hippo. *Homilies on the First Epistle of John*. Translated by H. Browne. Edited by Philip Schaff. Nicene and Post-Nicene Fathers, First Series 7. Grand Rapids, Mich.: Christian Literature Publishing Co., 1974.

———. *The Trinity*. Edited by John E. Rotelle. Translated by Edmund Hill. Brooklyn, N.Y.: New City Press, 1991.

———. *Confessions*. Translated by Maria Boulding. In *The Works of Saint Augustine* I/1, edited by John E. Rotelle. Hyde Park, N.Y.: New City Press, 1997.

———. *On Christian Doctrine*. Translated by J. J. Shaw. Mineola, N.Y.: Dover, 2009.

Dionysius the Areopagite. *The Divine Names and The Mystical Theology*. Translated by John D. Jones. Milwaukee, Wis.: Marquette University Press, 1980.

John of Damascus. *De fide orthodoxa*. Edited by Philip Schaff. Nicene and Post-Nicene Fathers, First Series 14. London: T and T Clark, 1980.

Anselm of Canterbury. *The Procession of the Holy Spirit*. In *Works*, vol. 3, translated by Jasper Hopkins and Herbert Richardson. New York: Edwin Mellen Press, 1976.

Richard of St. Victor. *On the Trinity*. Translated by Ruben Angelici. Havertown: James Clarke and Co., 2012.

Aquinas, Thomas. *Scriptum super libros sententiarum magistri Petri Lombardi*. 4 vols. Paris: Lethielleux, 1929–47.

———. *Summa contra Gentiles*. 4 vols. Translated by A. Pegis, J. Anderson, V. J. Burke, and C. J. O'Neil. South Bend, Ind.: University of Notre Dame Press, 1975.

———. *Summa Theologica*. Translated by the English Dominican Province. New York: Benziger Bros., 1981.

———. *Commentary on the Gospel of St. John*. 3 vols. Translated by Fabian R. Larcher and James A. Weisheipl. Washington, D.C.: The Catholic University Press of America, 2010.

———. *Super Boethium De Trinitate*. London: Aeterna Press, 2015.

Bonaventure. *Itinerarium mentis in Deum*. Edited by Philotheus Boehner and Zachary Hayes. Works of St. Bonaventure Series 2. Revised edition. Saint Bonaventure, N.Y.: Franciscan Institute, 2002.

———. *Collations on the Hexaëmeron*. Translated by Jay M. Hammond. Works of St. Bonaventure Series 18. Saint Bonaventure, N.Y.: Franciscan Institute, 2018.

Duns Scotus, John. *The Examined Report of the Paris Lecture: Reportatio*. Edited by Allan B. Wolter and Oleg V. Bychkov. 2 vols. Saint Bonaventure, N.Y.: Franciscan Institute, 2008.

———. *A Treatise on God as First Principle*. Whitefish, Mont.: Kessinger, 2010.

Simeon the New Theologian. *Eth*. 5. In *On the Mystical Life: Ethical Discourses*, vol. 2: *On Virtue and Christian Life*, translated by Alexander Golitzin. Crestwood, N.Y.: St. Vladimir's Seminary Press, 1996.

Catherine of Siena. *The Dialogue*. Translated by Suzanne Noffke. New York: Paulist Press, 1980.

Luther, Martin. *The 95 Theses*. In *The Roots of Reform*, vol. 1, edited by Timothy J. Wengert. Minneapolis, Minn.: Fortress Press, 2015.

Ignatius of Loyola. *The Spiritual Exercises and Selected Works*. The Classics of Western Spirituality 72. Edited by George E. Ganss. New York: Paulist Press, 1991.

Teresa of Avila. *The Collected Works of St. Teresa of Avila*. Translated by Kieran Kavanaugh and Otilio Rodriguez. 2 vols. Washington, D.C.: ICS Publications, 1976–80.

John of the Cross. *The Collected Works of St. John of the Cross*. Translated by Kieran Kavanaugh and Otilio Rodriguez. Washington, D.C.: Institute of Carmelite Studies, 1979.

Suárez, Francisco. *De sanctissimo Trinitatis mysterio*. Edited by A. D. M. André. In *Opera omnia*, vol. 1. Paris: Vivès, 1856.

Rosmini, Antonio. *Theosophy*. Translated by Denis Cleary and Terence Watson. 3 vols. Durham: Rosmini House, 2007–11.

———. *L'introduzione al vangelo secondo Giovanni*. Opere di Antonio Rosmini 41. Rome: Istituto di Studi Filosofici – Centro di Studi Rosminiani – Città Nuova, 2009.

Barth, Karl. *Church Dogmatics*, vol. 1: *The Doctrine of the Word of God*. Translated by G. T. Thomson. Edinburgh: T and T Clark, 1936.

———. *Church Dogmatics*, vol. 2: *The Doctrine of God*. Translated by G. W. Bromiley et al. Edinburgh: T and T Clark, 1957.

Florensky, Pavel. *The Pillar and Ground of the Truth.* Translated by Boris Jakim. Princeton, N.J.: Princeton University Press, 1997.

Bulgakov, Sergius. *The Bride of the Lamb.* Translated by Boris Jakim. Grand Rapids, Mich.: Eerdmans, 2002.

———. *The Comforter.* Translated by Boris Jakim. Grand Rapids, Mich.: Eerdmans, 2004.

———. *The Lamb of God.* Translated by Boris Jakim. Grand Rapids, Mich.: Eerdmans, 2008.

Stein, Edith. *The Science of the Cross.* Translated by Josephine Koeppel. The Collected Works of Edith Stein 6. Washington, D.C.: ICS Publications, 2002.

———. *Finite and Eternal Being: An Attempt at an Ascent to the Meaning of Being.* Translated by Kurt F. Reinhardt. The Collected Works of Edith Stein 9. Washington, D.C.: ICS Publications, 2002.

Rahner, Karl. "Il Dio trino come fondamento originario e trascendente della storia della salvezza." In *Mysterium Salutis: Nuovo corso di dogmatica come teologia della storia della salvezza*, vol. 3: *La storia della salvezza prima di Cristo*, edited by Johannes Feiner and Magnus Löhrer, 404–507. Brescia: Queriniana, 1969.

von Balthasar, Hans Urs. *Mysterium Paschale: The Mystery of Easter.* Translated by Aidan Nichols. San Francisco, Calif.: Ignatius Press, 2000.

———. *The Glory of the Lord: A Theological Aesthetics*, vol. 1: *Seeing the Form.* Edited by Erasmo Leiva-Merikakis. Translated by Joseph Fessio and John Kenneth Riches. San Francisco, Calif.: Ignatius Press, 1982.

———. *The Glory of the Lord: A Theological Aesthetics*, vol. 5: *The Realm of Metaphysics in the Modern Age.* Edited by Brian McNeil and John Riches. Translated by Oliver Davies, Andrew Louth, Brian McNeil, John Saward, and Rowan Williams. San Francisco, Calif.: Ignatius Press, 1991.

———. *Theo-Drama: Theological Dramatic Theory*, vol. 4: *The Action.* Translated by Graham Harrison. San Francisco, Calif.: Ignatius Press, 1994.

———. *Theo-Drama: Theological Dramatic Theory*, vol. 5: *The Last Act.* Translated by Graham Harrison. San Francisco, Calif.: Ignatius Press, 1998.

———. *Theo-Logic: Theological Logical Theory*, vol. 2: *Truth of God.* Translated by Adrian J. Walker. San Francisco, Calif.: Ignatius Press, 2004.

———. *Theo-Logic: Theological Logical Theory*, vol. 3: *The Spirit of the Truth.* Translated by Graham Harrison. San Francisco, Calif.: Ignatius Press, 2005.

von Speyr, Adrienne. *Das Wort und die Mystik.* 2 vols. Einsiedeln: Johannes Verlag, 1970.

Jüngel, Eberhard. *God as the Mystery of the World: On the Foundation of the Theology of the Crucified One in the Dispute Between Theism and Atheism.* Translated by Darrell L. Guder. Grand Rapids, Mich.: Eerdmans, 1983.

Hemmerle, Klaus. *Leben aus der Einheit: Eine theologische Herausforderung.* Edited by Peter Blättler. Freiburg i.B.: Herder, 1995.

. *Thesen zu einer Trinitarischen Ontologie.* Einsiedeln: Johannes Verlag, 1976.

Lafont, Ghislain. *Peut-on connaître Dieu en Jésus Christ.* Paris: Cerf, 1969.

Lubich, Chiara. *Essential Writings, Spirituality, Dialogue, Culture.* Translated by Tom Masters and Callan Slipper. Hyde Park, N.Y.: New City Press, 2007.

History of Trinitarian Theology Studies

Altizer, Thomas J. J., and William Hamilton. *Radical Theology and the Death of God.* New York: Bobbs-Merrill, 1966.

Ange, Daniel. *L'étreinte de feu: L'icone de la Trinité de Roublov.* Paris: Desclée de Brouwer, 1980.

Ayres, Lewis. *Augustine and the Trinity.* Cambridge: Cambridge University Press, 2010.

Benats, Bart. *Il ritmo trinitario della verità: La teologia di Ireneo di Lione.* Rome: Città Nuova, 2006.

Bernard and Joseph Wolinski, eds. *Le Dieu du salut: La tradition, la règle de foi et les Symboles, l'économie du salut, le développement des dogmes trinitaire et christologique.* Histoires des dogmes. Paris: Desclée, 1994.

Bernardi, Piergiuseppe. *Trinità e rivelazione: Le due economie in V. Losskij.* Rome: Città Nuova, 2004.

Blaumeiser, Hubertus. *Martin Luthers Kreuzestheologie: Schüssel zu seiner Deutung von Mensch und Wirklichkeit.* Paderborn: Bonifatius, 1995.

Bouyer, Louis. *The Eternal Son: A Theology of the Word of God and Christology.* Translated by Simone Inkel and John F. Laughlin. Huntington, Ind.: Our Sunday Visitor, 1978.

———. *Le consolateur: Esprit-Saint et vie de Grâce.* Paris: du Cerf, 1980.

———. *The Invisible Father: Approaches to the Mystery of the Divinity.* Translated by Hugh Gilbert. Petersham, Mass.: St. Bede's Publications, 1999.

Breuning, Wilhelm, and Eugen Drewermann, eds. *Trinität: Aktuelle Perspektiven der Theologie.* Freiburg: Herder, 1984.

Ciola, Nicola. *La crisi del teocentrismo trinitario nel Novecento teologico: il tema nel contesto emblematico della secolarizzazione.* Rome: Dehoniane, 1993.

Clemenzia, Alessandro. *Nella Trinità come Chiesa: In dialogo con Heribert Mühlen.* Rome: Città Nuova, 2012.

Coda, Piero. *Il negativo e la Trinitá: ipotesi su Hegel. Indagine storico-sistematica sulla "Denkform" hegeliana alla luce dell'ermeneutica del cristianesimo.* Rome: Città Nuova, 1987.

———. *L'altro di Dio: Rivelazione e kenosi in Sergej Bulgakov.* Rome: Città Nuova, 1998.

———. *La percezione della forma: fenomenologia e cristologia in Hegel.* Rome: Città Nuova, 2007.

Congar, Yves. *I Believe in the Holy Spirit.* Translated by David Smith. New York: Crossroad, 2001.

Crouzel, Henri. *Origène.* Paris: Lethielleux, 1985.

de Lubac, Henri. *La postérité spirituelle de Joachim de Fiore.* 2 vols. Namur: Culture et vérité, 1979–80.

de Margerie, Bertrand. *The Christian Trinity in History.* Translated by E. J. Fortman. Petersham, Mass.: St. Bede's Publications, 1982.

de Régnon, Theodore. *Études de théologie positive sur le Sainte Trinité.* 4 vols. Paris: V. Retaux et fils, 1892–98.

Dubarle, Dominique. *Dieu avec l'être: De Parmenide à Saint Thomas. Essai d'ontologie théologale.* Paris: Beauchesne, 1986.

Emery, Gilles. *La Trinité créatrice: Trinité et création dans les commentaires aux*

"Sentences" de Thomas d'Aquin et de ses precurseurs Albert le Grand et Bonaventure. Paris: Vrin, 1995.

———. *The Trinitarian Theology of Saint Thomas Aquinas.* Translated by Francesca Aran Murphy. Oxford: Oxford University Press, 2007.

Evdokimov, Paul. *La connaissance de Dieu selon la tradition orientale.* Lyon: Edition Xavier Mappus, 1967.

———. *L'Esprit Saint dans la tradition orthodoxe.* Paris: Cerf, 1969.

Fédou, Michel. *La sagesse et le monde: Le Christ d'Origène.* Paris: Desclée, 1994.

———. *La Voie du Christ: Genèse de la christologie dans le contexte religieux de l'Antiquité du II siècle au début du IV siècle.* Paris: Cerf, 2006.

Ferri, Riccardo. *Gesù e la verità: Agostino e Tommaso interpreti del vangelo di Giovanni.* Rome: Città Nuova, 2007.

———. *Il Dio unitrino nel pensiero di Tommaso d'Aquino: Dal Commento alle sentenze al Compendio di teologia.* Rome: Città Nuova, 2010.

Friedman, Russell L. *Medieval Trinitarian Thought from Aquinas to Ockham.* Cambridge: Cambridge University Press, 2010.

Gamillscheg, Maria Helene. *Die Kontroverse um das Filioque: Möglichkeiten einer Problemlösung auf Grund der Forschungen und Gespräche der letzen hundert Jahren.* Würzburg: Augustinus Verlag, 1996.

Garrigues, Jean-Miguel. "À la suite de la clarification romaine sur le *Filioque.*" *Nouvelle Revue Théologique* 119, no. 3 (1997): 321–34.

Gherardini, Bruno. *Theologia crucis: L'eredità di Lutero nell'evoluzione teologica della Riforma.* Alba: Paoline, 1978.

González, Marcelo. *La relación entre Trinidad económica e inmanente: el 'axioma fundamental' de K. Rahner y su recepción. Lineas para continuar la reflexión.* Rome: Libreria Ed. della Pontificia Università Lateranense, 1996.

Grillmeier, Aloys. *Christ in Christian Tradition: From the Apostolic Age to Chalcedon (451).* London: A. R. Mowbray and Co., 1975.

Hemmerle, Klaus. *Theologie als Nachfolge: Bonaventura – ein Weg für heute.* Freiburg: Herder, 1975.

Holzer, Vincent. *Le Dieu Trinité dans l'histoire: Le différend théologique Balthasar – Rahner.* Paris: Cerf, 1995.

Hunt, Anne. *The Trinity and the Paschal Mystery: A Development in Recent Catholic Theology.* Collegeville, Minn.: Liturgical Press, 1997.

Ide, Pascal. *Une Théo-Logique du Don: Le Don Dans la Trilogie de Hans Urs von Balthasar.* Leuven: Peeters, 2013.

International Theological Commission. *Theology, Christology, Anthropology* (1982). Available at www.vatican.va.

———. *God the Trinity and the Unity of Humanity* (2014). Available at www.vatican.va.

Kalaitzidis, Pantelis. "Theologia. Discours sur Dieu et science théologique chez Denys l'Aréopagite et Thomas d'Aquin." In *Denys l'Aréopagite et sa postérité en Orient ed en Occident,* edited by Ysabel de Andia, 457–87. Paris: Études Augustiniennes, 1996.

Kannengiesser, Charles. *Le Verbe de Dieu selon saint Athanase d'Alexandrie.* Paris: Desclée, 1999.

Kelly, John Norman Davidson. *Early Christian Doctrines.* London: Adam and Charles, 1968.

———. *Early Christian Creeds.* London: Routledge, 1982.

Krempel, A. *La doctrine de la relation chez Saint Thomas: Exposé historique et systematique*. Paris: Vrin, 1952.

Kretschmar, Georg. *Studien zur frühchristlichen Trinitätstheologie*. Tübingen: Mohr, 1956.

Lafont, Ghislain. *Structures et méthode dans la "Somme Théologique" de Saint Thomas d'Aquin*. Paris: Desclée de Brouwer, 1960.

Lambiasi, Francesco, and Dario Vitali. *Lo Spirito Santo: mistero e presenza. Per una sintesi di pneumatologia*. Bologna: Dehoniane, 1987.

Lebreton, Jules. *History of the Dogma of the Trinity: From its Origins to the Council of Nicaea*. Translated by Algar Thorold. Eighth edition. London: Burns, Oates and Washbourne, 1939.

Léthel, François-Marie. *Connaître l'amour du Christ qui surpasse toute connaissance: La théologie des Saints*. Venasque: Ed. du Carmel, 1996.

Lilla, Salvatore. *Dionigi l'Areopagita e il platonismo cristiano*. Brescia: Morcelliana, 2005.

Löhrer, Magnus. "Riflessioni dogmatiche sugli attributi e sui modi di agire di Dio." In *Mysterium Salutis: Nuovo corso di dogmatica come teologia della storia della salvezza*, vol. 3: *La storia della salvezza prima di Cristo*, edited by Johannes Feiner and Magnus Löhrer, 370–400. Brescia: Queriniana, 1969.

Lossky, Vladimir. *The Mystical Theology of the Eastern Church*. Crestwood, N.Y.: St. Vladimir's Seminary Press, 2002.

Madec, Goulven. *Le Dieu d'Augustin*. Paris: Cerf, 2000.

Maraldi, Valentino. *Lo Spirito e la Sposa: Il ruolo ecclesiale dello Spirito Santo dal Vaticano I alla Lumen Gentium del Vaticano II*. Casale Monferrato: Piemme, 1992.

Marengo, Gilfredo. *Trinità e creazione: Indagine sulla teologia di Tommaso d'Aquino*. Rome: Città Nuova, 1990.

Marinelli, Francesco. *Personalismo trinitario nella storia della salvezza: Rapporti tra la SS.ma Trinità e le opere "ad extra" nello "Scriptum super Sententiis" di San Tommaso*. Rome / Paris: PUL / Vrin, 1969.

Maspero, Giulio. *La Trinità e l'uomo: l'Ad Ablabium di Gregorio di Nissa*. Rome: Città Nuova, 2004.

———. *Essere e relazione: l'ontologia trinitaria di Gregorio di Nissa*. Rome: Città Nuova, 2013.

Mathieu, Luc. *La Trinité créatrice d'après Saint Bonaventure*. Paris: Editions Franciscaines, 1992.

Milano, Andrea. *Persona in teologia: Alle origini del significato di persona nel cristianesimo antico*. Naples: Dehoniane, 1984.

———. *La Trinità dei teologi e dei filosofi: L'intelligenza della persona in Dio*. Naples: Dehoniane, 1987.

Moingt, Joseph. *Théologie trinitaire de Tertullien*. 4 vols. Paris: Aubier, 1966–69.

Moltmann, Jürgen. *The Trinity and the Kingdom*. Translated by Margaret Kohl. San Francisco, Calif.: HarperCollins, 1981.

———. *The Crucified God: The Cross of Christ as the Foundation and Criticism of Christian Theology*. Translated by R. A. Wilson and John Bowden. San Francisco, Calif.: HarperCollins, 1991.

Mottu, Henry. *La manifestation de l'Esprit selon Joachim de Fiore: Herméneutique et théologie de l'histoire d'après le Traité sur les Quatres Evangiles*. Paris: Neuchâtel Delachaux, 1977.

Mühlen, Heribert. *Der Heilige Geist als Person: In der Trinität bei der Inkarnation und im Gnadebund: Ich-Du-Wir*. Münster: Aschendorff, 1963.

———. *Una mystica persona: die Kirche als das Mysteriu der Identität des Heiligen Geistes in Christus und den Christen: eine Person in vielen Personen*. München: F. Schöning, 1964.

Muscat, Noel. *The Life of St. Francis in the Light of St. Bonaventure's Theology on the "Verbum Crucifixum."* Rome: Pontificium Athenaeum Antonianum, 1989.

Obenauer, Klaus. *Thomistische Metaphysik und Trinitätstheologie: Sein, Geist, Gott-Dreifaltigkeit, Schöpfung, Gnade*. Münster: Lit Verlag, 2000.

Oberdorfer, Bernd. *Filioque: Geschichte und Theologie eines ökumenischen Problems*. Göttingen: Vandenhoeck and Ruprecht, 2001.

Orbe, Antonio. *La teologia dei secoli II e III: Il confronto della grande Chiesa con lo gnosticismo*. 2 vols. Casale Monferrato: Piemme, 1995.

Pannenberg, Wolfhart. "Die Subjektivität Gottes und die Trinitätslehre." In *Grundfragen systematischer Theologie: Gesammelte Aufsätze*, 2:96–111. Göttingen: Vandenhoeck and Ruprecht, 1980.

———. *Systematic Theology*, vol. 1. Translated by Geoffrey W. Bromiley. Grand Rapids, Mich.: Eerdmans, 1991.

Paris, Leonardo. *Sulla libertà. Prospettive di teologia trinitaria tra neuroscienze e filosofia*. Rome: Città Nuova, 2012.

Peterson, Erik. *Der Monotheismus als politischen Problem: Ein Beitrag zur Geschichte der politischen theologie im Imperium Romanum*. Leipzig: Hegner, 1935.

Pontifical Council for Promoting Christian Unity. "The Greek and Latin Tradition Regarding the Procession of the Holy Spirit." *Information Service* 89 (1995): II/III, 88–92.

Prenga, Eduard. *Il Crocifisso via alla Trinità: L'esperienza di Francesco d'Assisi nella teologia di Bonaventura*. Rome: Città Nuova, 2010.

Prestige, George. *God in Patristic Thought*. London: William Heinemann, 1936.

Rahner, Karl. "On the Theology of the Incarnation." In *Theological Investigations*, vol. 4: *More Recent Writings*, translated by Kevin Smyth, 105–20. New York: Seabury Press, 1974.

———. "The Death of Jesus and the Closure of Revelation." In *Theological Investigations*, vol. 28: *God and Revelation*, translated by Edward Quinn, 132–42. New York: Seabury Press, 1983.

———. *Foundations of Christian Faith: An Introduction to the Idea of Christianity*. Translated by William W. Dych. New York: Crossroad, 2004.

Rahner, Karl, and Wilhelm Thüsing. *Christologie Systematisch und exegetisch*. Freiburg i.B.: Herder, 1972.

Ratzinger, Joseph. *The Theology of History in St. Bonaventure*. Chicago: Franciscan Herald Press, 1989.

———. *Introduction to Christianity*. Translated by J. R. Foster. San Francisco, Calif.: Ignatius Press, 2004.

Robinson, John A. T. *Honest to God*. London: Westminster Press, 1963.

Sanchez Sorondo, Marcelo. *La gracia como participación de la naturaleza divina segun santo Tomas de Aquino*. Salamanca: Univ. Pontificias Buenos Aires, 1979.

Scheffczyk, Leo. "Dichiarazioni del magistero e storia del dogma della Trinità." In *Mysterium Salutis: Nuovo corso di dogmatica come teologia della storia della salvezza*, vol. 3: *La storia della salvezza prima di Cristo*, edited by Johannes Feiner and Magnus Löhrer, 187–278. Brescia: Queriniana, 1969.

Schmidbaur, Hans Christian. *Personarum Trinitas: Die trinitarsiche Gotteslehre des heiligen Thomas von Aquin*. St. Ottilien: EOS Verlag, 1995.

Schulz, Michael. *Sein und Trinität: Systematische Erörterungen zur Religionsphilosophie G.W.F. Hegels im ontologiegeschichtlichen Rückblick auf J. Duns Scotus und I. Kant und die Hegel-Rezeption in der Seinsauslegung und Trinitätstheologie bei W. Pannenberg, E. Jüngel, K. Rahner un H.U. von Balthasar*. St. Ottilien: EOS Verlag, 1997.

Sesboüé, Bernard. *Saint Basile et la Trinité: un acte théologique au IV siècle: Le rôle de Basile de Césarée dans l'élaboration de la doctrine et du langage trinitaires*. Paris: Desclée, 1998.

Soloviev, Vladimir. *Lectures on Divine Humanity*. Translated by Boris Jakim. Hudson, N.Y.: Lindisfarne, 1995.

Staniloae, Dumitru. *The Experience of God*. Translated and edited by I. Ionita and R. Barringer. 2 vols. Brookline, Mass.: Holy Cross Orthodox Press, 1994–2000.

Studer, Basil. *Trinity and Incarnation: The Faith of the Early Church*. Translated by M. Westerhoff. Edited by A. Louth. Collegeville, Minn.: Liturgical Press, 1997.

Tavard, Georges Henri. *The Vision of Trinity*. Washington, D.C.: University Press of America, 1981.

Tremblay, Réal. *La manifestation et la vision de Dieu selon saint Irénée de Lyon*. Münster: Aschendorff, 1978.

Ventimiglia, Giovanni. *Differenza e contraddizione: Il problema dell'essere in Tommaso d'Aquino: esse, diversum, contradictio*. Milan: Vita e Pensiero, 1997.

Vischer, Lukas, ed. *La théologie du Saint-Esprit dans le dialogue entre l'Orient et l'Occident*. Paris: Le Centurion, 1981.

von Löwenich, Walther. *Luthers Theologia Crucis*. Witten: Kaiser, 1954.

Zanghì, Giuseppe Maria. *Dio che è Amore: Trinità e vita in Cristo*. Third edition. Rome: Città Nuova, 2004.

Zizioulas, John D. *Being as Communion: Studies in Personhood and the Church*. Crestwood, N.Y.: St. Vladimir's Seminary Press, 1985.

———. *The One and the Many: Studies on God, Man, the Church, and the World Today*. Edited by Gregory Edwards. Alhambra, Calif.: Sebastian Press, 2010.

INDEX OF NAMES

From the Trinity: The Coming of God in Revelation and Theology
was designed in Garamond and composed by Kachergis Book Design
of Pittsboro, North Carolina. It was printed on 55-pound Natural
Offset and bound by Maple Press of York, Pennsylvania.